CHALLENGE AND CHOICE IN CONTEMPORARY EDUCATION

SIX MAJOR IDEOLOGICAL PERSPECTIVES

CHRISTOPHER J. LUCAS
University of Missouri-Columbia

MACMILLAN PUBLISHING CO., INC.
New York

To the memory of my father,
the late Marshal P. Lucas,
who made all things possible,
and to my son, Gregory,
who makes all things worthwhile,
this effort is gratefully dedicated.

Macmillan Publishing Co., Inc.
866 Third Avenue, New York, New York 10022

Collier Macmillan Canada, Ltd.

Library of Congress Cataloging in Publication Data

Main entry under title:

Challenge and choice in contemporary education.

   1. Education—Philosophy—Addresses, essays, lectures. 2. Education—United States—Addresses,
essays, lectures. I. Lucas, Christopher J.
LB41.C465   370.11   75-9702
ISBN 0-02-372180-4

Printing 1 2 3 4 5 6 7 8   Year: 6 7 8 9 0 1 2

PREFACE

This is a book about education and schools. Specifically, it is about the current phases of that perennial controversy that attends discussion of the most basic issues to be raised concerning education. These include disagreements over what ought to be the goals or objectives of the school system, which values should be served, how schooling should be conducted (if at all), and in a broad sense what knowledge educators should endeavor to impart.

Divisions of opinion on fundamental questions involving education are inevitable to a certain extent in a democratic society where ideas and values must compete for acceptance in the marketplace of ideas, and where there exists no substantial consensus on what should be taught or toward what ends. Structuring the schools to satisfy everyone, it turns out, is a practical impossibility. What happens, rather, is that various factions converge upon the schools armed with incommensurate proposals for change, animated by antithetic sets of values. Each group is unalterably persuaded, of course, that society's well-being depends upon the success with which the school is enlisted to help preserve its particular doctrines or cherished norms.

That the school as an institution is capable of sustaining itself under such a barrage of criticism and to function with some degree of effectiveness testifies to its resilience and powers of accommodation. On the debit side, some would argue that the price paid can be measured by the school's seeming imperviousness to needed reform, the degree of rigidity manifest in many of its curricula and instructional programs, and a certain deadening sterility brought on by schoolmen anxious not to offend or to provoke controversy. It does not seem too much to claim that the quite understandable tendency of most educators confronted by conflicting prescriptions for change has been to play it safe, to adopt a stance of neutrality, or, more often than not, to acquiesce before the demands of those groups within society wielding the greatest economic and political clout.

A necessary (though certainly not sufficient) condition for improving matters is unequivocal rejection of the pervasive trade-school mentality in teacher education today which advises that teacher candidates be trained like mechanical technicians, without much regard for the insight and broad understanding that should accompany the inculcation of teaching and classroom management skills. Lawrence Cremin summed it up best over a decade ago in *The Genius of American Education* (1965) when he remarked that "Education is too significant and dynamic an enterprise to be left to mere technicians; and we might as well begin now the prodigious task of preparing men and women who understand not only the substance of what they are teaching but also the theories behind the particular strategies they employ to convey that substance" (p. 59). More recently the same point was served in a comment of Bernier and Williams in their excellent study, *Beyond Beliefs, Ideological Foundations of American Education* (1973): "We cannot afford to unleash upon the schools teachers who act without thinking, who advocate change without understanding, or who support the status quo without sensitivity" (p. 2).

For reasons too complex to treat succinctly here, it is quite unlikely, however, that educators will act much differently than they have in the past unless or until they achieve a greater measure of professional autonomy. Meanwhile, lacking that minimal degree of intellectual independence and self-identity commonly associated with true professionalism, educators will probably continue to remain subservient to passing political persuasions or whatever metaphysical prejudices happen to be in fashion at any given moment. Time and time again, it can be shown, educational leaders are prone to succumb to the allure of arbitrarily stipulative definitions of teaching and learning, to surreptitiously persuasive definitions of education, and blatantly programmatic slogans designed to influence school decisions without regard for the logic and evidence which ought properly to come into play when choosing among alternative courses of action. Quite possibly no other semiprofessional group within society has proved itself so susceptible to the bandwagon mentality. On the other hand, considering how little time and effort are expended in both preservice and inservice training programs in assisting teachers, administrators, and counselors to develop some reasoned convictions about themselves and their tasks, it is remarkable just how well they do manage to acquire some grounded convictions about the management of education. In any event, relative political impotence affords no excuse for not thinking carefully about what one is doing. The point and purpose of the present work consequently is to acquaint prospective educators with some of the major arguments and lines of disagreement over basic issues in contemporary education.

The strategy employed herein begins by identifying six major ideological perspectives in education: those points of view that can be said to have exercised some significant influence upon the rhetoric of schooling and whose movements, upon occasion, have impacted directly upon the schools. Preceding what I hope is a judicious sampling of writings both supportive and critical of each movement, I have sketched out some relevant historical antecedents as well as the current pattern of development of each viewpoint. I have tried where possible to highlight the essential arguments advanced by proponents of each perspective and also the main lines of criticism.

It should go without saying that there is nothing authoritative or fixed about this particular six-fold classification scheme. Its validity will have to be judged solely in terms of its descriptive and explanatory utility to the reader. Nor do I suppose that a collection of readings is adequate to do justice to the range and complexity of opinions subsumed within each section. All that can be hoped for is that the reader will be left with a better feel for the major issues under consideration and a sense of the underlying values incorporated within each orientation. My primary purpose is not to engender commitment to any particular point of view—there is already an oversupply of ideologically rigid True Believers in education—but merely to provide materials for a more intelligent appraisal of the alternatives. I hasten to add that an educator who takes himself or herself seriously and who regards the work of education as a significant undertaking will have to come eventually to some reasoned and perhaps passionately held convictions about the issues involved. Eventual commitment should come, however, only as the terminus of an inquiry extending far beyond the confines of a readings book such as this. The initial exposure to the writings contained in this volume can only furnish a point of departure for a much longer journey toward professional self-definition. But if this work proves useful to some readers in their embarkation upon that effort, it will have been eminently worthwhile.

*   *   *

Appreciation is expressed to Lloyd C. Chilton, Jr., of Macmillan for his undoubted perspicacity in discerning the worth of my original proposal for a readings collection and to Dave Novack, for his assistance in shepherding the manuscript through the production process. I am grateful to the several authors, editors, and publishers cited elsewhere who extended permission to use previously published materials. Without their cooperation, needless to say, the project could not have been undertaken. I am especially indebted to my colleague Ralph Glauert, who graciously consented to review and critique the first manuscript draft and whose several suggestions proved most helpful. Special thanks are to be extended to Dacia Rzchowski for her patient labors in typing the manuscript. Lastly, I am grateful as always to my wife, Terrie, for her patience, understanding, and encouragement during the protracted gestation of this effort.

Columbia, Missouri   C. J. L.

CONTENTS

viii *Contents*

1
EDUCATIONAL CONSERVATISM AND THE LIBERAL ARTS TRADITION

The study of what man should be and what he should pursue is the
noblest of all studies.
Plato

THE GREEK CONCEPTION OF LIBERAL LEARNING

"At present opinion is divided about the subjects of education," Aristotle observed almost two and a half millennia ago in his *Politics*.
"People do not take the same view about what should be learned by
the young, either with a view to human excellence or a view to the
best possible life; nor is it clear whether education should be
directed mainly to the intellect or to moral character . . . whether the
proper studies to be pursued are those that are useful in life, or those
which make for excellence, or those that advance the bounds of
knowledge . . . Men do not all honor the same distinctive human excellence," he concluded, "and so naturally they differ about the
proper training for it." The situation is little changed today. Toward
what ends or goals ought the educative process be directed? What
criteria should apply in determining the subject matter of curricula,
and what standards for judging the outcomes of instruction? What
indeed constitutes the proper and appropriate direction of human endeavor generally; and how may education be employed in the realization of man's unique destiny? Such enduring questions still engage
the attention of thoughtful men in the contemporary world.

The Greeks of antiquity were the first to ponder deliberately
those perennial problems of education, to inquire about the nature of
the educative process, to ask how it ought to be conducted, and to

1

question what objectives it should serve. Though Aristotle's contemporaries did not always agree in specifics, nor draw identical conclusions concerning questions of pedagogy, learning, and the nature of human development, it seems fair to claim that among the classical Greeks there did gradually emerge nevertheless a kind of concrescent ideal of what education should be, a shared definition of its scope and content, and a consensual if oftentimes inchoate appreciation for the values by which it was to be defined, explained, and ultimately justified. If it is true, as John Stuart Mill once avowed, that the Greeks initiated almost everything prized in the Western cultural tradition, and their institutions and practices supplied its architectonic foundations, it is essential to examine briefly the intellectual origins of so vital and durable a tradition in educational thought. Embodied in its doctrines is a general perspective or point of view which still commands an important place in the contemporary marketplace of competing ideas and whose proponents with unflagging vigor aspire to shape modern schooling in light of the enduring values enshrined within that tradition.

The Hellenistic conception of "liberal" education derived originally from certain widely-accepted philosophic doctrines having to do with the nature of knowledge, knowing, and human reason itself. First was the notion that inherent in the mind is a natural propensity to inquire, to pursue knowledge, to seek to understand. As Aristotle observed in his *Metaphysics*, "All men by nature desire to know." To be human is to be possessed of an inveterate curiosity about the world and the manifold of impressions it offers the senses; and the attainment of knowledge satisfies and fulfills the mind which thereby realizes its own appropriate end or purpose.[1] The pursuit of knowledge, it was held, is an expression of the *raison d'être* of mind, and therefore, not only an essential element in the good life, but the chief means of its attainment. Since intellect is man's unique and distinctive possession, his defining trait as it were, and the quest for knowledge the natural fulfillment of rational intellect, it follows that man's highest purpose in life is to engage in those processes of inquiry, reflection, and contemplation which give full play to his intellectual or rational faculties.

Secondly, it was accepted among Greek philosophers that the human mind, rightly employed, is capable of apprehending the essential nature of reality. Reason is competent to discern within the transitory and always shifting currents of experience what is ultimately real, according to a hierarchical structure of knowing that

[1] Cf. Paul H. Hirst, "Liberal Education and the Nature of Knowledge," in Reginald D. Archambault, ed., *Philosophical Analysis and Education* (New York: The Humanities Press, 1965), pp. 113 ff. The interpretation closely follows Hirst's analysis.

commences with a finite understanding of sensory particulars in the
world and rises potentially to the realm of pure Being in and of itself.
Human knowledge may properly be regarded as a faithful reflection,
or at least a coherent reconstruction, of a harmonious and uniform
world order whose laws and principles are fixed and immutable.

From those doctrines there issued the ideal of education as a
process concerned simply and directly with the pursuit of objective
knowledge for its own sake.[2] Since the rational development of intellect through the pursuit of pure knowledge was thought of necessity to be its highest *summum bonum,* utilitarian considerations of
applied knowledge and skill played scarcely any significant role in the
Greek conception of formal education. The value of education as intellectual self-fullfillment was presumed to be intrinsic to the process
itself. To move from ignorance to knowledge, from error to truth,
from confusion to enlightened understanding, was understood as a
self-justifying good. And if any further rationale were required, it was
enough to show that because knowledge was the precondition of living the good life, liberal education was essential for understanding
how to live properly as a man as well as a member of some larger
social community.

Likewise basic to the Greek notion of education was a distinction, first introduced by Aristotle, between *liberal* education, suitable
for free men possessed of both the legal opportunity and economic
means to devote themselves of self-culture, and *illiberal* vocational
training, which Aristotle along with most of his contemporaries
regarded as fit only for a lesser breed of men, for slaves. Liberal education was the province of those desirous of freeing themselves from
error and illusion; manual training, in contrast (insofar as it was considered at all), was looked upon as a regrettable necessity for the common masses and therefore undeserving of further philosophic attention. This dichotomy was to persist down through the ages as the
difference between those forms of education having no ends or value
extrinsic to the act of knowing itself, and any type of training whose
worth is measured chiefly according to its economic or social utility.

The specific content of a liberal education, its subject matter as
opposed to the conception of its aim and value, has, as one might expect, admitted of many different definitions, depending upon the
time and place in question. Nor was the distinction between "liberal"
and "illiberal" education particularly troublesome until modern
times, mainly because the "liberal" studies of each age and culture
more often than not also served as the "practical" studies of that
age.[3] Thus, for example, whereas in antiquity the *artes liberales* for

[2] Ibid., p. 114.
[3] Lotus D. Coffman, *The State University, Its Work and Problems* (Minneapolis:
University of Minnesota Press, 1934), pp. 159–160.

the *liberi,* or freeman, encompassed rhetoric, dialectic, forensics, philology, grammar, philosophy, and the like—subjects regarded as useful in the law courts and political arena—succeeding centuries witnessed an extension or modification of the basic curricular schema to accommodate many new forms of knowledge. The proclivity of medieval man to compartmentalize and order his existence manifested itself in a tidy seven-fold division of liberal learning: the *trivium,* comprised by grammar, dialectic and rhetoric, and the *quadrivium,* or arithmetic, geometry, music, and astronomy. Yet, it is important to note, those subjects, the stuff and substance of formal training for physicians, lawyers, and theologians in the universities of twelfth to fifteenth-century Europe, were looked upon not only as the branches of knowledge essential for professional competence but likewise as the basic elements of liberal instruction.[4] Similarly, the innovations (chiefly language and literature) introduced by Renaissance humanists after 1400 had to fight for acceptance against the bitterest opposition, but the principle of intellectual utility remained the same.

THE SCIENTIFIC REVOLUTION

The rise of science and a consequent exponential expansion of knowledge, beginning at a time when the grand medieval synthesis of the scholastics had already begun to crumble, dealt the first major blow to one of the underlying tenets upon which the concept of liberal education had depended since the days of Plato and Aristotle: the idea of knowledge as certain, unchanging, and absolute. The rise of scientific modes of inquiry meant, first, that knowledge came to be looked upon as limited in scope, quantitative in its most adequate formulations, and probabilistic rather than immutable in character. Secondly, the scientific habit of mind encouraged a mechanistic view of the universe in which the old categories of plan and purpose and design seemed to play a decidedly less important part in the grand scheme of things. Thirdly, the growing scientific distrust of unprovable hypotheses and uncontrolled speculation had the practical effect of placing unprecedented importance upon the *utility* of knowledge. "The end of knowledge," Thomas Hobbes was to insist, "is power, and . . . the scope of all speculation is the performance of some action, or thing to be done." The venerable Aristotelian vision of pure intellectual contemplation began to give way to the point of view expressed by the seventeenth-century philosopher John Locke who asserted, "The principal end why we are to get knowledge here is to make use of it for the benefit of ourselves and others in this world."

[4] Cf. Francis H. Horn, "Liberal Education Reexamined," *Harvard Education Review,* **26** (Fall 1956), 303 ff.

It became increasingly evident from the seventeenth century onward that the inexorable growth of new scientific knowledge bid fair to annihilate all previous interpretations of the natural world founded upon reason, revelation, or ordinary experience. Traditional notions of solidity, permanence and reality slowly eroded away as one by one the great intellectual constructions of the universe, the *Weltanschauungen* of Genesis, Homer, Dante, Milton, Newton, and Goethe, each of which had in its turn conferred upon man some sense of his identity and place in the cosmos, disintegrated. In their absence, modern man has since plunged into a nightmarish quagmire of multi-dimensional continua, probability amplitudes, and abstract indeterminacies which far transcend the world of pure reason or sensory perception.[5] For the first time in the history of human thought there seems ample cause for wondering whether the universe *is* essentially knowable at all, or whether the mind is competent to apprehend directly its essential properties in any intelligible fashion whatever.

The logic of the nascent scientific revolution led perhaps inevitably to a conviction that the quest for objective knowledge of the natural phenomena of the world, however provisional and tentative in character, was the greatest, most vital, perhaps the exclusive business of the human mind. As against the great humanist tradition that insisted that the search for goodness, truth, justice, and beauty are paramount aims for man and that will, reason, and purpose are significant factors to be reckoned with in human experience, exponents of the emergent scientific tradition were forced to concede that empirical, quantifiable forms of knowledge yielded little or nothing in the way of ends, values, and moral judgments.[6] Accordingly, as Western culture hastened to embrace the fundamental postulates of the scientific-technological credo, concern for ends gave way more and more to a preoccupation with means, products to processes, objectives to methodologies. The distinction between fact and value widened into a veritable yawning chasm. Precisely as René Descartes and others had clearly foreseen as early as the 1600's, the rise of science accentuated the bifurcation of human life into two distinct and increasingly discontinuous realms or spheres: an objective world of sensory experience, of natural phenomena, and a subjective world of internal experience. Left unanswered in the relentless struggle for mastery over the physical world were questions about the status and basis of all those other forms of knowing whose stock in trade was "values" and

[5] Gerald Holton, "Modern Science and the Intellectual Tradition," *Science*, Vol. **161**, No. 131 (April 22, 1960), 1187 ff.
[6] John H. Schaar and Sheldon S. Wolin, "Education and the Technological Society," *The New York Review of Books* (October 9, 1969), 4.

which, lacking the characteristics of empirical knowledge, no longer seemed shareable as genuine knowledge.

One palpable result was a loss of confidence in practically any criteria by which to distinguish right from wrong, good from bad, the beautiful from the ugly. All that remained apparently were subjective preferences—the functional equivalents of values—feelings and private sensations. Even when it was conceded that so-called ultimate questions of moral and spiritual judgment were matters of supreme importance and self-commitment, it was tacitly assumed that these were necessarily subjective, personal, and in all likelihood unamenable to reasoned discourse. Consideration of the abiding mysteries of existence, the life of the spirit and of consciousness turned inward upon itself, was in effect consigned to the realm of the unknowable, or thrown over for the supposed certainties of an objective world of process and quantity. The Greek conception of a harmoniously ordered and hierarchically structured universe in which will and purpose were real and significant, in which facts and values alike were rooted in a common reality accessible to human intellect, had disappeared. With it went the old view of liberal education based on knowable truths, as opposed to uncertain opinions, beliefs, and subjectively derived values.

LOSS OF SHARED CULTURE

Yet another indirect consequence of the enormous accumulation of knowledge attendant upon the scientific revolution was the irreparable damage done to the classical ideal of a shared culture, or *paideia*, which had long been integral to the notion of liberal education. For the Greeks, man was the center and "measure of all things" in the universe. His primary aim was to achieve the fullest and most perfect development of personality. Like the sculptor fashioning his creation from raw clay, each man had as his task the modeling of the statue that was himself. "To make oneself," as H. I. Marrou, the famed historian of classical education wrote in characterizing the Hellenic ideal, "to produce from the original childish material, and from the imperfectly formed creature one may so easily remain, the man who is fully a man, whose ideal proportions one can just perceive: such is every man's lifework, the one task worthy of a liftime's devotion." [7] The outcome or result of that process of self-development was what had come to be termed in Hellenistic times "culture," or *paideia*. The truly educated man was one whose sensibilities were acute, his perceptions informed, his intellect developed to the highest level pos-

[7] H. I. Marrou, *A History of Education in Antiquity* (New York: Mentor, 1965), p. 146.

sible. *Paideia* was a form of personal life, what Plato termed "the most precious boon ever granted to mortal men." As understood by such writers as Varro and Cicero who translated the concept as *humanitas,* "culture" was at once the attribute of a cultivated mind and the object of its disciplined sensibilities. For Libanius and St. Gregory Nazianzen, *paideia* also meant a shared complex of beliefs, values, dispositions, and traditions to which every educated man was privy. Its possession was the one incomparable treasure of the human spirit, and a sure sign by which a cultivated mind could be recognized.

This concept of a culture of intellect held in common by educated men lasted for over a millennium and a half. Inevitably, however, it fell victim to the thousandfold increase in knowledge that took place in succeeding centuries, the fragmentation of intellectual culture into many discrete subcultures, and the concomitant demotion of values from the status of certain truths to subjective, private preferences. The accretions of the ages slowly but surely made the idea of any one single authoritative body of truths, values, and epistemological order more and more difficult to defend. By the early nineteenth century, specialization spurred by burgeoning new disciplines and subject matters spelled the breakdown in the idea of any one kind of liberal education that could plausibly be deemed necessary for all men regardless of the sort of careers or professions they might pursue. The growth of mass education offering instruction of bewildering variety to practically all classes of men simply exacerbated the problem further.

NEW DEFENSES FOR LIBERAL EDUCATION

There were several major figures in the nineteenth century who addressed themselves to the question of how to redefine liberal education for the modern age and how the humane values with which it was traditionally associated might best be preserved. Among those who essayed to resuscitate the concept of general or liberal education were Matthew Arnold, Ralph Waldo Emerson, and John Henry Newman. Newman's *The Idea of a University,* first published in 1852, was perhaps the most eloquent defense offered among them on behalf of the liberal arts tradition. Liberal education, he asserted, is not so much a body of subject matter as primarily a way of looking at things, an active involvement with knowledge such that the human intellect is trained, not to some specific trade or profession or to some particular study or science, but for its own sake, "for the perception of its own proper object, and for its own highest culture." It consists, properly speaking, of the training which permits one to view things in perspective, to relate things to one another and measure their respective values thereby, to free the mind so that the individual is afforded "a clear, conscious view of his own opinions and judgments" and learns "to see things as they are. . . ." [8] In the case of most men, Newman argued, once the intellect has been trained to "have a connected view of things," it "makes itself felt in the good sense, sobriety of thought, reasonableness, candour, self command, and steadiness of view which characterizes it." [9] Other "connatural qualities" of a liberal education assume the form of "a delicate taste, a candid, equitable dispassionate mind, and a noble and courteous bearing in the conduct of life." [10]

It was Aristotle, Newman believed, who best captured the meaning of the word "liberal" when he said that "Of possessions those rather are useful which bear fruit; those liberal, which tend to enjoyment. By fruitful, I mean, which yield revenue; by enjoyable, where nothing accrues of consequence beyond the using." [11] As applied to education, "liberal" signifies an education in which knowledge and understanding are sought for their own sake and not for any incidental benefits which might accrue. The cultivation of intellect, in short, is its own end. What Newman specifically was concerned to deny was the proposition that in order to claim that education is useful or valuable, one must be able to elucidate its specific vocational utility.

What was especially interesting about Newman's re-statement of the Aristotelian position was its emphasis upon process rather than content, on desirable qualities of mind and character presumed to accrue as outcomes from liberal study rather than upon an analysis of some specific scheme of knowledge. In one sense it was inevitable that proponents like Newman would have recourse to such an approach, not simply because of the already obvious disappearance of any one unifying *paideia* or culture of the intellect in Western society, but because serious doubts had long since been raised about the efficacy of any particular type of knowledge in developing the mind in desirable ways, and hence promoting the good life. And, moreover, if it seemed untenable to claim that knowledge is actually a faithful replication of the structure and pattern of some objective reality, insurmountable problems of definition and justification arose. Upon what basis was any one particular pattern or order of knowledge to be imposed upon a program of study if knowledge is only a partial, incomplete, and exceedingly provisional restatement of experience, rather than a hypothetical reality "out there"? Wherein lies the justification for those discrete moral virtues, habits of mind, and intellec-

---

[8] John Henry Cardinal Newman, *The Idea of a University* (London: Longmans, Green and Company, 1931), p. 173.
[9] Ibid., pp. xxxiv–xxxv.
[10] Ibid., p. 107.
[11] Ibid., pp. 97–101, quoting from Aristotle's *Rhetoric*, I, p. 5.

tual attributes stipulated as desirable results following upon the study of the liberal arts? Those questions, in various and sundry form, have confronted defenders of the liberal arts tradition ever since.[12]

By the midpoint of the last century attempts to closely identify any fixed and specific content or subject matter with a liberal education had been virtually abandoned. Colleges and universities, while yet insisting that their primary concern was to offer their students liberal instruction, began to experiment freely with electives, options within prescribed programs, and a variety of new curricula. From apologetics for the standard offerings in Greek, Latin, theology, ethics, and literature, spokesmen for general education turned for justification to the concept of curricular "breadth" or "scope" which, it was hoped, would help inculcate the habits of mind, catholicity of taste, refinement of judgment, and enlargement of spirit traditionally associated with the liberal arts. As for what one later commentator [13] aptly termed the problem of "a proliferation of facts and a *contraction of understanding*," American educators optimistically assumed that even when the various natural sciences were conceded their place in the curriculum, the humanities would continue to serve as the organizing and interpretive core of human knowledge.

Conceptions of how and why general education could be liberal differed. So long as higher learning was still linked to theology, the liberating effect of humane studies was yet understood in the biblical sense of "The truth shall make you free." Subsequently, when the academy found itself obliged to accommodate to a more secularized culture, that sense of "truth" was not abandoned altogether even after it grew virtually impossible to define. "It was still the case," as one observer notes, "that a student was *liberated* from intellectual parochialism by a *disciplined* study of his culture's *fundamentals*, analyzed in the context of *moral* maxims accepted as axiomatic: democracy is preferable to totalitarianism, high culture to pop art, rational discourse to coercion, marriage between loving partners to random mating, and so on. Criteria of worth, though debatable in marginal cases, were adamantine at their core; educational standards were not lessened by their separation from fundamentalist dicta." [14]

In the present century, attempts to elucidate the nature and function of liberal education continue unabated. The effort today is conducted against the background of a humanistic tradition very much on the defensive against the encroachments of scientistic and positivist philosophies, a rampant moral and intellectual relativism that rejects any sense of authority whatever, renewed polemics over

---

[12] The point is adapted from Hirst's argument, op. cit., pp. 116–117.
[13] Nevitt Sanford, *Where Colleges Fail* (San Francisco: Jossey-Bass, 1969), p. 201.
[14] William Peterson, "What Remains of Liberal Education?" *Change*, Vol. 45, No. 6 (Summer 1973), 46.

the disparity in modern culture between technical know-how and a lack of wisdom to direct its appropriate applications (so often the stuff of commencement speeches in liberal arts colleges), and, if anything, an aggravated split between what Charles Snow characterized many years ago as two distinct and antithetical cultures in Western society, the one humanistic and literary, the other scientific. "I believe the intellectual life of the whole Western Society is increasingly being split into two polar groups," he wrote, ". . . at the one pole we have the literary intellectuals—at the other, the scientists. Between the two, a gulf of mutual incomprehension. They have a curious distorted image of each other. Their attitude is so different that, even on the level of emotion, they can't find much common ground." [15] Finally, the case for the liberal arts as the core and organizing center of formal education has had to be made in opposition to ever-increasing demands for greater practicality, for more vocational training, and for what Thorstein Veblen contemptuously but ineffectually dismissed early in the 1900's as "matter-of-fact knowledge." [16]

Most notable of the many recent restatements of the ideal of liberal education was the 1945 Report of the Harvard University Committee entitled *General Education in a Free Society*. "General education," it was claimed (meaning something very close to Newman's idea of liberal education), is distinguished not by any particular subject matter but by method and outlook. It can encompass practically any discipline. The term "general" indicates that aspect of total learning which looks to the life of the individual as a responsible human being and citizen, as contrasted with "special" education whose concern is competence in some occupation. The Report went on to define liberal learning both in terms of the qualities of mind it ought to produce and the forms of knowledge with which it ought properly to be concerned (significantly, without achieving much success in showing any necessary connection or linkage of the two). Having distinguished three basic areas of knowledge, the natural sciences, the humanities, and social studies, the Committee claimed that each had a contribution to make in fostering the ability to think effectively, to communicate clearly, to make relevant judgments, and to discriminate among values.[17] After a lengthy discussion of these four abilities, an argument was offered to show how "the three phases of effective thinking, logical, relational, and imaginative, correspond roughly to

[15] C. P. Snow, *The Two Cultures and the Scientific Revolution* (London: Cambridge University Press, 1960), pp. 2–4.

[16] Thorstein Veblen, *The Higher Learning in America*. New York: Hill and Wang, 1957.

[17] Report of the Harvard Committee, *General Education in a Free Society* (London: Oxford University Press, 1946), pp. 64–65.

the three divisions of learning, the natural sciences, the social studies, and the humanities, respectively." [18] The Report closed with some general remarks on the connections between character formation, value choices, and education. Similar in intent if not in its particulars was the thesis advanced by Daniel Bell which claimed that liberal education, if indeed it is to be truly liberating, must concentrate upon teaching modes of conceptualization, explanation, and verification which are generalizable beyond specific areas of study.[19]

CURRENT DEFINITIONS

Definitions of what liberal education is supposed to encompass and what it should aspire to achieve abound in the literature of higher education. Writers as diverse in their views as Brand Blanshard, Lewis Mayhew, Earl McGrath, Russell Cooper, and a host of others appear to agree nevertheless on most of the following points: (1) general education can be "liberal" if it is sufficiently broad in scope to encompass a variety of disciplines and subject matters; (2) liberal learning is a basic preparation for all the nonvocational aspects of life such as intellectual endeavor, intelligent exercise of the prerogatives of citizenship in a free society, aesthetic enjoyment, personal adjustment, and effective participation in the common social life of society; (3) general or liberal education cannot be identified too closely with a specific body of subjects—its role in human development is more a matter of process and outcome; (4) among the hoped-for results of a liberal education must be counted a well-developed mind, a certain discernment of judgment, sensitivity toward others, breadth of intellectual and social vision, ethical and moral probity, refinement of taste, and intimate conversance with the cultural heritage; (5) the humanities, because they embody man's choices and feelings, are uniquely suited to occupy a dominant though not necessarily an exclusive position in the curriculum of a liberal education; and, finally, (6) liberal education is basic and essential for everyone, in as great an amount and for as long a period as the congruence of personal predilection and social circumstances will permit.[20] It remains to show how the concept of liberal-general education (however understood or defined) is typically associated with educational conservative thought as a whole.

[18] Ibid., p. 67.
[19] Daniel Bell, *The Reforming of General Education* (New York: Columbia University Press, 1966), pp. 7–8.
[20] Cf. John M. Purcell, "A Liberal Education in the United States," *The Journal of General Education*, Vol. **XXIII**, No. 1 (April 1971), 55–68.

CONSERVATISM IN EDUCATIONAL THOUGHT

Practically any systematic effort to tidy up the ideological cross-currents of American educational controversy invariably fails to do justice to the full range and complexity of the many points of view which historically have animated public discussion of the school—its aim and goals, its curricula, and its proper role in the social order. However, a case can be made for the thesis that there has been at least one abiding strain of thought whose historical antecedents reach back as far as the days of Thomas G. Carter and Horace Mann and the struggle to win support for a public common school system. That ideological strain was predicated upon the assumption that all children needed to be educated and that even within so pluralistic and heterogeneous a society as that of nineteenth-century America there were some learnings and values which all its members ought to share in common and to which formal schooling was a necessary means.[21] Educational conservatism, by which is meant loosely a viewpoint stressing the conserving function of education and the need for school curricula organized around an irreducible core of basic academic disciplines, subsequently evolved in the twentieth century as the expression of a concern to safeguard the intellectual rigor of schooling, to defend the concept of a common prescribed scheme of studies, and to buttress the role of education in the transmission of the Western cultural heritage. Under the rubric of "essentialism," conservative thought coalesced as an organized movement in the late 1930's under the leadership of such educators as William C. Bagley, Frederick Breed, Thomas Briggs, and Isaac L. Kandel, on behalf of the newly-formed Essentialist Committee for the Advancement of American Education. Basically it was directed as a protest against the alleged dominance of progressivism and the influence of Dewey's pragmatic philosophy upon prevailing educational thought. For reasons to be touched upon momentarily, conservative educational theory in the Thirties, and again in the Fifties and Sixties, lent significant if oblique support to the liberal arts tradition and the concept of general or liberal education.

A resurgence of conservatism in educational thought in the post-war period sounded many of the same themes advanced a decade earlier. Critics continued as they had before to assail the schools for allegedly anemic standards, vapid curricula, and ineffective discipline. Spearheading the advance were the National Council for American Education under Allen Zoll, and the American Education Association headed by Milo McDonald. True learning, by which was meant intel-

---

[21] Harry S. Broudy, *General Education: The Search for a Rationale* (Bloomington, Indiana: The Phi Delta Kappa Educational Foundation, 1974), p. 9.

lectual training and discipline, had been weakened, essentialists charged, by diversionary curricula emphasizing social and psychological adjustment or narrow vocational training. They observed a noticeable decline in academic rigor, and a falling away from the historic disciplines which had once served as the basis of formal education. Exceptionally able students were said to have been ignored or their special needs passed over because of a mistaken egalitarianism in pedagogy that treated all learners alike. Schools at all levels had abandoned their historic mission of transmitting the core values of the Western cultural tradition; and in giving up allegiance to the ideas of prescribed subject matter and mental discipline, it was said, had practically guaranteed the enshrinement of mediocrity as an educational norm. Education worthy of free men, conservatives insisted, should consist of intellectual training through rigorous application of the mind to the historic subject matters. Blistering criticism raged unabated into the decade of the late 1950's and early 1960's as commentators such as James B. Conant, Paul Woodring, Hyman G. Rickover, Albert Lynd, Rudolph Flesch, Arthur Bestor, Max Rafferty, and Mortimer Smith reiterated earlier demands for a return to an essential common core of subject matters, intellectual skills, and received values upon which the preservation of a free society and Western civilization was thought to depend.[22]

During roughly the same time period, there appeared a number of conservative critics who made higher education the special target of their criticisms and who inveighed against the utilitarianism, the social efficiency, and loss of identity they discerned endemic in the groves of academe. Most of them, like Mark Van Doren, Richard Livingstone, Jacques Maritain, Étienne Gilson, Irving Babbitt, Gilbert Highet, Mortimer Adler, and Robert Maynard Hutchins, were advocates, defenders, and apologists for the liberal arts tradition, urging a return to its ideals as the controlling principle for post-secondary education. While differing substantially in their respective philosophic underpinnings—essentialists, the intellectual heirs of Realist and Idealist traditions in formal philosophy, and perennialists, as the latter group were commonly referred to, indebted primarily to Neo-Scholasticism or Neo-Thomism—the programmatic proposals for reform advanced by both types of conservatives oftentimes proved mutually supportive. For their part, essentialists were not entirely immune to suggestions that school curricula should be geared to the social needs of the corporate state, and entertained a much broader conception of what a curriculum should encompass than did perennialists. The latter group tended to stress more rigidly an "intellec-

---

[22] Cf. Bernard Iddlings Bell, *Crisis in Education* (New York: McGraw-Hill, 1949), for a representative collection of writings.

tualist" education founded on certain ostensibly eternal truths derived from the Graeco-Roman and Judaic-Christian traditions, opposing on metaphysical grounds any suggestion that considerations of immediate social, political, or economic utility should figure prominently in an ideal educational system. Their differences notwithstanding, however, the thrusts of the two conservative movements have always shared a great deal in common.[23]

First, traditionalists or conservatives of varied persuasions have tended to agree that considerations of technocratic utility and efficiency should be subordinated to the paramount intellectual, spiritual, and ethical purposes of general education. Secondly, essentialists and perennialists concur that the crux of the educational enterprise is the transmission and assimilation of a prescribed body of subject matter, one incorporating the basic elements of the social cultural heritage. Thirdly, both groups acknowledge the cardinal importance of effort, discipline, and self-control in the learning process, as opposed to self-indulgent gratification of immediate needs and transitory interests. Fourthly, conservatives come together in endorsing the idea of curricular continuity: the foundations for a collegiate-level liberal education are laid in a systematic, planned, and sequential exposure to the rudiments of learning skills, beginning with the three R's in the elementary school, and extending through to an orderly introduction to the basic subject matter disciplines at the secondary school level.

THE SHAPE OF THE CURRICULUM

All in all, the approximate contours of a broadly-based educational program (for the lower schools at least) command a surprising degree of unanimity from educational conservatives of widely differing philosophic persuasions. For Arthur Bestor, writing in his influential *The Restoration of Learning* which first appeared in 1955, the school pro-

[23] For an opposing interpretation consider the following:

"It is important to understand that perennialism is not simply a kind of conservative philosophy of society and education, although it has on occasion been treated in the literature as if it were, just as some of the leading American spokesmen for the perennialist protest against American essentialism sometimes have been classified as educational conservatives. The protest of the perennial philosophy is not against simply the educational theories of the modern world . . . [but] a strong and continuing protest against the pattern of contemporary Western culture with its science and technology, its corporate industrialism, and its [secularized] political and educational institutions. . . . Perennialism is openly and frankly a proposal for cultural regression . . . and [its main thrust] is against the established American tradition in education, and the prevailing tradition in American education is essentialism." G. Max Wingo, *Philosophies of Education: An Introduction* (Lexington, Mass.: D.C. Heath and Company, 1974), pp. 234–235.

gram that the twentieth century inherited from the nineteenth was not some vestigial atavism of the past but the product of a penetrating analysis of the intellectual needs of the modern world. It was, Bestor asserted, a curriculum based upon an extraordinarily prescient forecast of what the great issues and concerns of succeeding generations were likely to be. It was a program not for the past or the present moment but for the century beginning. Bestor was to distinguish five major areas of disciplined study: (1) language and its uses (reading, writing, grammar, literature); (2) mathematics (with progress marked by a systematic progression from simple reckoning on to algebra, geometry, and calculus); (3) the sciences (particularly biology, chemistry, and physics); (4) history; and (5) foreign languages. Bestor's thesis has been echoed widely in the polemics of many other essentialist writers.

In a similar vein, Mortimer Smith, Executive Director of the Council for Basic Education, contends that liberal education embodies a definable heritage of transmissible knowledge with which all students should be conversant (though not all will master it at the same pace, in the same way, nor necessarily to the same degree). Basic general education accordingly begins with reading, writing, and simple computation; builds upon the organized knowledge represented by the physical sciences, algebra, geography, history, and the arts; and is fortified through exposure in high school to history (ancient, European, and American), English (prescriptive grammar, composition, and literature), foreign languages (both classical and modern), mathematics, the sciences (chiefly biology, chemistry, and physics), music, and the arts.[24] A true liberal education manages to preserve a balance between skills of analysis (facilitated especially by scientific study) and those involving intuition, insight, and imagination (inspired mainly by study of the humanities). Studies involving the basic disciplines, Smith insists, should be regarded for their intrinsic value and not simply as instrumentalities for extrinsic ends. The liberal arts, finally, are not "an adornment for an aristocracy, but a necessity for democrats" in a free society.[25] For Smith, the very fact that they are regarded in some quarters as standing in need of defense indicates the present perilous state of education.

Essentialists and perennialists alike would likely subscribe to the following often-quoted description of a basic curriculum:

> There is certainly a basic core of knowledge that every human person ought to know in order to live a genuinely human life. . . . First of all (a) the student should learn to use the basic instruments of knowledge,

[24] Mortimer Smith, "In Defense of the Liberal Arts," in Dwight W. Allen and Jeffry C. Hecht, *Controversies in Education* (Philadelphia: W. B. Saunders, 1974), pp. 26–33.
[25] Ibid., p. 26.

especially his own language. In order to understand it more clearly and objectively, he should gain some knowledge of at least one foreign language as well. In addition, he should be taught the essentials of humane logic and elementary mathematics. Then (b), he should become acquainted with the methods of physics, chemistry, and biology and the basic facts so far revealed by these sciences. In the third place (c), he should study history and the sciences of man. Then (d), he should gain some familiarity with the great classics of his own and of world literature and art. Finally (e), in the later stages of this basic training, he should be introduced to philosophy and to those basic problems which arise from the attempt to integrate knowledge and practice.[26]

PROSPECTS FOR THE RESTORATION OF LIBERAL EDUCATION

Differences among educational conservatives or traditionalists grow more pronounced in debate over the scope and content of collegiate education, to a considerable extent reflecting genuine divergencies of philosophic outlook among the respective protagonists. A diminishing number of hard-core classicists continue to insist that the languages and literature of ancient Greece and Rome are uniquely adapted for furnishing the basis of a liberal education to which everyone should be exposed before proceeding with more specialized pre-professional and professional training. Humanists of a more accommodating disposition have abandoned the notion that classical literature alone should frame the liberal curriculum, but remain adamant about the importance of the liberal arts (mainly the humanities) in general education. Still other proponents of the liberal arts tradition concede an enlarged role for the physical, biological, and modern social sciences, while stressing that although it is impossible to define precisely what specific range of subject matter may contribute the most to a genuinely liberal education, the purposes and goals of liberal learning are more *likely* to be realized through courses in philosophy and history than through, say, those in civil engineering, typing, or computer programming. Finally, some educational theorists are prepared to affirm that no particular subject is potentially devoid of liberal significance, and, conversely, no special course of study necessarily guarantees that the ends of liberal education will be achieved. The critical factor is methodology and intent; in a scientific-technological society especially, the most one can do is to make provision for exposure to a broad range of subject matters in the hope that breadth of content will somehow foster an appreciation for the humane values traditionally associated with a liberal education.

[26] John Wild, "Education and Human Society: A Realistic View," in John S. Brubacher (ed.), *Modern Philosophies and Education,* 54th Yearbook of the National Study for the Study of Education (Chicago: University of Chicago Press, 1955), p. 34.

Occupying a sort of middle ground are those like Mortimer Adler and Robert Maynard Hutchins who espouse a curriculum organized around the so-called "Great Books." Traditionalists of this persuasion are convinced that students should study those great works of literature, history, philosophy, and science which have passed the test of time by being acclaimed outstanding exemplars of their kind by successive generations of mankind. "The reading of these books," Adler explains, "is not for antiquarian purposes; the interest is not archeological or philological. . . . Rather the books are to be read because they are as contemporary today as when they were written. . . ." [27] Critics respond by claiming that combining two different criteria, the *intrinsic* (a classic of enduring esthetic or philosophic merit) and the *social* (a document which once figured importantly in the intellectual life of mankind but perhaps does so no longer), is arbitrary and overly restrictive.[28] Furthermore, it is sometimes alleged, there are insuperable pedagogical difficulties involved in accommodating a Great Books curriculum to the diverse needs of a heterogeneous learning population.[29]

There is no lack of difficulties, both theoretical and practical, with the ideology of educational conservatism and the liberal arts tradition. Some have been alluded to earlier. In addition, there is the question of whether it is reasonable or practical to insist upon general education for everyone. Does everyone need it? Is everyone capable of profiting from it? How general should the common curriculum attempt to be? Is there in fact a self-defining irreducible core of traditional skills and subject matter that must be transmitted by the school? According to what criteria shall it be defined or identified? Is "general" education necessarily or inherently "liberal"? What should be the role of the liberal arts in college and university education in view of increased demands for earlier and narrower specialization? Can general-liberal education actually make good on its claims to produce men of superior wisdom, judgment, moral virtue, and breadth of vision?

The enduring vitality of the general-liberal tradition in education, on the other hand, derives largely from the fact that it does speak to a set of very important and legitimate concerns, and seems to offer a needed corrective to parochial, illiberal points of view. At a

[27] Mortimer J. Alder, "The Crisis in Contemporary Education," *The Social Frontier,* Vol. V (February 1939), 63.
[28] Cf. Albert Guerurd, *The Education of a Humanist* (Cambridge, Mass.: Harvard University Press, 1949), pp. 128–132.
[29] In a somewhat different context, Broudy, op. cit. wryly notes that "it so happens that for the most part those children who can't seem to master the standard subject matter of the general education curriculum tend to be the ones who are alleged not to need it" (p. 19).

time when modern society seems intent on processing the young for preordained slots in its corporate System and the current vogue for narrow-gauged vocationalism finds advocates among exceedingly powerful and influential groups, it may seem all the more imperative to restore a better balance between career preparation and liberal self-cultivation. In a larger sense, it may well be that the last best hope for a humanity experiencing the dissolution of its ancestral order, the erosion of established authority, and a loss of existential meaning is educational institutions whose teachings extend beyond concern for mere factual acquisition. If proponents of the liberal arts are correct, the current manic preoccupation with technocratic competence, efficiency, and power are symptoms of an underlying spiritual malaise that threatens the very existence of civilization itself. It remains to be seen whether the restoration of liberal learning at the heart of education can or will effect the intellectual, spiritual, and moral transformation required for mankind's civilized survival.

What Are Schools For?

ROBERT E. EBEL
Michigan State University

When the history of our times is written, it may designate the
two decades following World War II as the golden age of American
education. Never before was education more highly valued. Never
before was so much of it so readily available to so many. Never
before had it been supported so generously. Never before was so
much expected of it.

But in [the present] decade of the twentieth century public education in this country appears to be in trouble. Taxpayers are revolt-
ing against the skyrocketing costs of education. Schools are being denied the funds they say they need for quality education. Teachers are
uniting to press demands for higher pay and easier working conditions.

College and high school students have rebelled against what
they call "the Establishment," resisting and overturning regulations,
demanding pupil-directed rather than teacher-directed education,
and turning in some cases to drink, drugs, and delinquency. Minorities are demanding equal treatment, which is surely their right. But
when integration makes social differences more visible, and when
equality of opportunity is not followed quickly by equality of
achievement, frustration turns to anger which sometimes leads to violence.

Surely these problems are serious enough. But I believe there
is one yet more serious, because it lies closer to the heart of our
whole educational enterprise. We seem to have lost sight of, or become confused about, our main function as educators, our principal
goal, our reason for existence. We have no good answer that we are
sure of and can agree on to the question, What are schools for?

It may seem presumptuous of me to suggest that I know the answer to this question. Yet the answer I will give is the answer that an
overwhelming majority of our fellow citizens would also give. It is
the answer that would have been given by most educators of the past
who established and operated schools. Indeed, the only reason the
question needs to be asked and answered at this time is that some influential educators have been conned into accepting wrong answers
to the question. Let me mention a few of these wrong answers:

—Schools are not custodial institutions responsible for coping

From "What Are Schools For?" *Phi Delta Kappan*, Vol. **LIV**, No. 1 (September
1972), 3–7. © 1972 by Phi Delta Kappa, Inc. Reprinted with permission.

with emotionally disturbed or incorrigible young people, for keeping nonstudents off the streets or out of the job market.

—Schools are not adjustment centers, responsible for helping young people develop favorable self-concepts, solve personal problems, and come to terms with life.

—Schools are not recreational facilities designed to entertain and amuse, to cultivate the enjoyment of freedom, to help young people find strength through joy.

—Schools are not social research agencies, to which a society can properly delegate responsibility for the discovery of solutions to the problems that are currently troubling the society.

I do not deny that society needs to be concerned about some of the things just mentioned. What I do deny is that schools were built and are maintained primarily to solve such problems. I deny that schools are good places in which to seek solutions, or that they have demonstrated much success in finding them. Schools have a very important special mission. If they accept responsibility for solving many of the other problems that trouble some young people, they are likely to fail in their primary mission, without having much success in solving the rest of our social problems.

Then what is the right answer to the question, What are schools for? I believe it is that schools are for learning, and that what ought to be learned mainly is useful knowledge.

Not all educators agree. Some of them discount the value of knowledge in the modern world. They say we ought to strive for the cultivation of intellectual skills. Others claim that schools have concentrated too much on knowledge, to the neglect of values, attitudes, and such affective dispositions. Still others argue that the purpose of education is to change behavior. They would assess its effectiveness by examining the pupil's behavior or performance. Let us consider these three alternatives in reverse order.

If the schools are to be accountable for the performance of their pupils, the question that immediately arises is, What performance? A direct answer to this question is, The performance you've been trying to teach. But that answer is not as simple or as obviously correct as it seems at first glance. Many schools have not been primarily concerned with teaching pupils to perform. They have been trying to develop their pupils' knowledge, understanding, attitudes, interests, and ideals; their cognitive capabilities and affective dispositions rather than their performances. Those who manage such schools would agree that capabilities and dispositions can only be assessed by observing performances, but they would insist that the performances themselves are not the goals of achievement, only the indicators of it. A teacher who is concerned with the pupil's cognitive capabilities and affective dispositions will teach quite differently, they point out, than one whose attention is focused solely on the pupil's performances. And, if performances are not goals but only indicators, we should choose the ones to use in assessment on the basis of their effectiveness as indicators. Clearly we cannot choose them in terms of the amount of effort we made to develop them.

But, if we reject performance goals, another question arises: What should be the relative emphasis placed on affective dispositions as opposed to cognitive capabilities? Here is another issue that divides professional educators. To some, how the pupil feels—his happiness, his interest, his self-concept, his yearnings—are what should most concern teachers. To others the pupil's cognitive resources and capabilities are the main concern. Both would agree that cognition and affect interact, and that no school ought to concentrate solely on one and ignore the other. But they disagree on which should receive primary emphasis.

In trying to resolve this issue it may be helpful to begin by observing that the instructional programs of almost all schools are aimed directly at the cultivation of cognitive competence. Pupils are taught how to read and to use mathematics, how to write and to express perceptions, feelings, ideas, and desires in writing, to be acquainted with history and to understand science. The pupil's affective dispositions, his feelings, attitudes, interests, etc., constitute conditions that facilitate or inhibit cognitive achievement. They may be enhanced by success or impaired by failure. But they are by-products, not the main products, of the instructional effort. It is almost impossible to find any school that has planned and successfully operated an instructional program aimed primarily at the attainment of affective goals.

That this situation exists does not prove that it ought to exist. But it does suggest that there may be reasons. And we need not look too far to discover what they probably are.

Feelings are essentially unteachable. They can not be passed along from teacher to learner in the way that information is transmitted. Nor can the learner acquire them by pursuing them directly as he might acquire understanding by study. Feelings are almost always the consequence of something—of success or failure, of duty done or duty ignored, of danger encountered or danger escaped. Further, good feelings (and bad feelings also, fortunately) are seldom if ever permanent possessions. They tend to be highly ephemeral. The surest prediction that one can make when he feels particularly good, strong, wise, or happy is that sooner or later he is going to feel bad, weak, foolish, or sad. In these circumstances it is hardly surprising that feelings are difficult to teach.

Nor do they need to be taught. A new-born infant has, or quickly develops, a full complement of them—pain, rage, satiety, drowsiness, vitality, joy, love, and all the rest. Experience may attach these feelings to new objects. It may teach the wisdom of curbing the expression of certain feelings at inappropriate times or in inappropriate ways. And while such attachments and curbings may be desirable, and may be seen as part of the task of the school, they hardly qualify as one of its major missions.

The school has in fact a much more important educational mission than affective education, one which in the current cultural climate and educational fashion is being badly neglected. I refer to moral education—the inculcation in the young of the accumulated moral wisdom of the race.

This change in our perception of the function of the school is reflected in our statements of educational objectives. A century ago Horace Mann, Herbert Spencer, and most others agreed that there were three main aspects of education: intellectual, moral, and physical. Today the main aspects identified by our taxonomies of objectives are cognitive, affective, and psychomotor. The first and third elements in these two triads are essentially identical. The second elements are quite different. The change reflects a shift in emphasis away from the pupil's duties and toward his feelings.

Why has this come about? Perhaps because of the current emphasis in our society on individual liberty rather than on personal responsibility. Perhaps because we have felt it necessary to be more concerned with civil rights than with civic duties. Perhaps because innovation and change look better to us than tradition and stability. Perhaps because we have come to trust and honor the vigor of youth more than the wisdom of age.

In all these things we may have been misled. As we view the contemporary culture in this country it is hard to see how the changes that have taken place in our moral values during the last half century have brought any visible improvement in the quality of our lives. It may be time for the pendulum to start swinging back toward an emphasis on responsibility, on stability, on wisdom. Older people are not always wiser people, but wisdom does grow with experience, and experience does accumulate with age.

Schools have much to contribute to moral education if they choose to do so, and if the courts and the public will let them. The rules of conduct and discipline adopted and enforced in the school, the models of excellence and humanity provided by the teachers, can be powerful influences in moral education. The study of history can teach pupils a decent respect for the lessons in morality that long experience has gradually taught the human race. Schools in the Soviet Union today appear to be doing a much more effective job of moral education than we have done in recent years. This fact alone may be enough to discredit moral education in some eyes. But concern for moral education has also been expressed by educational leaders in the democracies.

Alfred North Whitehead put the matter this way at the end of his essay on the aims of education:

> "The essence of education is that it be religious."
> "Pray, what is religious education?"
> "A religious education is an education which inculcates duty and reverence. Duty arises from our potential control over the course of events. Where attainable knowledge could have changed the issue, ignorance has the guilt of vice. And the foundation of reverence is this perception, that the present holds within itself the complete sum of existence, backwards and forwards, that whole amplitude of time which is eternity."

If these views are correct, moral education deserves a much higher priority among the tasks of the school than does affective education. But it does not deserve the highest priority. That spot must be reserved for the cultivation of cognitive competence. Human beings need strong moral foundations, as part of their cultural heritage. They also need a structure of knowledge as part of their intellectual heritage. What schools were primarily built to do, and what they are most capable of doing well, is to help the student develop cognitive competence.

What is cognitive competence? Two distinctly different answers have been given. One is that it requires acquisition of knowledge. The other is that it requires development of intellectual skills. Here is another issue on which educational specialists are divided.

To avoid confusion or superficiality on this issue it is necessary to be quite clear on the meanings attached to the terms *knowledge* and *intellectual skills*. Knowledge, as the term is used here, is not synonymous with information. Knowledge is built out of information by thinking. It is an integrated structure of relationships among concepts and propositions. A teacher can give his students information. He cannot give them knowledge. A student must earn the right to say "I know" by his own thoughtful efforts to understand.

Whatever a person experiences directly in living or vicariously by reading or listening can become part of his knowledge. It will become part of his knowledge if he succeeds in integrating that experience into the structure of his knowledge, so that it makes sense, is likely to be remembered, and will be available for use when needed. Knowledge is essentially a private possession. Information can be made public. Knowledge cannot. Hence it would be more appropriate to speak of a modern-day information explosion than of a knowledge explosion.

The term *intellectual skills* has also been used with a variety of meanings. Further, those who use it often do not say, precisely and clearly, what they mean by it. Most of them seem not to mean skill in specific operations, such as spelling a word, adding two fractions, diagraming a sentence, or balancing a chemical equation. They are likely to conceive of intellectual skills in much broader terms, such as observing, classifying, measuring, communicating, predicting, inferring, experimenting, formulating hypotheses, and interpreting data.

It seems clear that these broader intellectual skills cannot be developed or used very effectively apart from substantial bodies of relevant knowledge. To be skillful in formulating hypotheses about the cause of a patient's persistent headaches, one needs to know a considerable amount of neurology, anatomy, and physiology, as much as possible about the known disorders that cause headaches and a great deal about the history and habits of the person who is suffering them. That is, to show a particular intellectual skill a person must possess the relevant knowledge. (Note well at this point that a person cannot look up the knowledge he needs, for knowledge, in the sense of the term as we use it, cannot be looked up. Only information can be looked up. Knowledge has to be built by the knower himself.) And, if he does possess the relevant knowledge, what else does he need in order to show the desired skill?

Intellectual skill that goes beyond knowledge can be developed in specific operations like spelling a word or adding fractions. But the more general (and variable from instance to instance) the operation becomes, the less likely it is that a person's intellectual skills will go far beyond his knowledge.

Those who advocate the development of intellectual skills as the principal cognitive aim of education often express the belief (or hope) that these skills will be broadly transferrable from one area of subject matter to another. But if the subjects are quite different, the transfer is likely to be quite limited. Who would hire a man well trained in the measurement of personal characteristics for the job of measuring stellar distances and compositions?

Those who advocate the cultivation of knowledge as the central focus of our educational efforts are sometimes asked, "What about wisdom? Isn't that more important than knowledge?"

To provide a satisfactory answer to this question we need to say clearly what we mean when we speak of wisdom. In some situations wisdom is simply an alias for good fortune. He who calls the plays in a football game, who designs a new automobile, or who plays the stock market is likely to be well acquainted with this kind of wisdom—and with its constant companion, folly. If an action that might turn out badly in fact turns out well, we call it an act of wisdom. If it turns out badly, it was clearly an act of folly.

But there is more than this to the relation of knowledge to wisdom. C. I. Lewis of Harvard has expressed that relation in this way:

> Where ability to make correct judgments of value is concerned, we more typically speak of wisdom, perhaps, than of knowledge. And "wisdom" connotes one character which is not knowledge at all, though it is quality inculcated by experience; the temper, namely, which avoids perversity in intentions, and the insufficiently considered in actions. But for the rest, wisdom and knowledge are distinct merely because there is so much of knowledge which, for any given individual or under the circumstances which obtain, is relatively inessential to judgment of values and to success in action. Thus a man may be pop-eyed with correct information and still lack wisdom, because his information has little bearing on those judgments of relative value which he is called upon to make, or because he lacks capacity to discriminate the practically important from the unimportant, or to apply his information to concrete problems of action. And men of humble attainments so far as breadth of information goes may still be wise by their correct apprehension of such values as lie open to them and of the roads to these. But surely wisdom is a type of knowledge; that type which is oriented on the important and the valuable. The wise man is he who knows where good lies, and how to act so that it may be attained.[1]

I take Professor Lewis to mean that, apart from the rectitude in purposes and the deliberateness in action that experience must teach, wisdom in action is dependent on relevant knowledge. If that is so, the best the schools can do to foster wisdom is to help students cultivate knowledge.

Our conclusion at this point is that schools should continue to emphasize cognitive achievements as the vast majority of them have been doing. Some of you may not be willing to accept this conclusion. You may believe some other goal deserves higher priority in the work of the school, perhaps something like general ability to think (apart from any particular body of knowledge), or perhaps having the proper affective dispositions, or stable personal adjustment, or simply love of learning.

If you do, you ought to be prepared to explain how different degrees of attainment of the goal you would support can be determined. For if you can not do this, if you claim your favored goal is intangible and hence unmeasurable, there is room for strong suspicion that it may not really be very important (since it has no clearly observable concomitants or consequences to render it tangible and measurable). Or perhaps the problem is that you don't have a very concrete idea of what it is you propose as a goal.

Let us return to the question of what schools are for, and in par-

[1] C. I. Lewis, *An Analysis of Knowledge and Valuation* (LaSalle, Ill.: Open Court, 1946).

ticular, for what they should be accountable. It follows from what has been said about the purposes of schooling, and about the cooperation required from the student if those purposes are to be achieved, that the school should not accept responsibility for the learning achievement of every individual pupil. The essential condition for learning is the purposeful activity, the willingness to work hard to learn, of the individual learner. Learning is not a gift any school can give. It is a prize the learner himself must pursue. If a pupil is unwilling or unable to make the effort required, he will learn little in even the best school.

Does this mean that a school should give the student maximum freedom to learn, that it should abandon prescribed curricula and course content in favor of independent study on projects selected by the pupils themselves? I do not think so. Surely all learning must be done by the learner himself, but a good teacher can motivate, direct, and assist the learning process to great advantage. For a school to model its instructional program after the kind of free learning pupils do on their own out of school is to abandon most of its special value as a school, most of its very reason for existence.

Harry Broudy and John Palmer, discussing the demise of the kind of progressive education advocated by Dewey's disciple William H. Kilpatrick, had this to say about the predecessors of our contemporary free schools and open classrooms:

> A technically sophisticated society simply does not dare leave the acquisition of systematized knowledge to concomitant learning, the by-products of projects that are themselves wholesome slices of juvenile life. Intelligence without systematized knowledge will do only for the most ordinary, everyday problems. International amity, survival in our atomic age, automation, racial integration, are not common everyday problems to which common-sense knowledge and a sense of decency are adequate.[2]

Like Broudy and Palmer, I believe that command of useful knowledge is likely to be achieved most rapidly and most surely when the individual pupil's effort to learn is motivated, guided, and assisted by expert instruction. Such instruction is most likely to occur, and to be most efficient and effective, when given in classes, not to individuals singly.

If the school is not held to account for the success of each of its pupils in learning, for what should it be accountable? I would say that it should accept responsibility for providing a favorable learning environment. Such an environment, in my view, is one in which the student's efforts to learn are:

[2] Harry S. Broudy and John R. Palmer, *Exemplars of Teaching Method* (Chicago: Rand McNally, 1965).

1. guided and assisted by a capable, enthusiastic teacher;
2. facilitated by an abundance of books, films, apparatus, equipment, and other instructional materials;
3. stimulated and rewarded by both formal and informal recognition of achievement; and
4. reinforced by the example and the help of other interested, hard-working students.

The first two of these aspects of a favorable learning environment are unlikely to be seriously questioned. But perhaps a word or two needs to be said in defense of the other two. First, what of the need for formal recognition and reward of achievement as a stimulus of efforts to achieve?

In the long run learning may be its own reward. But the experience of generations of good teachers has shown that in the short run learning is greatly facilitated by more immediate recognition and rewards. This means words of praise and of reproof, which good teachers have used from ancient time. It means tests and grades, reports and honors, diplomas and degrees. These formal means and occasions for recognizing and rewarding achievement are built into our system of education. We will do well to retain them, to disregard the perennial advice of educational reformers that such so-called extrinsic incentives to achievement be abandoned—unless, of course, we are also willing to abandon excellence as a goal for our efforts.

Next, what of the influence of classmates in either stimulating, assisting, and rewarding efforts to achieve, or disparaging and ridiculing those efforts? In the experience of many teachers these positive or negative influences can be very strong. Of course a teacher's attitudes and behavior can tend to encourage or discourage learning. But much also depends on the attitudes the students bring with them to the class. If they are interested and prepared to work hard, learning can be productive fun. If not, learning is likely to be listless and unproductive.

There may be some teachers with a magic touch that can convert an uninterested, unwilling class into a group of eager learners. I myself have encountered such teachers only in movies or novels. Surely they are too rare to count on for solving the problems of motivation to learn, especially in some of the more difficult situations. For the most part, motivation to learn is an attitude a student has or lacks well before a particular course of instruction ever begins.

Going to school is an opportunity, and ought to be so regarded by all pupils. The good intentions which led us to enact compulsory schooling laws have trapped us. School attendance can be made compulsory. School learning can not be. So some of our classrooms are loaded with youth who have no wish to be there, whose aim is not to learn but to escape from learning. Such a classroom is not a favorable learning environment.

The remedy is obvious. No upper grade or high school young person ought to be allowed in a class unless he wants to take advantage of the opportunity it offers. Keeping him there under compulsion will do him no good, and will do others in the class harm. Compulsory school attendance laws were never intended to create such a problem for teachers and school officials. Have we the wit to recognize the source of this problem, and the courage to act to correct it?

Let me now recapitulate what I have tried to say about what schools are for.

1. Public education in America today is in trouble.

2. Though many conditions contribute to our present difficulties, the fundamental cause is our own confusions concerning the central purpose of our activities.

3. Schools have been far too willing to accept responsibility for solving all of the problems of young people, for meeting all of their immediate needs. That schools have failed to discharge these obligations successfully is clearly evident.

4. Schools are for learning. They should bend most of their efforts to the facilitation of learning.

5. The kind of learning on which schools should concentrate most of their efforts is cognitive competence, the command of useful knowledge.

6. Knowledge is a structure of relationships among concepts. It must be built by the learner himself as he seeks understanding of the information he has received.

7. Affective dispositions are important by-products of all human experience, but they seldom are or should be the principal targets of our educational efforts. We should be much more concerned with moral education than with affective education.

8. Intellectual skills are more often praised as educational goals than defined clearly enough to be taught effectively. Broadly general intellectual skills are mainly hypothetical constructs which are hard to demonstrate in real life. Highly specific intellectual skills are simply aspects of knowledge.

9. Wisdom depends primarily on knowledge, secondarily on experience.

10. Schools should not accept responsibility for the success of every pupil in learning, since that success depends so much on the pupil's own efforts.

11. Learning is a personal activity which each student must carry on for himself.

12. Individual learning is greatly facilitated by group instruction.

13. Schools should be held accountable for providing a good learning environment, which consists of a) capable, enthusiastic teachers, b) abundant and appropriate instructional materials, c) formal recognition and reward of achievement, and d) a class of willing learners.

14. Since learning cannot be made compulsory, school attendance ought not to be compulsory either.

Schools ought to be held accountable. One way or another, they surely will be held accountable. If they persist in trying to do too many things, things they were not designed and are not equipped to do well, things that in some cases can not be done at all, they will show up badly when called to account. But there is one very important thing they were designed and are equipped to do well, and that many schools have done very well in the past. That is to cultivate cognitive competence, to foster the learning of useful knowledge. If they keep this as their primary aim, and do not allow unwilling learners to sabotage the learning process, they are likely to give an excellent accounting of their effectiveness and worth.

To Know and To Do

MILTON MAYER

The Renaissance seems to have ended at Verdun, at least for the Europeans; and there are signs, finally, that the Americans are beginning to read the lesson that Europe learned on Mort Homme Hill: Man is not going to be an unqualified success. Progress is no longer axiomatic. Pessimism (or apathy, which is predigested pessimism) is becoming pervasive. Even the Communists' "new man" is nothing more than a ceremonial expression nowadays. This is the age—whatever else it is—of waning confidence.

As the age of confidence the Renaissance was more of a birth than a rebirth: Bacon's assertion that knowledge is power would have astounded all the men who had gone before him—the fallen Oedipus no less than the fallen Adam. They had been taught to expect Verdun. So had the prophet who said of the great nations of old, "They are wise to do evil, but to do good they have no knowledge."

Bacon was none the less right and the Renaissance none the less real. Knowledge *was* power. Man powered with knowledge was,

From "To Know and To Do," *Saturday Review* (February 15, 1964), 62–63, 83–84. © 1964 by Saturday Review, Inc. Reprinted with permission.

and is, as a god. But the power is proving to be independent of its generator. Like the Sorcerer's Apprentice, it needs no command to fetch water faster and faster. The water rises, and knowledge is a consternation: Rare indeed the commencement orator who does not wag his head over the discrepancy between man's moral and intellectual progress.

But what if morality is not progressive? And what if there is no necessary, or even probable, connection between morality and knowledge? What if (*horrible dictu*) the human crisis is first and last and always a moral crisis and not an intellectual crisis in the least?

When the late President Kennedy said that "science has no conscience of its own," he was doing more than quoting Rabelais; he was saying something revolutionary about education. He was saying (if science includes the highest sciences) that education is of conditional service to a man and of no service at all if the condition is not met.

Look at the general disorder of our time. When most men have less than a hundred dollars a year and the per capita expenditure on war in "peacetime" is forty, what is there that intelligence can tell us? When the most knowledgeable (and therefore the richest) societies, with the longest history of civilized institutions, lead the world in suicide, insanity, alcoholism, divorce, crime, and delinquency, what critical need have they (or, for that matter, the least knowledgeable societies) of knowledge? What is it the Communist needs to know who wants free elections in Mississippi but not in Germany, or the anti-Communist who wants bases ninety kilometers from Russia but not ninety miles from Florida?

The sovereign faith in education is everywhere in the world established now. What for Jefferson was the keystone of the democratic arch has become the keystone of the democratic and the non-democratic arches. If we can find a way to make use of universal education in the universal crisis, it would seem that we should do so. We would not make any such demand of bingo or tapdancing or swinging on the old front gate; we may make it of education because education is everywhere the great public enterprise.

We pedagogues have been willing to exploit the enterprise without examining its premise that the more of it there is the better off we shall be. Our trade secret consists in our being supposed to have a secret when we haven't. What we have is a skeleton in the multi-purpose closet in the form of the unexamined premise.

The public pressure that fills the schools with junk is irresistible, because we have nothing to resist it with. Why shouldn't driver training be compulsory? Driving is a moral problem, which the public thinks, mistakenly, can be solved by teaching. So, too, when the Russians launched their Sputnik: Out went the new humanities, in

went the new technologies, and up went the preprofessional preparation of technicians. Why not? Had the schools been doing anything
whose high purpose would justify their going on doing it? The Russians presented a moral problem—the *evil* of Communist success—
and the American people wanted it solved. The schools stood ready
to hand.

In the theocratic centuries the asserted object of teaching was
morality as a means to salvation. The object continued to be asserted
long after the age of the priests. Yale undertook to transmit not only
Veritas but *Lux;* Oberlin was consecrated by its charter to "the total
abolition of all forms of sin"; and the Haverford catalogue maintains
the primacy of the moral capacity to use the skills of learning for
worthwhile ends. Such private institutions have no legal impediment
to their transcendant aims; they are over the wall of separation upon
which the safety and security of the secular state rests like Humpty
Dumpty. But public education, at all levels, is forbidden by the First
Amendment to abolish sin, tamper with moral capacity, or ask which
ends are worthwhile.

What ever made us suppose that it could do these things even if
the law allowed? What evidence is there, now or ever, that even
under the most sacred auspices education could produce morality?
In its sacerdotal prime it made men good churchmen. Had the
churchmen been especially good men, Dante would have had to do
without the first two parts of his three-part comedy and Luther without all ninety-five of his Ninety-Five Theses.

The truly parochial schools still try to improve the adolescent
soul that will be known by its fruits. They make no bones about
meaning to make men good. And their alumni are all of them fine
fellows. But I do not know that they are finer than the alumni of Yale,
Oberlin, or Haverford—or of City College. And they should be, if
morality can be taught. Indeed, a weighted analysis should show that
college graduates are better behaved in later life than non-college
graduates and the top of the class than the bottom; and the Doctors
than the Masters. *Hélas!* as Sarah Bernhardt used to say.

Morality is action, and we know that action and knowledge are
wholly separable in, for instance, mathematics. But the separability
appears in the practitioners of all the other disciplines besides—in
the logician whose personal life is eccentric, in the gluttonous physi-
ologist, in the physicist who rounds a sharp curve at 80 m.p.h. One of
the great political scientists of our time dismisses civil disobedience
as anarchy because law is the indispensable condition of community—and asks a friend to slip a Swiss watch in through Customs.
"We imagined," said G. A. Borgese of Italian Fascism, "that the
universities would be the last to surrender. They were the first."

But mankind requires a moral purpose (or the color of one) in the institutions it supports, including war. There are no honest apostles of wickedness. Men want to be good and to live among good men, and if they have not found it feasible to be good themselves they want their children to be good. Al Capone, protesting that "Insull's doing it, everybody's doing it," was appealing his conduct to the moral standard of the community. For goodness alone is the bond of men, and unless knowledge can be shown to have a causal (or at least predisponent) connection with it, the best education is only an amenity.

Our search for the connection takes us at once to the epistemological commonplace that descriptive knowledge accumulates and normative knowledge does not. Twentieth Century man does not have to learn that the seat of fever is the blood—or that the world is flat—before he can learn that it isn't. He starts with the latest break-through. But there are no break-throughs in the moral realm: Relativity is new, but moral relativism is as old as Thrasymachus. The *Odyssey* takes us the long, long way home of the tired businessman who *really* loves his wife; the *Apology* assembles the Un-Athenian Activities Committee; and Sophocles owes his big Broadway hit to his study of Freud. Man the ingenious has no ethical or political ingenuity.

Why not? Why isn't moral advance as ineluctable as scientific, and moral fact as persuasive? Why isn't "righteousness by the Law"? The schoolmen thought that reason rules the intellect despotically but the appetite constitutionally; the appetite ("which moves the other powers to act") vetoes reason when reason threatens its closest interests. It is about *me* that I can't "think" straight—about me and my family and my friends, my race and my religion, my party and my country and my age. I insist upon comparing Albert Schweitzer with Attila instead of Bull Connor with Epictetus. I am the victim of what elementary psychology calls reflexivity, in which the subject and object of inquiry are one.

Whoever deals with himself deals unscientifically—including that hero of the endless serial, the Man in White. Not, of course, when we see him in Surgery. There he is working on an external organism. We stay the knife in his hand and ask him if this *man*—this Haman, this Hitler—ought to live or die. He says it is none of his business, and we ask him whose it is. He doesn't know; he suggests that we try the psychiatrist down the hall.

The psychiatrist down the hall replies by reading from his *New Introductory Lectures:* The physician "has no need to consider whether the patient is a good man, a suicide, or a criminal . . . It is not the business of the analyst to decide between parties." What is the business of the analyst? "To send them away"—he is still reading—"as healthy and efficient as possible." "But this is Haman!

This is Hitler." The psychiatrist—της ψυχης ιατρος, or doctor of the soul—shrugs and says, "Keep going down the hall."

Down the hall the judge is instructing the jury in that which is instructible: the law. But in that which is not—the good and evil of men that brings them into court—the jury is the judge. Twelve ordinary men whose only competence is their relative freedom from reflexivity. The petit juror, not the judge, is the judge of morals, just as the petit voter, and not the political scientist, is the judge of politics. What moral knowledge seems to want is the scientist's dispassion without the scientist's science.

With the Renaissance impact of secularism, pluralism, and science, moral doctrine lost the unity (and therefore the authority) with which it was so long advanced as the index, if not the compulsion, to action. Nowadays we have surveys of moral doctrines. The survey or peep-show has much to be said for it. It steers clear of the prerogative (no longer claimed by the church) to tell the child what is right and wrong. It avoids the parental storm that engulfs the teacher who presumes to teach (or even to have) a doctrine. And it keeps the moral philosopher out of the moral hole. The student in fourth (or fourteenth) grade who asks, "Why should I be honest?" or "Where do we go when we die?" can be sent down the long, long hall.

Natural science, unlike moral science, never did claim to be able to make men good. (To be sure, its practice fortifies such virtues as patience, initiative, and open-mindedness, but so do burglary, baby-sitting, and philosophy.) It teaches what it knows can be taught and delivers the goods—the goods that enable us in peace to live longer and less laboriously and in war to fight longer and more effectively. It doesn't try to tell us what to live or fight for, or whether labor is bad for us or longevity good. These are the "insoluble" problems that have to be taken to the man still further down the ever-lengthening hall.

Some of the designers of the atomic bomb pleaded secretly with Mr. Truman that it not be used, and some of them entrenched themselves behind the admirable scientific attitude of suspended judgment. (Mr. Truman, who had a sign on his desk reading, "The buck stops here," may have envied them their trench.) Apparently a scientific lifetime does not help a man decide whether or not to explode an atomic bomb. And in the summer of 1963 the nation's lawyers decided to straddle the civil rights issue as the only possible compromise between the Northern and Southern delegates to the American Bar Association. How learned must I be—and in what?—in order to know what to do about the atomic bomb and civil rights?

I am told that the modern world, with all its complexity, requires more learning of me than my forebears had. Not in my case;

I recall none of the crises of my life (there have been more than six) that I might have met better had I known more. But a little of my great-grandfather's incorruptibility might have come in handy. I have lied as a matter of course and cheated and stolen when I "had to." I have jettisoned principle when the wind howled and thanked God that I am as other men are. And on the occasions of unavoidable moral choice I have mobilized my good reasons for doing bad things and emerged as a trimmer whose object all sublime is to get on in the modern world.

I am told that the fortunate form of government under which I live requires a great deal of knowledge of me as a citizen. I have to understand public finance—which the public financiers, who don't have to understand anything else, dispute. I have to know whether Cambodia is east or west of North or South Vietnam and why we are fighting *there*. I have to have a judicious opinion on Guinea, Guiana, and Ghana. I am, in a word, producing more history than I can possibly consume. Without a righteous specialist in all these matters—or with an unrighteous one—I am lost.

Morality aside, I am told that I have to have more technological knowledge than my father, who didn't have an automatic transmission. Why isn't just the opposite true? The neighborhood crawls with automatic transmission men. And the work I am likely to get (if I am looking for work) requires me only to press the button every time the bell rings—a procedure which Pavlov's dog discovered long since is easier learned on the job than from books.

True, the conversion of knowledge to precept and precept to action is said to take prudence, and a man wants some sort of head for it; but as an excuse for helplessness it is one with the suspended judgment of the scientist who devises the bomb. A man lies bleeding by the road. Shall I use my automatic transmission to stop my car? The priest and the Levite were graduates of the Harvard Medical School, as the Samaritan was not. He misplaced the tourniquet. Too bad; but he was the only hope of him who had fallen among thieves.

We are asked if we mean to dispense with natural science. We reply: only with as much of it as we absolutely have to. It is nice to know that the earth goes round the sun, that man and a candle flame both metabolize, and that the angle of reflection is equal to the angle of incidence. It is nicer to know these things than to have to depend upon those who do. But the competence I want *and for which I can not depend upon another* is moral competence, and I can not get it from science.

Shall we then put a little more of our student's time into, say, esthetics? Music is said to have an inordinate power to soothe the savage breast—which comes closer to the moral crisis than all your metabolism. But we must aim at appreciation, not at theory: It is not musicology that soothes the savage breast. The trouble with the arts—music no less than medicine—is that a man may be both an artist and a swine. And this is true of the liberal artist too. Why, then, shouldn't we exhaust the possibilities of teaching decency (or at least exhaust ourselves looking for them) before we do our student the dubious favor of putting tools, even the finest tools, in his hand?

Watch out with your liberal arts, your arts of reasoning, or you will have equipped a monster to rationalize his monstrosities. You will have beefed up a part of a man—the part unique to men and to angels, and to fallen angels. Dewey may have been wrong in many things, wrongest of all to proclaim a science of pedagogy (as if a man could be *taught* to be a Dewey); but he was righter than he was wrong. He was right to insist, with Carlyle, that the end of man is an action and not a thought, however noble, and righter still to resist the compartmentalization to which the liberal, no less than the servile, arts are susceptible.

What is left, then, that may be taught to some possible moral advantage? What is left are, preeminently, the true humanities, the disciplines that deal with man as man: ethics, politics, psychology, sociology, social anthropology, history, natural theology, and the principles of metaphysics, jurisprudence, and economics. These are the studies, and they alone, that speak to the human crisis. What makes us think that they will be heard? Haven't we argued that knowledge does not compel action? The answer is that our parlous case must be made on the precarious faith that there may be a kind of post-nasal drip by means of which some of what goes into the head will find its way to the heart.

In this faith a studied acquaintance with man's moral struggle may commend itself to our crisis curriculum in several ways. It may urge sensitivity upon our student and intensify such sensitivity as he already has. It may sharpen his ability (though he may not be any the better for it himself) to tell a good man from a bad one. It may somehow, as Plato suggested, "anchor" the good man's goodness. Finally, his intercourse with the goodness and badness of men living and dead may exemplarily endear the one and dishearten the other to him.

The ancients had too few books. We have too many. But good books are better than bad books, and great books are great even though the two words are capitalized. Some of our texts may be remote in time or place, but so is progress; and their very remotion (so Alec Meiklejohn found at Amherst) may help our student escape the *Teufelskreis* of reflexivity. They will be masterpieces of the liberal arts, those tools of the verbal trade whose mastery constitutes a kind of graduate literacy. Why not teach the arts exemplarily too and use morality (the way the *Dialogues* do) as the material of their instruction? Some of our texts will be in foreign languages, which we can use to read them and to communicate with our fellow-men confronted around the world with the common human crisis.

The ancients took a cyclical view of the human condition. Men, even gods, soared and plummeted in a lifetime, in a single day, and "those cities which once were great are now nothing, while those that are great were once nothing." With the Renaissance behind us, the invalidity of the cyclical view is still to be demonstrated. It will not be demonstrated by new methods—not even when they are called methodologies—for teaching the irrelevant or by the construction of more stately mansions to shelter our cyclotrons.

We are not visionary these days, no more so (if no less) than our fathers who stoned the prophets. And our children, unless they are black, reject neither the image we present nor our preoccupation with images. There must be a reality somewhere. But the faith of the more recent fathers that education would disclose it turns out to be sterile. And its sterility illuminates the situation in which we find ourselves.

We are amputated Greeks. We have been cut off—cut ourselves off—from the mysticism that threaded Greek rationalism. An Italian in Thirteenth Century Paris, Aquinas by name, was the liveliest of all the Greeks; he undertook to prove the existence of God by reason alone. We dying Greeks undertake to prove we-care-not-what by reason alone and we wind up in the thrall of Emerson's Things and *their* meaningless mystique.

We know what goodness is, and we always have; Machiavelli knew, and Moses. But we do not know how to make men good. It is going on two-and-a-half millennia since the first discussion of education opened with the question, "Can you tell me, Socrates, whether virtue is acquired by teaching or by practice . . . or in some other way?" Perhaps the question is not to be answered; in which case we may concentrate on a succession (better yet, a continuum) of gaieties in contented conscience. But perhaps another two-and-a-half millennia of unrelenting inquiry will produce the answer; all the more reason for getting started at once.

Liberal Education and the Professions

LINDLEY J. STILES
Northwestern University

A liberal education is the tap root for all professional training and performance. It both nurtures growth and sustains life during drouths of uncertainty and the storms of controversy. Traditionally the liberal arts and sciences have served to sharpen sensitivity to the importance of knowledge for the mind and the relationship of knowledge to reality.[1] The ideal of an ordered or disciplined scholarship, which is a key goal of liberal education, is essential to the search for truth that all professions must pursue. The Romans had a word for it, *liber*, which not only meant *book* but a *free man*. The perception of liberal education as being the preparation of a free person, as contrasted to a slave, is a vision that every profession should cherish. It signifies that the mind has been freed to function, objectively and independently, to separate fact from fiction, error from reason, and right from wrong. What greater asset could any professional attain?

The contributions that liberal education can make to professional practice today are readily apparent. For example, how a person in a medical profession—doctor, nurse, or technician—responds to the moral questions related to abortion depends upon his type of education. What ideals motivate the engineer or scientist who wrestles with the newly-highlighted ecological equations is another example. Politicians who confront corruption in government, business people who are tempted to seek special advantage, economists who juggle monetary policies, educators who deal with integration, journalists who write contemporary history, military leaders who urge war or peace, and yes, lawyers who get caught up in their watergates—all have need to rely upon a liberal education for guidelines to wisdom and honesty.

Many dilemmas that professional people confront today, their controversies, and perhaps some of their notorious failures, result from too little liberal education, or perhaps from a failure of liberal education. But if liberal education has failed or, as some critics

From "Liberal Education and the Professions," *JGE: The Journal of General Education*, Vol. **XXVI**, No. 1 (April 1974), 53–64. Reprinted with permission.

[1] Paul H. Hirst, "Liberal Education and the Nature of Knowledge," in Cornelius J. Troost (ed.) *Radical School Reform: Critique and Alternatives* (Boston: Little, Brown and Company, 1973), pp. 91–114.

claim, become obsolete, the fault may not be with the concept itself. Other phenomena, such as the erosion of moral standards within the society, the loss of confidence in higher education, the confusion about what liberal education is and how it should be provided, as well as the elimination of liberal studies from professional programs may be to blame.

Moral erosion within the society.—The ideals and programs of liberal education have suffered from a moral erosion that tends to turn people away from their commitments to traditional values. New rebels have proclaimed that "God is dead" and that truth is nothing more than transitory illusion. The use of human reason and intelligence to solve problems has been replaced, time and again, by power and pressures. Expedience has become the criterion for action, with the ends justifying the means. In the process the ideal of the educated person has been replaced, all too often, by the glorification of the dogmatist. Intellectual inquiry has been scorned and thwarted almost to the point that an honest person might be classified among the endangered species.

Moral erosion, of course, is no new phenomena. It has been the Achilles heel of all civilizations. Nor are the recent threats to scholarship without historical precedence. Nevertheless, the shock of contemporary events almost immobilizes society because of the ranges and rapidity of the changes taking place. In the past decade, for example and to refresh our memories, dissident students—and some professors of liberal studies, I regret to note—have challenged the traditions of higher education by substituting activism for scholarship. Their demands for immediate relevancy made mockery of the study of art, music, history, language, literature, philosophy, and the basic sciences—learning that helps us to understand the sweep of civilizations, the meaning of knowledge, as well as such hard-won humanistic concepts as truth, freedom, and justice. As outlaw groups burned, bombed, and barricaded our campuses into submission, "free" and topical courses tended to replace organized subjects— with current events their content and extemporaneous "bull sessions" their technique. "Doing one's thing," unrehearsed and uninhibitedly, came to replace the kind of dedicated effort essential to real artistic and creative excellence. Standards became something on which protest placards were carried rather than guidelines for academic quality.

It is true that the percentage of students and professors who abandoned their scholarship for activist activities was relatively small. Nevertheless, their ends-justify-the-means tactics reached beyond campus boundaries to undermine the cohesiveness of our communities and to pollute our social, political, and commercial processes—even into the very highest echelons of business and government. Nor have the professions escaped the influence of these radical reformers. Old ethics are being challenged by "situation expediencies" espoused by new breeds of professionals who often do not appear to know right from wrong or care about the difference. Inescapably, professionals have an interest in joining with academic scholars to help repair the damage that such pragmatic behaviors have done to our programs of liberal education—and to the society for which they provide sustenance.

Loss of confidence in higher education.—Higher education is rapidly losing the confidence of people and, worse still, is losing confidence in itself. Changes have come so rapidly that neither laymen nor professionals understand all that is happening. Our doubts emanate from the fear that the modifications taking place may lead toward destruction rather than reform of higher education, as James A. Perkins has pointed out.[2] Among responses to loss of confidence that undermines liberal education are the increasing public and political demands for proof that higher education is doing its job properly. Our desperate efforts to prove our products—to be accountable—have created a climate that demands immediate validation in tangible terms.

In our anxiety to produce immediate, tangible results, we are developing assessment systems that spotlight instant replays of performance to prove that learning is taking place. The distorted behaviorism that is emerging emphasizes a kind of training that produces observable, overt responses. This type of programmed instruction—"programmed" whether by a machine or a human being—leaves no room for what we used to call the *concomitants* of learning experiences, those fringe benefits of reason, insight, inspiration, appreciation, and knowledge that unexpectedly emerge. Nor do these learning activities, limited to the acquisition of specific patterns of behaving, provide time or motivation for the achievement of other goals long associated with liberal education, such as the refinement of values, the stimulation of reflection, the cultivation of aesthetic responses, and the development of generalizations.

Advocates of behavioral objectives make broad claims for their approach. But when practice rather than theory is considered, the "behavioral-objective movement" fractionalizes learning at a level appropriate to the training of animals. For example, some professors, misled by the movement, have listed as many as 3,000 objectives for one English course! Students subjected to this type of program will be so busy learning to manifest the multitude of specific observable responses that they will have no time—or motivation—to think about

---

[2] James A. Perkins, *Reform of Higher Education: Mission Impossible?* (New York: International Council for Educational Development, 1971), pp. 12 f.

the meaning or interrelationships of any of them. They will be like the person who learned to read and speak six languages but could not think in any of them.

In trying to dispel doubts about its contributions, higher education may be falling into a trap, encouraging the type of animalistic behavior—individuals programmed to respond in specific ways to given stimuli—that serves business, the industrial world, and the military establishment in assembly-line types of jobs. What was once called "Watergate mentality" is, perhaps, an example of this kind of conditioned behavior. It is a manifestation of an old slogan, which can be restated:

> Ours is not to reason why
> When we're programmed with a lie;
> Ethics are for ancient times,
> Truth's no challenge to our crimes.

Lost in the process of projecting specific behavioral objectives are more comprehensive outcomes of education whose attainment cannot always be demonstrated instantly and overtly. I refer to goals that are typically stated in more general terms and evaluated over longer periods of time. They are outcomes that incorporate such intellectual and emotional capabilities as honesty, objectivity, creativity, appreciation, dependability, reflective thinking, respect for knowledge, empathy, social sensitivity, adaptability, diligence, insight, and such qualities as the ability to tolerate new ideas, other people, and one's self—the traditional ingredients that define an educated person. Such attributes differentiate human beings from machines or the lower animals. And they are capabilities that the emphasis on an instant replay of overt behavior may fail to promote. Ralph Tyler himself, the father of behavioral objectivism, recently observed that specific learning objectives are being confused with clear and appropriate educational goals. He made the point that everyone in higher education should heed: "an educational objective does not need to be specific in order to be clear, attainable, and capable of assessment." [3]

Other changes responsible for the loss of confidence in higher education and which have bearing upon both liberal and professional education include: the growth in size of institutions; the politicizing of colleges and universities; efforts to accommodate to new (or no) value schemes, particularly those of students; trends toward making our institutions instruments for social reform—urban renewal, environmental protection, racial integration—as well as for de-

[3] Kappan Interview, "The Father of Behavioral Objectives Criticizes Them: An Interview with Ralph Tyler," *Phi Delta Kappan* (Sept. 1973), pp. 55–57.

fense and industry. Open enrollments, individually designed student programs, the uses of mass communications media for instructional purposes, the growth of the community colleges, changed policies that make students accountable as citizens while on campus with diminishing responsibility for faculty members *in loco parentis*, and complex systems of governance—all these changes, and others, influence the relationships between liberal education and the professions.

Confusion about liberal education.—With all the changes taking place in higher education, the world of education—and much of the knowledgeable public—maintains unquestioned loyalty to the concept of liberal education.[4] Such confidence is similar to the way people feel about love, virtue, and beauty. All of us feel that a liberal education is good for an individual and beneficial to the society—but we cannot agree on what a liberal education is. Historically, the concept has been modified, or, depending on one's view, distorted, to accommodate new doctrines and intellectual thrusts, such as Christian theology, the renaissance of classical learning, and modern pragmatism. As new branches of knowledge and the complexities of life have spawned new professions, the tendency has been to shape the liberal-education base to each professional specialization.

Further confusion is generated by modifications made in the liberal arts college itself. This institution, a unique contribution to higher education by the United States, originally was intended to provide four years of liberal studies between the secondary and professional schools. The courses offered were supposed to contribute to general education rather than to specialized professional objectives. It did not quite work out this way. As professional fields developed and required collegiate preparation for entry, the tendency was to begin specialization within the liberal arts college rather than in the graduate school. With the exception of a few professional fields, this continues to be the pattern.

The growth of community colleges has brought a new image of

[4] In two studies of faculty attitudes toward liberal arts courses, made a few years ago, professors of liberal arts and those in professional schools agreed, almost unanimously (over 97 percent of each group) that all students should be required to take liberal arts courses. Almost as many (86 and 85 percent, respectively for liberal arts and technical professors) endorsed the view that people with both liberal and specialized training are better off vocationally. Yet, astonishingly, 90 percent of the liberal arts respondents and 84 percent of the professionals indicated that they saw no differences in the purposes of liberal and specialized education. Over half of each group indicated that they believed liberal arts courses *are* specialized. See: Paul L. Dressel and Margaret F. Lorimer, "A Comparison of Attitudes Toward Liberal Arts Requirements," in *Attitudes of Liberal Arts Faculty Members Toward Liberal and Professional Education* (New York: Bureau of Publications, Teachers College, Columbia University, 1960), p. 46.

a post-high-school institution, one which resembles neither the liberal arts college nor a university. One of the purposes of this new institution is to provide general or liberal education. But community colleges serve many students who will terminate their collegiate studies at the end of the two- or three-year programs; therefore, they place heavy emphasis on vocational and paraprofessional, as well as preprofessional preparation. The effect is to move specialization down into the first two years of collegiate study, years traditionally reserved for liberal education.

Another development has been the professionalization of liberal education courses themselves. In many colleges of arts and science, particularly those associated with universities, the first course in a subject field is the first step up the ladder to a Ph.D. program rather than the means to provide an organization of content that will contribute to the goals of liberal education. Included in the new professional specializations in liberal arts colleges that aim to prepare for employment are such fields as art, music, drama, sociology, economics, English, history, psychology, mathematics, political science, the modern foreign languages, as well as practically all the natural and physical sciences. About the only fields left that do not lean toward job preparation are philosophy and the classical languages.

As a consequence of these and related developments, the idea of a common or general education for all, a traditional goal, has become eroded to the point where liberal arts professors can describe liberal education only in the most general terms—courses that have no marketable value, or nonspecialized courses, or subjects that have general value. Lists of courses so designated usually allow for the most generous judgments, and students are given freedom to elect alternate specialized courses to meet degree requirements. So varied are the options that have evolved that two students can pass through the same program of *required liberal studies* without ever taking the same course. Each professional field may have its own list of courses prescribed for liberal education purposes which may range from only two or three courses to as much as two academic years of work. The truth is, what passes for a program of liberal education in a college or university today tends to be mere expediency, negotiated between liberal arts professors and their colleagues in professional schools and departments. In making such agreements, spokesmen for liberal education are forced to "deal from weakness" because both society and students, as well as leaders in professional fields, are heavily committed to utilitarian goals and, more important in a political sense, because they are outnumbered on their own liberal arts college faculties by professors whose loyalties are to specialized professional programs.

Elimination of liberal studies from professional programs.— Despite their endorsements of liberal education as an essential foundation for their various specializations, professionals in all fields tend to eliminate general education courses from their programs of preparation. Preprofessional requirements are loaded with courses that represent the beginnings of specialization, for instance biology, chemistry, and physiology for prospective medical students; economics, sociology, and political science for those preparing for entry into law schools; physics, mathematics, and computer sciences for pre-engineers. Rarely do these or other pre-professional students take courses in art, music, logic, foreign languages, linguistics, literature, or anthropology just to broaden their insights, appreciations, and general knowledge.

The field of teaching, in which I function as a professional, has often been criticized for requiring too many pedagogical courses and too few in the liberal education area. Yet, of all the professional programs, it perhaps provides the strongest emphasis in the liberal studies—as I believe should be the case. The prospective teacher, in most institutions, will take from 80 to 85 percent of his or her undergraduate programs in basic liberal arts and science courses. About half or more of these will be taken solely for general education purposes, with the rest concentrated in one or more subject majors, such as history, English, science, mathematics, or foreign language. No other professional field which begins professional preparation in an undergraduate school can compare with this emphasis on the liberal studies. Even law and medicine, whose professional programs begin after the bachelor's degree is earned, may not do as well because of the specifications made for specialized courses in preprofessional programs. While I am saying a kind word for the field of education, which it deserves but seldom gets, let me also point out that Master of Arts in Teaching programs typically require a student to take at least half of his or her work in a liberal-arts subject field. Many Ph.D. programs require prospective professionals in education to give a substantial emphasis to cognate courses in the social and behavioral sciences offered in liberal education programs.

NEED TO REDESIGN LIBERAL EDUCATION

The confusion about what liberal education is and how it should be provided, along with the forces distorting its effectiveness, suggest a need to redesign liberal education. Not since the Harvard report, *General Education in a Free Society,* published in 1946,[5] have we

---

[5] Report of the Harvard Committee, *General Education in a Free Society* (London: Oxford University Press. 1946).

had an in-depth look at the state of liberal education. Two studies at the beginning of the 1960s took samples of the attitudes of liberal arts faculty members and professors in technical schools concerning 20 propositions about the liberal arts.[6] In addition, a few individual scholars, notably Paul H. Hirst,[7] have written about the goals and nature of liberal education. Other treatises on higher education have focused more on the irrepressible problems at hand—protests, finances, governance, buildings, enrollments, control, minorities—with only tangential references to liberal education itself. Also, a few institutions, such as my own,[8] have examined the role and function of liberal studies programs as they have projected future plans. Such efforts, however, have produced no general agreements about what liberal education is or how it should be organized and provided.

I believe the need to redesign programs of liberal education to be the highest priority for higher education. It is so imperative that institutions and Boards of Higher Education in every state, interstate associations, national agencies and commissions, and professional schools—everyone concerned—should give attention to it. Liberal education is in trouble; we dare not allow it to deteriorate further. It is time to renew, to define goals, to project programs and instructional processes, and to evaluate results. We need to create new experimental models—think how long it has been since we have had any for liberal education—to validate different approaches to liberal education. We need a renaissance in liberal education, not necessarily a return to classical concepts.

Efforts to renew and redesign liberal education must, of necessity, give attention to the contributions that such studies can make to the professions. I would hope that they would be sensitive to the times as well as respectful of traditional values. They will need also to give attention to the interactions that are taking place between the society and its institutions of higher learning. They should take into account what we now know about teaching and learning and, particularly, the trends toward self-direction and individualization in instruction. Concerns that will emerge, also, will relate to how liberal education can provide a sense of usefulness for the individual and a degree of cohesiveness for the society, as well as equilibrium among

[6] Paul L. Dressel, Lewis B. Mayhew, and Earl J. McGrath, *The Liberal Arts as Viewed by Faculty Members in Professional Schools* (New York: Bureau of Publications, Teachers College, Columbia University, 1959). Also, P. L. Dressel and M. F. Lorimer, *Attitudes of Liberal Arts Faculty Members Toward Liberal and Professional Education* (New York: Bureau of Publications, Teachers College, Columbia University, 1960).
[7] Paul H. Hirst, "Liberal Education and the Nature of Knowledge."
[8] Report of Faculty Planning Committee, *A Community of Scholars*, Vol. I (Evanston, Illinois: Northwestern University, Sept. 1968).

the multitude of interdependent forces and factors that beset our social system.[9]

CONTRIBUTIONS OF LIBERAL STUDIES TO THE PROFESSIONS

Without agreement about what liberal education is or how it should be provided we can, with some degree of confidence, project some of the contributions liberal education should make to the professions. I suggest some here to stimulate our thinking, admitting freely that I am biased.

A literate person.—A first responsibility of liberal education should be to provide professional schools with talent that is literate— scientifically literate as well as generally literate—and at the level that I'll identify by the vague term "educated." It is ridiculous, I feel, for professional schools to have to teach their candidates to write well, as many are now doing. Nor should they have to devote faculty resources to such tasks as teaching students to use mathematical symbols, read maps, charts, graphs, or common scientific symbols, understand the scientific method, or abide by the rules of scholarship.

A precise mind.—By the time a student enters a professional school or department he or she should have learned from his liberal studies—much of which may be mastered at the precollege level, incidentally—to deal with information accurately, to think clearly, to reason carefully, and to organize logically.

A knowledgeable student.—The preprofessional student should gain from his or her liberal studies an understanding of the broad intellectual heritage of the human race. Such will come, I suggest, from the study of such branches of knowledge as the arts, sciences, philosophy, language, literature, and anthropology, as well as history.

An objective scholar.—Liberal education should teach respect for an appreciation of knowledge as well as the scholarly processes by which it is accumulated, classified, and applied. Every professional, in my opinion, should develop sound habits of objective scholarship in a discipline, as preparation for professional study, which will involve making applications of knowledge.

A curious and creative creature.—From research in recent years we now know that curiosity and creativity are malleable characteristics; they can be learned and taught. I believe that profes-

---

[9] See Harry D. Gideonse, "The Purpose of Higher Education: A Reexamination," in *The College and the Student*, edited by Lawrence E. Dennis and Joseph F. Kauffman (Washington, D.C.: American Council on Education, April 1966).

sional schools and departments have a right to expect the program of liberal studies to encourage, rather than discourage as they often have done in the past, their development.

An ethical individual.—No profession wants an unethical candidate. Programs of liberal education should by their pedagogy and recommendations emphasize the importance of ethical behavior for all—particularly those preparing for the professions.

A wholesome, well adjusted human being.—Discounting mental and emotional disturbances, which are matters for treatment by medical doctors, an individual's adjustment results from the experiences gained and the manner in which he or she interacts with others. Programs of liberal studies can contribute to the wholesome adjustment of students, particularly through the faculty-student and student-to-student relationships encountered, but also through the curricular opportunities made available.

An active and sensitive citizen.—Recent events—student activism, the renunciation of authority *in loco parentis* by college and university faculties, the lowering of the voting age—remind us that citizenship is not a responsibility that begins after graduation from college or a professional school. People are citizens from birth on. Liberal education, we agree, should hold as one of its major goals the development of active and sensitive citizens. Professional schools might well make civic competence a prerequisite for admission.

A leader.—Leadership inclinations and capabilities are learned, and every professional is looked to for leadership by the community as well as clients. The program of liberal studies should provide ample opportunities and encouragement for preprofessionals to develop leadership skills.

INTERDISCIPLINARY PARTNERSHIPS

Providing appropriate liberal education for professionals—and all other students—requires interdisciplinary partnerships that reach across traditional department, college, and school boundary lines. Ideally, professionals should be involved in setting the goals and projecting the outcome of liberal studies, and liberal arts professors can help professionals improve their own programs.

All professions are applied fields. They perform their service by making applications of basic knowledge to the problems of people. Much of the research that advances professional practice is done by scholars in the basic disciplines rather than by professionals themselves. Similarly, what a professional is and will become may be determined more by the foundation he acquires in the program of liberal education than in professional schools. Knowledge does not exist for itself alone but to be used. The scholar in a liberal arts college has an interest in seeing that the knowledge he or she helps to refine is used properly. Inescapably, professors of liberal studies and those in professional fields have common cause in the preparation of professionals. They should join as cooperating partners rather than as competing opponents—as is too often the case.

If liberal education is permitted to die, the professions will be the greatest losers. They cannot function without the knowledge base or the effective human traits that liberal education nurtures.

The Liberal Arts and Contemporary Society

EDWARD JOSEPH SHOBEN, JR.

When the question is posed baldly—What are the implications of the liberal arts for contemporary society?—the appropriate answer, unhappily, seems nasty, brutish and short: There are none. The basic reason can be stated with comparable roughness: The liberal arts, [presently], are unidentifiable.

Such talk meets stern and outraged resistance in academic circles, and the man who both wants to be heard and genuinely respects his potential opponents must hasten to explain his meaning. Two propositions (perhaps there should be twenty) are offered here: one is that the idea of the liberal arts has been eroded into functional nothingness by the forces of recent history; the other is that our culture is ground between two revolutions, one not yet complete and the other just coming to birth, that demand a wholesale revision of our notion of liberal education. The conclusion is that patchwork tinkering with the so-called liberal curriculum will accomplish little if anything of significance and that only a fresh image of the processes of liberation in our contemporary context will restore a constructive vitality to our campuses.

If we turn to our first theme, that of the erosion of the liberal arts and the conception defining their base, we need only remind ourselves of the subtle but far-reaching vicissitudes that have recently beset our academic faith. That faith held that the liberal arts were those whose practice became a free, a liberated, man. They

From "The Liberal Arts and Contemporary Society: The 1970's," *Liberal Education, Proceedings of the 56th Annual Meeting of the Association of American Colleges*, Vol. **XVI**, No. 1 (March 1970), 28–38. Reprinted with permission.

were the means by which an individual could transcend the parochialisms of his time and his society, both loosen and stock his imagination for the envisioning of better worlds than the one in which he actually lived, and exemplify in his style of life certain values of grace, responsibility, courage and interpersonal decency. In general, although put in a way that simplifies too much a complicated educational story, it is accurate to say that skill in the arts of freedom could be cultivated along two rather different avenues. One was exposure to the models of liberated human beings limned in the record of man's experience; the other was through the mastery of self by mastering such disciplines as those of music and mathematics, grammar and logic. The college curriculum therefore embodied literature and history, theology and then philosophy, mathematics and then the burgeoning sciences, as the means by which the goals of personal transformation might take place.

When one strips away a wishful nostalgia and the mellowness that rummaging the past frequently invokes, one finds it hard to say whether or not that faith was ever realized, or if it was, to what degree. In all probability, during the nineteenth century and decreasingly since about World War I, it was fulfilled in a significant fashion for a significant portion of those then attending college. In more recent decades, a number of influences have gutted the faith of substance, leaving only a rhetorical shell. Like so many forces at work in human history, these influences were neither the deliberate product of some villainous conspiracy nor have they been lacking in positive value, but the working out of their destiny has had deeply troubling consequences for American liberal education.

The first of these factors was the infusion of the German tradition into the Anglo-American pattern of higher learning. No one can sensibly argue about the enormous benefits that the United States has enjoyed from the establishment of *bona fide* universities, the development of graduate schools, and the professionalization of scholarship. Neither, however, can anyone blink the fact that the university has overwhelmed the college, that the graduate school has come to dominate baccalaureate programs, or that the professional scholar, understandably committed to this special field of study, has almost entirely replaced the teacher whose primary concern is with the development—the liberation—of students. Willy-nilly, the mission of undergraduate education has altered. The goal of providing a liberating experience has given way to the aim of advancing and, not quite incidentally, transmitting knowledge. Strongly reinforced by an increasingly technological society, this dynamism is, of course, the one so accurately described by Clark Kerr in *The Uses of the University*.[1]

[1] Clark Kerr, *The Uses of the University*. Cambridge, Mass.: Harvard University Press, 1963.

Second, associated with the transformation of institutional mission, major changes occurred in the two main paths to skill in the liberal arts. The exposure to great models of human conduct became formal literary study, a more "scientific" history, and the social sciences; the disciplines through the conquest of which one won a mastery over self became the specialized domains of science. In other words, the sources of liberating experience grew more exclusively cognitive, technical and professional. Even in the fields known as the humanities, the process of study focused far more on the training of potentially marketable abilities than on the development of the life-styles of free men. Obviously, these modifications in the academic *Zeitgeist* occurred over time and through complex channels, rarely demanding either-or decisions of an explicit sort by individual professors or by faculty units. Nevertheless, the trend was a strong one, showing no susceptibility to reversal.

Third, the nearly universal adoption of the Ph.D. as the qualification for professorial rank signaled not only the professionalization of faculty members as scholars; it defined a new set of expectancies for the college teacher. No longer was he supposed to reflect the values of a liberal education and to present himself as a practitioner of the liberal arts, a man for whom the cultivated intellect is a predominant tool in his engagement with aesthetic, moral and social issues; it was enough for him to project the image of the investigator, the technical man of knowledge, the specialist in a particular domain of complex abstractions. As a model for students in critical stages of personal development, the professor's role became increasingly occupational and decreasingly that of a kind of secular vicar, mediating between students and the sources of liberating experience. This change undoubtedly cleared the classroom air of a great deal of stuffiness, but for large numbers of undergraduates it also introduced an element of sterility and the strong odor of intellectual antisepsis.

Looked at in this fashion, two processes seem to have dominated our patterns of undergraduate education through the twentieth century, both moving at a steadily quickening pace. One has been the transformation of the liberal arts into highly professionalized and specialized fields of scholarship. The other has been the conversion of the college teacher from a guide to youth's involvement in traditional sources of self-realization and self-transcendence to a member of one or the other of a number of academic professions. The recent studies by Parsons and Platt [2] and by Gross and Grambsch [3] largely

---

[2] Talcott Parsons and Gerald M. Platt, *The American Academic Profession.* Cambridge, Mass.: Department of Social Relations, Harvard University, 1968.
[3] Edward Gross and Paul V. Grambsch, *University Goals and Academic Power.* Washington, D.C.: American Council on Education, 1968.

confirm common observations. Faculty members widely commit their primary allegiance to their domain of study rather than to an institution and its students; they think of their basic business as research or as service to such research-supporting bodies as funding agencies or their particular professional organization, and they view the teaching of undergraduates as fundamentally a means of either recruiting talented young people into their own academic craft or of creating a respectful and supportive audience for that craft.

As for the liberal arts themselves, if they ever really existed, they have died in the process of becoming professionalized disciplines. As the term "discipline" was used in the heyday of liberal education, it referred to the demands levied and the commitments required by a more or less objective set of skills for their mastery—classical languages, mathematics, music, grammar and logic. The point comes home in a famous passage of Thomas Hughes' insightful old novel in which Squire Brown is musing on sending his son Tom to Thomas Arnold's Rugby:

> "Shall I tell him to mind his work and say he's sent to school to make himself a good scholar? Well, but he isn't sent to school for that. . . . I don't care a straw for Greek particles or the digamma, no more does his mother. . . . If he'll only turn out a brave, helpful truth-telling Englishman, and a gentleman and a Christian, that's all I want," thought the Squire.

Although the quaintness of these reflections may strike many of us as funny, the article of faith is clear. Competence in the disciplines was only a means to an end; the student was expected to find himself by losing himself in exercises that firmed his character and instilled fundamental and widely honored values. Such a positive disciplining of the personality was abetted not only by exposure to the great human models of literature and of history but by the whole thrust of the institution—its athletic program, its arrangements for housing and dining, its code of conduct and the enforcement procedures supporting it, its patterns of interaction between faculty and students, etc.

This whole conception of a liberal education depended, of course, on a scheme of values in society that commanded broad respect and that held together at its center. It contrasts vividly with the value-free assumptions of today's highly professionalized academic disciplines, with the doctrine of institutional neutrality by which so many contemporary colleges try to live, and—perhaps most troublesome of all—with the evaluation of what might be called technical truth to the pinnacle of the academic value structure. With virtually all faculty members deriving from the graduate school and with undergraduate education increasingly conceived as a prelude to post-baccalaureate training of some sort, it is little wonder that personally meaningful conceptions of selfhood, ideas of bravery and gentleness, and notions of justice and morality hold hardly a candle among the norms of the academy to methodological proficiency and technical competence in the generation and handling of data. Whatever expands the frontiers of knowledge is an absolute good. As an isolated proposition, this one may be difficult to contend with, but it is a considerable distance from the propositions that, muzzily but persuasively, once defined a liberal education.

And it is here, of course, that one locates the current crisis in academic freedom. The unrestricted pursuit of knowledge and the enthusiastic application of the fruits of that pursuit have had in our time some bitterly ironic consequences. One has been nuclear weaponry, the outcome of one of man's most creative intellectual accomplishments, the unlocking of the atom's secrets of power. Another has been the explosion of population with all its attendant griefs and miseries of pollution, the decimation of wilderness areas, and urban decay. Here the determinants have been new discoveries and the invention of new technologies in agriculture, nutrition and food processing, in medicine and public health. Both the bomb and population growth define genocidal threats; and their omnipresence as a result of the constant and often dramatic rolling back of the frontiers of knowledge has raised grave and agitated questions about the linkages between truth and decency, between the pursuit of knowledge and the quest for morality, between extended research and extended human weal. The moral and social results of ungentle truth-seeking, the critics contend, are not only far from liberating; they flirt with downright catastrophe. And this capacity for disaster is rooted in the academic disciplines as they reach down from the graduate school into the undergraduate curriculum. No longer the paths to personal development, they have become the organized vehicles for creating or discovering facts and ideas that may well be true but are intolerably dangerous if they are untrammeled by humane concerns.

These observations bring us to our second large theme, the hypothesis that contemporary culture is caught between two major revolutions, one nearing its completion and the other just beginning.[4] The industrial revolution, dominating our lives for well over a century, has grown so familiar that we are inclined to forget the lineaments and dynamics of an industrial society, so radically different from those of its agrarian predecessors. Industrial cultures, regardless of their politics, focus on problems of producing and delivering the goods and services that are defined as real wealth. The

[4] Kenneth Keniston, "Historical Process and Psychological Development: Youth as a Stage of Life." Unpublished manuscript, 1969.

values of this focus crystallize around such characteristics of self-discipline, a prudent and foresightful orientation toward the future, work and economic success, and competitive striving. Institutionally, organizational patterns are judged primarily by the degree to which they support productivity rather than by the quality of participation that they invoke; rewards fall more to those who achieve than to those who occupy hereditary statuses, and rationality, the other side of which is emotional suppression and affective neutrality, is the prized mode of public conduct.

Despite its central concern with production, what is revolutionary in human terms about an industrial society is its distribution dynamics. As real wealth grows in volume, it must be widely delivered to be profitable. Because of a complex interaction among a variety of factors, delivery systems become both subtler and more involved with those intangibles that profoundly affect the quality of life for different component populations. The nautilus-like development from railroads to television illustrates the dimension of subtlety. The dimension of intangibility includes the delivery of rights, privileges and opportunities to wider and wider constituencies. What was once accessible only to an aristocracy is extended to the middle class and then to the white working class. The political and occupational chances falling first only to Yankees and Protestants are later delivered to immigrants and Catholics. The worlds available originally only to men are finally opened to women.

If the process moves slowly, jerkily, and most responsively when stimulated by internal expressions of discontent or even by the threat of violence, it still moves. In many ways, the relatively new militancy among populations that wear a racial uniform—preeminently blacks, but also browns, reds and (in a measure) yellow—represents the final phase of the industrial revolution as we have known it. We have reached a stage where to be poor, especially when poverty is combined with ethnic disenfranchisement, is no longer one of life's regrettable facts; it is an outrage. And the sense of outrage affects many who have never experienced deprivation, discrimination or oppression; merely witnessing these violations of deliverable justice and decency, particularly when a medium like television gives them pictorial impact and intimacy, is beyond bearing. Long-range goals become immediate rights among both the excluded and those for whom the values of an industrial culture have been deeply internalized, and the impatient—the properly impatient—cry goes out for justice and opportunity *now*.

But simultaneously, a new revolution, the post-industrial revolution,[5] has struck. For large numbers of Americans, relative afflu-

[5] Daniel Bell, "Notes on the Post-Industrial Society," *The Public Interest*, 1967 (Winter), No. 6, 24–35, and 1967 (Spring), No. 7, 102–118.

ence and basic political freedoms are no longer goals to be striven for; they are established and can be taken for granted. The ethic of production has lost its force, and the institutions, the norms and the reward systems of industrialism seem antiquated and constrictive. What matters is less success and security and much more the experience of joy, the stretching of personal consciousness, the free expression of self. The impulse life takes on new worth, and both change and conflict are celebrated for their accenting of diversity and their italicizing of authentic and unmediated interpersonal relations. The romantic and the Dionysian element is a powerful one; and for a time at least, it is unlikely that it can be denied. Its manifestation in hair styles and dress, in sexual mores, in the arts, and in altered states of consciousness, not only through drugs but through Eastern forms of meditation and various kinds of group interaction, shows its pervasiveness.

Participation clearly is one of the key terms in this new mode of life. On the one hand, participation specifies the conditions under which self-determination and identity can be experienced; on the other, it implies the involvement of all one's capacities as integrated characteristics of one's personhood. In education, it means the engagement of emotional and moral faculties as well as the intellect, and it means the extension of learning beyond the place of its occurrence—the testing of ideas learned in the classroom in off-campus settings, the checking of principles advanced in academic terms against the practices by which a college does its own business. Although it sometimes takes on the cast of sloganeering, the demand for participation suggests a quest for a new vision of possibilities: when economic security suggests a quest for a new vision of possibilities: when economic security and political freedom have been attained, what then for men? This question, which probably quite correctly assumes that man will not relax and enjoy his comforts when these ancient objectives are achieved, lies close to the heart of the post-industrial revolution.

Our world, then, may well stand at the juncture of two ages. As is the case where oceans flow together—Cape Horn, Good Hope—turbulence is intense. Though often politicized, that turbulence is much more concerned with a crisis in values, in cultural directions, and in the psychology of men in a changing time.

And what of the liberal arts in these times of clashing cultures? Here it seems necessary to distinguish between the goals of liberation and the means by which those objectives may be reached. As means, the liberal arts were severely crippled, at best, as the two major educational processes, exposure to the great human models of literature and history, and formation of character through subjecting oneself to the requirements of an objective discipline, were transmuted into professional fields of study. In outcomes, this transformation entailed a shift from the arts the practice of which becomes a free man to a set of skills the practice of which pays off occupationally. *Post hoc,* one can see how this development represents the working out of the late stages of industrial society under conditions of phenomenal technological and social change. There is little point, consequently, in discussing a possible revitalization of the liberal arts through improved teaching or through what are usually called interdisciplinary revisions of the curriculum.

As they are currently conceived, literature and history, psychology and economics, chemistry and botany are simply not facilitators of personal growth, mechanisms of self-transcendence or shapers of central values. Most of the professors who know them best are inclined to sneer when such a nostalgic possibility is broached. The academic disciplines are the bases of the academic professions; their improved teaching is likely to have no other significant result than the improved preparation of a new generation of academic professionals. Because both industrial and post-industrial cultures need professional scholars and well trained research people, such a result is worth cherishing; but reaching it takes us a long way from the liberal arts, and it leaves untouched the problem of a liberating curriculum for students without aspirations to donnishness or the scholar's occupational role.

Similar points hold for interdisciplinary programs of undergraduate study. When interdisciplinary approaches have proved most genuinely fruitful, scholars from different fields have found foci of common professional concern and generated something novel from their pooling of ideas and resources. Three examples: (1) recent studies in the physical chemistry of the cell; (2) the virtual creation of linguistics from a meld of philology, behavioral science and statistics, considerably helped by computer technology; and (3) area studies, in which historians, sociologists, geographers, economists and literary scholars join in attempts to describe and to account for the life of a region. Eventually, these developments find their way into the corpus of undergraduate offerings, but they do so as derivatives of professional scholarship, not because in some considered way they serve the strategies of personal liberation.

We probably need interdisciplinary conceptions of knowledge even more sorely than we realize; but if they are to have educational, developmental importance, then they almost surely must be cast in less professional forms, be more directly responsive to the interests of post-industrial students, and acquire a larger degree of problem-centeredness as problems are defined from the learner's point of view. Otherwise, an interdisciplinary curriculum can be as removed from the issues of personhood and community, as narrowly technical and professional, and as alienating to large numbers as is the present clutch of independent disciplines that fill our college catalogues. And as with the current curriculum, one seeking salvation through interdisciplinary forms can make the tragic error of attempting to transmit an industrial culture to a post-industrial generation. Nothing could be less liberating; nothing could more sadly or more shatteringly confirm the charges of sterility and irrelevance now hurled agains our institutions of higher education.

But if the historic conception of the liberal arts as means is a severely damaged one, the educational goals of liberation retain a high validity. Post-industrial society, like any society, is sure to have its particular parochialisms, to sort its values into a hierarchy in which some norms are more highly and more widely prized than others, and to comprise persons who search for more humane worlds. Perhaps even more than ever before, education will be expected to facilitate these processes of cultural transcendence, of embodying in one's person the best values of an age, and of imagining alternatives to the eternally inescapable present. It will probably remain the business of the college curriculum to promote these aims. It will probably be impossible to do so either by a return to the liberal arts as they once were conceived or by tinkering with our now dominant curricular machinery. The old liberal arts lack the cultural supports, the wholesale social agreements that Squire Brown voiced, which no longer give them attractiveness and meaning. The professionalized, value-free and technical disciplinary engines of the current curriculum are out of phase with the concerns and paramount interests of the most secure and informed generation of students yet to walk in academic halls.

Despite the wrench that it will cost most of us whose lives are bound up with colleges and universities, the pursuit of ancient liberating goals will demand new methods that are sure to have large and only partially predictable effects in our institutional life and in the relationships of higher education to the larger and rapidly and radically changing society. Room must be made for students to explore and to cultivate their affective and moral faculties as well as their rational skills. Credit will probably have to be given for experiences in psychotherapy, in encounter groups, in sensitivity training, and in other activities developed to reduce psychological inhibitions and to promote more direct apprehensions of self and more unmediated engagements with other human beings. To honor student needs for self-determination and participation, independent study, off-campus projects, and group-learning contracts are highly probable.

Because of the force of experience and the moral energies that are part of post-industrial culture, the curriculum must be geared more directly into the processes of rapid change in a highly urbanized world. Learning by participation in the immediacies and realities of that world is almost sure to become dominant over learning by vicarious, primarily bookish techniques. Intense debate over ethical and political questions will break out of the bull-session to become institutionalized as part of the curriculum. The arts will entail a more expressive and less appreciative form of involvement, and the sciences will be increasingly examined from the point of view of their dangers to human existence and of their moral and social implications. Above all, learning how to learn will supersede what is learned, and more attention will be invested in problem-formulation and in problem-solving as generalized processes than in mastering systematic bodies of knowledge.

This process will, of course, be a troubled and spiky one. There is the unfinished business of an industrial culture to complete at the same time as we get on to the enterprises of a post-industrial age. The new educational means to liberation will not be a savory cup of tea for all students, and the interests of those who trail in the movement toward a different culture must also be decently served. The limiting of intimidation and the channeling of romantic energies into the constructive channels necessary in an increasingly crowded and interdependent society will define problems to which history is only the most inexplicit guide. For the most part, faculty members are likely to lose status as mentors and masters of those who know, becoming, like books in a library, resources to be exploited at need, except in so far as they can display those human qualities in direct and egalitarian relationships that give them value beyond their knowledge and their expertise in the manipulation of symbol systems and ideas.

Because of its unfamiliarity, the view ahead for many of us connected with the American academy is not an alluring one. Shot through with potentially bruising uncertainties, marked by a variety of challenges that our personal histories have ill prepared us to meet, and likely to involve a style that most of us regard as shrill, demonic and graceless, it may be a far cry from the values and aspirations that led us into institutions of higher learning. In a sense, we are a little like the Indians of almost precisely a century ago—quite aware that the old ways were dying but at a loss to discover the means to grapple either comfortably or effectively with the new mores of a new culture. We may have a choice that our forebears did not give the Indian. We may elect, for a time at least, to retire to a few reservations in which the norms of industrialism still hold, or we may join in the shaping of post-industrial culture through the institutions which, although they are changing rapidly, we still know best. Schooled as most of us were, what we do may be the proper answer to the question of what the liberal arts have to say to contemporary society.

"Western Civ" After the Revolution

SCOTT EDWARDS
California State College, (Hayward)

Call it what you will—Western Civilization, Humanities I, Survey of World Literature—a course designed "to acquaint the freshman with his cultural heritage" is a standard offering in the undergraduate curriculum. It has been so for fifty years or more, ever since the classics were overthrown to give place to the sciences in their varied guises and the organizing principle of the academy became "the discipline." From the beginning, and in both its materials and its pedagogy, the general survey course in Western culture was an enclave of unreconstructed classicism and humanism in an institution that otherwise had little time for such things. It was, and it still is, all but identical with liberal education.

Western Civ endures, a modest outcropping on the mountainous bulk of the multiversity, nearly untouched by the curricular reforms which have altered or abolished so much that was merely traditional. Yet, it is highly doubtful that the course is in any way suited to the needs of the greatest number of those who take it. This judgment rests wholly on my personal observations as a teacher, and is therefore "subjective"; but I think that anyone who tries steadily to see Western Civ in the light of present realities must reach a similar conclusion. My purpose here is to say why.

But let us understand at the outset what kind of course Western Civ is. The aim is clear: to give undergraduates a beginner's grasp of Western art, literature, and philosophy in their broadest bearings and most general historical outline. And the methods are well settled: a student reads the great books, talks about them, and writes essays on the questions they raise; he listens to music and views painting and sculpture; once or twice a week he goes to a formal lecture and two or three times to an informal discussion where a professor and a handful of students make an attempt at dialogue. *Dialogue*—how beloved the word has been by the champions of general education (Hutchins, for instance), and how perfectly it expresses the pedagogical theory which has always animated Western Civ. To engage undergraduates in a dialogue after the Socratic example—that, as everyone allows, is the important thing.

Because of this emphasis on dialogue, teaching Western Civ has

From "Western Civ After the Revolution," *JGE: The Journal of General Education*, Vol. **XXV**, No. 3 (October 1973), 163–171. Reprinted with permission.

traditionally been attractive to a certain kind of academic man. Perhaps this is not obvious now, in a time uncongenial to distinctness of style; but no one who was an undergraduate before, say, 1960 will have difficulty forming a mental picture of the professorial type once common in Western Civ. He was, first of all, a "humanist" and a "generalist." To be sure, he had a discipline (history, English, philosophy), but if he was not quite contemptuous of "narrow specialization," his very presence in Western Civ proclaimed his to be a wider vision than that of his departmental colleagues, or The Association, or The Society. His air was a trifle unworldly, and he was somewhat eccentric in dress and manner—an appearance partly cultivated no doubt, but also partly an expression of the awkwardness actually felt by the humanist intellectual in a Disneyland civilization. He seemed, in Randall Jarrell's phrase, "a sad heart at the supermarket."

Students inspired him to mild affection, tempered by the feeling that they were more unsophisticated and less well read than they had to be, wrote badly, and were, often enough, sunk in Philistinism. Reflection on such things might occasionally give rise to small resentments about freshmen being allowed to wipe their feet on Plato and Shakespeare. But more often, the Western Civ professor took it to be his gratifying duty to flabbergast, overawe, and astonish. It was thought that students should come away from Western Civ with their native ignorance abated, their certitudes challenged, their complacencies not quite intact; they should become more intellectually mature, wiser. In achieving these ends, shock tactics like shows of atheism and political radicalism, or the most deliberately scornful treatment of middle-American verities were by no means ruled out.

Still, it was all essentially good-natured and, on balance, a fair approximation to the catalogue fustian about wide reading and the habit of critical reflection being the noblest of educational attainments. A student might come to see that the ironies of Socrates, the chill prescriptions of Machiavelli, and the acerbities of Voltaire had importance for *him,* that these lives and teachings and ideas mattered for the life he was himself living. Western Civ thus raised in the minds of both teachers and learners the expectation that, with effort, goods very much worth having might be obtained. It was one of the rare courses to which the too-much-used adjective "exciting" might fairly be applied.

Does the foregoing description offer a picture of things as they never were? One must no doubt be on guard against the fallacies of nostalgia. Surely, though it seems there are fewer of the type nowadays, the humanist-cum-iconoclast professor has not entirely disappeared from Western Civ. Yet something is missing. It seems fair to say that Western Civ no longer engages the minds of freshmen in the way that it once did. For the most part, the course now patently fails to liberate or enlighten, and so must be judged wanting by the measure of its own ideals. What explains this decline?

The answer lies in what everyone knows about higher education—that its expansion over the last twenty years has brought to the academy many students who have no great interest in traditional subjects (mathematics and languages, for example), and whose pre-college experience has not given them the "socialization" necessary for playing the academic game according to the traditional rules. Students these days do not defer readily to the ivory-tower fantasies of professors, nor are they willing to endure the psychological punishment of working for grades under great competitive pressure. Expansion, however, is not alone the cause of these changes. The truth of the matter is that our postindustrial culture has produced a new kind of student, one who, as we have been told at length by Charles Reich and others, possesses a new "consciousness."

Persons outside the academy may not be aware of it, but this new student is really not very much like the one imagined by the counterculturalists or the promoters of the Pepsi generation. He is in many ways like the student of old: he reads sparingly, has little independence, and doesn't take professors or academic work very seriously. Yet he *is* different. His difference, however, does not lie in his having an acute sense of social justice, or in being "involved." It lies, rather, in his deepest attitudes toward learning, which are the result of the persistent influence on him of the Saturday-morning cartoons, rock, megalopolis, limited war, and the popular celebration of the anarchic individualism implied in the notion of "doing your own thing." Not one of the institutions by which society preserves and transmits its beliefs about what is good and bad, beautiful and unbeautiful, important and trivial, real and unreal—not school, church, family, or body politic—has escaped the dissolving acids of pop culture. And not one any longer has the power of putting the young in a moral state sufficiently plastic to receive the imprint of traditional Western values—above all, respect for the *vita contemplativa.* It is having gone through childhood and adolescence in such circumstances, and not his possession of virtues unknown in any earlier generation, that makes the new student truly new.

These are the general facts which must be kept in view when trying to assess the contribution of Western Civ to the undergraduate curriculum. They show the need for a criterion of fitness to receive instruction in Western Civ—perhaps an "index of receptivity," akin to the notion of "reading readiness" by which teachers measure the aptitudes of preschool children. We lack such an index, but direct experience leads me to believe that the receptivity of the ordinary Western Civ student is minimal.

This low receptivity appears to have three causes. The most important of them is that many students lack even the rudiments of the kind of *experience* which would ready their minds for the study of Western culture, or even put them in sympathy with the project. They have read almost nothing; they are completely unaccustomed to talking about subjects of general interest—that is, about politics, morals, and religion; and they have been to high schools where the typical attitudes of students, teacher, and administrators alike generate indifference to things intellectual.

The real difficulty, however, has nothing to do with lack of intellect. It lies deeper: scarcely anything in their backgrounds gives these students a beginning purchase on the ideas which are the stuff of Western Civ. They are, for example, unable to make any sense of ancient conceptions of immortality, because they themselves have had no experience of religion. The meaning of an idea like ethics— conceived of as an inquiry about rational standards of conduct— eludes them because they have never before heard these matters discussed. They are embarrassed, ill at ease, and defensive when asked to express themselves on the nature of the gods, the meaning of justice, or the differences between *eros* and *agape,* because they have no foundation, no substratum of familiar impressions in which such ideas may be anchored. Any discussion of them is therefore a perilous venture into unknown and forbidding territory.

If the first cause of low receptivity in the new student is that he brings hardly any pertinent experiences to the study of Western culture, the second is that he frequently does bring to it a pronounced subjectivism. He appears settled in his belief that whatever is worth knowing about the past can be understood in *his* terms, as something "happening now." This attitude can become a powerful force, drawing Western Civ discussions toward banality, inanity, and just plain falsehood. Desiring to maintain a dialogue, and frustrated in the attempt to awaken the student to continuities, to the essential sameness of the human situation in every age, the professor finds himself yielding to the vagrant notions which naturally present themselves to minds locked in the present: Yes, Antigone could be seen as an antiwar activist; yes, Homer was a male chauvinist; yes, Augustine took up Christianity because he was a burnt-out case; and yes, *Love Story* may one day be seen as a classic comparable to the legend of Tristan and Iseult.

This habit of subjectivity, this acute concern with self and now, has not been accidentally acquired. On the contrary, it owes everything to the pedagogy of the lower schools, whose teachers—eager to make education open, nonlinear, cool, ecstatic—have for twenty years placed the highest value on "creativeness." Too often, this has meant giving a maximum of praise to work requiring a minimum of talent and effort; and it seems to have produced large numbers of students who are anxious for "payoffs" and irritable at any delay in getting them, who have little ability to wait while an idea unfolds, and who want the "right answer," without the tinsel of nuances or qualifications. It has produced, in short, students who are impatient. The slow, cautious pursuit of a subject is for them a kind of torture, and they are eager to steer discussions into the murky channels of "rapping" where there is no need to be consequent or coherent.

Antipathy to being in college at all is the third cause of low receptivity. No one can say how many, but a significant number of students sitting in classes do not want to be there. Oppressive circumstance, they feel, has thrust upon them a role they have no desire to play. It is true they come to college "voluntarily," but so did the draft-deferred students of a few years ago. This parallel is instructive: it was when government and academy began to collaborate in presenting college as a lesser evil than military service that the I'm-forced-to-be-here attitude became a respected undergraduate posture. The draft is gone, but, on the view that severe social penalties attach to not possessing the B.A. degree, many students persist in believing themselves unreasonably and unjustly compelled to spend four years fretting over units, grades, and requirements. To such students, Western Civ, though it may technically be an elective, is something imposed. Naturally, they resent having this burden forced on them, and therefore despise instruction.

All of this leads to uneasiness among professors, to a feeling that something ought to be done. Some hold the view that Western Civ should concern itself less with teaching books and ideas than with trying to be a "meaningful experience" for those taking the course. Purely academic goals, it is said, should be placed second to the purpose of creating lifestyles; and the professor should try to "share the consciousness" of the student, to help him discover "where he is at." It indeed appears that attempts at consciousness-sharing are being made. This is manifest in some small ways—for example, in the popularity of certain styles of professorial dress (painstakingly unconventional, occasionally groovy) and in ceremonious informalities like eschewing the classroom for circles on the greensward.

But a much more important attempt to share consciousness is to be seen in the giving of new twists to some old Western Civ themes. Since 1914, the decadence of the West has been taken for granted: machine civilization gone mad, dehumanization, the triviality of modern existence, incoherence in art, Prufrockism, the advent of mass man. One way of sharing consciousness is to connect these ideas with what currently agitates (or is supposed to agitate) the student mind—ecology, the population bomb, the evils of war and technocracy, the corruptions of "the system." Because ours is a time fatally attracted to simplisms, these concerns are easily merged with an outright indictment of science and technology. Quintessential expressions of the Western spirit, they are (it is said) a kind of moral insanity, the very substance of *hubris*. From this general thesis derives the dismal corollary that science and technology have no claim on the respect of intelligent and compassionate beings; and a critique of Western culture becomes an attack on reason as such. Hardly anyone asks whether these updatings of traditional themes are of any real help to the student in his effort to understand the world as it is, or even as we might wish it to be.

Unhappily (or happily, if one thinks them foolish and harmful) even the most heroic efforts at consciousness-sharing are not likely to engage the student's attention for long. This is because they are so patently inauthentic. Those who make such efforts may, however, take some comfort in the thought that the failure is not really theirs. It is just that the new student, as is said in an interesting corruption of the idiom, "could care less" about the similarities between Dante's descent into hell and an acid-trip, the anticipation in 19th-century romantic poetry of our soulless technocratic order, or a Western Civ discussion section being run as an encounter group. The truth is that such things bore him.

I am aware that these are sweeping judgments. To keep them in perspective, two points must be remembered. First, what I have said here rests on experiences at a large, public university and may apply with only diminished force, or not at all, to "elite" schools. Second, even under the least favorable conditions, there are *some* students whose receptivity to Western Civ is high and who greatly benefit from taking the course. When these things have been said, however, a salient question remains: Why should large numbers of students whose circumstances have not inspired in them a taste for reading, writing, and dialectics, or inclined them to Western Civ as "their thing," have such a course pushed on them? The question is fair and pertinent. It is not enough to reply that "the thing" in college is reading, writing, and dialectics, and that those who have no liking for them ought not to be students at all. This answer may sound entirely reasonable to traditionalists, but it addresses a world that does not exist.

No amount of wishful thinking will alter the fact that for twenty years or more, school counselors, governments at every level, and all the engines of publicity have labored to fix in everyone's mind the idea that the B.A. degree is an *economic* good. In consequence, it has actually become one; and because habits of thought die hard, many will continue to see it in this way even if (as now appears to have happened) the bottom drops out of the academic market. Besides, rational motives have long since given way to faith in schooling as the sovereign means whereby young men and women may "find" themselves. Going to college has become a rite of passage into the middle class, and as befits such a rite, our beliefs about it partake generously of myth. The *idea* of higher education, like the idea of passionate love, belongs to the fabric of our hopes: only those who have it can know true happiness. What else could be the reason that, by thousands, young people for whom reading and writing are distasteful chores sentence themselves to years of painful labor? Or that even those who rebel must set up their free universities, as though life were intolerable without the mediation of courses?

To see things in this light is to see that many students are driven by a powerful and irrational need "to be in school," and that there is therefore a strong element of truth in the claims of those who say society compels them to go to college. It is also to understand anew the prevailing demands for "relevance" in higher education. For all the cloudiness that has surrounded this notion, its plain meaning can only be that what students submit to in the classroom somehow connects with their self-chosen purposes and interests. Studying motorcycle mechanics is relevant to the racing of motorcycles and a course in mountaineering is relevant to seeing the world from conquered peaks. One who wants to do these things will without complaint suffer the trials of preparation and even find pleasure in them. But the key term is *wants:* if there is no wanting, there is no relevance, because there is nothing that teaching or learning can be relevant to. By this understanding of the term, Western Civ is the very prototype of irrelevance, for it serves no purposes which multitudes of those taking it recognize as their own.

Is Western Civ a waste of time? It probably is, except for a small minority of undergraduates. And because it would no longer *be* Western Civ if cut loose from its traditional moorings in talking, reading, and writing about the great books, there is no reform which could fit it to the needs of the day. This comes very close to saying that liberal education—the attempt to supply undergraduates with a common fund of (mainly) humanistic learning—is an enterprise which has seen its time. Its purpose was always to hold some small portion of the field against the narrowness and selfishness of the specialized disciplines, and, on the whole, it performed this task well. Liberal education could never quite be made to yield to the dominant ideals of organization and expertise; it has at last been slain by the arrival in force of students whose hopes, experiences, and states of mind it cannot touch.

Academic people are always talking about revolution. Indeed there has been a revolution, and its most important result is to be seen in the now established obligation of the academy to serve great numbers of those whom K. Patricia Cross calls the "new learners," students "who want to learn how to *do* things—as opposed to how to think about things." Perhaps, as Professor Cross suggests in her article, "The New Learners," *Change* (February 1973), "We might do well to give up our preoccupation with correcting the 'deficiencies' of New Students and concentrate instead on developing the new range of talents and interests that they bring to higher education." What seems beyond dispute is that the new student does not want his "cultural heritage" imposed on him; and under such conditions it is worse than folly to try to impose it. Our arrival at this pass may bring joy to some hearts and despair to others, but there is no turning back. And who cannot see that the road ahead is far different from the one already travelled?

No Possum, No Sop, No Taters: or, a Lack of Cash and a Failure of Nerve

O. B. HARDISON
Folger Shakespeare Library

I have borrowed the title of a poem by Wallace Stevens for this essay because it expresses, with saving irony, the current situation of the humanities in America. It is not a unique situation. Throughout our history, our attitudes toward the humanities have been ambivalent. We have ridiculed the humanities as useless, trivial, affected—even un-American—distractions from the real business of life. At the same time, we have accepted them as the basis of general education and as the core subjects around which the undergraduate curriculum should be organized.

Often the hostility and the respect have been curiously mingled. American innocents have never tired of making fun of the culture they found abroad, but neither have they ceased going abroad. And the same businessmen who have announced from the board room and the golf course that culture is a waste of time have, for the

From O. B. Hardison, *Toward Freedom and Dignity* (Baltimore: The Johns Hopkins University Press, 1972), pp. 3–27. © 1972 by The Johns Hopkins University Press. Reprinted with permission.

past century, been sending their sons to Harvard, Yale, and Princeton at great expense to learn French and German and read the classics from Plato to Kafka.

Today, however, the situation of the humanities is especially precarious. There are several reasons for this. Since the nineteenth century the standing of the humanities in relation to other disciplines has been declining. As new disciplines have emerged and older ones like physics and economics have expanded, the humanities have been pushed from the center to the side and even to the periphery of the curriculum.

More recently, the disruptions that began on the campus and in the city in 1965 had the effect of concentrating national attention on social issues. While the humanities continued to languish, showers of saint-seducing gold were rained on programs of social action. Concern for social problems also had its effect within the humanities. Traditional programs were attacked as irrelevant to current needs, and new ones, intended to meet the challenge of relevance, were introduced. In spite of some healthy reforms, the net effect has been widespread confusion and a deepening sense of futility among professional humanists.

While the humanities were still trying to adjust to the creed of relevance, the recession that began in 1969 changed the ground rules of American education. Everyone has suffered from the recession, but the humanities have been particularly vulnerable. With the replacement of educational philosophy by cost accounting, small classes have been eliminated, average class size has grown, research funds have been cut, and whole departments have disappeared with no other epitaph than "They didn't pay their way."

Given this situation, what is the future of the humanities? Are they relics of a pretechnocratic age? Vestigial organs that will atrophy as society evolves toward newer and presumably higher forms? Are they impediments to progress that should be demolished root and branch? Or do they represent a heritage so important that to lose it would be to lose the very qualities that make men greater than the systems they devise and mark the difference between a society of robots and a community of civilized human beings?

These questions are large and abstract. But they have immediate practical consequences. Our answers affect national policy, the allocation of government and private funds, the shape of the curriculum from kindergarten to graduate school, and ultimately, the shape of our culture. Should we train students broadly or narrowly—for life, as the progressive educators have it, or for jobs? Should education be understood as the assimilation of information—in which case, mass lectures, standardized testing, performance contracts, and a

"national video university" would be acceptable? Or should education be understood as the assimilation of values—in which case the
new English primary schools described in the Plowden Report of
1967, with their emphasis on small groups and intrapersonal relationships, might be a model? To turn from social policy to people,
since a student must choose among many courses and taking one
course means not taking another, should he be advised to register for
Shakespeare or Urban Sociology, a seminar in Plato or an introduction to computer programming? Will a future lawyer benefit more
from studying north Italian painting of the Renaissance or Keynesian
economic theory? A doctor from *Hamlet* or differential equations?
These are real choices. Over a period of four years they add up to the
kind of education a student receives and, by extension, to the values
that he takes from the academy into society.

In 1964 the Commission on the Humanities, a group sponsored
by the American Council of Learned Societies that included several
of the most distinguished American humanists then active, issued
the report that led to the establishment of the National Endowments
for the Arts and Humanities. The report included the following statement:

> During our early history we were largely occupied in mastering the
> physical environment. No sooner was the mastery within sight than ad-
> vancing technology opened up a new range of possibilities, putting a
> new claim on energies which might otherwise have gone into humane
> and artistic endeavor. The result has often been that our social, moral,
> and aesthetic development lagged behind our material advance. . . .
> The state of the humanities today creates a crisis for national leader-
> ship. While it offers cultural opportunities of the greatest value to the
> United States and to mankind, it holds at the same time a danger that
> wavering purpose and lack of well-conceived effort may leave us sec-
> ond-best in a world correspondingly impoverished by our incomplete
> success.

Today these words have a quaintness that we normally associate with kerosene lamps and Smith Brothers Cough Drops. Evidently, the members of the Commission harbored no doubts about
the basic soundness of the humanities. The chief problem was financial and the ingenious solution they hit upon was government
money. More money would presumably do the same thing for the
humanities that the National Science Foundation had done for the
sciences after Sputnik. In the academy this would mean more
courses, more teachers, more research, and of course, more influence. In society it would mean more artists, more dance companies
and orchestras, more theater companies, and more libraries. Everybody would be edified. Our "social, moral, and aesthetic development" would catch up to our material progress, and we would no

longer have to worry about being second-best or about our incomplete success contributing to international cultural deprivation.

The Commission was undoubtedly on the side of the angels and as American as cherry pie in proposing to solve its problems with government money, but it was wrong in assuming that the humanities were basically sound. Since 1965 they have been criticized and attacked from every conceivable angle. Apprehensions over their soundness are evident in the debate over teaching versus research and its cousin the publish-or-perish controversy; in the popularity of cost accounting, accountability, and performance contracts; in the appearance of "store-front schools," "free universities" and work-study programs based on the premise that the official curriculum is sterile and elitist; and in unprecedented—and unprecedentedly popular—experimentation with new courses, new degree requirements, new methods, and new subject categories cutting across previously impenetrable departmental barriers.

This turbulence is obviously not simply an educational problem. The academy has no control whatever over the growth of knowledge. Yet knowledge has grown geometrically since the beginning of the twentieth century. As the curriculum has expanded to keep up with this growth, the relative standing of the humanities has declined. In the period between 1901 and 1910, 28 percent of all Bachelor's degrees were in the humanities. In 1951–53 the figure had fallen to 15 percent. The corresponding decline in Doctoral degrees was from 33 to 16 percent. Thus, while absolute enrollment in the humanities has increased, the humanities have been steadily losing ground to other disciplines.

The loss per se is not especially worrisome. There is no reason why every college student should major in English or philosophy, just as there is no reason why a chemistry student should not appreciate (and even take courses in) literature or music or fine art. Along with the loss in status, however, has come an increasing tendency to question the idea of education posed by the humanities.

For the present I will refer to this idea as "general education." As recently as thirty years ago general education provided the rationale for the college preparatory track of the high schools and the first two years of undergraduate studies. Typically, it involved extensive work in English, foreign languages, and history, together with mathematics and a scattering of basic courses in the sciences. Only after an extended period of generalized study was the student allowed to proceed to a major. Often it was argued that students should not specialize at all, since education should prepare them for a variety of responsibilities rather than for a single vocation.

Memories of this tradition linger on. We read in the preamble of the catalogue of an exclusive New England college:

Whatever the form of experience . . . intellectual competence and awareness of problems are the goal of the program, rather than direct preparation for some profession.

Morris B. Abram, former President of Brandeis University, explains the ideal in a speech given at Davidson College:

Higher liberal education has, I believe, one primary and proper function: to teach those students who have the capacity and desire to learn from books *how* to learn. An education which accomplishes this in the student equipped for and desiring it is, I submit, always and thoroughly relevant. It provides the so-educated man or woman with the skills to make the learning relevant.

An example: At the outbreak of World War II, Oliver Franks, later Ambassador to the United States, was a tutor of moral philosophy at Queens College, Oxford. He was called from that post to become Permanent Secretary of the Ministry of Supply—the head of British war production industries.

What qualified him for the position was not any special training; it was, rather, having the mind, character, and ability to learn—in this case something as far afield from moral philosophy as the management of British industry.

Although the memories linger, the design has faded. The old courses and departments have been joined by a host of new courses and departments in fields like political science, anthropology, economics, sociology, public health, psychology, and city planning, to name the obvious ones. Many of these were not even listed in college catalogues thirty years ago. Our cultural perspective has also broadened. The original general education curriculum seldom strayed beyond the limits of Western culture. Today we think in terms of world culture rather than national culture, and in terms of the relation of disciplines rather than their separation. Meanwhile, the system of allocating the first two years of college to general studies and the last two to specialization, together with the network of requirements that prevented early concentration, has dissolved. Junior colleges tend to stress vocational training, and four-year colleges vacillate between the extreme of no requirements and the opposite extreme of permitting major work to begin during the freshman year. Instead of producing a more coherent curriculum, the demise of general education has left a vacuum. Shortly before the semester begins at a typical American college the student is presented with a catalogue listing hundreds of different courses. If he is lucky he may be able to arrange a fifteen-minute conference with a harried faculty adviser. If not, he does the best he can on his own. The humanities, in other words, no longer provide a core around which higher education—or even a two-year segment of it—is organized. Instead, they are one of a number of special-interest groups competing for programs, courses, students, and money.

Recent national and international events are as far beyond the control of the academy as the growth of knowledge. Yet these events also generate pressures that affect the curriculum. Most obviously, the pressure of events resulted, after Sputnik and the urban riots, in lavish financing of the sciences and social sciences. Administrators who paid lip service to the value of the humanities paid hard cash to attract faculty members whose work fell "within the national interest," to quote the magic phrase. This does not mean that the administrators were Philistines or hypocrites, merely that they were not free agents. They necessarily based their decisions on committee recommendations and money. As the number of humanists on their committees dwindled, the priorities of the committees changed. As for money, until very recently a faculty member whose work was in the national interest was an investment. He could usually raise more than he was paid, and the money he raised bought more facilities, more students, and more faculty members who, in turn, sat on the committees that made curriculum recommendations. The circle was not vicious because it was not consciously antihumanistic, but it was undeniably circular.

In 1960, the President's Advisory Committee on Science warned:

> While the report centers on the needs of science, we repudiate emphatically any notion that science research and scientific education are the only kinds of learning that matter in America. . . . Even in the interests of science itself it is essential to give full value to the other great branches of man's artistic, literary, and scholarly activity. The advancement of science must not be accomplished by the impoverishment of anything else.

Alas, during the New Frontier and the Great Society there was little time to ponder this warning. Congress supported the Peace Corps, the Job Corps, the Teacher Corps, the Space Program, the Model Cities Program, Medicare, the War on Poverty, and a whole alphabet of crash programs under the Department of Health, Education and Welfare. Typically, when the humanities were involved in these federal initiatives the programs were action-oriented. There was scant sympathy for the "artistic, literary, and scholarly activities" mentioned by the President's Committee. Within the government, the only bright spots in an otherwise bleak picture are the National Endowments for the Arts and the Humanities. As for the private sector, the major foundations have had their moments of generosity, but the pattern of their grants has resembled that of the federal government, with emphasis on international relations, minority problems, and the difficulties of the inner city.

The distortions introduced by lopsided funding have been exaggerated by human frailty. During the flush period of outside money, administrators often fell into the trap of competing for grants regardless of how they were to be used. Programs were created ad hoc or, alternately, they were sold to the academy by foundation hucksters dazzled by their personal theories of what was relevant or innovative or simply newsworthy. As the financial tide ebbed, many of these jury-rigged programs collapsed, and the colleges have been left to pick up the pieces. Since professors have tenure and hardware must be maintained even though nobody uses it, colleges have had to use operating funds to cover the cost of past venality. Institutional priorities have been warped to fit the realities of the budget. In contests between the Comptroller and the Dean of Humanities, it goes without saying who has usually won.

Confused by these excursions and alarums, students may be pardoned for failing to insist on the value of the humanities, and within the past few years there has been a shift away from them in favor of the more obviously "relevant" curricula of the social sciences. The out-migration has been accelerated by the disappearance of the entrance and degree requirements that made general education work. Foreign languages have been the chief immediate victims, but in the long run all studies that depend on the use of more than one language—and this includes most advanced studies in the humanities—will suffer.* Foreign languages were once officially considered "in the national interest." In spite of former government and foundation support and a great deal of pious rhetoric, we have evidently now concluded that they are a personal rather than a social concern.

If we turn from the political and social context within which the humanities exist to the humanities themselves, it is clear that outer pressures are complemented by inner stresses. Some of these are as old as education itself. Others—the most disturbing—are new.

Here, a little perspective will be useful. Educational philosophy has historically moved in three quite distinct directions. I will call these liberal, vocational, and aesthetic. Since I will be discussing them again later in this book I will limit myself to a brief sketch of each.

Liberal education goes back to the Renaissance, which in turn derived it from Greek and Roman sources. It was originally a curriculum for grammar schools rather than universities (which were un-

---

* Foreign language enrollments fell from 17.6 percent of all college enrollments in 1965 to 12.6 percent in 1970 and have continued to decline since then, while between 1965 and 1970 about 45 percent of American colleges abolished or reduced their foreign language requirements according to a survey by Richard Brod in the September 1971 issue of the ADFL *Bulletin.*

known before the Middle Ages), and the term "liberal" refers to the fact that this sort of education was considered appropriate for members of a particular social class, free citizens in contrast to slaves. Renaissance humanists made liberal education the basis of their curriculum because they wanted to create an intellectual elite. The Renaissance ideal of the *uòmo universale*—the man conversant with all aspects of his world—led them to stress general rather than specialized education, and the ideal of *mens sana in corpore sano*—a sound mind in a sound body—led them to insist that physical exercise, from wrestling and fencing to dancing, be a part of the curriculum. These ideas are still with us today—in the concept of *litterae humaniores*, the classics of literature, history, and philosophy that underlie the "great books" courses once common on American campuses, as well as in the physical education courses through which most of us suffered during freshman and sophomore years.

The most frequent explanation for liberal education, whether in the Renaissance or the twentieth century, is that it produces the ethical values and mental disciplines, necessary for leadership. (Recall Oliver Franks's exemplary ascent from a professorship of moral philosophy to the Ministry of Supply.) At its best, liberal education is an effort to live up to Plato's ideal in *The Laws*: "If you want to know what is the good in general of education the answer is easy: education produces good men and good men act nobly." In practice, the concern with ethics and leadership involves compromises. Liberal education typically thinks of leadership within the established order, and its modern strongholds have been establishment universities—Oxbridge in England and the Ivy League in America. It tends therefore to be conservative. Whatever its values, however, whether conservative or leftist, the more they are stressed the more liberal education tends to become a form of indoctrination. The subjects studied—in particular the liberal arts—become less important than the ideology they are used to convey.

Second, there is vocational education. Vocational education is as old as the apprentice system. It was institutionalized in the wake of the industrial revolution. According to the vocationists, liberal education is elitist. It is a gentleman's game. It does nothing to train people for jobs or to promote the greatest good for the greatest number. The proper task of education is to create economically useful skills. It helps people earn their livings, or to look at it from another angle, it provides recruits for expanding industries. Those with limited talents should be educated in trade schools, while the more promising should attend universities to be trained as engineers, chemists, physicians, architects, lawyers, and business executives. The legacy of this philosophy is evident in the United States in vocational schools, in the system of college majors oriented toward socially desirable skills, and in polytechnic universities, with MIT, Cal Tech, and VPI among the obvious examples.

Third, there is aesthetic education. I use the term for lack of a better one; in later chapters I will refer to it simply as humanistic education. The aesthetic point of view regards the experience of the individual as an absolute. It does not attempt to instill any particular ideology, nor is it interested in the economic utility of what is learned. Insofar as it has a curriculum it tends to emphasize the humanities. Its distinctive feature is not subject matter but its attitude toward subject matter. Beauty is its own excuse for being, and poetry makes nothing happen, but happens, itself, in a way that is important to the reader. From this point of view, the central value of education should be the freedom of the individual and the enlargement and enrichment of his inner life.

These three philosophies of education exist today in innumerable mixtures and variations. In general, the advocates of liberal education and the vocationists agree on a basic issue: the humanities exist to be used. If they neither teach an ideology nor create job skills they are not worth the effort. This is the opposite of the aesthetic position, which regards the humanities as self-justifying ends. You do not read *Macbeth* to learn about the evils of ambition and hence become a better committeeman or a less pushy second vice president. You read *Macbeth* because the experience is worthwhile. It is better in an absolute sense to have read *Macbeth* than not to have read it.

This brings us back to the pressure of events. If recent events have pressed in on the academy from the outside, they have also affected those within the academy. As demands for direct social action have become more urgent, there has been a loss of direction among humanists that is essentially a loss of confidence in the humanities as self-justifying ends. The burden of the complaint is that the humanities—or the humanities as taught—make no direct contribution to civil rights or ending the war in Viet Nam or the class struggle or Women's Liberation or whatever happens to be the cause of the moment.

In a widely publicized article in the March 1966 issue of *Harper's* magazine entitled "The Shame of the Graduate Schools," William Arrowsmith calls humanistic education "pathetically wanting— timid, unimaginative, debased, inefficient, futile." He adds that "the humanists have betrayed their subject" because they have permitted or encouraged a "gulf between one's studies and one's life, between what we read and how we live." If the times demand action, the argument runs, let the humanists become activist too. If they fail to do so they are escapist and irresponsible—"debased, inefficient, futile."

As the times have become more critical, the summons to action has become louder and the denunciations more vitriolic. For Louis Kampf, a former President of the Modern Language Association of America, Arrowsmith's "shame" has become an "open scandal." In "The Scandal of Literary Scholarship" published in *Harper's* of December 1967, Mr. Kampf announces the demise of his profession with grim satisfaction:

> Of the death of academic literary study as a serious enterprise few seem to be aware. Yet in spite of appearances to the contrary, it is a fact. . . . As one looks at the body it wriggles and twitches. . . . A closer examination reveals an army of vermin in frantic development.

Like Arrowsmith, Kampf demands a payoff from humanistic study:

> Today the idea of independent scholarship is a mask for the commercial activities of the academic bureaucracy. . . . If literary scholarship is to have an effect it must be committed to an end. . . . Commitment to what? Surely not to imprinting a static literary tradition on the minds of victims trapped in a classroom, nor to instilling in them a servile admiration for the glories of the past. Our devotion to criticism demands a willingness to destroy received dogmas, to rid ourselves of the deadening burden of history.

And again:

> For my students to react fully to the *Dunciad* . . . it may be more important for them to consult Marx's work on the cultural effects of Capitalism than Aubrey Williams' useful study of the poem's literary context; the former will channel their aesthetic perceptions into social understanding and (perhaps) action; the latter, into literary analysis.

Kampf's disdain for literary analysis leads to another point. The zeal aroused by the pressure of events has turned many humanists against themselves and their subjects. Fifty years ago, Irving Babbit, in many ways the finest literary critic of his generation, was led by his political conservatism to condemn the major French writers of the nineteenth century—among others, Victor Hugo, Baudelaire, Verlaine, and Balzac. Kampf's equally fervent Marxism leads him to reject the main tendencies of twentieth-century literature:

> The narcissistic obsession of modern literature for the self, the critical cant concerning the tragic isolation of the individual—these are notions which tie our hands and keep us from the communion necessary for meaningful action.

If these remarks seem extreme, they are no more so than a comment by Seymour Krim in *The New York Times Book Review* of April 14, 1968, which typifies both the attitude and the rhetoric of activism. Commenting on W. H. Auden's line "poetry makes nothing happen," Krim writes:

Mr. Eliot and Headmaster Auden want to stick [literature] under glass or in the freezer, in the over-civilized conceit that it is too good for action out in the riot-torn cities. . . . Perhaps the entire balance of our country and the new values we need to redeem ourselves as a once-decent people hinge on great and vengeful words that are also art.

The extent to which these attitudes have permeated the humanities is illustrated by statements made at a meeting of chairmen of English departments by John Fisher, Secretary from 1961 to 1971 of the largest organization of humanists in the United States. In 1969 Fisher told the chairmen that English departments are "inextricably bound in with an elitist principle" and that if this elitist principle is not accepted "the English department may be worse than useless. It may be the dead hand of the past inhibiting the development of the attitudes and ideas of a new society." He added, "The subject of English in this country has been used to inculcate a white, Anglo-Saxon, Protestant ethic. . . . My own feeling is that the game is just about played out." This is not the opinion of a political radical who accidentally blundered into teaching literature, but of a moderate and respected scholar who, at the time he expressed it, had been official spokesman for 30,000 humanists for eight years.

There is nothing new about the kind of anti-intellectualism that reduces all value judgments to questions of ideology. It is as old as Plato's decision to ban Homer from his ideal Republic because of Homer's impure religious and moral attitudes. It is unpleasant but harmless when expressed by a private individual. It is more disturbing when it is expressed by the chief officer of a major professional society, since it can hardly fail to demoralize half of his followers and turn the other half into instant Jeremiahs. When upheld by a powerful organization like the state, it becomes dangerous. It is the standard justification for censorship, the persecution of dissident artists, and the banality of official themes and styles. It has been invoked regularly to justify the imprisonment, exile, and execution of artists in totalitarian and Communist states; it has been invoked sporadically but often viciously in the United States, as, for example, in the persecution of leftist artists during the McCarthy period or the recent refusal by the American Academy of Arts and Sciences to award Ezra Pound a prize for literary achievement recommended by the Academy's own Committee on awards.

In spite of this fact, and in spite of the object lesson provided by the plight of Russian artists and the fatuity of official art, whether of the right or the left, the demand for relevance is widespread. Pursuits that do not promise immediate social benefits are unpopular. The effects of the external pressures on the humanities are thus magnified by the antihumanistic polemics of the humanists themselves.

So much for the possum and the sop. When we come to the

taters we encounter two additional problems—the multiplication of humanities courses and methodologies. For now, I will merely observe that a curriculum with a limited number of courses, few electives, and interdisciplinary reinforcement—so that, for example, a basic history course is coordinated with a basic literature course—may not be ideal but it is at least coherent. As course offerings multiply, coordination becomes increasingly difficult. A student spends more and more time on less and less. His courses, even within his major, become isolated and unrelated. Eventually it becomes possible to ask whether the program itself is not a myth; or whether, granted its existence, it adds up to anything worthwhile.

As for methodology, over the years the humanities have accumulated an almost embarrassing number of methods, but no single method has turned up that will answer all or even most of the questions that humanists like to ask. Faced with the options of philology, historical criticism, comparative criticism, *Quellengeschichte*, stylistics, genre theory, structuralism, contextualism, myth criticism, Freudian analysis, the sociology of literature, and phenomenology, to name only a few possibilities, most humanists are inclined to sympathize with the advice given by Henry James to a young man who asked him how one writes good novels: "Be very intelligent." To James's intelligence I would add a second criterion—sensitivity—if the two are not really different sides of the same coin.

But intelligence and sensitivity are not enough for critics of the humanities who want a single foolproof method and an objective way of measuring the payoff. At times almost everyone has gotten into this act with results ranging from high comedy to tragedy. An attractive and, in some ways, a very conservative critique is offered by Professor W. O. Maxwell in an article in the March 1968 issue of the *Bulletin* of the American Association of University Professors entitled "The Methodological Plight of the Humanities." Professor Maxwell asks:

> What is the nature of the link between the subject matter of the humanities and the goals they espouse? I suggest we don't know, and that from that fact stems, in large measure, the plight of the humanities.
> . . . Because of this methodological gap, research in the humanities lacks purpose and direction. . . . there are no set criteria with which to judge the method used in research of its results, so that much of this research is not cumulative.

And a little later:

> The . . . gap between the humanities and the goals of the humanities limits the ways in which curricula . . . can develop. . . . We cannot objectively specify the subject matters, mastery of which furthers these goals more than other subject matters.

Apostles of accountability to the contrary, a sympathetic student of the humanities might regard Maxwell's comments as the beginning of wisdom. He has stated an important truth about the humanities and specified quite clearly what they cannot do. But Maxwell is an adversary, not an advocate. From his point of view the humanities should have specific goals, a method for reaching these goals, and a way of measuring whether they have or have not been attained. What he fails to see is that for humanistic study his criteria are a liability. Any attempt to establish objective goals—as against subjective and individual ones—leads the humanities back in the direction of Irving Babbitt and Louis Kampf—to the elitist values of the right or the Marxist *Dunciad;* that is, to orthodoxy as the test of artistic excellence and propaganda in place of teaching.

In a way, this happens to Professor Maxwell. After debating with himself, he decides that the goals of the humanities should be wisdom and judgment. Wisdom and judgment are certainly good things. It is as hard to quarrel with them as it is (or used to be) to quarrel with motherhood. They recall the ethical values traditionally associated with liberal education. Whether or not they can be measured is beside the point since Professor Maxwell stipulates that the humanities can produce or at least augment them. "It is not denied," he writes, "that reading Chaucer makes one wiser . . . that a detailed knowledge of Bismarck would give our leaders enhanced ability to make decisions on national policy."

The point is that if it is not denied it ought to be. Reading Chaucer's "Miller's Tale" is undoubtedly fun. The reader learns a little about sex in the Middle Ages and a great deal about Chaucer's artistry, but surely he does not come away any wiser than he was before. Conceivably, he may become a little more foolish. By the same token, a biography of Bismarck will teach you something about Germany in the nineteenth century and more than you may want to know about the great Chancellor of Blood and Iron. But your judgment will probably remain unaffected. If it is affected, it may well be for the worse. I am told that Hermann Goering was an avid student of Bismarck. If his reading affected his judgment, it is at least arguable that he would have been better off with "The Miller's Tale."

The demand for simple goals and a pat methodology is a disguised form of the urge of liberal educators and vocationists to put the humanities to some practical use. From the point of view of the humanities themselves, to admit the validity of this impulse is to deny the basic values of humanistic experience—the free play of the mind and its corollary, an expanded sense of the self and its relation to the world. To deny these values would, indeed, be a problem, but it is a problem that disappears as soon as we accept the fact that neither the imagination nor works of imagination can be fitted neatly into the various abstract categories devised to explain them.

The humanities exist because they are native to the human soil. If they were banished today by government decree, they would eventually reappear. In fact, they always are reappearing, Proteus-like, in unexpected forms. The impulse to create large and harmonious forms that is manifested in the Gothic cathedral survives in the twentieth century in Paolo Solari's architectural fantasies. More practically, the universal human need for sculptured form emerges with astonishing force, if not always happy results, in the myriad shapes of the modern automobile, while as legitimate theater becomes a subdominant cultural form, it is replaced by cinema. To paraphrase Horace, if you push Nature out the front door, She comes in at the back.

On the other hand, the fact that the human spirit is resilient does not mean that the contemporary problems of the humanities are trivial. Societies can be life-enhancing or hostile to the free development of the spirit. The difficulties of the humanities within the academy are symptomatic of an illness that pervades modern society. As the role of the humanities in education diminishes, their potential contribution to society diminishes. I mean their potential contribution to the life of each individual and their potential contribution to the culture that is the summation of the lives of all individuals within the society.

NEO-POSITIVISM, EDUCATIONAL TECHNOLOGISM, AND THE TECHNOCRATIC REVOLUTION

The traditional distinction comes down to this: when we know what we are doing, we are training; when we do not know what we are doing, we are teaching. Once we have taken the important first step and specified what we want the student to do as the result of having been taught, we can begin to teach in ways with respect to which this outworn distinction is meaningless. In doing so we need not abandon any of our goals. We must simply define them. Any behavior which can be specified can be programmed.
B. F. Skinner

The student of the future will truly be an explorer, a researcher, a huntsman who ranges through the new educational world of electric circuitry and heightened human interaction just as the tribal huntsman ranged the wilds.
Marshall McLuhan

Our schools are, in a sense, factories in which the raw products (children) are to be shaped and fashioned into products to meet the various demands of life. The specifications for manufacturing come from the demands of twentieth-century civilization, and it is the business of the school to build its pupils according to the specifications laid down.
Elwood P. Cubberly

INTRODUCTION

Even the most casual observer of modern educational developments cannot fail to note how reform movements seem to follow an invariant and wholly predictable sequence, in well-defined successive stages of advancement. Initially the impetus for change comes with a wholesale indictment of education for its alleged failings and shortcomings. Critics denounce the schools because they fail to teach basic skills and ignore important cognitive learning. Or, it is said, schools badly neglect the affective, moral, and spiritual needs of learners. Others assert that the educational system needs to be reformed because it operates in a social vacuum, oblivious to its responsibility for meeting trained manpower needs and achieving pressing national goals. Or the system is rotten to the core because it serves as an inhuman screening, sorting, and selection mechanism for slots within the socio-organizational hierarchy. Whatever the reasons, schools are condemned as unrelievedly bad. Nothing less than a total, comprehensive overhaul of their basic purposes and processes will suffice.

The next phase is marked by enthusiastic advocacy of reform proposals, usually offered as a cure-all for the multiple ills said to afflict education. Proponents of change (curricular reorientation, instructional methodology, organizational format, or whatever), though scrupulously disclaiming they are touting a panacea, typically proceed to do precisely that. Only when the proper reforms are enacted, it is strongly implied, can the situation in the schools be improved. Contrariwise, unless the changes recommended are immediately forthcoming, calamitous results are sure to follow.

In the third phase, against a mounting chorus of reaction and counter-criticism, advocates of reform address themselves to the infinitely more difficult task of translating broad principles or concepts into specific proposals. The main thrust of the movement becomes implementation of workable programs capable of effecting desired change. This third stage may be characterized as the period when the new proposals—or more likely old ones dressed up for a return engagement—are divested of superfluous trappings. Educational practitioners (to change the metaphor) hammer out concrete means for applying the ideas, in process striking off or modifying the more extravagant claims advanced on their behalf. Finally there remains a useful core of ideological awareness and information which gets incorporated into prevailing pedagogical thought and practice. Alternatively, the movement is discredited and rejected, is fatally compromised, or enters upon a period of temporary quiescence lasting until it is resurrected in new guise at a later, more auspicious time.

Obviously, the foregoing smacks of caricature, but it does suggest a broad historical pattern of development characteristic of a considerable number of movements in education. To the extent that some such interpretive scheme is useful, it can be said that the many-sided, inchoate movement herein identified for want of a better inclusive term as educational "technologism" has tended in its emergence to reflect a pattern of strong criticism directed against existing practices, attended by a number of general reform proposals, followed subsequently by experimentation and exploratory improvisation. A number of specific innovations, programs, and processes presently associated with the movement are genuinely new. Some are of older vintage. A few of its defining characteristics trace far back into the history of education.

NEO-POSITIVISM AND EDUCATIONAL TECHNOLOGISM

The term "technologism," combining the Greek *technē* (skill, craft, technique) and *logia* (systematic treatment of; doctrine, theory, or science) with the suffix *ism* (denoting practice of, or doctrinal adherence) serves to denote under a single unifying heading a loose assemblage of diverse beliefs, values, and habits of mind which, though differing importantly in some respects, reveal themselves upon closer inspection to have much in common. To attempt to gather up all the tangled intellectual skeins of that ideological assemblage, to treat the historical and ideological antecedents of technologism in detail, lies far beyond the purview of a short introduction. It is enough simply to note that philosophically its orientation is materialistic and positivistic, while in its psychological bearings it tends to be behavioristic and reductionist. In its policy applications it characteristically fastens upon questions of technique and process, to the practical exclusion of consideration for ultimate goals, ends, or outcomes. The values it celebrates are instrumental ones of efficiency, economy, precision, and objectivity.

Positivism, the strain of philosophic thought with which technologism is most closely identified and which it finds most congenial, has its roots in the Greek Atomists of antiquity and their search for the constituent elements of phenomena manifesting a uniform regularity. It is to be discerned again in recurrent attempts throughout history to explain complex phenomena by isolating simpler elements and processes whose operations have been thought susceptible to mathematical formulation and prediction. Paradigm cases are supplied by the logico-analytic reductionism of Descartes in the seventeenth century and the method of "mechanic analysis" popular among eighteenth-century Newtonian scientists and philosophers. In modern times the term "positivism" was coined apparently by the early nineteenth-century French philosopher Auguste Comte (1798–1857) to emphasize his conviction that "positive" knowledge deals exclusively with that which is immediately observable. It therefore affords an immutable basis of fact compelling agreement because it is supplied prior to any inferences based upon it. In less technical terms, early positivism stood for the rejection of uncontrolled speculation and inference, a philosophic aversion to theology and metaphysics, and a programmatic refusal to consider anything but the operations of material phenomena and their mathematical correlations.

In his *Course of Positive Philosophy* (1831–1842), Comte argued that the scientific attitude alone affords real or "positive" knowledge. Through the quantitative reductions of the exact sciences, according to Comte, man is able to discover fundamental laws and relations which describe the natural world, doing so with a degree of sophistication and accuracy unequaled by more subjective modes of inquiry. The label "logical positivism" to denote much the same intellectual tendencies came to be applied to a philosophical perspective developed early in the present century by members of a group called the "Vienna Circle." It was an outgrowth of a seminar conducted by the Viennese philosopher Moritz Schlick. Its more prominent members beside Schlick included Otto Neurath, Philipp Frank, Rudolph Carnap, and later Herbert Feigel. The wedding of an "empiricist" philosophic tradition, going back to Locke and Hume, to the logical tradition associated partly with Comptian positivist thought was solemnized by the name "logical positivism" and later "logical empiricism."

Regarded as an attitude and habit of thought rather than as a formal doctrine, positivism has become extremely influential in modern life. Modern science, technology, and specialization have accustomed man to precision, have made him impatient with speculation regarding ultimate aims, origins, and causes.[1] The positivist, according to the German scholar Karl Jaspers, has little time for considerations of subjectivity, for internal feelings, for questions of causes, meanings, and consequences which resist quantification. Rather, he pointedly focuses upon verifiable knowledge, upon procedure and process instead of ends or intentions, on observation in place of speculation, on control rather than abstract understanding, on prediction in preference to insight. The positivist mentality is repelled by sentimentality and subjectivity.[2] It prefers uniformity, precision, rationality. Verifiability serves as its major criterion of significance. Order is exalted over disorder, and function is more interesting than purpose. In education, positivism finds expression in the current technologistic emphasis upon objectivity, external data, and manipulative control. Institutionalized roles are defined in terms of empirical expectations: teacher performance is gauged by pupils' scores on competitive tests, and student performance by observed changes in behavior. Further pedagogical assumptions reflecting the positivist

[1] Michael B. McMahon, "Positivism and the Public Schools," *Phi Delta Kappan,* Vol. LI, No. 10 (June 1970), 515.
[2] Karl Jaspers, *Man in the Modern Age,* translated by Eden and Cedar Paul (Garden City, N.Y.: Doubleday, 1957), pp. 47–49 ff.

mentality include the stress on replication as the best test of learning, and the pervasive use of objective tests for determining grades.[3] Finally, it is manifest in increasing reliance upon mechanized extensions of the teaching act and new modes of administrative management and control.

Technologism as the ideology most clearly expressive of the positivist mind-set in education is to be found in many guises and under the aegis of a number of different thrusts in contemporary education. The most significant of these are, in broad terms, (1) the application of behaviorist methodology to problems of pedagogical technique and evaluation; (2) increasing reliance upon electronically-based data storage, processing, and retrieval systems to supplement conventional modes of instruction; and (3) a technocratic revolution in methods of educational organization, administration, and management. Though discernibly different in a few respects, all tend to reflect implicitly the same basic ideological framework (or lack thereof), to approach problems on much the same general terms, and to assess educational phenomena according to similar canons of value. Behaviorism, with its emphasis upon overt public acts as opposed to subjective internal feelings and states of consciousness, places a premium on action, on doing. Modes of verification and assessment most consistent with the application of computer technology apparently have much the same effect. Newly-developed tools for organizing data relative to the management of teaching and learning are ill-adapted for considering subjective factors in decision-making. In all three cases the predominating concerns are those of technique, efficacy, and efficiency.

NEO-BEHAVIORISM IN THE CLASSROOM

The most pervasive and in some respects most important manifestation of educational technologism is the resurgence of interest in psychological behaviorism and its practical applications to teaching. Like philosophic positivism with which it is sometimes allied, the roots of behaviorism extend back well before the twentieth-century, reaching to the rise of scientific inquiry in the 1600's. Of all the consequences that followed from the early development of science, what must have seemed the most momentous was the inclusion of man within the scope of the natural universe. With the dawning realization that man as organism might be looked upon as subject to the same causal relationships governing physical phenomena, there grew a hope for a new "science" of humanity. It was expected that just as in physics, the application of certain deductive and mechanical methods to the

[3] McMahon, op. cit., p. 516.

analysis of a few simple cases would yield up fundamental axiomatic principles of behavior. From the first crude attempts to advance a mechanistic psychology by Hobbes and Descartes, to the orthodox deductive analyses of LaMettrie, Leibniz, and J. G. Herder, and continuing with the later systems put forth by Herbert Spencer, August Comte, and G. H. Lewes, the goal of deducing laws sufficient for defining man in terms of matter and motion remained essentially unchanged.

The father of modern American behaviorism is reckoned by most historians to have been John B. Watson (1878–1958), whose answer to the ancient question of whether psychology should deal with the data of consciousness or the data of behavior, or both, was that the nascent science of psychology should confine itself to the direct investigation of behavior. Like LaMettrie and others before him, Watson argued that it is unprofitable to try to study internal mental processes or states of mind which must always remain inferential since they cannot be observed directly. Positivism thus was to become, as Herbert Feigel noted, the *reductio ad actionem* of behaviorism; that is, operationally, psychological inquiry was to substitute for the purported object of observation (mind) its observational operations (behaviors). Though neither Watson nor his immediate followers went so far as to deny the existence of consciousness, they did claim that even introspection could be reduced to the operation by which it is observed and reported. As Watson put it in his *Behavior: An Introduction to Comparative Psychology* (1914), the whole of mental life could be studied and its laws formulated by eliminating "inaccessible states of consciousness" and confining attention to their "physico-chemical or functional correlates."

Behaviorism was further expanded and refined as a movement under the stimulus of such leading theoreticians as Edwin B. Holt, Max Meyer, Karl S. Lashley, Albert P. Weiss, and later on, Edward C. Tolman, Clark Hull, and Walter S. Hunter. Influenced both by Watson's pioneering work and that of the Russian investigator Ivan Pavlov (1849–1936), behaviorists came to regard psychology as a purely objective, experimental branch of natural science, whose proper area of inquiry is actually or potentially observable phenomena (that is, behavior), and whose major theoretical goal is the prediction and control of behavior. While they differed in their respective formulations of specific issues, early behaviorists and associationists as well shared a tendency to analyze the behavior of organisms, including man's, largely in terms of stimulus-response units, or "reflexes," and to fasten experimental attention upon the covariation of those two component elements of the reflex. Later, or neo-behaviorists, of whom B. F. Skinner is perhaps the best known, have greatly elaborated upon the original crude analyses of Watson and his disciples, and in some cases have gone far beyond their relatively narrow conceptual framework.

Behaviorism in education is expressed, first, by concern for the formulation of measurable instructional objectives in operant or behavioral terms; secondly, in calls for criterion-referenced types of instructional evaluation; and, thirdly, in the refinement of behavioral modification techniques for classroom management. Demands over the past decade for greater "accountability" in education, possibly more than any other single factor, have done the most to stimulate interest in the use of behavioral objectives and performance-based measures of assessment. The concept of accountability itself still lacks precise definition and denotation, but its general thrust is that the efficacy of schooling should and must be improved by fixing responsibility for instructional outcomes—for what children learn—upon those doing the teaching. As teachers are called upon to produce demonstrable results and to supply supporting evidence, the case for behavioral objectives becomes more persuasive.

Thus, it is usually argued that only by formulating objectives or goals in terms of intended behavior changes on the learner's part are adequate standards provided for assessing the extent to which instructional goals have actually been achieved. Loose talk about "insights" and "appreciations" and "understandings," the rhetoric commonly employed in defining teaching goals, does not lend itself at all to direct verification in precise, measurable terms. There is little hope of ascertaining, for example, whether a student "has insight into the principles upon which our nation's legal system is based." But if the objective employed states unambiguously the nature of learner behavior or product to be measured—that is, includes a description of a product to be achieved as a consequence of learner behavior—then the results of instruction are susceptible to independent checking. An example of an acceptably-defined objective would be: "When presented with three hypothetical descriptions of court decisions, the student will be able to select the one most consistent with an identifiable legal principle and adduce a minimum of three valid reasons for making that selection."

Proponents of behavioral objectives are prone to emphasize that the employment of operant measures is only a natural outgrowth of a learning theory widely supported by an impressive body of research. Theoretical consistency aside, by forcing teachers to specify their instructional goals in the explicit, detailed, and precise terms required by operational definitions, the effect upon classroom teaching, it is promised, will be salutory. Once teachers are obliged to define their purposes and expectations clearly in advance, they will be more effective in working toward them, with less attendant ambiguity or confusion for students.

For much the same reasons, instructors ought to be required in advance to specify the type of *evidence* acceptable for monitoring the learning they induce and for ascertaining the quality of instruction they presumably supply. Criterion-referenced grading, it is said, is a useful expedient in this regard. Old-fashioned norm-referenced measures of assessment have many valid uses, but their main utility is in gauging an individual student's performance in relationship to the performance of other individuals on the same measuring device. The meaningfulness of the individual's score emerges from its comparison with those of others. But for purposes of measuring high quality instruction, such standardized tests allegedly serve poorly, offering little evidence for making specific judgments about what individual students learn. More informative are procedures for measuring learning increments with respect to some specific criterion or performance-task. By taking stock before and after instruction is offered, the learning increment can be identified, and, further, can be measured against some specific set of achievement criteria. Only by ascertaining a learner's status with respect to those criteria (where the meaningfulness of the individual's score does not depend upon its being compared with others) can the true measure of instructional efficacy be taken.[4] Phrased differently, the argument is that a statistical distribution of test scores says little about the amounts of learning taking place or the quality of teaching going on, whereas individualized measures indicating progress toward predefined objectives *do* offer a basis for judgments about both the teaching and learning involved.

Critics of behavioral objectives nevertheless believe operant measures are unlikely to make more than a marginal contribution to the improvement of instruction. Their most frequent complaint is that only trivial learner behaviors can be operationalized, leading to neglect of more fundamental educational outcomes. Secondly, it is said that a rigid determination of operational goals discourages spontaneity in the classroom and discourages the teacher from taking advantage of unexpected learning opportunities or diversions. Some critics profess to see behavioral goal-setting as overly mechanistic and dehumanizing, especially in view of the fact that qualitative, as opposed to quantitative indices of learner performance, are notoriously difficult to come by. In such subject areas as fine arts and the humanities, opponents allege, it is virtually impossible to identify measurable pupil behaviors that are not innocuous, trivial, or irrelevant to the real learning that should be going on. They further argue that those who urge the preparation of instructional objectives in operational terms typically have very low cognitive levels of knowledge in mind, or pick

---

[4] The issue has generated an enormous literature. For two good discussions, consult W. James Popham, "Objectives and Instruction," in W. James Popham et. al., *Instructional Objectives, AERA Monograph 3* (Chicago: Rand McNally & Company, 1969); and Jason Millman, "Reporting Student Progress: A Case for a Criterion-Referenced Marking System," *Phi Delta Kappan*, Vol. 52, No. 12 (December 1970), 226–230.

illustrations from subjects where learning outcomes can be readily translated in terms of skills and performance tasks. Proponents, for their part, characteristically respond either by denying the validity of critics' arguments or by claiming *ad hominem* that dissident educators who oppose the quest for goal specificity in operant terms are simply looking for excuses to avoid thinking clearly and precisely about what they are trying to accomplish.

The rapid growth in popularity of behavior modification as an approach to classroom management represents a third major way in which psychological behaviorism has come to exercise an important influence upon education. Efforts to control and modify behavior theoretically could involve a number of divergent techniques, ranging from simple exhortation and persuasion, to those involving psychotherapy, subliminal conditioning and brainwashing, drugs, electronic implantations in the brain, and even genetic engineering. Less grandiose in its instrumentation and increasingly relied upon by educators is the technique of operant conditioning popularly associated with the work of B. F. Skinner. As an approach to managing the learning environment, the teacher is advised to observe what stimuli best reinforce desired behavioral patterns and to arrange for their systematic application so as to alter a learner's response pattern to conform with desired norms. Skinnerians claim that because positive reinforcements (rewards for doing something) are more effective behavior modifiers than are negative reinforcements (punishments for doing something other than what is desired), it is usually best to rely upon the former rather than the latter in shaping behavior toward specified outcomes. Proponents claim the systematic and consistent deployment of reinforcers offers the teacher a powerful tool for effecting learning, altering behavior, and maintaining order in the classroom.

Opponents are horrified over what they regard as the manipulative character of such behavior modification techniques. They question whether reliance upon extrinsic rewards—obedient pupils initially receive tokens which can then be exchanged for candy, money, or special privileges—does not thwart the development of intrinsic motivation or create undue pupil dependence upon external features within the learning environment. Some critics contemptuously dismiss the entire procedure as a form of "bribery" masquerading under a pseudo-scientific mantle of authority. Others have raised questions as to the long-range efficacy of behavior-shaping techniques. For example, when reinforcers in a carefully contrived situation are withdrawn does the conditioned behavior persist or is it quickly extinguished? Still others ask whether "learning" and "observable behavioral change" are actually synonymous, as most behaviorists allege, and if the focus of attention should be on behavior alone. Advocates of behavior modification respond that behavior-based technology is merely one more pedagogical tool to do more effectively what educators have always sought to achieve: to facilitate learning under controlled conditions so as to meet certain defined goals or objectives believed to be worthwhile.[5] Caveats about behavioral conditioning being an infringement upon the "freedom" and "dignity" of the human learner are regarded as inapposite or dismissed out of hand as literal nonsense.

COMMUNICATIONS MEDIA AND INSTRUCTIONAL TECHNOLOGY

The vastness of prevailing ignorance about both education and technology, as Anthony Oettinger points out, is matched only by acrimony of debate about the value of educational technology, a debate blighted by what he calls "a persistent confusion of ultimate promise with immediate possibility."[6] Enthusiasts point out that modern education cannot become much more labor-intensive than it is at present without inviting financial disaster; consequently there exists an urgent need to find new technologically-based ways of extending, supplementing, and complementing traditional modes of teaching and learning. One promising approach is through communications media: the various devices and processes which make possible the recording, storage, manipulation, retrieval, transmission, and display of information.[7] Having prepared the case for instructional technology, many proponents then move swiftly to speculative visions of classrooms as electronic learning laboratories equipped with global television, as well as computer-links with libraries and data banks around the world; of homes supplied with computer terminals and holographic television screens; of elaborate computer simulators, and various and sundry other programmed teaching devices. Only machines, supporters claim, can provide instant and unrestricted access to information with the infinite patience and accuracy required in a completely individualized learning format. Only through their installation can education be freed of the dreary, lock-step pattern consigned to it down through the centuries.

For their part, critics who remain unimpressed or skeptical about McLuhanesque visions of a utopian global village bound together

[5] A good general critique of behavior modification is to be found in Harvey Wheeler, "Social and Philosophical Implications of Behavior Modification," *Center Report*, Vol.5, No. 1 (1972), 3–5.

[6] Anthony G. Oettinger, *Run, Computer, Run: The Mythology of Educational Innovation* (Cambridge, Mass.: Harvard University Press, 1969).

[7] Seth Spaulding, "Advanced-Generation Educational Technologies in First Generation Education: An Inter-Disciplinary Crisis," in Julius Menacker and Erwin Pollack (eds.), *Emerging Educational Issues, Conflicts and Contrasts* (Boston: Little, Brown and Company, 1974), p. 323.

with communication linkages tend to view instructional technology as a threat to long-cherished human values. Many fear that education will become unduly depersonalized and mechanistic. Detractors project an Orwellian spector of brainwashing, of mass behavioral control, of a world in which students are trained like automatons and stamped out as copies of some master program. Mechanical artifice, it is claimed, can never match the spontaneity, versatility, and emotional caring of a human teacher.[8] Hence the conventional wisdom has tended to recoil from the prospect of a school technology based upon teaching machines, computer-assisted instruction, and other automated devices, fearing that cold, impersonal machines will not only mechanize but also dehumanize teaching.[9]

Supporters of a mechanized instructional technology here appear to have a cogent rebuttal. The assumption that traditional methods of instruction do not constitute a technology, they assert, is utterly indefensible.[10] Present methods do serve as elements of a technology though they may not always be recognized as such—a "Gutenberg" technology relying principally upon printed textbooks and upon chalkboards as the media of instruction. The resultant pedagogy is teacher-centered, group-oriented, and textbook-based. In terms of hardware, the addition of so-called "first generation" audio-visual aids such as record, wire and tape recorders, slide and film strip projectors, movie projectors and opaque or overhead projectors has not materially altered the conditions under which teaching and learning are conducted, except possibly to make learning more interesting. Nor have film loop cartridges, tape cassettes, prepared transparencies and other "packaged" software used in conjunction with mechanical contrivances shown the slightest sign of hastening the advent of a Brave New World.

The question is not *whether* a technology will be used, but *what* kind, in what ways, and for what purposes. Defined either in terms of apparatus, ranging from textbooks to television, or as a process by which objectives are achieved, educational technology is said by proponents to be relatively value-free. It can be used to pursue good objectives or unworthy ends. It is morally and philosophically neutral. McLuhan to the contrary, the message, not the medium, *is* only that, the message. To suppose then, defenders argue, that there is some inherent conflict between humanism and technology is to tilt at windmills. If the idea of a curriculum is looked at less in terms of a plan

[8] Howard A. Peelle, "Pygmalion's Computer," in Dwight W. Allen and Jeffrey C. Hecht (eds.), *Controversies in Education* (Philadelphia: W. B. Saunders Company, 1974), p. 238.
[9] Cf. Ronald Gross and Judith Murphy (eds.), *The Revolution in the Schools* (New York: Harcourt, Brace, 1964), pp. 10–11.
[10] David Engler, "Instructional Technology and the Curriculum," *Phi Delta Kappan*, Vol. LI, No. 7 (March 1970), 379 ff.

and more as the sum of what happens when a learner comes into contact with message and media, it seems obvious that there can be no curriculum—or learning—without some kind of instructional technology, some delivery system for the content imparted.

The situation becomes more ambiguous, however, in the case of so-called second and third-generation technological aids, whose use may eventually transform what the teacher is expected or required to do, in contrast with devices and materials designed primarily for the more efficient presentation and transmission of information in a conventional classroom setting. Examples of advanced-generation media might include broad-band communication systems utilizing coaxial cable, microwave relay, satellite transmissions, personalized video tape recorders, and, of course, computers. There may well be an important qualitative difference, for example, between the use of instructional television to broadcast a traditional lecture presentation and the use of computer-based programmed instruction involving a learner's real-time interaction with a terminal. As yet the computer technology in administration and management, on the one hand, and scientific and engineering applications, on the other, far exceed direct applications in education.[11] But if forecasters are correct in their assumptions and if the potential of computer-assisted instruction (CAI) is properly realized, the character and nature of education are likely to be radically altered. The nature of that expected transformation is what provokes so much heated debate between defenders and critics of electronic educational technology.

Automatizing devices, whether simple linear programmed textbooks or sophisticated branch-programmed electronic machines, have certain features in common. They depend for their effectiveness, first, on a micro-analysis of teaching-learning processes so as to render possible a precise order of problems or exercises through which the learner is conducted one step at a time. The behaviors to be taught are clearly defined, the necessary teaching steps developed, and appropriate learner responses throughout the sequence carefully identified. A student responds selectively in one fashion or another to the alternatives presented in a subproblem or exercise. The response varies depending on format, from filling in a blank or punching a hole in a card, to pulling a lever or pushing a button, typing out an answer on a keyboard, or touching an electronic stylus to a viewing screen. The machine then answers immediately, indicating whether the response was correct or not. If correct, the learner is permitted to progress to the next exercise, arranged usually in an ascending order of difficulty or complexity. By providing instant

---

[11] Phil C. Lange, *Programmed Instruction*, Sixty-Sixth Yearbook of the NSSE, Part II (Chicago: University of Chicago Press, 1967), p. 310.

feedback (correction and reinforcement), learning is supposedly greatly facilitated.

Arguments for and against the use of computers in instruction are familiar enough by now not to bear lengthy reiteration.[12] As a rule, those hostile to CAI argue it will impose a rigid regime of impersonal teaching; that it will lead to excessive standardization of educational materials; and contribute to the emergence of a dangerously concentrated mandarinate of programmers exercising grossly disproportionate influence over learning. Many are apprehensive that the role of the teacher will be downgraded. Others argue that computerized instruction is not a sufficiently "transparent" medium of communication; it unduly "colors" the learning context and can according to its own intrinsic logic end up dictating the purposes it ostensibly serves. Costs are prohibitive, existing machines have a low operating reliability, and available software leaves a great deal to be desired. The single biggest obstacle, many believe, is the lack of an empirically-validated theory of teaching for exploiting the computer's capabilities to the fullest. In the absence of a set of validated principles of instruction, it is almost impossible to make reliable judgments about how to construct teaching programs that serve with maximal effectiveness. Finally, a frequently-raised issue revolves around the requirements of precise specification and delineation of educational objectives in operant terms necessitated by computer programming. Critics question whether CAI will not end up accentuating once again the almost irresistible temptation to emphasize instructional outcomes that can be most easily measured with the degree of specificity that the system requires, to the disadvantage of important humanistic values that cannot be so defined.

On the other side, defenders of automated instruction argue vociferously that there is nothing inherently dehumanizing about computers—the programs fed into them can be dull and tedious, depending on who is doing the programming, or they can be playful and laced with humor. Far from leading to a stultifying standardization, computer-cased learning systems theoretically can be developed to provide almost unlimited diversity, just the opposite of uniformity. "Just as books freed students from the tyranny of overly simple methods of oral recitation," promises Patrick Suppes of Stanford, "so computers can free students from the drudgery of doing exactly similar tasks unadjusted and untailored to their individual needs." [13] Au-

---

[12] A discussion of the uses and abuses of educational technology, particularly with reference to computer-assisted instruction, appears in Charles E. Silberman, *Crisis in the Classroom* (New York: Random House, 1970), pp. 186–203.
[13] Patrick Suppes, "Computer Technology and the Future of Education," in Stephen C. Margaritis (ed.), *In Search of a Future for Education* (Columbus, Ohio: Charles E. Merrill, 1973), p. 106.

tomated media, so the argument has it, offer the last best chance under modern conditions of mass schooling to replicate the tutorial mode of one learner interacting with his own private teacher.

Prophets of the new technological revolution in instruction are fond of arguing that where practically every effort to individualize education formerly broke down was at the point of finding a technology capable of allowing a learner to proceed through content materials at a self-determined pace, working at times convenient to him, beginning instruction in a given subject at a point appropriate to past achievement, and with access to a wealth of instructional media from which to choose.[14] In the past, reforms failed precisely because they lacked a mechanism for altering the "ecological balance"—the web of relationships between and among learners, teachers, and the environment—which traditionally required a teacher to direct a group-based lockstep progression through the prescribed course of study.[15] But with the advent of computers capable of presenting concepts to individual learners at different times and affording each an opportunity for developing skill in their use through practice and drill, that goal of individualized instruction may be finally attainable. A new ecological balance in education may be brought about which will do more to make schooling an exciting and humane enterprise than all the cautionary humanistic rhetoric of latter-day Luddites can ever hope to achieve.

THE TECHNOCRATIC REVOLUTION IN EDUCATIONAL MANAGEMENT

Perhaps the most dramatic and in some ways portentous educational innovation wrought through the influence of technological ideology in recent years has been a thorough-going transformation of the processes and procedures by which school systems are organized, managed, and their functions evaluated. The cumulative changes in outlook and basic approach introduced within the last decade quite clearly amount to a genuine revolution in educational management and administration, one which extends beyond questions of curricular or instructional innovation within individual classrooms to encompass broader issues of how educational goals are formulated, how resources and personnel are allocated in the service of those objectives, and how results achieved are assessed. Looked upon both as a major causative factor and an emergent from the drive for greater accountability in education, the technocratic revolution in organiza-

---

[14] Harold E. Mitzel, "The Impending Instruction Revolution," in James A. Johnson, et al. (eds.), *Foundations of American Education: Readings,* Second edition (Boston: Allyn and Bacon, 1972), pp. 468–471.
[15] Engler, op cit., p. 380.

tion and management, together with a developing behavioral technology of instruction and new automated modes of teaching, promises to work major changes in popular attitudes toward schooling.

Calls for better accounting of professional educational practice over the last decade or so have been a function of many factors, most notably increasing pressure on tax dollars needed to support schools, and growing dissatisfaction with the quantity and quality of common school education. As the cost of education skyrockets, the public understandably has grown more critical of the schools and has issued demands for a better accounting of educational performance than has been traditional.[16] Almost inevitably those charged with responding to those demands have turned to the business community, with its reputation for efficiency and objectivity, for assistance in devising evaluation systems applicable in the public sector of the economy.

A pioneer at bringing business evaluative practices to the public sector was former Secretary of Defense Robert MacNamara, whose Program Planning and Budgeting Systems (PPBS), adapted from experiments begun at the Ford Motor Company and subsequently applied in the area of national defense planning and budgeting, early won him a reputation for efficiency, economy, and objectivity in matters of decision-making and executive administration.[17] It was not long before educators began to look with growing interest at the development of management procedures within business and industry which gave every appearance of registering dramatic gains in both the efficiency and effectiveness of production organizations.[18]

Basic to this approach is a type of strategic planning in which the organization's overall goals are made as clear-cut and precise as possible, the objectives for each production subunit within it spelled out, procedures for meeting goals delineated, and criteria agreed upon for guiding periodic appraisals of the attainment or progress made toward the goals specified. Beginning in the early 1960's, a growing number of educators began to question whether some such holistic approach might be applicable to educational planning. If it were possible, for example, to clarify what it is a school or system wants to achieve, it should be feasible to design a definite plan for achieving the sought-after ends, together with strategies for measuring what progress is being made, for diagnosing difficulties, and for modifying the basic plan if necessary as circumstances warrant.

Business leaders especially were attracted to the idea that ques-

[16] Julius Menacker and Erwin Pollack, "The Challenge of Accountability," in Menacker and Pollack, op. cit., p. 357.
[17] Ibid., p. 398.
[18] A good introduction to the topic is afforded by Leon M. Lessinger and Ralph W. Tyler (eds.), *Accountability in Education* (Worthington, Ohio: Charles A. Jones Publishing Company, 1971), pp. 1–6.

tions of educational management could be dealt with on a sound "business-like" basis. It was widely assumed, for example, that the task of specifying ends or goals in education was a fairly simple, straightforward undertaking, that tests could be devised readily for measuring whether objectives were being met, and that a consensus existed as to the norms or criteria by which the meaning and significance of results achieved would be evaluated with a view toward further improvements. In those assumptions, businessmen were joined by more and more educational administrators anxious to demonstrate their willingness and ability to be as "accountable" to their clientele as corporations are supposed to be to their stockholders and trustees.

What was particularly noteworthy, though troubling to many observers, was how the development of systems analysis in education came to depend more and more upon the combined style and nomenclature of the businessman and the mechanical engineer. Long accustomed to the use of mechanistic modes of thought for describing phenomena in the physical world and guided by criteria of predictability, precision, reliability, productivity, and organizational tautness, systems analysts soon began describing educational processes in terms of "inputs," "outputs," "entropy," "subsystem," and "suprasystems"—all the imagery of organizational management and physics. Talk about broad instructional intentions gave way to specifications for operant goals, and discussions of methods of instruction to "delivery systems," "cost-benefit ratios," "time-to-solution criteria," and "information management" processes. Far less was heard about the aims of education being to free the individual for comprehending himself, his world, and his moral and civic responsibilities, and more about manpower training, developing "human resources," and the improvement of schooling in terms of government and corporate-defined purposes.[19]

Much of the literature on accountability and systems design in education came to rely more and more upon the metaphor of the school as a malfunctioning machine needing repair, or as an inefficient, disorganized "production system" requiring readjustment. A common ploy was to talk about the school as a factory into which learners were to be sent for "processing." Another much-favored tactic was to conceptualize schooling as "capital" in a national investment scheme, with "dividends" in the form of better-educated peo-

[19] A good introduction to the topic and a still useful though dated bibliography is given in Bela H. Banathy, *Instructional Systems* (Palo Alto, Calif.: Fearon Publishers, 1968). For a critique, note John F. Cogswell, "Humanistic Approaches to the Design of Schools," in Arthur M. Kroll (ed.), *Issues in American Education* (New York: Oxford University Press, 1970), pp. 98–117.

ple.[20] Again, education has been looked at often in terms suggestive of a mechanical contrivance to which people are "hooked up" or "plugged in." Conspicuous by its absence has been much substantive consideration by technologists of questions whose treatment is not well-adapted to the rigorous language of educational engineering. A case in point is the philosophic issue of whether, as most techno-cratic managers tacitly seem to assume, the school *ought* to respond exclusively or even primarily to the narrow interests of the economic system and its political structure.

Even when dissident critics began to object that education was unthinkingly fueling the free enterprise drives of achievement, com-petition, profit, skill competency, and economic expansionism, there were few signs that technologists were paying much attention. Amidst a rising chorus of protest directed against a widely dispersed, faceless complex of warfare-welfare-industrial bureaucracies and control net-works, efficiency experts plunged ahead confidently with cost-effec-tiveness studies, operations analyses, and information-management systems predicated upon the very same instrumentalist values that came in for so much vigorous criticism only a few years ago.

Particularly noxious to many critics has been the prevailing ten-dency that developed early among many educational technologists to devise monolithic program planning and budgeting systems which, by their very construction, depend upon the assignment of quantita-tive values to the objectives they are designed to serve. Alex M. Mood, then with the Operations Analysis program of the U.S. Office of Education, was more forthright and candid than many when he conceded that systems planning eventually would necessitate cost-benefit judgments as to the *desirability* of many educational objec-tives. "Purists," he remarked, "will cringe at the thought of putting a dollar value on some aspects of education—the culturally enriched life, the soaring abstractions of the philosophers, the magnificent cosmological concepts of God's great universe, the homecoming games, or cavorting on the moon. Well," he suggested, "let's put a somewhat low value, maybe zero, on these things . . . and go ahead with it. There is, for one thing, an outside chance we shall find that we are not investing enough in education as a purely economic prop-osition. That would be a fascinating result, wouldn't it? And if it turns out the other way, we can then attach better values to the things mentioned." [21]

[20] Cf. H. Thomas James, *The New Cult of Efficiency and Education* (Pittsburgh: University of Pittsburgh Press, 1969), *passim*.
[21] Alex M. Mood, "The Operations Analysis Program of the U.S. Office of Educa-tion," in Werner Z. Hirsch et al. (eds.), *Inventing Education for the Future* (San Francisco: Chandler, 1967), p. 185.

Toward the close of the '60s, the lines of argument between technocrats and humanists were clearly drawn. Neglected, however, by both those who advocated the primacy of managerial principles stressing efficacy and objectivity in education and humanist critics who insisted first and foremost upon principles of subjectivity, was a body of literature which might have cast some light on the historical development of the issues under debate. Raymond Callahan's *Education and the Cult of Efficiency* (1962), for example, a study of the application of business and industrial values to education in the early decades of the twentieth century, showed clearly that latter-day proposals for output-oriented management methods, external evaluations and audits of schools, performance incentives, efficiency rating scales, and educational contracting had all been rehearsed in previous decades.

Strongly reminiscent of modern technologistic reductionism in discussion of educational goals and operations, to cite one instance, was the comment of Frank E. Spaulding in 1913 before a convention of school superintendents in Philadelphia: "Let us waste no time," he advised, "over the obvious but fruitless objection that the ultimate and real products of a school system—those products that are registered in the minds and hearts of the children that go out from the schools—are immeasurable, and hence incomparable." [22] Confident that "scientific management" techniques as developed for business by Frederick W. Taylor and others would prove effective in education, Spaulding joined with such self-professed "educational engineers" as James P. Munroe, William H. Allen, Franklin Bobbitt, and Ellwood P. Cubberley in urging the employment of scientific management in the schools. Cubberley, a highly influential voice in the field of educational administration throughout the 1920's, was unalterably convinced that completely "objective" standards needed to be devised by which the work of the schools could be determined, demonstrated, and communicated to the public.

Between 1911 and 1930, before the movement had run its course and the business-industrial gospel of efficiency had receded, numerous technologistic procedures were tried out. They included cost-efficiency studies, incentive programs, behavioral objectives, statistical surveys, tests and rating scales for teaching performance, task and bonus systems—and in one instance at least, a rating scale for measuring students' efficiency in which an item labeled "joy of learning" contributed five per cent to a total of one hundred per cent, or "perfect" efficiency. As sociologists Robert S. Lynd and Helen Merrell Lynd pointed out in *Middletown in Transition* (1937), the 1920's re-

---

[22] Quoted in Raymond E. Callahan, *Education and the Cult of Efficiency* (Chicago: University of Chicago Press, 1962), p. 68.

flected a period (like the 1960's) of ascendancy of business leaders to a position of ideological dominance in American society, the effect of which was to place an exaggeratedly high premium upon business-oriented values. It was only inevitable in such a context that some of the business-management ethos would be reflected in the ideology of schoolmen.

Much of the criticism leveled against the so-called technocratic revolution in educational management today rcalls that raised in opposition to what Callahan called the "cult of efficiency" a full half century ago. Most insightful of those who led the first campaign against a mechanistic technocracy were William C. Bagley and John Dewey, both of whom strongly opposed the inappropriate and simplistic application of industrial norms to the schools. They were joined in time by many others who tried to show that the "business" of educating students in a school could not be fairly compared, as Franklin Bobbitt had once attempted to do, with the manufacture of steel rails in a factory.[23] The exclusion of quality from studies of quantity, the making of educational decisions on pseudo-scientific and non-academic grounds, and the indiscriminate adoption of cost accounting processes, it was alleged, were "snares and delusions" in the search for good education.

After 1930, forceful opposition from many leading educators, plus growing popular disenchantment with business leadership which accompanied the Depression, helped relieve extreme overemphasis upon industrial-business management in education. For roughly two decades thereafter there was a cycle of withdrawal from mass-production methods and values. Not until the post-war period when several new governmentally-sponsored studies of management efficiency first appeared was there a noticeable resurgence of interest in analyzing social institutions, including schools, in terms of technologistic values. Throughout the 1960's and extending on through the 1970's, technocratic modes of organization and administration have continued to gain widespread support from many quarters, as judged by burgeoning interest in such recent innovations as integrated information management systems,[24] cost-effectiveness analysis,[25] computer simulation and gaming in budgeting,[26] performance-based and com-

[23] Ibid., p. 81.
[24] Cf. Thomas Mason, "Developing and Using Information Systems," in Paul L. Dressel et al. (eds.), *Instructional Research in the University: A Handbook* (San Francisco: Jossey-Bass, 1971), chapter 8; and Robert J. Parden, "Planning, Programming, and Budgeting Systems," in William W. Jellema (ed.), *Program Budgeting and Institutional Research* (San Francisco: Jossey-Bass, 1972), pp. 11–19.
[25] Note the discussion in Roy H. Forbes, "Cost-Effectiveness Analysis: Primer and Guidelines," *Educational Technology*, Vol. **XIV**, No. 3 (March 1974), 21–27.
[26] Cf. William H. Holloway, "Improved School Management and Planning: The Promise of Computer simulation," *Educational Technology*, Vol. **XIV**, No. 3 (March 1974), 33–36.

petency-based teacher education models,[27] and other appurtenances
of the generic systems analysis approach employed in business, industry, and the military. For reasons too complex to treat succinctly, it
seems probable that a congruence of political, social, and economic
factors in modern society will work to sustain and reinforce the underlying ideology of today's managerial revolution in education for
some time to come.

As yet there is little to suggest that the rift between humanists
and technocrats in education is closing. If anything, the two groups,
symbolizing conflicting points of view, have continued to drift farther
and farther apart, to the point where each finds the pronouncements
of the other camp literally incomprehensible. Educational technologists forever fail to see why demands for greater precision, objectivity, and control might be legitimately resisted by men of good faith.
On the other side, beleaguered defenders of the humanistic approach
to education cannot understand why technocrats remain oblivious to
the hazards, intellectual and spiritual, of mechanistic modes of
thought. Sociologist Edgar Friedenberg rather neatly hit upon a basic
psychological and philosophical difference between the two, however, one which goes far to explain if not to resolve the apparently ir-
reconcilable polarization prevalent in contemporary educational
thought and practice. Writing in his work *The Dignity of Youth and
Other Atavisms,* he observed:

> It makes a profound difference to the total personality and to the mean-
> ing one finds in life itself whether the subjective or the objective ap-
> proach to the world predominates; or whether, to speak in more fun-
> damental terms, one's sense of who one is in relation to the rest of the
> universe is felt to depend ultimately on one's dexterity and precision in
> responding to observable features of the environment.[28]

On balance, educational technologism has gone far to rid pedagogy of some of its obscurantist flavor, has streamlined a once-cum-
bersome, unwieldy conception of schooling, and promises in future
to serve as a galvanizing force for truly revolutionary change in the
areas of curricula and instruction. What remains unresolved at the
philosophical level, however, is the price to be exacted for greater objectivity, precision, and control. If, as promised, the new world of behavioral technology, computer-managed instruction, and accountability leads to positive gains, its advent can only be welcomed with

[27] Note W. David Maxwell, "PBTE: A Case of the Emperor's New Clothes," *Phi
Delta Kappan,* Vol. **LV**, No. 5 (January 1974), 306–311. See also W. Robert Houston and Robert B. Howsam (eds.), *Competency-Based Teacher Education* (Chicago: Science Research Associates, 1972).
[28] Edgar Z. Friedenberg, *The Dignity of Youth and Other Atavisms* (Boston: Beacon Press, 1966), p. 23. Cf. McMahon, op. cit., p. 517.

enthusiastic acceptance. But if the dark forebodings of humanists prove well-founded, and if in fact there are certain basic human values at stake in the struggle for dominance between two competing, antagonistic approaches to education, the ascendancy of neo-positivism, behavioristic, reductionism, and managerial technocracy will prove at best a very mixed blessing.

Behavioral Technology: A Negative Stand

JAMES F. DAY
University of Texas at El Paso

Behaviorism and its accompanying educational technology constitute a growing movement in American education. This movement largely stems from the behaviorist B. F. Skinner, his followers, the industrial ideology of scientific management, and dissatisfaction with teacher education programs and the public schools. Many terms are being used to label the movement: Skinnerism, behavioral technology, shaping, operant conditioning, behavior modification, behavior training, contingency management, programmed instruction, accountability, performance-based education, performance-based teacher training, competency-based education, and competency/performance-based education. These have tended to camouflage the phenomenon. What the next euphemism for Skinnerism will be, no one knows. Regardless of the label used, the strategies for controlling behavior remain constant, and thus make the variance in nomenclature of no importance. Always the strategy aims to control, manipulate, or shape behavior from outside the individual. No provision is made for feelings, attitudes, mind, or inner phenomenological choice. Thus, to many, the Skinner doctrine makes man into an "empty organism" whose only right is to respond to the rewards administered by the controller or shaper.

Today, many teachers are talking about the control and regulation of classroom learning through reinforcement. In a behavioristic way, performance contracting and accountability are shifting learning responsibility from student to teacher. Some educational centers, state departments of education, and schools of education have gone overboard in accepting Skinner's behavioristic-industrial model. Teaching machines, computers, modules, and various other gadgets and hardware are being introduced in the name of efficiency. According to some, the competency-based certification approach is to be a vehicle for promoting change within the educational establishment. Five states (Florida, New York, Minnesota, Texas, and Washington) are now working toward the implementation of competency-based teacher education. Many other states and their departments of education are beginning to show a similar interest. The U.S. Office of

From "Behavioral Technology: A Negative Stand," *Intellect,* Vol. **102**, No. 2355 (February 1974), 304–306. © 1974 by The Society for the Advancement of Education. Reprinted by permission.

Education's money grants have done much to stimulate the orthodoxy of behaviorism.

Many individuals and groups are reacting negatively to the trend of behavioral technology. They contend that teachers and professors do not need more controls and pressures. More time is required to be free and flexible in order to work properly with children and students. They maintain that students will be suffocated with the paraphernalia of technological gimmickry, behavioral objectives, behavioral modification, and the like. Statements are being made that the behavioristic-industrial model is a narrow, rigid, nonbookish, skill-centered curriculum which consists of trivial activities. Many other reasons are being offered for rejecting behavioral technology as the basis for education and teacher training. A rationale for a negative stand is given below.

For school learning, Skinner's theory is far too narrow. It emphasizes the one principle of external reinforcement to the ridiculous. When used in the classroom, it makes teachers into trainers, mechanics, and technicians, rather than professional guides of learning. For a learning theory to be adequate, it must take into account developmental processes, the effect of earlier learning on later learning, and the interrelationships of learning conditions and their applications to the acquisition of knowledge and understanding. Cognitive processes must not be ignored, as is done in operant conditioning. The behaviorists should realize that considerable research supports the position that the only subjects who are conditioned are those who are aware of the response-reinforcement contingency. Such research supports a cognitive theory and not the behaviorist contention that the effects of reinforcement operate automatically. Much more must be known about learning before American education should be dominated by operant conditioning with its one unproven law of reinforcement.

Teachers of all people should know better than to swallow a simple learning theory and a factory model of input-output efficiency. Tanner aptly states that, in performance contracting and accountability, "pecuniary values are attached mechanistically to education so that the processes of learning are regarded as machine processes, and the outcomes are regarded as industrial products." [1] Since the 1920's, many attempts have been made to solve the problems of education by using the factory model of scientific management, but these efforts have always failed.[2]

Skinnerism as a social philosophy is not in harmony with our republican democracy. It goes against the American concept of

[1] Daniel Tanner, "Performance Contracting: Contrivance of the Industrial-Governmental-Educational Complex," INTELLECT, 101:362, March, 1973.
[2] *Ibid.*

human freedom and individual opportunity. Left to the behaviorists, our traditional democratic concepts of the individual disappear. If there is one thing which can crush individuality in children, it is excessive control. Our salvation lies in maximizing freedom of choice. To exchange an individual's freedom for Skinnerian control would be to dehumanize individuals, institutions, and the schools.

Behaviorism, and especially Skinner's system, is externalistic. Individual choice is lost, since power flows from the one or ones in control. This does not result in individualized instruction as some have claimed. Actually, it is controlled or, at best, regulated instruction. We must not train students in our schools as animals are trained in the circus.

At best, competency-based education is a questionable doctrine; at worse, it is destructive to American education and our society. It rests on control and power, not freedom. The competency-based doctrine is now being forced by administrative decrees upon public school teachers and university professors. This is an abuse of power, and it is questionable that the legal capacity to make demands of this scope is possessed by state agencies of education. Also, questions of Federal constitutionality can be raised. University professors are expressing concern and negativism toward the several varieties of competency-based teacher education through their associations. The National Council of Teachers of English passed a resolution urging caution in the use of behavioral objectives.[3] In 1972, the American Historical Association went on record as opposing any attempt by any individual, agency, or center to control the content of academic history courses by requirements to conform to performance-based objectives or behavioral objectives.[4] The Texas chapter of the American Association of University Professors expressed concern regarding the Competency/Performance Based Education Program of the Texas Education Agency.[5] College professors are stating that a competency-based behaviorism would impose a straitjacket upon teaching and imperil the future of higher education and the country. Mowrer calls Skinner's system a "political dictatorship."[6] Others call it a straightforward form of fascism.[7] Many are saying that teachers do not need more controls and pressures. They need free-

[3] "Resolutions Passed by the National Council of Teachers of English at the Fifty-Ninth Annual Meeting," *College English*, 31:529, February, 1970.

[4] "American Historical Association Opposes Attempts by Outside Centers or Agencies to Control Content of History Courses," *Texas Academe*, 1:3, Winter, 1973.

[5] *Ibid.*, pp. 1–3.

[6] O. H. Mowrer, "Review of B. F. Skinner, *Beyond Freedom and Dignity*," *Contemporary Psychology*, 17:470, September, 1972.

[7] *Let's Take a Look at the Real Skinner* (Fort Worth, Tex.: The Institute for Epistemic Studies, 1973), p. 9.

dom to be flexible so that they can develop their own unique teaching styles. Increasingly, the tables are being turned—teachers are now saying that the behaviorists who talk of teacher accountability are the ones who should be held accountable for the effects their demands are having, and will have, upon education.

Behavioral technology will not lead the way to quality education, but will lead to narrowness and triviality. In behavioral-based education, the student studies the module and possibly other instructional packages and then is evaluated. If his score is adequate, he goes to the next unit or module. Both learning and assessment are a step-by-step controlled progression through discrete and often non-bookish units. Such education would be dominated by objectives that are readily quantifiable. Under such domination, education would be skill training, and professional teacher education would become apprenticeship training. The consequences would be disastrous.

One consequence would be a narrowness which ignores important objectives. An assessment which only considers the degree to which performance objectives are realized will be an inadequate evaluation. Many of the effects of education can not be stated in measurable objectives. In education—and especially in professional teacher training—the important objectives are not subject to measurement because they are complex, broad, and, in many respects, unique to each person. Performance assessment would ignore such important matters as understanding, patience, flexibility, ego development, attitudes, and character.

Another consequence would be to turn education into an industrial factory. The emphasis would be on bureaucratic efficiency and the end product. Education, one hopes, is concerned with what goes on within the school and not with just what is produced. Pace says: "A college or university is a habitat, a society, a community, an environment, an ecosystem. It should be judged by the quality of life that it fosters, the opportunities and exploration it provides, the concerns for growth, for enrichment, and for culture that it exemplifies. The question is not just 'what does your machine produce?,' but also 'how does your garden grow?' "[8]

A growing number of clinicians and counselors are rejecting Skinnerism from the standpoint of mental health. They contend that behavior modification techniques based on reinforcement hinder the development of mental health. Such techniques show utter neglect of the deep-seated origins of symptoms and disrespect for the meaning of symptoms from the individual's point of view. Some school

[8] C. Robert Pace, *Thoughts on Evaluation in Higher Education* (Iowa City, Iowa: American College Testing Program, 1972), p. 14.

children and students are greatly upset, and need help in the way of psychotherapy. The school should help in the treatment of these individuals by creating settings which convey acceptance, understanding, and respect for the emotional needs of students. For young people, humanistic thinking and planning is required, not behavioral tinkering and shaping which is devoid of feeling.

Both development and humanistic psychology supplement each other in making suggestions to education. Both are 180 degrees from behaviorism.

Developmental psychology is having a great influence on British schools, especially the infant schools. It is making for more informal, open education. The teacher is not concerned with controlling learning, but rather with being aware of each child's level of development, style of learning, and problems. There are no fixed seating arrangements. The teacher is a helper, a guide, a facilitator of learning of the child and of the group. Fortunately, mechanistic behaviorism has had little effect in England. Also, English school administrators are master teachers and give teachers freedom to be professionals in the classroom. The result is a humanizing atmosphere of teaching and not a rigid, skills-centered, controlled behavioristic form of instruction.

Humanistic psychology takes the position that, in order to understand behavior, we must take into account a great web of variables. Each person is unique and functions as a whole. Thus, he should be taught and studied as a whole, since his parts are closely interrelated. The teacher must accept, understand, and focus on the whole child. The humanistic attitude is basic to education and educators. It is an opposite and preferred orientation to the analytic and atomistic approach of behaviorism. Many would agree with Maslow's statement: "I have become more and more inclined to think that the atomistic way of thinking is a form of mild psychopathology, or is at least one aspect of the syndrome of cognitive immaturity." [9]

Teachers must satisfy student basic needs by putting more humaneness into our classrooms. A controlled behaviorist school and its many gimmicks such as performance contracting, voucher systems, and accountability should all be put out to a rocky pasture. Already, enough fragmentation of learning in the form of academic disciplines, subjects, and assignments exists in the traditional school. This artificial fragmentation will be a hundred times worse if the behaviorists take control. Educators should have enough sense to realize that important learnings and real growth are dynamic and complex and can not be accomplished with a prepackaged curriculum and by proceeding from skill to skill or from module to module. This

[9] Abraham H. Maslow, *Motivation and Personality*, 2nd ed. (New York: Harper & Row, 1970), p. xi.

is not education. Education comes through thought probing, exploring, and experimenting. American education needs the influence of developmental and humanistic scholars such as John Dewey, William James, Jean Piaget, Carl Rogers, Adolf Meyer, and the late Abraham Maslow, but not that of B. F. Skinner.

The history of America upholds professional teachers and traditional education. Certainly, our society does not support gimmickry without substance. Education can not afford to change in such wrong directions as behavioral technology. Should behaviorism continue to penetrate American education and professional teacher training, there soon will be no quality education—there will be factories concerned with skill training. Our people and culture will exist in a dehumanized desert with no learning, no understanding, and no freedom. Traditional education has changed gradually in attempting to meet student needs and social demands. Such education has survival value, while behavioral technology is untested. At present, educational research has not provided results showing what works best in education.[10] Research from a recent study conducted by a nonprofit research organization for the Office of Economic Opportunity (OEO) shows that the new experimental technology used in performance contracting proved to be no more successful than traditional classroom methods in school learning.[11] This OEO research places reinforcement theory and its hardware of gimmicks on the chopping block. If we stay with traditional education, all can agree that professional teachers are needed. Such teachers—with a sound understanding of theory, knowledge, and instructional procedures—can gradually lead the way to improvement. This will not result in the educational confusion and high levels of anxiety which have accompanied the sudden introduction of behaviorism and its accompanying educational technology to American education.

Many hopeful signs are on the horizon. The Board of Directors of the National Education Association recently resolved to fight simplistic approaches to accountability in our schools. The NEA contends that our schools are in an "accountability crisis," and places much of the blame for this crisis on the faulty belief that schools can be run like industry.[12] Robert Bhaerman, Director of Educational Research, American Federation of Teachers, has taken a negative stand on accountability.[13] Journals increasingly are containing articles which are opposed to Skinnerism. Teachers and university

[10] R. E. Schutz, "Methodological Issues in Curriculum Research," *Review of Educational Research*, 39:359–366, June, 1969.
[11] *The Office of Economic Opportunity Experiment in Educational Performance Contracting, Research Report* (Columbus, Ohio: Battelle Memorial Institute, 1972), p. 85.
[12] "NEA Board Launches Accountability Fight," *NEA Reporter*, 12:1, 5, March, 1973.
[13] Robert Bhaerman, " 'Accountability': A Short Course," *American Teacher*, 57:16, April, 1973.

professors are joining ranks to stop behaviorism from dominating American education. One now can be somewhat optimistic that Skinnerism and educational technology will be contained and soon will be a thing of the past. American education then will be able once again to make sense and move toward quality.

After the containment of behavioral technology, American education must turn in proper directions. Changes toward improvements and quality education must be gradual and not upsetting. Research, sound thinking, and the experience of professional teachers can provide cues to guide the way toward quality education which satisfies student needs and social demands. It can be expected that Piaget's developmental psychology, and other points of view will have their influence. Perhaps even a few elements from behavioral technology will be retained and assimilated into education in the future.

⌣ The Myth of Educational Technology

DAVE BERKMAN
American University

I

The myth of educational technology is the myth of the learning industry—which is itself a myth.

This assessment is based on two-and-one-half years with one of the largest of the knowledge industry conglomerates (the last year-and-a-half on its headquarters staff), plus six months in an executive capacity with one of the smaller learning outfits. Since it would serve little purpose, neither is identified by name; first, because each was typical of its competitors; second, because it might lend a self-defeating coloration of personal pique if the reader were to regard these observations as merely a "spite exposé," In fact, departure from each of these firms was on friendly terms, in both instances to accept a better position.

The term "learning (or knowledge) industry," was intended to connote an emerging class of corporate entities which would create the new, electronics-technology-based learning systems. It thus served to differentiate these new companies (many of them conglom-

From "The Myth of Educational Technology," *The Educational Forum*, Vol. **XXXVI**, No. 4 (May 1972), 451–460. Reprinted by permission of Kappa Delta Pi, An Honor Society in Education, owners of the copyright.

erates) from the traditional publishing and audio-visual houses which have always sold textbooks and miscellaneous educational films to the school market—and the most important of which they would soon acquire.

Considerable excitement was engendered by the promise of this new "industry" that it would become the prime mover behind the revolution necessary to reform an anachronistic, dreary, and all-too-often failing formal education structure.

But so far, nearly a decade, a couple of score of acquisitions, and an endless outpouring of verbiage later, all there is to show are the words!

Panel after panel, meeting after meeting, and convention after convention, together with increasingly frequent newspaper features, magazine pieces, and TV documentaries, are devoted to the theme that we have arrived at the threshold of a massive technological reformation of our schools and colleges. Unfortunately, any such claim can be dismissed as 90 percent gross exaggeration, nine percent outright untruth, and *maybe* one percent reality. For the most part, the claim rests on the existence of a massive miscellany of machines, incidental cartridges, and other such peripherals of "audio-viz ephemerality" which are displayed at the conventions, widely advertised in the professional journals, and occasionally even sold to gather dust in the storage rooms of schools all over America. Yet, none of these gizmoes, jimcracks, singly or in any contrived combinations, are in any way related to—if anything, they would seem the very contradiction of—that total systems restructuring of education which the learning industry promised to effect.

Thus we find the great educational technology revolution always being spoken of as "five years off." It was "five years off" in 1960; it was "five years off" in 1965, and it is still "five years off" today.

Part of the problem lies in the microscopic kernel of truth upon which the myth is based. There *is*, for example, a Nova High School, located in Florida's Satellite Alley, which is one of two or three which actually has attempted to introduce a technology-based restructure of the education it offers its students. Unfortunately the periodic obeisances to the myth of technologically mediated education which the Sunday supplements, "upper-middle-brow" magazines, and the TV documentary units pay to the myth only tell us about a Nova High which has done it. They neglect to mention the other 25,000 high schools which have not.

Fact: Despite the superabundance of technology which permeates the American environment, the formal education a student experiences today differs in no significant manner or degree from the schooling we experienced in 1920 or 1950.

Fact: About two weeks after Gutenberg wiggled that first block of movable type, Western education was locked into a system of schooling dominated by a talking-teacher-*cum*-textbook-plus-blackboard. And it has remained in this mold ever since.

Absolute, Overwhelming, All-encompassing, and Immutable Fact: A lot of people (they are known as "educators") have a lot of vested interest in perpetuating this five-centuries-old anachronism! (Which, to a considerable degree, is what the fight has been about when communities of urban Black and Spanish parents, such as in Ocean Hill-Brownsville, dare question the claim of a failing system of education that it has a professional *right* (!) to continue failing their children.)

II

The myth of educational technology which is, historically, largely the myth of the learning industry, can trace its beginnings to a set of "buzz concepts" and clichés immortalized by various electronics moguls given to *ex cathedra* utterances back in the early Sixties.

Forgetting that formal education had never made anything more than the most superficial use of a film medium which had been around for nearly 70 years; that it had all but ignored the potential of a radio medium entering its fifth decade; and was paying little more than lip service to television, which by then was already well past puberty, these electronics pontiffs painted a pastiche of promise and profit characterized by a logic which, on its surface, seemed irrefutable: If we hardware people who have all these machines get together with (i.e., acquire) all those software people who have all the stuff for us to display on our machines, why then this combination . . . better make that "Synergism" . . . why then, this synergism will lead to a knowledge industry which the *Wall Street Journal* was soon predicting would be the growth industry of the Seventies as TV was to the Fifties.

Thus was a glamor industry born.

Of course the clichés and buzzings did not end there.

"Knowledge doubles every ten years," someone said. And each of us dutifully repeated, "knowledgedoubleseverytenyears." The implication of this was a concomitant twofold increase in the density of facts and concepts contained in the curricula of formal education—and thus the need for new and more efficient formats and media to present them. For the sake of argument, however, let us assume this decennial doubling of knowledge is true: just how much of this new knowledge is of the relatively gross type of fact and concept with which the Grades 1–12 curricula are concerned? The writer had occasion not long ago to examine the New York State junior high school science curriculum. Science, it would seem, should be where this doubling of knowledge would have its greatest curriculum impact. Yet that curriculum was the exact same one which he suffered through in a Brooklyn junior high school 23 years earlier!

The irony here is that where there *are* increases in knowledge, or changes in fact that might *really* have some significance to youngsters—as in the areas of sex, drugs, or about a monolithic Communist menace that is no longer monolithic, and thus much less menacing— well, try packaging any of *this* new knowledge for cartridgized, computerized, electronicized, readout display, and see how much of it American schools will buy!

Before leaving clichés, some note should be made of what is perhaps the most ubiquitous of those which have their genesis in educational technology: "Multi-media." Most of the "multi-media presentations" which this observer has been privileged to attend have consisted of mis-matched, side-by-side slide displays, accompanied by poorly recorded, out-of-synch audio tape. In more than a few knowledge industry catalogues the heading "multi-media" will refer to silent filmstrips accompanied by a few pages of mimeographed material.

III

As a result of their uncritical acceptance of such superficial buzz-concepts as "hardware-software synergies," major American corporations, which *had to* know better—but obviously did not—entered into a frantic period of lemming-like acquisition activity in which company after company went out and bought at least one school publisher. Or, as their annual reports stated it, they "acquired a software capability."

In the process, they made but two errors, both bordering on the monumental: they completely misjudged what they were buying when they bought textbook houses; and they could not have been more wrong in what they assumed about the market to which these newly created learning combines would sell.

Whatever it is which one buys when he buys a book publisher, it is *not* something which, through the magical escalation of rhetoric, is mystically transformed into a "software capability;" which, in turn, will automatically program the reels, discs, and tapes which will fit his machines. Instead, the specifics came down to a relatively few things which are much more mundane: some printing plates containing old textbooks; a few gentlemen bearing the title of "editors," who boast the phone numbers of some other persons who can be called upon to write *new* textbooks; plus, most important, a cadre of "travellers," the corps of salesmen who actually do the selling.

And not a "software capability" in the lot!

The second error was even more grave. It rested on the supremely naïve assumption that in at least one very positive aspect, formal education was like the industrial market: As business leaped to buy electronic data processing systems and the new methods of copying, education would prove just as eager to buy new technologies which would make it not only more cost-effective, but—and most important to those who began to join the learning industry's working ranks—more learning- and learner-effective, as well.

That it did not, and is not, is a matter of record.

That it will not is a relatively safe prediction.

The knowledge industry was, of course, correct in seeing education as badly in need of more effective ways to foster learning. It ignored, however, that most basic of its own marketing axioms: that a potential customer's needs cannot be translated into sales, until he not only recognizes that such a need exists, but also demands something to fulfill it. A $50 billion education establishment is simply not going to admit to itself, let alone anyone else, that it is badly in need of new technology systems to rectify failure costing $50 billion a year!

IV

It is likely that the claims made here about the lack of any meaningful applications of technology within education will seem highly exaggerated to many readers who keep hearing about ITV, computerized instruction, learning carrels, etc.[1] However, according to the Report of the Commission on Instructional Technology—as close as we have to a definitive study of the impact which educational technology has had on our schools—"All the films, filmstrips, records, programmed texts, television, and computer programs do not fill more than five percent of the 1,250,000,000 pupil class hours a week. Some experts put the figure at one percent or less."[2]

Thus, for at least 19 out of every 20 school hours, it remains Talking Teacher Time, much as we, not to mention Gutenberg's kids, all knew it.

Take instructional television. If we know anything, we know that youngsters learn through TV. A dozen years ago, in what may

---

[1] A "learning carrel" being what most of us would call a schooldesk. However, add a few squares of acoustical tile perpendicular to the work surface, and through that previously cited semantical phenomenon of rhetorical escalation, it becomes a "learning carrel!"

[2] *"To Improve Learning,"* A Report to the President and the Congress of the United States by the Commission on Instructional Technology. March 1970. House Education and Labor Committee Print, page 21.

have been the largest mass experiment in the history of American education, the Ford Foundation spent tens of millions of dollars testing ITV. The results showed that regardless of grade level, or of subject discipline, students learn as much from televised instruction as from traditional face-to-face classroom teaching.

The proponents of ITV have argued that given the greatly varying abilities of teachers to present materials and because it is economically absurd for, say, 5,000 high school physics teachers to stand up in 5,000 separate classrooms and each duplicate the efforts of all the others, why not instead locate the best of these 5,000, record his presentations so that they can be played back through a television system, thereby freeing the other 4,999 to concentrate on small group and individualized follow-up? Here, then, TV would be assuming the basal or expositional function which it can do best—and the faculty would be free to perform the more individualized follow-up functions which teachers have always claimed they are best able to undertake.

And so, in 1956, with Ford underwriting, Hagerstown, Maryland, and the surrounding Washington County school system, became famous as the site of the demonstration which would prove the value of televised basal instruction.

Fifteen years later, Hagerstown is still the only one of some 20,000 school districts in the United States in which basal instruction via TV is offered on a *mandated* basis.

There is, of course, a great deal of supplementary and enrichment programming being televised around the country for classroom use on an optional basis. So much so that nine out of ten American youngsters attend a school within range of an ITV signal. Inherent, however, in any option to use, is the option to reject, and American teachers and administrators have overwhelmingly rejected televised instruction.[3]

V

The situation in which educational technology now finds itself is one dominated by a learning industry which will not risk the capital and the development dollars to produce technology-based learning systems, because formal education gives no reason to believe it will buy any of them. (Those few demonstrations which have received so much publicity, have virtually all been underwritten by Federal funding. Once the grants covering them expired, the programs died,

[3] For a detailed discussion of why there has been no learning industry entré into video instruction, see the writer's "The Learning Industry and ITV," *Educational Broadcasting Review*, June 1971.

leaving only the residue of the inevitable Sunday supplement feature on "Schools of the Future!") Thus, those isolated elements of formal education which *might* be disposed to incorporate technology into their educational programs find there is nothing for them to purchase. Nothing, at least, in terms of *systems,* as opposed to the bits and pieces which *are* being sold, and which go to make up *"Audio-Viz Time."*

Somewhat over a year ago while on the headquarters staff of a major learning conglomerate, the writer had occasion to visit the headquarters of a leading hardware manufacturer. The purpose of the visit was to discuss a potential mutual interest in a specific media system. It came as something of a surprise, however, to find that a whole morning had been set aside to describe and discuss an entirely different hardware configuration.

It seemed this company had developed a super-automated monster which could do just about anything an aberrated science fiction writer might conjure up. The central core of this behemoth ran $150,000, while individual user-stations could be strung out for $5,000 each. ("However, with mass production we could probably get that down to about thirty-five hundred!")

The problem which this company faced was simple: they had sold only one of the units, and that to a school district which paid for it with federal money.

They were still trying to sell the second.

They weren't quite sure why they were encountering such difficulty, although they revealed some glimmers of understanding that it might be due to the cost of the unit; also possibly to the fact there was no programming for it! (Which brings up another of those horrendous errors which the learning industry has refined to the state of a fine art: this absurd notion—especially endemic to its more hardware-oriented components—that schools would undertake to write their own software for any hardware they buy. As if schools ever wrote their own textbooks!)

VI

But what about *Computers???*

If, in discussing computers, what we are talking about is actual instruction *by* computer (also known as "computer assisted [or as 'computer aided'] instruction," or, "CAI" for short), then despite all we do hear about it, we are not talking of anything which our kids, their kids—and perhaps not even *their* kids—will experience.

At this point, however, the distinction should be made between CAI and CMI, or "computer *managed* instruction," not only because they constitute two distinctly different applications of the computer within education, but also because CMI distinguishes itself as per- haps the only reality-centered undertaking of potentially meaningful scope and significance which the learning industry has so far at- tempted.

What the proponents of CMI have done is apply the computer's data storage capability to the management of each individual stu- dent's work on a subject-by-subject basis. One of contemporary edu- cation's most common and inexcusable errors—inexcusable because it is so obvious—is to impute to youngsters a generalized level of ability which assumes an equal capacity to deal with all disciplines.

With CMI, a computer is fed data about each child's ac- complishments and difficulties on a daily, subject-by-subject basis, and the computer then prescribes what remedial, "regular," or ad- vanced instructional materials each of the students it is monitoring should be handed in each subject he or she is studying. The costs of such a system are relatively moderate. Many medium and virtually all of our larger-sized school systems already use their own or a shared computer to carry out various business and administrative tasks. Almost any of these computers could just as easily manage the administration of non-computerized instruction as well, if a period of time were set aside each day for them to perform this function.

However, it is CAI—that is, instruction *by* computer—and not CMI that the learning industry is attempting to convince the world is just around the corner.

Forgetting that CAI's proponents almost never consider the as- tronomical hardware costs necessary to implement CAI because of the numerous computers and hundreds of user-stations which would be necessary in any school of even moderate size if any significant part of its multi-grade, multi-subject curriculum were to be com- puter-taught; have any of those who so blithely predict the immedi- ate adoption of CAI ever bothered to examine the costs involved in the commercial preparation of just *one* one-semester or academic- year-length presentation of the basal content in just *one* discipline?

Bear in mind that the value of the computer as an instructional device lies in its capability to deal with open-ended responses. Oth- erwise, a 25¢ cardboard pulldown device, inserted in a book, which can accommodate a limited, four- or five-choice, fixed-response, pro- grammed instruction format would suffice. (The failure to recognize this, it should be noted, is what lay behind what even the learning industry itself will unhesitatingly admit has been its biggest fiasco: the "teaching machine" debacle of the early and mid-Sixties.)

The value of a computer-taught program is that it can respond *appropriately* to each of a large number of open-ended responses with which students can respond to any question or problem which the program presents. That is, not only can it tell a student that his response was right, in the case of the wrong answers it can explain specifically what was wrong with each of a large number of such incorrect responses.

Because a CAI program does have this ability to make virtually an unlimited number of responses, we would want to program it to do so for each of the erroneous responses which, for any given question, would account for, let us arbitrarily say, 95 percent of the total of incorrect answers which that problem will elicit. Let us then assume (also arbitrarily) that the number of wrong responses making up that 95 percent, regardless of subject or grade level, averages out to twenty. Let us totally ignore the research effort which would have to be mounted to determine what each of these twenty is. Then, to be even more conservative, let us cut that twenty figure in half. Let us also assume that a typical year- or grade-length CAI course in any given discipline at any given grade level requires an average of 5,000 frames. Because we are not even considering the cost of the just cited research effort, we will conservatively assume a developmental cost of $20 per response. What we now have, then, are 5,000 frames each requiring the programming of ten different responses at $20 per response. If, in order to make doubly sure that we are erring on the conservative side, we cut this $20 figure in half to $10, then we have 5,000 frames, times 10 responses per frame, times $10 per response, for a total cost per-course of one-half-million dollars.

Now, if we then contradict everything the past decade has taught us about the need to supply different programs to meet the differential needs of our varied socio-economic, ethnic, and racial groups and assume one standard course in each subject at each grade level to serve the whole country; and, if we further assume four disciplines per grade level for the first through eighth grades for a total of 32; plus another four-per-semester covering the eight semesters of the senior high grades for another 32, we end up with a grand total of 64 courses. Sixty-four course programs at a cost of a half million dollars per course gives us an aggregate figure *just for development* of $32,000,000! And this figure, bear in mind, takes *no* account of the sales, marketing, "g&a," and other costs—not to mention the implications for final pricing of the desired 25 to 30 percent pre-tax return on investment—all of which would double to triple the final outlay.

What learning company is ready to commit this kind of money to develop the materials for a curriculum-wide, computer-based instructional system, when no schools have the hardware through which CAI can be offered?

What school is ready to commit the millions in capital equipment dollars required to purchase the computer hardware for which programming does not exist?

So much for computerized instruction.

VII

The learning industry's latest in its series of periodic fascinations is with the new, "low-cost" video storage techniques.

Its leadership is certainly not dissuaded from its fantasizing in this realm when, say, a Jack Gould, or someone of like eminence, writes a column about how schools are all ready to begin making widespread use of these technologies to provide small group or individualized basal instruction via television. Certainly not when he does so with no attempt to examine the cost implications!

Conservatively defining "basal presentation" as requiring as little as twenty minutes of material per subject, every other school day, and figuring an 180-schoolday year, this means 90 twenty-minute cartridges per subject, per grade level. Taking CBS Labs' highly touted EVR [4] process to make our point, the out-of-pocket cost to the program material developer *just to duplicate* each set of 90, runs to approximately $2,000. Two thousand dollars merely for duplication—with no markup, no consideration of the expenditures necessary to develop the content and to mount the television production effort necessary to create the masters from which the copies can be duplicated; nor anything to cover sales and marketing.

How many schools are going to buy the requisite *multiple sets* of such video materials which are necessary so that they are available in the quantities needed for small group utilization, when the selling cost *per single set* would run between $6,000 and $8,000?

Yet when a Sunday column appears implying how EVR or the new and equally "inexpensive" formats will make TV-based small group instruction a reality, it is almost inevitable that on Monday the executive suites of the learning industry will be buzzing with talk about how video cartridges are going to transform education. . . .

Which raises a most intriguing phemonenon unique (?) to the learning industry: the adolescent-like, reactive psychology which seems to characterize the thinking of so much learning industry leadership. By analogy it would be as if the heads of Ford or GM depended on *Popular Mechanics* for *their* cues on what is new in the world of automobiles. In large measure this is because so many of those holding leadership positions in the knowledge corporations all too often *may* have come from Ford or GM! Those with first-hand education experience are relatively few. Indeed, one of the minor but continuing frustrations encountered by the professional educator working within the knowledge industry is having to convince his superiors that whatever may have transpired most recently within the

---

[4] In the interim since this was written, CBS has itself seen the light, and given up the EVR ghost. The same costs, however, would apply to the ½" videotape casette formats which are being touted as enthusiastically this year as EVR was the past four!

Darien, Scarsdale, or New Canaan school systems cannot be projected as typical of American education!

VIII

Is there any hope?

This observer sees three possibilities—all, admittedly, relatively slim—whereby educational technology could begin to make the impact it is capable of effecting on American schools.

The first rests on the assumption that as taxpayers continue to revolt against higher school costs, the collective bargaining organizations (mainly the NEA and the AFT) which represent professional educators, will find they have to agree to a "tradeoff:" acceptance of cost-effective, technology-based learning systems for higher salaries and job protection for those already employed. Thus, we may reach a point where education *has to* become less labor-intensive and is forced to let technology take over some of the burden if only to save money.

Such a thesis as this could, however, contain some of the very naïveté which has been ascribed to the knowledge industry, insofar as it ignores that the middle-American mentality which votes down increased school expenditures, is also least likely to appreciate such concepts as "cost-effectiveness tradeoffs." It is not difficult to imagine the initial capital bond outlay for an eventual cost-reducing ITV system being rejected, for example, because "ITV is TV and-TV-is-that-fun-thing-we-watch-at-night-and-the-schools-have-got-to-stop-wasting-money-on-all-those-frills-and-get-down-to-teaching-the-3Rs!"

The second hope lies in the changes which will result from the gradual assumption by Blacks of control over urban education—control which, if it doesn't come this year or next through community takeovers, will come before the decade is out as a result of the inevitable Black takeovers of whole cities. To Blacks, whose children have been all but totally failed by the traditional print-based system of education, the promise of media-mediated, technology-based basal learning systems are not just a luxury, but perhaps a matter of survival. (Why is it we heard so much about all the turmoil in Ocean Hill-Brownsville—and virtually nothing about the intensive degree of experimentation that community-controlled school system undertook in order to test new educational ideals and techniques?) Related to this is the turn to technology which Roman Catholic education is making as a matter of immediate survival. (Case in point: while the rest of education has virtually ignored the special set of frequencies known as the Instructional Television Fixed Service[ITFS], which the FCC set aside exclusively for instructional—as opposed to "educational" or Public—TV, seven of the ten largest Catholic school systems are operating ITFS systems.)

Third, and perhaps the best hope of the three: the fallout from *Sesame Street*. A generation of youngsters are entering our kindergartens and first grades this year who could prove to be as different from those who entered last fall as we are from our grandparents. Over half these youngsters have watched *Sesame* on a regular basis. If they turn off as quickly to the uninspired, laboriously-paced, mind-debilitating tedium which passes for early grade education, as one can reasonably expect they will after their *Sesame* exposure, then something drastic just could happen. (When it's *"our"* kids, and not "those Black kids" whom the schools begin to turn off and fail in large numbers, then that—pardon a mixed metaphor—is a failure of a different color!)

For the present, however, the reality is that any meaningful application of educational technology within our schools exists only in the rich verbal traditions of the learning industry—and, unless things change drastically, this mythology may prove to be about *all* that it has produced.

On Educational Accountability

MOHAMMED A. A. SHAMI
Maryland State Department of Education

MARTIN HERSHKOWITZ
Resource Analysis Division, Operations Research, Inc.

KHALIDA K. SHAMI

Much has been written about the subject of accountability, but few writers have appreciated the global impact of the accountability concept. Many models of accountability have been suggested and, in some cases, implemented. One major weakness in most of these models is their limited scope of design. In this respect, Glass makes the following point:

> There are at least six separate activities to which the term accountability is currently applied: 1) input-output analysis relating educa-

From "Dimensions of Accountability," *NASSP Bulletin*, Vol. **58**, No. 383 (September 1974), 1–12. © 1974 by the National Association of Secondary School Principals. Reprinted with permission.

tional resources to educational outcome; 2) school accreditation programs; 3) program planning and budgeting system; 4) behavioral statements of objectives reference testing: 5) school voucher systems; and 6) performance contracting. None of these activities embodies all of the elements of an accountability relationship. Each fails in one or more respects to hold the schools truly accountable to the public.[1]

This basic weakness in establishing a fundamental framework for accountability has led to incomplete approaches to accountability implementations. The concept of accountability is both encompassing and complex. Without indepth knowledge of this concept, misguided efforts towards accountability will be not only fruitless, but may be damaging as well.

The literature abounds with both broad and limited definitions of accountability. For the purposes of this paper, two mutually reinforcing definitions, one by Glass and the other by Lessinger, form the basis for identifying an accountability system.

Glass states:

> An accountable relationship between seller and buyer involves three elements: 1) *disclosure* concerning the product or service being sold, 2) product or performances *testing*, 3) *redress* in the event of false disclosure or poor performance.[2]

Lessinger expands this by addressing time and resource use in his definition:

> Accountability is the product of a process. At its most basic level, it means that an agent, public or private, entering into a contractual agreement to perform a service will be held answerable for performing according to agreed upon terms, within an established time period, and with a stipulated use of resources and performance standards.[3]

In addition to being a highly complex concept, accountability is also a very sensitive issue, fraught with confusion, interpersonal conflicts, and a potential for confrontation between special interest groups. In order to implement a logical, systematic and, above all, realistic system of accountability which will incorporate these concerns and issues, it is necessary to address the following dimensions of accountability:

- What are the goals for which education is accountable?
- What are the measures of accountability?
- Who is responsible for what?

[1] G. V. Glass, "The Many Faces of Educational Accountability," *Phi Delta Kappan,* *LII*(10), 1972, p. 637.
[2] Glass, p. 636.
[3] L. Lessinger, "Engineering Accountability for Results in Public Education," *Phi Delta Kappan, LII,* 1970, p. 217.

- To whom is education accountable?
- What are the different levels of accountability?
- What kind of data should be collected in an accountability system?
- How should the results of accountability be used?

WHAT ARE THE GOALS FOR WHICH EDUCATION IS ACCOUNTABLE?

It is not uncommon to find schools and school systems lacking clear statements of their goals. Even in those schools that do have clear goal statements, the statements are generally global and seldom relate to what goes on in classrooms. Thus, typical goal statements do not provide any direction and are rarely more than an exercise in semantics. "Goals of education" is almost a virgin territory, and unless this area is futher developed, efforts towards accountability will not attain their objectives. It is necessary to know who is responsible for establishing goals of education, how these goals may be established, and what the different levels of goals are.

- Who should establish goals of education? The public, including all the special interest groups, has the authority and responsibility to establish goals of education.
- How should the goals be established? The Committee method, Delphi method, and Survey method are generally employed to establish education goals. Under the Committee method, representatives from various public groups establish goals. The Delphi method compels a consensus of opinion among participants by repeatedly asking them to reconsider their opinions in line with the majority opinion. The Survey method establishes goals by contacting representatives of various public groups.
- What are the different levels of goals of education? Four levels can be immediately identified, each carrying with it its own level of specificity: state, system (or district), school, grade by subject. Each of the methods suggested above can be used to define goals for each of the identified levels, so long as the goal statements become more specific and program oriented as the level approaches the classroom milieu. It is best, however, to first obtain goals at the state level.

WHAT ARE THE MEASURES OF ACCOUNTABILITY?

There are two types of accountability: 1) *outcome accountability*, which is concerned with the end-product or result of an education program and 2) *transactional accountability*, which is concerned with the processes involved in conducting an educational program. *Product evaluation,* with reference to the attainment of knowledge and mastery of skills, is the measure of outcome accountability. This measure is highly sensitive to the definition of "outcome." *Process evaluation,* with reference to the program's material and its presentation, is the measure of transactional accountability. This measure is sensitive only to the specificity of the transaction.

It is one thing to define accountability and quite another to implement it. In particular, product evaluation is currently possible only in a very limited sense. For years, educators have been measuring outcome in terms of concept knowledge and skill mastery for a restricted number of subject matter goals, but few dependable instruments exist for measuring the attainment of higher-order goals.

Another problem, even for those few cognitive outcomes for which instrumentation exists, is the question of the validity of standardized or norm-referenced instruments. Educators are beginning to claim that the norm-referenced test does not assess all that they teach in the classroom; hence, these tests are not valid in terms of content. Popham has summarized this growing concern over standardized tests:

> . . . For the purposes of measuring results reflecting high quality instruction, standardized tests are usually inappropriate. They were designed, developed, and refined with a totally different purpose in mind, namely, to permit us to distinguish between different learners.[4]

In response to these concerns there is a decided trend toward the development of criterion-referenced testing. Carver, for instance, has been a leader in calling for criterion-referenced tests in reading.[5] Title II of the Elementary and Secondary Education Act of 1965, as amended, has encouraged state education agencies to develop similar intruments for assessing outcome with reference to higher order affective goals.

The final argument against accountability centers on the untested validity of the teacher education programs. Most of the course work and teaching practices considered essential for teacher education are based either on conjecture or on research that is poorly conducted, inconclusive, and conflicting. Thus, knowledge of instruction is very limited and educators are not in a position to put confidence in their teaching strategies, especially for children from minority groups. Under these circumstances, holding teachers responsible for

[4] W. J. Popham, "The New World of Accountability: In the Classroom," *NASSP Bulletin,* 56(364), 1972, p. 28.
[5] R. P. Carver, "Special Problems in Measuring Change with Psychometric Devices," Proceeding of the *American Institutes for Research Seminar on Evaluative Research: Strategies and Methods,* Pittsburgh, Pa., 1970.

the outcomes, when the teaching methods recommended to them in their teacher education programs may be invalid, would be unfair.

However, the concept of transactional accountability implies that the roles, functions, and duties of each professional in the educational system can be specified. Transactional accountability specifies that information regarding the performance of these duties by each professional be collected and evaluated at appropriate intervals. For each professional role a frame of reference must be developed from which the details of function and duty can be specified and a level of acceptable performance established.

Several schemes have been suggested to satisfy the need for a frame of reference for each professional role. Nicholson presents a skill-strategy matrix for the principal's role, where the skills are technical, humanistic and conceptual, and the strategies are of control, implementation, evaluation, and development.[6] Barrilleaux presents another scheme for identifying principal behavior, classifying it as diagnostic, prescriptive, implementative, and evaluative.[7] For the role of the teacher, several classroom interaction scales are available, such as Amidon and Flanders' "Interaction Analysis Scale"[8] or Vincent's "Indicators of Quality."[9] Similar schemes exist or can be created for the educational researcher, curriculum designer, and material innovator.

Outcome accountability provides information on the extent to which a program is meeting its stated goals and objectives. If a definition of value or educational worth is available, then outcome accountability can provide information on the extent to which a change in status is "good" or "bad." Transactional accountability provides information on the extent to which educators perform their roles (with respect to their functions and duties) in accordance with established program standards.

WHO IS RESPONSIBLE FOR WHAT?

Responsibility is the key issue in the accountability controversy. Teachers have been threatened the most by accountability, and their concerns are genuine. They feel that they may be held responsible for something over which they do not have total control.

[6] E. W. Nicholson, "The Performance of Principals in the Accountability Syndrome," *NASSP Bulletin*, 56(364), 1972.

[7] L. E. Barrilleaux, "Accountability Through Performance Objectives," *NASSP Bulletin*, 56(364), 1972.

[8] E. J. Amidon and N. Flanders, "Interaction Analysis as a Feedback System," [E. J. Amidon and J. E. Hough (eds.)] *Interaction Analysis: Theory, Research, and Application* (Reading, Pa.: Addison-Wesley Co., 1967).

[9] W. S. Vincent, "Indicators of Quality," *Institute of Administrative Research Bulletin*, 7(3), 1967.

Schools have more influence on some products than on others. Likewise, some professionals' contributions to student learning can be more easily assessed than others'. In particular, the contribution of school superintendents, subject matter supervisors, and school principals affect the learning environment, but rarely affect the student directly. Psychologists and social caseworkers directly affect the student, but there is little, if any, knowledge of the effects of their contribution on the learning environment. Obviously, at the present time the responsibility of each professional toward the attainment of different educational outcomes cannot be adequately determined.

In spite of the fact that teacher and other professional responsibility for outcome accountability cannot be precisely established, the demand for teacher accountability has been often raised. Popham first defines accountability in a very narrow sense:

> . . . In general the concept of educational accountability involves the teacher's producing evidence regarding the quality of his or her teaching, usually in terms of what happens to pupils, then standing ready to be judged on the basis of the evidence.[10]

He then suggests two methods for establishing teacher accountability: 1) criterion-referenced measures, and 2) instructional mini-lessons. By providing criterion-referenced measures, the teacher can more readily monitor the quality of instruction in relation to student progress and, insofar as resources permit, make individual diagnoses and prescriptions for different learners.

The instructional mini-lesson offers a more explicit method of teacher accountability by providing a specific instructional objective along with a sample measurement item showing how the attainment of the objective will be assessed, then testing the student on his attainment without the teacher's knowledge of the result.

It would appear that the concept of outcome accountability is too broad to be associated with an individual; *outcome responsibility* is collective and extends beyond the boundary of the instructional environment. On the other hand, the concept of transactional accountability can be directly associated with individuals through *transactional responsibility*. It follows, then, that the educator should be accountable for the functions and duties of his specific role, while the educational system and its surroundings should be accountable for the result.

TO WHOM IS EDUCATION ACCOUNTABLE?

An initial response to this question might be that the system is accountable only to those who pay the bill—the public. Insofar as the

---

[10] Popham, p. 26.

public is composed of the involved special interest groups, this is true; however, accountability to the public is only one facet of this issue. In a very real sense education is accountable to the future. That is, the students of today will hold the system accountable in the future for the experiences they encounter today. Thus, accountability is both real and perceived.

In order to implement the accountability concept, it is necessary to identify and become familiar with the involved public groupings. Knowledge of their opinions, beliefs, and perceptions help to establish a frame of reference from which needs can be defined and accountability oriented.

WHAT ARE THE DIFFERENT LEVELS OF ACCOUNTABILITY?

Accountability can be implemented at different levels, that is, from accountability of a lesson plan to accountability of a teacher, and thence to program accountability in a school, accountability in total, to school system accountability, and finally to accountability at the state level.

Lack of distinction between these concentric levels of accountability has resulted in unnecessary conflicts between teachers and other groups. For the most part these conflicts arise due to a misunderstanding of specific responsibilities. For instance, teacher accountability entails the individual teacher's responsibility for his instructional performance.

Program accountability involves the joint responsibility of different professionals with regard to specific functions of the program. School accountability involves the more complex joint responsibility of the administrators, specialists, teachers, and other staff members with regard to the overall worth of those programs within the school and the specifics of the instructional processes. School system accountability involves the even greater complex responsibility of two levels of administrators and specialists, as well as teachers and other staff members with regard to the coordination, leadership, and worth of the totality of educational programs within the system, along with the specifics of the instructional processes. State level accountability follows the same principles as school system accountability involving, in addition, the joint responsibility of each of the school systems within the state and the state department of education.

WHAT KIND OF DATA SHOULD BE COLLECTED IN AN ACCOUNTABILITY SYSTEM?

Accountability systems do not have to be identical, but can vary over the range of school systems and their unique requirements. This can be extended to the program level, where variations in evaluative data requirements exist, for example, between conventional classroom programs and open-classroom, team-teaching programs. The major objectives of the accountability system, the type of accountability (i.e., outcome or transactional) and the level of accountability will dictate the specifics of the data. In general, data should be collected on those variables which are classified according to the following:

- Taxonomy of educational outcomes (i.e., variables which can be measured or assessed in the cognitive, affective, and psychomotor domain)
- Taxonomy of educational transactions (i.e., variables which describe the functions and duties of the professionals with respect to the program processes)
- Taxonomy of educational inputs (i.e., variables which describe and measure the system—e.g., pupil-teacher ratio, instructional materials and facilities, etc.)
- Taxonomy of context variables (i.e., variables which describe and measure the environmental context of the community— e.g., social, economic, political, educational, etc.).

In addition, it would be desirable to collect data from the community on value and from the educational system on cost and on cost/tradeoff relationships. As time progresses and outcome accountability becomes feasible, this data will enable value-versus-cost tradeoff analyses so that a new concept of accountability may be implemented, *community accountability*. That is, an informed community and its legislative representatives should be responsible for and held accountable for voting on and enabling legislation based on value-versus-cost tradeoffs which can affect educational transactions; the community should be accountable for its legislative decisions here as well.

HOW SHOULD THE RESULTS OF ACCOUNTABILITY BE USED?

Although outcome accountability cannot now be implemented, product evaluation should still be performed. Product evaluation should be used to provide feedback to educators for improving and redirecting educational programs in order to meet stated goals. On the basis of this information, educators can estimate the strengths and weaknesses in programs and can reinforce or take corrective action wherever needed. In a similar manner, through the setting of goal priorities, the community can exert its influence on the educational system to construct and maintain its programs to meet these goals.

A second use of product evaluation would be to provide a valuable data base for basic research which otherwise would be very difficult to acquire. Such a data base would allow these programs to be simulated, tested, and refined *before* they are implemented in a live classroom environment.

Transactional accountability *can* be implemented at the present time. Its purpose is to provide feedback on how the program's activities are proceeding and how the plan meets the the actual and perceived needs of the community. This feedback allows the program's characteristics to be enforced so that product evaluation, in conjunction with transactional accountability, will afford comparisons among programs designed to accomplish the same or similar results.

Transactional accountability augmented by the collection of product evaluation data is valuable, since it provides comprehensive information for improvement of instructional programs as well as data badly needed for research. A comprehensive inferential analysis on this data bank will yield:

- control over the out-of-school variables in order to determine the effect of the learning environment on student achievement
- control over the out-of-school variables in order to determine the relative effectiveness of different program designs.

Finally, with the implementation of a meaningful accountability system and the establishment of a community value index on educational outcome and of cost/tradeoff relationships, accountability data can be presented to the public, who can then exercise their franchise based on intelligence rather than myth and subjectivity.

RECOMMENDATIONS FOR IMPLEMENTING ACCOUNTABILITY

The dimensions of accountability presented above should orient the educator to the various facets of accountability, the problems involved in its implementation, and the extent to which he may expect a meaningful accountability system to function. In response to the concepts and limitations presented here, the accountability implementor must focus on two issues: 1) current practices in accountability and 2) instrumentation for product evaluation.

The socio-political pressures to implement an accountability system have placed the educator in the vulnerable position of having to implement a system where there is often a misinterpretation between product and process; where teacher, administrator, curriculum innovator, researcher, and community responsibilities are not yet well defined and often overlap; where present evaluative tools exist only for a limited few areas; where goals are rarely stated in a manner suitable for accountability or with public approved priorities among them.

Under these circumstances, the educator often succumbs to the

accountability proposal which applies a few tests, employs a data retrieval system, points the finger of responsibility and "Voilà, Accountability!" Why is it that war and space deserve a thorough systems analysis and systems design, but educators are willing to
support the "quick trick"?

There is one possible reason for funding the quick-trick project.
Such a project offers a public relations visibility that relieves the accountability pressures during the life of the project. When the project
results in little success or in dismal failure, the system becomes the
center of a brief but bitter controversy until the next "cure-all" project can be funded, ad nauseum. Who has not seen this game,
whether intentionally or otherwise, played over and over again?

In recent years the controversy over norm-referenced versus
criterion-referenced tests as a suitable instrument for product evaluation has pervaded educational philosophy and educational research.
One complication, which further confuses the issue, is the fact that
criterion-referenced tests can be "standardized" and can be
"normed." Indeed, the standardizing and norming process is needed
for quality control on the developing criterion-referenced tests; thus,
the semantic issue compounds the technical issue. In order to clarify
this situation, Carver introduces the concept of *edumetric:*

> "Edumetric" refers to the current focus upon measuring *progressive
> within individual gains* of high relevance to education. This revolu-
> tionary edumetric approach to standardized test construction may be
> contrasted with the traditional psychometric approach which tends to
> focus upon the *static between individual differences* of high relevance
> to psychology.[11]

And, in a paper on how to tell the difference between psychometric
and edumetric tests, Carver further states:

> Psychometric tests are the wrong tests for evaluating the quality of ed-
> ucation, and the rate at which they are approaching bankruptcy is not
> nearly fast enough for the good of education.[12]

The edumetric concept would appear to be more suitable for determining individual progress, while not being as directly related to the
behavioral objective as the criterion-referenced concept. It would
follow then, that edumetric tests satisfy the need of outcome accountability for product-evaluative instrumentation.

We advocate that both process and product evaluation should
be conducted simultaneously. However, only process evaluation

[11] R. P. Carver, "Reading Tests in 1970 Versus 1980: Psychometric Versus Edumetric," *The Reading Teacher,* 26(3), 1972.
[12] R. P. Carver, "The Bankruptcy of Psychometric Tests in Education: How to Tell a
Psychometric Test from an Edumetric Test," AIR. Silver Spring, Md., 1973.

should currently be used for accountability, while product evaluation should be used as a supplement. In this way transactional accountability can be implemented initially.

As knowledge about the use of product evaluation for outcome accountability becomes more dependable, the emphasis should be shifted from transactional to outcome accountability. In general, implementation of a total accountability system must include the following stages:

- goals validation
- needs assessment
- priority of needs
- responsibilities determination
- formal transactional accountability system
- edumetric (i.e., standardized, normed criterion-referenced)
- test development
- product evaluation schemes
- formal outcome accountability system
- community value index development on outcome accountability criteria
- cost/tradeoff relationships on outcome accountability criteria
- formal community accountability feedback system.

Teacher Accountability— A Fallacious Premise

ALTON HARRISON, JR.
Northern Illinois University

In a recent study, the U. S. Office of Economic Opportunity reported that the educational achievement gains made by students in performance contracting programs were not significantly greater than those made in traditional public school programs.[1] Much of the fanfare that was initiated by the vast resources of industry (money and technological developments) have been applied to selected educational problems and while some gains were made the overall results are not encouraging.

From "Teacher Accountability—A Fallacious Premise," *The Kappa Delta Pi RECORD*, Vol. 9, No. 3 (February 1973), 75–76. Reprinted by permission of Kappa Delta Pi, An Honor Society in Education.

[1] O. E. O. Pamphlet (3400-5) *Experiment in Performance Contracting, Summary of Preliminary Results*, Office of Planning, Research, and Evaluation (February 1, 1972).

Just prior to the optimistic advent of performance contracting the federal government was making an assessment of its massive aid to selected programs in compensatory education. Again, the results were most discouraging.

Actually, none of these negative results should be surprising. As early as 1966, Coleman [2] in an impressive national study of 600,000 school children, reported that such items as per pupil expenditure, number of children per class, laboratory space, and number of volumes in the school library were of negligible significance in a child's educational achievements. He also reported that home background was the most important element in determining how well a child does at school. This finding was confirmed in a more recent study by Scriven. "Thus, in comparison to the home or family influence, the school has relatively little impact in determining the dominance of cognitive needs and interests and, hence, the degree of high or low motivation in the school milieu." [3] Within the school milieu, Coleman reported that the most important factor in a child's educational achievement was not teacher qualifications but peer group influence. Scriven also concluded that, "As teachers and administrators it is not unnatural, despite evidence to the contrary, to cling to the notion that our influence over youth is potent. But of the hordes of children who annually swarm through the classrooms, there is only a small percentage upon whom the teacher makes a significant impact." [3] Research by Bronfenbrenner [4] has also revealed that peer group influence has a marked effect upon the educational achievement of children.

All of the available evidence indicates that the student's attitude toward learning is the crucial factor in educational achievement and that the schools—teachers, except for a few dramatic exceptions, have a negligible influence on the formation-modification of these attitudes. It was the recognition and acceptance of this vital principle which prompted A. S. Neill to write:

> *We have no new methods of teaching because we do not consider that teaching in itself matters very much. Whether a school has or has not a special method for teaching long division is of no significance, for long division is of no importance except to those who want to learn it. And the child who wants to learn long division will learn it no matter how it is taught.* [5]

[2] James K. Kent, "The Coleman Report: Opening Pandora's Box," *Phi Delta Kappan* (January 1968).

[3] Eldon G. Scriven, "Motivation—Beyond the Teacher's Control?" *School and Community* (January 1970).

[4] Uri Bronfenbrenner, "The Split-Level American Family," *The Saturday Review* (October 7, 1967).

[5] A. S. Neill, *Summerhill* (New York: Hart Publishing Co., 1960).

This is such a simple, logical truth but educators refuse to accept its validity and continue to behave as if learning can be imposed on students. Not only is this type of approach ineffective; it also creates a crippling dependence on the part of students.

As Illich writes, there must be a transformation of consciousness about the nature of learning. "This means, above all, a shift of responsibility for teaching and learning. . . . Only when a man recovers the sense of personal responsibility for what he learns and teaches can this spell be broken and the alienation of learning from living be overcome." [6]

Each person must assume the major responsibility for what he learns. Learning, after all, is a highly personal and individual matter. In a discussion of his personal thoughts on teaching and learning, Rogers stated, "It seems to me that anything that can be taught to another is relatively inconsequential and has little or no significant influence on behavior. . . . I have come to feel that the only learning which significantly influences behavior is self-discovered, self-appropriated learning." [7] Learning cannot be packaged and peddled to students. "We must now recognize the estrangement of man from his learning when it becomes the product of a service profession and he becomes the consumer." [6] Learning is not something that one person (teacher) does to another (student). As Rogers asserted, "Self-discovered learning, truth that has been personally appropriated and assimilated in experience, cannot be directly communicated to another." [7]

In reality, learning is and should be the primary responsibility of the learner. To be sure there are other factors such as teachers, instructional materials, physical facilities, etc., which can enhance or facilitate the learning process but the accumulated evidence, thus far, indicates that these influences are minimal. The critical factor is the student's attitude toward learning which is directly related to family background and peer group influence. Thus, the attempt to hold a teacher responsible or accountable for what a student learns is both illogical and futile. If we really want to identify and hold responsible those factors most influential in the educational achievement of a child, then, the accounting must be rendered by his family and peers. Obviously, this would be most impractical if not impossible. Certainly those docile public servants, teachers–administrators, would be much easier to control and manipulate. Could this be the reason that we persist in trying to hold them accountable for student learning despite the fact that their influence is minimal?

[6] Ivan Illich, "The Alternative to Schooling, *The Saturday Review* (June 19, 1971).
[7] Carl R. Rogers, *Freedom to Learn* (Columbus, Ohio: Charles E. Merrill Publishing Co., 1969).

It would be possible to hold teachers accountable for learning if parents would turn their children over to the schools shortly after birth. While this may seem to be a radical suggestion, it is by no means an original proposal. The Soviet Union has certainly been receptive to such an educational concept, and the rapid growth of early childhood education in the United States may be a move in this direction.

The Systems Approach and Education

JOHN L. HAYMAN, JR.
Pennsylvania State University

Such terms as "systems approach" and "systems analysis" have appeared more and more in the educational literature in recent years, and we are likely to see more of them as time passes. What do these terms mean, and what is their value likely to be in education?

First, they imply a holistic and comprehensive problem-solving approach, an approach which is complex and exacting. In trying to increase reading ability in a school, for example, one would not look merely at the reading instruction received; he would examine all of the factors which influence reading ability, and which are influenced by reading ability; he would identify a reading "system" and examine it from the perspective of general system theory. This requires more effort than we are accustomed to investing in particular problems. However, the failure to approach problems from this perspective accounts for much of our frustration. We tend to be piecemeal and shortsighted in our efforts, and we oversimplify. We seem to think that any result can be achieved in the space of a single year. Obviously, we must learn to be more effective, and this will require greater effort than we have previously invested—the kind of effort required by the systems approach. What is the systems approach?

THE SYSTEMS APPROACH

Von Bertalanffy states that it involves problem solving from the system viewpoint; and this means proceeding as follows:

From "The Systems Approach and Education," *The Educational Forum*, Vol. XXXVIII, No. 4 (May 1974), 493–501. © 1974 by Kappa Delta Pi, An Honor Society in Education. Reprinted with permission.

A certain objective is given; to find ways and means for its realization requires the system specialist (or team of specialists) to consider alternative solutions and to choose those promising optimization at maximum efficiency and minimal cost in a tremendously complex network of interactions.[1]

Working from the theoretical framework described as general system theory, the system specialist solves problems through four general stages:

1. states or is given objectives; determines what ends are to be achieved;
2. analyzes the "tremendously complex" network of interactions in the relevant system, i.e., conducts a system analysis;
3. outlines alternative solutions to the problem;
4. determines which alternatives provide the best solution at maximum efficiency and minimal cost, i.e., performs a system synthesis.

The systems approach has been defined in various ways in educational writings. Examples of two descriptions of it are illustrated in Figure 1.

FLANAGAN [2]	CORRIGAN AND KAUFMAN [3]
1. Define the objectives in specific terms.	1. Problem identification.
2. Develop tests and performance standards to measure the attainment of the objectives.	2. Specification of detailed goals and subgoals.
3. Identify or develop the types of procedures which indicate the most promise for the achievement of the objectives.	3. Identification and selection of alternatives for achieving the goals and subgoals.
4. Implement the system.	4. Design and utilization.
5. Evaluate the effectiveness of the system and revise the system to improve its performance.	5. Evaluation.
6. Continue the implementation, evaluation, and revision cycle (1971, p. 2).	6. Required revision (1966, p. 127).

FIGURE 1. Two Descriptions of the Systems Approach

[1] Ludwig von Bertalanffy, *General System Theory: Foundations, Development, Applications* (New York: George Braziller, Inc., 1968), p. 4.
[2] John C. Flanagan, "The Plan System for Individualizing Education," *NCME: Measurement in Education* 2 (January 1971).
[3] R. E. Corrigan and R. A. Kaufman, *Why System Engineering* (Palo Alto, Ca.: Fearon Publishers, Inc., 1966).

These examples from the educational literature miss a central and crucial point: that the relevant system must be carefully analyzed so that the complex network of interactions can be understood. The CIPP model, developed by Stufflebeam and his associates, comes much closer to the mark by dealing with context, input, process, and product.[4] As in the systems view, the relevant universe is divided into system and environment (context), and both must be analyzed; there is context evaluation (the environment and its influences on the system are analyzed) and process evaluation (the internal workings of the system are analyzed). This model assumes an open system, and it provides for analysis of inputs (controllable elements from the environment which are fed into the system) and outputs (the condition of certain system components or of the total system after a certain degree of system operation). Inputs can include money, materials, instructional processes, staff, training programs, or any other items which are controllable. Outputs, or "outcomes" as they are sometimes called, are most often in terms of the degree to which stated goals and objectives have been met, and in local educational systems these usually concern learner characteristics. There are many outcomes in addition to those related to stated goals and objectives, however, and these additional outcomes (sometimes called "side effects") must be considered to understand system operation fully and its consequences. This systems oriented evaluation model is illustrated in Figure 2.

Suppose one were going to attempt to solve some learning-related problem at the local school district level, and he was going to use the systems approach. How would he go about it? First, he would follow a process which, in the manner of Flanagan, Corrigan, and Kaufman, can arbitrarily be defined as a sequence of steps. These steps are as follows:

1. Identify the problem
2. Perform a system analysis
   a. Describe the system and its environment; describe current structures, functions, and roles
   b. Describe target groups and their characteristics
   c. Conduct a needs assessment
   d. Identify constraints, including budgetary limitations
3. Specify detailed goals and objectives, that is, specify intended outcomes
4. Outline and evaluate alternative courses of action

[4] Daniel I. Stufflebeam et al., *Educational Evaluation and Decision Making* (Itasca, Ill.: F. E. Peacock Publishers, Inc., 1971).

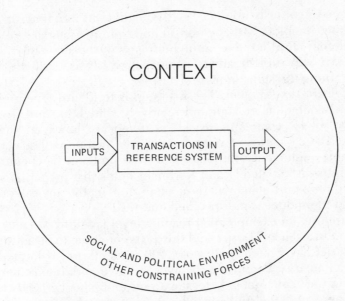

FIGURE 2. A System-Oriented Evaluation Model

5. Perform a system synthesis
   a. Design or redesign the relevant system, with specifications for:
      i. Inputs
         —Processes
         —Materials
         —Facilities and equipment
         —Personnel
      ii. Procedures and transactions within the system, including decision and control mechanisms
      iii. Supporting components, including information subsystems
   b. Construct or modify system components, according to the design
   c. Begin operating the system according to the design
   d. Conduct process evaluation
   e. Conduct product evaluation
   f. Assess, revise, and recycle through as many steps as necessary

The systems approach appears so logical, some have been moved to claim it is nothing more than common sense. Silvern has made the point, however, that the systems approach is not just "common sense rigorously applied." [5] It is, rather, an inquiry area and a discipline, complete with theoretical underpinnings and a developed methodology. Furthermore, applying many of the steps turns out to be an extremely difficult and exacting matter. Let us clarify this point by examining the steps in more detail.

Identify the Problem. The first step is to identify the problem. This seems obvious enough and relatively straightforward. It is apparently not so "common sensical" as it appears, however. Kaufman has noted as a "source of amazement" that "people will select, produce, and implement solutions before the problem has been identified and substantiated" [6] and Kerlinger holds that preparing a mission (or problem) statement is a vital step in the logical process required to produce some specified end result. [7]

Suppose, for example, that reading level is felt to be lower than desirable in a school district, and this is the problem to be addressed. The district has a membership of 6,000 students and is located in a metropolitan area. Parents on the average have middle incomes, and they hold blue collar jobs. At least, parents and school officials would like 50 percent of the students to be above national norms on reading achievement tests. This is the level of generality of problem statement which is likely to exist when application of the systems approach begins.

Systems Analysis. Step two is to perform a system analysis. This involves first describing relevant aspects of the system and its environment, looking at current structures, functions, and roles, and the way these interrelate. A special subset of system components consists of the people involved, and description of target groups and their characteristics is extremely important. It would also be important to conduct a needs assessment, and this can be seen as a part of the description of the system. It is singled out because of its particular importance in approaching learning-related problems. A recent set of USOE guidelines [8] indicated that needs assessment should be concerned with such things as:

> The proportions and actual numbers of students who fall below desired performance standards;
> Physical location where problems are most difficult;

[5] L. C. Silvern, "Introduction," *Educational Technology* 9 (June 1969): 18–23.

[6] Roger A. Kaufman, "System Approaches to Education: Discussion and Attempted Integration," *Social and Technological Change: Implications for Education*, Part III, p. 154.

[7] Fred N. Kerlinger, *Foundations of Behavioral Research* (New York: Holt, Rinehart and Winston, Inc., 1965).

[8] U.S. Office of Education, "A Manual for Project Applicants and Grantees," Guidelines for Title III, section 306, Elementary and Secondary Education Act of 1965, mimeographed (Washington, D.C.: U.S. Office of Education, 1970), pp. 35–37.

Hypothesized reasons performance falls below standards in different locations;

Characteristics of facilities, of staff, and of programs in relevant areas;

General population characteristics in the area of concern;

Implications of the needs assessment for the entire system, including areas where the problem is less severe or does not exist.

The last step in system analysis is identifying constraints. Cook [9] and others have noted that a constraint and a resource are often the same thing; it depends on how one looks at them. In identifying constraints, one examines the resources available—money, personnel, facilities, and the like—and determines their status. He also examines such things as the relevant political forces.

The systems literature generally recommends model building as a part of or as a next step after analyzing the system. In fact, an informal model has been generated in the steps outlined above. In any event, much of the work has been done in the analysis by identifying relevant components of the system and its environment and the interrelationships among them. Stating these in formalized fashion so that the complexities and influences are made explicit and operational outcomes can be predicted is part of the model building exercise. Mathematical models are desirable because of their preciseness in predicting outcomes; they have not been applied with much success in education. Formal verbal models can be highly useful, however, in organizing thought and in expressing complex situations parsimoniously and understandably.

To continue with the previous example, the relevant system—the unit of concern—includes everything in the district which influences reading ability. The influence of a number of factors are fairly obvious here: teacher experience and skill, instructional methodology used for reading at different grade levels, facilities, ability level of the children, past performance and current reading level of the children, the home environments and their characteristics, other nonschool environments, money available to the district, and the like. At least some of these are often examined in analyzing reading problems. What is not so obvious, and what is often neglected, is the interrelationship of reading with other academic subjects and the total effect reading ability has on self-confidence and on self-esteem as a learner. The learner needs materials at appropriate reading levels in all subjects, and he needs success experiences in reading in a variety of situations. The systems orientation tells us that the total range of interrelationships must be considered if the reading problem is to be solved.

[9] Desmond Cook, *Educational Project Management* (Columbus, Oh.: Charles E. Merrill Publishing Company, 1971).

In approaching the problem in this manner, the analyst would have defined the relevant components of the reading system and would have determined, at least at a verbal level, the relationships among components. Also, he would have defined the environment and determined the relevant influences from it. In effect, he would have constructed a model, a model which might be purely descriptive or which might be enhanced through graphic representations. The model in this case aids greatly in understanding the reading system and how it operates. It also must have some predictive power; it will aid later in deciding what changes are likely to result in more desirable outcomes.

Model-building in education is seldom engaged in consciously. The systems orientation indicates that important influencing factors are almost certain to be neglected without it and attempts to produce specific changes in outcomes stand a good chance of failure.

Stating Goals and Objectives. The next step in systems analysis is to lay out a specific set of goals and objectives. So much has been written about this area that we will not elaborate on it here.

The most important thing about goals and objectives is their placement in this description of the systems approach. A good deal of careful work must be accomplished before one is ready to talk about what he wants some program or some organizational change to accomplish. This seems elementary, but in practice it almost never happens, partly because the system analysis step is seldom taken. The set of goals and objectives must be comprehensive. For an instructional system, it must include all of the behavioral changes, the information, and the attitudes and values the learner is to acquire.

Setting goals and objectives is not just a matter of determining the current area of interest among the target audience at different levels and in different locations, and deciding on the basis of realistic expectancies how this differs from what should be. The values and desires of the target audience and of relevant others such as parents and the broader community must also be taken into account and some concensus reached.

When one arrives at this stage he will have details on the people with whom he is to work, he will know what he wants them to be like or to do as a result of the changes he is planning, he will know the relevant characteristics of the system he is working with and of its environment, and he will know about the constraints under which he is to operate. He will know a great deal about what he wants to happen, in other words, and he is ready to be serious about how he gets it to happen.

Identifying and Evaluating Options. There will always be a number of alternative ways in which the desired outcomes might be achieved. The problem is to pick the one which is most likely to succeed best in the system which has been analyzed and described. Making decisions requires knowledge of the relevant characteristics of each alternative, and here it is essential that theory, past results, and practical experiences be brought into play.

This step involves making predictions. The more accurate such predictions are at this point, the less redevelopment will be necessary later. The question is, given the system which exists—or rather the model of it which has been constructed—how can the system itself be restructured and how can controllable inputs be changed to produce the desired outcomes? In the example used above, there will obviously be many options, varying from broad restructuring such as open education to use of specific reading instruction methods in different locations and with different learners. One must match the characteristics of the existing model with those of the alternatives. What does theory say and what does hard evidence say about operation of the different alternatives under the circumstances which exist? Note that feasibility and practicality will be operating; identification of constraints is a part of systems analysis, and planning must take these into account.

System Synthesis and Evaluation. The final stage of the process involves system synthesis; putting together what seems to be the optimum solution. After the best-appearing alternative is selected, the relevant system is designed or redesigned, with specifications for:

1. Inputs
   a. processes
   b. materials
   c. facilities and equipment
   d. personnel
2. Procedures and transactions within the system, including decision and control mechanisms
3. Supporting components, including information subsystems.

One decides, on the basis of the information collected, how the relevant system is actually to be structured and to operate. He determines what its components will be and how they will be fitted together. He must also be concerned at this stage with how the system he is developing or changing will fit into the larger suprasystem, that is, with that part of the environment with which there are more formal relationships.

In the reading example, the system is likely to be defined as operating largely within classrooms or at the level of learner-teacher interactions. In this case, the school can be seen as a suprasystem, the district as a suprasystem at the next higher level, etc. Relations with these suprasystems obviously affect operation of the reading system, and must be given special consideration in the planning.

One next proceeds to construct new system components or modify old components, and to put the system together according to his design. Then he begins to operate the system, and conducts a process evaluation or, as Scriven [10] calls it, a formative evaluation. The concern is with determining how well the components of the system are operating in practice and discovering problem areas, including the reasons they exist. Some piece of equipment may not be working as intended, for example, or classroom teachers may not be behaving as desired. Supporting subsystems may not be functioning properly so that equipment is not delivered on time, administrative leadership is not maintained, or a computer is down so often that it interferes seriously with operation of the program. Problem areas must be identified and their causes understood if corrections are to be made and the system moved toward the optimum. Also related is the task of conducting a product evaluation, or a summative evaluation, as Scriven calls it.[11] The task is to determine the extent to which objectives are being met.

The final step, assessing, revising, and recycling, can now be taken. The information at hand must be carefully analyzed, process and product evaluation data related and their implications determined, and operational weaknesses and their causes identified. Unless some miracle has occurred, the system will not have performed exactly as intended, and its objectives will not have been fully met. Some of the reasons for this will be known if the preceding steps have been carefully followed, and recycling will be in order. The system must be reanalyzed and the model which represents it restructured. One or more additional cycles through the process may be required. The notion of iteration, that is, of cycling back through the series of developmental steps so that a convergence between intended outcomes and obtained outcomes occurs, is an essential of the systems approach. This idea is described graphically in Figure 3.

When is one finished with the development of a system? Ideally, when the discrepancy between achieved outcomes and intended outcomes has reached some acceptable level, and evidence indicates that maximum efficiency at minimal cost has been achieved. Sometimes he is finished when developmental resources are exhausted. In another sense he is never really finished. He may cease developmental activities in a particular area but as Kaufman has stated:

> No system or procedure is ever the ultimate system. A particular system like any other tool should constantly be challenged and evaluated

[10] Michael Scriven, "The Methodology of Evaluation," *AERA Monograph Series on Curriculum Evaluation,* vol. 1 (Chicago: Rand McNally and Company, 1967), pp. 39–83.
[11] Ibid.

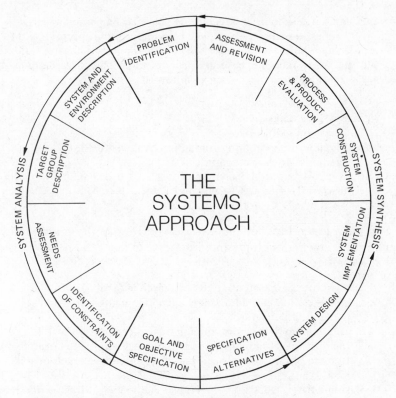

FIGURE 3. The Systems Approach in Program Development

relative to other alternatives and should be revised or rejected when other tools are more responsive and offer greater utility.[12]

SYSTEMS TOOLS

A number of special "tools" are used in the application of system theory, and use of these tools is often mistakenly identified as the "systems approach" or as "systems analysis." A planner may make a PERT chart to outline his intended activities, for example, and pronounce himself engaged in systems analysis. A finance director may begin installation of program budgeting, and may consider himself to be following the systems approach. As Kaufman notes, what they are really doing is using tools which have been developed as a part of systems methodology.[13]

. . . "System(s) Approaches" are a number of tools and techniques that have much to offer in the quantitative improvement of educational

[12] Kaufman, "System Approaches," p. 142.
[13] Ibid., p. 162.

outcomes. These tools and techniques have accompanied a marked shift in educational activities away from an intuitive approach and towards an empirical and even an evaluative framework for the systematic and measurable improvement of education. The most common of these tools and techniques are as follows:

1. Needs Assessment
2. System Analysis
3. Behavioral Objectives
4. Planning-Programming-Budgeting Systems (PPBS)
5. Methods-Means Selection
6. Network-based Management Tools, such as Program Evaluation Review Technique (PERT) and Critical Path Method (CPM)
7. Testing and Assessment (p. 162).

From a much broader framework, von Bertalanffy enumerates a number of "novel" developments intended to meet the needs of general system theory: [14]

1. Cybernetics, based upon the principle of feedback or circular causal change providing mechanism for goal-seeking and self-containing behavior;
2. Information theory, introducing the concept of information as a quantity measurable by an expression isomorphic to negative entropy in physics, and developing the principles of its transmission;
3. Game theory analyzing, in a novel mathematical framework, rational competition between two or more antagonists for maximum gain and minimum loss;
4. Decision theory, similarly analyzing rational choices, within human organization, based upon examination of a given situation and its possible outcomes;
5. Topology or rational mathematics, including nonmetrical fields such as network and graph theory; –
6. Factor analysis, i.e., isolation, by way of mathematical analysis, of factors in multivariable phenomena in psychology and other fields.

A major difference in the Kaufman and von Bertalanffy statements is the emphasis on mathematical techniques in the latter and the nonmathematical nature of the former. Most writers in the education literature speak very little of mathematical approaches when discussing "systems analysis" or "the systems approach." Outside of education, however, system theory has been preeminently a mathematical field, closely linked with computer science. This difference in emphasis seems partly related to certain intrinsic characteristics of education (e.g., the enormous complexities involved and

[14] von Bertalanffy, *General System*, pp. 90–91.

the lack of a comprehensive theory of instruction), but it is also due to the fact that applications of system theory and use of the systems approach in education are of recent origin and are still in a relatively primitive state.

CONCLUSIONS

This article has attempted to define the systems approach and to discuss how it might be applied in education. A very important point is that the approach derives from and is closely related to a broader perspective, the systems orientation, or still broader, to general system theory. The systems approach itself is a problem solving process or set of processes applicable at various levels in education. As the discussion makes clear, it is both complex and rigorous, and very demanding and costly. On the other hand, the systems approach is powerful and appears capable of systematically producing change. It has proven these qualities in applications in other fields, and it almost certainly has an important role in the future of education.

The question is: Do we have the patience and fortitude to learn the theory in all of its ramifications and to develop the skills needed to apply the approach?

The Systems Approach: For Education a Mixed Fit

ARNI T. DUNATHAN
University of Missouri-Columbia

In less than a decade, from the middle '50s to the middle '60s the United States space program moved from a point where it could only with great difficulty launch a grapefruit-sized satellite into shallow orbit to a high where three men in multiple spacecrafts were transported to the moon and back. How this seemingly impossible task was accomplished has fascinated men almost as much as the feat itself.

Putting a man on the moon called for a large-scale, coordinated approach to human and technological problem-solving unique in two important respects. First, the multiplicity of problems to be solved

This paper was prepared specifically for inclusion in this volume.

called for an organizational approach which could identify, monitor and complete thousands of individual tasks, in an order and on a time schedule that would permit attainment of the project goal at the earliest possible time. Second, the initial fund of information from which to begin was so pitiably small that decision-making could not be paced with traditional techno-scientific methods for producing provable data. What was needed was a method for making decisions about unknowns from unknowns: in other words, on the basis of prediction.

The resulting method was characterized by (1) detailed specification of objectives and priorities; (2) generation of multiple strategies; (3) decisions based upon best available data from applied research and simulation; (4) reduction of entropy via continuous monitoring of feedback.

The product became known as the manned spacecraft *system;* the method that produced it: *the systems approach.*

Long before the project was completed the system concept captured public acceptance. All that was required to enhance any human enterprise was to attach the word "system" to it. Thus an automobile muffler became an "exhaust emission control system" and simple soap a "clothes brightening system." On Madison Avenue and network TV, "system" became generic for "new-improved-effective."

In like fashion the word has been bantered about the education community. In the search for new-improved-effective processes in education, some have simply added the word to traditional practices. Authors and distributors market everything from textbooks to T-Squares as instructional systems. Kits of the '60s became systems of the '70s.

In slightly more serious attempts to apply systems approaches to educational processes and innovations, advocates have snipped off one or another bit of the concept in an attempt to make improvements. This decade's easy answer is the same as the last's: the production of behaviorally-stated objectives are the best "system" for providing ". . . more effective guidance to teacher planning and student learning." [1]

Of course the specification of objectives behavioral or otherwise falls short of being a system. Producing objectives is simply one of a number of predecessor events [2] which may or may not lead to more effective education. At its best the production of behaviorally-stated

---

[1] Wayne Dumas. "Can We Be Behaviorists and Humanists Too?" *The Education Forum,* 3, (1973), 303–306.

[2] Federal Electric Corporation. *A Programmed Introduction to PERT.* New York: John Wiley & Sons Inc., 1961.

objectives require following a widely distributed, well known and subtle art akin to cookery.[3,4,5]

And it is the very simplicity of the objective-stating task that is its greatest asset and liability, attracting multitudes of easy converts who feel, wrongly, that by writing objectives they have rubbed up a genie only to later find, rightly, that they still do not know how to get the teaching task accomplished. There is more to systems approach than suggesting that specifying the desire for a pile of wood is a system for chopping it.

Before outlining the characteristics of a system and the systems approach, it should be pointed out that there is unnecessary confusion over the term *system* and *systems approach*. A system can be defined as any interacting set of functions directed toward the accomplishment of a particular task. Thus both the interacting set of functions that resulted in the building of a manned spacecraft and the spacecraft itself, another set of interacting functions, are both systems. But the same systems approach could have been taken to making peanut butter, in which case the resulting process would be the system and the peanut butter the product. In other words, the systems approach to problem-solving necessarily produces a system as its by-product on the way to producing the target product (attaining the specified objective).

A system has particular characteristics, all of which must be present in any process if it is to qualify as a true system. In addition to the basic quadrad identified previously (specification of objectives; generation of alternative strategies; data-based decision; self correction), systems are usually large, complex, precise, technologic, and expensive.

The latter characteristics are understandable because the effort involved in mounting a true system is seldom expended unless the task to be accomplished is difficult and sufficient talent and money is available to address the problem. In addition the need for data demands applied research and simulation activities calling for heavy investments in electronic technology.

What then of education? Do the schools constitute an educational system, or is the term applied from recent fad or long habit? Space does not permit more than a cursory evaluation of the issue, but some data strongly suggest that education has only some characteristics of a system.

[3] Robert Mager. *Preparing Instructional Objectives.* Palo Alto: Fearon Publishers, 1962.
[4] Grant E. Barton. "Designing Competency Statements," *Audio-visual Instruction,* **2,** (1972), 16–18.
[5] Thorwald Esbensen. "Writing Instructional Objectives," *Phi Delta Kappan,* **1,** (1967), 246–247.

There are 64,020 public and 14,372 private elementary schools; 23,572 public and 3,770 private secondary schools; 1,780 K-12 schools; 1089 public and 1,467 private colleges in the United States.[6] If enormity is a criterion, education is a system. Total expenditures for public elementary and secondary education in the United States totaled $40,683,428,000 in 1970.[6] If high cost is a criterion, education is a system.

On the other hand, if specified objectives are a criterion, there is some question whether education qualifies. The ability of individual states to wipe out illiteracy, for example, varies widely from a high of 6.3 percent illiterates in Louisiana to a low of 0.7 percent in Iowa.[6] In a broader indicator of literacy as well as general knowledge, the percentage of draftees failing to méet minimum mental standards for induction into the armed services varies from percentages as high as 35.2 in Mississippi to a low of 1.9 in Minnesota. Unless the specific objectives for reducing illiteracy and providing basic knowledge is markedly different from state to state, education broadly taken does not resemble a system.

Less frequently-mentioned objectives, like providing equal educational opportunity, raise other doubts about education as a system. For example, the 370,786 pupils who attended school on curtailed sessions in 1971 were spread over 20 states and territories. Curiously, some states having a large number of pupils on curtailed sessions were among those who abandoned the largest number of classrooms in the same year.[6]

Statistics pointing out wide variations in governance and expenditures are myriad. For example, the Chief School Officer is in some states elected, in others appointed, and in others hired by the state board of education.[7] Clearly, the intent of the "system" varies. The percentage of money spent on administration and instruction calls forth further variance with some states spending as much as ten cents on the instructional dollar for administration while others spend less then five cents.[6]

The point is that it makes little sense to talk about *the* objectives, *the* strategies, or *the* anything else of our educational system. It is not a system and those characteristics it has in common with systems are secondary: enormity, complexity, and high cost.

What gains could be expected in education if a system approach were used to accomplish its tasks? The following is a synthesis of those advantages of systems most often cited.

[6] Bance W. Grant and George C. Lind. *Digest of Educational Statistics, 1973 Edition.* OHEW Publication No. (OE) 74-11103. Washington, D.C.: National Center for Educational Statistics Office of Education, 1973.
[7] Sam P. Horris. *State Departments of Education, State Boards of Education, and Chief State School Officer.* OHEW Publication No. (OE) 73-07400. Washington, D.C.: U.S. Government Printing Office, 1973.

1. The specification of goals and objectives focuses effort and clarifies for all parties involved what the process is directed to accomplish. Objectives not included in the specifications cannot be expected to be attained. For education this means a purposefulness of effort at all levels and a particular gain in the perceived relevance of teaching by faculty and learning by students.
2. The provision for multiple strategies provides flexibility as well as fail-safe backup. The system can continue to function when some routines are blocked. In education this promises provision for individual differences not only among learners but among other participants in the system.
3. The commitment to data-based decisions allows the system to function rationally in accord with facts and outside the constraints of opinion, intuition, and emotion. It promises to make a reality of accountability and allow education to demonstrate with hard evidence its accomplishments.
4. The provision for evaluation and feedback consciousness allows the system to be programmed for both designer oversights and changing objectives. Responsiveness to change could be an educational strength or advantage under a systems approach.

In other words, education could by using a systems approach to its tasks become a smoothly operating process in which objectives, methods and evaluation proceeded according to data-proved routine. One can conceptualize a high degree of success for each student individually and a high degree of success for groups of students as a whole. Depending upon the goals established for the system, education could become more or less expensive, more or less individualized, more or less satisfying for all involved personnel, and a host of other things which we now only hope for.

On the other hand, systematizing educational process could have some disadvantages. To understand these, it is useful to use a less exotic example than manned space flight. The crafts business in this country, painting by number included, has grown into a multimillion-dollar industry. Its growth has been largely due to the ability of those in the industry to reshape what had previously been specialized creative activities for an elite few to the status of popular creative activities for the masses. As a result, millions today do leather crafts, beadwork, stitchery, ceramics, painting and other artwork successfully.

Systematizing arts and crafts involved an approach similar to that which might be taken in systematizing instruction to the schools. First, the goal of arts and crafts needed to be reworked. The new goal of art and crafts was not to make works for the masses, but to make feasible the production of art by the masses. Secondly, objectives had to be reworked; a typical objective would be to have the average untrained adult produce a recognizable pastoral scene in oil when given suitable materials and instruction. Thirdly, strategies had to be mounted in such a fashion that success would be guaranteed for even the most inept consumer. Basically the strategy chosen was the self-instruction module in which all materials, instructions and evaluation (examples) were coordinated into one kit: paints, palettes, brushes, art board, sketches, instructions, and finished examples. Evaluation was built-in two ways: the numbered sketch allowed for GO/NO GO decisions and the finished examples showed the consumer what he was to produce before and after he produced it. The advantages from both the producer and consumer standpoint are obvious. The temptation to transfer guaranteed-success zero-failure systems to education is great. Why then has the systems approach to instruction not been adopted wholesale by educators in the schools?

The answer is multilayered. First, the conversation of traditional schooling methods to those just discussed is neither inexpensive nor easy. Research and development time is great even for modularization of the most simple learning task. Moreover, the talent and training for accomplishing the authorship of these modules is not widely available to education. Teacher training institutions are not widely training pre-service and inservice teachers in module preparation.

This is one reason the application of systems approaches to instruction has not been all that its advocates hoped. In too many instances, the quadrad had been translated to mean: (1) confront the learner with a miniscule task; (2) provide some encounter with content or experience; (3) measure acquisition and grade. This kind of system approach to instruction has produced boxfuls of boxes (believe it or not often shoeboxes) called learning kits. Affluent schools buy them ready-made from publishers, others less fortunate make them up during afternoon and weekend workshops.

Secondly, and more importantly, the educational process cannot be arrested while the changeover is made. Pupils still come to school everyday, teachers still instruct everyday. The modularization task must then be accomplished as a part time effort by personnel who are already occupied full time. Even when modules are being constructed in parallel with traditional instruction, the opportunity to field test and validate is limited by time and money. Thus where systemization is being attempted, it proceeds at an agonizing slow pace.

A third and often overlooked disadvantage is perhaps the most serious. A system approach to the development of anything, whether it be spacecrafts or arts and crafts, necessarily prohibits efforts outside of the constraints imposed by goals and objectives. Creativity can occur only within the narrow limits prescribed by the system. Thus the paint by number artist can substitute some colors for those specified, but he can only with great difficulty produce a painting entirely different from the one sketched. In the same way, the manned spacecraft program could not produce any interstellar vehicle other than some form of rocket. In other words, when the purpose of systematizing is to gain predictability and reliability, the obvious loss is variance.

It is the loss of variance in system approaches that is presently concerning more than teachers. Scientists are currently much disturbed at the emphasis upon applied research. In the research on cancer, funding agencies are supporting only those proposals directly linked to the search for a cure. Necessarily, much research which appears to be only peripherally related or research which is nondirectionally "pure" cannot for lack of funds proceed. The concern of many is that the key knowledge needed to solve not only the problem of cancer, but other scientific problems as well may never be discovered within the constraints imposed by applied research.

A related concern is expressed by those who ask whether systems approaches to education reduce the scope of instruction to a point short of concern for values. While it may be true that applications of systems approaches to education seem thus far to be limited to psychomoter and lower level cognitive tasks, there is nothing inherent in the systems approach that prohibits values oriented goals and objectives. The fact seems to be that designers are unable to mount strategies that are successful for getting at the values questions objectives. The highly successful and widely known systems of some evangelists and transcendentalists might suggest that the limitation is more fancied than real.

In attempting to assess the utility of the systems approach to educational problems it is important to understand that there is no single system approach; that any process for planning, developing and validating procedures that includes the quadrad discussed here can be called a systems approach. Said another way, any process for solving educational problems that results in the establishment of a true system is a systems approach. This is more than double talk for it emphasizes the real contribution of the systems approach: that the product is more important than the process. It is curious to realize, in fact, that the often heard condemnation of the systems approach, that the means justify the ends, is directly opposed to the message of the approach: the ends justify the means.

And the ends of education ought to be of such wide import that they justify the most effective means for attaining them. The systems approach may be that mean.

RELATED REFERENCES UNCITED

AACTE. *Final Report PBTE Regional Conference.* Washington, D.C.: mailed to conferees, July 3, 1973, p. 7.

Banghart, Frank W. *Educational Systems Analysis.* London: Collier-Macmillan Limited, 1969.

Bundy, Robert F. "Accountability: A New Disneyland Fantasy," *Phi Delta Kappan,* **LVI,** No. 3 (1974), 176–180.

Davies, Ivor D. *The Management of Learning.* London: McGraw Hill, 1971.

Frontz, Neven B., Jr. and Gary L. McConeghy. "Individualized Instructional Systems for Industrial Education," *AV Instruction,* **2,** (1972), 19–23.

Garloff, David A. "Instructional Development in Health Science Education," *AV Guide,* **10** (1972), 5 +.

Haney, John B., et al. "The Heuristic Dimension of Instructional Development," *AV Communication Review,* (Winter 1968), pp. 358–371.

Lawson, Tom E. "Influence of Instructional Objectives on Learning Technical Subject Matter," *Journal of Industrial Teacher Education,* (Summer 1973), pp. 5–14.

Ramsey, Curtis. "Interview," *AV Forum,* **1** (1970), No. 3.

Schoffer, Susan. "Before Objectives: Goals," *AV Forum,* **1** (1970), No. 10.

Toye, Michael. "Training Design Algorithm," *Training in Business and Industry,* **10** (1970), 36 +.

Trow, William Clock. "The Systems Approach," *Strategies and Tactics in Secondary School Teaching: A Book of Readings.* New York: Macmillan, 1968, pp. 27–31.

Intellectualism and Professionalism

DANIEL E. GRIFFITHS
New York University

A recurring topic of discussion among educators is the need for professional education to assume truly professional proportions. What does it mean to be professional? Are we professionals? How can we become more professional? Attempts to answer these questions generally fail because they deal with the external manifestations of professionalism, not with its essence. At the heart of any profession is intellectualism, and educators have been unwilling to address themselves to the intellectual dimensions. Quite to the contrary, in fact, professional education has had a definite anti-intellect line since its birth.

Reprinted by permission from *New York University Education Quarterly,* **V,** I, (Fall 1973): 1–6. © by New York University.

ANTI-INTELLECTUALISM IN EDUCATION

Hofstadter observed that "The appearance within professional education of an influential anti-intellectualist movement is one of the striking features of American thought." [1] The truth of this statement should be apparent to any observer. What passes for a professional literature, the speeches at educational conventions, the dialogue among practitioners, and in many cases the quality of teaching in classrooms can hardly hold up as intellectual. The question one must ask is not so much whether or not professional education is anti-intellectual, but rather how did it come to be this way and why does it remain so. In the vein of social Freudianism, I do believe there is a degree of causation between beginning states and present conditions. America began as an anti-intellectual country and today largely continues to be so. It would be great fun to deliver stories of the anti-intellectualism in American life, as, for instance, President Eisenhower's definition of an intellectual as "a man who takes more words than are necessary to tell more than he knows," [2] but we are restricted to exploring intellectualism in relation to professional education.

Professional education grew out of generations of public school teachers. The status and quality of the early teachers did much to set the tone both for public perception of teachers and for the quality of those who entered teaching. Hofstadter cites Elsbree as the source of discussing colonial schoolmasters in terms of drunkenness, slander, profanity, lawsuits, and seductions.[3] Wittlin, writing in *The Professions in America*, notes, "The low opinion of the rank and file schoolmaster in Europe spread to the New World, and a seventeenth-century Rector of Annapolis recorded that on the arrival of every ship containing bondservants or convicts, schoolmasters were offered for sale but that they did not fetch as good prices as weavers, tailors, and other tradesmen." [4] She refers later to the Annual Report of 1842 of the State Superintendent of Instruction in Michigan, which declared that "an elementary school, where the rudiments of an English education only are taught . . . requires a female of practical common sense, with amiable and winning manners, a patient spirit, and a tolerable knowledge of the springs of human action." [5] A profession that begins this way has a long uphill battle. What of today?

[1] Richard Hofstadter, *Anti-Intellectualism in American Life*, New York: Knopf, 1963, p. 323.
[2] Ibid., p. 10.
[3] Ibid., p. 313.
[4] Alma S. Wittlin, "The Teacher," in *The Professions in America*, Kenneth S. Lynn, ed., Boston: Houghton Mifflin, 1965, p. 96.
[5] Ibid., pp. 96–97.

It seems to me that anti-intellectualism is still prevalent in both old and new forms. Certainly the great recognition both in the general public and among professional educators of the critics of education must be construed as the ascendancy of meddlers who lack true understanding of the professional challenge. Critics such as Kozol and Holt are clearly not intellectuals. Illich, who must be considered an intellectual, is not really a critic of education but of American society. Actually he judges the schools to be too successful. Jencks too is not really a critic of education but rather a socialist who now realizes that he cannot accomplish his revolution through the schools. Silberman's critique makes intellectual overtures, that is, he attacks the lack of purpose and the "mindlessness" of teachers, and he reports the tradition of John Dewey. However, his advocacy of the English integrated day as a model for American elementary education is not made because children learn more in the English open-classroom, but because they seem happier there.

THE FAULTS OF COMPETENCY-BASED TEACHER EDUCATION

The major development in teacher education at the national level is competency-based teacher education (CBTE). With so much being said and written about it (the American Association of Colleges for Teacher Education recently published its twelfth booklet on the subject), one would think it easy to define. This is not the case. Schmieder, one of the founders of the movement, recently published a seventy-seven-page booklet in which he successfully avoided coming to grips with a definition.[6] As I understand it—many tell me I do not—competency-based teacher education is an attempt at creating a system that ties together the school of education (professors and students), the public school, the teachers, and the community in the definition of teacher performances (competencies, behaviors, or skills—all terms which are used interchangeably) that are then to be related to student learning. This is called "putting it all together." At present, all that has been put together is the process, the relations among the various groups. No one has yet related a teacher's behavior to a student's learning. There is some doubt that this will ever be done. For example, the Florida State Education Department, always among the first on an educational bandwagon, has published a thick catalog of teacher competencies. One of these is tolerating lengthy periods of silence in the classroom. The research trick is how to relate the teacher behavior, tolerating silence, to student learning.

I submit that competency-based teacher education as it is pres-

---

[6] Allen A. Schmieder, *Competency-Based Education: The State of the Scene*, Paper No. 9, Washington, D.C.: American Association of Colleges for Teacher Education, 1973.

ently proposed is the height of anti-intellectualism. It presumes to reduce teaching to a set of performances that can be imitated by relatively untrained people such as paraprofessionals. Competency-based teacher education as it appears to be conceived and practiced is quite the opposite of the professional approach to teaching, that is, the education of teachers who are conceptualizers, who understand their tasks in a broad, theoretical framework.[7] When the advocates of CBTE are confronted with this argument, they label the theoretical components as performances whether or not those components can be reduced to overt observable behaviors. For instance, deriving the mean of a distribution is called a competency at the University of Toledo. This, Broudy tells us, is transubstantiation by semantic incantation.[8] It is a typical reaction of professional educators: what they are doing has so little intellectual rigor, they use words they like to describe their work. While this manifestation of anti-intellectualism in CBTE relates to the product and to the implications of the movement for education, a second manifestation relates more directly to general anti-intellectualism. Competency-based teacher education completely ignores its own historical bases. During the 1920s there was a similar movement called elementalist psychology, which took teacher education by storm. In this instance the idea was to take what the child was to learn and break it up into very small pieces. In geometry, for instance, a theorem might be divided into a hundred bits and each taught to the child. I suppose the concept was related to the idea of a division of labor in factories where difficult tasks performed by skilled mechanics are subdivided and little pieces are taught to unskilled laborers. While the work got done, no one expected the unskilled laborers to become skilled mechanics. But in education it was anticipated that children taught by elementalist psychology would become mathematicians, historians, and the like. It was quickly found that while the children did learn the elements, they had no idea what it meant when they had learned all the bits. The sum of the parts did not equal the whole. As could be expected in a field which had and still has no theoretical base, professional education immediately swung to the opposite—Gestalt psychology—an equally fruitless approach to teaching. As if these failures were not enough, during the 1950s the Cooperative Program in Educational Administration sponsored by the Southeast Center of the Kellogg Foundation spent hundreds of thousands of dollars on the competency approach to training school administrators. Needless to say, that also was a complete failure.

Competency-based teacher education as a movement is anti-in-

[7] Harry Broudy, *A Critique of PBTE*, Paper No. 4., Washington, D.C.: American Association of Colleges for Teacher Education, 1972.
[8] Harry Broudy, *Why Oppose PBTE?*, mimeo paper, 1973.

tellectual because it ignores the lessons of history and it is attempting to move ahead with no adequate theoretical base. But it does not need to continue this way. The emphases on field-relatedness, involvement with teachers, and materials development, which characterize so many competency-based programs, is highly desirable. But more programs need to seek out theoretical rationales for what is taught. The approach employed at New York University and described in Part II of this report is but one of many that could be used. Competency-based teacher education would make more progress if its advocates would stress substance rather than process, if they would insist on competencies having a theoretical rationale, and if they would actually relate teacher competencies to student learning.

INTELLECTUALISM

Enough for anti-intellectualism. What is intellectualism? It has, of course, been defined in many ways over the years, the definition reflecting the biases of the interpreter. Eric Hoffer, for instance, says, "By intellectual I mean a literate person who feels himself a member of the educated minority." [9] The context in which he writes gives the definition the meaning of "literate snob," certainly not an acceptable way of using the term. There are other more useful ways of talking about intellectuals. Shils offers a highly operational definition, which at first hearing strikes the listener the way all operational definitions do—circular, obvious, and a bit silly. He says: "Those who produce intellectual works are intellectuals. Those who engage in their interpretation and transmission are intellectuals. Those who teach, annotate, or expound the content of works are intellectuals. Those who only 'consume,' for example, read intellectual works in large quantities, and who concern themselves receptively with works are also intellectuals." [10] The three intellectual functions correspond roughly to the types of intellectuals: productive, reproductive, and consumer.

But this does not help us to understand the concept or to use it more wisely. Shils goes further, however, and asserts: "Any intellectual work is produced in a setting of intellectual tradition or traditions. . . . Any intellectual tradition exists in a stock of works which those who participate in the tradition 'possess,' that is, assimilate into their own intellectual culture and to which they also refer." [11]

It seems to me that this statement marks the distinguishing characteristics of an intellectual. He is a person who lives and works within a line of thought that is public, that exists so anyone who is interested can read and verify the referents. In the field of education, for instance, a philosopher might claim to be a pragmatist of the John

[9] [Ed. note: Footnote omitted in the original.]
[10] Edward Shils, "Tradition of Intellectuals," *Daedalus*, Spring 1972, p. 22.
[11] Ibid., p. 23.

Dewey mold. Pragmatism has a long and distinguished history, a literature replete in both substantive contributions and criticism. A philosopher who identifies himself as a pragmatist is instantly recognized as a participant in an established intellectual tradition. It is expected that he will make references to the literature of pragmatism as he establishes his own position. It is not expected that he will always stay within the established tradition, but the reader of his works will always be able to interpret what the pragmatist is saying because he understands the tradition.

PROFESSIONALISM

What does intellectualism have to do with professionalism? The point is that unless one deals first with intellectualism and then with intellectualism in relation to professionalism, professionalism has little or no meaning. It is because we in professional education have been unwilling to connect the two that our efforts at attaining full professional status have met with so little success.

First consider a document written by Charles C. Mackey, Jr., Associate in Teacher Education of the New York State Education Department. He states that the distinguishing characteristics of a profession are these:

—dedication to service
—the assumption of responsibility for quality of service
—a selective process which will ensure competence of membership
—individual growth of members within a profession
—respect for law and authority
—a higher priority for duties and responsibilities than for rights and personal welfare.[12]

Where did these characteristics come from? Certainly they are not related to the long line of studies of the professions. Therefore, they do not have any relationship to traditional ideas about the professions. In fact, they appear to be more applicable to barbers or plumbers than to teachers. What is appropriate for a craft only touches the minimal requirements for a profession without getting at the essential ingredient. Mackey's list lacks what is most necessary, the intellectual aspect. It is simply impossible to talk about a profession without talking about its intellectual base.

Whitehead's approach to the need for an intellectual base for a profession can be seen in the distinction that he draws between a craft and a profession. A craft, he says, is "an avocation based upon customary activities and modified by trial and error of individual practice," while a profession is "an avocation whose activities are

---

[12] Memorandum from the University of the State of New York, The State Education Department, Division of Teacher Education, February 15, 1973.

subject to theoretical analysis and are modified by theoretical conclusions derived from that analysis." [13] This is the distinction which must be made. A profession rests upon theoretical bases. By theory, one generally means a set of assumptions from which are deduced by logical and/or mathematical means hypotheses which, in turn, can be tested. It is through this process that a body of verified knowledge is established. Practice can then be compared with knowledge, whereupon it receives a degree of legitimacy. Whitehead is saying that the essence of professionalism is intellectual in the sense that I have been using the term.

At the present time, teaching is, by Whitehead's definition, a craft. Most, if not all, teachers perform according to their customary procedures and occasionally try something new. The test of the new is highly personal: Did the teacher like the new approach? Did the children like it? Did the children seem happy? Did the teacher think the children learned better?

It is possible for teaching to become a profession provided the necessary knowledge base is built. A beginning has been made in that a number of recent researchers have contributed valuable knowledge to teacher educators. Bloom's review of almost one thousand studies of selected human characteristics pointed up the tremendous importance of early education. The significance of his work has been reflected in Head Start, in the interest in nursery school and kindergarten education, and in a revival of concern for primary education. One of the many ideas that Guilford's work on the "structure of the intellect" has led to is that learning is the discovery of information, not merely the formation of associations. Suppes' research on principles of learning utilizing advanced computer technology promises to open new vistas for teacher educators. The effects of the environment on child development have been explored by Martin and Cynthia Deutsch in Harlem schools, with the result that reading scores of disadvantaged children have been substantially improved. Clearly, research in the past ten years indicates that, given sufficient support, a knowledge base can be established which will give full professional standing to teaching.

Research in the next decade should build upon that mentioned above and should address itself to critical educational questions. Previous studies clearly point to the socioeconomic level of the child's family as the most significant factor in his school success. The crucial question is not, what is the correlation, but rather, why is there a consistently high positive correlation regardless of who studies the problem? What is there about the socioeconomic level of the family that makes for school success? If the elements of the factor can be determined, these might be duplicated for deprived children.

[13] Lynn, p. v.

After nearly a century of psychological research, educators still know little about how children learn. Since virtually all schooling takes place in groups it may be that studies should be sociological and anthropological rather than psychological. Certainly we cannot shrug off a hundred years of failure; it is time for a change.

The third urgent concern is more along development than research lines, but as the task unfolds research topics would emerge: Can the school be reconstructed as a social institution? Enough is known about the behavioral sciences to design schools in which children can live and learn much better than they do now. As the model for the new school develops there will be a need to know more about the classroom as a social system; about the way unionism affects relations between teachers, administrators, and school board members; how schools should be administered given the increasing professionalism of teachers; how schools relate to other social systems; and, of course, what should be taught in the schools.

This is not an exhaustive list of research and development questions. If, however, answers could be found to these questions, the education profession would be well on its way toward establishing an intellectual base.

PROFESSIONAL TRAPPINGS ARE NOT SUFFICIENT

Two other points are always discussed in connection with teaching as a profession. The first is status. Teacher organizations go to great extremes to gain status for their members—passing special laws generally called professional practices acts, insisting on being called professional, and the like. Certainly it is true, as Hughes has said, "A profession is an occupation that has attained a special standing among occupations." [14] Status, however, cannot be mandated or legislated, it must be earned. The United Federation of Teachers in New York City is a good case in point. It has now achieved great power through political action. Its leadership is well aware, though, that this power has not moved its members one inch closer to recognition as a profession at the same level as medicine and law. The leadership realizes that there is virtually no knowledge base for teacher practice, and they are aware that the public knows it too. The UFT is therefore turning its efforts toward improving the knowledge base for teaching, and the rest of us should join with them to achieve full professional status.

There has also been the idea that a professional is one who sets his own hours and working conditions and, in general, is an autonomous entrepreneur. While it is true that some doctors, lawyers,

[14] Everett Cherrington Hughes, *Men and Their Work,* Glencoe, Ill.: Free Press, 1958, p. 157.

architects, and others are independent, far more professionals work within institutions. Hughes goes so far as to say, "Most of the new professions, or would-be professions, are practiced only in connection with an institution." [15] By new or would-be professionals he meant nurses, librarians, social workers, and teachers. Further, more and more doctors are joining together in clinics or work for business, industry, the armed forces, and other institutions. It is probably correct to say that more lawyers work for law firms than operate individually. The trend appears to be toward professionals working in the context of a great variety of institutions. In this sense, they will become more like teachers. Certainly it can be said that autonomy is not a necessary requirement for professional status.

In summary, the argument has been made that while teaching is one of the oldest careers it lacks full professional status. It is still ranked with nursing, social work, and the other emerging professions. This is so because the intellectual foundations have not been established, largely because of the anti-intellectual stance of professional educators. There is nothing inherent in the nature of teaching or in the conditions under which it is practiced that prevents the acquisition of professional status. The weakness is in those who teach, those who teach the teachers, and in the material that is taught to the teachers. There has, however, been enough new knowledge developed in the past twenty years to be optimistic about the possibilities of building the necessary intellectual base for a profession of teaching.

[15] Ibid., p. 133.

New Threats to Teacher Autonomy

THOMAS R. BERG and LOUIS SPINELLI
University of Northern Iowa

In the eighteenth and nineteenth centuries, rationality was identified with freedom. The ideas of Freud about the individual, and of Marx about society, were strengthened by the assumption of the coincidence of freedom and rationality. Now rationality seems to have taken on a new form, to have its seat not in individual men, but in social institutions which by their bureaucratic planning and mathematical foresight

This paper was read originally before a session of the American Educational Studies Association, Chicago, Illinois (February 21, 1974) and is reprinted with the permission of the authors. Also by permission of *The Journal of Thought* for its use as "Contemporary Threats to Teacher Autonomy," *The Journal of Thought*, 9, 4 (November, 1974), 230–236.

usurp both freedom and rationality from the little individual men
caught in them.
C. Wright Mills

The reaction of educationists to the many critics who have
claimed that schools are ineffective and inessential is beginning to
shape up as a frantic scurry to demonstrate that schools *are* important, that they *are* productive, that measurable results *are* being
achieved. This justification process is being done systematically and
with a vengeance, for it is felt that the schools must produce results
that are visibly demonstrable, quantifiable, and amenable to assessment. The inefficiencies of former educational practices and loosely
organized schools composed of autonomous, unreliable, and distinc-
tively unscientific teachers must be corrected. Thus we have seen, in
the past several years, the rapid rise of a "systems approach" to education, including such programs as Individually Guided Education
(I.G.E.), Individually Prescribed Instruction (I.P.I.), Individual
Mathematics System (I.M.S.), and the various behavior modification
systems which are being adopted at an ever-increasing rate. The defenders and salesmen for these educatioal programs argue that they
are educational techniques which rationalize and systematize what
all good teachers are now doing. The systems approach, so the argument goes, merely permits these techniques to be used with greater
consistency and reliability. The position to be taken here is that the
generalized trend toward these kinds of systematic approaches, program packages, and behavior modification systems is in itself a threat
to the autonomy of teachers. Furthermore, these programs will result
in an inevitable transformation of the definition of what a teacher is,
resulting ultimately in the exclusion of subjectivity from the teaching
act.

As a reaction to the turbulence of the sixties, many teachers and
administrators have come to believe that the concept of "education
as liberation" has reached its limits. The desirability of conflict between interest groups in a democratic society has become suspect.
Order, stability, and a hassle-free life are becoming more important
than a risky commitment to encouraging freedom and autonomy and
accepting the possibility of disorder. Abstract ideals are easily replaced by tangible behavioral "outcomes." Because of what they felt
to be the outrages of the New Left during the past decade, even
many intellectuals have become embarrassed about advocating freedom, and the program developers and learning-system hustlers have
begun to fill the gap with promises of order *and* learning. The difficulty is that with most of these programmed and behavioral systems, the problem of discovering the general will is supplanted by
the slickness of a packaging-advertising approach to gaining ap-

proval, consensus, and cooperation. Education as liberation is replaced by education as manipulation and social control.

These teaching systems are doubly attractive to administrators. First, they establish the grounds for systematic accountability procedures; and second, they permit the exercise of greater knowledge of and control over what each individual teacher is doing and achieving. Holding teachers to personal professional integrity is simply less effective than holding them to the demands of a technical pedagogical system. This is not a case of ruthless administration, pitting its intimidating force against the teachers, but rather the subtle imposition of technique as the standard of judgment and accountability. We will no longer rely upon faith in autonomous, knowledgeable, creative persons, but rather on effective implementation of technical and behavioral systems to get the educational job done. Diversity and pluralism must be eliminated, since they are antagonistic to the ends of effective management and the refinement of technique. The implications of this new emphasis on technique become clear when one considers such systems as I.G.E., which will not "permit" a school to implement its program without the absolute commitment of all teachers and all classrooms to the I.G.E. method. Apparently, even the *possibility* of criticism, dissent, or perhaps competition will impair the effectiveness of the program. It appears that the critical faculties must be suspended for the successful implementation of this system. Scientific faith is apparently a suitable substitute for the more primitive faith in reason, diversity, and dissent.

The shift in emphasis from human qualities (knowledge, style, intelligence, spirit, humor, soul) to technique has the effect of diminishing the possibility of unity among teachers; and the effect of treating the individual as the "sole sociological unit" (as Ellul points out) diminishes freedom. The breakdown of traditional unity opens man up to change, "innovation," and manipulation, and thus administrators have a vested interest in the individualized technical approach. Traditional groups resist "progress," and a plastic society is "possible only when the individual (is) completely isolated." [1] The managed environment is possible only when human beings are fully integrated into the overall system, and this is attainable only when the person is subservient to technique, and other loyalties are weakened through individuation. Adherence to technique ultimately technologizes its user.

Just as necessity generates technique, technique generates ideology. Out of a desire for order and predictability comes a technology that presupposes its own goodness. The obstacle to order is not technique, but man. Technique can be perfected, but man can-

---

[1] Jacques Ellul, *The Technological Society* (New York: Vintage, 1967), p. 51.

not; thus man must be accommodated to process. The new educational elite has assumed the burden of "assessing individual needs" and responding with appropriate educational programs. This kind of technical expertise with respect to discerning needs will lead to the imposition of "appropriate" styles, levels, and kinds of education, to which the individual will respond. Social class will increasingly be a function of the ability to plan the futures of others.

There is no guarantee that these techniques will or will not be used to oppress, control, or brutalize man. The central issue is that we are choosing to believe that mistreatment at the hands of teachers is more likely than mistreatment arising from the faulty application of technique. The technologists, administrators, and behavior managers are betting that technique is more humane and reliable than philosophy.

Public school teachers ought to realize that the planner, not the implementer, is in control; for the planner moves on, making his previous innovations obsolete, keeping one step ahead of the implementers. And if the programmed systems do not standardize the students, they certainly enhance the control and manipulation of the teacher. Administrators who do not trust teachers to manage their jobs (and few do) are strong advocates of systems which diminish teacher autonomy. Administrators turn to this approach both as a means of increasing the reliability of pedagogical "production" and of improving the image of teaching as a scientific, rather than a freelance, enterprise. When the managerial ethos becomes an end in itself, technique, rather than substance, is the means of achieving recognition and control.

The impetus to control, to manage, to manipulate the environment is the outgrowth of a loss of faith in the person and in education. These goals have nothing to do with the art or craft of teaching, but rather with a growing desire to eliminate the problematic side of human existence. The dangers of this enterprise have been pointed out by Bernard Mehl who wrote that in the near future, "Psychic imperialism will take the place of economic and political imperialism. Well-being will be the exportable product. Those who refuse well-being must be insane." [2] Teachers who prefer the unmanaged environment and the unprogrammed teaching act will have no place in education.

> The right use of technology is to simplify the environment, not clutter it; to provide necessities and conveniences, not gimmicks; to tailor itself modestly to human functioning, not to overbear it and straightjacket it. [3]

[2] Bernard Mehl, *Classic Educational Ideas* (Columbus: Charles E. Merrill, 1972), p. 211.
[3] Paul Goodman, *Like a Conquered Province* (New York: Vintage, 1967), p. 386.

Peter Schrag prophesied and documented the decline of the WASP who had for decades set the standards which the ethnics and populists had sought to emulate. They had led out of their competence, courage, and cussedness. But in these sophisticated educational times, people are not so easily led and are increasingly reaching their own conclusions. However, this has not humbled those who rush to fill the leadership gap, equipped, not with real competence, but with slogans, banners, and an abiding faith in public relations.

Increasingly, the significant difference of perspective seems to lie between real performance and public relations. Where the demand and come-on of technique (in the sense that Ellul gives us) requires some brashness and offers in its standardization to rid us of our problems while taking care of our insecurities, the public-relations programmer offers us gimmickery and faddishness at their lowest levels.

Where the excesses and irresponsibilities of the young of the 1960's might be explained by an overweening idealism, mis-matched expectations, and a general environment of mass revolutionary fervor, how can one explain similar behavior legitimatized and institutionalized on the part of many in management and administration? This has to be one of the strangest flip-flops in history. The turmoil of the late 1960's forced most to call for a re-emergence of those who knew and knew how-to-do. But those who have answered the call have shown us only corporate irresponsibility, human insensitivity, and an unbelievable immaturity of significant experience. This forces most of us, citizen and teacher, back to the ethic of self-reliance. The WASP as a national direction is dead, and the new managers and programmers are only hustlers institutionalized.

The real teacher has always known that his contact and interaction with his class and his ability to summarize and learn from these personal experiences were always greater guides to the precious process of learning than any sloganeer could offer. But maybe there existed some superintendents or school principals who had earned their wisdom from years in the classroom and thus were able to pass on to the incoming teacher some helpful suggestions. And maybe the incidence of this was enough to reinforce a confirmed and common belief that positions that claimed expertise actually proved such expertise in performance. After all, if you can't trust the experts, whom can you trust? The events of our day point increasingly toward a Protestant world of personal decisions and a feeling of "who is minding the store?"

Has our faith in inevitable progress blinded us to the flim-flams perpetrated in the name of "innovation" or "needed change"? As Peter Schrag points out in his *The End of the American Future,*

Having acceded to power on the basis of promises that were economically and ecologically beyond fulfillment, the new priests of science and technology were likely to try to hold on with the argument that they were the only people who could hold off a technological apocalypse and that the rest of us had better come along if we didn't want to face total destruction. Given the context and the tone in which it was made, the call for a "reordering of priorities" sounded more like a way of keeping intellectuals occupied than an expression of confidence in resolving genuine social problems.[4]

Where is the much-expected backlash and American anti-intellectualism? Maybe the growing criticism of administration and government is a healthy sign of populist accountability. Why should we ever have counted on technicians and sloganeers in the first place? Maybe, as Schrag points out, "Common sense lost its nerve and Main Street its self-confidence; the magic and the power now rested not in the dynamo of Henry Adams' era, but in the laboratories. . . . And where the magic was, there also was the future."[5]

More specifically, in education, after a brief affair with humanism and during a time of declining enrollments, the cult of efficiency is making a comeback in terms of thinly-guised threats such as "accountability" or "performance-based" or "competency-based" education. Again, promoted by administration and critics alike, it seeks to denigrate teaching as wasteful, inefficient, boring and haphazard. The very notion that the development of the human mind and character can so easily lend itself to such uninformed manipulation reflects among those who promote it either a staggering human callousness or a total lack of real experience in teaching. All of this continues to reflect either a complete lack of educational humility or an exuberant immaturity on the part of those who run across a new concept and immediately seek to impose it. Thus the drive to "innovate" and "implement" demands a constant criticism of what is or has been, and in this way is an insult to the professional teacher who, in his drive for craftsmanship or art, needs time, room, and support from those who really seek to improve education. But what the teacher encounters is abuse, criticism, glibness, and arrogance from those who only promise and plan but never have much time to teach.

Paul Goodman, in his *Like a Conquered Province*, sums up the contrast between technical management and the American spirit in teaching in this way:

it has no warrant of legitimacy, it has no tradition, it cannot talk straight English, it neither has produced nor could produce any art, it does not lead by moral means but by a kind of social engineering, and it is held

[4] Peter Schrag, *The End of the American Future* (New York: Simon and Schuster, 1973), p. 267.
[5] Ibid., p. 259.

in contempt and detestation by the young. The American tradition—I
think the *abiding* American tradition—is pluralist, populist, and libertarian while the Establishment is interlocked, mandarin, and managed.
And the evidence is that its own claim, that it is efficient, is false. It is
fantastically wasteful of brains, money, the environment, and people. It
is channeling our energy and enterprise to its own aggrandizement and
power, and it will exhaust us.[6]

Thus educational administration and management plans and
promotes while teachers must perform and thus either work miracles
or face the cutting sword of merit threats. The drive for teacher autonomy has never been more called for, and teachers, in general,
have never been more deserving. Overloaded, underpaid, abused
and harassed from above, teachers have sought, out of a sense of
duty, to implement what was demanded of them. But this must
change. The very programmers and innovators who threaten accountability are the least accountable and the most wasteful. Those who
represent responsibility, stability, and competence have become the
Establishment revolutionaries, hippies, and know-nothings of the
1970's. If someone is to be counted upon to mind the classroom,
knowledge and reality demand that it be the craftsman-teacher. Education is developmental and demanding of time, commitment, and
knowledge. It is not a game or a slick phrase. Education is not a
product of magical slogans, but a long and very human process of interaction with content and probing minds.

This is the final and absolute strength of the teacher and the
only real solution to ignorance and confusion. That teachers recognize and act on this is a necessity. The one vital truth that continues
to assert itself in a programmed world is that there is no alternative
to good teaching. Theory-into-practice has become a literal exercise
and a slogan of relevance, much in the line of McLuhan's "You become what you behold." The process of education is not Xerox, slick
style, or technique. Erik Erikson's profound truth must be maintained by those who teach and who know education personally and
professionally from their daily commitment to those seeking information, education, and wisdom. As Erikson tells us:

> man *needs* to teach, not only for the sake of those who need to be
> taught, and not only for the fulfillment of his identity, but because facts
> are kept alive by being told, logic by being demonstrated, and truth by
> being professed. Thus, the teaching passion is not restricted to the
> teaching profession. Every mature adult knows the satisfaction of ex-
> plaining what is dear to him and of being understood by a groping
> mind.[7]

[6] Paul Goodman, op. cit., p. 370.
[7] Erik Erikson, *Insight and Responsibility* (New York: W. W. Norton and Co., 1964),
p. 131.

Combating the Efficiency Cultists

STEPHEN K. BAILEY
American Council on Education

Whatever the present shortcomings of our colleges and universities—and there are many—the increasingly recurrent response to setting things right is "accountability." Or "productivity," "efficiency," "fiscal responsibility," "better management systems," "cost effectiveness" or simply a "businesslike" approach.

We have heard it before: if we could just run our universities as General Motors is managed, most of our educational problems would vanish. The management scientists are having a field day, and perhaps higher education deserves what is coming its way. There has been, and there remains, a lot of fat in academic management. I have little patience with faculty and students who demand 9:00, 10:00 or 11:00 A. M. classes only, Monday through Friday—leaving a vast amount of expensive academic plant unused during half the workweek. All of us get upset, or should get upset, by institutional egoisms that preclude regional efficiencies in library acquisitions and computer sharing. College investment policies have tended to gyrate between portfolios of penury and wild orgies at the racetrack. Faculties have resisted the introduction of educational technology, various forms of nontraditional studies and outside calls for a more precise definition of academic goals, and this resistance has understandably worn thin the patience of those called upon to finance higher education—seemingly at ever higher rates. Too many presidents and chancellors balance their budgets on the corpse of deferred maintenance.

Quiet huzzahs will fill the air of trustee meetings as the ratios of full-time equivalents to units of usable floor space improve by the smallest of incremental fractions. Smiles of stoic satisfaction will presumably greet the announcement that because of small enrollments, Greek mythology and the senior seminars on Milton and on Chinese music have been dropped from the catalog. Each faculty member will be forced to state his or her course objectives clearly and develop measures of productivity to determine whether learning objectives are being met, and how well. All of this information—computerized, naturally—will become part of the management information system aimed at improving cost-benefit determinations that undergird next year's budget allocations.

From "Combating the Efficiency Cultists," *Change Magazine*, Vol. 5, No. 5 (June 1973), 8-9. © 1973 by *Change Magazine*, Vol. 5, No. 5. Reprinted with permission.

By at least 1984, if we work hard we can make education supremely efficient and accountable. Efficiency is what we render unto Caesar, and we hardly need reminding that Caesar has his legions. But the very awesomeness of the powers and principalities of the cult of efficiency compels me to argue with some fervor that there are limits to accountability, limits to efficiency, limits to slide-rule definitions of educational productivity. Surely the ultimate philistinism of our culture would be totally to impose management science upon the educational process. Though I am not opposed to faculty unionism, unless carefully guarded it could well exacerbate the secular drift toward education's domination by efficiency cultists. Faculty, like the rest of us, are not incapable of selling their souls for a mess of pottage. Trade-offs of higher salaries for the faculties' submission to the calipers of CPAs and systems analysts may well be the contractual paradigm of the next decade.

If so, we may well lose what we are trying to save. Perhaps we have lost it already. Perhaps the halls of academe killed it from within by the aridity, sterility and arcane quality of much of our research. Perhaps we lost it in our struggle for parking-lot status, or through our incapacity to distinguish between student anguish and student bullying. Perhaps we lost our essence in the contradictions we allowed to develop between our claims to academic freedom and the intemperate and irresponsible politicking we indulged in under the protection of its cloak.

What is that essence? It may defy description, but what we cannot define, perhaps we can illustrate.

For example, the discipline of mathematics has many useful instruments. A working knowledge of those instruments in pure and applied form is amenable to test and measurement, and hence to some cost-benefit model of pedagogic effect. But how can one measure that ineffable moment, known to every math professor worth his salt, when a student's eyes wander unfocused and luminous past the teacher and the blackboard in the sudden discovery of the symmetry, the wonder and the principled beauty of the universe?

A working knowledge of vocabulary can be tested. We can measure how many words a student can define in September, and how many more he knows in June. Fairly precise "program objectives" can be set for syntax and for spelling. But how does one measure the mounting excitement of a student who, in catching the cadence of a line from Yeats, suddenly knows Innisfreedom?

For reasons of cost effectiveness we can, of course, lop off a course in Greek mythology because of low enrollments. But it is just possible that if one or two statesmen had read about Promethean hubris prior to our excursions in Vietnam, the world might have been spared ten or twenty years of the anger of the gods.

We can stop faculty junketing to academic conferences by holding down travel budgets or multiplying travel forms, but the search for truth can suffer if the faculty is not exposed to both catalysts and critics.

And what of the dividends of faculty-student friendships? Remember the lovely confession of E. B. White? "When I was an undergraduate," he once wrote, "there were a few professors who went out of their way to befriend students. At the house of one of these men I felt more at home than I did in my own home with my own father and mother. I felt excited, instructed, accepted, influential and in a healthy condition."

Surely if we have a responsibility to insist that what we render unto Caesar we render efficiently, we have an equal if not superior responsibility to ensure that what we render unto God we render effectively. This may mean that in some circumstances narrow canons of efficiency are the enemy of effectiveness. Academia needs some spiritual, physical, intellectual and temporal space, uncluttered by the artifacts of management logicians and quantitative doodlers. If we would be true defenders of the faith, we must be willing to promote efficiency while protecting effectiveness. And we must learn when these concepts are compatible and when they are not.

How, in fact, can the current and foreseeable demand for accountability be meshed with the subtler aspects of academic need? Alas, there are no gimmicks. In protecting the life spaces of the learning process, trustees and chancellors and deans and department heads can demonstrate, by the questions they ask and the trade-offs they reject, their devotion to true academic effectiveness. Sometimes this will take the form of protecting an "uneconomic" small course; sometimes it will manifest itself in protesting at a budget hearing, or before a legislative committee, against abolishing out-of-state travel allowances for faculty; occasionally it will appear as a defense of an assistant professor who is a mediocre lecturer but a superb student adviser; frequently it will express itself as defense of faculty and student time for reading and reflection upon important matters.

When cost accountants or budget specialists ask for the economic justification of such "frills," they should be reminded of the late Glenn Frank's response to a rural member of the Wisconsin legislature when it showed signs of shock in hearing that University of Wisconsin faculty taught only nine hours a week. President Frank responded, "Sir, you are famous for your stud bulls. Would you judge their value by the number of hours a week they work?"

Part of the job of trustees is to make their friends in the legislative and executive branches of the national and state governments understand that it is essential to support those aspects of education not amenable to tight schedules of efficiency. Perhaps academic budgets can be divided into "measurable items" and "nonmeasurable items." In regard to the former, responsible officials should insist that accountability be rigorous, quantified and detailed. In regard to the latter, officials should be asked to recall the moments in their own education that in retrospect meant most to them. I have confidence that public servants will respond to this approach. During the campuses' dark days of the late 1960s, a few politicians in the legislative and executive branches of our state and federal governments preserved education from the imposition of barbarous external constraints upon academic processes. We owe these politicians much. I wonder if we ever took the time to thank them.

For most of mankind, life is a dirty trick. For others it is lived, in Thoreau's term, in quiet desperation. The promise of education is that through knowledge of nature and knowledge of self, people can fashion a temporary habitat on this whirling planet that can cater with some felicity to the impertinent claims of their restless souls. We get seduced into narrow definitions of education's function: the development of job skills, which we need; the mastery of specific disciplines, which is important; the capacity to communicate, which is indispensable; the uncovering of new knowledge and the refining of old knowledge, which is essential. These are, for the most part, measurable goals of education.

But I submit that the prime function of education is not measurable. The ultimate business of education is human freedom. And if human freedom means nothing but the sad and sorry flow of existence upon a well-documented darkling plain, the charge to university graduates should be to push the button when they have the chance. If the human race has, in fact, been caught up in an irreversible ebb tide, if Matthew Arnold's transient mood at Dover Beach has become an eternal reality, then it is irrelevant whether the missiles fall. For the option is an endless melancholy, a sullen ennui—deaf to the song of the thrush, blind to the evening sky and indifferent to the creative wonders of man's mind and hand.

Education today must affirm the promise of human life. It must help us see citizens and public officials not as instruments of survival or of mere security, but as possible instruments of human freedom—to see the good society as an arrangement of institutions and laws that help to free men from the bondage of fear, loneliness and injustice, and from the crushing impersonalities of life. It must promote all that is ennobling and creative in the human psyche. It must help us posit a society whose ultimate dividends are joy and variety and vitality within the bounds of community, a society in which humanistic critics postulate man not just as he has been or as he is, but as he can be.

The great philosopher-President of prewar Czechoslovakia,

Thomas Masaryk, once defined our supreme task for us. After decades of struggle in the harsh arena of public life, Masaryk summed up his philosophy. "You see how it is the method must be absolutely practical, reasonable, realistic, but the aim, the whole, the conception is an eternal poem."

Our supreme function is not to improve managerial efficiency in education. We cannot countenance obvious waste, and we have obligations to the public to see that money is not used frivolously. But our supreme obligation is to remind ourselves and our public and private benefactors that a partially unquantifiable and inherently untidy system of higher education must routinely make legitimate demands upon the treasuries of the purse in order to nourish the treasuries of the mind and spirit. For freedom is the condition of nobility, and knowledge is the condition of freedom.

III

HUMANISM AND THE SCHOOLS: THE OPEN EDUCATION MOVEMENT

Teachers almost invariable take their pupils as they find them; they turn them, beat them, card them, comb them, drill them into certain forms, and expect them to become a finished and polished product; and if the result does not come up to their expectations . . . they are indignant, angry, and furious. And yet we are surprised that some men shrink and recoil from such a system. Far more is it a matter for surprise that anyone can endure it at all.
Johann Amos Comenius

INTRODUCTION

Mention of the word "school" to most adults conjures up memories of rows of desks and chairs bolted to the floor, all facing the front of the classroom, where the teacher stood with chalk and pointer in hand droning over the lesson. Students anchored in their seats leafed desultorily through the pages of their readers, surreptitiously passed notes to one another across the aisle, or simply stared apathetically out the window, longing for the world of freedom outside. Most often the teacher is remembered as a blurred nonentity whose day was given over to checking attendance, enforcing discipline (by which was meant imposing silence and immobility), and barking out instructions in a stentorian tone calculated to intimidate all but the most obdurate. Only the ambitious or well-prepared among the class ever strained to answer the teacher's questions or voluntarily participated in the forced "discussion" of the day's assignment. Most lounged listlessly in their chairs, watching the hands of the clock crawl toward recess, or resignedly awaited their turn at recitation.

Formal education was a world defined by order, discipline, and regimentation, by hall monitors and passes, tardy slips, detentions, and report cards. There were times of course when school life did have its brighter moments, though they usually had nothing whatever to do with academics or formal classwork. And while corporeal punishment was officially banned, the calculated employment of its equally potent psychological equivalents—fear, anxiety, guilt—lent credence to the old song about "readin' an' writin' an' 'rithmetic, taught to the tune of the hickory stick." School, all things considered, was never a particularly pleasant affair.

The closing years of the 1960's and the opening years of the decade following brought a remarkable upsurge of protest against that age-old pattern of boredom and repression, coupled with strong interest in what came to be known as "open education" or "the open classroom." As characterized by Charles E. Silberman, who more than anyone was responsible for popularizing the movement, the new shift in interest involved "a change in atmosphere—toward more humaneness and understanding, toward more encouragement and trust." Schools did not have to be destructive, sterile, and authoritarian, he and other critics argued; they could be pleasant, supportive, even challenging places in which to pursue knowledge. Open education was understood to imply also a basic change in learning style "away from the teacher as the source of all knowledge to the teacher as the facilitator of learning, away from the traditional whole-class orientation to more concern with individualized learning." [1] Both changes, in environment and learning style, were regarded as critical to the work of humanizing education.

Publication in 1970 of Silberman's *Crisis in the Classroom,* a Carnegie Corporation-commissioned study of American education, marked the culmination of years of mounting criticism of schools for their alleged repressiveness and regimentation. "Because adults take the schools so much for granted," its author charged, "they fail to appreciate what grim, joyless places most American schools are, how oppressive and petty are the rules by which they are governed, how intellectually sterile and esthetically barren the atmosphere, what an appalling lack of civility obtains on the part of teachers and principals, what contempt they unconsciously display for children as children." [2] It need not be so, Silberman insisted, if professionals and laymen were not so prone to "mindlessness"—the failure or refusal to question established practice. The solution he proposed was a greater infusion of purpose in the schools, and more careful consideration of the ways in which technique, content, and organization might be

[1] Charles E. Silberman, *The Open Classroom Reader* (New York: Vintage, 1973), p. xvi.
[2] Charles E. Silberman, *Crisis in the Classroom* (New York: Vintage, 1971), p. 10.

mobilized to facilitate joy in learning, to allow for aesthetic expression, and to encourage the development of character—in rural and urban slums no less than in the more prosperous suburbs.

This was no utopian dream, Silberman emphasized, but a practical program for educational transformation. Given viable alternatives stressing activity, joyfulness, and spontaneity, such as those provided in the example of certain innovative English infant and junior schools, most Americans, he felt, would opt for a system where learning was made more humane, attractive, and interesting. In place of authoritarian, overroutinized, and demeaning mental prisonhouses of the mind, schools could become true centers for learning and growth. Besides being attractive, they would become vastly more effective.

Silberman's critique was widely acclaimed in the early 1970's as the most important book on education to appear since the heyday of John Dewey. The favorable response it received from parents, teachers, school administrators, superintendents, professional teacher associations, and university educationists prompted Joseph Featherstone, an influential journalist likewise instrumental in popularizing school reform, to observe of Silberman's litany of complaints that "what was once a point made by a handful of radical cultural critics is now very close to being official wisdom." Yet scarcely two years after Silberman's book was published, the Dean of the New School of Behavioral Studies at the University of North Dakota, himself a pioneer in the open education movement, already was voicing his fear that it might eventually become just "another fad, a new gimmick to sweep over the American landscape, only to end up a few years from now on the educational junk heap of once-promising reforms." [3]

Indications not long afterwards appeared to bear out his prophetic misgivings. Whereas the heady rhetoric of humanistic reform had won ready adoption by the very educational Establishment that had been the target for so much invective and criticism, apparently the correlative imperatives for substantive changes in schools had not. Observing a widening gap between rhetoric and reality, between the public professions of schoolmen and the education they actually superintended, many felt prospects for meaningful reform were entirely illusory. Cynics who had warned against the futility of trying to work "within the system" felt vindicated in their assertion that sloganeering had been made to substitute for actual change. Reform proposal after proposal disappeared into obscurity or was frustrated in its applications once its radical implications were grasped by educational traditionalists.

Some critics ascribed the precipitate decline in popular support

[3] Vito Perrone, *Open Education: Promise and Problems* (Bloomington, Ind.: Phi Delta Kappa Educational Foundation, 1972), p. 7.

for humanistic learning to weaknesses, ambiguities, and contradictions inherent in the open education movement itself. Others
wondered if its incipient eclipse could fairly have been predicted by
the fate of the not altogether dissimilar progressive education movement a quarter century earlier. Still others discerned a conspiracy to
co-opt and disarm the activist youth movement of the late 1960's by
confining its attention to matters of school pedagogy and curriculum.

Yet for all the inevitable compromises and accommodations inevitable in the translation of reformist fervor into programmatic reality, there was at least some evidence to show that efforts were being
made to make schools more humane, to personalize and individualize instruction, to render curricula more flexible and responsive to
the diverse needs of students. Detractors might dismiss reforms as
mere "cosmetic" alterations whose practical effect was to leave the
underlying ideological substructure intact and the basic cultural milieu untouched (which was true for the most part), but to a greater extent than many were willing to admit, education *was* being "human-
ized." Rigid authoritarianism in the school setting was gradually being
replaced (in some areas at least) by more democratic and egalitarian
modes of organization and administration. More and more the old
lockstep pattern was giving way to ungraded classrooms. Students
were slowly but surely assuming a greater voice in determining their
own destiny. Teachers and administrators alike began evidencing a
greater receptivity to change, more toleration for individual differences in values and lifestyle, a heightened concern for heretofore
neglected affective elements in the learning experience. Educators as
a group appeared more willing than ever before to respect diversity
of opinion and to help sustain the conditions necessary for genuine
independence of thought.

It remains to observe that the campaign to humanize schooling
through "open" classrooms is still very much an important feature of
the current educational scene, although its earlier phases which were
marked by so much angry protest and criticism have for the most part
been left behind. It is unclear whether the gains registered over the
last half dozen years or so are destined to be lost in the scramble after
different social goals lately coming to the fore, or whether the new
humanism can exert a lasting influence upon schools in years ahead.
Whatever its future course of development, supporters and critics
alike might better understand its present predicaments and perhaps
its long-range prospects by looking to some of the major historical
antecedents of today's open education, especially in the two distinct
but interrelated currents of thought from which it is chiefly de-
scended: the romantic tradition of Rousseau, Pestalozzi, Tolstoy,
and A. S. Neill, on the one hand, and the progressivist tradition popularly associated with Dewey and his disciples on the other.

In diverse and sometimes contradictory ways, proponents of contemporary humanistic education are deeply indebted to both traditions.

THE ROMANTIC TRADITION IN EDUCATION

Even a cursory look to the history of education suggests that down through the ages, for every schoolmaster who sought earnestly to make school a pleasant experience and who worked to render learning palatable, there have been a thousand pedagogues who brutalized their charges, relying upon the whip and cane to compensate for lifeless curricula and a woefully unimaginative pedagogy. St. Augustine in his *Confessions* is typical in his reminiscences of the "miseries and mockeries" of childhood. "Nor did they that forced me to my book do very well," he recalled, "for no man does well against his will. . . ." He chafed at the discipline of his schoolwork: "One and one make two, and two and two make four was a harsh song to me, but the wooden horse full of armed men and the burning of Troy and the ghost of Creusa was a most delightful spectacle. . . ." He disliked Greek intensely precisely because it was forced upon him by his tutors: "I believe that Virgil is no less harsh to Grecian children when they be compelled to learn him, as I was to learn Homer: for to say truth, the difficulty of learning a strange language, did sprinkle as it were with gall all the pleasures of those fabulous narrations. For I understood not a word of it, yet they vehemently pressed me and with most cruel threatenings and punishments to make me understand it."

The imposition of incomprehensible subject matter was bad enough in every century, but the error was invariably compounded by cruelty and beatings. The autobiography of the twelfth-century monk Guibert, Abbot of Nogent, for example, offers a vivid picture of an ignorant teacher inflicting himself upon a sensitive, painstaking youth. Guibert relates that almost every day he was pelted with a hail of blows and curses as his incompetent mentor tried to force him to learn. "He took vengeance on me," Guibert recalled, "not knowing what he knew not himself; he ought certainly to have considered that it was very wrong to demand from a weak little mind what he had not put into it. Six years passed without reward. . . ." Something of the spirit of medieval learning is distilled in rules for the supervision of oblates and novices at Canterbury School, as described in the *Constitutiones Lanfranci*. Students, it was ordered, "shall . . . sit separate from each other; shall never leave the place in which they are kept, except with the monk who has charge of them. . . . No youth is to talk with another, except so that the master may hear and understand what is said by both of them." Penalties for the slightest infraction were harsh.

Erasmus of Rotterdam (1466–1536) was unsparing in his criticism for school tyrants, agreeing with Augustine's rueful admission that were he faced with the choice of death or being compelled to return to primary school, he would choose death. He had little patience with schoolmasters who "expect their little pupils to act as though they were but diminutive adults," and who senselessly hammered grammatical rules into children's uncomprehending heads. They caused children "to hate learning," he fumed, "before they know why it should be loved." In an almost Rousseau-like passage Erasmus recognized the value of flexibility and patience on the teacher's part: "Lead the beginner to face his unfamiliar matter with self-confidence," he urged, "to attack it slowly but with persistence. We must not underrate the capacity of youth to respond to suitable demands upon the intelligence. . . ." "The child," he continued, "like every other creature, excels in the precise activity which belongs to it . . . follow nature, therefore, in this, and so far as is possible take from the work of the school all that implies toilsomeness, and strive to give to learning the quality of freedom and enjoyment."

Michel de Montaigne, the sixteenth-century French humanist, heartily concurred. In his various essays he repeatedly returned to the theme of educational repression. "We direct all our efforts to the memory and leave the understanding and the conscience empty," he complained. "Like birds which go forth from time to time to seek for grain and bring it back to their young in their beaks without tasting it, our pedants go gathering knowledge from books and never take it further than their lips before disgorging it. And what is worse, their scholars and their little ones are no better nourished by it than they are themselves." Rote learning, Montaigne insisted, "is no knowledge, and signifies no more but only to return what one has intrusted to our memory."

It is important to allow the child an active role in his own learning. "By depriving a pupil of liberty to do things for himself we make him servile and cowardly." Good pedagogy avoids implanting fear in the heart of the child. By the same token, effective teaching, Montaigne claimed, depends upon its being "carried on with a firm gentleness, quite contrary to the practice of our pedants, who, instead of tempting and alluring children to study, present nothing before them but rods and ferrules, horror and cruelty. Away with this violence! Away with this compulsion." Nothing more dulls and degenerates character, he alleged. "How much more respectable it would be to see our classrooms strewn with green boughs and flowers than with bloody birch rods. . . ." He roundly condemned "all manner of violence in the education of a young spirit, brought up to honor and liberty. There is," Montaigne observed, "a kind of slavishness in churlish vigor, and servility in compulsion; and I hold that that which

cannot be compassed by reason, wisdom and discretion, can never
be attained by force and constraint."

Despite repeated pleas from a minority of enlightened theorists
who argued for the replacement of fear with love, of rigid lessons
with diverse, flexible curricula, and the abolition of physical punishment, the overwhelming majority were agreed, as Philoponus put it,
that a school should be "a place void of all fruitless play and loiter-
ing." Richard Mulcaster expressed prevailing opinion when he urged
the liberal use of the rod to spur students on. It "may no more be
spared in schools than the sword may in the prince's hand," he declared. A "sharp master who will make boys learn what will afterwards
be of service even though they are unwilling at the time is to be
preferred to the vain shadow of a courteous master." Most teachers
accepted John Brinsley's grim counsel in his *Ludus Literarius* to foster
a "meet and loving fear, furthered by wise severity to maintain discipline."

Not until the seventeenth century did there appear any substantial body of educational theory openly defending spontaneity, interest, or freedom in learning. In the writings of Archbishop François
Fénelon (1651–1715), for example, there are some glimmerings of the
view explicitly developed much later by Jean-Jacques Rousseau: that
instruction ought not to be unduly coercive, and that the teacher
should rest content with following and assisting the child's own natural development. For Fénelon, the young student's attention span is
like a candle guttering in the wind; it is enough to answer questions
as they arise, to help satisfy youthful curiosity with simple responses,
and to allow the pupil to mix recreation with instruction. His main
prescription is to replace formal lessons with *"conversations gaies"*;
anything that stimulates the child's imagination is to be pressed into
the service of the teacher. "Let us change the [usual] order," he suggested, "let us make study agreeable; *let us hide it under the appearance of liberty and of pleasure"* [emphasis added].

For Johann Amos Comenius (1592–1670), the great Moravian educational reformer, it was imperative that instruction be arranged according to the order and course of nature, that teaching be conducted without violence, that uniformity be sought in method, the
curriculum organized in an orderly, graduated sequence of studies,
and students led inductively where possible from sensory experiences to more abstract learning. In fact, the central idea of his *Magna
Didactica* is to "follow the footsteps of nature" in offering knowledge
to the learner. The mind should not be compelled to any study "to
which its natural bent does not incline it in accordance with its age
and the right method." Comenius abhorred the use of punitive discipline. "No discipline of a severe kind should be exercised in connection with studies or literary exercises," he declared. "For studies,

if they are properly organized, form in themselves a sufficient attraction, and entice all . . . by their inherent pleasantness. If this be not the case, the fault lies, not with the pupil, but with the master, and if our skill is unable to make an impression on the understanding our blows will have no effect. Indeed, by any application of force we are far more likely to produce a distaste for letters than a love for them. Whenever, therefore, we see that a mind is diseased and dislikes study, we should try to remove its indisposition by gentle remedies but should on no account employ violent ones. . . . Such a skillful and sympathetic treatment is necessary to instill a love of learning into the minds of our pupils, and any other procedure will only convert their idleness into antipathy and their lack of interest into downright stupidity." [4]

Without question it was Jean-Jacques Rousseau (1742–1778) who most fully synthesized and elaborated the views of humane educators before him, and whose writings most clearly influenced the development of what is commonly called the "romantic" tradition in educational thought. Before him educators had tended to look upon nature basically in terms of defects which education had to convert, as chained powers and faculties which training had to liberate, as dormant human values which instruction was supposed to arouse.[5] Rousseau, however, unequivocally proclaimed his faith in human nature, and tried to show how the supposed deficiencies of the child's nature enclose in embryonic form later developments or potentialities. He was convinced it was vital to get beyond the old questions having to do with making learning pleasant or techniques for amusing children. Where his predecessors had viewed the central problem of education as one of getting the learner to conform to the strictures of a preordained curriculum, and to subordinate the child's impulses to the teacher's desires and objectives, Rousseau advanced the more revolutionary idea that education, in order to be effective in the forming of good human beings and through them of a good society, must be thoroughly child-centered. Those before him had stressed the need to take account of the child's point of view, but invariably they had conceived children as limited, imperfect creatures requiring refashioning after the adult pattern.[6] Rousseau subordinated that view to a general principle of "following nature," that is, of giving free play to the faculties and impulses of the child as they develop, according to an internal logic. "Natural" education, which implies no external

[4] M. W. Keatinge, trans., *The Great Didactic of John Amos Comenius* (New York: Russell & Russell, 1907), p. 250.
[5] Cf. William J. McCallister, *The Growth of Freedom in Education* (London: Constable & Company, 1931), p. 231.
[6] William Boyd (ed.), *The Emile of Jean-Jacques Rousseau* (New York: Teachers College Press, Columbia University, 1960), p. 180.

imposition in the guise of authority or benevolent intervention, was, Rousseau announced in the Preface to his great educational romance, *Émile,* not only "intelligible and feasible in itself," but "adapted to the nature of things."

Integral to Rousseau's view of education was his conviction that man in himself, man as a natural being, is innately good. It follows that the child cannot become intelligent by having his natural inclinations suppressed or his desires thwarted—in the long run coercion is unproductive even when it succeeds because it brings about undue submission to the values and feelings of others—and the second-hand learning served up in a conventional school setting is almost always injurious. Since the child originally is born innocent, it is the vices and errors of a malformed social order that frustrate natural human development: "Everything is good as it comes from the hands of the Creator but degenerates once it gets into the hands of man." Children are living, growing beings who at every stage of their development are persons in their own right, capable of being properly prepared for later maturity only through the active interests of their own age and condition.[7] The cardinal pedagogical sin, therefore, consists of imposing ready-made habits, values, and beliefs on the child before he is capable of understanding them or of framing his own judgments.

The specifics of Rousseau's essentially romantic theory of education are less important in the present context than the basic underlying themes which fed into the thinking of his successors. The notion of learning readiness, of faith in the basic goodness of the child's nature, of trust in its untrammeled expression and development, of opposition to uncritical or purely verbal learning, the idea of growth and discovery made possible through the absence of inhibiting constraints, the stress of freedom, the place accorded intuition, feeling, individuality—they were just some of the major elements in the romantic tradition advanced first by Rousseau. They were elaborated upon by a host of pedagogical theorists and practitioners, especially by Rousseau's sensitive disciple, Johann Heinrich Pestalozzi (1746–1827).

In a characteristic passage the latter succinctly summed up the spirit and concern of humanistic pedagogy in his advice to teachers:

> Be thoroughly convinced of the immense value of liberty; do not let vanity make you anxious to see your efforts producing premature fruit; let your child be as free as possible, and seek diligently for every means of ensuring his liberty, peace of mind, and good humour. Teach him absolutely nothing by words that you can teach him by the things themselves; let him see for himself, hear, find out, fall, pick himself up, make mistakes, no word, in short, where action is possible. What he

[7] Ibid., p. 178.

can do for himself let him do; let him be always occupied; always active, and let the time you leave him to himself represent by far the greatest part of his childhood. You will then see that nature teaches him far better than men. But when you see the necessity of accustoming him to obedience, prepare yourself with the greatest care for this duty. . . . Make sure of his heart and let him feel that you are necessary to him . . . If he often asks for something you do not think good, tell him what the consequences will be, and leave him his liberty. . . . Should he leave [the right way] and fall into the mire go to his rescue, but do not shield him from the unpleasant results of having enjoyed complete liberty and of not having listened to your warnings.[8]

With due allowance for stylistic differences, Pestalozzi's views, penned originally in the eighteenth century, might just as easily come from the writings of such contemporary radical humanists as Homer Lane, Bertrand Russell, or A. S. Neill.

Still other elements precursive of twentieth-century educational romanticism are to be found in the work of the Russian novelist Lyóf Nikoláyevitch Tolstoy (1828–1910) whose experimental village school at Yasnáya Polyána in the mid-1800's represented a remarkable attempt to explore the limits of freedom in education. "All are agreed," he wrote, "that schools are imperfect; I, personally, am convinced that they are noxious." He was much impressed with the contrast between the child he observed as a "vivacious, inquisitive being with a smile in his eye and forever seeking information for the sheer pleasure of it" *outside the classroom,* and that same child *in school,* where he became "a weary shrinking creature repeating merely with his lips someone else's thoughts in someone else's words, with an air of fatigue, fear and restlessness: a creature whose soul has retreated like a snail into its shell." Tolstoy termed that strange unhappy condition the "school state of mind," which consists "in all the higher capacities, imagination, creative power and reflection yielding to a semi-animal capacity to produce words without imagination or reflection."

In his own school, the cardinal rule was freedom: "The only criterion of pedagogy is freedom . . . ," he asserted, and "the less the children are compelled to learn, the better is the method; the more— the worse. . . . In instruction [there can be] no necessity of compelling children to learn anything that is tiresome and repulsive to them, and that, if necessity demands that children be compelled, it only proves the imperfection of the method." For two years he conducted his school on the basis of the maxim that "the method which does not demand an increase of discipline is good; the one which demands greater severity is bad." Having begun without any preconceived theories about education, according to his own testimony, Tol-

---

[8] Roger DeGuimps, *Pestalozzi: His Life and Work,* translated by J. Russell (New York: Appleton-Century-Crofts, 1895), pp. 47–48.

stoy was driven by his own personal experience to conclude that the only kind of education fit for human beings was a "natural" one wholly free of constraints, compulsion, authority, and drudgery.

It would be incorrect to claim that recent supporters of open education have simply adapted the thinking of earlier romantics; indeed, contemporary critics leave the impression that their calls for more freedom in education are altogether novel. The single greatest weakness in current humanistic rhetoric in this regard perhaps *is* a lack of historical perspective, an apparent indifference to whatever counsel and guidance might be afforded by a thorough perusal of relevant historical precedents. Unfortunately, as has so often been the case involving educational controversy, demands for change typically have been expressed in the evangelical mode, with little regard for what has gone before.

THE PROGRESSIVIST TRADITION IN EDUCATION

Besides the romantic tradition with its abiding faith in human nature, its appreciation for spontaneity and joy in learning, and its deeply-rooted aversion to formalism and imposed order, the current expression of humanism in the movement for open education bears a close affinity with the progressive movement of the early 1900's. Progressivism had its origins in a broadly-based liberal crusade for social, political, and economic reform in the last half of the nineteenth century, the educational manifestations of which focused upon questions of curricular and instructional reform. As a historical phenomenon, progressivism was, as one commentator notes, a movement of vast and untidy proportions. It was eclectic in character, in some of its aspects incurably romantic and even sentimental about childhood, and frequently inconsistent in its theoretical underpinnings. What early progressives shared in common, nevertheless, was a profound dislike for the traditional school and for many aspects of the society supporting that school.[9] In tone and relative emphasis, it differed significantly from educational romanticism on many points.

As a reaction against prevailing educational usage at the turn of the century progressivism took as its special targets rigid classroom convention and the divorce of formal learning from its surrounding social context. "The realm of the classroom in the 1890's was totally set off from the experience of the child who inhabited it," notes historian Oscar Handlin. "The teachers' lessons encrusted by habit, the seats arranged in formal rows, and the rigid etiquette of behavior all

[9] G. Max Wingo, *Philosophies of Education: An Introduction* (Lexington, Mass.: D. C. Heath & Company, 1974), p. 148. Cf. also Lawrence A. Cremin, *The Transformation of the School* (New York: Alfred A. Knopf, 1962), chapter 1.

emphasized the difference between school and life. Hence learning consisted of the tedious memorization of data without a meaning immediately clear to the pupil." [10] What the reformers hoped to do therefore was to bridge that gap between life and learning, to bring the school back into the mainstream of social life. If schools were authoritarian and undemocratic, they needed to be made more democratic. If instruction had grown mechanical and rigid, the time was ripe for innovation. Curricula stood in need of overhaul so that proper account could be taken of new advances in the experimental sciences. Schools were to be made more responsive to the individual needs of students, and, more broadly, to the larger needs of a changing society.

Armed with a buoyant faith in social progress and confident that critical human intelligence would eventually prevail over both institutional and ideological inertia, educational progressives waged a spirited, many-sided campaign to transform the country's system of schools. At Marietta Johnson's Organic School at Fairhope, Alabama, at Junius Meriam's laboratory school at the University of Missouri, and at its better-known predecessor at the University of Chicago, in Caroline Pratt's Play School at New York, the Kindergarten at Teachers College, Columbia, and at Colonel Francis Parker's Cook County Normal School, there were intimations of how progressive pedagogy would develop. Students participated actively in helping to plan the activities and procedures of these schools. Children enjoyed much greater freedom than ever before, and under vastly improved conditions for real learning. Physical plants were designed for activity, for mobility, not simply for lecturing and reciting. Greater attention was given over to individual growth and development. The emphasis was upon "learning by doing," so as to forge a new unity between education and life. As John Dewey explained, the curriculum of the New Education had to be based upon a student's interests and his active involvement in learning activities "if the pupil is to understand the facts which the teacher wishes him to learn; if his knowledge is to be real, not verbal; if his education is to furnish standards of judgment and comparison." [11]

The pluralism and diversity of the growing progressive education movement soon proved to be as much a major weakness as a strength in its drive for acceptance. Dewey foresaw the difficulty early when, speaking of progressive educators, he observed, "If they do not intellectually organize their own work, while they may do much in making the lives of children . . . more joyous and more vital, they contribute

[10] Oscar Handlin, *John Dewey's Challenge to Education* (New York: Harper & Brothers, 1959), p. 42.
[11] John Dewey and Evelyn Dewey, *Schools of To-Morrow* (New York: Dutton, 1915), p. 294.

only incidental scraps to the science of education." The founding of the Progressive Education Association in 1919 represented a response to that caveat when, under the able leadership of Stanwood Cobb, what had formerly been a rather loosely defined revolt against educational formalism now gained a vigorous organizational voice.[12] Over the next few years the polyglot system of ideas combining vague doctrines of freedom, self-expression, and psychological adjustment, was refined and articulated with increasing clarity by theorists like Harold Rugg, Ann Shumaker, John Childs, and of course, by John Dewey.

By the beginning of the 1920's the main outline of progressive pedagogy could be discerned. Briefly, it encompassed the following: (1) concern for the child in all his complexity—his interests, needs, desires, feelings, and attitudes; (2) recommendation of an advisory rather than authoritarian or directive role for the teacher; (3) advocacy of problem-solving techniques of instruction in preference to those stressing pupil passivity, rote memorization, and deductive learning; (4) strong rejection of the doctrine that education is a preparation for living rather than a part of the process of living; (5) emphasis upon a warm, supportive, humane classroom environment from which all cruel punishments were banished; (6) advocacy of patterns of educational organization encouraging cooperative, communal experiences through which pupils would actually practice democratic modes of behavior; and (7) curricula geared to the maturational level of each student, based upon canons of interest, pupil initiative, creative self-expression, and individual personality development.[13] Running through all specific questions of technique was a thread of protest against the idea of education solely as transmission of subject matter, and a strong hope that the school as a social institution would serve as a catalyst for societal progress and for the extension of democratic ideals to all peoples. Dewey's seminal contribution, more than anything else, was the development of a body of pedagogical theory which could encompass, refine, and sharpen that diverse assemblage of progressivist ideas and values.

Dewey shared with Rousseau a conviction that education was not something to be imposed from without. It involved rather a process of growth, in accordance with the felt needs and interests of the learner, and organized around learning activities regarded by the student as meaningful and relevant. Always, the emphasis was supposed to be upon activities and concrete experiences, not as ends in themselves but as means of evoking stimulating questions which would

---

[12] Cf. Lawrence A. Cremin, "John Dewey and the Progressive Education Movement, 1915–1952," in Reginald D. Archambauldt (ed.), *Dewey on Education, Appraisals* (New York: Random House, 1966), pp. 10–25.

[13] Cf. Christopher J. Lucas, *Our Western Educational Heritage* (New York: Macmillan, 1972), p. 529.

then set the stage for further development.[14] Dewey himself defined the new progressivist strain as hostility to "imposition from above," to "learning from texts and teacher," to "acquisition of isolated skills and techniques by drill," to "preparation for a more or less remote future," and to "static aims and materials." Against those assumptions of the nineteenth century, he called for the "expression and cultivation of individuality," for "learning through experience," and for "acquaintance with an ever-changing world." [15] Though the progressive tendency accorded with the romantic emphasis upon the needs and interests of children (in the tradition of Rousseau, Pestalozzi, Froebel, and Tolstoy) as developed by Dewey it was colored and given the cachet of scientific authority by his frequent appeals to an empirically-based psychology of learning and behavior.

Dewey did not simply call for freer classrooms and the abandonment of adult authority, but rather argued on psychological grounds that a school closely geared to the world of its students could dispense with discipline in the old-fashioned sense of keeping order through external force. Children whose interest was actively engaged in learning tasks would require no policing, he confidently asserted, basing his argument on an elaborate epistemology and a theory of learning. They could be allowed maximum freedom to assume increasing responsibility for their own actions, the performance of which would evoke order from within.[16]

As for the aims and goals of education, Dewey believed that they were inevitably relative to time and place and learner. Objectives are not something separate and apart from the dynamic intentions and desires of students; they necessarily grow out of a combination of social circumstances, pupil interests, and the immediate set of prevailing conditions. "An educational aim," he wrote, "must be founded upon the intrinsic activities and needs . . . of the given individual to be educated. . . ." [17] In a larger sense, education can have no end extrinsic to or beyond itself: "Since growth is the characteristic of life, education is all one with growing; it has no end beyond itself. The criterion of the value of school education is the extent in which it creates a desire for continued growth and supplies means for making the desire effective in fact." [18]

On the question of methodology or pedagogical technique,

[14] E. C. Moore, "John Dewey's Contributions to Educational Theory," in *John Dewey, the Man and His Philosophy* (Cambridge, Mass.: Harvard University Press, 1930), p. 23.
[15] John Dewey, *Experience & Education* (New York: Macmillan, 1938), p. 56.
[16] John Dewey, *The School and Society* (Chicago: University of Chicago Press, 1899), pp. 124–125; and John Dewey, *Democracy and Education* (New York: Macmillan, 1916), p. 138.
[17] *Democracy and Education*, p. 126.
[18] Ibid., p. 62.

Dewey argued as did most progressivist theorists that what was wrong with static "assign-study-recite" forms of instruction with all its accoutrements of pupils at attention, fixed desks and chairs, and a stern disciplinary attitude on the teacher's part, were that they failed to elicit interest, to stimulate motivation, or to promote meaningful learning.[19] Good methodology, on the other hand, involved a process of building upon the native powers, interests, and desires of the learners involved, under whatever conditions proved most effective in stimulating them to develop habits of critical reflection and disciplined thought. The student cannot be looked upon as some passive cipher; he is an active, dynamic, curious, purposive, willful, experiencing organism, seeking to better control, direct, and understand his further experiences through the use of intelligence. He is in a state of constant interaction with his environment, of which the school is an important part. Hence, from Dewey's viewpoint, the teacher should seek to uncover ways of assisting the learner to deal ever more effectively with his environment. The teacher is a guide, a resource, and an arranger of experiences. Far from leaving the child free to do whatever momentary impulses and whims dictate, the teacher assumes an active role in working with, advising, and stimulating him. Methodology is simply another name for the varied ways in which learners are helped to develop and broaden themselves, to test their skills, to nurture their abilities so they become more adequate, better-adjusted human beings.

Subject matter in a curriculum, according to Dewey, should not be thought of in terms of rigidly defined, isolated bodies of knowledge, nor can it be divorced from considerations of process or methodology. It should be understood in wholly dynamic terms, relative to the varying needs of learners, and arising out of their individual experiences and inquiries. Students should study "whatever is recognized as having a bearing upon the anticipated course of events" in their lives, he asserted. Subject matter, phrased differently, should consist of "those things actually acted upon in a situation having a purpose." In his famous essay on curriculum, Dewey wrote: "The source of whatever is dead, mechanical, and formal in schools is found precisely in the subordination of the life and experience of the child to the curriculum. It is because of this that 'study' has become a synonym for what is irksome, and a lesson identical with a task." [20] Over and against the traditional notion of a school curriculum as something to be acquired passively, Dewey taught that subject matter for learning

[19] Cf. Reginald D. Archambault (ed.), *Dewey on Education, Selected Writings* (New York: Modern Library, 1964), pp. xxiii–xxiv.
[20] John Dewey, "The Child and the Curriculum," in Martin S. Dworkin (ed.), *Dewey on Education, Selections* (New York: Teachers College, Columbia, 1964), pp. 95–96.

should be built around active "occupations" or "enterprises" having genuine educational import. "The problem of the educator," he said, "is to engage pupils in . . . activities in such ways that while manual skill and technical efficiency are gained and immediate satisfaction found in the work, together with preparation for later usefulness, these things shall be subordinated to *education*—that is, to intellectual results and the forming of a socialized disposition." [21]

During the 1920's and increasingly in the '30's and '40's, Dewey grew apprehensive over the directions the progressive education movement seemed to be following, so much so that by 1938 when he wrote *Experience and Education* he had become more of a critic of certain progressivist practices than an advocate. In a 1938 address before the Progressive Education Association, Dewey prefaced his criticisms by conceding the positive advances made by progressive schools over their forebearers. They were, he said, more informal, freer, more inclined to respect individuality and to build upon the nature and experience of children instead of imposing external standards and subjects; they emphasized activity as distinct from passivity; and they encouraged socialization to a greater extent than had formerly been the case. He then went on to question, however, whether romantic oversimplifications had not infiltrated into progressivist thought, whether pedagogy had succumbed to the dangers of aimlessness and unrestrained permissiveness. It was time, Dewey announced, to introduce a greater measure of intellectual rigor and clarity into educational theory, to consider more carefully the conditions under which learning takes place most effectively, and to build up a systematic science of education. Without this, he implied, progressivism was destined to failure if it hoped to effect permanent reform within American education.

THE REACTION AGAINST PROGRESSIVISM

By the late Thirties reaction had set in, prompted in part by the evident weakness and ambiguities of progressive education which Dewey had warned against a full decade earlier. Essentialists led by Isaac Kandel and William Chandler Bagler were in the forefront of a battle against the progressivist movement, alleging that the prevailing "life adjustment" thrust of the U.S. Office of Education had done irreparable harm to academic standards, and that recent pronouncements of the Educational Policies Commission in support of progressivist ideology constituted a prescription for social disaster. Again in the post-war period, the offensive against the progressive education movement was renewed, marked most notably by publication of Ber-

[21] *Democracy and Education,* p. 231.

nard Iddings Bell's *Crisis in Education* (1949) and Mortimer Smith's
And Madly Teach which appeared the same year. Spurred by the need
for technically trained manpower, conservative critics excoriated the
schools for loose standards, watered-down curricula, and ineffective
discipline—just as Dewey had foreseen.

The 1950's and early 1960's witnessed new diatribes against progressivist thought, with popular disaffection reaching an almost hys-
terical pitch in the wake of the Soviet Union's successful orbiting of
Sputnik in 1957. Alarmed at the apparent failure of the United States
to compete successfully in the international technological arena,
critics issued strident calls for the total revamping of American education.[22] The various exposes and studies of Hyman Rickover, Max Rafferty and James Conant, among others, underscored the view that
schools ought to be looked upon as instruments of national policy,
and employed as weapons in the international Cold War. It followed
from this that the best thing schools could do was to produce inspired scientists and competent technicians as expeditiously as possible.[23] Calls went out for a massive infusion of science and mathematics into the curriculum.

The work of reconstruction began with the now-famous Woods
Hole Conference of 1959 when strategists led by Jerome Bruner of
Harvard and Jerrold Zacharias of MIT started looking for ways to
render instruction more efficient and economical. The single most
widely read book on education of the period was Bruner's *The Process of Education* (1960), which popularized such themes as "inductive method," "spiral curriculum," "discovery learning," and "disciplinary structure." New programs and curricular packages soon
spewed forth in profusion: a New Math, New Science, New English,
New Social Studies. Throughout, the tacit assumption of most school
reformers in the early Sixties engaged in building new programs was
that there was nothing basically wrong with the school as an institution or with its objectives; what was needed, it seemed obvious, was
a much improved instructional technology, more rigorous curricular
packages—"teacher proof" if possible so that their implementation
could not be frustrated through incompetent instruction—and more
efficient systems of administration and control.

THE OPEN EDUCATION MOVEMENT

Ironically, at the same time educational technocrats were busily devising ever more monolithic systems of education management, a rising

[22] Cf. Christopher J. Lucas, "The Invisible Dissenters," *Educational Studies*,
Vol. **2**, No's 1/2 (Spring/Summer 1971), 1–4.
[23] Neil Postman and Charles Weingartner, *The School Book* (New York: Dela-
corte Press, 1973), p. 5.

chorus of critics who had come to reject practically all of the assumptions upon which prevailing pedagogical wisdom depended, began insisting that something was radically wrong. For evidence they pointed to skyrocketing drop-out rates among the nation's youth, to signs of rampant disaffection in suburbia and alienation in ghetto schools, to the myriad ways in which educational institutions were failing to educate their charges. Schools do not enlighten, they charged, they indoctrinate. Passivity is dressed up as social adjustment, and conformity interpreted as respect for authority. Teachers confuse learning with discipline, giving more attention to rules and regulations than to the curriculum. The basic underlying trouble with public education, they alleged, is that schools miseducate: they provide children with practically no opportunity or freedom to practice the very behaviors expected of them as reasonable, mature adults. Thus, educators preach democracy and practice depotism. They laud creativity but reward pedantry. They endorse divergent, original thinking, but penalize students whose work betrays signs of it. What was needed was not greater efficiency and control, but a thorough-going reappraisal of the basic objectives and goals of the schools.

The first phase of humanistic protest began with an inchoate sense of revulsion and moral outrage at the destruction of the hearts and minds of "disadvantaged" youngsters, as reported graphically by Nat Hentoff's *Our Children Are Dying* (1966), Herbert Kohl's *36 Children* (1967), Jonathan Kozol's *Death at an Early Age* (1967), and James Herndon's *The Way it Spozed to Be* (1968). Each in its own way bore eloquent testimony to the rigid authoritarianism, the classroom repression of natural humanity, and the systematic suppression of real learning characteristic of ghetto schools. John Holt uncovered the same tyranny, albeit in more subtle forms, in suburban schools, and shared his anger in the bestselling *How Children Fail,* published in 1964. Before long the trickle of protest had become a deluge, as writers, journalists, psychologists, and sociologists, not to mention many practicing classroom teachers, rushed into print with fiery denunciations of the school. Important works of the period include Paul Goodman's *Compulsory Mis-education* (1962), William Glasser's *Schools Without Failure* (1969), Postman and Weingartner's widely-read *Teaching as a Subversive Activity* (1969), Jerry Farber's profane *The Student As Nigger* (1970), George Leonard's *Education and Ecstasy* (1968), and George Dennison's poignant *The Lives of Children* (1969).

Historians and sociologists will one day likely judge the school criticism of the Sixties as one expression of a much broader protest movement, just as educational progressivism before it originated as part of a larger, more broadly based movement of liberal social, economic, and political reform. Whatever the specific associations, that first phase of the humanistic movement was coincident with civil rights activism on the domestic scene and rising protest against military adventurism overseas. In addition, many radical critics of the school clearly drew their inspiration and style from an emergent youth counter-culture militantly opposed to the dominant lifestyle and values of Middle America. To claim, as many detractors did, that the school had become an ancillary service agency to the dominant interlocking bureaucracies of society was practically tantamount to saying that it was hopelessly degenerate beyond hope of cure, because society itself was thought to be beyond redemption, short of total revolution. Other less radical critics, agreeing that schools were creatures of an alienating and corrupt social order, held out hope they could yet be transformed. The quest for alternatives, for a new pedagogy, framed the second phase of the new wave of school reform.

Humanistic pedagogy in its present state defies any single neat characterization. Especially in so diverse a movement, sweeping generalizations about beliefs and practices held in common are likely to be extremely misleading. Differences notwithstanding, the basic themes upon which many reformers do seem to have found a measure of agreement might be summarized as follows:

The learner. Young children are innately curious and will engage in exploratory behavior without benefit of adult intervention. Children seek to understand, to make sense out of their environment. They do so in a variety of ways, depending upon their individual styles and rates of psycho-social development. Children choose to engage in activities of high interest to them, sometimes learning individually and sometimes cooperatively in groups. The felt needs, expressed desires, and interest of children ought to furnish guides for the conduct of educational endeavor. The dignity and worth of every learner should be respected. Trust in children is basic.

The learning process. Among young children, learning is not easily distinguishable from play. Children, young and old alike, usually prefer active exploratory kinds of learning experiences, with opportunities to make use of manipulative materials, as opposed to a static, passive instructional format. Learning is "a personal matter that varies for different children, proceeds at many different rates, develops best when children are actively engaged in their own learning, takes place in a variety of settings in and out of school, and gains intensity in an environment where children—and childhood—are taken seriously." [24]

The curriculum. It is difficult if not downright impossible to specify a fixed body of knowledge which it is essential for everyone to

[24] Perrone, op. cit., p. 8.

acquire. The educator's chief concern should not be for a particular collection of information or set of skills so much as for the processes by which anything is taught and the conditions under which it is imparted. Certain literacy skills are important, but should never be taught in isolation from other learning experiences. The old-fashioned organization of knowledge and skills into separate subjects is counter-productive; ways must be found to integrate knowledge, skills, and values more closely.

Instruction. Memorization and rote learning should be de-emphasized in favor of inquiry and problem-solving modes of instruction. Information-giving encourages passive acceptance. Teaching should aim to assist individual learners to inquire, investigate, explore, generalize, verify, and apply data. There is no one set of techniques for instruction applicable for all situations or for all students.

Assessment. The knowledge possessed by a learner is personal and highly idiosyncratic. It is a function of how each individual synthesizes his own unique experiences. Those aspects of a person's learning which are susceptible to objective assessment are not necessarily the most important. Moreover, it is possible, even likely, that an individual can possess knowledge of something without necessarily being able to demonstrate that awareness to others. Knowledge resides with the knower, not in its public expression. Conventional standardized tests are poorly adapted to measuring important kinds of learning.

The learning environment. The school as an institution should not be run like a factory according to mechanical processing procedures. Classrooms "must be decent, pleasant places in which to spend time; for childhood and adolescence are not simply corridors through which children should be rushed as rapidly as possible to get them to the next stage." [25] The learning environment must permit trial-by-error learning, the freedom to make mistakes. It should be individualized, flexible, child-centered, and rich in a broad variety of learning resources. Above all, it must be humane, and psychologically as well as physically attractive.

The school in society. Schools should not be screening, sorting, and selecting mechanisms; nor should they serve primarily as credentialing agencies to other institutions within society. They are not tools to be used to generate trained manpower, or to further broad social, economic, or political purposes extrinsic to learning itself. The school is a place for the affective, cognitive, social, spiritual, and moral growth of individual human beings. It exists to assist people in an adventure of self-discovery and fulfillment.

[25] Silberman, *The Open Classroom Reader*, p. xix.

A third phase in the effort to reform schools was, properly speaking, the open education movement itself. Having analyzed the faults of the nation's educational system and delineated an alternative set of assumptions about processes and purposes, the next and more difficult challenge confronting reformers was to effect actual programmatic changes within the schools. That work, begun late in the 1960's, continued throughout the decade of the 1970's.

A "typical" open classroom (if indeed there is any such thing) is organized around four or five operating principles. First, the room itself is decentralized: desks, if any, are grouped in clusters and space divided into "learning areas" broken up by dividers, screens, or bookcases. Each area is supplied with materials suitable for the activities or types of inquiry to which the space is devoted. Thus, for example, a reading area is generously supplied with books and magazines; a math area or corner comes equipped with cuisinaire rods, rulers, and other counting and measuring devices; an art center contains easels, paints, chalk, and the like for painting, sculpting, or whatever.

Secondly, ample provision is made for physical mobility. Children are free to converse with one another, to move about individually or in groups, and to choose their own activities according to a very fluid schedule.

Thirdly, the classroom environment is rich in learning resources, including many different kinds of media for various activities such as reading, cooking, sewing, arts and crafts, scientific experimentation, listening to music, play-acting, writing, and so on.

Fourthly, the teacher and his or her aides work most of the time with small groups or with individuals. Rarely does the teacher convene the entire class except possibly for issuing instructions or suggestions at the beginning of the day. "The teachers begin with the assumption that the children want to learn and will learn in their fashion; learning is rooted in firsthand experience so that teaching becomes the encouragement and enhancement of each child's own thrust toward mastery and understanding. Respect for and trust in the child are perhaps the most basic principles underlying the open classroom." [26]

SOME PROBLEMS

Open education possesses no one single orthodoxy or ideal program: it takes many varying forms, depending upon the individual

[26] Ewald B. Nyquist and Gene R. Hawes (eds.), *Open Education, A Sourcebook for Parents and Teachers* (New York: Bantam, 1972), p. 10.

teachers, children, schools, and communities involved. And, as might be expected, the degree of true "openness" differs greatly, ranging from the almost totally open-ended programs offered in a certain few experimental or "alternative" free schools (whose numbers have diminished drastically in recent years) to highly-structured models organized on a "systems" basis, such as the Kettering Foundation's IGE (Individually Guided Education) program.

Predictably, enthusiasm for open education has oftentimes degenerated into faddism, particularly when well-intentioned school administrators attempt to impose it by fiat on unwilling or uninformed teachers without adequate preparation or consultation. Sometimes too an open classroom program is adopted with a very simplistic understanding of its fundamental principles, as when a school faculty deludes itself into thinking its successful implementation depends upon nothing more radical than the abolition of the self-contained classroom. At the opposite extreme, strongly reminiscent of progressivist excesses, open education has been allowed to degenerate into aimlessness and license where teachers lacked the competence to create new structures for learning.

All too often an anti-intellectual strain has developed among open education proponents, as evidenced by assertions that children must be left entirely on their own, or that the imposition of standards for achievement and evaluation are unfair or inappropriate. Adding to the problem is a lack of reliable evidence to show what evaluative processes are best suited for measuring the kinds of learning that open classrooms develop especially well. After a decade of controversy on the question of how open educators are to be held "accountable" for the results of their labor, there is little agreement on the instruments or standards of assessment that should be employed.

Finally, innovative programs for open education are geared primarily to the needs of children in the elementary school, but even yet there has been little further practical applications of the open education concept for middle and upper secondary-level schools. Colleges and universities, unsurprisingly, have scarcely been affected at all by the movement.

FUTURE PROSPECTS

The fate of open classroom reforms at the present juncture appears unclear. Much of the early enthusiasm seems dissipated, and already signs of a reaction against the subjectivity and individualism characteristic of open education are in evidence. On the other side, the number of school systems across the country endeavoring to overthrow long-established pedagogical traditions and to humanize instruction is probably considerable. Curricula have been revamped, promising new multi-media approaches to learning are still being developed, and novel forms of classroom management are being introduced. Above all, the hallmarks of open education—respect and trust for children, openness, flexibility, diversity—have gained widespread acceptance among influential groups of teachers, parents, and administrators. It remains to be seen whether the basic values of educational humanism can survive amidst the conflicting ideological cross-currents of American life, or whether they will recede temporarily into the background, awaiting revival at some future date when the realization dawns once again that schools, first and foremost, should be for children.

Can Human Rights Survive the Classroom?

MORREL J. CLUTE
Wayne State University

Citizens of the United States have been shocked (and if not, they should be alarmed or at least deeply concerned) over the recent dramatic increase in the callous disregard for human life and the human rights of others. Not only is this disregard reflected in an ever increasing rate of crime in all categories, but more specifically in an increase in crimes against people, which are characterized by brutality and senseless destruction of life.

Life, liberty, and the pursuit of happiness, once considered inalienable rights, are in such jeopardy that many people fear walking alone and no longer feel secure in their own homes.

People, in general, seem to have become less accepting of deviation and more demanding of conformity in behavior.

It is a time of confusion, uncertainty, suspicion, fear, and anxiety. Explanations of what has brought about such damaging human conditions are now available and solutions are not clear.

It is, however, clear that we are living in a period of technological change that has outraced our ability to cope with the problems which such rapid change creates for increasing numbers of people struggling to live together. There is also evidence that a technological and scientific revolution focuses primarily on *processes* and *things* and that *people* thus tend to feel less human, less worthy, and less needed. This is particularly true for young people who find it difficult to understand why the older generation has been so apathetic and callously indifferent to the physical and psychological devastation of the world which they have inherited.

One cannot help but wonder whether or not as a nation we have done what we could toward helping people develop greater respect and concern for human life. It is natural too that we should look to the school which for almost a century we have believed could help develop citizens who would believe that the personal rights to life, liberty, and the pursuit of happiness depended upon zealously protecting those self-same rights for others.

A more serious effort to overcome the dehumanizing effects of

From "Can Human Rights Survive the Classroom?" *Educational Leadership*, Vol. **31**, No. 8 (May 1974), 681–684. Reprinted with permission of the Association for Supervision and Curriculum Development and Morrel J. Clute. Copyright © 1974 by the Association of Supervision and Curriculum Development.

the emphasis upon products and processes is imperative. A fundamental issue of these times has become the issue of human and constitutional rights of citizens, and the courts have made it clear that students are citizens with rights.

PROPER USE OF HUMAN RIGHTS

If schools are really to make a commitment to help students find personal meaning in the concepts of freedom, dignity, rights, and responsibilities, a base is needed for developing programs and processes which have high success probability.

Research provides some fundamental data relative to human functioning that should be tremendously helpful. Much of this research data, however, seems to imply educational practice which is contradictory to past practice.

A review of sources of the research makes this point clear. Only recently have we come to appreciate the significance of past experience as a determiner of meaning in the processes of learning. Adelbert Ames, Jr., made great contributions to this understanding through his research in visual perception.[1] Ames' work provides sound research evidence to support what teachers have always known intuitively: Past experience is all we have with which to make meaning from our perceptions (all that is selected by our sensory organs for input). What we are able to see, hear, taste, smell, and feel is dependent for its selection and its meaning upon past experience. We reach out from the center of our universe, which is the space we occupy as defined by our skin, amd make our external world. The personal meaning we make out of each clue or situation is limited and modified by the experiences we have known and the purposes we have evolved. As we alter, change, or add to the background of experience, we increase a child's potential for making meaning or learning. The most significant "breakthrough" in learning theory of the past decade is, no doubt, the recognition that intelligence, as human talent, is as alterable as other human talents.

The past decade too has provided us with an abundance of research evidence as to the significance of feelings in human functioning. We know that self-concepts—feelings about one's own worth and dignity—are inextricably related to all aspects of human behavior. We know too that most of significant behavior is more often the outward manifestation of "right feelings" than it is "right reasons." Behavior that is damaging and destructive to people and property is most often seen as outcomes of degraded feelings—feelings of worthlessness, frustration, despair, and anxiety. Positive behavior grows

[1] Earl C. Kelley. *Education For What Is Real.* New York: Harper & Brothers, 1940.

out of positive feelings. A child cannot respect another person unless he has some reason for respecting himself.

RESPECT FOR SELF AND OTHERS

If the child is to understand the issue of rights and responsibilities, he must not only experience respect for his own human and civil rights but he must be helped to understand that these rights exist for him only as they are protected for all others. It is not enough for a child simply to know what his rights are but he must also know what the consequences are when human rights are violated.

Responsibility cannot be learned in the absence of freedom; nor can respect for law and order be learned in the absence of respecting experience. If damaging behavior is the result of inadequate feelings about one's self and one's chances, then the classrooms of American schools must become places where children in their formative years come to know from experience what respect for rights of citizens really means. Teachers must be freed from continuing school and classroom practices which demean, diminish, and/or destroy a child's feelings of worth. Most of the teaching practices or methods which characterize American classrooms evolved in the pre-scientific days. Much of what we do, we continue to do simply because we always did it that way.

The time has come for us in education to apply the same strict standard to educational practice that the federal government applies to the pharmaceutical industry in terms of knowing the side effects before a drug can be released on the market. Teachers must be free to depart from tradition when that tradition has damaging side effects on a child's growth or it represents unsound practice.

A Canadian teacher in a graduate class, as a result of looking at the side effects of some present day practice, wrote the following:

> Reflection on these situations brought back memories of many things that I have done to children during the years of my teaching. My actions were well-intentioned; I had no desire to act toward them in any negative way; I simply did what I did either because I thought it was educationally sound, or because I didn't think at all.
>
> I had long insisted upon a highly disciplined milieu where students spoke to each other only during "appropriate" times, usually through teacher-originated discussion topics, where seat-work activities were conducted on an individual, non-communicative basis, where retention of facts and development of cognitive skills were by far the most important aspects of education, where aesthetics were restricted to those areas of the curriculum, such as art, music, and literature, that provided for them, and where the effective learning, if any, took place without any help from me, during the lunch hours and after-school time.
>
> I have, in the past, either praised or punished students on the basis

of how I perceived their behavior. Through my lack of understanding, I praised mindless obedience and thoughtless acquaintance to authority because I perceived it to be "cooperation." I have rewarded factual regurgitations of what I have taught, and criticized creative but different interpretations. I have punished students whom I perceived to be "fighting" when they were actually "playing," "inattentive" or "disruptive" when they were either bored or engaged in some other activity that was more valuable and meaningful to them. I have become frustrated when children did not learn what I thought I had taught, and I have vented my frustration on their "stupidity" when I was really the one at fault.

These memories fill me with regret, to be sure, but my regret is even greater when I consider the vast number of teachers who have done precisely the same things to generations of children. How I wish that all of us could have had an opportunity, many years ago, to see some of these "educational" practices through the eyes of the students! [2]

There is evidence too that traditional classroom practice almost totally ignores the human and constitutional rights of students. A survey by John Babcock [3] replicating the study reported in the September 1973 issue of *Phi Delta Kappan,* "Student Perceptions of Teacher Violations of Human Rights," [4] revealed shocking statistics. Not only were the findings corroborated, but an even greater percentage of students in an urban and suburban high school perceived their own human rights had been violated. Ninety percent felt that their own opinion did not count. An even higher percentage felt that they had not been consulted or had been uninvolved in helping to plan some aspect of class work.

STUDENTS' RIGHTS ARE IGNORED

It is strange, indeed, that young people who are responsible enough to walk a mile to school are not viewed as responsible enough to walk through a school corridor or use the restroom properly. Students report that they are denied the right to question their punishment, feel that they are degraded or treated with disrespect, and report that the school does not tell students of their rights as citizens in a democratic social order. Feelings are real and whether or not we agree with these findings, the fact that thousands upon thousands of students both young and old feel degraded, that their opinions do not

[2] Ron Patrick. "Reflections." Unpublished master's paper, Wayne State University, December 1973.
[3] John Babcock. *Some Teachers Are Letting Students Down.* Unpublished master's paper, Wayne State University, December 1973.
[4] T. Buxton and K. Pritchard. "Student Perceptions of Teacher Violations of Human Rights." *Phi Delta Kappan* 55: 66–69; September 1973.

count and that their teachers perceive them as unable to be responsible for their own behavior, becomes a self-fulfilling prophecy.

Further research, particularly that of Rosenthal and others, indicates that there is a direct relationship between the teacher's expectations and student growth. In the September 1973 issue of *Psychology Today*, Rosenthal offers new evidence to support his theory that "students live up or down to their teacher's expectations of them. Teachers communicate their opinions of students consciously and unconsciously in word, grimace, posture, and gesture." Rosenthal finds four common characteristics of teachers who expect good things from their students and usually get it.

They appear to: "create a warmer social-emotional mood around their 'special' students; give more feedback to these students about their performance; teach more material and more difficult material to their 'special' students; and give their 'special' students more opportunity to respond to questions." [5]

The matter of student rights and responsibilities is not so much a curricular issue as it is a total school commitment to human development as the all-purpose goal of education.

If children are to grow up to understand the personal meanings of rights and respect of others; if they are to understand the meaning of freedom, then they must grow up with people who are themselves free. Students need to be consulted, involved in working out their own destiny, respected as citizens with rights, and perceived as valuable human beings.

Teachers must be freed from the use of degrading and demeaning practices which are destructive to a child's own feeling of worth. The practices of comparative grading, ability grouping, and standardized achievement testing are examples of traditional practices that have a destructive potential.

We must eliminate the fallacy that has existed for so long in education—the belief that one person teaches, that a teacher transfers his knowledge and his wisdom to his students. No one person ever really teaches another. Every individual teaches himself; he gives himself to learning or he withholds himself from it. Every learner is in complete control of his own learning. Belief in content to be taught (transferred) demands single right responses to questions asked.

It is probable that there is no single teaching practice that does more to destroy interest in learning than does the excessive use of "single right answer questions." The excessive use of such questions is destructive to interest in learning and in feelings of worth, and ultimately results in a hostile rejection of all organized education.

[5] Robert Rosenthal. "The Pygmalion Effect Lives." *Psychology Today* 7 (4): 56–58; September 1973.

In spite of the apparent damage which can come from this kind of teaching strategy, it still dominates classroom practice throughout the schools of America.[6] Teachers must be freed from expectations of this kind.

Children must live with and experience freedom if they are to understand it. Most of the learning we do (all of us) comes from the mistakes we make, but this is only true when it is safe to examine the causes and understand the consequences of mistakes.

Only as we treat students as citizens with rights can they become citizens with responsibility.

Impact of Learning Failure, See:

William Glasser. *Schools Without Failure.* New York: Harper & Row, 1969.
John Holt. *How Children Fail.* New York: Pitman Publishing Co., 1964.
Carl Rogers. *Freedom To Learn.* Columbus, Ohio: Charles T. Merrill Publishing Company, 1969.

[6] John I. Goodlad and Frances M. Klein. *Behind the Classroom Door.* Worthington, Ohio: Charles A. Jones Publishing Co., 1970.

Tempering a Fad

JOSEPH FEATHERSTONE
The New Republic

Word of English schools reaches us at a time of cultural and political ferment, and the American vogue for British reforms must be seen as one element in a complex and many sided movement. Within our schools, there is nearly a pedagogical vacuum. Few reformers have come forward with practical alternatives; even fewer have deigned to address themselves to working teachers. The grassroots nature of the English reforms, with their emphasis on the central importance of good teaching, has a great appeal for people who are victims of the general staff mentality of our school reformers and managers. Blacks and other minorities are interested in new approaches simply because they reject all the workings of the schools as they stand; some of the best of the community control ventures, such as the East Harlem Block Schools, have been promoting informal methods, as have some of the parent-controlled Head Start programs. And there are growing numbers of middle and upper middle class parents

From *An Introduction* by Joseph Featherstone. © 1971 by Schools Council Publications. Reprinted by permission of Citation Press, a division of Scholastic Magazines, Inc.

in favor of "open" and "informal," not to mention "free," schooling, even though they are vague on the pedagogical implications of these terms.

The most cogent chapters in Charles Silberman's *Crisis in the Classroom* are a plea for American educators to consider the English example. Silberman's book is interesting as a cultural document, as well as a statement in its own right, for it registers an important shift in opinion. Silberman is arguing that too many American schools are grim and joyless for both children and teachers. What was once a point made by a handful of radical critics is now very close to being official wisdom. Silberman, it should be added, distinguishes himself from many critics of the schools in that he is deeply sympathetic to ordinary classroom teachers and has a clear sense of the crucial importance of the teacher's role in creating a decent setting for learning.

By now I've visited a fair number of American classrooms working along informal lines. The best are as good as anything I've seen in England; the worst are a shambles. In the efforts that look most promising, people are proceeding slowly, understanding that preparing the way for further improvements and long-term growth is more important than any single "innovation." (As I've noted, there are too few entire school environments run along informal lines.)

Understanding the need for slow growth and hard work with teachers and children, many of the informal American practitioners I've talked to are alarmed at the dimensions of the current fad for "open" schools. There are reasons for skepticism. From today's perspective, which is no doubt morbid and too disheartened, it seems that our successive waves of educational reform have been, at best, intellectual and idealogical justifications for institutions whose actual workings never changed all that much. At the worst, the suspicion is the past reform movements, whatever their rhetoric, have only reinforced the role schools play in promoting social inequality. The realization that schools alone cannot save the social order—which should have been obvious all along—has prompted some to despair over ever getting decent education.

Added to these sobering reflections is a fresh sense of dismay over the outcomes of the past ten years of "innovation." For we have finished a decade of busy reform with little to show for it. Classrooms are the same. Teachers conduct monologues or more or less forced class discussions; too much learning is still rote; textbooks, timetables, clocks set the pace; discipline is an obsession. The curriculum reform efforts of the 1960's brought forth excellent materials in some cases—materials still essential for good informal classrooms—but they took the existing environment of the schools for granted. Perhaps because so many were outsiders, the reformers failed to engage teachers in continual thought and creation, with the result that the teachers ended up teaching the new materials in the old ways. Being for the most part university people, specialists, the reformers were ignorant of classrooms and children: of pedagogy. They concentrated on content—organized in the form of the standard graduate school disciplines—and ignored the nature of children and their ways of learning. Too often children were regarded as passive recipients of good materials, and teachers as passive conduits. The reformers lacked a coherent vision of the school environment as a whole, a sense of the entire curriculum and the necessary human climate for learning. It was characteristic of the movement that it ignored the arts and children's expressiveness.

In the philosophical chaos of the curriculum projects, the proponents of precision had a debater's advantage. They were able to state their goals in precise, measurable, often behavioral terms. For a time, this false precision encouraged a false sense of security. And for a while, the behaviorists and the education technology businessmen were allies: They imagined that a new era of educational hardware was dawning, promising profits commensurate with those in the advanced defense and aerospace industries. Now that the bubble has burst, it seems evident to more and more people that this curious alliance had all along been talking about training, not education. Training means imparting skills. It is an aspect of education, but not all of it. I suggest a reading example: If I teach you phonic skills, that is a kind of training. Unless you go on to use them, to develop interests in books, you are not educated. This ought to be the common sense of the matter, but it isn't. Our technicians conceive of reading as a training problem on the order of training spotters to recognize airplane silhouettes. If a sixth grader in a ghetto school is reading two years below grade level, as so many are, the problem may not be reading skills at all. A fourth grade reading level often represents a grasp of the necessary skills. Part of the problem is surely that the sixth grader isn't reading books and isn't interested.

Another reason why some practitioners are dubious about "open" education reflects a further skepticism about the evangelical American mode of reform, with its hunger for absolutes and its weakness for rhetoric. Our "progressive" education movement often neglected pedagogy and the realities of life in classrooms and instead concentrated on lofty abstractions. It will be essential in promoting good practice today to abandon many old ideological debates. Yet the English example is now part of a whole diverse American cultural mood, which means that it is already ranged on one side of an ideological debate. The American milieu is polarized culturally and politically; this polarization conditions American responses to accounts of informal teaching. The responses tend to fall into the stereotyped categories of a cultural cold war raging between the hip, emancipated upper middle class and the straight middle and working class. It is a class and cultural conflict, and it takes the form of battles between those who see life as essentially a matter of scarcity—and defend the virtues of a scarce order, such as thrift, discipline, hard work—and those who see life as essentially abundant—and preach newer virtues, such as openness, the cultivation of feelings, and spontaneity. Hip people like the idea of open classrooms, because they seem to give children freedom; straight people fear the supposed absence of order, discipline, and adult authority.

If I portray this conflict in highly abstract terms, it is because it seems to me remote from the concerns of good American and British practitioners actually teaching in informal settings. Take the issue of freedom, for example. Letting children talk and move about is helpful in establishing a setting in which a teacher can find out about students; it helps children learn actively, to get the habit of framing purposes independently, and of using their own judgment. But this freedom is a means to an end, not a goal in itself. As a goal, freedom is empty and meaningless—"a breakfast food," as e.e. cummings once put it.

There are always those who argue that freedom is something negative—freedom from—and those who argue that freedom is a positive thing. From authoritarians like Plato to libertarians like Kant and Dewey, the second line of argument has linked freedom with knowledge—the free use of reason or intelligence and, sometimes, action with knowledge. Whatever the merits of the positions in this fascinating, perpetual debate, it is surely more appropriate for educators of the young to conceive of freedom in the second sense, not a momentary thing at all, but the result of a process of discipline and learning. Informality is pointless unless it leads to intellectual stimulation. Many children in our "free" schools are not happy, and one suspects that part of the reason is that they are bored with their own lack of intellectual progress. As William Hull remarks in a trenchant critique of the current fad for "open" education: "Children are not going to be happy for very long in schools in which they realize they are not accomplishing very much."

Or take the issue of authority. That it *is* an issue is a mark of deep cultural confusion, as well as a reflection of the frequent misuse of legitimate authority in America. Whatever their politics, good practitioners assume as a matter of course that teachers have a responsibility to create an environment hospitable to learning, that there is what might be called a natural, legitimate basis for the authority of an adult working with children. In his superb little book, *The Lives of Children*, George Dennison outlines some aspects of this legitimate authority: "Its attributes are obvious: Adults are larger, more experienced, possess more words, have entered into prior agreements with themselves. When all this takes on a positive instead of a merely negative character, the children see the adults as protectors and as sources of certitude, approval, novelty, skills. In the fact that adults have entered into prior agreements, children intuit a seriousness and a web of relations in the life that surrounds them. If it is a bit mysterious, it is also impressive and somewhat attractive; they see it quite correctly as the way of the world, and they are not indifferent to its benefits and demands. . . . [For a child] the adult is his ally, his model—and his obstacle [for there are natural conflicts, too, and they must be given their due]."

Disciplinary matters and the rest of the structure of authority in American schools work against the exercise of legitimate authority. And thus, in reaction to the schools, the education opposition movement foolishly assumes that all adult guidance is an invasion of children's freedom. Actually, in a proper informal setting, as John Dewey pointed out, adults ought to become more important: ". . . Basing education upon personal experience may mean more multiplied and more intimate contacts between the mature and the immature than ever existed in the traditional schools, *and consequently more rather than less guidance.*"

If you remove adult authority from a given group of children, you are not necessarily freeing them. Instead, as David Riesman and his colleagues noted in *The Lonely Crowd's* critique of "progressive" education, you are often sentencing them to the tyranny of their peers. And unacknowledged adult authority has a way of creeping back in subtle and manipulative ways that can be more arbitrary than its formal exercise.

Another fake issue in the debate on open education is the distinction between education as something developed from within, and education as something formed from without—the old, boring question of whether to have, as they say, a child-centered or an adult-directed classroom. There are, to be sure, certain respects in which the best informal practice is child-centered. The basic conception of learning, after all, reflects the image of Piaget's child-inventor fashioning an orderly model of the universe from his varied encounters with experience. The child's experience *is* the starting point of all good informal teaching. But passive teaching has no place in a good informal setting, any more than passive children do. Active teaching is essential, and one of the appeals of this approach to experienced teachers is that it transforms the teacher's role. From enacting somebody else's text or curriculum, the teacher moves toward working out his own responses to children's learning. The teacher is responsible for creating the learning environment.

Still another confusion on the American scene lies in the notion that liberalizing the repressive atmosphere of our schools—which is worth doing for its own sake—will automatically promote intellectual development. It won't. We need more humane schools, but we also need a steady concern for intellectual progress and workmanship. Without this, it is unlikely that we will get any sort of cumulative development, and we will never establish practical standards by which to judge good and bad work.

Some American practitioners question the utility of slogans such as the "open school," or "informal education." The terms are suspect because they become clichés, because they don't convey the necessary values underlying this kind of teaching, because they suggest a hucksterized package, and because they divide teaching staffs into the "we" who are doing the open approach and the "they" who are not. Some imitate the philosopher Charles Saunders Pierce, who changed his "pragmatism" to the much uglier-sounding "pragmaticism"—in order, he said, to keep his ideas safe from kidnappers. They prefer an awkward and reasonably neutral term like "less formal." A brave few are modestly willing to march under a banner inscribed "decent schools."

This suspicion of slogans can be carried to ludicrous extremes. But at the heart of such evasiveness it is an important point: Educating children or working with teachers is an entire process. A good informal setting should not be thought of as a "model" or as an "experiment," but as an environment in which to support educational growth in directions that have already proved to be sound.

Some observers fear the manner in which our schools implement reforms—a manner that destroys the possibility for further development of teachers. (There are already instances where principals have dictated "open education" to their staffs.) There is a deep—and I think altogether justified—mistrust of the conventional channels of reform from the top down: pronunciamentos by educational statesmen, the roll of ceremonial drums, the swishing sound of entrepreneurs shaking the money tree. Most of the serious American informal practitioners are self-consciously local in their orientation. They are interested in planting themselves in Vermont, Philadelphia, New York City, North Dakota, or wherever, and working at the grassroots. They imagine that it will take a very long time to get good schools, and they do not believe that big-wig oratory or White House Conferences on Education are any substitute for direct engagement with teachers and children in classrooms.

The changes they are starting are small but they have large implications. All teachers, no matter how they teach, suffer from the climate of our schools, and every serious attempt at reform will soon find itself talking about lunchrooms, toilet passes, the whole internal control structure of the schools, relationships to parents, relationships to supervisory staff, the ways in which supplies are ordered, the links between an individual school and the central bureaucracies; ultimately issues of politics, power and money.

As schools move in informal directions, there will be an increasing criticism of our system of training and credentialing teachers and administrators. (Here, with the exception of outstanding institutions like London's Froebel Institute, the English do not have examples to emulate: Their teacher colleges are improving, but they have trailed behind the work of the best schools.) The training of administrators will come under attack, and in some places separate training programs for administrators will be abolished. The inadequacy of teacher training will also become more evident, although it is far from clear how to improve it. What we do know is that theory has to be reunited with practice. Without a solid grounding in child development, much of our informal teaching will be gimmickry; and without a sound base in actual practice in classrooms, theory will remain useless.

The enormous variety of the American educational landscape makes it difficult to speak in general terms. In certain areas, education schools willing to restore an emphasis on classroom practice may unite with school systems ready to move in informal directions. In other areas, where the education schools are unable to change their mandarin ways, school systems will have to assume more and more of the responsibility for training and credentialing teachers. Whichever the pattern, a central feature of successful programs will be periods of work in good informal settings. Thus a prerequisite to any scheme of training will be the existence of good schools and classrooms and classrooms to work in. The single most important task in the reform of schools and classrooms, for good informal classrooms provide the best teacher training sites.

Whether the current interest in informal teaching leads to cumulative change will depend on many things. Two are worth repeating: whether enough people can understand the essentially different outlook on children's intellectual development which good informal work must be based on, and whether our schools can be reorganized to give teachers sustained on-the-job support. I'm somewhat optimistic, about the first: the ideas are in the air, and many teachers, on their own, are already questioning the assumptions behind the traditional classroom. The second question will be much harder to answer satisfactorily. In some places, the schools are ripe for change; in others, change will come slowly and painfully, if at all; and in others, the chances for growth are almost zero. Those promoting informal teaching ought to be wary of working in institutional settings where real professional growth is out of the question. In such a setting, all obstacles mesh together to form what people rightly call the System.

Right now, it seems unlikely that the System in our worst school systems will ever permit teachers to teach and children to learn. But things may have looked that way to some British educational authorities in the 1930's, too.

A final word on the faddishness of our educational concerns. The appearance of new ideas such as the clamor for open, informal schools does not cancel out old ideas. "Open education" will be a sham unless those supporting it also address themselves to recurring, fundamental problems, such as the basic inequality and racism of our society. The most pressing American educational dilemma is not the lack of informality in classrooms: It is whether we can build a more equal, multiracial society. Issues like school integration and community control have not disappeared, to be replaced by issues like open education. The agenda simply gets more crowded. It will be all the more essential, however, to keep alive in troubled times a vision of the kind of education that all wise parents want for their children.

Open Education, Are High Schools Buying It?

JAMES W. BELL
Arizona State University

In his book *Crisis in the Classroom*, Charles Silberman [1] states his belief that our most pressing educational problem is to help create and maintain a humane society. He charges that schools are dull, lifeless institutions which oppress children and he feels that how we teach and how we act are even more important than what we teach.

These views are not necessarily new, at least to some people; however, a renewed effort is being made to make practical applications of more humane ways of educating. The new approach, called open education, has its historical antecedents in the progressive movement of the 1920's and 1930's. Progressive education concepts, as espoused by John Dewey, advocated the importance of the individual and that the teacher should be a guide in the learning process.

From "Open Education, Are High Schools Buying It?" *The Clearing House*, Vol. **48**, No. 6 (February 1974), 332–338. © 1974 by The Clearing House, Fairleigh Dickinson University. Reprinted with permission.

[1] Silberman, Charles, *Crisis in the Classroom*, New York: Random House, 1970.

Unfortunately for those who believed in this philosophic approach, there was very little change in American public school methods of teaching or understanding of learning. Some followers distorted the concepts and advocated complete permissiveness in the schools. The failure of educators to help students develop the responsibility necessary for a workable permissive atmosphere and the general public's lack of understanding and desire to accept radical changes in schools led to the derailment of progressive education as a movement toward more humane schools. Individual teachers did implement many of the basic concepts and have continued in their efforts to improve schooling for their students.

OPEN EDUCATION

The new movement in the United States toward more informal education has drawn heavily on the work accomplished in the elementary schools of England. The Plowden Report,[2] a study of English Primary Schools, was published in 1967 and has had wide influence on school reformers in England and the United States.

Open education seems to be the most prevalent name in the literature for this movement; however, it is also known as informal education, integrated day, free day, Leicestershire Plan, and other titles. Some people also refer to open plan or open space schools. Advocates of open education write that it is an attitude and an approach to teaching rather than a facility; therefore it is more than an open space school. It is generally agreed, however, that a physical environment which is open will facilitate open education.

To define or conceptualize open education is a difficult task. Most of the advocates and writers on the topic have identified major ideas as they see it. A most comprehensive effort by Walberg and Thomas [3] listed eight themes around which the role of the teacher is conceptualized and approximately 90 characteristics of open education.

The themes are:

(1) Instruction—it is to be highly individualized.
(2) Provisioning—the providing of a wide range of materials and equipment.
(3) Diagnoses—the teacher continually watches each child and makes plans accordingly.

[2] Plowden, Lady Bridget *et al.*, *Children and Their Primary Schools: A Report of the Central Advisory Council for Education*, London: Her Majesty's Stationery Office, 1966.
[3] Walberg, Herbert and Susan Thomas, "Characteristics of Open Education—A Look at the Literature for Teachers," *Education Development Center Inc.*, Newton, Mass., 1971.

(4) Evaluation—the teacher gathers information about each child's growth and learning that will help him gain his goals.
(5) Humanness—a respect and trust in the individual.
(6) Seeking—the teacher's responsibility for personal growth.
(7) Self-perception—the teacher views herself and must believe in what she is doing.
(8) Assumptions—the beliefs held about children and the process of learning. (Assumptions include a warm accepting atmosphere, reasonable rules, a dependable source of authority, and a faith in children's curiosity and ability to explore on their own.)

Rathbone [4] discusses the rationale of open education under six subheads.

(1) How children learn. It is an active process and direct experience is central.
(2) A view of knowledge. Knowledge becomes real only when it is personalized. The idea of covering a certain amount of the school curriculum is rejected.
(3) A perspective on schooling. School represents the larger world and open education begins with the needs and concerns of the individual child. The setting and attaining of goals which will include the learning of facts and knowledge are encouraged, but the emphasis is on learning how to learn—to develop independence, self-reliance, trust, and responsibility.
(4) The teacher's role. The teacher is primarily a facilitator and resource person. She must diagnose individual needs and provide a rich environment for learning to take place.
(5) The psychological-emotional climate. The classroom is a place of trust and openness. The expression of feeling is encouraged and accepted and as a result mutual respect and toleration are increased.
(6) The moral context. The child has rights, obligations, is free to choose, and is to be treated with kindness and respect. The teacher has the responsibility to make issues clear in any study and to help the child accept his responsibility.

Another source [5] has identified the major objective of open education as developing an individual with positive self-image, a confident approach to problem solving, an acceptance of responsibility for his own growth, and a desire to explore and experiment. The process is inductive with the teacher guiding, supporting, and motivating.

To summarize some of the ideas mentioned above and others from the literature, it seems that the open education classroom is

[4] Rathbone, Charles, *Open Education*, New York: Citation Press, 1971.
[5] Baughman, M. Dale and Robert Eberle, "The Open Classroom," *The Clearing House*, Vol. 39, No. 7, March, 1965.

both student centered and teacher centered. The student is encouraged and helped to plan what he wants to learn and how it will
be accomplished. A major key to open education is individualized instruction. Individuals vary in the way and rate at which they learn.
The open philosophy involves movement, communication, creativity, and the development of self-direction. Basic skills are fundamental and are dealt with, but not in isolation from other learning.
The attempt is to integrate learning around problems of concern to
the child. In order to take advantage of children learning from other
children, heterogeneous grouping is advocated and at times a vertical grouping of different age groups.

Open education teachers are responsible. It is not a place
where anything goes. Rules are established and the teacher must
uphold them and see that each student is able to move, explore, and
choose freely. Although the teacher has final responsibility for making decisions and handling discipline, the atmosphere of mutual
trust leads to an individual and group responsibility. The teacher has
to plan a variety of programs, sometimes one for each student, and
then be flexible enough to change plans on the spot with a changing
situation. The teacher will give information when it is needed to an
individual student, a small group of students, or the total class. The
teacher is basically a stimulator, guide, and evaluator.

The teacher provides and structures the physical environment.
It may be a single traditional-sized classroom or an open area of several traditional-sized classrooms. The area will have many materials
and equipment and will have learning centers around the room. Students are free to move within the classroom and to other areas in the
building and outside the building. Team teaching is essential for the
larger open areas.

Evaluation is a major area of concern for proponents of open education. Most feel that objective achievement measures are inappropriate and may have a negative effect on learning. Evaluation should
be in terms of each student's progress. Observation of the the student's interaction with materials and people and what he produces
should be the basis for the evaluation and it should cover a long
range of time. It is subjective in nature.

Reports of studies which have compared students in open education classrooms with students in more traditional classrooms show
that in general the academic achievement is about equal. There is reported a greater horizontal growth by students in open classrooms. It
is also reported that students from open classrooms are better able to
identify and solve problems, have more self-direction and self-
responsibility, have a more positive self-concept, and are better able
to use inquiry skills.

SECONDARY SCHOOL VISTATION

Most of the advocates of open education and the literature on the topic have referred to elementary school education. The change in English schools has been almost exclusively at the elementary level, although Charity James in her book *Young Lives at Stake* [6] does refer to some experiments in English secondary schools. Much of the practical application of the open education concept in the United States has also been at the lower grade levels.

However, some writers have made special reference to secondary schools and specific schools are mentioned which are purported to be following open education concepts. Brunetti [7] reports in a survey of buildings constructed in 43 states from 1967–69 that approximately 52 per cent were of the open design and about equally divided as to elementary, junior high, and senior high school. However, most of the high schools classified as open facilities were open in only a part of the building such as the English or social science departments.

Because of my special interest and position I visited secondary schools, both junior high and senior high, in various parts of the country. Sixteen schools in eight states were visited. Ten of these schools were senior high, four were junior high, one was a junior-senior high, and one was K-12. Schools visited were some of those mentioned in the literature or were identified by letters from the state department of education as working with open education.

An attempt was made to gather data in areas identified by the proponents of open education. There was no structured questionnaire to be followed; however, I did have an outline of things to look for. Materials were collected from schools and notes kept on each visit.

The most prominent finding of the visits was the wide variety of things that were going on or provided in these schools that claim, at least in part, to be open education schools.

However, there were common points found in many if not all of the schools.

(1) There was some kind of openness to the building. This varied from one end of the classroom being open to a space which typically would have had 4 to 8 classrooms being completely devoid of inner walls.

(2) A library or media center which was very open to entry and use.

(3) More variety of courses being offered than had previously been

[6] James, Charity, *Young Lives at Stake*, Agathon Press, 1972.
[7] Brunetti, Frank, *"Open Space: A Status Report,"* School Planning Laboratory, Stanford University, August, 1971.

offered at these schools. Thus students have a greater choice of courses to take.

(4) More team teaching.
(5) Schedules that are more flexible.
(6) Students have more choice in how to spend their unscheduled time. This varied from being able to go to the student commons area to being free to leave campus.
(7) Provision in the building for a student commons area or gathering place.
(8) Students very favorable toward the changes.
(9) Teachers are sharing more with other teachers and utilizing the media center more.
(10) A problem had developed with considerably higher loss and/or destruction of materials in the open media center.

Listed below are some other points that were found in one or more schools but not in a majority.

(1) Students choose their own schedule and the teachers they work with.
(2) A large block of time provided in all junior high schools and two senior high schools.
(3) Learning packages being used.
(4) Vertical grouping of students.
(5) Letter grades replaced with some other reporting system.
(6) A tendency to have more independent study within courses and to use some form of contract with students.

It should be noted that most of the points in the two lists above could be accomplished by innovative teachers in traditional schools or by any school that wants to try something new. The openness of the facilities, of course, requires a new building or removal of walls from an older building.

When one compares the findings from school visits with the proponents concept of open education, as for example Rathbone's six areas, a trend toward open education can be noted in #1 how children learn, #3 a perspective on schooling, and #6 the moral context. There seems to be very little change from traditional schools in the other areas identified by Rathbone.

There were two notable exceptions where it seemed to me that these schools had incorporated much more of the open education rationale.

(1) The Wilson School on the campus of Mankato State College, Mankato, Minnesota. In this school of grades K-12 students have four curriculum options from almost complete independent study to more structure for those who want it. There are no preplanned courses and students chose their advisors, the subject areas they want to work in, and the teachers to work with. The student sets

up a goal sheet with his teacher and decides when and how long he will work in a subject area. Students keep a folder in some areas to record time spent and things done. The school is non-graded and in some subject areas a 7-year-old and a 15-year-old student may be seen working together. Teachers will be primarily working with individual students. Evaluation is a written report rather than letter grades. The building is not new and does not have large open space areas.

(2) Marjorie French Junior High, Topeka, Kansas. The school is experimenting with 140 students in a three-hour block of time. The program is non-graded but students represent the typical seventh, eighth, and ninth grades. The building has large open areas on each side of an open media center. A student commons area was provided and is used for large group instruction, independent study, lunch, and student activities. Four teachers, two each in language arts and social studies, are assigned to the block and each student is assigned to one of the teachers.

Each student is responsible for planning a weekly schedule which is approved by his base teacher. The time block is divided into 15 minute units. All students are required to schedule certain units such as a minimum of 15 units per week in language arts and 15 in social studies activities. All are required to schedule 4 units per week in introspection, which is an open reading and creative writing activity. The student may schedule part of his time in the area of science, physical education, art, music, industrial arts, and home economics. Each Friday a time is blocked out for the Town Meeting where all 140 students meet together to discuss grievances, make suggestions, and set rules.

Folders are provided for each student in basic study areas, independent study, and introspection. Many entries for the folders are made by the students.

The teachers and the students are very enthusiastic about the program. Students reported that they were more interested in their studies and attained more depth of understanding. Teachers say the students seem more mature and courteous to each other. The only negative comment by students was that it was a little noisy at times.

PROBLEMS AND QUESTIONS

Some of the more important problems and questions relating to open education will be listed and briefly discussed.

(1) *The attitude of educators and parents.* It takes considerable time and effort to effect important changes. Teachers need to be innovative and successful and then have training prior to the change and follow-up help during the change. Parents must be informed, in-

vited to visit and participate, and secure feedback from their children.

(2) *How much do you trust the students.* Most students thrive on responsibility (although many need help to arrive), but some find it very difficult to cope with. Why are open schools losing so much material from media centers? Most schools have moved to much stricter controls in this area. One school visited was a notable exception on this point since the media area was completely open and the loss had been minimal. The only difference that could be identified between this school and others visited was that the entire district was open and had been for a number of years, thus the students of this school had come through open elementary schools.

(3) *Student evaluation.* This problem has been discussed previously. The proponents of open education must help develop measures for assessment more compatible with the goals. Student achievement and other valid objectives should be evaluated.

(4) *A concern for structure and the coverage of subject matter.* Most if not all proponents and practitioners agree there is a need for structure to provide a sense of order and meaningful options. The integration of subject matter around problems and inquiry is a major characteristic of open education, but very little of this is actually happening in the secondary schools visited. The following quote by Renfield seems to summarize the open education philosophy on this point.

> The knowledge explosion gives hope. It may eventually overwhelm those who suffer from a compulsion to plan curriculum. They may lose faith in their assumed ability to shrink the world's knowledge down to manageable size. The schools, set adrift in a turbulent ocean, will no longer be able to ladle out a tidy pool of knowledge and to define their activities in terms of subject matter. They will be free, at last, to pursue the goals they always claimed to be pursuing anyway—and their pupils will learn more subject-matter than ever before.[8]

(5) *Securing materials and helping students select appropriate material for their use.* Only a few of the schools visited, all of which had federal money help, had well stocked department learning centers and school media centers. Many schools had severely limited materials for learning.

(6) *Noise level.* Some teachers and a few students perceive this as a problem; however, a research study [9] found no significant difference in sound levels in open plan and conventional plan schools.

[8] Renfield, Richard. *If Teachers Were Free,* Washington: Acropolis Books, 1969, p. 158.
[9] Kyzar, Barney, *Comparison of Instructional Practices in Classrooms of Different Design,* ERIC report ED 048669, January, 1971.

SUMMARY

Secondary school educators in many parts of the United States are attempting to make their schools more humane and more interesting places for students to learn in. The open education movement, although centered in the elementary schools at present, is making an impact at the secondary level. The impact seems to be mainly in facilities, organization, and course offerings; very little has been changed in other key concepts of open education such as individualized instruction, integration of content, vertical grouping, creativity, and self-direction.

Some of the concepts and practical applications of open education at the elementary level may need to be changed or adjusted for secondary education. For example, some integration of subjects can be accomplished, but how much is desirable? Should there be a balance between individualized instruction and group interaction? Is the role of the teacher the same? These and other questions should be experimented with and researched carefully.

Changes come slow in education for many reasons both good and bad. The changes being advocated by proponents of open education are basically the right ones and although there are many problems ahead, let us hope that the movement is not derailed by overconservative detractors or by overzealous advocates.

Humanism and Educational Reform—The Need for a Balanced Perspective

ALTON HARRISON, JR.
Northern Illinois University

I have been an eager, receptive reader of most of the critics of traditional education. My thinking has been especially influenced by the humanist movement. Writers like Rousseau, Emerson, Neill, Goodman, and Rogers, to name a few, have had a significant impact on my instructional methods and teaching style. The dissatisfaction I had with my own experiences as a traditional student and later as a

From "Humanism and Educational Reform—The Need for a Balanced Perspective," *The Educational Forum*, Vol. XXXVIII, No. 3 (March 1974), 331–336. © 1974 by Kappa Delta Pi, An Honor Society in Education. Reprinted with permission.

traditional teacher provided a favorable climate for the growth and development of many of their ideas.

I have come to believe that each person is born with a unique potential and that education should not only respect this individuality, but create programs conducive to its growth. I believe that learning is natural for man; that every individual is motivated by natural curiosity and a desire for inner peace or happiness. Like Emerson, I am convinced that learning could and should be an enjoyable experience. While recognizing the importance of cognitive development in education, I regard affective development to be of equal importance.

As this basically individualized-humanistic philosophy of education grew and shaped itself in my thinking, I compared it to what was actually happening in public schools and particularly in my own classes—both were found lacking. For the most part, schools appeared to be repressive factories whose main purpose at the elementary level was custodial and at the upper levels utilitarian. Children were raw material that was mass processed to fit into a limited number of molds bearing the U.S. stamp of approval. Individuality was not just ignored but openly discouraged. Conformity was richly rewarded. Learning did not seem to be especially joyful; in fact, it appeared to be a grim business.

As the comparative discrepancies grew, so did my disenchantment. Since I taught at the university level, I enjoyed a considerable amount of freedom in terms of my own personal approach to teaching. I began to make changes designed to give the students more choices and, thus, hopefully, increased involvement in formulating course requirements related to their own individual needs and interests.

The results were less than spectacular. But the experience was exhilarating, in a way, since I was at least experimenting and some students did seem receptive and responsive. In any case, no irreparable damage seemed to have been done. However, as the semesters came and went I lost much of my initial exhilaration and the number of responsive students did not increase appreciably. A major source of frustration was the conflict between the individualized approach and the traditional process of evaluation. Individualization and affective development do not lend themselves to objective measurement. But the registrar continued to require that not only should the goats be separated from the sheep, but also the half-goats and half-sheep. Grades definitely seemed to be an obstacle to the kind of honest relationships I sought to establish.

My commitment to individualism-humanism was also shaken by students who used their newly gained freedom to work for more demanding professors or to engage in some form of recreation-relaxation, but I would comfort myself by saying their behavior was to be expected in view of their long years of conditioning in traditional classes. And, if that did not work, I would add that arbitrary requirements might force them to go through the motions and, thus, salve my ego, but the end results, in terms of useful learning, probably would be no greater.

It was about this time that a new group of education critics appeared on the publishing horizons, and I began to read writers like Holt, Dennison, Silberman, Postman-Weingartner, and Kozol. It was reassuring because their ideas of educational reform were very supportive of the changes I had been trying in my classes. Thus, armed with the wisdom of a new generation of critics, I became bolder in the reforms I had initiated in my own classes. I had already eliminated tests but had substituted other forms of evaluation which involved the students. I had utilized individual conferences in which the student and I attempted cooperatively to weigh the available evidence and come up with an honest, fair grade. However, if an agreement could not be reached, I always retained the authority to make the final decision. For the most part, these were awkward bargaining sessions in which students frequently asked for a grade higher than I thought was just. Grades, of course, are extremely important to students—even to those who say they do not care. Grades are critically important in determining whether or not a student can stay in school, get a degree, enter graduate school and get an advanced degree. This in turn has a considerable influence on the type of job he can acquire and the way he will be viewed by his family, friends, and society. In other words, grades have a critical effect on a youngster's self-esteem. No matter how I tried to deemphasize evaluation, students, logically, continued to be extremely grade conscious. And as long as I retained the right to sit in judgment and decide their grades, their major objective was, as it always had been, to figure out what I wanted and to give it to me. I was prepared to take that decisive step which would enable students to cast aside the game of "give the teacher what he wants." I was ready to relinquish my evaluation authority and permit students to make the final decision in the determination of their grades. It was not an easy decision to make. I did a considerable amount of fretting and agonizing. What if a student did not do anything and gave himself an "A?" So, what if he did? Would the integrity of the university be undermined? Would the earth stop turning on its axis? I decided to try it!

I spent the first three class meetings of the new semester explaining how the course would be conducted. I told the students that in order to eliminate the evaluation threat, they would be permitted to assign their own grades at the end of the semester. I emphasized the freedom they would have to pursue topics, issues, and projects related to their own individual needs and interests. I discussed my role in terms of advising, facilitating, participating, guiding, and consulting. I talked about the class as a cooperative learning endeavor—not just for them, but for me. I indicated that each person had a significant contribution to make and a responsibility for making it.

Initially, everyone floated aimlessly back and forth to class each day waiting, somewhat expectantly, to see what I would do next. The majority clearly wanted me to give them some specific assignments. I refused to do this, and attempted to coax them into taking advantage of the opportunity to develop a meaningful course related to their own individual needs and interests. As their puzzlement and frustration increased, I agreed to throw out some suggestions and possibilities. At that point about one third of the class immediately adopted the suggestions and began to work on them as course requirements. Another third, approximately, continued to drift, waiting for more definite directions, and the other third faded in and out doing virtually nothing.

The semester ended in disappointment but not regrets. It was a worthwhile experiment, and I had finally gone "all the way" by eliminating teacher evaluation—a process which I had previously considered a major obstacle to individualized-humanistic learning. But the results fell far short of my expectations, and I considered the experiment a failure.

Initially, I identified three major factors which seemed to cause success to elude me. One which has already been discussed was teacher evaluation. However, as I indicated above, the replacement of teacher evaluation with student evaluation seemed to be relatively inconsequential. A second factor that received consistent blame was the conditioning effect of traditional education. For years students had been told exactly "what to do" in school, "how to do it," and "when to do it." Thus, it was no wonder that students were incapable of handling freedom-responsibility. So the argument went, and most students were quick to use it. However, I noted that the majority of students gave this excuse at the beginning, middle, and end of the semester. I have no difficulty accepting this argument at the opening of the semester and even at midsemester, but after that its logic deteriorates rapidly. The student who is still using this excuse at the end of eighteen weeks is exhibiting a behavior pattern which must be attributed to something other than conditioning effects. After all, he is not a white rat! So much for factor number two.

A third factor which seemed to be an obstacle was the institutional setting. Obviously, the design and arrangement of nearly all classrooms is for the traditional "tell 'em and test 'em" approach. Classrooms, like hospital rooms, are sterile and impersonal; not at all conducive to the development of warm interpersonal relationships leading to a sense of community which seems to contribute so much to the learning process and the ultimate success of a course. I still regard the insitutional environment as a handicap in changing from a traditional to a more humanistic approach in education. However, I do not think it is crucial or insuperable.

In essence, the three factors analyzed above have been rejected as major causes of failure. It occurs to me at this point that I have been referring to my attempts at educational reform as having ended in failure. But what constitutes failure? What criteria were used to make this decision? Was the changed approach to learning a failure compared to the traditional approach? The answer is definitely negative. In fact, I would judge the new approach to be somewhat better than the traditional. Certainly, it is no worse. And even if it were judged to be a draw, it could not be called a comparative failure.

Apparently, the reason I have considered the reforms to be a failure is because they did not measure up to my expectations. I had expected an overwhelming response of enthusiasm to my changes, and I did not get it. But that does not constitute failure. However, it does constitute disappointment, and I realize, now, that this is a more accurate term than failure. Actually, it's my dissatisfaction and frustration that needs to be analyzed.

In retrospect, I realize that I indulged myself in a fantasy that seems to be common among educators, especially reformers. First of all, I kept looking at educational reform in terms of *my* experiences, *my* needs, and *my* interests. Then, I began to generalize from my experiences to the total population. I began to view students the way I viewed myself and, thus, my needs were the same as theirs. When stated bluntly in this fashion it sounds like a terribly stupid thing to do. But you must realize that this is a subtle process that occurs just below the level of consciousness. It is a trap that is easy to fall into, and it requires concentrated thinking to bring it to the awareness level. In any case, the result of approaching educational reform in this fashion is that you do "connect" with a certain number of students—those who are, in fact, similar to you. This compatibility results in a comfortable if not productive relationship with those particular students. But what about the other students who possess a different behavior pattern based on a different set of values? Herein, I think, lies the seeds of my disappointment and frustration. Under a given set of conditions and circumstances I find learning to be exhilarating and extremely gratifying. I assumed that if I could create those conditions and circumstances in my classes, all or vitually all students would react in the same way. Wrong! Similar reactions came from only those students whose values and behavior patterns coincided with mine, and this was never a sizeable number. Some students wanted and needed structure and direction and supervision. Others did not want either freedom or structure, but they would do whatever was necessary to get the credits required for a degree. A few always tried to get through by doing as little as possible, and if they could get something for nothing, so much the better.

These last two groups make humanist reformers squirm uncomfortably, and most deny their existence. But reality refutes their illusions. In fact, there are a sizeable number of students in every school (be it free or controlled, liberal or conservative) who are there for some reason other than to learn. In my opinion, no amount of reform will change this. I believe this not only because of my recent experiments with education reform, but also because of the mounting psychological and educational research indicating that certain basic attitudes and behaviors are developed early in life and that educational components (teachers, instructional materials and methods, physical facilities, etc.) seem to have a negligible effect in the modification of these basic behavior patterns. Family background and peer influence seem to be the most potent forces in the formation and modification of the behavior patterns.[1]

As a teacher, this is a bitter pill to swallow. After all, we are in the behavior-changing business. Still, the evidence [2] is hard to ignore, and Etzioni provocatively displays much of it in a recent article titled, "Human Beings Are Not Very Easy to Change After All." [3] This is the primary reason that our society has found it necessary to identify the objectives most desired by the greatest number of people—namely material wealth and prestige—and then decree education as a prerequisite. By doing this, we are able to keep in school greater numbers of students for longer periods of time, but the vast majority of students consider education as a distasteful interlude to life. And any candid teacher will readily admit that there are very few who leave with any great love or enthusiasm for learning and a desire to continue it. In other words, we can force students to exhibit certain kinds of behavior in order for them to get something else they desire. Students are familiar with this practice, and refer to it as "playing the role," but this does not modify their basic behavior patterns. It is true that for a small percentage of students, their behavior is altered, sometimes dramatically, while in school. However, a careful investigation would probably reveal that the alteration was not directly related to classroom experiences. Or, if it was, the students were already predisposed in the direction of the change. I have noted that the little influence I seem to have on students has been to reinforce a propensity, not to reverse it.

[1] James K. Kent, "The Coleman Report: Opening Pandora's Box," *Phi Delta Kappan* 49 (January 1968).
[2] Massive financial support of programs in compensatory education and performance contracting has produced disappointing results.
[3] Amitai Etzioni, "Human Beings Are Not Very Easy to Change After All," *Saturday Review*, 3 June 1972.

Apparently my disappointment in educational reform is also related to the fact that I attempted to initiate humanistic changes which run counter to the materialistic values that dominate our culture. Despite the optimistic speculations of writers such as Reich [4] and Revel [5] about a growing counterculture with a humanistic bent, we are still living in a highly materialistic society in which success is measured on an economic scale. Most of our youth are extremely conscious of this and act accordingly. My observations of university students, including the campus radicals, indicate that the vast majority are there because they perceive education as having an economic value. I readily admit that my own education was pursued for this purpose. Through education I acquired intellectual and economic security, and *after* this I began to develop a humanistic orientation. Most students are still seeking this security, and not surprisingly, exhibit little more than a superficial concern for humanism.

Thus far, I have painted a rather grim picture for the reformer in education, especially those with a humanistic tendency. In fact, it does not stack up very well for any teacher who desires to have a significant influence on the majority of his students. But perhaps the grimmest picture of all would be the realization of these desires. When you consider the great number and variety of teachers to whom students are exposed, wouldn't they be a mess if they were significantly influenced by each one? Perhaps, we should be grateful that students are not easily influenced by their teachers.

It is also very possible, perhaps probable, that a teacher's influence on students is neither immediate nor dramatic and, hence, its assessment difficult to make. The teacher's influence may be part of a cumulative effect that occurs over a long period of time. It is highly probable that the student may not realize the extent of a teacher's influence until after a considerable lapse of time. And it is even more probable that he will never communicate this information to the teacher.

In any case, it seems to me that I must give up the practice of measuring my worth as a teacher in terms of the number of converts I am able to make. Since learning is the primary concern of my trade and the activity in which I am most interested, maybe I need to focus greater attention on my own involement in the learning process. If what I say is true—that I find learning exciting, enjoyable, and gratifying—then perhaps my exhibition of this as a practitioner or live model is the greatest service I can render, not only to my students, but to myself.

[4] Charles A. Reich, *The Greening of America* (New York: Random House, Inc., 1970).
[5] Jean-Francois Revel, *Without Marx or Jesus* (New York: Doubleday and Company, Inc., 1970).

The Free and Happy Student

B. F. SKINNER
Harvard University

His name is Emile. He was born in the middle of the eighteenth century in the first flush of the modern concern for personal freedom. His father was Jean-Jacques Rousseau, but he has had many foster parents, among them Pestalozzi, Froebel, and Montessori, down to A. S. Neill and Ivan Illich. He is an ideal student. Full of goodwill toward his teachers and his peers, he needs no discipline. He studies because he is naturally curious. He learns things because they interest him.

Unfortunately, he is imaginary. He was quite explicitly so with Rousseau, who put his own children in an orphanage and preferred to say how he would teach his fictional hero; but the modern version of the free and happy student to be found in books by Paul Goodman, John Holt, Jonathan Kozol, or Charles Silberman is also imaginary. Occasionally a real example seems to turn up. There are teachers who would be successful in dealing with people anywhere—as statesmen, therapists, businessmen, or friends—and there are students who scarcely need to be taught, and together they sometimes seem to bring Emile to life. And unfortunately they do so just often enough to sustain the old dream. But Emile is a will-o'-the-wisp, who has led many teachers into a conception of their role which could prove disastrous.

The student who has been taught *as if he were Emile* is, however, almost too painfully real. It has taken a long time for him to make his appearance. Children were first made free and happy in kindergarten, where there seemed to be no danger in freedom, and for a long time they were found nowhere else, because the rigid discipline of the grade schools blocked progress. But eventually they broke through—moving from kindergarten into grade school, taking over grade after grade, moving into secondary school and on into college and, very recently, into graduate school. Step by step they have insisted upon their rights, justifying their demands with the slogans that philosophers of education have supplied. If sitting in rows restricts personal freedom, unscrew the seats. If order can be maintained only through coercion, let chaos reign. If one cannot be

Reprinted by permission from *New York University Education Quarterly* IV, 2 (Winter, 1973): 2–6. Copyright by New York University.

This paper was prepared with support from a Career Award from the National Institute of Mental Health.

really free while worrying about examinations and grades, down with examinations and grades! The whole establishment is now awash with free and happy students.

DROPPING OUT OF SCHOOL, DROPPING OUT OF LIFE

If they are what Rousseau's Emile would really have been like, we must confess to some disappointment. The Emile we know doesn't work very hard. "Curiosity" is evidently a moderate sort of thing. Hard work is frowned upon because it implies a "work ethic," which has something to do with discipline.

The Emile we know doesn't learn very much. His "interests" are evidently of limited scope. Subjects that do not appeal to him he calls irrelevant. (We should not be surprised at this since Rousseau's Emile, like the boys in Summerhill, never got past the stage of a knowledgeable craftsman.) He may defend himself by questioning the value of knowledge. Knowledge is always in flux, so why bother to acquire any particular stage of it? It will be enough to remain curious and interested. In any case the life of feeling and emotion is to be preferred to the life of intellect; let us be governed by the heart rather than the head.

The Emile we know doesn't think very clearly. He has had little or no chance to learn to think logically or scientifically and is easily taken in by the mystical and the superstitious. Reason is irrelevant to feeling and emotion.

And, alas, the Emile we know doesn't seem particularly happy. He doesn't like his education any more than his predecessors liked theirs. Indeed, he seems to like it less. He is much more inclined to play truant (big cities have given up enforcing truancy laws), and he drops out as soon as he legally can, or a little sooner. If he goes to college, he probably takes a year off at some time in his four-year program. And after that his dissatisfaction takes the form of anti-intellectualism and a refusal to support education.

Are there offsetting advantages? Is the free and happy student less aggressive, kinder, more loving? Certainly not toward the schools and teachers that have set him free, as increasing vandalism and personal attacks on teachers seem to show. Nor is he particularly well disposed toward his peers. He seems perfectly at home in a world of unprecedented domestic violence.

Is he perhaps more creative? Traditional practices were said to suppress individuality; what kind of individuality has now emerged? Free and happy students are certainly different from the students of a generation ago, but they are not very different from each other. Their own culture is a severely regimented one, and their creative works—in art, music, and literature—are confined to primitive and elemental materials. They have very little to be creative with, for they have never taken the trouble to explore the fields in which they are now to be front-runners.

Is the free and happy student at least more effective as a citizen? Is he a better person? The evidence is not very reassuring. Having dropped out of school, he is likely to drop out of life too. It would be unfair to let the hippie culture represent young people today, but it does serve to clarify an extreme. The members of that culture do not accept responsibility for their own lives; they sponge on the contributions of those who have not yet been made free and happy, who have gone to medical school and become doctors, or who have become the farmers who raise the food or the workers who produce the goods they consume.

These are no doubt overstatements. Things are not that bad, nor is education to be blamed for all the trouble. Nevertheless, there is a trend in a well-defined direction, and it is particularly clear in education. Our failure to create a truly free and happy student is symptomatic of a more general problem.

THE ILLUSION OF FREEDOM

What we may call the struggle for freedom in the Western world can be analyzed as a struggle to escape from or avoid punitive or coercive treatment. It is characteristic of the human species to act in such a way as to reduce or terminate irritating, painful, or dangerous stimuli, and the struggle for freedom has been directed toward those who would control others with stimuli of that sort. Education has had a long and shameful part in the history of that struggle. The Egyptians, Greeks, and Romans all whipped their students. Medieval sculpture showed the carpenter with his hammer and the schoolmaster with the tool of his trade too, and it was the cane or rod. We are not yet in the clear. Corporal punishment is still used in many schools, and there are calls for its return where it has been abandoned.

A system in which students study primarily to avoid the consequences of not studying is neither humane nor very productive. Its by-products include truancy, vandalism, and apathy. Any effort to eliminate punishment in education is certainly commendable. We ourselves act to escape from aversive control, and our students should escape from it too. They should study because they want to, because they like to, because they are interested in what they are doing. The mistake—a classical mistake in the literature of freedom—is to suppose that they will do so as soon as we stop punishing them. Students are not literally free when they have been freed from their teachers. They then simply come under the control of other conditions, and we must look at those conditions and their effects if we are to improve teaching.

Those who have attacked the "servility" of students, as Montessori called it, have often put their faith in the possibility that young people will learn what they need to know from the "world of things," which includes the world of people who are not teachers. Montessori saw possibly useful behavior being suppressed by schoolroom discipline. Could it not be salvaged? And could the environment of the schoolroom not be changed so that other useful behavior would occur? Could the teacher not simply guide the student's natural development? Or could he not accelerate it by teasing out behavior which would occur naturally but not so quickly if he did not help? In other words, could we not bring the real world into the classroom, as John Dewey put it, or destroy the classroom and turn the student over to the real world, as Ivan Illich has recommended. All these possibilities can be presented in an attractive light, but they neglect two vital points:

(*a*) No one learns very much from the real world without help. The only evidence we have of what can be learned from a nonsocial world has been supplied by those wild boys said to have been raised without contact with other members of their own species. Much more can be learned without formal instruction in a social world, but not without a good deal of teaching, even so. Formal education has made a tremendous difference in the extent of the skills and knowledge which can be acquired by a person in a single lifetime.

(*b*) A much more important principle is that the real world teaches only what is relevant to the present; it makes no explicit preparation for the future. Those who would minimize teaching have contended that no preparation is needed, that the student will follow a natural line of development and move into the future in the normal course of events. We should be content, as Carl Rogers has put it, to trust

> the insatiable curiosity which drives the adolescent boy to absorb everything he can see or hear or read about gasoline engines in order to improve the efficiency and speed of his "hot rod." I am talking about the student who says, "I am discovering, drawing in from the outside, and making that which is drawn in a real part of me." I am talking about my learning in which the experience of the learner progresses along the line: "No, no, that's not what I want"; "Wait! This is closer to what I'm interested in, what I need." "Ah, here it is! Now I'm grasping and comprehending what I need and what I want to know!" [1]

[1] Carl R. Rogers, *Freedom to Learn*, Columbus, Ohio: Merrill, 1969.

Rogers is recommending a total commitment to the present moment, or at best to an immediate future.

FORMAL EDUCATION AS PREPARATION FOR FUTURE REWARDS

But it has always been the task of formal education to set up behavior which would prove useful or enjoyable *later* in the student's life. Punitive methods had at least the merit of providing current reasons for learning things that would be rewarding in the future. We object to the punitive reasons, but we should not forget their function in making the future important.

It is not enough to give the student advice—to explain that he will have a future, and that to enjoy himself and be more successful in it, he must acquire certain skills and knowledge now. Mere advice is ineffective because it is not supported by current rewards. The positive consequences that generate a useful behavioral repertoire need not be any more explicitly relevant to the future than were the punitive consequences of the past. The student needs current reasons, positive or negative, but only the educational policy maker who supplies them need take the future into account. It follows that many instructional arrangements seem "contrived," but there is nothing wrong with that. It is the teacher's function to contrive conditions under which students learn. Their relevance to a future usefulness need not be obvious.

It is a difficult assignment. The conditions the teacher arranges must be powerful enough to compete with those under which the student tends to behave in distracting ways. In what has come to be called "contingency management in the classroom" tokens are sometimes used as rewards or reinforcers. They become reinforcing when they are exchanged for reinforcers that are already effective. There is no "natural" relation between what is learned and what is received. The token is simply a reinforcer that can be made clearly contingent upon behavior. To straighten out a wholly disrupted classroom something as obvious as a token economy may be needed, but less conspicuous contingencies—as in a credit-point system, or possibly in the long run merely expressions of approval on the part of teacher or peer may take over.

The teacher can often make the change from punishment to positive reinforcement in a surprisingly simple way—by responding to the student's successes rather than his failures. Teachers have too often supposed that their role is to point out what students are doing wrong, but pointing to what they are doing *right* will often make an enormous difference in the atmosphere of a classroom and in the efficiency of instruction. Programmed materials are helpful in bringing about these changes, because they increase the frequency with which the student enjoys the satisfaction of being right, and they supply a valuable intrinsic reward in providing a clear indication of progress. A good program makes a step in the direction of competence almost as conspicuous as a token.

Programmed instruction is perhaps most successful in attacking punitive methods by allowing the student to move at his own pace. The slow student is released from the punishment which inevitably follows when he is forced to move on to material for which he is not ready, and the fast student escapes the boredom of being forced to go too slow. These principles have recently been extended to college education, with dramatic results, in the Keller system of personalized instruction.[2]

THE RESPONSIBILITY OF SETTING EDUCATIONAL POLICY

There is little doubt that a student can be given non-punitive reasons for acquiring behavior that will become useful or otherwise reinforcing at some later date. He can be prepared for the future. But what *is* that future? Who is to say what the student should learn? Those who have sponsored the free and happy student have argued that it is the student himself who should say. His current interests should be the source of an effective educational policy. Certainly they will reflect his idiosyncrasies, and that is good, but how much can he know about the world in which he will eventually play a part? The things he is "naturally" curious about are of current and often temporary interest. How many things must he possess besides his "hot rod" to provide the insatiable curiosity relevant to, say, a course in physics?

It must be admitted that the teacher is not always in a better position. Again and again education has gone out of date as teachers have continued to teach subjects which were no longer relevant at any time in the student's life. Teachers often teach simply what they know. (Much of what is taught in private schools is determined by what the available teachers can teach.) Teachers tend to teach what they can teach easily. Their current interests, like those of students, may not be a reliable guide.

Nevertheless, in recognizing the mistakes that have been made in the past in specifying what students are to learn, we do not absolve ourselves from the responsibility of setting educational policy. We should say, we should be *willing* to say, what we believe students will need to know, taking the individual student into account wherever possible, but otherwise making our best prediction with

[2] *P.S.I. Newsletter*, October, 1972 (published by Department of Psychology, Georgetown University, J. G. Sherman, ed.).

respect to students in general. Value judgments of this sort are not as hard to make as is often argued. Suppose we undertake to prepare the student to produce his share of the goods he will consume and the services he will use, to get on well with his fellows, and to enjoy his life. In doing so are we imposing *our* values on someone else? No, we are merely choosing a set of specifications which, so far as we can tell, will at some time in the future prove valuable to the student and his culture. Who is any more likely to be right?

The natural, logical outcome of the struggle for personal freedom in education is that the teacher should improve his control of the student rather than abandon it. The free school is no school at all. Its philosophy signalizes the abdication of the teacher. The teacher who understands his assignment and is familiar with the behavioral processes needed to fulfill it can have students who not only feel free and happy while they are being taught but who will continue to feel free and happy when their formal education comes to an end. They will do so because they will be successful in their work (having acquired useful productive repertoires), because they will get on well with their fellows (having learned to understand themselves and others), because they will enjoy what they do (having acquired the necessary knowledge and skills), and because they will from time to time make an occasional creative contribution toward an even more effective and enjoyable way of life. Possibly the most important consequence is that the teacher will then feel free and happy too.

We must choose today between Cassandran and Utopian prognostications. Are we to work to avoid disaster or to achieve a better world? Again, it is a question of punishment or reward. Must we act because we are frightened, or are there positive reasons for changing our cultural practices? The issue goes far beyond education, but it is one with respect to which education has much to offer. To escape from or avoid disaster, people are likely to turn to the punitive measures of a police state. To work for a better world, they may turn instead to the positive methods of education. When it finds its most effective methods, education will be almost uniquely relevant to the task of setting up and maintaining a better way of life.

Educational Critics Have Been Wrong All Along: Long Live Tradition!

S. SAMUEL SHERMIS
Purdue University

For the last 15 years or so a coterie of education critics have been almost unanimous in their charges. Schools are impersonal factories: large, cold, efficient, inhumane. Teachers and administrators are criminally callous in respecting the rights of students. The curriculum is irrelevant and boring. Children, especially minorities, have joy and spontaneity crushed out of them. Here are some illustrative quotations.

Talking about his initial experience in a classroom, Herbert Kohl says:

> I tried for the next six weeks to use the books assigned and teach the official curriculum. It was hopeless. The class went through the readers perfunctorily, refused to hear about modern America, and were relieved to do arithmetic—mechanical, uncharged—as long as nothing new was introduced. For most of the day the atmosphere in the room was stifling. The children were bored and restless, and I felt burdened by the inappropriateness of what I tried to teach. It was so dull that I thought as little as the children and began to despair.[1]

Not too many years ago, apparently in a fit of anger, I wrote:

> Granted, the temptation to accuse history teachers of *deliberately* boring hell out of their students, of *knowingly* brainwashing them, may seem well-nigh irresistible. But, it is best to assume that they do these things not out of malice prepense, but simply because they have accepted a batch of assumptions which turn out to be myths.[2]

If the official curriculum is irrelevant and teachers are dull, then what of the mainstay, the textbook? Jonathan Kozol talks about his experiences in the Boston schools:

> The attitudes of many teachers, I suppose, are derived over the course of years from the kinds of books they use. Many of the books we

From "Educational Critics Have Been Wrong All Along: Long Live Tradition!" *Phi Delta Kappan*, Vol. **LV**, No. 6 (February 1974), 403–406. © 1974 by Phi Delta Kappa, Inc. Reprinted with permission.

[1] Herbert Kohl, *36 Children* (New York: New American Library, 1967), p. 16.
[2] S. Samuel Shermis, "Six Myths Which Delude History Teachers," *Phi Delta Kappan*, September, 1967, pp. 9–12.

had at schools were very bad for many reasons, and none of them I
recall was very good.[3]

The texts, Kozol observes, "outstripped" the usual criticism
made of social studies books. They completely ignored prominent
black historical figures, were dated in their scholarship, were offen-
sively middle class in their bias, and ignored important moral issues;
the authors of one text could not even bring themselves to offer a
judgment on slavery, so dedicated were texts to blandness and moral
neutrality. A more tedious, irrelevant, distorted compendium of nonsense, Kozol clearly implies, could scarcely be devised by the mind
of man to degrade black children and blunt the appetite of all children for the study of history.

In a study of a process they called "ressentiment"—defined as
resentment, impotence, frustration, a desire for revenge—Nordstrom,
Friedenberg, and Gold thought that they had been able, at least partially, to identify characteristics which "seriously interfere" with a
"strong and forceful character." They said:

> In our preliminary judgment ressentiment operated to stifle enthusi-
> asm, to undermine fortitude, and to discourage the development of
> self-mastery; and to the degree that this is true we saw ressentiment as
> insidious when endured, difficult to fight, and stultifying in its conse-
> quences.[4]

These quotations—and there are thousands more like them—
suggest that those of use who tend to be critical of what we designate
traditional educational practices should conclude that schools in general and social studies in particular are dysfunctional. They do not,
we have been saying, cultivate the capacity to think critically; they
encourage acceptance of distortions, mythology, and bias; they
repress student expression; they strengthen dull conformity.

While it may seem absurd to challenge the validity of these criticisms, I submit the hypothesis that those practices normally labeled
irrelevant, dull, indoctrinative, unjust, mechanical, and depressing
are, in actuality, extremely useful. The irrelevant and dull are useful
and important because they serve to prepare students for life in a realistic and accurate manner.

If schools exist, as William James alleged many years ago, to
prepare students for life, then it can be argued that those schools
whose internal conditions are most like what students will find outside prepare students best.

Hence I here recant my intemperate words of six years ago and

---

[3] Jonathan Kozol, *Death at an Early Age* (Boston: Houghton Mifflin, 1967), p. 61.
[4] *Society's Children: A Study of Ressentiment in the Secondary School* (New York: Random House, 1967).

state that the task lies in persuading Kozol, Kohl, Friedenberg, et al. that there is a marvelous Catch-22 aspect of schools we have not hitherto perceived: The dull is useful, the irrelevant is entirely relevant, the trivial is important, the unjust is needed.

Ritualism—One of the most striking features of traditional studies is its ritualistic quality—and one can generalize further and talk about the ritualism that pervades entire schools. Neither students nor teachers seem deeply involved in what they are doing. There is little effort to seek significance. Teaching comes to resemble the religiously inert—mumbling, rising, kneeling, refraining, repeating—with no sense of meaning, merely a desire to comply. It matters little what the topic is or the age of the students—How a Bill Becomes a Law, Community Helpers, the New Deal, State History, the Judiciary—one can imagine himself 2,000 miles away or 50 years back in time, for it is all the same. Teachers repeat the same behavior, introducing the topic in the same way, pressing home the same concepts, testing in the same manner.

As frequently as the comments above are made, critics also point to the irrelevance of much of what goes on. A good deal of the content of social studies is held to be irrelevant—and, although "relevant" is rarely defined, it appears to mean that the curriculum is not related to the goals, concerns, or interests of students. The curriculum is handed to kids in so many discrete lumps. Students are asked to incorporate these lumps without asking the question, In what way does this relate to me? Why ought I to take a wholehearted interest in this?

I suggest that there is a relationship between irrelevance and ritualism. Ritualism is a substitute for relevance. Since it has been decided that the curriculum is fixed in advance, and since it is not possible to relate it to students' concerns, mechanical coverage of tradtional topics is predictable. Teachers' energies are devoted to organizational problems and not to instructional problems. The continuing question is not, What should students know and how ought I to teach it? The question is, How do I organize students for doing what they have been doing all along?

Both the ritualism and the irrelevance of the curriculum are functional. It would seem that what schools are saying is, *What* you learn is not significant. It is that you have *learned to endure* which really counts. The work is boring, but then it was never designed to be anything else but boring. To have survived hour after hour of boredom is in itself the goal. Children who have gone through 12 years or more of repetition, ritual, and irrelevance and who have learned to tolerate it respectfully and politely have fulfilled the school's objective. It would seem as if the capacity to endure is really good preparation for life out of school.

A recently published report, *Work In America,* describes research done on employee satisfaction. What seems to emerge from this report is that most workers—and the report describes both blue- and white-collar workers—are not content with their jobs. The report quotes Robert Kahn:

> For most workers it is a choice between no work connection (usually with severe attendant economic penalties and a conspicuous lack of meaningful alternative activities) and a work connection which is burdened with negative qualities (routine, compulsory scheduling, dependency, etc.).[5]

The individual, given such a choice, says Kahn, "has no difficulty." He works.

We work, then, because we have nothing better to do and because we need the money. However, the work that we do is, to use the restrained academic prose of Kahn, "burdened with negative qualities." Note these negative qualities: routine, compulsory scheduling, dependency. They are precisely the characteristic of schools in which the teaching process is reduced to ritual.

What better way of preparing children to work in circumstances where their hours are rigidly scheduled, where they are made dependent on someone higher in the "hierarchy of authority"? There is, then, no intrinsic meaning to work, if we believe the report. Work is a means to an end—a salary. School is, similarly, a means to an end—diploma or degree testifying that one had endured and is therefore certified capable of enduring further. If enduring is the objective, relevance is not relevant. Ritual is.

Critical Thinking—Much has been written about the need for critical thinking in schools. The arguments supporting the need to teach an intelligent and discriminating approach to issues was made first in the early 1900s by a series of commissions. It was summarized by John Dewey in 1910 in his famous *How We Think.*[6] It was popularized by Dewey's disciple, Boyd Bode, in the 1920s and 1930s and since that time by an uncountable number of philosophers, psychologists, and curriculum makers. Indeed, it is almost axiomatic by now: A self-governing society requires a high caliber of decision makers, for only an intelligent and discriminating populace can make the kinds of decisions that are needed.

For the sake of developing my argument, let us assume the opposite. Our society is so organized that the last thing it needs is an intelligent and discriminating citizen. There is too much invested in

[5]*Work In America,* report of a Special Task Force to the Secretary of Health, Education, and Welfare (Cambridge: The MIT Press, no date).
[6] Described at length by Robert Barr in his doctoral dissertation, "The Changing Role of History in the American Public Schools," Purdue University, 1969.

a docile, confused, and impressionable populace ever to seriously educate it toward intelligence and discrimination. Begin with economics.

If John Kenneth Galbraith's thesis—described originally in *The Affluent Society* and elaborated in his latest book, *Economics and the Public Purpose*—is correct, the ability of manufacturers has far outstripped the capacity of the people to consume or even effectively to dominate production, as traditional economic theory has it. Galbraith sees a kind of "planning system" which, in effect, generates wants and demands—as contrasted with the traditional belief that the market simply responds to the public's effective demands. Manipulation of the public's wants has yielded a powerful advertising industry; almost unlimited expansion of credit and something called planned obsolescence. In effect, the public is manipulated to consume by business and industry.

If there were indeed an intelligent and critical buying public, the manipulative aims of manufacturers would be identified, with the likely consequence that people would not be seduced into buying and would be able to resist the invitation to expand their credit beyond what they can afford. In short, if Galbraith is correct, our economy rests upon a consuming populace whose wants and needs are deliberately created and molded by the interests of manufacturers. The last thing, therefore, that is needed is a populace capable of deciding autonomously what it really wants and what it can afford to pay for satisfying its wants.

In the area of politics, a questioning and discriminating populace is equally undesirable. Individuals who have blamed the nation's race problems on either "northern agitators" or "black militants" would realize that this is a silly evasion that has nothing to do with the broad problem of inequality in a democracy allegedly committed to equal opportunity. A skeptical citizenry would not have been bamboozled into committing 30 billion dollars a year in Southeast Asia on the dubious premise that our national security depended upon intervention in an ancient and complex Vietnamese conflict. It would not be to the benefit of President Nixon, whose television performance in 1973 was clearly based upon the proposition that the nation could be deceived by a tissue of evasion and duplicity presented in a sincere manner, to be confronted by an alert and discriminating population. In short, except for a couple of generations of social studies textbook writers and a few other theoreticians, we do not, as a culture, need to have young people trained to be alert and skeptical inquirers.

And for this reason, social studies classes ignore serious contemporary problems and, when they do touch on an issue, dish it up in a gutless *My Weekly Reader* format which carefully avoids the point. Given the necessity of manipulating society, there is little need for what Postman and Weingartner called "built-in crap detectors."

Procedure—That much of any school day is taken up with various kinds of meaningless procedure is a fairly evident fact of life. Philip Cusick documents this quite effectively, asserting that it is easy to

> . . . make the point that a large part of the student's day may be spent in spectatorship in which he simply watches and waits. Consider just the first 35 or 40 minutes of the morning . . . , add the 35 for the total day devoted to passing in the halls, the additional 40 minutes devoted to lunch, the time spent in getting ready in each of the classes, a conservative estimate of which could be at least five minutes; add five minutes more for the time taken out of class for more passing of papers, books, worksheets, or directions. Add at least half of the study hall period in which something other than academic activity is taking place, and judging from the observed study halls, that too is a conservative estimate. Add an additional period when a student is engaged in something other than academic activity, that is, time spent with administrators, counselors, nurses' activities, looking for someone, or going somewhere. The total is 200 minutes a day, or over three hours of the total time spent in school in which any single student can be expected to either spend his own time on procedural and maintenance details or wait while others tie up the class on their own.[7]

Why the extraordinary emphasis on procedure and administrative detail? The obvious response is, What else would you expect from a bureaucracy in which there are rules and regulations to which all must adhere? However, considering the obvious notion that schools are supposed to educate and not take up the time of students with nonacademic procedure, it is conceivable that the real purpose is not to educate but to acclimate students to enduring procedure. And if this is a tenable explanation, what is the ultimate payoff in making students endure 200 minutes a day of procedure?

Learning to cope with bureaucratic and administrative details is excellent training for a vocation which, if one has the normal experience, will require him to put up with a vast number of requirements, forms to fill out, waiting, directions to follow, etc. It is important for students to finish 12 years of education without either becoming depressed and whipped by bureaucracies or, on the other extreme, defiant and rebellious. Hence schools are perfecting plans made originally in the nineteenth century, plans that cast schools in the mold of a factory or business.

According to Raymond E. Callahan in *Education and the Cult*

[7] *Inside High School: The Student's World* (New York: Holt, Rinehart and Winston, 1973), pp. 48, 49.

of Efficiency, and a more recent work by Stanley Schultz, *The Culture Factory,* as our society became more industrialized, more pervaded by business values, more influenced by technology, it seemed reasonable for schools to see themselves as existing to prepare students to assume their rightful place in such a society. Schultz describes the thinking of Boston's first superintendent of schools:

> Bishop knew that effective administration depended upon effective organization. Just as reformers and other educators had argued for the reorganization of schools on a factory model, so did Bishop. A school system could, and should, be rationalized along the lines of business experience. Bishop was certain that in organizing a system of popular education, the same practical judgment is to be exercised in making special adaptations of means to ends as in any manufacturing or other business enterprise.[8]

In this discussion of the early origins of Boston's educational bureaucracy, the author argues that, faced with the need to educate large numbers of children whose parents could not afford private schooling, Boston community leaders rather naturally drifted into an industrialized model for schools. They copied the concerns of business and industry for low cost per unit of production, interchangeable roles and parts, cost accounting, quality control, and uniformity. Schools were deliberately built so as to realize these goals. The boxcar rooms, grades, uniform curricula, textbooks, state licensing procedures, and centralized administration—later in the twentieth-century uniform, nationwide testing—all reflected the business and industrial model.

The question arises, Of what value is it to make kids endure endless, repetitive procedure? The answer is, Because only by learning to endure endless, repetitive procedure can students fit into an industrialized, bureaucratized society in which endless, repetitive procedure is required for all. That schools developed along business and industrial lines, as Schultz and Callahan make persuasively clear, was scarcely accidental or unplanned. It reflected the wisdom of our nineteenth-century ancestors who understood that if students were to survive in our rapidly industrializing society, then schools should prepare them for such a society. Schools not only modeled themselves along the lines of business and industry because to do so was more efficient, schools created themselves as a miniature of the larger society. The critics who dwell on spontaneity, joy, absorbing activity, and the natural curiosity of children do not understand why these are irrelevant to the organization of public schools. If they did

---

[8] From Schultz, *The Culture Factory, Boston Public Schools 1789–1860* (New York: Oxford University Press, 1973). This quotation is taken from a chapter titled "A Want of Symmetry: The Beginnings of Bureaucracy," pp. 132–53.

realize this, they would recognize the inadvisability of joy, individuality, and curiosity in a system designed for quite another reality.

Injustice—The prevalence of various forms of injustice traditionally practiced against students has, by now, been well documented. Thomas Buxton and Keith Prichard document many such examples of injustice, describing the extent and character of such practices as flagrant teacher suppression of student expression, teacher refusal to allow restroom use, administration veto of student proposals, dress codes, capricious punishment. They introduce their discussion of injustices with the by-now common-sense observation:

> Thus the issue of due process, the concept that school children must be granted the same legal and constitutional guarantees that are accorded adult citizens, may be the most perplexing problem confronting our schools.[9]

Despite the clear mandate of the Supreme Court that "suppression of underground newspapers critical of a school's management can be justified only when motional and substantial disruption of normal school activities occurs," [10] the practice of forbidding underground newspapers and harassing the editors and writers is fairly widespread. John Birmingham has documented this with a series of editorials, letters, anecdotes, and vignettes in a book he wrote during his senior year of high school. His book is a dreary compilation of reports on the violations of what is called "human rights" or "constitutionally protected rights" that so many of us like to talk about.[11]

The sheer number of such violations may compel us to wonder why, in view of the very consistent Supreme Court decisions, have administrators and teachers shown themselves so callous concerning student rights? Unfortunately, phrasing the question this way ignores the extraordinary difference between the philosophical frame of reference of school people and that of civil libertarians.

Given the underlying goal of transmitting to students a set of values, attitudes, and beliefs concerned with respect for adult authority, conformity, obedience, and docility, school people do not perceive certain behavior as simply constitutionally protected freedom of expression. Such behavior is seen as extremely threatening to the institution and ultimately to the stability and viability of society. To criticize principals, superintendents, boards, and teachers means—in an authoritarian framework—that young people, who have no right to do so, are calling into question the very rules and procedures which keep our society from sliding into chaos and anarchy.

[9] Thomas H. Buxton and Keith W. Prichard, Student Perceptions of Teacher Violations of Human Rights," *Phi Delta Kappan*, September, 1973, pp. 66–69.
[10] Ibid., p. 66.
[11] John Birmingham, *Our Time Is Now: Notes from the High School Underground* (New York: Praeger, 1970).

It follows, then—that is, it follows given this assumption—that those who flout authority, dress bizarrely, use provocatively foul language, and express contempt for accepted social wisdom deserve no better than to be repressed. That such repression is condemned by a few as capricious, whimsical, extreme, or cruel is not really important. If the Supreme Court ever understood what the presence of critical nonconformists does to a school and to the community, they would immediately alter their permissive and libertarian policies.

The point is that what libertarians perceive as repressive violations of democratic, constitutionally protected rights is simply and clearly the adult authority's attempt to perpetuate the vitally important patterns which the larger community in fact wishes to maintain. Even though Kohl, Kozol, Silberman, et al. perceive the problem as repression, and even though they are critical of schools for not teaching the skills of critical thinking and inquiry, this is simply not the way adults look at the problem. Ironically, in the same issue of the *Kappan* in which the just-cited article on repression of student rights appeared, a Gallup poll reveals that the number one problem mentioned by the public is "lack of discipline." [12] A plausible inference is that parents are more concerned that schools make kids mind than they are that schools help kids to think critically about problems.

The critics to whom many of us have listened intently seem to have missed the underlying reality. In their emphasis on the dull, fixed, ritualistic, conformist behaviors that prevail in schools, the critics cited above have not seen that these would never have persisted unless they had tangible, vital connection with the dominant culture. Those who have focused on joy, spontaneity, inquiry, meaning, and relevance have simply not perceived the point that if schools are to prepare children realistically for life, then life in school should be consonant with what exists in the culture.

Criticism leveled against schools and the education establishment, therefore, is misdirected. It is not to schools, curriculum, teachers, and administrators, etc., that critics should aim their barbs. It is rather to the dominant culture. If the curriculum is irrelevant and ritualistic, if there is disproportionate emphasis on procedure, then it is not to schools but to the reality of work that critics should look. If traditional education subverts students' constitutional rights in the interest of inculcating conformist behavior and instilling respect for duly constituted authorities, then critics should ask another kind of question, viz., Is not the definition of a good citizen one who conforms to expectations, who obeys all laws, who participates in a prescribed way? Has not the nonconformist been defined not as one

---

[12] George H. Gallup, "Fifth Annual Gallup Poll of Public Attitudes Toward Education," *Phi Delta Kappan*, September, 1973, pp. 38–51.

who marches to a different drummer but as a subversive? If these are
the accepted definitions, why lash schools for punishing kids who
wear armbands, publish underground newspapers, question their elders, and insist upon asserting their opinions in class? Schools are
doing only what they ought to do. Of course, if one concludes that
subverting democratic procedures is too high a price to pay for ex-
tracting conformity, respect, etc., then one had better engage in a
kind of cost-benefit analysis and thereby determine which societal
values are more important.

In sum, what goes on in schools is neither accidental nor was it
forced upon them by a willful minority of educators, as the critics of
20 years ago thought. Schools for the most part accurately reflect the
cultural values and patterns found in the larger society. That schools
have been so resistant to reforms urged since 1900 ought to have suggested that, by and large, Americans feel that their schools are functional and that in some valid sense they prepare young people for
work, for higher education, and for assuming their proper roles in society. Those of us who have been arguing that schools were remiss in
their essential purpose have apparently misperceived the purpose. If
the purpose of schools is construed as preparation for life, then
schools have functioned quite well indeed. If we are unhappy with
what schools have been doing to children, then our scrutiny ought to
be directed toward the larger society which directs and controls what
happens in schools.

The Open Schoolroom:
New Words for Old Deceptions

JONATHAN KOZOL

In the past few years there has been a massive media campaign
to popularize the idea of a painless revolution in the U.S. public
schools via something known as "open-structured education." The
enthusiastic reception which this notion has received in liberal circles, above all in the upper-class schools which wish to have an innovative and attractive image, suggests the desperation that is felt by

From "The Open Schoolroom: New Words for Old Deceptions," *Ramparts*, Vol. **II**,
No. 1 July 1972), 38–41. © 1972 by Jonathan Kozol. This article also appears in Kozol,
The Night Is Dark and I Am Far From Home (Boston: Houghton Mifflin Company).
Reprinted by permission of Noah's Ark, Inc. (*Ramparts*), the author, and Houghton
Mifflin Company.

those who recognize incipient stirrings of an insurrectionary nature in the consciousness of children and young teachers. It is not possible to leave such stirrings undomesticated. Ethical strivings in the consciousness of youth constitute a solemn danger to an unjust nation. The public school, as the custodian of youth, can not allow this kind of ferment to go unrecognized and unconstrained.

All governments and administrative hierarchies will, if they are skillful and astute, find a means to undermine any danger they find themselves in. In other societies, less skilled and practiced than our own, the only methods known are often those of frank repression. In this society, two decades of experience in counter-revolutionary tactics have educated the kinds of men who handle power in the best of ways for neutralizing and de-fusing controversy. Napalm and high-flying aircraft may in certain cases be acceptable for use in foreign nations, but not in our own. Such methods run directly counter to the pretense of unmanaged intellection and of unmanacled expression of ideas that our society is built upon. It is only in emergencies, then, or in the context of those sections of the population where our instincts of abhorrence are abated somewhat by the sense of biological discrimination, that methods of this kind will be employed.

In most cases, what we do in public schools in the United States today is not to suppress but to buy out the revolutionary instincts of our children. We offer them "independent research," "individualized learning," "open-structured education," "non-directive class-discussions." Each child, in the standard code-word of the fashion, learns "at his own pace." Teachers are present not as educators but as "resource-people." The children "do their own thing." Everybody "tells it like it is" and tells other people "where it's at. . . ." It is all fashionable, fun and "innovative" . . . It is intelligently marketed and publicized. It is remarkably well-packaged.

It would, of course, be careless and inaccurate on my part to indicate that all of these innovations constitute overt or even indirect deception. It would also be inaccurate to suggest that they do not make *some* things different, and some situations less manipulative and less painfully oppressive than they were before. There is unquestionably a lower level of direct indoctrination and direct manipulation of a child's thinking now than in the old-time classroom. A number of things are much more fun, and there is far less of the sense of lockstep-motion and of inevitable non-stop perseverance than before. These are real differences and to a small degree they represent a lessening of the sense of desperation and of straight-line perseverance which enslave and paralyze so many children in the course of twelve years of sequential labor in the more traditional classrooms of the old-time schools.

It is my belief, however, that these changes do not seriously undermine the overriding purposes and operations of a public school, but have at best the function of adorning servitude with momentary flashes of delight and secondary avenues of unimportant deviation. At no point do these kinds of changes touch upon the basic anesthetic character of public school, its anti-ethical function, its chauvinistic fealties, its inculcation of the sense of vested interest in credentialized reward, its clever perpetration of a sense of heightened options in a closed and tightly circumscribed arena. At no point is there honest confrontation with the mandate of a man's · or of a woman's, sense of justice. At no point is there actual, concrete, vivid provocation of that sense of justice. This sentence is the one, for me, which sums up all the rest: children are not free in any way that matters if they are not free to know the price in pain and exploitation that their lives are built upon. Stated differently, just children cannot be educated in an unjust school. A school which constitutes an island of self-etherized and of self-serving privilege within a land of pain is not a just school, whatever the games the school board authorizes, whatever the innovative slogans it may ply.

A KIND OF DMZ

The notion of the "open-structured" school most often involves four or five associated notions, all of them wholly or in part erroneous: (1) that a proper and effective answer to the injustice and to the devastation of the time in which we live is constituted by an individual and self-directed search for Love and Satisfaction; (2) that the child who "freely" chooses one out of the fifty things selected in advance by teacher, School Board, EDC or IBM should be persuaded to believe that he is really "doing his own thing," that he is "exercising freedom"; (3) that we can, or ever do, "spontaneously" go from BEING GOOD AND LOVING to our (nearby) friends to BEING GOOD AND LOVING to our (distant) victims, especially if we have no means of finding out they *are* our victims or have no words or concepts to articulate this kind of truth; (4) that in face of pain, in face of hunger, in face of misery on every side, each man has the right to tend to his own needs, and to advance his own enlightenment, reward, self-interest, postponing into an indeterminate and into an unknown future the time at which he worries about those whom he does not see; (5) that a major change in the relationships between rich men and poor can ever come about without a solemn confrontation of some form. Stated differently, it is the notion that is now so much a part of North American mythology concerning progress: the fantasy that we can ever get real goods without authentic payment, that anything that matters ever comes scot-free.

It is upon this basis, I believe, that the whole notion of the open-structured class must finally depend. To the teacher, most of all, it carries the consoling message that there is no solemn need to stand up and take sides: "We do not sustain; we do not subvert; we just stroll pleasantly through the class with an inductive glow and, now and then, we stop and smile. . . ." If there is a single phrase to summarize this notion, it is one like this: No one (even a committed man or woman) needs to take sides. No one needs to put his or her body on the line. The classroom does not need to be a counterfoil; it is sufficient if it constitutes a kind of island or a kind of DMZ.

The virtue of the "open-structured" classroom and of the so-called "non-directive" teacher, from the point of view of the society at large, is clear and quite straightforward. If it does not constitute overt cooperation with the ideological wishes of the state, at least it stops one step this side of open and direct rebellion. Battles can be fought on all sides of a DMZ: there is no danger here of rear-guard actions.

From the point of view of social change, or educational upheaval, open-structured education is less easily defended. For this statement I would like to offer two related arguments: one in relation to the teacher's role as a neutral or non-neutral force; the other in regard to the surrounding context.

First, in regard to the surrounding context, the point, I think, needs to be made that "neutral education" or a "neutral classroom"—or a classroom "open," as it were, to winds of truth and falsehood in the world outside—has little meaning in a managed framework of controlled ideas and preference-manufacture such as that which the industrial success of the United States now totally depends upon. There is a great deal more at stake within the school, and in the context of that school, than words and deeds of individual teachers. The physical structure, previous history, sequential character and complex interlock of school itself convey a body of explicit or implied directions, mandates, and requests. The "medium," as it were, of "school and schoolyear" carries with it an overriding and important message, regardless of what may be conveyed by words and textbooks. The message is largely one of dull, benevolent and untumultuous assurance. It is the message of a world which has been built, not like TV and other public media, on active lies, but on discreet negations. Strong colors, deep emotions, soaring passions are left out, and, in the leaving out, a fraudulent image of the world is perpetrated.

The overall picture is a little like the message flamboyant preachers used to call "The Good News." The good news of school, in essence, is the news that life is nice, that people are okay, that poverty is unreal or, if real then fortunately unrealizable in the young imagination. Whatever the individual teacher does or does not say, all of the rest of this will still be present in the air around us, in the other classrooms, in the previous and succeeding years of school, as well as in the simple, physical persuasion of the architecture and of the flag outside the building. There is also, of course, the body of manipulated views and managed wants and manufactured aspirations that come with every child into this school-building from the outside world. These biases and aspirations, views and yearnings, for the greater part, come from TV and radio, daily press and picture magazines, as well as from one another, older friends, and older brother, sister, father, mother: in short, from all of those people who have been already muted and contained, modulated, styled, quieted, by their own prior course of mandatory public school indoctrination.

It seems to me that "neutral" education, in a time like this and in a land like ours, is less than honest, and less than "neutral" too, if we already recognize too well the presence of a uniform body of controlled and managed stimuli and viewpoints. The notion of the "neutral classroom" and of the "non-directive" teacher depends upon the prior existence of a neutral field, or at least a neutral pocket of unmanipulated and unmanaged intellection. To believe in this (and it is a gentle and appealing notion) is to believe in children who have lived their lives within a sweet and unplowed meadow. But we know very well our children do not live in a sweet meadow: they live in a mine-field crossed by electronic beams and planted with high-voltage speakers. To play the game of "non-directive educator" in this context is perhaps to fill a more attractive and less openly manipulative role than that of conscious salesman or saleswoman for a weary catalogue of patriotic notions. It is, moreover, a less demeaning role in that at least it frees the teacher from the obligation to say things which he or she, in fact, does not believe. Only in this sense does it represent a less debilitating posture, in that it represents a lower level of direct deception. It is deception, nonetheless.

The myth, the wishful thinking or the amiable deception, that lies beneath the notion of the open-structured classroom is the imagined "authenticity," the "spontaneity," and the "autonomy" of the child's intellectual initiatives. "Elicit the wishes, questions and directions from the child, unimpeded and unhindered and without much adult interference." But what is the meaning of a statement of this kind if we know very well that we, and all our children with us, are living in a closed kingdom of confined and narrow options, guided stimuli and calculated access to alternative ideas? A child does not spontaneously "ask" to learn of things that he has not first been allowed to hear of, nor does he innocently ask to learn what he has been already trained to view as inappropriate or awkward or unpopular or dangerous, or morally contaminated.

For the teacher to acquiesce in recognitions of this kind, to silence her own convictions, sit down on the floor, smile her inductive smile and await the appearance of "spontaneous desires" on the part of children, may look to us, or to a uninformed observer, to be open and unbiased, "innovative," "honest," and relaxed. It may be innovative, but it is not open. There is a deep and powerful area of self-deception working here: one that attempts to tell us that the child's offerings are *really free*. The vested interest that we hold in this belief is in direct accord with the more powerful vested interest of our faith in our own freedom. The insistence of these notions in the face of all that we have read and comprehended and believed is index of the threat we feel when faced with the reality of our oppressed condition. It is similar to the way a patient feels in psychotherapy at times of imminent, but endangering insight.

It may well be that there was once a time, ages ago, in some other land or even in our own, when thoughts were free and wants were largely self-created. Today, whatever we wish to say, we know it is not so. The wants of the young, like those of their elders, are relentlessly controlled. "It is the essence of planning," Galbraith has said, "that public behavior should be made predictable. . . . The management to which we are subject is not onerous. It works not on the body but on the mind. It first wins acquiescence or belief: action is in response to this . . . conditioning and thus devoid of any sense of compulsion. It is open to anyone who can to contract out of this control. But we are no less managed because we are not physically compelled."

The foregoing deals with what I call the "field," or context of ideas, in which the classroom stands. There is also, however, an additional question about the teacher's role and function. In the long run there is, and can be, no such thing as an unbiased education or a neutral teacher. No teacher, no matter what he does or does not do, can fail in certain ways to advertise his bias to the children in his care—even if it is only by the very vivid lesson of avoiding a field fraught with ethical significance and with the possibilities for moral indignation. What the teacher "teaches," after all, is not only in what he says but at least in part in what he is, in what he does, in what he seems to wish to be. In the classroom, the things a teacher does not wish to say may well provide a deeper and more dangerous and more abiding lesson than the content of the textbooks or the conscious message of the posters on the wall. The teacher who does not speak to grief, who cannot cry for shame, who does not laugh and will not weep, teaches many very deep and memorable lessons about tears, laughter, grief *and* shame. When war is raging, and when millions of black people in our land are going through a private and communal Hell, no teacher, no matter what he does or does not do, can fail to influence his pupils in some fashion. The secret curriculum is the teacher's own lived values and convictions in the lineaments of his expression and in the biography of passion or self-exile that is written in his eyes. A teacher who appears to his children to be anesthetized, sedated, in the face of human pain, of medical racism, black infant-birth, or something so horrible and so quintessentially evil as the massacre at My Lai, may not teach children anything at all about medical racism, birth mortality or My Lai, but he will be teaching a great deal about the capability of an acceptable and respectably situated North American adult to abdicate the consequences of his own perception and, as it were, to vacate his own soul. By denying his convictions in the course of class-discussion, he does not teach *nothing:* he teaches *something.* He teaches, at the very least, a precedent for non-conviction. For these reasons, then, apart from all the others, it seems apparent that a teacher cannot, no matter what he does or does not do, maintain a neutral posture in the eyes of children. It is just not possible for us to disaffiliate entirely from the blood and the stench of the times in which we live.

NEW WINE, OLD BOTTLES

"The social worker," Freire has written, "has a moment of decision. Either he picks the side of change . . . or he is left in the position of favoring stagnation." The open-structured classroom is a means by which the teacher is enabled to imagine that he does not need to choose. In truth, he chooses (for non-direction, non-participation, fashionable non-intervention) but he does not wish to tell himself that he has made this choice. Most teachers who have been in situations of this kind are well aware of the co-optive nature of the process in which they have come to be involved. Most of these teachers, for example, understand and can predict extremely well the kinds of things their pupils will select when they are "freely choosing" areas of study. They know very well the kinds of things they will "conclude" when they are working on their "independent research." They write down in advance, on Sunday afternoon, in lesson-books, the things their children will "discover" Wednesday morning in "small group discussion." The open-structured classroom may be "child-centered," but it is also "teacher-written," "IBM-predicted," "School Board-overseen." Nobody ever really discovers anything within the confines of a well-run public school in the United States which someone somewhere does not give him license, sanction and permission to discover. It is just a better form of salesmanship than we have ever used before. In olden days we had to *tell* the children what to think, handing them, as it were, the bottle and the spoon. Today, we lead them, by a pretense of free inquiry, to ask for it themselves. It is the same old bottle.

Teachers in open-structured situations speak of matters of this kind with one another frequently: they do not say the same things to the children. There is a way, for instance, known to many teachers in the open-structured situation, of opening up a controversial issue with the children in the classroom, in a manner that seems un-managed, conscientious, honest, open-minded, and leaves us later on with a sense of having "faced the issue but only, as it were, to tell ourselves we had. This is the way in which most dangerous ideas are now de-fused in innovative classrooms. Teachers pretend to open up an issue when what they really do is close it more emphatically than it has ever been closed before. The teacher who encourages this sense of artificial confrontation with a painful issue is denying more to the pupil than a teacher who avoids the issue altogether; for the latter, whether he knows it or not, has left at least the possibility that the pupil, in rebellion, will search out the forbidden area at a later time and find something in it to enrich or challenge him. But the pupil who has had the false sense of meeting the issue in a classroom that was stacked against it has seen the issue sterilized forever.

All of the points that I have been trying to make come down at last to one important, over-riding and intensely unattractive bit of truth: In an unjust nation, the children of the ruling-classes are not free in any way that matters if they are not free to know the price of pain and exploitation that their lives are built upon. This is a free-dom that no public school in the United States can willingly give children. Businessmen are not in business to lose customers; public schools do not exist to free their clients from the agencies of mass-persuasion. "Innovative schools" with "open-structured" classrooms speak often about "relevant learning-processes" and "urban-oriented studies," but the first free action of such a class of honest children in an unmanipulated, genuinely open classroom in a segregated school within an all-white suburb, would be to walk out of class, blockade the doors and shut down the school building. School serves the state; the interest of the state is identified for reasons of survival, with the interests of industrial dominion. The school exists to turn out man-ageable workers, obedient consumers, manipulable voters and, if need be, willing killers. It does not require the attribution of sinister motives, but only of the bare survival instincts, to know that a mono-lithic complex of industrial, political and academic interests of this kind does not intend to build the kinds of schools which will em-power pint-sized zealots to expropriate their interests. It is in the light of considerations such as these that all innovations, all liberal reforms, all so-called "modern" methods and all new technologies ought to be scrutinized: Do they exist to free consumers, to liberate citizens, to inspire disagreement, inquiry, dissent? Or do they exist instead to quiet controversy, to contain rebellion and to channel inquiry into accepted avenues of discreet moderation? Is it conceivable that public schools can serve at once the function of indoctrinating agent and the function of invigorating counterfoil? I find this quite improbable and view with reservations of the deepest kind such genteel changes as may appear to offer broader liberties to captive children.

The only forms of educational innovation that are serious and worth consideration in this nation in the year of 1972 are those which constitute direct rebellion, explicit confrontation or totally independent ventures, such as networks, storefronts, Free Schools and the like, which stand entirely outside of the public system and which at all times labor to perform the function of provocateur and counterfoil. The *New York Times* can tell us what it likes of "open-structured education." The Carnegie Foundation can pay its parasitic program officers what it wishes to propagate the notion of "alternatives within the system." There are no such alternatives so long as the system is itself the primary vehicle of state control.

It is time to raise the stakes and open up our minds. It is time to look with deepened insight and scepticism on the innovative cliché and the high-priced pacification of the open-structured school: *There is a price to be paid, and a struggle of inordinate dimensions to be undertaken.* There is no way in which a serious man or honorable woman can escape the implications and the dangers of this statement.

IV

THE NEW VOCATIONALISM: CAREER EDUCATION

The kind of vocational education in which I am interested is not one which will "adapt" workers to the existing industrial regime; I am not sufficiently in love with the regime for that. It seems to me that the business of all who would not be educational timeservers is to resist every move in this direction, and to strive for a kind of vocational education which will first alter the existing industrial system, and ultimately transform it.
John Dewey

It is flatly necessary to begin to construct a sound, systematic relationship between education and work, a system which will make it standard practice to teach every student about occupations and the economic enterprise, a system that will markedly increase career options open to each individual and enable us to do a better job than we have been doing of meeting the manpower needs of the country.
Sidney P. Marland, Jr.

NEW DEMANDS FOR VOCATIONAL EDUCATION

Critics of education, it has been said, can be divided into four categories: (1) those who complain that schools neglect the individual, (2) those who allege that schools are not maintaining sufficiently high academic standards, (3) those who criticize educational institutions for not using the most effective forms of organization and techniques of instruction, and (4) those who allege schools do not place enough emphasis upon the most important subjects, skills, or types of learning.[1] With due allowance for overlapping, it can be said humanist advocates of individualized instruction, open classrooms, or alternative schools most nearly belong to the first group. Educational conserva-

[1] Cf. the analysis in H. J. McNally and A. H. P. Passow, *Improving the Quality of Public School Programs* (New York: Teachers College Press, Columbia, 1960).

245

tives who demand more rigorous, disciplined instruction can be assigned to the second category. Those who fall in the third group would include technologists, behaviorists, and the new breed of managerial technocrats. In the fourth group might be counted those critics who today argue that, in the allocation of educational resources, insufficient attention has been given to the hard social reality that sooner or later practically everyone must seek gainful employment. Consequently, so the argument goes, preparation for the world of work—equipping people with saleable skills needed in the market economy—ought to be of paramount concern among educators. Proponents of the new vocational movement in education, however, go well beyond traditional arguments in favor of more vocational training. They now vigorously claim that work and preparation for work should become a *primary* emphasis of school curricula at all levels of the school structure. "Occupational awareness, orientation, exploration, and preparation for careers," it is argued, "have to become *central rather than peripheral in the curriculum.* Regardless of school-leaving age, individuals should possess saleable skills and have the opportunity to return without stigma or penalty to the educational enterprise for instruction which will advance them on career ladders." [2]

The basic outline of vocationalist ideology is as follows: The institution of schooling is in serious trouble. Its root assumption, that formal intervention during the formative years of childhood and adolescence is essential for teaching youngsters how to become adults and to assume their roles in society, is itself under assault. Disaffection among the young is well-nigh universal. Boredom, resentment, and occasionally outright rebellion characterize the attitude of many, perhaps most, youngsters confined to the nation's classrooms. Criticism of the school has never before been so harsh or so ubiquitous. Reform proposals, ranging from new regimens of traditional subjects to massive transfusions of expensive technology, are bound to fail because they depend upon conventional assumptions about the school's basic purposes. [3] For much the same reasons, neither do such innovations as team teaching, modular scheduling, differentiated staffing, open classrooms, sensitivity training, or independent study, promise significant relief. They do not alter the basic philosophical framework of education. [4] At best they are short-range expedients designed to shore up a decaying system on the verge of collapse.

[2] Larry J. Bailey and Ronald W. Stadt, *Career Education: New Approaches to Human Development* (Bloomington, Ill.: McKnight Publishing Company, 1973), pp. 3–4, 51.
[3] Ibid., pp. 1–2 ff.
[4] Jack Hruska, "Vocational Education—All the Way Or Not at All," in Dwight W. Allen and Jeffrey C. Hecht (eds.), *Controversies in Education* (Philadelphia: W. B. Saunders Company, 1974), p. 48.

Equally misguided, according to vocationalists, are those allegedly radical critics who prescribe alternate forms of experience or new delivery systems for learning. They too are obsessed with finding ways of doing the same old job better. Despite the best efforts by educators to respond to the avalanche of criticism that threatens to inundate them, schools remain basically the same. Children stay dissatisfied and unhappy; and public education is in jeopardy.

From the vocationalist viewpoint, important danger signals in society that point to a fundamental weakness in the educational system include growing unemployment, a dramatic increase in the number of people on welfare, and a swelling segment of the population that lacks useful skills. The rate of unemployment among younger persons especially is staggering, the reason being they cannot sell anything the labor market wants to buy. At the root of the school's failure has been its long-standing neglect of vocational training. The system does not meet the occupational needs of the overwhelming majority of students in school, and thus helps create the dropouts, the juvenile delinquents, the unemployables, and the welfare recipients. The typical curriculum is deficient because it offers individuals little help in planning careers, making decisions, or preparing for eventual employment.[5] The college preparation program found in most high schools only prepares students for more schooling—or for unemployment. As for the so-called "general" education track, it is a strictly dead-end proposal, leading neither to school or to a job. Because the school system is captive to elitist intellectual academics, it has grown snobbish, impractical, and undemocratic. It feeds upon itself in demands that people stay in school longer. Meanwhile, educators fail to respond in any practical way to social problems created through their neglect of job-related instruction, refusing to assume their rightful responsibility for the vocational needs of the nation's youth.

The solution to the problem of widespread social malaise according to James A. Rhodes, twice governor of Ohio and author of a widely-read tract entitled *Alternative to A Decadent Society*, rests in jobs, employment, and the security which these provide.[6] "The problem of the poor, the disadvantaged, and the ghetto," Rhodes asserted confidently, "can be solved in a large measure by providing vocational education for jobs." [7] In fact, Rhodes contended, the single greatest challenge confronting education today is the successful implementation of a universal policy providing occupational education for everyone, to the end that no student drops out of school who is not prepared to enter the world of work, that no student graduates

---

[5] Bailey and Stadt, op. cit., p. 57.
[6] James A. Rhodes, *Alternative To A Decadent Society* (Indianapolis: Howard W. Sams and Company, 1969), p. 10.
[7] Ibid., pp. 10–11.

who does not possess marketable skills or talents, and no adult denied an educational opportunity to become properly employable.[8] Today's students grow restless, bored, and apathetic because they quite properly cannot see any relevance to their lessons. Those who last beyond high school are forced in college to "wade through" two years of general academic theory before being allowed to pursue a more specialized course of instruction leading to employment. In a properly ordered system, students would be encouraged, even compelled, to begin acquiring saleable skills at a relatively early point in their education. "Youth must be prepared to carry forward the technological and political society in which we live," Rhodes argued; "The forward movement of our society is not as dependent on our enjoyment of the arts as it is on the investment of ourselves in that society through our work." [9]

HISTORICAL ANTECEDENTS AND DEVELOPMENTS

Rhodes' argument for more vocational education is typical in its insistence that educational quality is correlated with utility, with the degree to which schooling directly prepares people for life in shops, offices, and factories. While some look for the ends of education in conventional academic terms, or in terms of psychological adjustment and self-fulfillment, a number of highly vocal critics like Rhodes believe the goals and purposes of education ought to be related closely to job preparation, and to the meeting of industrial manpower needs.

In order to better understand the current phase of this perennial controversy, it is helpful to recall that few of the contemporary arguments include much that is new or original. The basic underlying issues in the debate between those who would use schools primarily for purposes of employment training and those who view education as a process engendering total human growth have been debated several times over the past few decades. As will be shown, the contemporary career education movement does introduce at least one novel element into the controversy, but the basic alternatives and values are substantially those argued over repeatedly by vocationalists and their opponents in years past.

Until modern times and the advent of the industrial revolution, vocational education rarely if ever occupied a place in formal school curricula. Traditionally, job-training requirements were met in a highly informal manner through direct observation and first-hand imitation or through some type of apprenticeship. The first known refer-

---

[8] Ibid., p. 16.
[9] Ibid., p. 14. Rhodes' argument reduces to the familiar thesis that students who do not enjoy or do well in academic subjects are likely to do well in vocational studies—a proposition for which there is scant supporting evidence.

ence to an apprenticeship system appears in the ancient Babylonian Code of Hammurabi which stipulated that "If an artisan takes a son for adoption and teaches him his handicraft, one may not bring claim against him. If he does not teach him his handicraft, the adopted son may return to his father's house." [10] Among the Greeks of antiquity, Solon's rules exonerated children for failing to support their parents in their old age if the latter had not troubled themselves to bring up their children in a trade. Talmudic literature abounds with injunctions to school the young for gainful employment. "Whosoever does not teach his son a trade," according to one Jewish saying, "teaches him to be a thief." Apprenticeship continued to be the primary method of vocational instruction down through the centuries, reaching a particularly advanced level of development in the guild system of the late medieval period when masters in a particular trade or occupation, in exchange for service rendered, instructed apprentices in the elements of their craft. In England and later in colonial America, apprenticeship was the main route of entry into most vocations and the various professions.

Concern for the practical education of the working classes and for manual training evolved gradually in America. Thomas Budd, an early Quaker, was among the first (1685) to submit that there should be public schools established to teach useful trades and handwork skills together with other subjects. In 1745, the Moravians opened an industrial school near Philadelphia which proved to be only the first of many founded throughout the eighteenth century. Benjamin Rush, a physician from the Philadelphia area, applauded a number of the vocationally-oriented schools of his day (1745–1813), and is credited with influencing Dr. John de la Howe of Abbeville, South Carolina, to bequeath a large tract of land for an agricultural school in 1797, the first such institution of its kind in the United States.

In Europe during the same period, a number of important educators addressed themselves to questions of vocational education. Johann Julius Hecker (1707–1768) at Halle stated that the basic aim of his famed *Realschule* was "to develop the tendencies of such young people as are not destined for studious pursuits but whose talents would fit them for business, for agriculture, for the industrial and fine arts, and so on, and to afford them an introductory training for these pursuits." [11] Jean-Jacques Rousseau (1712–1788), the author of *Émile*, lent his support to the role of manual work in education. "Of all pursuits by which a man may earn a living," he wrote, "the nearest to a state of nature is manual labor." The character Émile in his educa-

---

[10] A. B. Mays, *Principles and Practices of Vocational Education* (New York: McGraw-Hill, 1948), p. 6.
[11] Adapted after the quotation supplied in L. F. Anderson, *History of Manual and Industrial School Education* (New York: D. Appleton-Century, 1926), p. 43.

tional romance, Rousseau asserted, "will learn more by one hour of manual labor, than he will retain from a whole day's verbal instruction." [12] Especially influential was his recommendation that boys be taught a trade in a specially constructed workshop, on the theory that knowing a trade would pay dividends by making the boy independent and helping engender a sense of respect for menial labor. "It is important to learn a trade," Rousseau claimed, "less for knowing the trade than for overcoming the prejudices which despise it." [13] Indicative of Rousseau's influence was the fashion followed by many late eighteenth-century German and French nobility in building home workshops for their sons.

Others of the same period who favored the introduction of manual arts, commercial training, and vocational education included Rousseau's disciple, the Swiss educator Johann Heinrich Pestalozzi (1746–1827), who thought a vocational course of instruction the best means of alleviating the condition of the poor; and Philipp Emanuel von Fellenberg (1771–1844), a Swiss pioneer in the trade and agricultural school movement, whose educational views took root in early nineteenth-century America in the form of manual labor colleges and academies. With a breakdown of apprenticeship systems, so-called mechanics' institutes modeled after Fellenberg's ideas won growing acceptance among early industrialists and educational philanthropists. Friedrich Froebel (1782–1852), founder of the kindergarten, for example, was convinced that work in and of itself possessed enormous moral and educational significance.

Without entering upon a detailed historical analysis, it should be noted that the emergence of what Max Weber in 1904 called the "protestant work ethic" was also an important formative influence upon the development of vocational education. Ernst Troeltsch, in his classic *Protestantism and Progress,* notes that Protestantism— especially Calvinism—encouraged the competitive businessman's ethic of diligence, frugality, and thrift. By condemning sloth as sinful and endorsing work as a positive virtue, the Puritan insistence on unremitting toil and diligence enjoined the amassing of wealth as practically a sacred duty. [14] In particular, the Calvinist notion of "vocation" as an occupational choice to be pursued strenuously and exactingly with a sense of religious purpose imbued capitalists and workmen with the values of frugality and self-application. Together they helped provide an ideological basis for industrial development in the

[12] Jean-Jacques Rousseau, *Émile* (London: J. M. Dent & Sons, 1911), p. 158.
[13] R. L. Archer, *Rousseau on Education* (London: Edward Arnold, 1912), p. 169.
[14] Cf. the discussion in Christopher J. Lucas, *Our Western Educational Heritage* (New York: Macmillan, 1972), p. 243.

western world.[15] In America, an early and enthusiastic advocate of the work ethic was that homely moralist Benjamin Franklin whose maxims and preachments helped mold the attitudes of successive generations toward work, leisure, and vocation.[16] Franklin's support for practical trade schools, business schools, and formal skill-training mark him as a significant leader in the advancement of vocational education in the United States.

One major consequence of the industrial revolution was a shift in production from cottage to factory, from home handicrafts to power-driven machinery. Such a drastic change in production methods soon demanded a radical readjustment in trade or vocational education, the effect of which was to finally destroy the old apprenticeship system. In contrast with the handworker who was acquainted with an entire course of manufacture, from the procurement of raw material to the distribution and sale of the finished product, a machine worker seldom if ever became acquainted with more than a fraction of the total production process. His skills were at once more specialized and more limited. As vocational training ceased to be an incident of production and more an explicit responsibility of the producer, the trend developed of looking to the school as an agency for fostering skills, values, and work habits required in the industrial system. Pragmatic necessity, coupled with the growing economic and political complexity of industrial capitalism, made it inevitable that vocational training would be elevated to the status of a formal school subject.[17] Thus, the stage was set for later controversy over whether schools should be looked upon mainly as vehicles of general education or as institutional tools for preparing people for the world of work.

The nineteenth century brought a steady increase in both private and public trade schools, mechanical and agricultural institutes, and industrial colleges. The first part of the century witnessed efforts to open elementary trade schools for poor and pauper children where they might be taught a trade. In 1825, for example, the Welsh industrialist and émigré Robert Owen, whose sponsorship of schools in

---

[15] As presented the argument is overly simplistic, but it suffices to identify the source of the work ethic. Cf. Rupert N. Evans, *Foundations of Vocational Education* (Columbus, Ohio: Charles E. Merrill, 1971), p. 88.

[16] Ibid., p. 89. Evans offers an interesting argument that the predatory excesses of capitalism helped discredit the ideals of the protestant ethic in the twentieth century, but that their eclipse has also been largely a function of the secularization of the common school. Cf. loc. sit., pp. 89–90.

[17] John S. Brubacher, *A History of the Problems of Education,* second edition (New York: McGraw-Hill, 1966). The foregoing is borrowed from Brubacher's exposition.

connection with his model textile mills had attracted so much widespread attention, introduced a manual arts curriculum in his school at
New Harmony, Indiana. During the latter half of the century, there
were renewed attempts to develop schools responsive to the importunate needs of industrialism and commercial trade, as revealed by
passage of the 1863 Morrill Act lending federal support for collegiate-
level agricultural and mechanical education. The relationship between the social and economic well-being of society and skilled
manpower was repeatedly enunciated throughout the late 1800's by
such men as Calvin M. Woodwork, Dean of the Polytechnic School of
Washington University, and John D. Runkle, President of the Massachusetts Institute of Technology. Added impetus for the expansion
of vocational training in the schools came through the influence of
Victor Della Vos of the Russian Imperial Technical School in Moscow
whose system of training mechanics was demonstrated at the Centen-
nial Exposition in Philadelphia. In many U.S. cities, manual training
programs for both sexes in high schools emulated contemporary Fin-
nish and Swedish efforts to combine work and learning. Around the
same period, and for much the same purpose, many elementary
schools were experimenting with manual arts training in the upper
grades.

By the turn of the century, demands to make academic programs
in the school more practical had practically assumed the stature of a
popular crusade, together with an intensive campaign to introduce
and extend vocational education in the public schools. William James,
in his *Talks to Teachers,* spoke for many when he remarked, "The
most colossal improvement which recent years have seen in secondary education lies in the introduction of the manual training
schools; not because they will give us a people more hardy and practical for domestic life and better skilled in trades, but because they
will give us citizens with an entirely different intellectual fibre." [18]
More characteristically, however, the rationale for vocational education was that offered by the President of the National Association of
Manufacturers in 1910 when he stressed that "trade schools . . . [are]
more and more demanded as means of recruiting the ranks of skilled
mechanics . . . as well as to checkmate militant organized labor on
its policy of obstructing the free employment of apprentices." [19]
Whatever the motives involved, the new emphasis upon the practical
in education struck a responsive chord in most Americans, a people
who having carved out a civilization in the wilderness of a new
world were well aware that the secret of their success, and the key to

[18] William James, *Talks to Teachers* (New York: Norton Library, 1958), p. 40.
[19] Quoted in Joel H. Spring, *Education and the Rise of the Corporate State* (Boston: Beacon Press, 1972), p. 42.

material acquisition, had not been "book larnin' ".²⁰ Most traced their ancestry from the underprivileged classes of Europe, and lacking any tradition of learning or scholarship of their own, tended to overreact to the scorn and condescension of a cultured literate elite in American society. That reaction was to manifest itself repeatedly in the form of popular anti-intellectualism, as revealed in such epithets as "mere book learning" and "scholastic education." For Andrew Carnegie, to cite one well-known example, the term "academic" was practically synonymous with "useless." In a typical comment, Carnegie denounced the study of Greek and Latin as of no more practical use than Choctaw.²¹

The most specific outcome of business pressure upon education was the expansion of new vocational schools and the elaboration of vocational courses in existing schools. Especially after 1905, mounting fears of German industrial competition led American businessmen to urge wholesale adoption of Germany's rigorous system of industrial schooling, in the belief that it, more than any other single factor, accounted for their spectacular successes in trade and industry. By the end of the century's first decade, the drive for manual training, for trade-training courses, and for classes in home economics, agriculture, and commerce had reached into the discussions of almost every major educational association. As one speaker put it before a session of the annual meeting (1909) of the National Education Association, "The program of this association bristles with the topic." No less a personage than the U.S. Commissioner of Education told the NEA delegates to the meeting that industrial-vocational education was a major priority requiring their attention in years ahead.²²

The first vocational education movement (1906–1917) in the present century may properly be said to have begun in 1906 with the widely-circulated report of Massachusetts' Governor Douglas's Commission of Labor. In its report, the Commission came out strongly on behalf of elementary-level instruction in agriculture, mechanical arts, and homemaking. At the high school level, there was to be ample provision made for elective courses in industry-related subjects. Among its other recommendations were numerous proposals for day, part-time, and evening trade and vocational schools. The year 1906 also marked the founding of the National Society for the Promotion of Industrial Education, under the impetus of Dr. James P. Haney, the

²⁰ Raymond E. Callahan, *Education and the Cult of Efficiency* (Chicago: University of Chicago Press, 1962), p. 8.
²¹ Ibid., p. 9.
²² Ibid., p. 13. At the risk of pointing out the obvious, note the parallel with the 1971 address of Commissioner Sidney Marland before the National Association of Secondary School Principals in which the concept of "career education" was first set forth.

Director of Art and Manual Training of New York City, and Charles R. Richards, a professor of manual arts at Teachers College, Columbia University.[23] So great was the pressure generated for more course offerings to meet the complex skill needs of industrial America that by 1913 William H. Maxwell, Superintendent of Schools for New York City, was moved to lash out at what he called the "arrogant unreasonableness" of critics who demanded that education be made totally ancillary to business and industry. He lamented the fact that "the educational world is now seething for the introduction of industrial or trade teaching in the public schools," and attributed the origin of pressure on educators to manufacturers who, having abandoned the apprenticeship system as too costly, wanted to persuade the state to assume the burden through the public schools.[24]

The widespread agitation for more vocational education culminated in 1917 with the Smith-Hughes Act which, in its final form, provided public support for a variety of vocational training programs. Through the combined efforts of the National Association of Manufacturers, the American Federation of Labor, and a number of major farm organizations, federal aid for vocational education in both agricultural and industrial occupations, was well established. Two prominent leaders in the movement were David Snedden, a leading light in the related "educational efficiency" movement, and Charles A. Prosser, the Executive Secretary of the National Society for the Promotion of Industrial Education and later first Executive Director of the Federal Board of Vocational Education.

Then as now the debate that grew up over vocational education pitted defenders of social and economic utility in learning against proponents of general education for well-rounded social, intellectual, and spiritual development. It may be too much to claim, with Arthur G. Wirth, that the choice was and is whether schools are to become servants of technocratic efficiency or whether they can act "to help men humanize life under technology." [25] But it is clear that the goal of people like Prosser was to make vocational training central in the nation's schools. Traditional "scholastic" education, he maintained, was aimed at preparing citizens for leisure. In the modern age, such

---

[23] For a more complete discussion, consult Arthur G. Wirth, "Philosophical Issues in the Vocational-Liberal Studies Controversy (1900–1917): John Dewey vs. The Social Efficiency Philosophers," *Studies in Philosophy and Education*, Vol. VII, No. 3 (Winter 1974), 1969–182. The organization was changed in 1918 to the National Society for Vocational Education, and in 1926 joined another state organization to form the American Vocational Association, a lobby group which moved vigorously to secure the support of labor and business for trade-related schooling.

[24] Callahan, op. cit., pp. 13–14.

[25] Wirth, op. cit., 169.

an education was hopelessly outmoded and irrevelant. It should be replaced, Prosser argued, by a type of education designed according to a detailed job analysis of the needs of industry. "Vocational education," he noted with some satisfaction, "only functions in proportion as it will enable an individual actually to do a job." [26] Against the conservative social philosophy put forth by Prosser and Snedden, the best-known critic and opponent was John Dewey who, while agreeing that study of "occupations" had a useful role to play in education, vehemently denied that social efficiency, economic utility, or business applicability should be relied upon as *major* criteria for deciding what should be taught in schools.

Above all, Dewey strongly resisted efforts to build a dual educational system with one school for job training, and another for academic subjects. But neither did he believe that vocational education by itself was a viable alternative:

> Instead of trying to split schools into two kinds, one of a trade type for children whom it is assumed are to be employees and one of a liberal type for the children of the well-to-do, [a new type of general education is required which] will aim at such a reorganization of existing schools as will give all pupils a genuine respect for useful work, an ability to render service, and a contempt for social parasites. . . . It will indeed make much of developing motor and manual skill, but not of a routine or automatic type. It will rather utilize active and manual pursuits as the means of developing constructive, inventive and creative power of mind. It will select the materials and the technique of the trades not for the sake of producing skilled workers for hire in definite trades, but for the sake of securing industrial intelligence—a knowledge of the conditions and processes of present manufacturing, transportation and commerce so that the individual may be able to make his own choices and his own adjustments, and be master, so far as in him lies, of his own economic fate. It will be recognized that, for this purpose, a broad acquaintance with science and skill in the laboratory control of materials and processes is more important than skill in trade operations. It will remember that the future employee is a consumer as well as a producer, that the whole tendency of society, so far as it is intelligent and wholesome, is to an increase of the hours of leisure, and that an education which does nothing to enable individuals to consume wisely is a fraud on democracy. So far as method is concerned, such a conception of industrial education will prize freedom more than docility; initiative more than automatic skill; insight and understanding more than capacity to recite lessons or to execute tasks under the direction of others.[27]

[26] Charles A. Prosser and Thomas H. Quigley, *Vocational Education in a Democracy*, revised edition (Chicago: American Technical Society, 1950), pp. 215–220, *et. passim*.

[27] John Dewey, "Learning to Learn," in *Education Today* (New York: G. P. Putnam's Sons, 1940), pp. 131–132; quoted in Wirth, op. cit., 180–181. Curiously, Dewey's remarks, especially if taken out of context, seem to offer a very apt description of what career educators assert they are trying to accomplish today.

Again in the immediate post-World War II period (coinciding significantly with a resurgence of political conservatism), new demands
were set out for more vocationalism in school curricula. There are
several striking parallels between the controversy then and present
demands for job-related learning. In 1945, the Division of Vocational
Education of the U.S. Office of Education, responding to a committee
headed by the same Charles Prosser who had served as ideologue for
the vocational education movement three decades earlier, launched
an ill-fated program on behalf of what was labeled "life adjustment
education." Like the career education movement begun under federal auspices in the early 1970's, life adjustment education was presented at a response to social unrest and popular discontent with the
schools. The two movements also resemble one another in that both
were defended as expressions of democracy in action, both essayed
to offer school programs suitable for meeting the needs of practically
everyone, both encapsulated a strong interest in careers and employment. The two were further alike in that both were promoted through
the pronouncements and policy statements of official spokesmen
rather than by individual educational theorists or critics speaking in a
purely private capacity.[28] In each case, furthermore, opponents of the
respective movements complained that they were designed to preadapt people through education to the existing social, economic, and
political order.

The drive to render schooling more responsive to the needs of
business and industry early in the twentieth century was accompanied
by vigorous efforts to foster the corporate-industrial values of economy, efficiency, and control in the conduct of education. It should
come as no surprise, therefore, that the current manifestation of educational vocationalism in the form of career education should appear
at a time when the industrial values of precision and cost-effectiveness accountability have once again won a large following among
educators. What distinguishes today's career education movement
from its predecessors is that its supporters (at least the more thoughtful spokesmen) do not necessarily aspire to make all formal education
vocational in character. They do insist, however, that merely adding
more vocational elements within a basically unchanged curriculum,
or expanding existing but separate courses in practical and industrial
arts, is not enough. For too long, the attitude has prevailed that vocational education is acceptable only when it is intended for someone
else's children, with a resulting tendency to employ occupational education as a "dumping ground" for the academically unfit. The time

[28] Cf. H. R. Douglass (ed.), *Education for Life Adjustment* (New York: Ronald
Press, 1950). It might be added that in its usual reflexive way, the National Education Association warmly endorsed both movements at the height of their influence.

has now come, vocational spokesmen insist, to close once and for all the gap between academic and vocational education.

Typical in its expression of a more positive and aggressive stance, one directly precursive of career education, was the Annual Report (1968) of the National Advisory Council on Vocational Education:

> It is time that we ended the artificial cleavage between vocational education and so-called academic education. All of our citizens require education to function effectively as citizens and to realize their potentials as human beings. Moreover, we know that literacy and the basic skills which should be developed in any educational process are also necessary for people to learn work skills properly and to advance in their jobs.
>
> We also regard it as nonsense to have an imaginary line separate the individual's academic education and his participation in his life's career. Academic education would be enhanced, not compromised, if vocational preparation were introduced into our general school system. Moreover, an increase in vocational education might help to end the false hierarchy of values which educators have consciously or unconsciously introduced through their treatment of vocational education, the notion that preparation for a life career is a second-class activity for second class citizens.[29]

The following year brought new expressions of support for a sweeping recasting of education in vocational terms. The summary recommendations of a landmark conference report sponsored by the U.S. Office of Education in Atlanta, Georgia, urged a wholesale merging of academic and vocational curricula, one aimed at nothing less than making career or job awareness the central organizing principle of all schooling. Its specific proposals included the following:

> Vocational education should be structured as a developmental and sequential process from elementary through post-secondary and adult vocational programs.
>
> Vocational education should be viewed as the responsibility of the total school.
>
> Vocational experiences should be incorporated in the teaching of basic academic skills.
>
> Each student at the point of separation from school should be provided with a saleable skill as well as a basic educational preparation.
>
> Career development efforts should begin at the elementary school level.
>
> Career exploration programs should not be seen as a mining operation strictly concerned with the selection of certain talents for the purpose

---

[29] Quoted in Grant Venn, *Man, Education and Manpower*, revised edition (Washington, D.C.: National Association of School Administrators, National Education Association, 1970), pp. 80–81.

of meeting particular manpower needs, but rather as a farming approach in which all individuals are provided with opportunities to grow
and develop.

Career development experiences should be subsequently organized
from the elementary grades through high school.

Schools should assume responsibility for all pupils until they successfully make the transition from school to work. . . .

Schools should more fully cooperate with business and industry in the
development of basic habits of industry on the part of students.[30]

The position advanced at the Atlanta Conference was echoed in
an important speech delivered by Assistant Education Secretary James
E. Allen before the 1970 annual meeting of the National Association of
Secondary School Principals. On that occasion, Allen called for a "recasting of the entire education system" to favor vocational education
and career development in relation to manpower demands. The following year Commissioner Sidney P. Marland Jr., of the U.S. Office of
Education, swung the full prestige and authority of his office behind
the concept of "career education" in remarks delivered at the NASSP
meeting in Houston, Texas. Marland opened his now famous address
by suggesting that educators get rid of what he termed "irrelevant
general education pap." They should, he urged, divest themselves of
lingering academic snobbery, and substitute a true blending of academic and vocational curricula for the "fallacious compromise" of
academic liberal arts and vocational training. The goal, Marland
avowed, was a system in which every graduating student would be
prepared by the the twelfth grade either for higher education or for
useful and rewarding employment.[31] Although he did not offer any
specific explanation of what career education should be, his promises
of substantial federal support for programs and models based upon
the concept of career education practically assured it an enthusiastic
reception. Marland's remarks were iterated in numerous speeches
and articles thereafter, subsequent history of the career education
movement being mainly an account of efforts to implement in practical programs his goal of bringing career awareness and formal learning closer together.

To claim, as some critics have done, that career education is

[30] Cited in G. Bottoms and K. B. Matheny, *A Guide for the Development
and Implementation of Exemplary Programs and Projects in Vocational Education* (Atlanta: Georgia State Department of Education and Division of
Vocational Education, 1969), pp. 23–26.
[31] For amplification and initial reaction to Marland's original speech, entitled
"Career Education Now," consult Sidney P. Marland, Jr., "Criticism, Communication, and Change," *College and University Journal*, Vol. **10**, No. 4 (September 1971), 17–19; and Marland, "Educating for the Real World," *Business Education Forum*, Vol. **26**, No. 2 (November 1971), 3–5.

nothing more than a new and pretentious label for old-fashioned vocational training fails to do justice to their differences, even though the distinction is sometimes hard to preserve. Career education, as defined by the Associate Commissioner for Adult, Vocational and Technical Education, was termed "a lifelong systematic way of acquainting students with the world of work in their elementary and junior high school years and preparing them in high school and in college to enter into and advance in a career field of their own choosing." It is similar to vocational education, he conceded, but there is a fundamental distinction. "For while vocational education is targeted at producing specific job skills at the high school level and up to but not including the baccalaureate level, Career Education embraces all occupations and professions and can include individuals of all ages whether in or out of schools." [32]

Continuing confusion over the meaning of career education was partly attributable to Marland's reluctance to offer any simple, clear-cut definition. As he phrased it some two years after his original 1971 NASSP address, "we have conscientiously avoided trying to lay down a precise definition for career education." [33] What he had tried to express, he explained, was his concern at the "continuing failure of the schools to serve fully a third of the young people attending them"—what he characterized as "the swelling numbers of young . . . boys and girls listlessly, apparently helplessly, entering their names on the roles of the unemployed, not because they lack talent, but because the schools have not given them a decent or fair preparation for the hard, competitive business of life—including, of course, adequate job skills. . . ." [34] The basic objective of career education, Marland explained, was to inculcate among youth an understanding of what to do with themselves when the transition to adulthood is completed.

On various occasions, Marland spoke of career education "as a new educational unity," as an approach to reform in vocational education, and as a "true and complete reform of the high school." In a speech before a 1971 gathering of vocational educators, he spoke briefly of several "models" for implementing career education, but offered little to clarify its explicit meaning.[35] Again in 1973, while de-

[32] R. M. Worthington, *The Implications of Career Education for Adult Education in the United States.* Paper presented at the Third UNESCO International Conference on Adult Education, Tokyo, Japan (July 25–August 7, 1972), 3–4.

[33] Sidney P. Marland, Jr., "Career Education: A Report," *NAASP Bulletin*, Vol. 57, No. 371 (March 1973), 3.

[34] Ibid., p. 2.

[35] Sidney P. Marland, Jr., "Career Education: More Than a Name," in Keith Goldhammer and R. E. Taylor (eds.), *Career Education: Perspectives and Promises* (Columbus, Ohio: Charles E. Merrill, 1972), pp. 43–52.

nying emphatically that career education meant all education should become vocational in nature (although vocational education was termed an important part of career education), Marland restricted himself to very broad characterizations and generalizations. Career education, he claimed, in its most philosophical sense, is really "a change of mind and a change of heart" directed against the divorce between things occupational and things intellectual. It seeks to erase "the snobbish distinction between the vocational learner and the college preparatory learner." Marland quoted with evident approval Whitehead's famous dictum that the antithesis between a technical and a liberal education is fallacious:

> There can be no adequate technical education which is not liberal, and no liberal education which is not technical; that is, no education which does not impart both technique and intellectual vision. In simpler language, education should turn out the pupil with something he knows well and something he can do well.[36]

Arguing that education divorced from its proper ends and uses withers into "irrelevancy," Marland noted that he was far from being the first to urge that the educational experiences of youth should fit subsequent employment, James B. Conant, for one, in his book *Slums and Suburbs* (1961) had advocated a type of education providing a smooth transition from full-time schooling to a full-time job, whether the transition was made after the tenth grade, after high school graduation, or upon completion of one's college or university education. Others, like Erich Fromm, had long championed the same goal.

Kenneth B. Hoyt, an early exponent of career education, defended Marland's definitional imprecision on the rather peculiar ground that, like many other vague or undefined ideas in education, the meaning of career education was to grow out of controversy and debate about it.[37] Left unclear was how conceptual imprecision might contribute materially to debate about educational goals and objectives. Hoyt's own definition (more nearly an interpretation) suggested that career education he looked upon as "the total effort of public education and the community to help all individuals become familiar with the values of a work oriented society, to integrate these values into their personal value structure, and to implement those values in their lives in ways that make work possible, meaningful, and satisfying to each individual." [38]

[36] Alfred North Whitehead, *The Aims of Education,* quoted in Marland, "Career Education: A Report," op. cit., 4.
[37] Kenneth B. Hoyt, *Career Education Resource Guide* (Morristown, N.J.: General Learning Corporation, 1972), p. 5.
[38] Ibid., p. 6.

Similar in tone were the many official pronouncements, position statements, and explanations advanced in the early 1970's by various professional associations and governmental agencies involved in popularizing the career education idea. What they shared in common was a pervasive desire to link work, career awareness, job preparation, and classroom learning. Most proposed definitions and interpretations reflected agreement with six major objectives delineated early in 1971 in a conference discussion paper issued by the U.S. Office of Education's Division of Vocational and Technical Education. Listed as basic priorities for the decade of the 1970's were the following objectives: (1) providing every high school graduate with a saleable skill and assured entry to further education or training, (2) providing an equivalent experience for students who left school prior to graduation, (3) offering career education orientation, with subsequent guidance, counseling, and placement services, to all students at all educational levels, (4) emphasis on and enlargement of post-secondary and adult vocational and technical education programs, and (5) reforms whereby general education would be replaced by career education.[39] Career education it was implied, would begin as a general concept and gradually become more specific, so that somewhere halfway through high school "entry level skills" to a vocation or occupation would be gained, and in the last years of high school, more specific work skills. According to another publication issued through the American Vocational Association, career education was to be defined as "the development of a *lifelong* [emphasis added] learning process that provides for a broad approach to preparation for citizenship; provides job information and skill development; and, also helps individuals develop attitudes about the personal, psychological, social and economic significance of work in our society." [40]

CRITICISM OF CAREER EDUCATION

It was precisely the all-encompassing generality of career education that most troubled Harold Howe, Vice-President of the Division of Education and Research in the Ford Foundation. Speaking at a conference sponsored by the Educational Testing Service in May of 1972, Howe shared some of his misgivings about the career education concept and its implementation. He noted that to him the very lack of controversy and criticism at the introduction of the idea rendered its

[39] E. L. Rumpf, *Vocational Education for the 1970's* (Washington, D.C.: United States Office of Education, Division of Vocational and Technical Education, 1971), pp. 2–3.
[40] "Career Education: Perspectives; New Perspectives for Industrial Arts: An Introduction," in *Career Education: New Perspectives for Industrial Arts* (Washington, D.C.: American Vocational Association, 1972), p. 5.

initial formulation suspect. The very fact that so many educators of diverse social, economic, and educational viewpoints appeared unanimous in their support suggested several undesirable possibilities: people had not taken the notion seriously, they did not understand what it meant, or they failed to grasp its revolutionary implications.[41]

Above all, Howe deplored what was to later become a distinguishing characteristic of the rhetoric advanced on behalf of career education: its intellectual imperialism. The trouble, he decided, lay with exaggerated claims, with an overemphasis upon vocationalism, and with the tacit assumption that career education is broad enough to incorporate within itself a very wide range of entirely legitimate educational concerns having little to do with jobs or vocational awareness. As a case in point, Howe cited a USOE pamphlet entitled "Career Education" which read:

> The fundamental concept of career education is that *all* educational experiences—curriculum, instruction, and counseling—should be geared to preparation for economic independence and appreciation for the dignity of work.[42]

Howe disagreed, claiming that a considerable proportion of the educational effort should be geared not just to economic man—linking work and education—but to the roles of men as citizens and as private individuals. Career education is insufficient as a total response to the reforms needed in American education, Howe went on to explain, because basically it is concerned only with the problems of man as economic producer and consumer. To some extent it therefore deserves support, but to claim that there are no *other* aspects to human existence which should be served by education is narrow and unlovely. To claim that career education is an appropriate conceptual vehicle for the channeling and expression of those many other concerns is unrealistic or disingenuous.

In that observation, Howe anticipated a type of criticism leveled often in subsequent years against career education enthusiasts. Reminiscent of Whitehead's observation that educators tend to lower their ideals to the level of their practices, critics complained that the educator's goal of life preparation (protests to the contrary notwithstanding) were being reduced by career education to job preparation.

---

[41] Harold Howe II, "Remarks Regarding Career Education," *NASSP Bulletin*, Vol. 57, No. 371 (March 1973), 45.

[42] Quoted in Howe, op. cit., 47. The original version, delivered in Assistant Commissioner R. M. Worthington's Tokyo address, continues as follows: "[Career education's] main purpose is to prepare all students for successful and rewarding lives by improving their basis for occupational choice, by facilitating their acquisition of occupational skills, by enhancing their educational achievements, by making education more meaningful and relevant to their aspirations, and by increasing the real choices they have among the many different occupations and training avenues open to them." Worthington, op. cit., 3–4.

Having failed to educate, it was claimed, too many were now willing to settle for simple training.

Marland himself cautioned vocational educators against seizing upon the concept of career education in the mistaken belief that their day had come and that all education was soon destined to become occupationally-related. It had never been his intention, Marland emphasized, to undertake a rejection of the liberal, humanistic tradition of education in favor of a strictly pragmatic, utilitarian approach focused entirely on employment and income.[43] But for Howe and others, career education had little to say about the need in school to expose students to the pressing issues of the day—not just to the big issues of war and peace, environment, and human relations, but to the difficult local issues of taxation, racism, zoning, and governance. Schools should also afford access to the past, to 5,000 years of civilization with its rich philosophic, literary, and esthetic inheritance. Cultural transmission, in its own way, is every bit as vital and urgent a task as career training or awareness. And while it may seem reasonable to ask that humanities bear some relation to the world of work, their contribution to human life, it was said, cannot be limited solely to themes revolving around a work ethic.[44]

Some critics professed to see in the career education movement an implicit conspiracy to limit rather than to enhance the opportunities of minority groups by relegating their children to vocational instead of academic schooling. Others took exception to the notion that, given the diversity of school curricula and aims, career education could ever aspire to unify all aspects of public education, especially with respect to its somewhat vague proposal that educational programs be organized around various career job groupings or "clusters." Another form of criticism centered on the movement's educational legitimacy, not that it was addressed to a spurious need (even the harshest critics concede the reality of the problem of occupational preparation), but that career education was based upon a social and political rationale rather than an educational one. Purchasing a commitment by the use of federal funds, a "carrot" to attract allegiance to federal educational policies, smacks of bribery, some alleged, and affords a very shaky basis for educating people. Still other critics objected to career education's strained attempt to reanimate the work ethic in a dawning post-industrial era, an age in which the classical form of that ethic may no longer be viable.[45]

Even on its own terms and presuppositions, career education

[43] Marland, "Career Education: A Report," op. cit., 2.
[44] Marland, "Meeting Our Enemies: Career Education and the Humanities," *English Journal*, Vol. **62**, No. 6 (September 1973), 900–906.
[45] Cf. Kenneth B. Hoyt et al., *Career Education and the Elementary School Teacher* (Salt Lake City: Olympus, 1973), pp. 67–69. Many of the criticisms cited are discussed in selections reprinted in the present volume.

was to come in for heavy criticism from opponents. The assumption that there exists a shortage of trained manpower in the country at the level of entry open to school drop-outs and high school graduates was strongly questioned, as was the argument that job training in secondary school might help create jobs. Possibly, critics said, the real shortage lies with jobs themselves. Nor it is likely at present levels of funding and support that secondary schools can be refashioned to offer as high-quality career training as might be made available elsewhere under other institutional arrangements. As for the proposals to foster career awareness in the elementary grades, critics wondered if it was either useful or desirable to encourage children to contemplate possible career choices when statistics reveal the average person changes jobs five times in his lifetime, when occupational schools are quickly outdated, and when on-the-job training may be the most efficient way of fostering both career awareness and occupational competence.[46]

The problem with the concept of "career," as Donald E. Super pointed out, is that it connotes a kind of occupational permanence or stability that is increasingly rare among the nation's work force. Except for certain comparatively stable professions like law, medicine, and upper-echelon business management, few occupations offer the continuity and possibilities of self-fullfillment implied by the somewhat elevated notion of *career* with its overtones of commitment, calling, and life-long vocation. The truth of the matter is most people simply work at jobs—oftentimes a series of unrelated and often depersonalized positions lacking much semblance of continuity or common purpose.[47] Whereas it may be advantageous and highly desirable to plan for a stable, conventional "career," it may also be unrealistic. If more than half the working population is to have discontinuous careers, in an unpredictable and always shifting market economy, is it possible, opponents asked, either to train for a specific job, for skills generic to a "career cluster," or even for awareness of jobs that might not exist five, ten, or twenty years hence? Discontinuity and change in the economy foster a need for great adaptability and frequent retraining. Career educators were challenged to demonstrate how they proposed to meet that need in their programs. On the one hand, if career education instruction remained very general in character its practical applicability in the world of work seemed limited. On the

[46] Hruska, op. cit., p. 50. A separate but related issue is the propriety of the school's providing industrial training at public expense.

[47] Donald E. Super, "The Changing Nature of Vocational Guidance," in Arthur M. Kroll (ed.), *Issues in American Education* (New York: Oxford University Press, 1970), pp. 139–155. As Gerard Piel points out, much work, whether in office or factory, is mostly boring and repetitive; and offers few of the psychological satisfactions ideally associated with a vocational occupation. Cf. Venn, op. cit., p. 35.

other, it was not clear to critics how career education could, in fostering specific entry-level skills to jobs, avoid the dangers of irrelevancy or obsolescence. Similar considerations may have dictated the decision in 1974 of The National Advisory Council on Vocational Education to recommend in its Eighth Report that the distinction between vocational and career education be carefully preserved. Career education, it was said, had so far failed to benefit those for whom it was intended or to face squarely the problems confronting its effective implementation. To date, the Report stated, it was "over-promised and under-delivered." [48]

PRESENT PROBLEMS AND FUTURE PROSPECTS

In the years since career education was first introduced, a number of federally-supported model programs have been instituted throughout the country. Most of the initial pilot programs are organized on a so-called "school-based" model for career orientation activities; some are functioning to test a "rural-residential" model intended to serve disadvantaged youths living in areas geographically distant from major population centers; a few are experimenting with a "home-based" model originally suggested by Sidney Marland; and in one or two cases efforts are underway to explore a business or employer-based career education model. At the same time, a great amount of effort is being expended in government-funded university projects to develop new conceptual frameworks and alternative ways of realizing the goals of career education.

Some of the criticism heaped upon career educators in recent years seems undeserved or beside the point, though it must be emphasized once again that much of it *has* served to raise important and entirely legitimate questions about the viability of the underlying concept. Already disillusionment and reaction have developed in some quarters, most likely in response to overblown claims advanced in the first burst of enthusiasm accompanying the movement's inception and in the aftermath of its inevitable failure to work instant miracles.

Whether career education can in future somehow achieve the benign synthesis of vocational and academic or general education remains an open question. What is painfully obvious is that even if it turns out that education of *any* kind proves unsuccessful as a way of intervening directly in social problems, the problems to which career education is intended as a response will in all likelihood remain for the foreseeable future. They may grow worse. At the present time, over a million young men and women under age twenty-two who

[48] The National Advisory Council on Vocational Education, *A National Policy on Career Education: Eighth Report* (September 1974).

have left school are unemployed. Well over a third of today's high school dropouts are classified as unemployable, and even among high school graduates, almost one in five were jobless at the decade's midpoint. It is estimated that less than five percent of the current work force is engaged in unskilled work, while room in a depressed labor market for the undereducated and unskilled is shrinking daily. At the other end, there are literally thousands of so-called "overqualified" college graduates who are enjoying no better success in effecting a smooth transition from school to work, and are forced into menial tasks they have been taught to regard as degrading and demeaning. To many thoughtful observers of American education, an answer to the problem of melding human resources and life-fulfilling employment, if it exists at all, still lies with the schools and with career education.

Career Education Now

SIDNEY P. MARLAND, JR.
U.S. Office of Education

What are we educating our children for?

Educators, it seems to me, too often have answered: We simply are not sure.

Uncertainty is the hallmark of our era. And because many educators have been unsure as to how they could best discharge their dual responsibility to meet the student's needs on the one hand and to satisfy the country's infinite social and economic appetites on the other, they have often succumbed to the temptation to point a finger at vocational educators and damn them for their failure to meet the nation's manpower requirements, doubly damning them for their failure to meet the youngster's career requirements, not to mention his personal fulfillment as a human being.

GENERAL EDUCATION—NEITHER FISH NOR FOWL

There is illogic here as well as a massive injustice. How can we blame vocational educators for the hundreds of thousands of pitifully incapable boys and girls who leave our high schools each year, when the truth is that the vast majority of these youngsters have never seen the inside of a vocational classroom? They are the unfortunate inmates, in most instances, of a curriculum that is neither fish nor fowl, neither truly vocational nor truly academic. We call it general education. I suggest we get rid of it.

Whatever interest we represent—federal, state, or local—whether we teach or administer, we must perforce deny ourselves the sweet solace of claiming that it is the other fellow who is in the wrong. We share the guilt for the generalized failure of our public system of education to equip our people to get and hold decent jobs. And the remedy likewise depends upon all of us. As Grant Venn said in his book, *Man, Education, and Manpower:* "If we want an educational system designed to serve each individual and to develop his creative potential in a self-directing way, then we have work to do and attitudes to change."

From "Career Education Now," *NASSP Bulletin*, Vol. **55**, No. 355 (May 1971), 1–9. © 1971 by The National Association of Secondary School Principals. Reprinted with permission.

This selection is an extract from the speech delivered before an annual meeting of the National Association of Secondary School Principals by the U.S. Commissioner of Education, in which the author first introduced the concept of "career education."

The first attitude that we should change, I suggest, is our own. We must purge ourselves of academic snobbery. Education's most serious failing is its self-induced, voluntary fragmentation, the strong tendency of education's several parts to separate from one another, to divide the entire enterprise against itself. The most grievous example of these intramural class distinctions is, of course, the false dichotomy between things academic and things vocational. As a first step, I suggest we dispose of the term *vocational education,* and adopt the term *career education.* Every young person in school belongs in that category at some point, whether engaged in preparing to be a surgeon, a brick layer, a mother, or a secretary.

A NEW GOAL PROPOSED

How absurd to suggest that general knowledge for its own sake is somehow superior to *useful* knowledge. "Pedants sneer at an education that is useful," Alfred North Whitehead observed. "But if education is not useful," he went on to ask, "what is it?" The answer, of course, is that it is nothing. All education is career education, or should be. And all our efforts as educators must be bent on preparing students either to become properly, usefully employed immediately upon graduation from high school or to go to further formal education. Anything else is dangerous nonsense. I propose that a universal goal of American education, starting now, be this: that every young person completing our school program at grade 12 be ready to enter either higher education or useful and rewarding employment.

Contrary to all logic and all expediency, we continue to treat vocational training as education's poor cousin. We are thereby perpetuating the social quarantine it has been in since the days of the ancient Greeks, and, for all I know, before then. Since U.S. vocational fields were originally defined shortly before World War I as agriculture, industry, and homemaking, we have too often taught those skills grudgingly—dull courses in dull buildings for the benefit of what we all *knew* were young people somehow pre-judged not fit for college, as though college were something better for everyone. What a pity and how foolish, particularly for a country as dependent upon her machines and her technology as America. The ancient Greeks could afford such snobbery at a time when a very short course would suffice to teach a man how to imitate a beast of burden. We Americans might have been able to afford it even a half century ago when a boy might observe the full range of his occupational expectations by walking beside his father at the time of plowing, by watching the farmers, blacksmiths, and tradesmen who did business in his home town.

But how different things are today and how grave our need to reshape our system of education to meet the career demands of the astonishingly complex technological society we live in. When we talk of today's career development, we are not talking about black-smithing. We are talking about the capacity of our people to sustain and accelerate the pace of progress in this country in every respect during a lifetime of learning. And nothing less.

The question seems to be fairly simple, if we have the courage and creativity to face it: Shall we persevere in the traditional practices that are obviously *not* properly equipping fully half or more of our young people, or shall we immediately undertake the reformation of our entire system of secondary education in order to position it properly for maximum contribution to our individual and national life?

I think what our choice must be is apparent. Certainly continued indecision and preservation of the status quo can only result in additional millions of young men and women leaving our high schools, with or without benefit of diploma, unfitted for employment, unable or unwilling to go on to college, and carrying away little more than an enduring distaste for education in any form, unskilled and unschooled. Indeed, if we are to ponder thoughtfully the growing charge of "irrelevance" in our schools and colleges, let us look sharply at the abomination known as general education.

Of those students currently in high school, only three out of 10 will go on to academic college-level work. One-third of those will drop out before getting a baccalaureate degree. That means that eight out of 10 present high school students should be getting occupational training of some sort. But only about two of those eight students are, in fact, getting such training. Consequently, half our high school students, a total of approximately 1,500,000 a year, are being offered what amounts to irrelevant, general educational pap!

In pained puzzlement they toil at watered-down general algebra, they struggle to recollect the difference between adjectives and adverbs, and they juggle in their minds the atomic weight of potassium in non-college science. The liberal arts and sciences of our traditional college-preparatory curriculum are indeed desirable for those who want them and can use them. But there must be desire and receptivity, and for millions of our children, we must concede, such knowledge is neither useful nor joyful. They do not love it for its own sake and they cannot sell it in the career market place. Small wonder so many drop out, not because they have failed, but because we have failed them. Who would not at the earliest convenient and legal moment leave an environment that is neither satisfying, entertaining, or productive? We properly deplore the large numbers of young men and women who leave high school before graduation. But, in simple truth, for most of them dropping out is the most sensible elective they can choose. At least they can substitute the excitement of the street corner for the more obscure charms of general mathematics.

NEW EDUCATIONAL UNITY REQUIRED

I want to state my clear conviction that a properly effective career education requires a new educational unity. It requires a breaking down of the barriers that divide our educational system into parochial enclaves. Our answer is that we must blend our curricula and our students into a single, strong secondary system. Let the academic preparation be balanced with the vocational or career program. Let one student take strength from another. And, for the future hope of education, let us end the divisive, snobbish, destructive distinctions in learning that do no service to the cause of knowledge, and do no honor to the name of American enterprise.

It is terribly important to teach a youngster the skills he needs to live, whether we call them academic or vocational, whether he intends to make his living with a wrench or a slide rule or folio editions of Shakespeare. But it is critically important to equip that youngster to live his life as a fulfilled human being. As Secretary Richardson said, "I remind you that this department of government more than anything else is concerned with humaneness."

Ted Bell, now Deputy Commissioner for School Systems in OE, made the point particularly well in a recent speech to a student government group. He was speculating on the steps a young person needs to take not just to get a diploma or a degree today, but to make reasonably sure he will continue to learn in the years ahead, to be an educated man or woman in terms of the future, a personal future. Mr. Bell said:

> Here the lesson is for each person to develop a personal plan for life-long learning: learning about the world we live in, the people that inhabit it, the environment—physical and social—that we find around us; learning about the sciences, the arts, the literature we have inherited and are creating; but most of all, learning the way the world's peoples are interacting with one another. If one educates himself in these things, he will have a pretty good chance of survival and of a good life.

In other words, life and how to live it is the primary vocation of all of us. And the ultimate test of our educational process, on any level, is how close it comes to preparing our people to be alive and active with their hearts and their minds and, for many, their hands as well.

INTERIM STRATEGY—FOUR MAJOR ACTIONS

True and complete reform of the high school, viewed as a major element of overall preparation for life, cannot be achieved until general education is completely done away with in favor of contemporary career development in a comprehensive secondary education environment. This is our ultimate goal and we realize that so sweeping a change cannot be accomplished overnight, involving as it does approximately 30 million students and billions of dollars' in public funds. Until we can recommend a totally new system we believe an interim strategy can be developed entailing four major actions.

First, we are planning major improvements in the vocational education program of the Office of Education. This program, as you know, involves the expenditure of nearly $500,000,000 annually, and our intention is to make the administrative and programmatic changes that will enable the states to use this money to make their vocational education efforts more relevant to the needs of the young people who will spend their lives in careers in business and industry. We intend to give the states new leadership and technical support to enable them to move present programs away from disproportionate enrollments in low-demand occupations to those where national shortages exist and where future national needs will be high.

Right now state training programs fill only half the jobs available each year. The other half are filled by job seekers with no occupational job training of any kind. We do better in some fields than in others, of course, particularly production agriculture where we are able to come closer to meeting the total need because it is a relatively static job market with little growth projected. About 70 percent of the demand in farm jobs will be met with trained help this year compared with only about 38 percent in the health occupations and 35 percent in various technical fields. This is nice if you happen to own a farm, not so nice if you run a hospital or laboratory.

We obviously require greater emphasis on such new vocational fields as computer programmers and technicians, laser technicians, and jet mechanics. We particularly need qualified people in health occupations such as certified laboratory technologists, dental assistants, occupational therapists, and the like. And, of course, we badly need men and women to service capably the rapidly growing environmental industries. Though when we speak of new occupations, it is always useful to remind ourselves that even some of the newest, such as computer programing, for example, will very likely be obsolete in 20 years or so, affirming once again the need for a sound educational base underlying *all* specific skill training.

Second—here I speak of all cooperating agencies of education and government—we must provide far more flexible options for high school graduates to continue on to higher education or to enter the world of work rather than forever sustain the anachronism that a youngster must make his career choice at age 14. This demands that we broaden today's relatively narrow vocational program into something approaching the true career education we would eventually hope to realize. Vocational students need much more than limited specific skills training if they are to go on to post-secondary education, whether at the community college or four-year level. And young people presently drifting in the general education wasteland need realistic exposure to the world of work, as well as to the option of general post-secondary schooling.

Third, we can effect substantial improvement in vocational education within current levels of expenditures by bringing people from business, industry, and organized labor, who know where the career opportunities are going to be and what the real world of work is like, into far closer collaboration with the schools. Eventually, further subsidies or other encouragement to industry to increase cooperative education and work-study could greatly enhance these programs. Efforts should be made by people in educational institutions offering occupational courses to get nearby employers to help in the training. This will not only aid the students but employers as well by providing these cooperating firms a ready supply of skilled workers well prepared for the specific demands of their particular fields. I would add only this caveat: that these work experience arrangements be accepted and operated as genuine educational opportunities, of a laboratory nature, not simply as a source of cheap help for the business and pocket money for the student. Youngsters should be given the opportunity to explore eight, ten, or a dozen occupations before choosing the one pursued in depth, consistent with the individual's ambitions, skills, and interests.

Fourth, we must build at all levels—federal, state, and local—a new leadership and a new commitment to the concept of a career education system. For we require leaders willing to move our schools into more direct and closer relationships with society's problems, opportunities, and its ever-changing needs. I believe these leaders will come primarily from the ranks of organizations such as yours. Not only will the present vocational-technical education leaders be partners in change, but general educators, long dedicated to the old ways, must become new champions of the career program. . . .

Educating for the Real World

SIDNEY P. MARLAND, JR.
U.S. Office of Education

The success of education in the United States can best be measured by the individual fulfillment it brings to the lives of those who are products of our schools and colleges. From that viewpoint, it is evident that we need to substantially improve our performance. We need to particularly improve our ability to teach vocational skills at the high school levels for those not going on to college. And, we need to guide the understanding of those who are going on to higher education so that they will take a degree with some definite purpose in mind, not simply—as is so often the case—for something to do. And for all students, whatever their ultimate destination, we need to provide a solid understanding of our free enterprise system and of the opportunities and obligations that the system holds out to each of us. We have failed to impart either broad understanding or specific skills to tens of thousands of young Americans. Many are as a consequence unemployed or underemployed and obviously can know very little personal fulfillment. They are a reproach—and a continuing challenge—to our capacity to educate.

Bluntly speaking, vocational education has not made it in America for a variety of reasons. Our high schools have not been able to make sure that every young man and woman who receives a diploma is qualified either for immediate employment or further education. American business, individually and through organizations such as the Chamber of Commerce, has repeatedly expressed and demonstrated its faith in education. That faith, I am sorry to say, too often has found us wanting.

A special report on public education in California put out by the Pacific Telephone Company in 1968 is an example of the kind of support the business community is prepared to provide. The report said in part: "No force helping the individual or the nation to grow is stronger than education. If a society is to lead, flourish, and perhaps even survive, its people must grow steadily in knowledge and understanding."

I hope Pacific Telephone is still on our side, though I wouldn't

From "Educating for the Real World," *Business Education Forum*, Vol. 26, No. 2 (November 1971), 3–5. Reprinted with the permission of the National Business Education Association.

Excerpted from an address delivered by the U.S. Commissioner of Education to a national convocation of the National Business Education Association.

blame them if they were a bit discouraged. Recently the president of the company, Jerome Hull, was quoted in the public press to the effect that 4 out of every 10 high school graduates who come his way are inadequately trained in the fundamental skills of reading, writing, and arithmetic. Mr. Hull reports that out of the 300,000 job applicants interviewed each year, almost half "will not meet even our modest basic requirements."

The grave failure of this nation to prepare its young for work is not the fault of the vocational educators, since only about 12 percent of our high school students have traditionally been exposed to some kind of skill-producing training, though that percentage has gone up in the last year due to the larger amount of federal funds being made available to the field.

Alongside this small percentage we must place another statistic of the current educational scene—that fully half of all high school students enroll in college after graduation. Superficially that sounds fine. But too many take this step, I fear, because a pernicious conformism infecting our society forces them to flock to campuses to get credentials many really don't need—or, at least, shouldn't need. Given the inflexible law of supply and demand, the flood of bachelor's degrees has inevitably reduced their value as an entree to a good, professional job primarily because there simply aren't that many jobs in the American economy that require a college education. And we now have a dangerous oversupply in some professional fields—teaching for one, the aerospace industry for another. During this decade, according to the Bureau of Labor Statistics, only 2 of every 10 jobs will require a college degree, leaving the other 8 jobs open to a high school diploma or perhaps some nondegree post-secondary training.

Finally, in addition to the vocational and academic tracks, there is a third group of students, those locked into the ill-conceived, unproductive general curriculum. The general curriculum, for those of you not familiar with it, is a fallacious compromise between the true academic liberal arts and the true vocational offerings. It is made up, as its name suggests, of generalized courses, possessing neither the practicality and reality of vocational courses nor the quality of college-preparatory offerings. Watered down mathematics, nonspecific science, "easier" English—such is the bland diet offered in the name of the general curriculum—not much to chew on, not much to swallow.

We normally think of discrimination as an illegal separating-out process based upon racial and ethnic considerations. I regard the general curriculum as just as discriminatory and just as outrageous.

Students in this track have little likelihood of attending college where their immaturity, confusion, and indecision about a career can be masked for a few more years. And, given the vagueness of their high school preparation, they have no prospects for a decent job when—and if—they graduate. The "if" is a large one. About 750,000 youngsters drop out before graduating from high school each year, most of them from the general curriculum. Nearly all of our youthful unemployed—those between the ages of 16 and 23—are victims of this shame. America, richest of all nations, has the additional crude distinction of the highest youth unemployment rate in the world, a frightening amount of it concentrated among the minorities and urban poor.

Career education would provide the training these students require for successful employment, and it would give them the education they need to bring personal fulfillment into their lives. It would teach reading, writing, and arithmetic as the fundamental skills. It would at the same time stress the ability to think, decide, and judge—the "survival skills." While career education will necessarily and properly embrace many of the vocational-technical education's skill-producing activities, it will also reach a large percentage of students presently unexposed to the usual vocational offerings.

Career education, in sum, would reflect a far broader understanding of the purpose of education in today's highly sophisticated, technical, change-oriented society—the need not only to fit a person to function efficiently but to make him aware of why he is doing what he is doing, and to bring relevance to our classrooms for many who, with reason, now find them irrelevant.

It is no longer enough for a man or woman to know only that there is a button to be pushed, or a bolt to be tightened, or a needle to be threaded. To maintain our democratic and technological equilibrium, it seems to me that every American must be aware of the full ramifications of his work in both the physical and social environment. He must share with the rest of our society a workable set of human values against which progress is a personal sense and community sense can be measured. He must be able to evaluate and use new developments. In short, he must be educated, not just trained.

Because I am so convinced of the urgency of this matter, the Office of Education research staff is giving major emphasis to the design of a workable career education system that can be tested at a number of federally financed pilot installations and, when satisfactorily developed, offered to the entire country. We have begun to develop three model programs—one for use in schools, a second to be generated within the business community, and a third to take place in the home. These models represent the first attempt to devise a career education system for virtually all Americans from which the learner spins off at any level of maturity, whether as an auto mechanic or a physician, at the level of growth he chooses.

The school-based model is oriented directly toward the school setting from kindergarten through junior college. Its basic objective will be to guide each student either to a job at the completion of high school or to further formal education.

The home-community model is designed to reach and teach individuals, especially adults, with little formal schooling or with limited skills that hold them back from job opportunities or advancement. We believe occupational training of this sort can be effectively transmitted by television in emulation of the highly successful *Sesame Street* preschoolers' program, beaming directly to home television sets information on such matters as career options and job conditions, followed by access to cassette video tapes for home learning, and procedures for reentry into systematic skill learning.

The third of the three career education plans is the employer-based model. This is the most radically new of the three plans in that it proposes establishment of an alternative education system, separate for all practical purposes from the public schools, enrolling students on a completely voluntary basis, and supported by the public school system by contract.

The model system would be created, developed, operated, and supervised primarily by an organized group, or consortium, within the community. Groups of this kind are to be found in a number of American cities where businessmen have turned the talents and expertise of their corporations to the needs of the schools. The idea is to systematize and greatly expand such cooperative effort between business and education. Though typical existing arrangements are small and involve only a handful of local businessmen and educators, they indicate a pattern of mutual concern that can be applied nationally.

In December of 1968, I chaired a meeting of schoolmen and businessmen called for the purpose of exploring the further development of their relationship. Superintendents and school board members talked with executives of many of the nation's largest corporations. Some from the very same cities met at that conference for the first time.

Participants repeatedly expressed the need for a strong new partnership in education between schools and industry. The question was how to bring that partnership about. How can school and business leaders gain ready access to each other? If these powerful institutions are to make common cause after a long history of independent and dissimilar operations, how are they to agree on common goals?

The answers to these questions may be contained in the employer-based career education model. As we now conceive of it—recognizing that our ideas may be significantly changed as time goes by—we think that enrollees would be in the 13-to-18 age group and mainly of two types—those rejected by the traditional classroom and those who themselves reject the traditional classroom. This latter type, as you recognize, is increasingly common. The younger generation feels free to express a dissatisfaction that in the past was more often felt than expressed.

Our present concept is that the learning program would contain three basic elements. The first would be a common or core program centered around the academic fundamentals and aimed at achieving the level of knowledge demanded for satisfactory employment in the business concern sponsoring the program and suitable to the needs of comparable corporations in the technological employment market. The second element would be an elective program offering a range of studies to complement the core program. I'm talking about a learning environment of computer programing, creative writing, business management, laboratory techniques, manufacturing skills, production standards—instruction that addresses not only career-related and college-related interests but also provides skills and knowledge needed for living a rewarding life in the real world of work.

The third element would be the learning program's most critical component—a series of diversified work experiences specifically designed to give the student a taste of a number of possible careers, the live options that are open to him. For example, a student might be assigned to work in the parts department of an automobile dealership where he would use parts catalogs, handle inventory sheets, and deal with real records, reports, purchase orders, and the like.

Exposure to an actual working environment would involve the students in relevant learning—give them an opportunity to view that world in terms of their own needs and aspirations and challenge them to put their interests and abilities to practical test. Far from providing such down-to-earth experience, the typical school shuts the child into an artificial world far removed from the pressures and expectations of adulthood.

I must stress that this model program is in an exploratory stage. We are certain only that something needs to be done to correct the failure of schools to prepare many students for useful careers, and with the cooperation of the business community, the models now being designed in the Office of Education appear to have a decent promise of eventual accomplishment. . . . Actual operation of each project will very likely be delegated by the consortium to a firm of professional managers working in cooperation with the local school system. A close relationship with school authorities will obviously be essential to insure that the academic components of the program meet state legal requirements and to guarantee that graduates of the system receive certification of high school equivalency.

Many questions must be answered before we invite inquiries from communities that may be interested in obtaining planning funds from the Office of Education in order to design a projected employer-based system. We will within the coming year, however, have a fairly good idea of what such a system should accomplish. In designing our model, we are looking for the ideas of men and women who are intimately familiar with the conditions at the local level to tell us how the program might most effectively be operated. We do not see this as something for industry to do without compensation. It would be a large new social arm of industry as a government partner.

Career education is the goal. It remains for all of us who are concerned with the employability of America's student population as businessmen and educators to discover the new ways to meet tomorrow's needs not only of industry but also of the many young people who are unsuited to the schools as they exist.

Rationale for Career Education

RUPERT N. EVANS
University of Illinois-Urbana

In an interdependent technological society, the development of competence to produce a fair share of commodities and services is a major objective of any realistic educational system. So is the development of ability to earn income. Competence to pursue civilized leisure and to fulfill the general obligations of responsible citizenship are equally important and closely interrelated objectives.

Emerging concepts of "career education" can be viewed as one basic part of the process by which an educational system pursues all of those objectives. Clearly, work and the products of work help make life satisfactory. Such work, in itself, can be psychologically rewarding. Useful work can also help people fulfill a major portion of their civil obligations. Income derived from work can enlarge opportunities for individuals and their families to enjoy leisure. Adequate income also enhances individual self-respect and provides opportunities to consume fair shares of the commodities and services produced by fellow citizens.

For these reasons, career education has the potential for becom-

From "Rationale for Career Education," *NASSP Bulletin*, Vol. **57**, No. 371 (March 1973), 52–61. © 1973 by the National Association of Secondary School Principals. Reprinted with permission.

ing more than the catchword of the latest Commissioner of Education. In other places [e.g., Hoyt, Evans, Mackin, and Mangum, *Career Education: What It Is and How To Do It* (Salt Lake City: Olympus Publishing Company, 1972)] it has been pointed out that each of the components of career education exists in some form in the schools today. They need to be brought together into a coherent whole, extending from early childhood education, through post-secondary education of many types, to education for retirement.

In order to form a coherent whole that is clearly related to other aspects of education, career education needs a rationale. This rationale is beginning to take shape, through speeches, books, articles, and conversation among concerned educators and other citizens. This article is an attempt to add to the development of such a rationale by examining four of its related parts: (1) need for practice in career decision making, (2) motivation for learning the material in the school curriculum, (3) the importance of work to society, and (4) the need for preparation for work.

PRACTICE IN CAREER DECISION-MAKING

Much of the current school program actually discourages decision making by students. Each year of school is designed to prepare for the next, the curriculum is largely predetermined, and the only real decision in school is the decision of whether to meet the school's expectations. Even here, the full force of society is marshaled to force compliance.

Most youth make tentative occupational choices several times before they enter high school. If a child of age seven or 17 announces that he wants to be a lawyer or a truck driver, we may be reasonably sure of three things: (a) this tentative decision is made on the basis of inadequate knowledge of his own characteristics and of the demands of the job; (b) the school has done little to provide either type of knowledge; and (c) the school will say, in effect, "You are too young to concern yourself with such things. They should be decided later."

Every college has graduates who are about to complete the baccalaureate serenely confident that a decision about the type of work to be sought or any other important decision can be postponed still longer. This continual deferral of decision making is not true of all other cultures and need not be true of this one. Avoidance of decisions can be taught as can ability to make decisions.

The recent literature on career development makes it clear that ability to make adequate decisions in this field is learned behavior. The term "occupational choice" is no longer favored, because it seems to imply a one-time irreversible decision. Careers are built through a series of experiences, which affect sequences of decisions, most of which are revocable, occurring throughout life. Obviously these decisions can be planned; they can occur by chance, or some combination of planning and chance can be involved. Most of the research in career development suggests that most careers in our society follow one of the latter two patterns. This type of research is descriptive, and concentrates on describing what types of careers are actually followed by people who have different types of careers.

It is not enough, however, to be able to describe typical patterns of careers which exist today. By any standard, many careers are unsatisfactory to the individual, and many careers contribute little to the goals of society. Such careers are not the goal of career education. Rather, the goal is the development of *ideal* career.

From the standpoint of the individual, an ideal career may be defined as a succession of work experiences, each of which is personally more satisfying than the one which precedes it. Such an ideal career is much more likely to be reached if it has a firm base in career education; if the student, whether youth or adult, learns that satisfactions are built on more than immediate earnings; if the student learns more and more about his or her interests and capabilities in relationship to the needs of society, and if he or she is taught that there are preferred ways of securing and evaluating jobs.

Some educators seem to have an almost irrational fear of teaching decision making in relationship to work. They seem to feel that such instruction will lead to early, irrevocable occupational decisions which will minimize future student options. This attitude seems a bit like that of the parent who does not allow a youth to have dates until reaching the age of 21. The intention is to keep the youth's options open; the effect is often the opposite—a liaison with the first person available after the bars are let down.

Career choice involves some of the most important decisions of a person's life. It does much to determine his standard of living and, even more importantly, his style of life and much of his happiness. A decision as important as this should not be left to chance or have no base in education. Adequate career development demands a series of choices, extending over a period of time, and education has a vital role to play in facilitating these decisions and enabling them to be made on a more rational basis.

MOTIVATION FOR LEARNING WHAT THE SCHOOL TEACHES

The series of tentative occupational choices which students typically make can be used to provide motivation for learning much of what the school has to teach. For some students, there is too little motivation to learn in school. The standard motivational ploys used in the school are "Learn it! You'll like it!" or Learn it! It's good for you!" These motivations suffice for some of the pupils most of the time, but not for all of the pupils all of the time. One way to build intrinsic motivation is to show ways in which the material to be learned is relevant to the needs of society. It is possible that young people today are more concerned about service to others than any previous generation in our society. Career education provides a means for demonstrating the social relevance of most school learnings by showing their relationships to socially relevant careers and, indeed, to the continued existence of society.

Perhaps an even more important motivator is provided by showing the ways in which material taught and competencies developed in the school are relevant to the individual goals already held by the student. The tentative occupational choices made by most students provide a natural vehicle for demonstrating relevance. Most school subjects can contribute something to success in each occupational field. All school subjects can contribute a great deal to success in some occupational fields. If the student can be shown how the subject is relevant to his or her personal interests, motivation to learn is enhanced.

There are two common, but contradictory, objectives to using student occupational choice as a motivational force for school learning: (a) the choice made by the student is almost certain to be changed and, therefore, does not provide a stable base for motivation; (b) the school, by using the student's choice of occupation as a motivating factor, is locking the student in and decreasing his or her options. The first of these objections assumes that stability is desirable, while the second assumes that it is not.

Career development involves a series of tentative occupational explorations, each of which appears to the individual at the time to be highly important and worthy of further study. Whether the occupational choice will be the same in a month, a year, or 10 years is not important from a motivational standpoint. In order to learn to read or write, one must read or write about something. Too often the teacher wants each student to read or write about the same things, but learning would certainly be enhanced if each student reads or writes about those things in which he or she is interested. If that interest changes next month, the student will still retain the basic skills learned in the process. It is important to design instruction so that reading and writing (and other school subjects) make sense while they are being learned. By capitalizing on tentative early vocational choice an additional factor can be provided.

It is also important, however, to note some of the by-products of such learning. It is no minor accomplishment to learn enough about an occupation and about oneself to be able to decide whether or not to continue in that field of interest. Neither is it a small matter to be able to come to a decision, rather than postponing it. Nor is it inconsequential to be able to research a topic and come to a conclusion.

All of this assumes, of course, that the teacher knows enough about the applications of his subject to be able to be of some assistance to a learner, and that the teacher is willing to allow students to pursue different interests while still learning common subject matter.

THE IMPORTANCE OF WORK TO SOCIETY

It has always been true that no society can exist without work. Any one individual may elect not to work, but work has to be performed to furnish food, shelter, and other necessities of life for the individual and to enable society to move toward the achievement of its goals. Throughout history, there have been predictions of a society in which no one will have to work because slaves or machines will take over. Such predictions overlook the work needed to secure and subjugate slaves, and to build and maintain machines and to supply energy to them. They also overlook the psychic effects of dependency on human or non-human slaves. Work, by some, if not by all, will continue to be one of life's necessities, and for many people it will remain one of life's rewards, because it provides self-fulfillment and another good reason for existence.

In recent years, however, the nature of work has changed. One of the most important changes has been that unskilled jobs have decreased sharply in number while skilled and professional jobs have become far more complicated. At the same time the number of youth has increased markedly. This has had the effect of sharply increasing youth unemployment. (In the 1930's youth unemployment was one and one-half times as high as general unemployment. For forty years it has increased steadily, and now it is more than three times as high). Youth who have had vocational education (a part of career education) have unemployment rates only equal those of the general population.

Unemployment rates do not tell the whole story, however. In order to be unemployed, one has to be looking for paid work. An increasing proportion of youth are not looking for work, and hence are not counted among the unemployed. Some of these people have looked for work, could not find it because they had no saleable skills, and stopped looking. The part of career education that develops saleable skills obviously could have helped them. An even more basic problem is developing, however. There is a youth subculture which rejects work, largely because its members do not understand the contributions of work to society and to individual well-being in more than a monetary sense.

It is a well-known fact that attitudes are first shaped early in life, and that attitudes toward work are formed as are other attitudes. For example, first-graders have clear attitudes as to which occupations are desirable for men and which for women, and these attitudes often do not change between the first and sixth grades. These findings suggest that the part of career education that has to do with attitudes toward work (e.g., the dignity of all productive work) needs to start in early childhood. Moreover, these findings suggest that the present elementary school program is having little effect on changing attitudes toward work.

PREPARATION FOR WORK

When the concept of career education began to take form, there was considerable confusion over the role of preparation for work in such an educational plan. Some vocational educators have assumed that specific preparation for work constitutes nearly the whole of career education. Contrariwise, some general educators appear to have assumed that when career education is implemented fully, vocational education will become passé and that preparation for work will no longer be the responsibility of the schools. Neither position seems defensible.

The existing situation is that the formal education structure provides extensive preparation for work in certain occupations and little or none in most occupations. Society provides a great deal of moral and financial support for university graduate schools. Each program in these schools has as a central focus the preparation of people for work. Graduate school is the capstone of education for vocations in many of the academic and professional disciplines. Recently there has been some concern that graduate schools may be turning out more workers than the labor market can absorb, but there has been no controversy over whether or not this type of vocational training is a proper role for publicly supported educational programs. We recognize that we need those who will push the frontiers in the liberal arts, sciences, and professions. We feel that formal preparation for these occupations is desirable for society and for the individual being educated.

Similarly, a high proportion of students in four-year colleges are engaged in programs which prepare them for work as journalists, teachers, nurses, engineers, farm managers, etc. For all of these students there is substantial tax support. (In "public" schools this support is more visible; but fellowships, tax exemptions, buildings, materials, and services for which the public pays are vital to private schools as well.)

Far fewer opportunities are available for preparation for work in occupations requiring less than a four-year college degree for entrance. Although only 20 percent of jobs require the baccalaureate, more than half of high school students are preparing for college work, and only 25 percent of high school students receive preparation through vocational education for the remaining 80 percent of the jobs. Some of this vocational education is of very high quality, but some of it is obsolete or inefficient. Virtually none of it is available to students who choose to drop out of school at age 16 or whenever there is an alternative. Clearly, vocational education in high schools and community colleges is a vital ingredient in career education, and must be expanded in scope so that every student who needs it and wants it can have access to high quality vocational education in the field for which he or she wishes to prepare.

The remainder of the labor force is trained in quite different ways, each of which may have disadvantages for the trainee:

a. For certain jobs in the largest firms, the company itself conducts the training, and passes the costs on to the consumer. With the exception of apprenticeship, which graduates less than one percent of the annual additions to the labor force, the content and extent of the training is controlled by the company. Sometimes the options of the trainees are enhanced, but this is not the goal of the training.

b. Similar comments may be made about military training, except that the taxpayer foots the bill. There are relatively few civilian jobs needing the skills of a thoroughly trained infantryman. In technical fields, if the re-enlistment rate drops because too many trained personnel find jobs in the civilian economy, training courses have been redesigned to decrease trainee options outside the military.

c. Proprietary schools train sizable proportions of workers in a few fields and a few workers in each of many fields. Quality of training varies greatly from one school to another, and cost is a bar to certain students who most need help.

d. All jobs require skills related to finding employment and working with others, but some jobs require little or no specific preparation. The proportion of such jobs has decreased enormously as technology has eliminated the need for unskilled and semi-skilled workers whose jobs can be performed efficiently by machines.

A portion of every job is learned at the work place, through trial and error, with the consumer eventually paying the bill, both in money and in frustration. In the school, specific preparation for work can be justified only if the instruction there is more efficient *or* if student options are increased, relative to those provided by other training methods.

Preparation for work, both in the school and on the job, is a vital part of career education. If it is not available in sufficient quantity, or if it is designed in ways which fail to increase student options, of if it is restricted only to certain prestigious occupations, many students will suffer. Lower class students suffer the most because schools are concerned with occupations typically entered by middle class students and ignore the occupations usually staffed by persons of low socioeconomic status. To add insult to injury, our middle class society then proceeds to convince lower class students that this type of occupational discrimination is good for everyone.

The need for preparation for a broad range of occupations does not stop with entry into employment. People change jobs, and jobs change in ways which require additional knowledge. Each change requires additional awareness, exploration, and preparation, and hence career education. Society has every reason to facilitate these adjustments to work change, and career education offers an effective vehicle for this facilitation.

SUMMARY

A rationale is a reason for existence. Before career education can be fully accepted, it needs such a reason for existence. A rationale is also an examination of underlying principles. Such an examination is needed in order for career education to develop parts which are complementary, rather than antagonistic.

This paper has suggested that many, if not most, students need practice in decision making and added motivation for learning the material in the school curriculum. It suggests that as presently constituted, schools often encourage students not to make even tentative career decisions, and rarely teach decision making. It suggests that while some students are motivated to learn because the school says they should learn, other students need to see the social and individual relevance of material in order to learn it efficiently. Career education should and can be designed deliberately to minimize these deficiencies.

Further, this paper has suggested that not only is work important to society, but also that a major goal of education should be to teach the dimensions of the importance of work to all students. Career education provides a natural vehicle for this instruction and for formation of an individual work ethic that is grounded on more than hedonism.

Finally, it is noted that our society requires that most individuals be prepared for work. We have organized our schools so that they provide preparation for occupations which typically are occupied by the middle and upper class. The great majority of occupations, especially those performed by the lower socio-economic class, are virtually unmentioned in the school. Specific preparation for careers which emphasize these latter occupations is turned over to employers and to proprietary schools, where those least able to pay must pay either in reduced earnings or in substantial fees. Employers and proprietary schools have important roles to play in occupational preparation, but the rationale for career education suggests that the site and method of financing for occupational preparation should be determined on the basis of efficiency of instruction and on maximization of student (rather than instructor) options.

If this rationale is effective, career education programs which are designed with it in mind should be more internally consistent, more nearly geared to increasing student options, more readily accepted by all parts of the community, and more effectively evaluated.

Life Career Development: An Educational Investment

EARL J. MOORE
NORMAN C. GYSBERS
University of Missouri-Columbia

Educators are faced with an investment problem. It is similar in many ways to a typical financial investment problem; the return on a previous investment has dwindled and a new investment possibility has some risks. Life career development is the new educational investment possibility and content-centered learning is the previous investment.

CONTENT-CENTERED INVESTMENT

Content-centered learning is the traditional educational methodology used most frequently in education today. It emphasizes the content that individuals are expected to learn.

> In this view of education and child training, mastery of content, whether it be English, mathematics, social manner, or religion, be-

This paper was prepared specifically for inclusion in this volume.

comes the standard or criterion by which development is defined and measured. . . . One of the central aims of formal education, from this viewpoint, is to increase the amount of knowledge acquired and to raise the level of performance achieved in whatever the particular content or "subject" area may be.[1]

Education has a heavy investment in the teaching of content and it was made with good cause. Content learning was justified "in terms of its social utility, that is, in terms of its benefits to society as a whole."[2] At one time in our country's growth and development, we needed this type of education. Coleman noted that at the turn of the century, our educational resources were placed in a system that provided people with vicarious experience and abstract knowledge about the greater world. It was the school's responsibility to furnish content. The teacher acted as a storehouse of information.[3] Coleman described this process as the "pitcher principle." The teacher was seen as a pitcher pouring the milk of knowledge into students who at examination time, poured back the knowledge into the pitcher.[4] Rewards were given for outstanding performance in the abstracting skills. Reading particularly was valued highly.

Unfortunately, what once seemed to be a realistic approach to education, no longer seems as valid today. Individual needs and societal conditions have changed substantially since those early years and yet most educational practices are still rooted firmly in past conditions. The consequences of this are many. Children who cannot learn abstract skills such as reading soon understand that they are not valued. Glasser contends that these children are subtly informed they are failures.[5] If children do not read well, they are grouped and remediated. They quickly get the message that they are not living up to expectations. Under the press to reach grade level in reading immediately, many other features of their competence and worthwhileness are forgotten. Reading competence is extremely important as are the other basic skills, but they should be seen as facilitators of feelings of self worth and success in children, not as ends in themselves.

[1] Harold M. Schroder, Marvin Karlins and Jacqueline O. Phares, *Education for Freedom* (New York: John Wiley and Sons, Inc., 1973), p. 10.

[2] Dunn, James A. et al., *Career Education: A Curriculum Design and Instructional Objectives Catalog* (Palo Alto: American Institutes for Research, 1973), p. 4.

[3] James S. Coleman, "Education in Modern Society," in N. Gysbers, H. Drier, and E. Moore (eds.), *Career Guidance: Practice and Perspectives* (Charles A. Jones Publishing Company, 1973).

[4] James S. Coleman, *Report of a National Seminar: Toward a More Relevant Curriculum* (Dayton, Ohio: IDEA, Inc., Far Hills Branch, 1971).

[5] William Glasser, *Schools Without Failure* (New York: Harper and Row Publishers, 1969).

Content Set in Concrete

The content-centered investment forced teachers into an omnipotent role, since they were the repository of knowledge that was to be imparted to students.[6] Students were viewed as objects to be brought up to grade level in basic content areas by the end of the school year. The classroom was designed with the teacher at the front of the room to control the delivery of content. The efficiency of transmitting the breadth and depth of content became the concern of administration. Administrators modeled themselves after their industrial counterparts who took pride in the production and efficiency of their operations. Lesson plans were used to insure systematic and efficient coverage of subject matter. Teachers were encouraged to specialize in content areas and were organized into departments to build content expertise.

Even new innovations and educational changes such as programmed learning and closed-circuit TV were merely refinements of the content-centered approach. Libraries and media centers became central features of content-centered schools. Adjustment specialists such as reading diagnosticians and learning disability consultants focused on the abstracting skills. Professional education groups were organized around content areas and professional conferences emphasized special methods to deliver content-based knowledge and skills. The grading and standardized testing system also was designed to assess the amount of knowledge acquired in a content area.

College Preparatory Pride

As the public schools continued to invest more resources in content-centered learning, the college preparatory curriculum flourished and was expanded. Higher education specialists encouraged intensified programs in their respective content areas. Public schools were rewarded for their college preparatory program. Administrators pridefully reported the percentages attending college, master teachers usually taught the college preparatory classes, and counselors, with the mandate of NDEA of 1958, were engrossed in identifying the academically talented and providing information about colleges and universities. Grade point average calculation, scholarship application completion and the writing of personal recommendations for college admissions became administrative priorities.

Counselors built their content-centered expertise around standardized testing and occupational and educational information. In some instances, counselors participated in the efficiency operation of

---

[6] Harold M. Schroder, Marvin Karlins, and Jacqueline O. Phares, *Education for Freedom* (New York: John Wiley and Sons, Inc., 1973).

the school as an extension of the principal's needs. Often the counselor would serve as a buffer between the school and community. Personal-social counseling usually meant adjusting the student to the content-centered school system.

The school curriculum placed emphasis on intellectual development. College attendance figures and achievement test profiles were used to furnish evidence of intellectual development. Students became scholars—at least the good ones did. Youth became abstract rich and action poor.[7]

Paying the Consequences

Although there is still some return from the content investment, the price paid has been heavy. Some students have become alienated and are involved in power struggles with parents and teachers. Others complain of the dehumanizing effects of school and the need for programs that foster identity and stress uniqueness.[8] Observers note rigidity and noncreativeness in graduates. A content-centered school tends to create a passive, dependent student who may be apathetic, irresponsible, or rebellious.[9]

In the past, the return on the content investment has been great enough to overshadow such consequences as increased dropout rate and delinquency, particularly since the students involved in such activities were viewed as misfits who could not make it in school anyway. Recently, however, there has been discontent expressed by content capable students who have become disenchanted with their schooling. The achieving student's involvement in the drug scene, subsequent value collisions with teachers and parents, and a realization that there seems to be less economic return from college training than expected has created considerable uneasiness in the school and community.

Unfortunately, however, as educators we continue to invest heavily in the content-centered approach to education. Our answer seems to be that what is wrong can best be corrected by intensifying the content investment. As a result, we may be doing a better job delivering content but could it be that we are doing the wrong job? Could it be that we have forgotten about the need to make the educational system more responsible, sensitive and functional in helping students resolve their needs in the context of society's demand? If this is so, then what may be needed is a broader conception of the

[7] James S. Coleman, "Education in Modern Society," in N. Gysbers, H. Drier, and E. Moore (eds.), *Career Guidance: Practice and Perspectives* (Worthington, Ohio: Charles A. Jones Publishing Company, 1973).

[8] Carl Rogers, *Freedom to Learn* (Columbus, Ohio: Charles E. Merrill, 1970).

[9] Earl J. Moore and Norman C. Gysbers, "Career Development: A New Focus," *Educational Leadership*, December 1972.

educational process which can serve as an organizer for all of the emerging and expanding purposes and goals of education.

LIFE CAREER DEVELOPMENT INVESTMENT

What kind of conception of the educational process can be expected from a life career development investment? What might be the outcomes? Gysbers and Moore have conceptualized the Career Conscious Individual Model for Education [10] as an outcome oriented model designed to create career consciousness in all individuals at all educational levels, to help them develop necessary life competencies, attitudes and values, to assist them in visualizing possible life career roles and to analyze and relate these roles to their present situations.

> Included within the idea of consciousness is a person's background, education, politics, insight, values, emotions, and philosophy, but consciousness is more than these or even the sum of them. It is the whole man; his "head"; his way of life. It is that by which he creates his own life and thus creates the society in which he lives.[11]

The Career Conscious Individual

The Career Conscious Individual Model is based upon life career development concepts and principles. The word life indicates that the focus is on total persons, on all aspects of their growth and development over the life span. The word career identifies and relates the many settings in which people find themselves—home, school, occupation, community; the roles which they play—student, worker, consumer, citizen, parent; and the events which may occur in their lifetime—entry job, marriage, retirement. The word development is used to show that people are continually changing over their

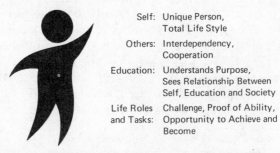

Self:	Unique Person, Total Life Style
Others:	Interdependency, Cooperation
Education:	Understands Purpose, Sees Relationship Between Self, Education and Society
Life Roles and Tasks:	Challenge, Proof of Ability, Opportunity to Achieve and Become

FIGURE 1. The Career Conscious Individual

[10] Ibid.
[11] Charles Reich, *The Greening of America* (New York: Random House, Inc., 1970).

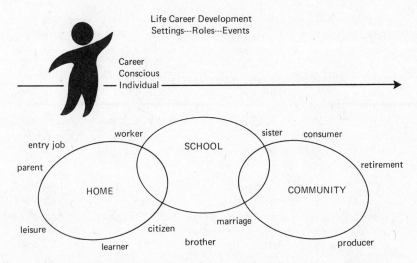

FIGURE 2. Life Career Development Settings—Roles—Events

lifetime. We are always in the process of becoming. When used in sequence, the words life career development bring these separate meanings together in sequence. Taken collectively, they describe whole persons—unique persons with their own life style. Life career development is defined as self development over the life span through the integration of all the roles, settings and events of a person's total life.

Life Career Centered Education

Life career development as a perspective on human growth and development can serve as the basis for a new educational investment. The life career development focus on human development has the potential to restructure the processes and activities of education, modify the values and attitudes of educators and maximize the opportunities for individual involvement and responsibility. Life career development can become the lens through which educators view and understand individuals. Life career development concepts can become the organizer for the total curriculum.[12] When this is done, education becomes life career centered and has investment potential.

The life career development perspective puts a premium on individuals as persons—on personalizing education to make it meaningful. Dunn et al. stress this point in their discussion and definition of career education.

---

[12] Earl J. Moore and Norman C. Gysbers, "Career Development: A New Focus," *Educational Leadership,* December 1972.

The increasing sophistication of education in accommodating individual differences in personal interests, abilities, goals, and ambitions, coupled with a growing social concern for the maintenance of individuality in an increasing dehumanized and technological society, appears to be resulting in a strong pressure for schools to become more concerned with serving the individual. Implicit in this is the assumption that the schools can best serve society by serving the individuals who constitute that society. This places the school in a position markedly different from that which it held a generation or two ago. The school is becoming, in effect, a responsive resource rather than an institutional arbiter of social need. . . .

In brief, career education exists for the benefit of the individual, recognizes the inherent dignity of the individual, attempts to increase the relevance of the curriculum to specific career needs of individuals, and attempts to demonstrate to the individual the relevance of the school curriculum to his goals in life.[13]

Life Career Centered Curriculum

Specifically, what makes up valid life career centered curriculum investments? What are the basic thrusts? A life career centered curriculum does *not* exclude abstract skill development such as reading and mathematics. On the contrary, abstract skill development is placed in perspective and emphasized along with other human development skills. From a curriculum viewpoint, the life career perspective emphasizes the following features.

1. An *authentic curriculum* of basic studies.

Basic knowledges, skills and attributes needed for individuals to deal with their present and future needs in society must be developed based on an understanding of their personal background of experiences and needs. Entwistle suggested that preparation for the present and preparation for the future are equally important for learning to be meaningful to the learner.

> The problem is not therefore one of choosing between academic subjects of a life curriculum, so much as teaching the academic disciplines through concrete exemplar situations drawn from life, whether from contemporary life, life in the past, or life as it may be imagined in the future.[14]

[13] James A. Dunn, Lauri Steel, Judith M. Melnotte, David Gross, John Kroll, and Stephanie Murphy, *Career Education: A Curriculum Design and Instructional Objectives Catalog*, American Institutes for Research, April 1973.

[14] Harold Entwistle, *Child-Centered Education* (London: Methuen and Company, Ltd., 1969), pp. 138–139.

Entwistle also noted that developing the best that is in an individual requires a correlative insistence upon the individual's obligation towards social responsibility; the claims of social education have to be set against the emphasis upon the child as an individual.[15]

2. The *hidden curriculum* of morals and values.

As the purposes of education are being directed increasingly toward personalizing education, attention to the hidden curriculum of morals and values is crucial. Kohlberg focused attention on moral education,[16] Raths and Simon discussed values clarification [17] and Sprinthall and Mosher included morals and values in their discussion of the need for deliberate psychological education.[18] These authors have observed that presently morals, values and the conception of self and others develop in individuals without specific attention in the curriculum. The life career centered focus emphasizes the importance of morals, values and conception of self and others and provides a vehicle to integrate these areas into the total curriculum in a comprehensive and systematic way.

3. The *omitted curriculum* of process skills for living and learning.

There is a need for "facilitating the development of thinking and feeling skills essential to adaptive and productive living in modern society." [19] Specifically, Toffler suggested that education stress learning how to learn, learning to choose and learning how to relate to others.[20] Schroder, Karlins and Phares identified intrinsic motivation, which is based on information processing skills, adaptability to change, and self-determined value judgments, which comprise what others might describe as decision-making skills.[21]

Cole's review of process education examined various processes, programs, and proposals. The processes that were

[15] Ibid.
[16] Lawrence Kohlberg, "Understanding the Hidden Curriculum," *Learning,* December 1972.
[17] Harmin L. Raths and S. Simon, *Values and Teaching* (Columbus, Ohio: Charles E. Merrill, 1966).
[18] Norman A. Sprinthall and R. L. Mosher, "Deliberate Psychological Education," *The Counseling Psychologist,* **2**, 4, 1971.
[19] Henry P. Cole, *Process Education* (Englewood Cliffs, N.J.: Educational Technology Publications, 1972), p. xi.
[20] Alvin Toffler, *Future Shock* (New York: Random House, 1970).
[21] Harold M. Schroder, Marvin Karlins, and Jacqueline O. Phares, *Education for Freedom* (New York: John Wiley and Sons, Inc., 1973).

discussed included productive thinking, inquiry, problem solving, expressive behavior, social interactive behavior, affective and creative behavior.[22] That part of process education dealing with human relationship skills is receiving systematic attention from such authors as Carkhuff,[23] Randolph [24] and Bessell.[25]

THE PROSPECTUS

Since we are all products of the content-centered curriculum, it may be difficult to visualize a life-career centered perspective for education. Nevertheless, the prospectus for investing in life-career centered education has real potential for meeting the educational challenges of today and tomorrow.

1. In life-career centered education there is investment potential for everyone. Life-career centered education is not the property of a vested group. Consumers and professionals can relate equally to the basic concepts. There is common relevance for all.

2. Other movements in education having similar purposes and goals such as process education, values education, open education, individually guided education, confluent education and psychological education can be integrated into the life-career centered education framework.

3. Cultural crisis and problems in living such as drug abuse, human sexuality and human rights can be approached directly and comprehensively without creating curriculum appendages.

4. Linkage to the home and community can be accomplished naturally. A program for continuing and adult education is not only implied but expected.

5. Investing educators can proceed at their own rate. The size of step will depend upon a school district's commitment and each educator can explore on his own or in small groups.

---

[22] Henry P. Cole, *Process Education* (Englewood Cliffs, N.J.: Educational Technology Publications, 1972).

[23] Robert Carkhuff, *Helping and Human Relations* (New York: Holt, Rinehart and Winston, 1969).

[24] Norman Randolph, *Self Enhancing Education* (Santa Clara, Calif.: 1971.) Unpublished monograph.

[25] Harold Bessell, *Methods in Human Development* (El Cajon, California: Human Development Institute, 1970.) Unpublished monograph.

The New Vocationalism

JAMES HITCHCOCK
St. Louis University

Almost every institution in American society has suffered confusion and demoralization in the past decade. Probably none has suffered more than the university, precisely because it is expected to provide enlightenment and leadership, to stay on the path of wisdom when everyone else has strayed. Now the universities have confessed that they no longer see clearly where the lamp of reason is leading, and it is ironic that they have undertaken to prescribe the remaking of society at a point in time when they seem to have no clear notion of their own purpose.

Educational change has been advocated under a rubric which is generally "leftist" or "radical," with no very precise idea of what these terms mean used in such a context. Almost everything which appears to be new, which breaks noticeably with existing patterns, which can in some sense be deemed "relevant," has achieved automatically an aura of desirability.

This can result in some rather bizarre positions, such as a leftist professor arguing against foreign-language requirements on the ground that "all educated foreigners speak English anyway"; a dean urging more personal attention to students in order to weed out potential troublemakers; another administrator advocating a new personalism so that alumni will have pleasant memories of the school and will make larger donations ("they don't remember ideas, just people"), a professor urging "community service" programs because "the signals from the White House are that this is where the money will be."

In each case what is superficially presented as a radical point of view proves on inspection to be reactionary. The mystique of innovation is at present a formidable one, however, and nearly any educational philosophy that diverges from the traditional can expect to gain a following and a measure of credibility.

The key to present educational confusion is the fact that, for all the ridicule that has been heaped upon the concept, there is no longer any pedagogical absolute except relevance. "Relevance," however, is indefinable, since it is whatever the individual perceives as meaningful to himself, and such perceptions are constantly changing.

From "The New Vocationalism," *Change*, Vol. 5, No. 3 (April 1973), 46–50. © 1973 by Educational Change, Inc. Reprinted with permission from Change Magazine, Vol. 5, No. 3.

From the election of John F. Kennedy until the Democratic convention of 1968, relevance tended to be equatable with political awareness. Students were said to be impatient with studies remote from social needs. Traditional disciplines, including the formerly prestigious sciences, began to lose ground to political science and sociology, and practitioners of the older disciplines sometimes attempted to salvage them by demonstrating their political relevance. Initially, ecological studies were perhaps such an attempt on the part of natural scientists, and many humanists took pains to show the recurrence of Marxist themes throughout history, philosophy and the arts.

As political concerns began to wane for various reasons, and as the "soft" counterculture began to replace the "hard" revolutionary ideologies, relevance tended to change its meaning also—from the objective, outward-looking scrutiny of society to the intensely subjective scrutiny of self.

The greatest irony of the educational history of the past decade is the fact that relevance has now turned full circle and is coming to apply precisely to what five years ago almost everyone agreed was fundamentally the wrong function of higher education—"processing students for the System." In short, the newest version of relevance is vocationalism.

When student rebellions first erupted on the campuses, almost all commentators—from philosophers to Sunday-supplement writers—accepted the often shouted student assertion that young people were tired of being forced to spend years in school, during which they were treated like IBM cards, solely in order to fit into an occupational slot marked out by the capitalist-technocratic society. Education, according to the rebels, was supposed to be humanistic and humanizing, divorced from occupational requirements, so that students would have leisure and space to think, experience and criticize.

This view of education, which was consistent with the philosophy of the traditional liberal arts if not always with their practice, still survives, just as do the older notion of the liberal arts and the notions of education for radical political activity and for personal probing. The dominant voices in education, however, now increasingly speak of vocationalism as the necessary way of the future, the path the universities must follow if they wish to make themselves relevant.

It is a point of view articulated, for example, by Joseph P. Cosand, United States Assistant Commissioner of Education (see "Washington," *Change*, June 1972), and it was given strong emphasis in the Newman Report on the reform of higher education, which has attracted much favorable attention in both governmental and educational circles. The need for education to be oriented toward some kind of useful work has been advanced also, in different ways, by educational "radicals" like Michael Miles and traditional humanists like the classicist William Arrowsmith and the medievalist Barnaby Keeney, former head of the National Endowment for the Humanities.

Cosand has argued for an educational system which, from kindergarten to graduate school, concerns itself with career choices and vocational training, so that students can drop out at any point and find themselves with some remarkable skills. He is troubled by the phenomenon of large numbers of students apathetic about future careers (the same students who a few years ago were being praised for their refusal to be "co-opted by the System") and by the universities' failure to train students for jobs which are satisfying and remunerative (the two do not necessarily coincide, of course).

Clearly a man in Cosand's position does not speak merely for himself, and he has also indicated that the Office of Education intends to fund and encourage vocationally oriented education all over the United States. This program means "for one thing . . . the gradual elimination of the 'general' high school curriculum now being taken by about 50 percent of the students." This in turn has important implications for the universities, which will have to accommodate an increasing number of students with specific vocational objectives and which may be required to grant credit for prior nonacademic activity such as employment experience, military service and voulunteer social work.

Since Cosand, whatever his personal political views, is an official of a conservative Republican administration, it is tempting to speculate that neovocationalism, cloaked in a radical rhetoric (". . . cannot remain aloof from these new realities . . . adapt to change . . . learn how to learn . . . develop personally"), is part of a general conservative reaction against the present state of the universities. The new emphasis on vocationalism no doubt builds on the awareness that, in general, students training for a specific career were much less likely to rebel or to become radicalized a few years ago than those in the liberal arts who contemptuously rejected vocationalism as an educational goal. Career orientation, with a realistic prospect for gainful employment at the end, might be an effective way of ensuring a permanent return to tranquillity on the campuses. It would also ensure a greater measure of outside control on the universities, since they would be educating students in accordance with the demands of the market. The conservative bias also reveals itself in the hard economics of the situation. In the postwar years, until about the early 1960s, educators often had to defend the expenditure of money on "useless" kinds of education. The "radical" stance in those years was an affirmation of general humanistic values in education as opposed to vocational purposes. Now, however, the humanities are coming to be seen as a luxury the country cannot any longer afford, whatever their value. If taxpayers, parents and students themselves are going to have to pay more and more for education, they will increasingly demand evidence of measurable economic benefits. In the past, educators justified expenditures for economically unproductive disciplines by making exaggerated claims for the necessity of a highly educated labor force. Recent studies have cast doubt on whether highly educated persons necessarily perform better at most jobs than do high school graduates.

It would, however, be a serious mistake to regard neovocationalism as solely the program of political conservatives. The tendency of recent educational radicals to take student desires as the ultimate criterion of correct pedagogy works to the same end, because by definition one cannot tell a student what is relevant to him. If he finds the promise of a well-paying career the best motivation for education, there is no way short of a revived paternalism that can deter him. The student rebellions of the past few years gave enormous impetus to student rights and the need for universities to be responsive to student desires. If many students now evaluate their educations in hard economic terms, this is just as legitimate as for other students to evaluate theirs in terms of political or personal relevance.

The democratizing of higher education through the admission of more students from minority groups, and the general penetration of higher learning by the white working class through community colleges and state university branches, tends especially to this end. Radicals of the 1960s assumed that the admission to college of large numbers of the disadvantaged would force higher education in the direction of radical political activity, to the point of encouraging exotic and revolutionary programs in black studies, for example. It is now clear, however, that minority students want and need a practical education, either for personal advancement or community leadership. As in the past, students from a disadvantaged background generally prefer educational programs that appear to promise tangible career benefits rather than those emphasizing personal development or knowledge for its own sake.

There are other ways too in which radical attitudes of the past now tend to support conservative educational goals. Many young people whose consciences were aroused in the 1960s are concluding in the 1970s that passion and acute theoretical understanding are less valuable than specific skills—law, medicine, engineering—for dealing with social problems ranging from racism to pollution. If conservative businessmen and the ambitious children of the poor tend to regard the traditional humanities as expensive irrelevancies, many white social activists do also.

The deflation of the counterculture tends to the same end in that the areas of that culture which are proving enduring—viable communes, for example—seem to depend on the acquisition of usable or salable skills. There is a disenchantment with vague dreams and theories and a new respect for professional competence. Many radical young parents would probably not send their children to school, for example, except to learn usable skills. There is a general distrust, on both the Right and the Left, of the mere intellectual who is unable to do anything. Administrators, faculty and students now all abjure the ivory-tower concept of education and speak of the obligation of the universities to address themselves to society's needs. Under this vague exhortation a multitude of both radical and conservative goals are concealed, many of them mutually contradictory.

The resurgence of vocationalism fills the vacuum left by the general loss of self-confidence on the part of the chief practitioners of the traditional humanities and sciences—the professors. James Q. Wilson, the Harvard political scientist, has pointed out how the liberal arts, by encouraging endless questioning and suspension of commitment, tend finally to discredit themselves and even to give rise to antiliberal tendencies. As the humanities were undermined in the late 1960s, what survived of them was almost solely the impulse to question and challenge—not the methods of discipline and scholarship and the attitudes of civility they were supposed to cultivate. The questioning attitude is still strong, but there is a good deal of disillusionment even with it. There is a new desire for certitude among young people, as evidenced by occultism and the religious revival. Some will find certitude in a renewed dedication to career.

Certainly at present humanities and science professors tend as a body to lack the will and the conviction to challenge such a trend, whereas they did challenge it rather effectively fifteen or twenty years ago. There is a widespread conviction in the universities that liberal arts education has failed and needs to make way for something else, whatever that might be. Rather than having failed, however, it is possible that the liberal arts are the victims of their own success. In the 1950s professors railed at students to shake them out of their unquestioning, career-oriented complacency; in the 1960s they reaped the whirlwind. Obviously a generalized humanistic education was not the sole or perhaps even the major cause of student idealism in the past decade, but it was undoubtedly an important contributing factor. An education oriented toward questioning, toward social awareness, toward a concern for great problems, certainly bore significant fruit in the 1960s, even if not all of it was sweet. The "irrelevancy" of the humanities lies in that, having brought students to perceive social problems, they appear able to contribute little to the problems' solution. Their value, however, has always been in the attitudes and habits of mind they create, the spirit they engender, and not in their practical usefulness. It is worth asking what society will be like if, even at the university level, there is a retreat from the ideals of humanistic education.

That there will be such a retreat seems evident, despite the disclaimers of the apostles of vocationalism. The removal of all or most course requirements by many colleges does not, for the most part, enable students to follow imaginative, personally tailored programs of self-development but allows them to pursue rather narrow and often rigid career objectives. At a time when knowledge proliferates geometrically, the colleges are paradoxically reducing the time required to achieve a degree, which inevitably sacrifices "unnecessary" courses unrelated to the student's major interest. As private colleges (and some public colleges) are forced more and more to compete for students, there is a strong temptation to offer programs that impede as little as possible the student's purposeful march toward a closely defined educational goal. Joseph Cosand acknowledges the possibility that the new vocationalism may foster a narrow provincialism. His remedy is a pious hope that the student has "the intention of picking up a broader education later."

There is, however, a good deal to be said on behalf of vocational education, whatever its dangers. It is a dubious procedure to force into the academic mold young people who have little taste for intellectual things, although humanities professors also know that some members of this captive audience are awakened in the process. Many students will in the long run probably be happier and wealthier if they settle on a reasonable career and follow it.

It is especially questionable to continue requiring a general education when the general educators are themselves so confused and demoralized. Innumerable teachers now evidence a deep lack of respect for their chosen disciplines. On some campuses humanities courses have degenerated into vague, purposeless, self-indulgent "happenings" that waste students' time and money and may do great personal harm. Other students are subjected constantly to their teachers' political harangues. By contrast, vocational training appears healthy.

No establishment ever loses its credentials entirely without cause, and the decline of the humanities can have a good effect if it forces professors to make their courses "relevant" in the best sense—by addressing themselves to important and meaningful questions. In their golden era the liberal arts produced the certified expert who, because of his scholarly celebrity, was regarded as having few obligations to his students or his university, and teachers of all ages and degrees of competence whose chief pedagogical ambition was to teach the narrowest possible specialty.

There is now the possibility, however, that not only will students not be required to partake of a general education but that academic pressures will work against it. Students are already turning away from disciplines in which it seems unlikely that they will find teaching posts and are turning to secondary career choices where employment seems possible. Meanwhile the deemphasis on general education reduces the need for teachers still further, thus reinforcing a continuous downward spiral. Vocational programs will be able to set their own requirements, which tend always to increase; and as the three- and even two-year degrees become common, students may simply have no time for general education even if they desire it. A growing trend toward giving credit for work experiences will have the same effect.

Curiously, the United States Constitution might itself become an obstacle to humanistic education. In *Griggs* v. *Duke Power Company* (1971) the Supreme Court ruled unanimously that a company may not require education as a qualification for employment unless it can show the relevance of that education to the particular job. The full implications of this judgment are not yet clear, but presumably it would allow a company to require training in a "useful" discipline like accounting or engineering while possibly excluding any requirements pertaining to general knowledge. Majors in philosophy or English literature might find their degrees stripped of all economic value except for nonexistent teaching jobs.

Advocates of the new vocationalism are no doubt sincere in asserting that it is not their intention that career programs be narrow and philistine, but that they aim for students, through practical disciplinary training, to learn useful skills and also acquire the perspective and motivation to use them for the common good. But the long-term prospects are doubtful. Many professional persons are indifferent to larger social questions, not through moral failure or lack of intelligence but because the time required to learn and maintain their professional abilities prevents them from acquiring a sophisticated awareness of larger issues. Students of law and medicine came to a social commitment some time after it had burgeoned in the liberal arts colleges, and other professions have not come to it yet.

Perhaps unintentionally, the apostles of vocationalism may also intensify class distinctions in higher education. It is unlikely that the most prestigious schools will commit themselves to vocationalism to any significant degree; a general education will continue to be the hallmark of the most privileged students. The greatest demand for vocational training, and the greatest response, is likely to be in the community colleges, the state schools and lesser private schools struggling to survive. There may come to be a division between academic and vocational institutions at the highest level comparable to that which has long existed at the secondary level.

The resurgence of interest in vocationalism coincides with reports of a new conservatism, or at least a new quietism, on the campuses. To the degree that vocationalism proves acceptable to students, it will help to bury yet a little deeper the many myths circulated about "the young" in the 1960s, especially their alleged rejection of the goals of money and success. (This is not to say that vocationalism may not now be tinged with a larger dose of altruism than was formerly the case.) Student interest in vocational education is in large measure stimulated by the poor employment prospects that now face liberal arts graduates, indicating that an indifference to the marketplace was common only so long as students felt that they could find employment if they should ever want it. They no longer possess this assurance.

It is also noteworthy that the "needs of the students"—whether for political relevance, personal exploration or now for marketable skills—have generally been interpreted and propagated in the educational community by older persons, some of whom have had axes to grind (as defenders of the liberal arts also have axes to grind). Since "student opinion" has never been monolithic despite efforts to make it appear so, it is always possible for adult educational crusaders to find students who do indeed support the latest educational nostrums. Despite their proclaimed critical intelligence, the universities are extraordinarily susceptible to sales campaigns—first on behalf of "academic excellence" and "the humanities," then for "revolution," then for the "development of students as persons," now on behalf of jobs.

The abandonment of the liberal arts as the core of higher education has implications far beyond mere pedagogy. The tradition of liberal arts education rested on the assumption that Western culture has a common base, a common tradition that should be accessible to all persons living in the culture, so that communication and a sharing of common values and perceptions are possible. It was considered the individual's necessary starting point in his search for self-definition. Now this assumption is both explicitly and implicitly denied in favor of a radical individualism that sees each person as hopelessly locked within himself, able to articulate only in terms of his own feelings, his own perceptions, his own ambitions and desires.

The frantic search for "community" often masks a deeply rooted self-centeredness. The universities were perhaps the last institutions that kept alive the older ideal of meaningful and civilized discourse founded on a common culture. The educational changes of the past half decade—whether predicated on the individual's need to discover who he is or merely on his need to find a suitable job—proclaim an end to that ideal. On the campus as elsewhere, each person is now left to do his own thing, while the forces of the whole culture touch and mold him in ways he can only dimly understand and scarcely at all control.

Career Education: Program on a White Horse

ANTHONY LADUCA
LAWRENCE J. BARNETT
University of Illinois at the Medical Center, Chicago
Center for Educational Development

Over the past few years, the name *career education* has sent a tremor through the American educational corpus that set its curricular teeth chattering. The federally stimulated vibrations were particularly strong during the presidential election year of 1972. However, the signs and symptoms of withdrawal from the initial career education spasm have been clearly discernible.

But before we discuss its fall from favor, it seems worthwhile to reflect on career education's meteoric rise. Where did the name come from? What gave it its magic? What have been the results of its persistent incantation? Will it pass into the education index graveyard along with such predecessors as Education for Life Adjustment, Gestalt Education, Quality Integrated Education, and so many others? Or, will the slogan have greater durability than either its inventor or its host of aphoristic antecedents?

A MASTER SEMANTIC STROKE

First, let us consider where the slogan came from. Until 1970 when Sidney P. Marland became the nominee of the executive branch for U.S. Commissioner of Education, the term "career education" was not part of the lexicon of such fields as vocational guidance, vocational and technical education, industrial arts education, distributive education, or business education. The most popular and durable terminology then found in the literature of these groups, at the same

From "Career Education: Program on a White Horse," *New York University Education Quarterly*, Vol. V, No. 3 (Spring 1974), 6–12. © 1974 by New York University. Reprinted with permission of the publisher and authors.

level of abstraction as career education, were such rubrics as "education for the world of work" and "occupational education." In search of wider acceptance for their fields, many professionals had adopted those terms during the sixties. They were thought to evoke fewer aversive middle-class reactions than perhaps more candid and concrete labels such as "job training" or "trade and industrial" education. Yet even this new terminology did not appear to contribute appreciably to the growth of the population of high school youth involved in vocational pursuits. This population was variously estimated during the sixties as 7 to 10 percent, not including pupils in industrial arts classes. Of course, the reasons for the relatively small numbers of pupils involved in vocational courses are much more complex than can be explained by mere nomenclature. The American middle class (which may in a functional definition include those who hold and are motivated by the values of that class) are well known as aspiring to ever higher social and economic status. They are predictably less than pleased at the prospect of their progeny learning a trade. To do so would be to risk being declassed and would negatively reflect on their adequacy as parents. For different reasons such groups as blacks, Chicanos, Puerto Ricans, and other minorities have also rejected vocational education. Principally, these groups have viewed such educational pursuits as yet another majority strategy to keep them from access to the payoff—power positions in a free enterprise society. The professions, business, and politics have been accurately perceived by minorities as more direct avenues to those vantage points.

Thus, the Commissioner's appeal resided not so much in his polemic against America's sorting system of vocational, academic, and so-called general education tracks, but in his selection of the term "career" and its linkage with education. The derivation of the word *career* is connected to motion. Such motion in contemporary usage is understood as upward progression, generally through such socially esteemed occupational areas as medicine, the law, science, business, and the performing and plastic arts. One does not ordinarily refer to one's "career" as a hod carrier, garbage collector, lathe operator, garage mechanic, or dishwasher. That is, unless one has used those pursuits as springboards to ownership or management of the construction company, waste disposal corporation, machine tool business, automotive dealership, or restaurant chain. With those job status conditions as end states, the romance and myths of the work ethic coupled with the effects of natural and nurtured potential are secure.

Dr. Marland then, with a master semantic stroke, accomplished virtually overnight what vocational educators had failed to do in over fifty-three years of effort. This selection and dissemination of the words "career education" resulted in widespread and warm reception of the vocationally vectored, yet unspecified term by large segments of the private and public sectors of the American body politic.

BANDWAGON

Other factors also influenced the rise of the previously unknown career education shibboleth. As later revealed in events associated with the Watergate and the Ellsberg burglary episodes, a high-intensity social and political paranoia appears to have been pervasive among top echelon administration figures. In the light of these recent revelations, we believe that many actions of the administration during that period were motivated by fear and reinforced by arrogance. The president's fears about the condition of the nation, including the educational system, were displayed in his declarations about the revival of the "work ethic"; his vice president's unrelenting attacks on dissidents; the frightening local violence with which he responded to demonstrations against U.S. violence abroad; and his threats and actions against institutions of higher education, which he seemed to perceive as the locus of indigenous threats to national security. We conclude that these events were instrumental in developing an executive mind-set for a crash educational reform strategy. The central goal of such reform would be the socialization of children and youth in ways that would make them more likely to run with, rather than against, the conservative corporate stream. At the least, it would neutralize them.

Additional segments of the population from school administrators and policy makers, to parents of fiteen-year-old runaways, and citizens dismayed by the apparently thoroughgoing irreverence of youth comprised, in many instances, a receptive constituency for the anchorage in old verities offered by Dr. Marland:

> How absurd to suggest that general knowledge for its own sake is somehow superior to *useful* knowledge. "Pedants sneer at an education that is useful," Alfred North Whitehead observed. "But if education is not useful," he went on to ask, "what is it?" The answer, of course, is that it is nothing. All education is career education, or should be. And all our efforts as educators must be bent on preparing students either to become properly, usefully employed immediately upon graduation from high school or to go on to further formal education.[1]

---

[1] Sidney P. Marland, Jr., "Career Education Now." Address given at the 1971 Convention of the National Association of Secondary School Principals, Houston, Tex., January 23, 1971. In Keith Goldhammer and Robert E. Taylor, eds., *Career Education: Perspective and Promise*, Columbus, Ohio: Merrill, 1972, p. 35.

In his State of the Union Message to Congress on January 20, 1972, President Nixon gave special and unusual emphasis to the emerging career education program, advising Congress that

> Career education is another area of major new emphasis, an emphasis which grows out of my belief that our schools should be doing more to build self-reliance and self-sufficiency. . . . Too many of our students from all income groups have been "turning off." . . . The present [educational] approach serves the best interests of neither our students nor our society. We need a new approach and I believe the best new approach is to strengthen career education. . . . To help spark this venture I will propose an intensified federal effort to develop model programs which apply and test the best ideas in this field.[2]

Meanwhile, in the U.S. Office of Education (SUOE) the word was out that programs of career education would have to be put in proper geopolitical place before the upcoming presidential election in November of that year. As Director (Barnett) and Assistant Director (LaDuca) of Career Education at the Center for Urban Education in New York City during the pre-election period 1971–1972, we were in continuing and intimate contact with personnel and developments occurring within the special USOE Career Education Development Task Force created to expedite progress and meet the political deadline. Several "get-it-done" types previously imported from the private sector were put in charge of that special career education apparatus. Running roughshod over the bureaucratic maze of USOE and utilizing the device of "sole source" contract letting, which does not require competitive bidding, they got it done.[3] By September, 1972, six "school-based" programs, four "employer-based" programs, a "home-community-based" program, and one "rural-residential" program were visible, albeit dimly in some instances. (School-based programs are understood to mean any career education curricular entries that occur principally within the K-12 formal school apparatus. Employer-based programs are understood as career education experiences that occur principally within and or through employer structures, which are generally broadly defined to include any possible employing person, agency, or institution. The home-community-based program is an attempt to inform individuals about existing work and training opportunities in the community and to apply the mass media in reaching selected homebound populations. The rural

[2] U.S. Congress, House, *Congressional Record*, 92d Cong., 2d sess., 1972, 118, pt. H 158.

[3] A "sole source" contract is one which is let to a contractor who has "unique qualifications" for the accomplishment of some specified tasks. Such a contract, when allowed, obviates competitive bidding and provides a much more rapid route than the normal process of proposal announcements, guidelines publication, review and evaluation, and eventual contract awarding.

residential model is an attempt to prepare whole families for various work roles. Its population is principally rural, poor, and of minority status. Entire families are brought to live and receive training on a former Air Force base.) The geographic spread was as follows: (a) school-based programs in Mesa, Ariz.; Los Angeles, Calif.; Jefferson County, Colo.; Atlanta, Ga.; Pontiac, Mich.; Hackensack, N.J.; (b) employer-based programs in Portland, Ore; Charleston, W. Va.; Philadelphia, Penn.; Oakland, Calif.; (c) home-community program in Newton, Mass.; and finally (d) rural-residential program in Glasgow, Mont. Sixteen regional workshops involving industry, labor, civic, ethnic, and other special-interest groups were also included in that first year. More than 1,200 spokesmen from some thirty national organizations ranging from AFL-CIO to the NAACP met with federal, state, and local school officials to talk about ways to further the career education salient. The speed and compass of the entire effort was extraordinary for education.

Since that time, a genuine bandwagon phenomenon has developed. For example, as recently as November, 1973, a Gallup poll indicated that 90 percent of the nation's adults support career education.[4] Thus, there is hardly a school system anywhere that cannot present either plans or programs bearing the name *career education*.

However, in many instances, what is identified by that name used to be known by some other name. Industrial arts, technical or vocational education, cooperative education, field trips to the firehouse, all have often been transformed overnight into career education. Frequently this has occurred with the stroke of a pen, consensus at a meeting, or just persistent iteration. In fact, it is extremely difficult to arrive at conclusions about the authenticity of career education programs. The principal reason behind this difficulty lies in the fact that it has been so variously and openly defined. A summation of its definitions leads inescapably to the conclusion that it is everything in education, both formal and informal, which bears on one's total life. Then, all of these infinite numbers of things are somehow caused to be related to the dependent variable, career. As Commissioner Marland and other spokesmen have put it, it is "all encompassing." In short, it is everything. Of course if it is everything then it is at once anything and nothing. The reader may confirm this confusion by even a random sampling of the continually increasing entries into the huge pile of career education literature. Contributions emanate from such varied sources as the local suburban or rural coordinator of career education to the research, development, and evaluation formidables from the mega-universities and "think tanks." Included as well are position papers from a variety of

[4] *National Assessment of Educational Progress Newsletter*, 6, 8 (November 1973):2.

national business, labor, and professional organizations. These range from the American Vocational Association to the AFL-CIO.[5]

However, a most important, influential and widely disseminated piece of work carried out by the Center for Vocational and Technical Education at Ohio State University deserves special scrutiny. This seminal career education effort has been heavily supported by the USOE since 1971.[6] Intended as the underpinning of the so-called Model I school-based K-12 programs, its formulations and rhetoric can be noted in the content of the emerging career education program documents from hamlet to metropolis. Its widespread propagation has made it the basis for decision making and program design in school-based career education. Thus, examination and analysis of this particular work is in effect examination and analysis of much of what is practiced and preached in schools across the nation under the rubric career education.

COMPREHENSIVE CAREER EDUCATION MODEL

The Ohio State University Center for Vocational and Technical Education (CVTE) established the nationwide network of previously identified school districts to collaborate in the development of the Comprehensive Career Education Model (CCEM). This project's purposes were stated in the following words:

> The CCEM seeks to restructure curriculum in terms of knowledge of career and human development. Because basic attitudes and competencies begin to develop at an early age and are modified over time, use of the model encompasses all grade levels. Use of the model will require extensive cooperative involvement on the part of the community, parents, and students and will stress the placement of every departing student in either an entry-level job or in the next step of educational preparation.[7]

The completed model was seen as promoting "career awareness" during grades K-6, "career exploration" during grades 7–9, and "career preparation" during grades 10–12. These three phases were elaborated through preparation of pupil goals cross-referenced by school year. Eight "key elements" were also identified as recurrent

[5] For example, see "Task Force Report on Career Education," *American Vocational Journal*, 47 (January 1972):12–14.

[6] Precise levels of support are virtually impossible to determine. However, in an interview published in *The New York Times*, August 8, 1971, then-Commissioner Marland stated his intention to provide $50 million in discretionary funds for R&D in career education.

[7] Center for Vocational and Technical Education, *Developmental Program Goals for the Comprehensive Career Education Model*, Columbus, Ohio: Ohio State University, 1972.

in the approximately 1,500 pupil goals. Together with their associated "pupil outcomes," they are listed below.

Comprehensive Career Education Model

Key Elements	Pupil Outcomes
1. Self-Awareness	1. Self-Identity
2. Educational Awareness	2. Educational Identity
3. Career Awareness	3. Career Identity
4. Economic Awareness	4. Economic Understanding
5. Decision Making	5. Career Decisions
6. Beginning Competency	6. Employment Skills
7. Employability Skills	7. Career Placement
8. Attitudes and Appreciations	8. Self-Social Fulfillment

Each "key element" was associated with varying numbers of "themes" and "goal statements" for all grade levels. So, for example. *Self-Awareness* for the kindergarten pupil was associated with six themes and twenty-two statements. The following summarizes the relationship between *Self-Awareness* in kindergarten and its component themes and goals:

> The student becomes aware of his interest in certain toys and play activities. He recognizes family roles and the influence of other people. He becomes aware of his body-space relationships and cultural differences.

By grade 3:

> The student becomes aware of his interest in tools and his abilities to perform specific tasks. He becomes aware of his body's physical capabilities and spatial relationships. He recognizes that people with similar roles may behave similarly. He recognizes the importance of his achievements. He recognizes cultural differences and the uniqueness of himself and others.

For grade 6 the summary statement reads:

> The student becomes aware that his interests, aptitudes, and achievements will influence his future occupational goals. He recognizes the relationship between his health and physical development and recognizes his cognitive, psychomotor, and affective capabilities. He becomes aware that role expectations influence his development. He becomes more selective about his interests and understands how they relate to his development of values.

By grade 10:

> The student internalizes the meanings of his values and emerging goals in relation to his present and projected life-style. He understands

personal needs when setting goals and monitoring progress. He is sensitive to his interactions with other people.[8]

CONTRADICTIONS IN THEORY AND PRACTICE

Statements of CCEM purposes reveal a shocking and fatal lack of awareness of previous efforts at large-scale curriculum development. The curriculum reform movement of the 1950s and 1960s was identified with generally elaborate, multi-year, multi-million dollar projects. Each was intended to revise one-year courses in, for example, secondary science. These projects tended to operate where a well-defined course of study had been traditional, like biology or physics, and where a supporting academic discipline already existed.[9] The difficulties of revising individual high school courses pale in contrast to CCEM's stated intention to reform all school subjects, in all grades, and in the absence of any recognizable supporting academic discipline. This is not to suggest that previous curriculum reforms deserve uncritical imitation. However, the lessons learned in these subject-matter revisions are valid indicators of both the complexity of successful curriculum reform and the magnitude of investment in personnel and resources needed to achieve far less ambitious goals. It is difficult to believe that a careful reading of the history of the curriculum reform movement would not have given reason to ponder the feasibility of the entire CCEM undertaking.

The vehicle for accomplishing reform through CCEM is identified as the fusing of educational theory and career development theory. But fusing theoretical constructs demands a great deal more than assertions. Not only is this imprecise—just what is "educational theory" anyway—one finds that the initial reference to educational theory appears to be the last. Moreover, nowhere in CCEM goals can one find explicit reference to learning theory, pupil performance parameters, model diffusion strategies, evaluation schemas, or teaching methods.

If CCEM gives short shrift to contemporary educational practice, it does violence to career development theory. Consider, for example, the requirement that pupils make career choices before grade 10. Implicit is the assumption that career development is a simple, continuous process during which adolescents experience a linear reduction in the number and range of career preferences. While research indicates that the adolescent's understanding of his interests

---

[8] *Ibid.*

[9] It has been reported that the Physical Sciences Study Committee received $5 million from NSF between 1957 and 1960. The Biological Sciences Curriculum Study received $10 million for the years 1958 to 1968.

and occupations improves with age, the ability to crystallize preferences has been shown to be greatly influenced by ego development. Merely providing information about careers does not automatically lead to early valid and definitive choice. Indications are that the full range of significant variables extends far beyond the influence of the school. In addition, research in vocational psychology has shown that the career preference process is not continuous, but marked by significant discontinuity. This usually begins around age thirteen and extends to age sixteen. Between these ages, adolescents experience a period of occupational confusion, associated with an *increase* in expressed vocational choices.[10] The explanation of this discontinuity relates to the effect of increased awareness of the influence of realities on adolescent decision making. The adolescent becomes cognizant of limitations of which he was not formerly aware. In the resulting reevaluation of career plans he displays uncertainty and confusion.

School-based career education as represented by CVTE puts itself squarely in conflict with these findings. It does so by requiring reduction in preferences to a single definitive career choice at precisely the ages where significant numbers of adolescents are incapable of making such decisions. This flaw is highly significant since adolescent career choice is a highly valued feature of career education. It would appear that an effective program in career awareness and exploration should encourage increased vocational uncertainty among adolescents. More and better information about careers and a better understanding of the self should in turn promote productive occupational confusion. The CCEM plan precludes this outcome. This fact casts serious doubt on the efficacy of career education as a means of promoting appropriate career selection among adolescents. The assertion that CCEM "combines in one conceptualization the important aspects of career and educational development theory" could be described as hyperbole. In our view the assertion is vagrant, i.e., without visible means of support.

CAREER EDUCATION AND THE WORLD OF WORK

Most behavioral scientists agree that work functions as one of the most important criteria by which our society defines identity and assesses human worth. This belief is discernible in all segments of the population. Thus, emerging evidence of widespread worker dissatisfaction is extremely significant. Nixonian efforts have ascribed worker dissatisfaction to an erosion in the "work ethic." However, scholarly analysis identifies the real culprit as the alienation that

[10] John O. Crites, *Vocational Psychology*, New York: McGraw-Hill, 1969.

characteristically arises from work that is depersonalized, provides few opportunities to complete any job, and prevents any sense of participation from which pride of accomplishment could be derived.[11] Technological advances have made humane changes in the conditions of work a realizable goal.[12] Yet such alterations have not accompanied the decline in the need for maintaining alienating work. This is especially true where such work is highly automated.[13] Recent labor difficulties at the General Motors assembly plant at Lordstown, Ohio, and the issue of voluntary overtime in the Chrysler-United Auto Workers contract negotiations are both related to the unwillingness of workers to forgo job satisfaction in return for purely material rewards. Moreover, there is a candid realization among a broad range of ages and occupations, white collar and blue collar, that too many work situations are unnecessarily undignified.

Career education advocates have been mute on this issue. To do otherwise would call into question certain basic assumptions. Rather than treating the problems of worker alienation, they construct instead a *Snow White* world in which millions of career-educated dwarfs skip gaily off to their dignified and redemptive jobs in the mines, mills, and restaurants of the nation.

Not only have career educationists contradicted career development theory and research, they have also failed to do reality testing of their own constructs. Their educational schemes require at a minimum that there be a job available for every career education alumnus. Moreover, the practice of referencing career preparation choices to locally determined manpower needs, as frequently occurs, does little to guarantee such a high level of employment.

SOCIAL PHILOSOPHY AND CAREER EDUCATION

When confronted with this inventory of logical inconsistencies and misrepresentations, even the most charitable reviewer would probably experience confusion and dismay. What is career education really supposed to do? In response, one prominent career educationist put it this way: "The ultimate goals of career education are individuals with stable work personalities who are (*a*) adjusted to and sa-

---

[11] See, for example, Special Task Force on Work, *Work in America*, Washington, D.C.: U.S. Department of Health, Education, and Welfare, 1972, and Georges Friedmann, *The Anatomy of Work*, New York: Free Press, 1961, pp. 139–145.

[12] Herbert Marcuse uses the term "pacification of existence" to describe this consequence of technological improvements in means of production. See his *One-Dimensional Man*, Boston: Beacon, 1964, p. 16.

[13] For a critique of management approaches to worker dissatisfaction see Peter F. Drucker, "Beyond Stick and Carrot: Hysteria over the Work Ethic," *Psychology Today* 7,6 (November 1973):87–92.

tisfied with their occupational role and with their roles in society; (*b*) satisfactory to both their employers and to the society of which they are a part; and (*c*) employed in an occupation contributing to a balance in the supply and demand for professional and nonprofessional manpower." [14]

In defining the role of the individual in our society as *employee,* such goals identify the paramount task confronting the student as assimilation into the present social order. The goals reveal a persistent authoritarian social philosophy underlying career education. The essential purpose of schooling, then, is not the highest development of human potential, but the creation of submissive workers with marketable skills.

SCHOLAR REACTION TO CCEM

Examination of program evaluation literature is possible but difficult for several reasons. Little work of this nature has been either launched or completed. This is understandable considering the relatively short history of the enterprise, not to speak of the basic definitional difficulties encountered as noted above. The second source of difficulty lies in the general unavailability of such evaluation efforts as have been completed. One example, *A Review of the Developmental Program Goals for the Comprehensive Career Education Model* ,[15] provides the results of two conferences which were held to review and assess the basic "School-Based Model" career education work of the CVTE.

The Institute for Educational Development under contract to NIE conducted the two conferences. Conference I saw "Nine Scholars Assess the Quality of the *CCEM Developmental Program Goals* as an Intellectual Product." This group included Professors Egon G. Guba, David W. Ecker, Donald E. Super, Dorothy H. Eichorn, W. James Popham, Joseph J. Schwab, Elliot W. Eisner, Raold F. Campbell, and Scott Greer. Conference II saw "Six User Groups Assess the Acceptability and Usefulness of the *CCEM Developmental Program Goals.*" Users comprised state legislators, local school board members, employers, state teachers' association representatives, school superintendents, and union leaders. With the exception of union leaders who occasionally demurred, the user groups reacted with consistent favor to the work of the CVTE. However, in our view, the conference results of most significant valence are those deriving from the intensive intellectual analyses of the scholars.

---

[14] Frank C. Pratzner, "Career Education," in Goldhammer and Taylor, p. 178.
[15] Institute for Educational Development, *A Review of the Developmental Goals for the Comprehensive Career Education Model*, New York: IED, 1973.

Moreover, it appears less than useful, and perhaps paradoxical, to report the attitudes of "users" who have not in the main been involved in use.

Our reading of the comments of the nine scholars reveals an unmistakable and unanimous dissatisfaction with the CVTE cornerstone career education work. The "Research Base" of the *Program Goals* was evaluated by Super. He noted the following:

> A reader who knows the research in several related areas can recognize the implicit research base in many instances, the unsupported propositions in others, and the assumptions which are contradicted by available evidence in still others. The early expectation of self-awareness, the shocking shortness of the exploratory process, the premature postulating of definitive decisions and the poor provision for reassessment and reevaluation, are examples of failure to make good use of the research base, failures which should make a cautious user of the *Goals* question every assumption.

Popham, asked to reflect on "Utility in Curriculum Selection," offered this:

> Developing the CCEM set of goals was far too ambitious. One suspects that this project represents the classic syndrome of the federal government's providing immense financial resources while failing to recognize that it takes time—a long time—to assemble a sufficiently large talent pool to accomplish the intended tasks. It appears that the project staff embarked on a tremendous effort sans requisite talent.

Remarking on the "Acceptability to the Profession and to the Public" of the *CCEM Development Program Goals*, Campbell wrote:

> I think the CCEM goals are an example of over-reach, over-promise, and over-kill. *Over-reach* is found in the attempt to make career education the total school program. I do not believe that all of education should be utilitarian in nature. There is a world of art, of music, of thought, as well as a world of work. *Over-promise* appears in the words "a new educational strategy that will ensure that upon leaving school students will be prepared for career pursuit whether it involves direct employment or continuing education." I see no way by which the outcome can be guaranteed for all persons. *Over-kill* exists in the 1,500 goal statements. The generation of themes, cells, and items seems to have become a game, perhaps satisfying to the developers but completely unworkable to the teachers.
>
> I am concerned about the assumptions which appear to underlie the goals. Here are several I would reject:
> 1. Our industrial system and the work arrangements in it are given. The system itself is not to be questioned. Rather, persons are to be prepared to plug into it.
> 2. The world of work seems to constitute the whole of life. Apparently, there is no place for the world of leisure, the world of aesthetics, or the world of thought.

3. Education is to be completely utilitarian in nature: the school is to make preparation for work its central thrust.
4. Learning is a matter of direction; there is almost no mention of learning as a matter of discovery.
5. Curriculum makers will decide what is to be taught and teachers will be told to teach it. There seems to be no place for the teacher as a wise adult, as a diagnostician, as a program planner, as an arranger of the environment, or even as a warm person.

Greer reflected on the "Future Relevance" of the CCEM goals. Among his comments were these:

. . . the program is weak in that it does not really tell a neophyte how to make it or, failing that, how to make out. We should be quite candid about what makes our system work, alerting the neophytes to such factors as these:

1. A basic assumption of all bureaucracies is that the preservation of the control system takes precedence over any objective output of the system. A basic assumption of all bureaucrats is that the preservation of their own place in the role system takes precedence over all objectives of the system.
2. Unofficial rewards are what makes the system go. If you want individual contributions, you have to reward them. All organizations do by graft, corruption, or more generally favoritism.
3. Promotion is not usually a result of what grades you make on a test; "non-universal" criteria frequently determine whether or not you make it. We should teach neophytes how those criteria can kill them.
4. Age, sex, ethnicity, and education can work for you, or against you in the world of work. For instance, women and men always operated in a world in which the dimensions of sexual attractiveness is a factor.
5. Corporate groups control jobs, protect their assets, and organize privilege. Take the Rockefellers and Datanga. Take the labor unions.

I had the terrible feeling as I read the goals that we were dealing with a system within which the docile taught docility, but a competitive docility. It could teach conformism yet have little place for the collective good, the public interest, the human race. . . . Are we to continue an education which increases man's knowledge without increasing his wisdom?

EPILOGUE

On the occasion of its birth in 1972, NIE inherited along with selected USOE staff some of the research and development baggage of that office as well. Among this collection, career education and its accumulation of effects were notably included. NIE's first and predictable organizational response was to declare a reflective hiatus—a retreat in effect—to a position of protection from what they prudently suspected may have been the "over-reach, over-promise, and over-kill of career education. Two years later their suspicions appear to have been confirmed.

The NIE Task Force on Career Education found, for instance, that a precise definition of career education did not exist; consequently, no clear sets of problems were identified. And without the problems, cause and effect relationships had not been established or hypothesized. Also the NIE staff believed that many educators and laymen considered career education to be a panacea for their troubles. Premature expectations, it seemed, were being raised before adequately tested strategies and products could be developed and made available. . . . NIE decided to concentrate its limited r&d resources on two target groups most affected by problems of career entry and progression: youth and midcareer adults, particularly women.

The NIE has lowered the volume on its career education music, reinforced by Congressional reduction of NIE funding by more than 50 percent. However, programs with developed momentum outside the purview of NIE have not experienced hard times. As noted previously, in schools across the nation the din of career education increases, supported by an undiminished flow of vocational education funds, and the case with which current offerings can fit under the career education umbrella. At the same time, these vocational programs remain both unnumbered and unevaluated. In the absence of systematic review, one suspects they retain the full array of deficiencies and confusion of the CCEM. Despite NIE efforts, the Nixon-Marland educational juggernaut will not be easily deterred from its alarming course, nor will the magic of its name be readily dispelled.

V SOCIAL RECONSTRUCTION AND EDUCATIONAL FUTURISM

Human history becomes more and more a race between education and catastrophe.
H. G. Wells

Education must shift into the future tense.
Alvin Toffler

FUTURISM AND UTOPIANISM

Man's fascination with the future is as old as civilization itself. Among the diviners of Neolithic China, a tortoise shell was heated over a fire in the belief that the shape of things to come could be discerned in the pattern of hairline expansion cracks formed across the carapace. Seers of a later period cast fortunes with the aid of the milfoil plant or pored over the hexagrams of the mysterious *I Ching* for clues to the future. Documents such as the *Eloquent Peasant* and the *Book of the Dead* offer testimony to a like interest in prognostication among the ancient Egyptians. The Greeks looked to the famed oracle of Apollo at Delphi for premonitory advice; while the Romans had their own soothsayers and augurs who observed the flight of birds across the sky and examined the entrails of sacrificed animals in hopes of deciphering the course of future events. Medieval seers experimented with Tarot cards, consulted the stars, or delved into the forbidden black arts of the necromancer for the same purpose. Modern man reads the syndicated astrology columns in his newspaper.

The attitude of men in earlier periods toward the future might fairly be said to have been essentially one of supine passivity, inasmuch as it was believed that little could be done to alter the course of future events except possibly by addressing petitions to benign deities or offering up propitiatory sacrifices to placate malevolent spirits.

Modern man, in contrast, over the past several centuries has entertained a burgeoning hope that his future is not something fixed and
immutable, but instead is amenable to modification and subject to
redirection as a consequence of decisions made and actions initiated
in the present. Toward that end, man has enfranchised a new magic,
scientific rationalism, to help forecast the future and, indeed, to assist
him in achieving mastery over it.[1] Within the past decade or so, moreover, increasing attention has been paid to the *educational* significance of the future, both as a proper and legitimate focus for study in
the school and as an object of systematic inquiry by eduational planners and policy-makers.

Closely bound up with man's perennial interest in the latent
possibilities of the future has been a fundamental impulse toward
social reform. Beginning with Plato who drafted his Republic as an
ideal against which to judge the flawed society of fourth-century Ath-
ens, and extending through a tradition defined in the writings of
Thomas More, Francis Bacon, Robert Owen, Samuel Butler, Edward
Bellamy, H. G. Wells, and B. F. Skinner, utopian visionaries across the
centuries have been moved to project into an imagined future (or a
geographically distant and remote present) their hopes and aspirations for a transformed world—one in which existing evils have been
eliminated and dreams of a fuller, richer, more abundant life ultimately realized. Alternatively, certain modern dystopian writers such as
Aldous Huxley in his *Brave New World* or George Orwell in *1984,* seek
to forestall social nightmare by highlighting or satirizing certain omi-
nous trends within existing society. The great mission of the utopia,
as Ernst Cassirer perceptively noted some years ago, has been to
overcome the natural inertia of mankind and to endow humanity with
a heightened capacity for deliberately reshaping its own destiny.[2]

Basic also to much utopian thought has been the place of importance accorded education as a precondition for bringing about a
more perfect social order and for preserving it inviolate once
achieved. The Platonic Republic includes an elaborate system for the
upbringing and training of the guardians and prospective philos-
opher-kings; More *Utopia* makes provision for universal and compulsory education; Skinner's *Walden II* depends upon a systematic
application of techniques of behavioral engineering to reinforce the
social integrity of the community. Because most utopians have be-

[1] The point is developed in Michael Marien and Warren L. Ziegler (eds.), *The Po-
tential of Educational Futures* (Worthington, Ohio: Charles A. Jones Publishing
Company, 1972), p. xi. Cf. also Stephen P. Hencley, "Why Futurism?" *Journal of
Teacher Education,* Vol. **XXV**, No. 2 (Summer 1974), 98.
[2] Cv. Lewis Mumford, *The Story of Utopias* (New York: Boni and Liveright, 1922);
Karl Mannheim, *Ideology and Utopia* (London: K. Paul, Trench, Trubner, 1936);
and Karl Mannheim, *Man and Society in an Age of Reconstruction* (London:
K. Paul, Trench, Trubner, 1940).

lieved that social reconstruction requires nothing less than a comprehensive transformation of society's basic institutions, they have, by
and large, emphasized educational endeavor as an indispensable
means of fostering a consensus of opinion for radical change as well
as a vehicle for adjusting men to the altered society.[3] Within the last
quarter-century, the utopian strain of educational thought referred to
as reconstructionism and a developing interest in techniques for anticipating and predicting the future have tended to coalesce as a
movement calling for—more precisely, demanding—that schools be
enlisted in the struggle to build a better society and that education be
oriented more closely toward helping people prepare themselves for
a world of constant change.

SOCIAL RECONSTRUCTION AND THE SCHOOLS

Current interest in exploiting the potential of education to assist in
the implementation of and adjustment to needed social change has
strong roots in the American past. Historically, faith in the power of
education to help achieve major social goals has been an archetypal
element in American social and political thought. Until very recently
in fact, the power and effectiveness of education has been considered practically infinite, both as cure for various social, moral, economic, and political maladies and as the means for the enforcement
of overarching social values.[4] Early colonists looked to education for
the creation and preservation of a truly sacral society; the founding
fathers expressed concern for a system of education to buttress the
infant republic; Jacksonian democrats turned to popular education to
help dislodge an allegedly aristocratic residue within early republican
institutions; and post-Civil War progressives worked hard to enlist
the schools in the struggle for social reform. For Horace Mann, who
more than any other single individual helped create an expansive national educational mythology, common schooling was to serve as "a
great equalizer of the conditions of men, the balance wheel of the
social machinery. . . ."[5] In addition to such pedestrian tasks as fostering literacy and assisting in the maintenance of social control, late
nineteenth-century schools were looked to for help in the accultura-
tion of an immigrant population, the promotion of a strong work
ethic, the fostering of public morality, the inculcation of patriotic virtue, and the enlargement of a democratic society. Deweyean educa-

[3] Howard Ozmon, *Utopias and Education* (Minneapolis: Burgess Publishing
Company, 1969), p. ix.
[4] Consult Rush Welter, *Popular Education and Democratic Thought in America*
(New York: Columbia University Press, 1969), pp. 3 ff.
[5] For a fuller treatment, note the discussion in Lawrence A. Cremin, *The Transformation of the School* (New York: Alfred A. Knopf, 1961), pp. 228 ff.

tional progressivism, as an early twentieth-century reform movement aimed at humanizing and transforming the schools, stood squarely in the America tradition that linked looked-for social change with renewed educational effort.

By the late 1920's there began to emerge within the mainstream of progressivist educational thought a distinct current emphasizing the importance of the social context in the formulation of policy for the schools and the role of education in the cause of social reform. Over and against a "child-centered" wing of progressivism which retained its primary interest in the psychological growth and development of the individual, a small but important coterie of progressivist educational theorists turned from their earlier preoccupation with questions of freedom for children in the schools to consider more fully the *social* conditions upon which such freedom was thought to depend. A "social reconstructionist" wing of progressivism subsequently grew out of the activities of an informal discussion group that gathered around the figure of William Heard Kilpatrick, and included such luminaries of the day as George S. Counts, John L. Childs, R. Bruce Raupp, Harold Rugg, and Goodwin Watson. The group met intermittently over the next decade or so, giving public expression to its views chiefly through the Educational Policies Commission of the National Education Association, the American Youth Commission of the American Council on Education, the pages of the progressivist journal *The Social Frontier* (1934–1943), and the 1933 yearbook of the National Society of College Teachers of Education, entitled *The Educational Frontier*.

The central thesis held by practically all members of the group was that experience-centered, pupil-planned activity schools in the original progressivist mold had proved inadequate in the Depression era. The central task of education, it was said, should be "to prepare individuals to take part intelligently in the management of conditions under which they will live, to bring them to an understanding of the forces which are moving, [and] to equip them with the intellectual and practical tools by which they can enter into a direction of these forces." [6] The key to meeting the changing imperatives of society was in alerting teachers and students to the pressing social issues of the day. Whereas earlier it had seemed sufficient to afford opportunities for creative self-expression and growth through a curriculum based largely upon the felt needs and interests of individual pupils, social reconstructionists now argued that the development of critical intelligence required informing students about the larger economic, political, social, and ideological forces operative within society, about the problems and dislocations endemic in laissez-faire capitalism, and

[6] Quoted in ibid., pp. 229–230.

about the apparent failure of existing modes of production to guarantee a stable economic order.[7] Their plea was for a new, more directive kind of education that would send into society persons better able to understand it, to live intelligently as effective citizens within it, and upon the basis of an intelligent appraisal of its future needs, to change it to suit the vision of a better life for all. Periodically the suggestion was advanced that the public school might be used as a deliberate instrument of social reconstruction in order to bring about a new form of social organization grounded in intelligent foresight and rational planning. Educational changes would necessarily be "correlative and interactive" with political alterations, social reconstructionists conceded, but there was no doubt that they regarded the former as fully coextensive with the latter.

A sort of credo for the early reconstructionists was furnished by George S. Counts in his manifesto-like *Dare the Schools Build a New Social Order?* (1932). Progressive education, he alleged, was as dimless as a baby shaking a rattle, "utterly content with action." Preoccupation with the methodology of problem-solving, Counts claimed, had led to a fatal neglect of goals or objectives, of the values and social purposes for which education was indispensable. Coupled with a demand for more structured and didactic teaching methods was his claim that although schools could not be the primary shapers of an industrial civilization, they most emphatically could become tools for the advancement of certain ideological ends within it.

Harold Rugg, an equally vocal critic of conventional progressivism, denounced prevailing school theory for being "obsessed with the halo of the past, blind to the insistent problems of the present, and impotent to project alternative solutions" to society's pressing needs for the future.[8] What was needed, he claimed, was a totally revised curriculum built "directly out of the problems, issues, and characteristics of our changing society." With remarkable prescience, Rugg identified as the major concerns of the years ahead such issues as overpopulation, unplanned urbanization, the growth of scientific technology, doubts about the viability of capitalism as an economic system, rising nationalism, the increasing interdependence of world trade and culture, and the dangers of acquisitive materialism. When critics alleged that social reconstructionists were really trying to use the schools for the promotion of noneducational objectives, Counts

---

[7] A useful analysis is provided in Robert E. Mason, *Contemporary Educational Theory* (New York: David McKay Company, 1972), pp. 94–104.
[8] Writings of the period that amplified this theme included Harold Rugg, *Culture and Education in America* (New York: Harcourt, Brace and Company, 1931); *American Life and the School Curriculum* (Boston: Ginn and Company, 1931); and *That Men May Understand* (New York: Doubleday, Doran and Company, 1941).

replied acidly that an educational system which did not attempt to shape learners toward definite ideological and social objectives was a contradiction in terms. To Counts' challenge, John Dewey responded by saying that in a heterogeneous, pluralistic society, the school could never be the main determinant of political, intellectual, or social change. "Nevertheless," he added, "while the school is not a sufficient condition, it is a necessary condition of forming the understanding and the dispositions that are required to maintain a genuinely changed social order." [9]

Society is in a process of change, Dewey noted, and it is a commonplace to observe that the schools tend to lag behind: "We are all familiar with the pleas that are urged to bring education in the schools into closer relation with the forces that are producing social change, and with the needs that arise from these changes." He then went on to observe that there was little consensus as to what the schools were supposed to do or how they should do it. Some claimed that schools should simply reflect social changes that had already occurred, while others with equal vehemence insisted that schools should take an active part in *directing* social change.

The fact is, Dewey argued, schools already do take part in the determination of a future society because they follow and reflect changes in the existing social arrangement. Furthermore, they *discriminate* with respect to the social forces that play upon them, emphasizing certain values, dispositions, behavior patterns and beliefs to the exclusion of others. Nor does the effect of that selection and organization of elements within the social milieu end at the classroom door—it affects the structure and movement of life far beyond. The real question is not whether the schools shall or shall not influence the course of future social life, but in what direction they shall do so and how: "whether they . . . do it blindly and irresponsibly, or with the maximum possible of courageous intelligence and responsibility." Educators collectively may elect to perpetuate confusion and possibly increase it. Or they may choose intelligently to try and make the school a conserving force which maintains the old order intact against the impact of new forces. Thirdly, Dewey asserted, they may select from the scientific, technological, and cultural forces that operate for change, may estimate their likely direction and outcome, and seek to ally educational endeavor with them.

Under the third alternative, Dewey concluded, the biggest problem would be in developing the insight and understanding that would enable "youth who go forth from the schools to take part in the great work of construction and organization that will have to be done, and

[9] John Dewey, "Education and Social Change," *The Social Frontier,* Vol. **III**, No. 26, (May 1937), 237.

to equip them with the attitudes and habits of action that will make their understanding and insight practically effective." [10] The only course of action *not* open to educators is one of ideological neutrality. "Perhaps the most effective way of reinforcing reaction under the name of neutrality," he insisted, "consists in keeping the oncoming generation ignorant of the conditions in which they live and the issues they will have to face. This effect is the more pronounced because it is subtle and indirect; because neither teachers nor those taught are aware of what they are doing and what is being done to them. Clarity can develop only in the extent to which there is frank acknowledgment of the basic issue: Where shall the social emphasis of school life and work fall, and what are the educational policies which correspond to this emphasis?" [11]

Post-World War II efforts to build upon the social-activist strain in Dewey's thought by developing educational theory committed to societal change found expression in the declarations of a considerable number of pedagogical reformers, but nowhere so eloquently as in the writings of Theodore Brameld, one-time Vice-President of the Progressive Education Association (1941–1942) and a nationally prominent professor of educational philosophy. Echoing complaints against progressivism raised by Rugg, Childs, and Counts a decade or more earlier, Brameld criticized the older child-centered pedagogy for being "dilatory" and "inefficient." The most vulnerable aspect of progressive education, he declared, was that it had not clearly or unequivocally focused upon either the content or meaning of educational goals. Like the American culture with which it was ideologically allied, progressivist thought had been much more concerned to delineate an effective methodology of pedagogy than to formulate appropriate educational goals. "The fear that any kind of substantive commitment to ends will lead to dogmatism and then to immoral means for achieving them has haunted progressivists," Brameld wrote. "My opinion is that progressivists sometimes avoid and evade the responsibility [for affirming definite objectives] . . . because they are conditioned perhaps often quite unconsciously by the milieu of a culture which has actually discouraged even defensible commitments in favor of the more comfortable and safer stance of methodology and process." [12]

For Brameld and his followers, as for Karl Marx, the real point of philosophic endeavor is not to interpret the world but to change it. As cultural "tools" for first organizing and then directing experience, competing philosophic positions should be judged on the basis of

---

[10] Ibid., p. 238.
[11] Ibid., p. 238.
[12] Unpublished private correspondence with Richard J. Anderson (November 30, 1965).

whether they fulfill the basic needs of the cultural situation they propose to serve, what quality of life they make possible, and whether
they can be translated into concrete programs of action to accelerate
the thrust of man's efforts to build a better world. Especially in an age
of upheaval and almost cataclysmic change, the only adequate philosophic orientation for education, it was claimed, is one which fixes
the attention of schools upon the future.[13] The queries which ought
to shape and define school curricula at all levels accordingly include
the following: What kind of world do we want and what kind of world
is achievable? What quality of life should prevail? Toward what directions should human civilization be moving in order to meet the challenges of the future?

Reconstructionists led by Brameld began to claim anew that the
central task of education was to prepare men to assume active charge
of the future. "The central critique of modern culture contends that
. . . the major institutions and corresponding social, economic, and
other practices that developed during preceding centuries of the
modern era are now incapable of confronting the terrifying, bewildering crisis of our age," Brameld argued. The human species has
reached a crisis in its long struggle to satisfy basic physical and emotional needs. Technology has developed to the point where a truly
utopian order of existence lies within the grasp of man, providing that
the same technological capacity is not employed to reduce human
civilization to a smoking, radioactive heap of rubble. Because the
major political, social, and economic institutions in the world are
based upon destructive, exploitive uses of technological power and ·
consequently are tending to lead mankind closer and closer to the
brink of cataclysmic disaster, they must be radically reconstituted if
the inertial drift of the world toward chaos is to be reversed. Education in an age of impending catastrophe can do no less than to help
people participate fully and actively in the dynamics of cultural reconstruction, to transform the existing social order, and so prevent its
eventual annihilation. Society must be reconstructed, not simply
through political action, but more fundamentally through the education of its members to the grave dangers of the present situation as
well as to a vision of a new and more viable social order. Education,
Brameld claimed, should "attempt to build the widest possible consensus about the supreme aims that should govern mankind in the
reconstruction of world culture."

What is needed ultimately is "a world in which the dream of
both ancient Christianity and modern democracy are fused with mod-

---

[13] Van Cleve Morris, *Philosophy and the American School* (Boston: Houghton
Mifflin Company, 1961), p. 375.

ern technology and art into a society under the control of the great majority of the people who are rightly the sovereign determiners of their own destiny." [14] The fundamental goal is "a world civilization and an educational system which in all ways support human dignity for all races, castes, and classes; self-realization; and the fullest vocational, civic, and social cooperation and service." [15]

Reconstructionists insisted that the new civilization envisioned would have to be realized or brought into being democratically, with scrupulous regard for democratic processes of decision-making. "The majority of peoples should, through their freely chosen representatives, control all fundamental economic, political, and social policies, and they should do so on a planetary scale. This is the supreme goal of education for the current decades," Brameld claimed.[16] Under a principle of "defensible partiality," the educator need not maintain a sterile neutrality with respect to the issues around which the present cultural crisis revolves, but instead should in process of freely accepting divergent ideas, examining the evidence, and pondering alternative solutions, help define the basic thrust of proposed changes. As Brameld phrased it, "Reconstructionists . . . seek to determine what obstacles lie in the way of our objectives and to determine how *the largest possible majority of people* can find strength and intelligence to remove these obstacles. Above all, reconstructionists try to make certain that any design to be transformed, and any practices that may be implemented in building it, are rooted in defensible beliefs about reality, knowledge, and value. However gigantic this undertaking [the creation of a planned world civilization capable of providing economic abundance, better health, better education, richer aesthetic enjoyment, and other wants of all people, achieved through organized democratic machinery], they are convinced that Western Civilization is at an end if man fails in them." [17] A basic refashioning of both the means and ends of education to confront the imperatives of the future, finally must seek to allow all members of the human race, without regard for present national boundaries, to share without hindrance in the projection of utopian goals for all mankind, to test those goals in the light of the best evidence available, and, ultimately, to engage in concerted action to achieve the goals to which a convergent mankind becomes committed. Far from

---

[14] Theodore Brameld, *Education for the Emerging Age* (New York: Harper and Row, 1965), p. 25.
[15] Theodore Brameld, *Education As Power* (New York: Holt, Rinehart and Winston, 1965), p. 103.
[16] Ibid., p. 6.
[17] Theodore Brameld, *Patterns of Educational Philosophy in Culturological Perspective* (New York: Holt, Rinehart and Winston, 1971), p. 356.

being "utopian" in the pejorative sense of unattainable or impractical, only a reconstructed education can possibly meet the challenge of a world in crisis.[18]

Critics of reconstructionism typically argue that Brameld's faith in education as a primary instrument of social change and social welfare is grossly misplaced. It may be wholly unrealistic to expect teachers in the school to initiate or lead the wholesale ideological and social revolution required for cultural reconstruction. Fragmented by the same political, economic, and social forces that divided other groups within society, the teaching profession is like-wise subject to the identical corporate forces and influences that apply in other sectors of the socio-political economy. Lacking any operational consensus on goals and objectives, educators are unlikely to come together with a single coherent strategy for a future-oriented curriculum.

The reconstructionist rejoinder is to reiterate in the starkest terms possible that the alternative to social reconstitution, quite likely would be global chaos and the eventual obliteration of human civilization itself. In other words, if the reconstructionist analysis of a culture in crisis is substantially accurate, there is *no* acceptable alternative to a radical restructuring of the major social, economic, and political institutions of society if it is to survive. Education as an institution either will be used to thwart change and obscuring the urgent necessity for far-reaching societal transformation, or it will be enlisted in the cause of effecting society's positive and orderly transition into the future.

EDUCATING TOWARD THE FUTURE

More recently a growing body of opinion among educators has inclined toward Dewey's original judgment that it is naive to anticipate that institutionalized education can ever serve in the vanguard of a major social revolution. However, with Dewey, many social reconstructionists have come to share his belief that the school is nevertheless a *necessary* condition of "forming the understanding and the dispositions" required for adaptation to rapid change. Education can apprise people of the best informed judgment concerning what the future holds in store, and to assist students in coping with the sometimes wrenching adaptations essential for dealing with change. Although the schools cannot directly initiate social change, they can help prepare people to respond in a forthright and intelligent man-

---

[18] James E. McClellan, *Toward an Effective Critique of American Education* (Philadelphia: J. B. Lippincott Company, 1968), p. 133. McClellan was one of many commentators to offer devastating criticisms of Brameld's position.

ner. As long as it was reasonable to assume that the future would basically resemble the past, there was perhaps no critical need to orient curricula toward the future. However, if that assumption has become invalid, no schools can now sensibly claim to educate its students adequately unless it makes available to them whatever knowledge exists about the future world in which they will live, and the problems they will likely confront:

> The children of this decade will be inhabitants of the 21st century— our future, but *their* present. If, like past generations through the recorded history of mankind, we could still safely assume that the future will be like the present, we could rest easy with the application of past verities to the existential present. But there is a growing suspicion among some teachers, students, administrators and policy makers that the future is going to be sufficiently unlike the past to raise a portentous question about the present aims, contents and structures of education.[19]

The need for a future-oriented education gains special urgency from the historically unprecedented *rate* of current social change. As Margaret Mead predicted many years ago, to the multiple traditional functions of an educational system such as cultural transmission, the teaching of skills, and the inculcation of time-honored values which sufficed in a slowly changing society, a quite new function which will have to be added is educating for "rapid and self-conscious adaptation to a changing world." For the most vivid truth of the new age dawning, she claimed, is that "no one will live all his life in the world into which he was born, and no one will die in the world in which he worked in his maturity. . . ." [20] The traditional "vertical" transmission of knowledge, from an older generation to its successor will shortly be superseded in the "prefigurative" culture of a fast-changing world by what Mead calls the "lateral" sharing of knowledge by the informed with the uninformed, whatever their respective ages.[21]

Yet for all the rhetoric about studying the future and the need to help people survive the buffeting of rapid and continuous change, "what passes for education today . . . ," declared Alvin Toffler in his 1970 best-selling book, *Future Shock*, "is a hopeless anachronism. Parents look to education to fit their children for life in the future. Teachers warn that lack of an education will cripple a child's chances

[19] Warren L. Ziegler, "The Potential of Educational Futures," Chapter I in Marion and Ziegler, op. cit., p. 3; cf. also Chris Dede and Draper Kauffman, Jr., "The Role of Futuristics in Education," in Dwight W. Allen and Jeffrey C. Hecht (eds.), *Controversies in Education* (Philadelphia: W. B. Saunders Company, 1974), pp. 206–212.
[20] Margaret Mead, "Why Is Education Obsolescent," *Harvard Business Review*, Vol. 36, (November–December 1958), 23.
[21] Cf. Margaret Mead, *Culture and Commitment* (New York: Doubleday and Company, 1970), *passim*.

in the world of tomorrow. Government ministries, churches, the mass media—all exhort young people to stay in school, insisting that now, as never before, one's future is almost wholly dependent upon education." The root of the problem, he alleged, is that "schools face backward toward a dying system, rather than forward to the emerging new society. Their vast energies are applied to cranking out Industrial Men—people tooled for survival in a system that will be dead before they are." [22]

Popular interest in Toffler's thesis subsided fairly quickly in the first few years following publication of *Future Shock,* though the arguments he advanced proved durable in subsequent discussions of futurism.

In preindustrial "stagnant societies," Toffler maintained, "the past crept forward into the present and repeated itself in the future." It was sufficient to school the young in the skills, techniques, knowledge, and values of the past in those societies—until the advent of the Industrial Revolution created the need for a new kind of man, one possessed of new skills, new values, and a drastically altered time-sense. Mass education was the device constructed by industrialism to preadapt people for "a new world of repetitive indoor toil, smoke, noise, machines, crowded living conditions, and collective discipline." [23] The new education system simulated this industrial world: it assembled masses of students (raw material) for processing by teachers (workers) in a central school (the factory) run by an administrative bureaucracy modeled after the structure of industrial bureaucracy. Even the organization of knowledge into fixed disciplines was grounded on the assumptions of industrialism.

"The inner life of the school," Toffler claimed, "thus became an anticipatory mirror, a perfect introduction to industrial society. The most criticized features of education . . . the regimentation, lack of individualization, the rigid systems of seating, grouping, grading and marking, the authoritarian role of the teacher . . ." were and are precisely what made mass public education so effective for its place and time.[24] Those who were processed through the educational machine entered an adult society whose structure of jobs, roles, and institutions was not dissimilar to that of the school itself. Children did not simply learn material for subsequent use; they lived as well as learned a life resembling the one they would lead in the future.

Now however, according to Toffler, the pace of life in an emerging postindustrial era is quickening at an ever-increasing rate, the scope and magnitude of changes are growing larger, and the acceler-

---

[22] Alvin Toffler, *Future Shock* (New York: Bantam, 1971), pp. 398–399.
[23] Ibid., pp. 399–400.
[24] Ibid., p. 400.

ative thrust of society is toward still greater change. "Future shock" serves as a label for the shattering stress and disorientation many people suffer by being subjected to too much change in too short a period of time. It is "the disease of change." For education the lesson is clear: "its prime objective must be to increase the individual's 'cope-ability'—the speed and economy with which he can adapt to continual change." The more change, Toffler wrote, the greater the need to extend one's attempts to cope with the environment into the future:

> It is no longer sufficient for Johnny to understand the past. It is not even enough for him to understand the present, for the here-and-now environment will soon vanish. Johnny must learn to anticipate the directions and rate of change. He must . . . learn to make repeated, probabilistic, increasingly long-range assumptions about the future. And so must Johnny's teachers.[25]

In *Future Shock* and later publications, Toffler spelled out in detail the essential features of what he characterized as a "super-industrial education" devoted to helping people generate successive, alternative images of the future: assumptions about new types of jobs and professional vocations, changing human relationships, shifting ethical norms, sociological and technological innovations, and novel life styles. "It is only by generating such assumptions," he insisted, "defining, debating, systematizing and continually updating them, that we can deduce the nature of the cognitive and affective skills" needed to survive the onslaught of tomorrow.[26] Assailing the current curriculum as "a mindless holdover from the past," Toffler argued that nothing should ever be included in a required curriculum unless it could be incontrovertibly justified in terms of the future. What was needed, he alleged, was a move to "ad-hocratic" forms of educational organization, management and administration stressing dispersal, decentralization, mobility, and flexibility. Curricula should be revamped completely. New contingency programs, the teaching of new skills under the most imaginative circumstances possible, the fostering of new values better adapted to a fast-changing world, a comprehensive reorientation of the schools from their past-oriented focus to concentration on the future—these he cited as major imperatives confronting educators in the modern world.

Further aggravating "the dizzying disorientation brought on by the premature arrival of the future," as Toffler phrased it, is the sheer *magnitude* of the problems confronting mankind and the urgency of finding solutions to them. The futurist-reconstructionist litany of

---

[25] Ibid., p. 403.
[26] Ibid., p. 403. Cf. also Alvin Toffler (ed.), *Learning for Tomorrow, The Role of the Future in Education* (New York: Vintage, 1974).

problems, challenges, and impending disasters has become frighteningly familiar.

(1) *Imminent eco-catastrophe.* Overpopulation breeds poverty, ignorance, scarcity, aggravates pollution of the biosphere, and hastens consumption of the planet's irreplaceable natural resources. Existing patterns of social organization and ideology in the industrialized nations are maladaptive to the future because they are predicated upon an unrealistic expectation of continuous growth and limitless expansion. As nations run afoul of iron Malthusian limits and starvation becomes widespread, attendant social unrest generates a need for greater and greater social control. Age-old notions of the intrinsic dignity and worth of the individual succumb to the imperatives of a police state.

(2) *Global maldistribution of resources.* A grossly disproportionate consumption of energy and raw materials by developed nations has created a widening gap between the standard of living sustained in industrially advanced states and that characteristic in underdeveloped nations. The haves and the have-nots are becoming antagonistically polarized as the rising expectations of the poor go unfulfilled. International economic blackmail exacerbates global tensions. Neither classical laissez-faire capitalism or Communist-style state capitalism can survive the hammer blows of political revolution and successive economic upheavals. Worldwide economic depression may assume the status of a norm.

(3) *Threat of nuclear war.* Overhanging every ineffectual effort to secure peace among nations and to preserve as "balance of terror" is the Damoclean sword of thermonuclear holocaust which, once released, makes likely the annihilation of civilization and very possibly all intelligent life on the planet.

(4) *Tribalism.* In all its myriad forms—racism, cultural ethnocentricity, class prejudice, sexism, chauvinistic nationalism—tribalism continues to exert its seemingly irrational hold over the minds of men, threatening social instability, injustice, civil conflict, and conceivably even outright genocide.

(5) *Soulless technology.* Advances in the various physical, biological and social sciences render the human environment ever more subject to purposive control and manipulation. Cybernetics and developmental microbiology suggest the eventual possibility of deliberately altering the genetic, biological, or psychological make-up of individuals, quite possibly for purposes of exploitation at the hands of others. Automation engenders mass unemployment or at least severe economic dislocations as workers repeatedly have to be trained for new tasks. The physical landscape is reworked, its scenic beauty obliterated by unchecked urbanization and industrialization. Increased

longevity poses problems of productive employment, induces new patterns of schooling, and poses questions relating to the satisfying use of leisure. The environment is growing out of human scale and suffers from progressive aesthetic impoverishment.

(6) *Value crisis.* Technocracy threatens the extinction of certain critical humanistic values. The decline of the Protestant work ethic, a falling away from once-prevalent norms governing personal conduct and morality, and advancing secularism coincident with a decline in the authority and influence of religious institutions are contributory to a pervasive individual and social malaise unprecedented in modern times. The moral imperialism of yesterday's ethical absolutes has disappeared. New value systems capable of restoring to man a sense of identity and purpose are lacking. Western civilization has entered upon a transitional phase, and the moral outlines of tomorrow remain unclear. Youth lacks an attractive, meaningful, future-focused role within society.

(7) *Challenges to democracy.* Totalitarianisms of the political left and right continue to exercise a potent appeal for millions, particularly among the oppressed peoples of the Third World. Questions as to the relevancy and efficacy of democratic processess are raised with increasing frequency, even within the democratic nations.

(8) *Ignorance.* Functional illiteracy is on the increase, both in relative and absolute terms. Opportunities for formal learning are systematically denied millions. Ignorance helps perpetuate greater ignorance, rendering more difficult the search for solutions to mankind's dilemmas.

Futurists of a more sanguine disposition of course are prone to stress the *positive* future benefits of technology and to emphasize the limitless possibilities for the improvement of the human condition attendant upon the expansion, refinement, and application of new knowledge. All agree, however, on the need to study alternative future possibilities and to project answers for tomorrow's questions. Data must be sharpened and new techniques devised for "researching" the future, for anticipating the factors that will need to be taken into account in the formulation of long-range policies.

Techniques for the exploration of alternative futures have advanced considerably since Voltaire first coined the term *prévoyance* to describe the process of simple linear extrapolation as a means of deriving from the present state the most probable developments in the future. Beginning with the relatively crude pioneering work of such eighteenth-century futurists as J. L. Favier (1711–1874) and Pièrre-Louis Maupertius (a contemporary of Voltaire), and continuing on down through experimentation in the Fifties with much more elaborate methodologies by the RAND Corporation and various other "think tanks," by the late 1960's and early 1970's futurists could lay claim to a broad array of well-developed forecasting techniques. Included in the arsenal of projection tools refined by major business corporations were alternative scenarios, contextual mapping, the Delphi and Monte Carlo systems, various statistical models and surveys, cross-matrix analysis, force analyses, Markov chains, relevance trees, Bayesian mathematical model systems, and a host of other research implements.

Whatever the specific methodology or research design, the basic intent in applying any set of forecasting strategies to education is said to be, first, to identify new social developments or trends and to estimate their probable implications for education; secondly, to provide a basis for judging how proposed educational changes might generate other long-range political, social, and cultural consequences; thirdly, to determine more precisely cause-effect linkages between current educational decisions and the subsequent achievement of future goals; fourthly, to refine techniques of analysis utilized in assessing educational outcomes; and, fifthly, to generate data about the differential effects, or net consequences over time of competing approaches to operations analysis, program budgeting, and needs assessments. A multitude of other more specific purposes may well be served through future research, but the above-mentioned aims tend to be cited most frequently as basic concerns by recent futurist literature. Other possible uses will likely be found for forecasting techniques in the areas of vocational guidance, international education, and instructional media, in the design of new delivery systems and institutional arrangements for formal learning, and in long-range curricular planning.

At the level of present-day school curricula and instruction, advocates of educational futuristics see several important ways of making the study of the future a major element or component in the education of all students. Studies in such diverse fields as anthropology, economics, political science, psychology, sociology, and philosophy should incorporate consideration of likely trends and developments, with particular attention paid to the ways in which new discoveries are likely to impinge upon existing disciplines and organized bodies of subject matter. Every opportunity should be seized to encourage students to make projections into the future through games and simulations, the analysis of serious science fiction literature, and encounter groups. There should be courses devoted to war and peace, value clarification, leisure, population control and eugenics, utopianism, megastructural engineering and technological forecasting, ecology, urban planning, business administration and management, theology, history, home economics, biology, physics, mathematics, and all the barely imaginable cross-disciplinary hybrids still in process of intellectual gestation. Futuristics courses dealing with a broad range of philosophical, psychological, historical, linguistic, political and social issues can and should be instituted at all levels from kindergarten through graduate school.

At present, it is still too early to judge whether any systematic concern for the study of the future will infiltrate into school instruction and curricula, or whether educational systems will respond to the challenges inherent in such study. Proponents are convinced that futurism offers an excellent opportunity to re-examine the meaning and significance of what has been learned, to test the relevancy of the historic subject matters, to refocus the direction of educational research, and to infuse schooling with a purpose and direction it has often lacked. To look ahead is to examine resistances to change, to endeavor to build new modes of nonlinear consciousness, and to foster creative responses to psychological stress. Above all, futurists are supremely confident that the impetus toward future orientation in education is not simply a passing fad easily dismissed:

> Futurism is neither super-gadgetry nor salvationist ideology. It does not traffic in hysterics or lullabies. It does not seek to change human nature in manipulative fashion, but rather to encourage awareness of the rich changes inherent in its own multiplicity. Above all, futurism does not now and never will, possess an assured or fixed body of content that exists apart from what it seeks to comprehend. Indeed, in the final analysis, what recommends futurism is its inclusiveness, its capacity to generate synthesizing and unifying ways of looking at man. . . .[27]

Traditionally, the humanist of the Western cultural tradition has professed a deep and abiding concern for the whole man or woman and for his or her growth and development in and through the social environment. The individual separate and apart from the world is not whole. Neither is the individual whose orientation toward life is directed exclusively to past and present. For futurists, the ancient humanistic ideal of education for wholeness cannot survive without adequate and proper consideration of the future as well.

[27] Irving H. Buchen, "Humanism and Futurism: Enemies or Allies?" in Toffler, *Learning for Tomorrow*, p. 140.

A Call to the Educators of America

FREDERICK L. REDEFER
New York University

The year 1932 was a troubled time for America. The country was shaken by a severe depression, unemployment was high, business was stagnant, and veterans of World War I, unable to fine jobs, had encamped in Washington. The concept of a planned society in the USSR caused many Americans to question the free-enterprise system.

In February 1932 Prof. George S. Counts startled the educational profession by his address to the annual convention of the Progressive Education Association (PEA), in which he asked, "Dare the schools build a new social order?" Counts left no doubt that he believed a new social order was necessary. He challenged the progressive schools because they were the most promisimg movement for change on the educational horizon. Counts contended that if schools were to build a new social order, they would have to drop their Deweyan child-centeredness, come to grips with planning an education for social change, cease to allow the individual child to do only what he wanted to do, and help young people to understand and cope with the problems of the times. In this way, schools would be building for a new social order.

The boldness of Counts's address startled the conference and stirred delegates deeply. The dinner meeting ended with groups forming and talking—some of them discussing Counts's challenge into the wee hours of the morning. In the history of education no other speech has had such an impact on the educational profession.

But how do schools go about building a new social order? Counts was not specific as to how it should be done or what the curriculum should be. He was even less specific about the new social order, except that privilege was to be stripped from the few and that democratic planning would create a society with low unemployment, better housing, and better health.

The PEA had no ready answers to the questions Counts raised, and the debate that ensued divided the movement as to whether a new social order could be achieved through education without indoctrination or whether, if teachers resorted to indoctrination, they would cease to be educators.

A committee issued "A Call to the Teachers of America," writ-

ten largely by Counts; but by 1936, when this report was submitted
to the members for study, the New Deal, under Roosevelt's leadership, was tackling more vigorously the problems of unemployment,
housing, and the welfare of the people. As a result, it became clear
that the schools would not attempt to build a new social order.

The educational situation today is not too different from that of
1932, although our problems are not solely economic. They still include not only housing and health but also overpopulation; pollution
of air, sea, and land; the wanton destruction of the earth's resources;
war; and/or atomic annihilation. What is new about today's critical
problems is that none of them can be solved on a national basis. Our
international organizations are not equipped to tackle them when the
minds of statesmen and citizens are still nationally provincial.

Higher education has not educated youth for this new world. A
few professors in individual courses facing the present and future
have reached a small percentage of the total student body. These
scattered courses do not add up to much, and colleges, whose major
concern is the professional preparation of students, have expressed
little interest in the crisis mankind faces. Without the challenge of
what a new world could be like, students become socially apathetic.

The challenge to higher education presented by Ivan Illich's
Deschooling Society, in which he proposed that all schools and colleges be closed, has not been taken seriously. The revolt of college
students of the Fifties and Sixties produced little fundamental
change. Pass/Fail grades in place of the old marking system have not
brought change in the curriculum. Student-organized courses, enjoying a brief flurry of interest, have been submerged by faculty power.
"Universities without walls" show little concern with the problems
of mankind. The voluminous study of higher education conducted by
the Carnegie Foundation inspired no purpose for higher education
other than supporting the status quo, while the grants of the Ford
Foundation have sidestepped any fundamental change. American
education faces a world situation that it seems unwilling to look at,
and today it is higher education, rather than childhood education,
that needs to be challenged to build a new world order.

Higher education is in a crisis far more complex than mere lack
of funds. The loss of faith in our colleges and universities as agencies
for social improvement is clearly evident in the apathy of students,
and a "withdrawal" is spreading in an expressed cynicism among
graduate students. Robert Maynard Hutchins has given up reforming
higher education and calls for reforming society first. But does this
not require a better-educated citizenry and a different education
among the faculty itself? Colleges no longer express an educational
effort to achieve definite purposes.

In the past two decades the traditional program of liberal arts in undergraduate education has crumbled—a victim of graduate school specialization, of emphasis on excessive vocationalism, and of the revolt of youth against any restrictive requirements. A state of educational chaos has resulted. This is particularly true for the first two years of the traditional four-year college. These years no longer have meaning for students. Advanced standing and early admission of students indicate that these years are no longer considered essential for education, even by the faculty. In most colleges these are the years to be avoided for teaching assignments by the more experienced professors. More and more colleges have become a "holding operation," and they do little for young people and contribute less to society as a whole.

Are colleges and faculties ready for change? The answer is no, because faculties are participants in a built-in system protecting the time-encrusted administrative arrangements and practices of higher education that inhibit change.

There are, however, pockets of younger and older teachers who realize that change is necessary. The world confrontation, the shock of Watergate, the lack of ethics in high places, and the commercialization of American culture have convinced some that a new education is necessary if we are to educate a younger generation that is concerned, committed, and prepared to create a better society. These pockets of educational leadership need to be discovered, encouraged, and supported. If given encouragement, they could create a purpose for higher education.

A new purpose for higher education must be directed toward the future, making students aware of the dangers of the present drift; the crucial shortages the world will face in energy, resources, foods; the effects of overpopulation; pollution of water and land as projected in the recent report by the Club of Rome. Higher education must prepare students for a life far simpler than they now live, for satisfactions less dependent on technological machines.

Such a purpose requires design and experimentation to create the kind of man needed by the world into which we are moving so rapidly. The traditional liberal arts are no longer relevant to this end. Rational thought needs to be applied to daily living, and a knowledge of the past must be applied to contemporary problems. An education limited to the study of the Western world is an anachronism. The traditional courses of the history of Western civilization, the appreciation of Western art, Western music, and Western literature omit more than half of the world of man. It is such courses, repeating what is sketched in secondary schools, that have helped to turn students off, causing them to drop out in order to discover who they are. The new approaches in anthropology, economics, geology, and international relations need to be brought together in new patterns. The

East and West need not be separated in courses or departments. Interdisciplinary designs are necessary if students are to receive the background essential for informed citizens of the world. Before one becomes a lawyer, a doctor, a business executive, or a teacher, one needs to be a *man*—who knows himself and others, who thinks of himself as a man before he thinks of himself as a citizen of any particular country, or an example of any racial strain, or as a member of any religious or non-religious group. He needs to be a man prepared to live and share with others the planet earth and to be vitally concerned about the destruction of any man or any part of that earth. It is clearly evident that such men are not plentiful today and even more evident that educators do not do what they could to develop such men.

Educators would do well to re-examine the successful project sponsored by the Progressive Education Association in the depression years (1932–41) known as The Eight-Year Study.

This study approached the problem of college admission with a view to freeing secondary schools to plan a better educational program and, at the same time, to prepare students for college. It aimed at breaking up the rigid plan for college admission based on grades received and examinations passed in required subjects. For eight years practically all colleges in the United States allowed 30 secondary schools freedom from specific college-admission requirements. They were free to plan a new education for youth.

The Eight-Year Study was one of the few successful experiments in American education, and it demonstrated there is no *one* way of preparing for college. It proved that a variety of patterns could be followed and that graduates of the participating schools achieved as high a level of success in college as did matched students from schools following traditional courses. Unfortunately, World War II, the flood of GIs into our colleges in the post-war years, the tremendous expansion of higher education, the fears of communism of the McCarthy era—all contributed to lessening the benefits that should have been derived from this study. Most unfortunately, the colleges of the Thirties concluded—from the examples of these young people who had been educated differently—that there was little need for change.

America is now questioning its values and is more aware than ever before that changes must come. Is this not the time to develop purposes for education and to create a new education for some students in some schools and colleges by some of the faculty? Is it not a time when a social purpose for education can be found and a commitment to an improved world accepted? Must we wait for society to change before colleges do?

A new eight-year study involving *secondary schools and col-*

leges is needed. It should focus on the first two years of college, before specialization sets in, and on the last two years of the secondary school—periods that are now floundering. Faculties of colleges and secondary schools should plan together for four years of education with an arrangement for admission to college similar to that which existed in the original Eight-Year Study. Such a proposal of a "new" four-year unit has been made before and has a sound psychological basis in the stage of development of young people.

A national committee could explore such a proposal with the college and secondary-school associations that now exist in the eight geographical regions of the United States to discover their interest in establishing an eight-year study in their respective areas. Wherever there is an interest, a committee could be established in each region to contact the faculties of colleges and secondary schools and to select those that are prepared to participate. What one region designs for such an education need not be identical with what another region plans, nor does it follow that what a college does in its first two years or what a secondary school does in its last two years would be similar to what all other schools and colleges in that region are doing. Designs for the education of man living on the planet earth ought to produce diversity, for there must be many paths to this goal. Regional committees could select the most promising college and secondary-school plans and be responsible for communication among the participating institutions to improve, evaluate, and advance plans in the course of eight years.

A single foundation need not support this proposal, but many of them cooperatively could make such a project possible. The original Eight-Year Study, involving 30 schools, required a grant of less than $2 million over eight years. This proposal might call for $20 million over an eight-year span, and this is a small amount to devote to meet the needs of American education.

The creativeness of educators can meet the challenge if innovative colleges and imaginative teachers are sought out—rather than those merely with reputations and status. In this spirit, the educators of America are summoned to answer the challenge of this age and to create an education for the man who must build a new world order.

Whither Goest the Curriculum?

LOUIS J. RUBIN
University of Illinois–Urbana-Champaign

The future has always held a strange fascination. We not only examine the present but look backward in the past so as to sharpen our judgments regarding the future. But despite our keen desire and increasing sophistication in reading social signs, prediction remains a hazardous enterprise. It is particularly hazardous when simple cause and effect relationships are confounded by other complicated phenomena, as is the case in societal evolution. Predicting the future of schools, consequently, is not only difficult but in some aspects impossible.

DIFFICULTIES OF EDUCATIONAL FORECASTING

The difficulties of prediction span a broad spectrum. To begin with, despite advances in our social forecasting techniques, the probabilities of inaccuracy remain high.

On another count, social interconnections become increasingly complex as human aspirations increase. Years ago, a curriculum decision could be made with reference to its impact upon youth in general. But now a decision's implications must be assessed with respect to taxpayers, minority groups, teacher organizations, and budget controllers. How could we have predicted, a decade or so ago, that women's quest for equality would require organizing interscholastic athletic competition for girls, or that ethnic chauvinism would lead to decentralized governance in the school systems of large cities?

Yet, for all these vicissitudes, the indisputable fact remains that planning is necessary. Although our best estimates of problems on the horizon may go astray, although our shrewdest plans may eventually falter, the failure to anticipate and forearm often results in much larger catastrophes. There are, happily, some blessings which help matters. Educational forecasting—the projection of likely developments—has several virtues which help offset its evils. First, contingency planning is possible. We cannot bet the whole of our marbles on a given eventuality. Put another way, there is little to prevent us from constructing optional provisions so that changes can be initiated.

From "Whither Goest the Curriculum?" *Journal of Teacher Education* Vol. **XXV**, No. 2 (Summer 1974), 113–118. © 1974 by the American Association of Colleges for Teacher Education. Reprinted with permission.

Second, it is possible that some of our projections will be right rather than wrong. For example, larger amounts of leisure will probably characterize lifestyles of the future. While the probabilities of these circumstances cannot be guaranteed, the odds are good. Should we choose to assume that the curriculum of 1980 must reckon with such a possibility and equip ourselves accordingly, the chances favor our being correct rather than incorrect.

Third, we cannot do anything in the way of preventing undesirable long-range developments, unless we decipher the meaning of present trends and speculate about inhibiting mechanisms. It is not difficult to reason that however effective our efforts to conserve energy are, it would also be wise to acquire new and more plentiful sources if the conveniences we presently enjoy are to continue. Similarly, since we know that extended population growth will lead to a variety of difficulties, we can begin to counterbalance the trend with appropriate corrective measures.

Fourth, there are short-run and long-run dimensions of social forecasting. And the former influence the latter. It follows, then, that dealing with the future can have its most pragmatic inception in the problems of the present. Nevertheless, in speculating about the future we cannot overlook the fact that our education system does not yet teach all children to read, or that present configurations of schooling do not yield successful experience for all youngsters, or that the offspring of the rich usually receive a better education than those of the poor. For many reasons, it is less than rational to contend that prediction, or at least thoughtful forecasting, is the business of fools and lunatics.

CONFLICTING THEORIES OF EDUCATION

A brief review of ongoing disputes among theorists regarding the current difficulties of education is instructive. Intense debates now rage over the desirability of compulsory education, the comparative advantages and disadvantages of free and open schools, the morality of moral education, and the usefulness of conventional pedagogy. Resolution of these disputes will have a profound impact upon educational events and their forecasting.

Consider Graubard's distillation of the rationale underlying free schools that children are inherently curious and—given a stimulating environment and sensitive guidance—will learn of their own accord. Good education, in short, is inhibited by a set curriculum, preplanned lessons, and arbitrary standards. Freedom is all. Graubard states: The most important condition for nurturing this natural interest (of children) is freedom supported by adults who enrich the environment and offer help. In contrast, coercion and regimentation only inhibit emotional and intellectual development. It follows that almost all of the major characteristics of public school organization and method are opposed—the large classes, the teacher with absolute power to administer a state-directed curriculum to rigidly defined age groups, the emphasis on discipline and obedience, the constant invidious evaluation and the motivation by competition, the ability tracking, and so forth [1].

However, Broudy and Palmer seriously question whether an informal, random approach to learning will produce future generations able to cope with social dilemmas.

> Such a society simply does not dare leave the acquisition of systematized knowledge to concomitant learning, the by-products of projects that are themselves wholesome slices of juvenile life. Intelligence without systematized knowledge will do only for the most ordinary, everyday problems. International amity, survival in our atomic age, automation, racial integration, are not common everyday problems to which commonsense knowledge and a sense of decency are adequate [2].

Pondering the same theme, Bereiter states that whereas child care and training are both desirable, one should not be confused with the other. Training is designed to induce a specified performance ability; child care, on the other hand, is designed to provide a safe and attractive environment. "The need for training," he says, "arises from the incompleteness of normal experience. To try to reshape the ordinary experience of children so that it includes all that is necessary for the natural acquisition of reading and numerical skills is to produce an absurdly artificial environment [3]."

Katz, contrasting the competing ideologies of theorists who champion a humanistic environment and those interested in schooling that leads to a more stable society, ends up demolishing the arguments of both:

> . . . . the purpose of the school people has been more the development of attitudes than of intellect, and this continues to be the case. It is true, and this point must be stressed, of radical reformers as well as of advocates of law and order. The latter want the schools to stop crime and check immorality by teaching obedience to authority, respect for

[1] Graubard, Allen. "The Free School Movement." *Harvard Educational Review* 42 (August 1972): 352.
[2] Broudy, Harry S. and John R. Palmer. *Exemplars of Teaching Method.* Chicago: Rand McNally and Co., 1965, p. 161.
[3] Bereiter, Carl. "Schools without Education." *Harvard Educational Review* 42 (August 1972):406.

the law, and conformity to conventional standards. The former want the schools to reform society by creating a new sense of community through turning out warm, loving, non-competitive people . . . [4].

The human qualities that radical reformers seek in and through the schools are very beautiful ones; if achieved, they would give us a worthier and lovelier society. But it is no more realistic to charge the schools with the creation of such qualities than it is to expect them to fulfill traditional moralistic aims. . . . Despite substantial financing and a captive audience, the schools have not been able to attain the goals set for them, with remarkably little change, for the last century and a quarter. They have been unable to do so because those goals have been impossible to fulfill. They require fundamental social reform, not the sort of tinkering that educational change has represented . . . [5].

The moral should be clear. Educational reformers should begin to distinguish between what formal schooling can and cannot do. They must separate the teaching of skills from the teaching of attitudes, and concentrate on the former. In actual fact, it is of course impossible to separate the two; attitudes appear in any form of practice. But there is a vast difference between leaving the formation of attitudes untended and making them the object of education . . . the attempt to teach patriotism, conventional morality, or even their opposite in a *compulsory* public institution represents a gross violation of civil rights. . . . My point is that educational theory should define strictly educational tasks and that schools should concentrate on those [6].

Convinced that much of the existing curriculum is questionable, Katz believes that students should have a variety of options in moving from childhood to adulthood. These options, moreover, cannot be provided by the present system because of its excessive bureaucratization, rigidity, and traditional value orientation. He finds the problem of values particularly acute.

Without yet speculating as to what is right or wrong in the preceding arguments, we can consider three primary issues on which the debate hangs: (a) *Should the prescribed curriculum go beyond basics?* That is, would we do better to incorporate in our curriculum the development of moral values, creative thought, and democratic attitudes, or should we restrict ourselves to a limited number of fundamental intellectual skills? (b) *However we resolve the first issue, can effective learning take place in an informal (unstructured) setting, or must we teach children through systematized instructional procedures?* It seems clear that learning of some kind probably

---

[4] Katz, Michael B. "Trust the Present Moment in Educational Reform." *Harvard Educational Review* 41 (August 1971):355.
[5] Ibid.
[6] Ibid., pp. 355–6.

occurs whenever and wherever a child is involved in a meaningful activity. But the deeper question is: If we wish to cultivate the ability to read, are structured methods better than spontaneous ones? (c) *Can good education contribute, in any significant way, to the improvement of the society?* Since the affairs of society are directed by those in power, the question thus becomes: Are the values of the power elite influenced by their school experiences?

To further enrich the mix, let us listen briefly to a few other voices. Junell has a different perspective:

> Let us not delude ourselves. It is feeling, not reasoning that keeps alive many of our most widely held moral beliefs and provides us with the motivation for following their precepts. . . . any attempt to induce new modes of behavior that does not utilize the emotional component as the primary anchor point in the learner's experience is by and large doomed to failure . . .[7].

> The fact remains that in the realm of attitudes and values we find ourselves in a quicksand world where good or evil so often hinges on mere impulse, right or wrong on simple conviction, and truth or falsehood on the heart's desire. As inadequate for making judgments as these criteria may be, we cannot entirely escape them [8].

To follow Junell's prescription, "deliberately inculcating our very young children with a few attitudes calculated to ensure a more humane use of reason [9]," we would need to make a number of value choices. What attitudes, in particular, ensure a humane use of reason? What ideals are consistent with happiness and survival? And, of greatest moment, How do we reconcile Junell's willingness to deliberately inculcate with Graubard's conception of freedom and Katz's concern for student's civil rights?

Yet Bassett, attacking the problem from still another quarter, sees the possibility of inculcation as hopeless:

> So then, if we cannot through prescriptive education predetermine the future (either of the individual or of society)—if we cannot by teaching produce a manipulable citizenry—if it is not possible for education to solve on demand society's problems—if people's behavior cannot be modified—if education cannot guarantee national survival, liberty and justice for all, peace, virtue, and kingdom of God—then we can afford to relax about these palpable misses and turn our sights on what education can do [10].

---

[7] Junell, Joseph. "The Limits of Social Education." *Phi Delta Kappan* (September 1972):14.

[8] Ibid., p. 15.

[9] Ibid.

[10] Bassett, T. Robert. "It's the Side Effects of Education That Count." *Phi Delta Kappan* (September 1972):17.

What it can do is help the individual make himself into the kind of person he wants to be. To help him we must first induce him to the use the educational opportunities we are able to supply, which means (for starters) changing the school from being grim, joyless, and unrewarding to being appetizing, satisfying, and happy-making, a congenial place to live and work in, free of imposed goals and requirements, ready with a wide variety of learning situations to select from and complete freedom of choice in selecting them. We must grant him, with respect to his education, the basic human right of self-determination. We must treat him, not as a future citizen, but as a present human being; not as a means of social betterment, but as an end in himself. Besides embodying the democratic concept of the primacy of the individual person, this philosophy would almost certainly promote the solution of many school problems, which as Emerson counseled, "solve themselves when we leave institutions and address individuals [11]."

It is hardly necessary to observe that Junell and Bassett, both of whom have a hand in training teachers, would not only have a lively time over a cup of coffee but, in all probability, strive to shape rather different breeds of teachers. Bassett is convinced that education can neither resolve social problems nor modify people's behavior. Like Katz and Bereiter, he believes that education has labored in vain toward impossible dreams. But he parts with them in that, instead of emphasizing fundamentals, he (like Graubard) would have the schools provide an environment of freedom, granting each student almost total self-determination.

Finally, let me cite two more points of view. Ebel says:

Feelings are essentially unteachable. They cannot be passed along from teacher to learner in the way that information is transmitted. Nor can the learner acquire them by pursuing them directly as he might acquire understanding by study. Feelings are almost always the consequence of something—of success or failure, of duty done or duty ignored, or danger encountered or danger escaped. . .[12]. The remedy is obvious. No upper grade or high school young person ought to be allowed in a class unless he wants to take advantage of the opportunity it offers. Keeping him there under compulsion will do him no good, and will do others in the class harm. Compulsory school attendance laws were never intended to create such a problem for teachers and school officials. Have we the wit to recognize the source of this problem, and the courage to act to correct it [13]?

Schools ought to be held accountable. One way or another, they surely will be held accountable. If they persist in trying to do too many things, things they were not designed and are not equipped to do well,

---

[11] Ibid.
[12] Ebel, Robert L. "What Are Schools For?" *Phi Delta Kappan* (September 1972):4.
[13] Ibid., p. 7.

things that in some cases can not be done at all, they will show up badly when called to account. But there is one very important thing they were designed and are equipped to do well, and that many schools have done very well in the past. That is to cultivate cognitive competence, to foster the learning of useful knowledge. If they keep this as their primary aim, and do not allow unwilling learners to sabotage the learning process, they are likely to give an excellent accounting of their effectiveness and worth [14].

Strongly persuaded that schools have become hopelessly enmeshed in a chaos of priorities, and convinced that emotional growth cannot effectively be nurtured through classroom experience, Ebel nonetheless believes that moral education is essential.

Schools have much to contribute to moral education if they choose to do so, and if the court and the public will let them. The rules of conduct and discipline adopted and enforced in the school, the models of excellence and humanity provided by the teachers, can be powerful influences in moral education. The study of history can teach pupils a decent respect for the lessons in morality that long experience has gradually taught the human race [15].

Thus, Ebel argues that "teachers can be powerful influences in moral education [16]," whereas Katz, diametrically opposed, earlier contended that the attempt to teach conventional morality in a compulsory school was a violation of civil rights.

Theodore Brameld sets forth one last proposition:

To come straight to the point, our most voluble advocates of the "free school movement" offer us an astonishing array of glittering half-truths. Because uncertain and confused about the meaning of the very freedom that they glibly assume, these advocates largely avoid any adequate role of prophecy—that is, of transformative personal-and-cultural designs which alone can provide the shape and substance of freedom itself . . . [17].

Does not education acquire at least major responsibility to help students appraise and implement the prophetic role of full employment and racial egalitarianism? Are not international sovereignty and global community, regulated control of population through UNESCO and other international programs, esthetic and religious communion between East and West, completely democratic management of both natural resources and megatechnology—are not these prospects of freedom at least equally revelant to "classroom" experiences [18]?

[14] Ibid.
[15] Ibid., p. 4.
[16] Ibid.
[17] Brameld, Theodore. "Education as Self-fulfilling Prophecy." *Phi Delta Kappan* (September 1972):10.
[18] Ibid., p. 11.

Agreeing with Broudy, Palmer and Ebel, Brameld questions the long-range efficacy of the free school movement. But he also disagrees with Ebel, Katz and Bassett when he extolls the virtues of citizenship education: "Education already projects and thereby reinforces whatever habits of personal and cultural life are considered to be acceptable and dominant [19]." Putting the point even more strongly, he asks: "What prophecies shall education be obliged to consider if not the expectations and aspirations that everyday people deserve to confront and to achieve within the less than three decades that remain in this century [20]."

FUNDAMENTAL QUESTIONS REGARDING SCOPE AND TECHNIQUE OF EDUCATION

Having sampled these disparate voices, what can be said in the way of getting things together? Summarizing the ideas of Graubard, Broudy and Palmer, Katz, and Bereiter, three predominant issues come to the fore: (a) *Should the prescribed curriculum go beyond basics?* (b) *Can effective learning take place in an unstructured setting?* (c) *Can education contribute to improvement of the society?* Now, having reviewed the additional propositions of Butts, Junell, Bassett, Ebel and Brameld, three further issues arise: (d) *Should we seek to indoctrinate values?* Attitudes and beliefs shift with the times. Yet reason would suggest that some values are universal, and that schools are the only organized institutions through which adults can transmit to their young the life ideals they most treasure. (e) *Should the content of education deal with personal development, social problems, or both?* The choice is between striving for the nurture of competent individuals, in the belief that such competence will enable them to deal with whatever social problems occur—or striving to familiarize those on the verge of adulthood with critical problems of society and with prospective solutions. Lastly, to touch upon the most basic issue of all, (f) *Should education be compulsory?* In short, should schooling serve individual or societal interests?

These six issues are points of departure for making curricular decisions for the future. Whether the coming decades bring an increasing polarization of political ideas, a new concept of the work ethic, or a prolonged period of social violence, the obligation to resolve the issues we now face cannot be escaped. In a manner of speaking, then, the present *is* prologue and today's difficulties are inexorably linked with those of tomorrow.

[19] Ibid., p. 9.
[20] Ibid., p. 11.

IMPLICATIONS FOR THE FUTURE

Much has been written of the future. Social scientists, deploying a large number of forecasting techniques, have laid upon us a panoply of probable developments. To be sure, we cannot count upon these projections as certainty, but we can assume their likelihood. Hence, if we hold the issues of the present in bold relief, we can look forward into the future so as to identify probable trends and clarify some of the fuzziness surrounding desirable courses of action.

It is possible that we will witness the growth of a new humanism, the evolution of a lifestyle increasingly preoccupied with the inner person, a rekindling of idealism, and a realignment of balance between material acquisitiveness and serving the human good. Should these circumstances occur, our traditional notions regarding the work ethic may change and a period of broad social experimentation will arrive. These events should spawn greater social confrontation and violence. Hence, the issues surrounding public schools will be thrust into the political arena.

With respect to curriculum, young people will continue to mature earlier. Instruction will need to address the ubiquitous problems of population control and environmental conservation. Despite a continued interest in career education (if only during the short run), learning and self-growth will be viewed increasingly as ends in themselves rather than as means to an end. School people will seek to orchestrate instructional programs so that more content is acquired outside school. As vested interest groups become increasingly cognizant of the true power of education, the clamor for reform will continue. And curriculum designers will continue their speculations regarding *the* pivotal question: What knowledge is of most worth to students who will mature in an uncertain and unstable society?

We are well advised to restrict ourselves to what might be termed knowable aspects of the time ahead. The immediate tasks before us are sufficiently compelling that—in conceptualizing the curriculum we need—it would be prudent to restrain ourselves to the sorts of issues outlined earlier, and to those evolutions which already are plainly in process. It is not that the radical changes necessary in the long run are not vital; it is that those in the short run will heavily influence what comes later.

RECOMMENDATIONS FOR CURRICULA

When we learn that a technocratic power structure and a machine-dominated society are in the offing, a number of realistic curricular implications come to mind. Since it is not the machine but man's misuse of the machine that must change, it may be possible for us to restructure our social patterns to accommodate new cultural needs. With this societal end in mind, one can locate certain curriculum underpinnings relating to social awareness, value priorities, and decision-making skills that lend themselves to schooling. Thus, a question we might ask ourselves to ascertain which future trends have a legitimate bearing upon our task is: What social crises could be reduced or eliminated by learning experiences—in and out of school—that help shape social sophistication and involvement?

It is difficult to set forth specific recommendations for specific curriculum areas. When the objectives for the short run are considered, it seems apparent that the indispensable elements in a curriculum for the future are universals; they must, in short, be a part of all that goes on in school. Recommendations are directed toward identifying a sane and rational transition between what *is* and what *should be*.

In the period ahead we will need a curriculum based more upon active and less upon inert knowledge. Subject-matter content that is purely decorative or steeped in tradition must be abandoned in favor of knowledge that helps the young to better understand their world. Not only do we know too little about how learning occurs in schools, we know next to nothing about the way it occurs outside. We cannot achieve optimal integration between schooling and the education acquired in the larger environment until the integrating mechanisms are clearer. The efforts of the past decade to reform instruction, as well as the alternative schools they generated, have opened a number of useful vistas. Until, however, we devise a variety of options through which students can learn and know what is relevant, true alternatives to the present system are improbable.

The school of the future must emphasize decision-making skills. The goal is hardly new; indeed, one might say, as Chesterton remarked of Christianity, that it was not tried and found wanting, it simply was not tried. The importance of decision making, naturally, increases in proportion to the number and degree of decisions made. It is precisely because the citizenry of the future will be called upon to make agonizingly difficult choices in priorities, lifestyles, and social aspirations that the instructional program of the schools must treat, in varying contexts, the processes through which people examine problems, gather evidence, project probable consequences, and reach decisions.

The young not in school will find it necessary during adulthood to make difficult decisions regarding scarce natural and economic resources, the distribution of power, and their own identities. They can be prepared for these obligations by a curriculum which affords practice with real events. The study of history can contribute (by exposing students to the problems and decisions of earlier citizens), and the study of drama can similarly contribute (by familiarizing students with the works of the theater that provide a penetrating commentary upon the human condition). It is not the title of the subject, or the collection of man's accumulated wisdom it embraces, that will make the difference. Rather, it is the particular ideas and exercises—extracted for the purpose of developing decision-making skills—that are crucial.

Decisions depend upon a body of underlying values. As a consequence, value education must also have a large place in the curriculum of the future. If our social scientists are correct, the future will require individuals to take fundamental positions with respect to personal versus group identity, leisure versus material affluence, formal versus informal learning, and other issues. Other kinds of values will be constructed to fit the circumstances. The curriculum we need must transmit, at least for consideration, the dominant values of the present society and—at the same time—afford practice in the fabrication of new value systems.

To achieve these ends it may be necessary to provide different kinds of schools for different purposes, to extend the interaction between schools and the society at large, to explore new possibilities for learning through work, and to penetrate deeply into noncognitive aspects of human choice.

Forecasting barometers indicate that we are moving toward a period of pluralism in human beliefs and ambitions. In view of this value diversity, decision-making skills take on even greater importance. If ethnic and other group aspirations conflict, if the distribution of desirable goods and services becomes a matter of dispute, internicine political wars are possible. The nonviolent resolution of these disputes and conflicts, therefore, serves to establish a curricular target. Children's learning experiences must encompass the techniques of compromise and negotiation, the ability to empathize with other points of view, and the willingness to grant others the privilege of difference.

Another imperative derives from the profound need to familiarize the young with ongoing social problems. Curriculum designers have explored the potential of simulated learning. The lessons of real life have more to offer.

These imperatives give rise to the probability that we will need to explore new forms of education, devise new criteria for evaluating educational outcomes, and train new kinds of teachers. Our best designs are at the mercy of the teacher's knowledge and skill. If we choose to follow the prescriptions of various scholarly groups who have studied needed reforms—introducing learning experiences in human interdependence, expanding our treatment of global education, and using commercial television programs to facilitate our instructional objectives—our obligation to update and refurbish teaching techniques will grow correspondingly.

Finally, the future curriculum may well come to embrace an entirely different role. In lieu of serving as the vehicle for dispensing knowledge and skills which we deem essential, it may become a kind of integrating clearinghouse that organizes, directs and orders the knowledge and skills that students obtain throughout their lives. Closely related to the constructs of Coleman, such a curriculum would not only account for the imperatives I have listed above, but others as well [21].

The curriculum is in turmoil, and the time is ripe for action. We would do well to remember that it is not our proprietary possession; lawmakers, parents, students, and interested citizens have a great stake in its destiny.

[21] Coleman, James. "The Children Have Outgrown the Schools." *Psychology Today* (February 1972):72.

Education for the Future

HERBERT J. MULLER
Indiana University

Among the many novel ideas that soon become commonplaces at a time of fantastically rapid change is the vogue of futurism. The future has long been a subject of speculation or dreaming, of course, but never before have its uses been so insistent as they have become in recent years. Immense sums spent on research and development represent a systematic way of shaping it. Specialists banded in commissions, councils and institutes are busy at equally systematic efforts to anticipate what it may hold in store; they have elaborated a score of new techniques for the so-called science of "futurology." And of late dozens of universities have been offering all manner of "future-oriented" courses, as the fashionable jargon has it. Alvin Toffler, author of the best seller *Future Shock*, has been going up and down the land addressing university audiences on the primary need of "education in the future tense." Henceforth, he writes, "we must search for our objectives and methods in the future, rather than the past"—the past that has traditionally provided the subject matter of education.

From "Education for the Future," *The American Scholar*, Vol. 41, No. 3 (Summer 1972), 377–388. © 1972, Herbert J. Muller. Reprinted with permission of the author and the United Chapters of Phi Beta Kappa.

Now, Toffler is so completely sold on the new vogue that he exemplifies its most extravagant tendencies. He writes in a breathless style that may make one wish he would pause now and then to take a deep breath. He is fond of such coinages as "Ad-hocracy" to define a basic need of properly future-oriented people, who may then assist in the creation of the brave new "Super-industrial" world he anticipates. In education he reflects the popular faith in technology by welcoming the prospect of "a whole battery of teaching techniques," including the inevitable computerized programs. With Ad-hocracy must come provision for "life-long education on a plug-in/plug-out basis." And so on.

Yet I propose to take his thesis seriously, on the assumption that the new vogue is by no means another passing fashion. Toffler is uncommonly well informed about the whole subject, having consulted all kinds of specialists. However naïve, his faith in technology is something that educators have to reckon with, especially since many of them, too, are pleased with all the new educational hardware. Even so, he has many sensible things to say in his diagnosis of contemporary life, including sound criticism of our schools. And even in his extravagances—or just because of them—he forces fundamental questions that are too often overlooked in the universities.

One could say this of his basic proposal that we should look to the future rather than the past for our objectives and methods. To my mind it is obviously no question of "rather than," but of "as well as." In reading Toffler I found myself adhering more firmly to some old-fashioned notions about a liberal education, and rising to the defense of the uses of the past, as represented by not only history but literature, the arts, and philosophy. To these uses, especially for the purposes of value judgments, I shall give the last word. At the same time, much that has come down from the past in the universities is of questionable value for contemporary needs, and has been unquestioned simply because it has long been customary, as comfortable to academics as old habits, and as mindless as the ivy on the college walls. I have myself supported the common complaints of students about the irrelevance of too much of their education, and have pointed to the need of education for the future. This need I think should get the first word.

Then we perforce begin with the commonplaces about revolutionary change and radical discontinuities that have antiquated much traditional policy and practice. Certainly our curriculum has not focused enough on the most relevant use of the past, a better understanding of the extraordinary present, or of who we are, where we are, how we got this way, and where we may be going. Considering specifically our radically new kind of society, with its drive to technological "progress" that has generated out major problems, one has only to ask: How many students acquire an adequate understanding of how the drive got started, how it gathered such terrific momentum and accelerated the pace of change, even though most people do not really like living in a revolutionary world? And why does it nevertheless seem irresistible, bound to continue?

So we move into "futurology," which is naturally based on an extrapolation of current trends. Specialists in it have made popular the year 2000—and be it noted, with nothing like the apocalyptic visions that the year 1000 A.D. once inspired in many Christians. For our students, speculation about what life will be like in that year is not at all idle or academic: they will be in their prime then. To be sure, prediction is necessarily uncertain, for reasons they had better understand clearly. But immediately we have to face the confidence with which Herman Kahn and Anthony Weiner can list a hundred important technological innovations that they say are almost certain to appear by the year 2000. I, for one, am quite willing to take their word for it, inasmuch as scientists and technicians are already busy on the job of realizing these possibilities. Given the common assumption that education should prepare young people for life, one recognizes that it should now make them aware of major developments that are strong probabilities, or even virtual certainties.

This task is all the more important because of the uncertainties about the future, which involve the social and cultural consequences of all the scientific discovery and technological innovation looming up. In view of the compulsive drive to acquire systematically ever more knowledge, and with it more power, the question is: What will man do, or ought he to do, with his new powers? Some of them have obviously beneficent possibilities, which appear in the radiant visions of the future offered by the more naïve scientists and apostles of technology. Others are obviously frightening, for instance, the development of more thermonuclear and chemical weapons. Many have alarming possibilities as means of manipulating people, controlling behavior, even transforming personality. But almost all these powers, including potentially beneficent ones, raise complex social and political problems. It is the problems that most concern serious forecasters, the prospect of still more problems for our policymakers—who right now, let us add, are not up to dealing effectively with the many grave ones already confronting us.

Hence there is a wide field for courses on the future. Time and space do not permit a review of the many possibilities, but let us take a look at the already popular subject of the environmental or biological crisis, aggravated by the population explosion. Ecologists tell us that if current trends continue we are headed for disaster, conceivably a world that will become uninhabitable. Together with the possibility of a thermonuclear war, these trends make human survival a problem for the first time in history. Meanwhile we are faced with such immediate threats as the increasing pollution and the urban crisis, the steady deterioration of the central cities in the sprawling metropolitan areas. And behind all these problems is the accepted national goal of indefinite economic growth, even though Americans already consume many times their proportionate share of the world's dwindling natural resources. While one may doubt that such growth can continue indefinitely, neither business, government, nor the public is prepared to accept a program of national austerity, which scientists are insisting is necessary. Almost all economists have assumed that steady growth signifies a healthy economy; only of late have some begun to question it. I would welcome courses in economics for the future.

All this brings up a basic problem for educators that troubles me much more than it apparently does Toffler and most other futurists. In a course on modern technology I set students to exploring independently a wide variety of problems, and those who did the most thorough job of research uniformly reported pessimistic conclusions about our prospects. What troubled me was the difficult effort to maintain a nice balance. On the one hand, young people need to be clearly aware of what they are up against, the very real dangers, the good reasons for alarm about the future. On the other hand, they need to retain a hopeful spirit if there is to be any hope for the future. The most that I could say to my students was that the growing alarm was the best reason for hope. They were accordingly heartened by the defeat of the S.S.T. program, the first dramatic success in halting the drive to what most Americans regard as progress. Only they then pointed out that President Nixon at once assured the public that despite this temporary setback America would retain its technological leadership of the world, and ensure further progress.

In more familiar terms, young people have more need of being flexible, adaptable and resourceful than any generation before them. Education should accordingly help to make them so, immediately through a fuller awareness of their fast-changing world, and then by developing their powers of choice. Some of the new courses on the future, I gather, attempt to do this by games presenting them with possible alternatives. For, although the drive of science and technology will force adaptation to much change, like it or not, they still have plenty of vital options—a point that Toffler rightly emphasizes, in view of the stereotypes about our standardized mass society. More freely than any previous generation they can set their own goals and life-styles, as many have been doing in unconventional ways. As citizens they can hope to have some say about their future by influencing policy-makers. And on both counts I am led to my particular concern—the role of the so-called humanities in education for the future.

So far the specialists in efforts at forecasting have been mostly assorted social or behavioral scientists. Literary men, philosophers, and even historians have contributed relatively little to this whole enterprise, presumably because they are not equipped with the necessary specialized knowledge and techniques. Nevertheless, I believe they have much to offer. We might recall that more than a generation ago, before the vogue of futurology, Aldous Huxley offered an imaginative forecast in *Brave New World*, in which, without benefit of fancy techniques or methodology, he was remarkably prophetic about some developments.

As for formal education, humanities departments could offer relevant courses just because of their traditional preoccupation with the past. An obvious example is a study of utopias, which have been a distinctive product of Western civilization from the Renaissance on, and as a tradition, strengthened by the rise of the idea of progress, have had a growing influence on its history, most conspicuously through Karl Marx's vision of a classless society. Such studies might illuminate the revulsion against the utopian tradition, as in *Brave New World, 1984,* and much science fiction. Then they might make clear that utopianism is nevertheless by no means so dead as it is reputed to be outside the communist world. It survives not only in the apostles of technology but also in such humanistic thinkers as Paul Goodman and Lewis Mumford. Altogether, visions of ideal possibilities—however improbable—are especially pertinent in view of our fabulous technological means.

But my main concern is a more fundamental one. Toffler writes approvingly of "the people of the future," the small minority—even in the advanced industrial societies—who are well adjusted to the increasingly rapid pace of life, in a "short-order" or "instant" culture. They live faster, they regard transience and novelty as normal, they welcome change—in short, they are "the advance agents of man," who are already "living the way of life of the future." Education, it follows, should concentrate on molding many more such people, with specific preparation for changes to be expected. "Even now," Toffler writes, "we should be training cadres of young people for life in submarine communities."

Here I shuddered, and the more so because some of the young people conceivably may have to live in such communities, or in the underground cities envisaged by other futurists. I would concentrate instead on efforts to give the young a better idea of what civilized life has meant and can mean at its best, so that they might help to shape a future in which people would not be condemned to so unnatural a life. The "people of the future" who welcome change are not disposed to think hard enough about the fundamental questions: Is all the change really necessary? Is it *desirable?* If so, by what standards? Such questions raise the abiding issues of permanence and change, of the natural life or the good life for man, of basic human values. While Toffler recognizes the necessity of value judgments in developing powers of choice, I doubt that even whole batteries of the latest techniques can do the job well enough. My thesis is that the most important contribution the humanities could make to education for the future is a basic study of the problems of human values and value judgments—judgments that students are not trained to make in the social or behavioral sciences, whose approved methodologies do not lend themselves to such purposes, but rather support the common illusion that true science is "value-free"; and judgments that call for more knowledge of the past than these up-to-date scientists usually have.

So let us consider more commonplaces. Transience is plainly the order of the day, above all in America, where it has invaded all spheres of daily life. Americans have grown accustomed to impermanence in their surroundings because of their mobility and the constant demolition and new construction; few live out their lives in the houses in which they were born. Their economy features throw-away goods, planned obsolescence, the latest models, the latest fashions; a major purpose of the immense advertising industry is to make them dissatisfied with old possessions. In their cities the seemingly so solid new skyscrapers that keep replacing old buildings are not built for keeps, as men used to build. Lewis Mumford, although a harsh critic of our technological society, has himself celebrated "the death of the monument," in which all societies expressed their aspirations to the everlasting; to this symbol of "death and fixity" he opposed the value of a capacity for vital renewal in civic life. Behind Mumford lay the philosophies of Becoming, from Hegel on through John Dewey, that have largely supplanted the traditional philosophies of Being, based on assumptions of fixities, immutable essences, eternal verities. For Dewey the main end of education was growth—a good word for change. And I should add that a survey of the long ages of man may give one a deeper appreciation of some important respects in which the human race has grown in its pursuit of truth, beauty and goodness.

Yet man could not have grown aware of change, of course, except for a background of unchanging realities. Permanence remains a basic condition of his life in the natural world, including the uniform fate of mortality. As Mumford knew, a capacity for renewal itself implies biological and social constants. These have made possible the enduring values that man has wrested from his endless travails, which have likewise been a constant in his history. Today the extraordinary pace of change may obscure the underlying continuities and uniformities, the elementary truth that change is not the only constant in our time. While I happen to cherish old possessions, prefer the old cities of Europe, and admire many of the great monuments of the past, I also write as a conscientious relativist who came to conclude that, short of eternal verities or life everlasting, there are permanent values, absolute goods, which must be considered in any aspiration to the good life—and especially today, above all by "the people of the future."

These goods bring up immediately the issue of the "natural" life for man. The study of history makes plain that we cannot talk easily of such a life for a creature who moved from the cave to the life of the soil, later from the village to life in cities, and who all along developed a remarkable diversity of cultures that alike seemed natural to the people brought up in them. His record shows that man is an extraordinarily adaptable creature. So in adapting himself to an industrial society radically different from all previous ones, he learned among many other things to live by the mechanical clock instead of the natural rhythms of night and day and the seasons. I assume that most people could adapt themselves to life in submarine communities. Conceivably, too, man may in time be made still more adaptable by not only systematic conditioning, such as B. F. Skinner aspires to impose on the whole society, but such imminent possibilities as new wonder drugs, genetic surgery and engineering, and biochemical controls of the nervous system. Another eminent psychologist rejoices in the prospect that by biochemical means "we will achieve the ability to change man's emotions, desires, and thoughts."

Yet "we" would mean in practice the various specialists in social or human engineering. If I am myself too set in my ways, or too content to go on with my own thoughts and feelings, laymen in general cannot simply trust to the wisdom of these technicians. In any case, no educator can stake his all on such future possibilities. Meanwhile we have to deal with young people who have the same biological and psychological needs as their ancestors have had through the ages. We must consider too the plain reasons why modern life may in some respects be legitimately called unnatural. Certainly life in a noisy, congested, polluted environment is not natural for man, or good for man, or good for him, even if people get used to it; quiet, sunshine, fresh air, open space, and greenery are among the elementary natural goods. When René Dubos, speaking as a biologist, calls for a "new social ethic" based on the idea of living in harmony with nature instead of forever exploiting and "conquering" it, we might be reminded that this is a very old idea, common not only in folk cultures but in ancient Greece, Confucian China, Buddhist Japan, and much Western literature. In a historical view it is the technological drive to exploit and conquer, at any cost to the natural environment, that is strictly unnatural, as now its menace to human survival also suggests. So too is the American rage for endless acquisition and consumption to satisfy "needs" created by admen, often at the plain expense of mental health. The more adventurous young people are themselves seeking more "natural" ways of living.

There remain the higher needs of the life of the mind, developed during the history of civilization, which are the special concern of the humanities. Embracing aesthetic, ethical, intellectual, broadly spiritual values, they lead us to the issues of the good life. Needless to say, we shall never agree on this. It would be most unfortunate if democratic educators ever did approach agreement, inasmuch as their task is to assist their students in deciding for themselves what the good life for them is. Then the young people might settle for the life of the superindustrial future as pictured by Toffler. But first I would like to widen their range of choices in possible futures, for both themselves and their society, and to develop their powers of judgment, by making them think hard about the perennial questions, how to live and what to live for—the right questions even though, or again just because, they cannot be given conclusive answers by scientific or any other methods.

Any such effort would call for some introduction to the wealth of possible answers suggested by the diverse cultures of the past, in both East and West, embodied in the great works of art and thought that the human race has hung onto. I doubt that most thoughtful, independent students would welcome Toffler's vision of a superindustrial technology that will manufacture experience instead of mere commodities, since so many are bent on having their own experience, doing their own thing; but for this reason, too, they need to be acquainted with the kind of experience provided by Shakespeare, Rembrandt and Beethoven, and by such rebels against the modern world as Dostoevski, Nietzsche and D. H. Lawrence. In their common quest of significance, ways of ordering life and giving it meaning, they need as well more time sense than is provided by an instant culture that prizes immediacy. With all this they might get too some tragic sense of life, a deeper sense of the abiding realities of the human condition—a spirit lacking in Toffler and in most other futurists, who may, therefore, often seem superficial.

Again space does not permit a survey of the many ways in which the liberal arts may promote a full development of capacities for growth, self-realization and self-determination. (I am assuming that most young people are still not ready to let B. F. Skinner determine the kind of self everybody should have.) Here I would stress in

particular the importance of aesthetic education, commonly neglected in both contemporary practice and futuristic theory. In a society whose business is business, it is more necessary than ever before
to develop sensitivity of perception, refine powers of choice, and
enrich ideas of desirable futures. It could make more meaningful and
effective the standard complaints about the quality of American life.
Now that President Nixon has added this cliché to his stock, it is fair
to remark that he is only typical of our society in that on his record
he has a pretty vague or vulgar notion of the standards of excellence
the phrase implies, including aesthetic standards, and has displayed
little awareness of the deterioration in quality during the phenomenal economic growth of the nation. For young people the aesthetic
judgment is more pertinent because it accordingly enters as well into
judgment of the life-styles they are experimenting with.

Now, all such old-fashioned talk may seem still more academic
and ineffectual because of the facts of professional life in the so-
called humanities. I have myself dwelt wearily on the too many
thousands of Ph.D. dissertations and learned articles in the professional journals, the great bulk of them written by specialists only for
other specialists, with little relevance to basic issues of value judgments, still less to education for the future. For different reasons contemporary art may make talk about permanent values seem as irrelevant. Here transience is the order of the day in the form of the
fashions that keep sweeping over the arts, often with the announcement that old styles or art forms are dead. In this welter of novelty
there is indeed much imaginative work of merit, perhaps of promise
for the future, but most conspicuous is the element of mere fashion,
the latest "ism," the rage for novelty. Mostly short-lived, the fashions
support Toffler's belief that the values of the future will be more
ephemeral than the values of the past.

I suppose he may be right, especially because all the signs are
that the pace of change will continue to accelerate. As he writes
briskly that "permanence is dead," so the historian J. H. Plumb
writes soberly that "the past is dead." But if so, I should still say so
much the worse for the future. Meanwhile, at any rate, permanence
is not actually dead, nor is the past. We still have plenty of earnest
students who are not so wedded to transience and novelty as Toffler's people of the future. The actual problem for educators aware of
the challenges posed by the pace of change is much more difficult
than fighting a rear-guard battle in a steady retreat. It is to create a
more selective, usable past, by instilling more reverence for its great
works of art and thought that can still speak meaningfully to us, but
also by recognizing its too common tyranny, in both the world of
thought and the political world; and by instilling an appreciation of
both the enduring values it created and the values of change and

growth, recognizing the inveterate unreasoned tendency of most people to resist change, but now also the too common tendency to accept it as unthinkingly. In short, a perpetual balancing act, in which educators can never be sure that their timing and emphasis are right.

They face a related problem of balance in the judgment of science and technology, in particular because of the animus of many literary intellectuals against them. It is obviously futile to treat them as simply a curse, inasmuch as we now could not possibly live without them. Quite apart from all the material benefits flowing from them, they too have inspired great imaginative works, while contributing the indispensable scientific spirit to the values developed by our civilization. Today humanists have no more effective allies than the many life scientists who are deeply concerned over the problems of not only human survival but survival in a decent environment, fit for fully human beings to live in. At the same time, humanists have to contend against the popular faith that science can give us all the answers. Although they may find allies too among behavioral scientists who know better, they have to keep pointing out that too many others have an excessive faith in the latest techniques, or in a methodology that, far from answering the fundamental questions, tends to obscure them or rule them out. Toffler, an ardent pupil of the behavioral sciences, is typical when he calls for a "science of futurism," the establishment of more "scientific futurist institutes," scientific "measures" of the quality of life, social experiments with "the most rigorous, scientific analysis of the results," and so forth. He is too sophisticated to believe that all this could give us positive answers, but the magic word remains "scientific"; so it is necessary to emphasize that he is using it in a not at all rigorous sense.

Finally, however, I would emphasize chiefly that any serious concern for the future demands first of all thoroughgoing criticism of the present state of America, to which both scientists and humanists have been contributing. The root of our troubles is the American way of life, with business as usual, politics as usual, consumerism more than usual. I think that education for life in that year 2000 might do no better than turn out more Ralph Naders.

Education to Meet the Psychological Requirements for Living in the Future

GLEN HEATHERS

Research for Better Schools (Philadelphia)

A major consequence of current and future societal changes is that they place new or intensified demands on individuals in the psychological realm. Such demands require schools to make appropriate changes in their programs and also require education personnel to receive special preparation for planning and conducting the needed program changes. This paper examines major features of changing society that are shaping the future, identifies psychological demands such changes place on the individual, and lists types of changes in education called for to meet these demands.

UNIVERSAL CHANGE IN SCIENTIFIC-TECHNOLOGICAL SOCIETY

At least since World War II it has been evident that our society and all other societies throughout the world are undergoing an ever-accelerating tide of change. Change in all aspects of living is so massive, so rapid that it threatens to overwhelm the individual. Francis Chase warns: "Changes in the technologies through which man adapts himself to his environment are so rapid as to justify the oft-repeated assertion that, for the first time in history, change has become an ordinary occurrence, and adaptation to a succession of changes has become a necessity for survival [1]."

Interpreters of today's "scientific-technological" society are in general agreement as to its essential features and their probable projections into the future. The slogan terms are all familiar: mass production, mass communication, automation, efficiency, bureaucracy, impersonality, complexity, rapid change, and unpredictability.

From "Education to Meet the Psychological Requirements for Living in the Future," *Journal of Teacher Education*, Vol. **XXV**, No. 2 (Summer 1974), 108–112. © 1974 by the American Association of Colleges for Teacher Education. Reprinted with permission.

[1] Chase, Francis S. "School Change in Perspective." Chapter 11 in John I. Goodlad, ed., *The Changing American School*. 65th NSSE Yearbook, Part II. Chicago: University of Chicago Press, 1966, p. 275.

FEATURES OF SOCIETAL CHANGE REQUIRING THAT PEOPLE CHANGE

Economic Effects of Automation

The massive and rapid changes in knowledge, technologies, and social forms that characterize society today have vital implications for the individual as worker, citizen, and person. With respect to vocational requirements, increasing automation tends to eliminate routine jobs and to retain or create jobs requiring communication skills, planning ability, and problem-solving competencies. Increasingly, "The premium, is . . . not on skills per se, but on the capacity to acquire skills, to modify them, and perhaps to begin again. Adaptability and flexibility are the qualities demanded for today's worker [2]."

Broudy offers a safety valve to the predicament of worker morale:

> The very system that has reduced the individual's freedom occupationally may help to free him from it psychologically. With automation and new forms of power, earning a living may well become a peripheral rather than a central principle of life and one's key significance may not be sought there [3].

Another central aspect of change in Western societies has been the mechanization of agriculture and other land-based industries and the migration of millions into the inner cities, where many who lack the education to obtain employment must live in a "culture of poverty." Frank Jennings doubts that the great problems of our urban centers can be relieved except by bringing all our resources to bear on them. "The forces that are roiling in our cities cannot be harnessed by education alone. . . . It is possible that the new critical mass will blow down all the school walls and let the whole of urban society into the classroom. Perhaps the cities themselves must be recreated as giant learning centers [4]."

Political Pressures

The effects of the scientific-technological revolution are as pervasive and powerful in the political and social aspects of society as in the economic. These areas too are characterized by mass organiza-

---

[2] Gow, J. Steele, Jr., Burkhart Holzner, and William C. Pendleton. "Economic, Social, and Political Forces." Chapter 7 in Goodlad, ed., *Changing American School*, p. 185.
[3] Broudy, Harry S. "Art, Science, and New Values." *Phi Delta Kappan*, November 1967, p. 116.
[4] Jennings, Frank G. "It Didn't Start with Sputnik." *Saturday Review*, September 16, 1967, p. 97.

tion, intense pressures toward conformity to group norms, rapid change, and great uncertainty. Under these circumstances, individuality tends to be stifled and choices reduced to a few group-sanctioned alternatives. Yet, if individuals are to retain or regain control of society and their own lives, they must learn to exercise social influence and political power. "The alternatives to tyranny by experts or mindless nose counting in such a society is political education . . . [5]."

The role of instant mass communication, particularly television, in influencing political decisions is of special importance. Increasingly, the politician needs a charismatic TV image to win elections. Citizens, confronted with the growing complexity and uncertainty associated with all aspects of our changing society, are in such a state of insecurity and anxiety that they are easy targets for the techniques of mass persuasion. Learning to interpret and gain control of the uses of the communications media is essential if citizens are to maintain, or reestablish, orderly democratic processes.

Social Change

Changes in the political realm are only a part of the cataclysmic changes taking place in all our institutions and social processes. A valuable listing of trends of change in our social institutions, mores, and folkways occurs in a 1972 report of the Commission of Educational Planning of Alberta, Canada entitled *A Choice of Futures*. The list includes "declining influence of marriage and the family, religious institutions and the work-ethic," "continuing relaxation of the norms governing personal behavior," "decreasing emphasis on values pertaining to law and order, patriotism and cultural identity," "mounting tension between major groups in society," and "growing need for government regulation in inter-personal and inter-group relations [6]."

Street crime and group violence have become commonplace; some feel "law and order" reactions to continual violence may be turning the country into a police state. The impact on the individual of the myriad changes in our institutions and social norms has been dramatically summarized by Toffler:

> To survive, to avert what we have termed future shock, the individual must become infinitely more adaptable and capable than ever before. He must search out totally new ways to anchor himself, for all the old

[5] Broudy, Harry S. "To Regain Educational Leadership." *Studies in Philosophy and Education* 2 (1962):156.
[6] Commission on Educational Planning of Alberta. *A Choice of Futures*. Alberta, Canada, 1972.

roots—religion, nation, community, family, or profession—are now shaking under the hurricane impact of the acceleration thrust [7].

Effects of Change on the Individual

The influences of societal transformation go beyond the changes it imposes on the individual's economic, political, and social roles. It profoundly influences his view of his world and of himself and leads to various types of effort to find meaning, emotional security, and self-expression. The "youth culture" represents the search of young people for identity, personal integration, values, and self-expression that they do not find by identifying with, and looking ahead to participating in, the adult world of work, community, and family.

Toffler, in an analysis of the "psychological dimension" of future shock, sees a widespread turning away from a faith in rational ways of coping with one's experience:

> The assertion that the world has "gone crazy," the graffiti slogan that "reality is a crutch," the interest in hallucinogenic drugs, the enthusiasm for astrology and the occult, the search for truth in sensation, ecstasy and "peak experience," the swing toward extreme subjectivism, the attacks on science, the snowballing belief that reason has failed man, reflect the everyday experience of masses of ordinary people who find they can no longer cope rationally with change [8].

Toffler's catalog of retreats from reality applies to people of all ages in all walks of life who are searching frantically for answers, when accustomed ways of adapting are no longer functional.

One of the most pervasive changes in modern society has been the tremendous development of the psychological sciences and their techniques for analyzing and modifying individual personality and interpersonal relationships. We are daily bombarded with "psychologizing" in the communication media. As a result, many millions have learned to look inward toward the self, examining their needs, capabilities, feelings, values, and adjustment problems. This turning toward inner experience is constructive when it enables the individual to know himself better, contributes toward his self-improvement, enlarges his experience, and increases his capacities to relate to others. Such a development of personal resources is what Riesman, Glazer, and Denney termed becoming "inner-directed" as opposed to "other-directed [9]." In future, it may become necessary for individuals to find meanings and satisfactions increasingly in private experi-

[7] Toffler, Alvin. *Future Shock*. New York: Random House, 1970, p. 35.
[8] Ibid., p. 365.
[9] Riesman, David, Reuel Denney, and Nathan Glazer, *The Lonely Crowd*. New Haven: Yale University Press, 1950.

ence and in the company of intimate companions, since world over-population and the depletion of natural resources may restrict individual space and geographic mobility (if not physical posses-sions).

Yet neither the needs of individuals nor the demands of society can be met by those who retreat into self and build walls against others, since human beings are inherently social and interdepen-dent. Maintaining a free, yet manageable human society in the face of the many forces toward social disorganization and anarchy requires that individuals develop higher capabilities for mutual re-sponsibility and cooperation.

The psychiatrist Karl Menninger makes the claim that a loss of moral values combined with a social conscience is a key to society's problems. In *Whatever Became of Sin?*, he holds that the loss of a sense of personal and social responsibility (though a sense of guilt remains) is at the root of our major social crises—corruption, vio-lence, and the pervading sense of depression, gloom, and fear [10]. Guilt, or a sense of sin, results from doing what one feels is not right, which usually means what one believes others would disapprove or punish.

With the rapidly declining influence of organized religion and the decline in adherence to conventional standards respecting sexual conduct and obedience to arbitrary authority, the bases for con-science and guilt are being transformed. Menninger's point, ob-viously, is that social controls depend greatly on governors of indi-vidual conduct that consider the effects of one's acts on others. If religion, parental authority, laws, and police are not to be the sources of restraints on conduct, what will replace and, let us hope, improve on them? The social education of individuals—at home, in commu-nity, at school, and in other agencies—needs to be restructured to provide an effective balance of freedom for self-realization combined with responsibility for others. It must take into account new norms of conduct allowing for greater diversity of values and behavior than are permitted by traditional ethics. In this country, this means re-placing the Puritan ethic.

Social controls based on the fear of punishment, while neces-sary, should be counted on less than controls that "accentuate the positive," that is, controls based on empathy and a sense of common purpose with others. A number of recent techniques offer means whereby individuals can learn effective mutual relationships and ways of gaining satisfactions through acts that benefit others. Two such popularized techniques are group psychotherapy and group dy-namics with its "T-groups," in which people learn to function in

---

[10] Menninger, Karl. *Whatever Became of Sin?* New York: Hawthorn Books, 1973.

groups. Recently, encounter groups have provided an agency for people to resolve various problems—drug addiction, difficulties in sex, or inabilities to form close friendships; communes have had a particular appeal to youths who seek richer experiences in cooperative living; while in the universities, the co-ed dormitory offers students an education in living intimately with members of the opposite sex.

Learning to relate to members of groups different from one's own is an evident need in view of the historic polarization of society into conflicting units. Louis Lundborg, board chairman of the Bank of America, confronted this purpose in response to an antibank rebellion directed at the officers of his company. He invited leaders of the opposition group to lunch to learn their views and to work out ways of achieving solutions of the conflict. His book, *Future Without Shock*, proposes methods of negotiation between opposed groups as a way of resolving issues.[11] Schools could introduce similar means for students to learn to participate constructively in intergroup relations. A total-community approach to education could confront the generation gap by offering genuine intergenerational education programs. Intergenerational courses could bring adult community members representing different backgrounds and roles together with elementary or secondary students for the serious study of local or national problems. The results would be increased mutual understanding across the generations as well as steps toward devising solutions to the problems studied.

PSYCHOLOGICAL REQUIREMENTS FOR LIVING IN THE FUTURE

What chief demands on the individual does societal change impose? These demands challenge education to make changes that will meet them, insofar as education can contribute toward satisfying such difficult requirements.

In the *economic* realm, there is an increasing demand for workers possessing competencies in problem solving and in human relations, and for individuals who are capable of relearning their jobs or preparing for different jobs. The industrial worker's tasks increasingly will be those of creating programs for machines and troubleshooting problems that were not anticipated in automated programs. The need for greater skills in human relations results from the increasing proportion of jobs in service occupations—teaching, work in interpersonal and intergroup relations, social welfare occupations, jobs in government, recreational work, etc. Special provisions are

[11] Lundborg, Louis B. *Future Without Shock.* New York: W. W. Norton, 1973.

needed to prepare many millions in our inner cities to obtain jobs in industry or service occupations.

In the *political* sphere, there is the need for every citizen to become prepared for responsible participation in dealing with the many critical societal problems that exist now and are certain to become more acute in the years ahead. The alternative is for our citizens to abrogate democracy through permitting control of our society by whatever special-interest groups can seize power—Fascists, technocrats, generals, unions, or corporations. Enlightened self-interest in dealing with issues and problems is at the heart of citizenship in a democracy. But effective democracy demands citizens who recognize that their interests can be served best when, through negotiation and compromise, the interests of many different groups are served.

Citizens respond tardily to events, becoming aroused to action only after problems have become acute. Thus, learning to look ahead—to see local, national, and world-wide problems in their early stages and to take preventive political action—is becoming increasingly essential for survival. An educated citizenry should be prepared to influence the direction and pace of change, rather than adjusting defensively to changes that have already taken place.

In view of the great powers of mass persuasion in the hands of the communication media, citizens have a particular need to learn to delay decisions related to their vital concerns until they have obtained and judged the evidence on issues.

In the *social* realm, the increasing need is for individuals to acquire the attitudes, values, and skills required for effective interpersonal and intergroup relations. Our society is becoming increasingly split into conflicting groups that are both unprepared and disinclined to find common purposes through negotiation. Ways must be found to break through the communication barriers separating young and old, black and white, affluent and poor.

Central to the individual's social life are close relationships with other individuals in family, work, community, and recreational roles. The growing disorganization of society, in the view of most students of human behavior, has resulted from serious shortcomings in the area of our ability to form and maintain emotionally satisfying relationships with others. Distrust, hostility, and rejection toward one's associates are foundation stones for intergroup and international conflict.

Skills in intergroup relations are as vital as interpersonal skills. An effective community requires that various groups work together to meet common needs, including education, jobs, transportation, recreation, personal services, and physical safety. To counter the growing disorganization of communities, community members generally need to become active participants in groups representing different constituencies that are committed to finding humanistic solutions to problems of common concern.

The same skills necessary to interpersonal and intergroup relations are needed in relations with people in other countries. The prevailing myth that America and Americans are best, and all other countries and peoples inferior, is a poor basis for building international understanding, good will, and cooperation. Racial bigotry toward fellow Americans is paralleled by a readiness to treat people in other countries as less-than-human. Labeling Orientals as "gooks" and "monkeys" because of their small stature, dark skin, and pajamas made My Lai possible, as it made napalm bombing of noncombatants tolerable to many Americans. Education for international living must begin now.

In the *personal* sphere, each individual needs to develop qualities of individuality than can withstand societal pressures toward becoming what Mills has labeled "The Cheerful Robot." [12] The individual must learn to tolerate or cope with the complexities, contradictions, and uncertainties of mass society. He should become able to achieve personal satisfactions and have meaningful human relationships despite the impersonal qualities of an automated society. And, since personal man provides the foundation for social man, the individual needs to acquire empathy, tolerance, and the will to work with others for mutual benefits.

The increased leisure most individuals will have as a product of automation offers the opportunity, as Broudy puts it, to choose between "self-cultivation" and "distraction or boredom." [13] Education for productive and enjoyable uses of leisure becomes a critical requirement since few people spontaneously develop their capacities for rich and active leisure pursuits.

Achieving an integrated and personally satisfying set of values and interests is an especially difficult thing under conditions of very rapid societal change. Learning to look at oneself objectively and to examine the consequences of various courses of action, then to choose and act upon what promises to yield a sense of personal worth as well as satisfying experiences, are critical requirements for arriving at personality integration emphasizing freedom and expression rather than passive conformity to external pressures.

Building a rich inner life is an important purpose at any time. It may become even more important if the future brings greater regimentation and restriction of outward freedoms, as seems likely. The

---

[12] Mills, C. Wright. *The Sociological Imagination.* New York: Oxford University Press, 1959.
[13] Broudy, "To Regain", p. 139.

"psychological revolution" in today's society points the way and offers methods of getting there. The turning of many toward eastern society for models in Yoga and other disciplines is not merely escapist; it offers a way of slowing down, exploring unfamiliar resources, and learning skills of body, mind, and emotional control.

"Communing with nature" cannot be denied us unless we come to live in concrete bunkers below ground. Books, art, and music offer avenues to private experience. Failing these, there remain the resources of direct sense experience, meditation, and imagination. Our Western society has largely blocked these out in a preoccupation with the world outside ourselves. People in "undeveloped" countries have skills and habits of living in this private world that exceed ours. It is a fine paradox that our industrial society may require us to return to a more primitive communication with nature and our inner being for psychological survival.

A key point in developing the personal sphere is that allowances must be made for a great diversity in individual values, interests, and styles of coping with the world. Not everyone will elect to follow a model suited to paragons of self-knowledge, autonomy, and active participation in private and social worlds. Some will choose to conform to outward influences. Some will stress emotional rather than intellectual outlets. Others will emphasize sense experience. Others will seek to express themselves primarily in social relationships. Still others will seek outlets in creative activities. To assume that any one style of life will suit everyone is arrogant presumption, entirely contrary to the history of human society.

An aspect of individuality that will need to be provided for in future as well as today is cultural identity, that is, identification with the traditions, values, and customs of one's ethnic or cultural group. Being a black, a Jew, an Italian, a Quaker, a Baptist, or a Mohammedan is a central part of a person's identity. Society in the future must allow for cultural diversity and permit individuals to associate freely with members of their groups of choice. Totalitarian regimes that have severely restricted freedom of association and expression have found it virtually impossible to destroy a cultural tradition. When external expression is denied, group identifications remain as an important part of inner experience.

PROVISIONS NEEDED IN EDUCATION FOR THE FUTURE

Based on the analysis of psychological requirements for living in the future, the following aims should receive emphasis in educational programs:

1. Teach all students competencies in problem solving in the various curriculum areas. Skills should be taught in iden-

tifying and analyzing problems, then devising and testing solutions, using both academic and real-life situations.

2. Offer all students career education involving study of various occupations that includes work sampling in real or simulated situations. Regular individual career counseling should be offered as a basis for planning the student's program of studies.

3. Offer all students systematic citizenship education including the analysis of issues and societal problems in terms of values involved and consequences of alternative decisions. Students should participate in political processes through student government and through taking part in real or simulated elections and government activities.

4. Teach students competencies in interpersonal relations, group participation, and intergroup relations. This instruction should give particular attention to studying and interacting with individuals and multicultural groups differing in race, national origin, sex, age, and other characteristics.

5. Involve all students in community study and participation in community activities. This school-in-community approach should provide for a regular interaction of the school with both formal and informal community agencies and organizations.

6. Teach all students to understand and appreciate people and cultures elsewhere in the world, with emphasis on industrially less-developed countries in Africa, the Middle East, the Orient, and South America. Stress should be placed on teaching how individuals grow from infancy to adulthood in the different societies, using data obtained by cultural anthropologists.

7. Offer all students education directed toward self-knowledge, a positive self-concept, an integrated set of values, and qualities of initiative and independence enabling them to accept challenges and take needed risks.

8. Teach all students to develop leisure-time interests and skills including physical, intellectual, and esthetic expression and giving attention to both social activities and private experiences.

9. Individualize or personalize each student's educational program in terms of courses of study, learning goals, learning methods, and rate of advancement. Instruction should stress the full development of the student as an unique individual.

10. The schools should treat each student as a person of worth and dignity, recognizing that, at any age, the student is the

client whose interests the school's staff serves. Students should participate in decision making about the school program as fully as their maturity allows.

Calcutta: A Vision of the End of the World

WILLIAM VAN TIL
Indiana State University

To paraphrase T. S. Eliot's *The Hollow Men,*

This is the way the world ends
Not with a bang but a cheeseburger.

Concerning India, I have encountered two persuasions. There is a boastful type who pays no attention to health precautions, apparently drinking out of any nearby fountain and eating "whatever the people eat," or the more credible type who uses boiled and bottled water solely, shuns the uncredentialed vegetables, and generally behaves as though Pasteur hadn't made it all up after a bad night. As science-respecting people, we accept the latter interpretation of the universe and hence ate carefully in Calcutta, India, in March, 1974. But naturally, because the world is a place of shades and shadows, and life is a set of floating hazards and unpredictabilities, I got a contaminated cheeseburger at one of Calcutta's best hotels. After four good intercommunicating speeches to educators, many of whom really cared about humanity, at the University of Calcutta, Birla College, American University Center, and Ramakrishna Institute, I dropped like a stunned ox in my own bloody vomit.

If you're going to be sick in Asia, better be sick in a city where you are working for the United States Information Service. I realize it is not fashionable to say anything good today of the government of the United States and totally *de trop* to say anything kindly of the bureaucracy. But you haven't been sick—I hope—in Asia. Put the ugliest face on it and point out that it isn't good publicity for the Foreign Service boys to have somebody die on their hands while practicing his specialty abroad. Point out that their houses abroad allow them to live beyond the style to which they would be accustomed at home. But when you're struck down you're glad that the USIS and the American Embassy are there with their characteristic

From "Calcutta: A Vision of the End of the World," *Phi Delta Kappan*, Vol. **LV**, No. 10 (June 1974), 699–700. © 1974 by Phi Delta Kappa, Inc. Reprinted with permission.

foreign service names like Holbrook Bradley. Their loyalty to you is total. They have a magnificent Indian USIS staff doctor, Dr. Wats, who comes to your hotel where you're vomiting away your life blood in the middle of the night. They have access to a small hospital, handicapped technologically yet suffused with kindness and caring. They have a compound in which they live, guarded by constantly patrolling Indian soldiers, with an apartment where your wife can wait it out and where you, too, if you manage to survive, can contemplate recuperation. However, we took a three-plane, 30-hour sleepless journey back to the United States for diagnosis and treatment.

All this takes place in Hell—my only descriptive word that comes close to describing Calcutta. Yes, I've seen the Victoria Memorial and the art galleries and mansions too, but my pervading memory of Calcutta is the unimaginably dense-packed streets. Incredible numbers of human beings are born, live, and die on the squalid streets. Naked babies lie in the dust and the sacred white cows drop their loads beside the little heads. The old sit and wait for death. Outside the Department of Education of the University of Calcutta is a vast garbage dump in which the ravaged bodies of what once were human beings compete with the sacred cows for a morsel of food.

If you want to change an intelligent and sensitive man's attitudes on a problem, I suggest you send him to Calcutta. Don't give him any temporary shelter, such as my bureaucracy with its little glass box cars. . . . Send some of the living room liberals from America who worry over a currently fashionable problem which always, strangely enough, has some mild impact on their own physical comfort. Worldlings that they are, they will be acquainted with culture shock, could in fact deliver lectures on it. But see if the massive uncaringness, part of the armor, the self-imposed blindness of many of the Indian and American intellectuals, doesn't just for a moment grab their hearts so that they cry in the streets like crazy prophets, "Someone must see! Someone must do something! Someone must care!" before they go back to explaining to themselves that India has tried all faiths, all philosophies, all reforms, all revolutions, and that none of them work. So the armor and blindness are restored and culture shock is neatly filed and categorized, and they can go their way again, caring not about these hordes of people but only about selected problems which will affect their own comfort and convenience.

What I experienced in my Calcutta illness was culture shock perhaps—yet different too. It may have been a version of future shock, but not the kind that Toffler writes about. My version of future shock was a prophetic one. Under doctor-administered drugs, it came to me that Calcutta represents what the cities of our world may sometime die of. Not the bright plastic world of some of the futurists, such as Herman Kahn. Not the world of silent abandonment and desolation in Rachel Carson's *Silent Spring* or Nevil Shute's *On the Beach*. The apocalypse coming for the human race may be a slow, noisy death of the big cities.

I felt it in 1974 in Calcutta as the poor publicly foraged and died while the rich drove sightlessly and unheeding through the streets. I felt it when the "low shedding," a severe shading down and brownout of power any time of the day or night, began unanticipated at any moment. In huge areas of the city all power would go off. Cars continued to move tensely and dangerously through the streets, flashing their lights momentarily as required by law, then roaring head-on toward each other in the darkness. The telephone system flickered and died, flickered and died, then briefly roused. Transportation stopped and resumed. The city was noisily dying.

My vision was that Calcutta today presaged a likely future after energy use-up, environmental breakdown, widening gaps between rich and poor, the collapse of old religious caring, and the incapacity to achieve new social caring. The poor would die first, after desperate attempts at rebellion, sometimes succeeding, more often failing. Hanging on to the end would be the patricians in the native population who had their own built-in enclaves. They would buy what they could. The poor would go first when they used up their edible garbage; some would hang on longer than others. The rich would go last when they used up their life-lines. Then silence would come over the clamoring, sweltering, exuding, contrasting city. Life would no longer pulse in the garbage eaten by the poor. The last air conditioner would go off, the last bulb hidden in the last refrigerator would shed no more light for the patricians.

So in Calcutta I witnessed in future shock through my drugged visions the end of the world of the cities. When? Someday. Don't ask me what my horror vision means to educators. Because if you don't know that it means that there must be a colossal gathering of forces for *caring* and *survival*, then my journey to the end of the night and my witness to the end of the world will have no meaning to you.

In my vision of Hell, the last emaciated patrician came out of his house. He saw no poor people. But since he had never seen the poor people throughout his life, this was not unusual. But now he looked for the poor to teach him where to dig in the garbage. But the poor people were all dead. He fell on his face on the garbage and began clawing. After a while there was no movement at all on the vast garbage dump as the world ended in Calcutta and maybe in your city. So went my vision.

Why? Because not enough people CARE. Some do. But not enough by far. And that is why humankind today is in deep, deep trouble.

VI

EDUCATION WITHOUT SCHOOLS: DESCHOOLING SOCIETY

Learning is but an adjunct to ourself,
And where we are our learning likewise is.
William Shakespeare

The belief that a highly industrialized society requires twelve to twenty
years of prior processing of the young is an illusion or a hoax.
Paul Goodman

THE END OF THE "IMPOSSIBLE DREAM"

Americans traditionally have shared an almost unbounded faith in the
power of the schools to work for individual betterment and social
amelioration. Enshrined in the national mythology (as noted in a previous section) has been a belief that schooling can be a potent tool
for fostering equality, justice, and universal prosperity for all. The
myth further held that schools enabled society to remain immune
somehow to the economic inequities and social malaise found among
mankind elsewhere; schools were thought, among other things, to
guarantee an open, free society and to offer the best means for individual social mobility.[1] In particular, formal education was considered
one of the most acceptable ways of employing national wealth to provide the poor and disadvantaged with a chance for economic and
social advancement—doing so, significantly, without offending or
threatening the comfortable. As Horace Mann, Secretary of the Mas-

---

[1] Cf. Godfrey Hodgson, "Do Schools Make a Difference?" *Atlantic Monthly*, Vol.
231, No. 35 (March 1973), 36; Christopher J. Lucas, "Historical Revisionism and
the Retreat from Schooling," *Education and Urban Society*, Vol. 6, No. 3 (May
1974), 335–356; and Peter Shrag, "End of the Impossible Dream," *Saturday Review*, Vol. **LIII**, No. 38 (September 19, 1970), 68.

sachusetts Board of Education, phrased it in his annual report of 1848, the common school for children of all social classes and backgrounds is "a great equalizer of the conditions of men, the balance wheel of the social machinery. . . . It does better than disarm the poor of their hostility toward the rich: It prevents being poor. . . ." [2]

Historically, the range of functions assigned schools was extraordinarily broad. Schools were called upon to inculcate respect for authority, to foster obedience and self-discipline, to instill patriotic sentiment, and to nurture love of country. They were expected to preach the virtues of hard labor, of thrift, of cleanliness, and to warn against the evils of tobacco, alcohol, and later of sex and communism. They were called upon to help acculturate the immigrants who inundated the nation's shores in successive waves, to furnish each new generation with marketable vocational skills, and to produce a high level of literacy among the general population. With characteristic satisfaction, historian Henry Steele Commanger once observed that no other nation "ever demanded so much of schools and of education [and] none other was ever so well served by schools and its educators." [3]

More recently, however, as the national mood has become less expansive and more cautious, a pervasive disenchantment with the fruits of schooling has apparently set in, accompanied (it seems only fair to add) by a more general erosion of confidence in the power of other institutions within society to offer easy solutions to age-old problems of poverty, inequality, and injustice. If it is true, as many have claimed, that education has always been the true American religion and the school (with its bright and shiny promise of entry into a certificated meritocracy) its church, clearly there has been a noticeable loss of faith in recent years on the part of many people and a corresponding falling away from the institutionalized expression of that faith. That so many observers have become convinced that the school as an institution has failed—at least as judged by the inflated standards of the past—signals what Peter Schrag aptly termed some years ago the end of the "impossible dream," the end of the apparent delusion that schooling is a panacea for social ills.

Despite, or possibly because of, heavy demands placed upon schools, the nation's educational system has never lacked critics of its failures or shortcomings. What renders the current phase of educational criticism historically unique is its direct frontal attack against the institution of schooling itself. Until very recently, the desirability of schools and of compulsory attendance by the young were more or less taken for granted by friend and foe alike. Even the harshest critics, those most dissatisfied with the status quo and desiring

[2] Quoted in Shrag, loc. cit., p. 68. The discussion follows Shrag's treatment.
[3] Ibid., p. 68.

change, aspired somehow to improve the condition and operation of the schools rather than do away with them entirely. Nowadays, however, not only has the traditional faith in formal education as an instrument of social change been challenged, but the basic viability of the school as a social institution is under question. While earlier detractors indicted the schools for their failings and issued demands for reform, virtually all critics operated on the assumption that schools as such, however much altered, would endure. It was assumed that after reforms were enacted, schoolhouses and classrooms and teachers and lessons and some form of compulsory attendance would still remain once the dust had settled.[4] But, lately, it has become a commonplace in some circles to argue, not that schools should be improved, but that they should be abolished. Allegedly, the real imperative is not to *change* schools so much as it is to end our dependence upon them as institutions for carrying out the work of education. The time has come, it is claimed to "deschool" society.

FROM REFORM TO DISESTABLISHMENT

One major challenge to the public school mystique, in particular to popular faith in schools as the foundation of a free and democratic society, was the charge levied by radical critics of the mid-1960's that in reality schools were neither free nor democratic. Assailing them for being excessively authoritarian, repressive, antidemocratic, and positively miseducative, critics lashed out at what they characterized as the emptiness, spiritual brutality, boredom, and sheer waste of human potential to be found in traditional classrooms. The strident polemics of writers such as Nat Hentoff, Herbert Kohl, and James Herndon exposed the rigidity, the pervasive racism, and the sometimes unwitting but nevertheless debilitating suppression of real learning endemic in decaying urban schools. John Holt, Edgar Friedenberg, and Charles Silberman, to name a few of the more widely-read reformers of the period, extended the attack against prevailing abuses in middle-class suburban schools. At the same time, a host of militant critics of higher education, such as Paul Goodman and Jerry Farber, were mounting an assault against the establishmentarian groves of academe. Disaffection became rampant, generated by successive indictments of the schools for their alleged emphasis upon conformity instead of creativity, on discipline rather than independence, on regimentation rather than the requirements of genuine learning. Yet, through it all, most radical proponents of "open"

---

[4] Philip W. Jackson, "A View from Within," in Daniel U. Levine and Robert J. Havighurst (eds.), *Farewell to Schools???* (Worthington, Ohio: Charles A. Jones, 1971), p. 60.

classrooms and a "humanistic" pedagogy continued to accept as an implicit premise the assumption that progressive educational policies, once acted upon, would prove sufficient to effect meaningful, substantive change.

Frustration over resistance to change in the public schools, however, inevitably led some reformers to look for alternatives in the form of educational institutions ostensibly freed of the inertia and vested interests of public school bureaucracies. Uninhibited by the ideological commitments and political restraints of existing public or private schools, proponents argued hopefully, independent "alternative" or "free" schools might yet offer a more flexible and humane type of education for those ill-served by traditional educational institutions. Accordingly, the alternative school movement in its initial phase often was directed toward creating schools which would more effectively serve those students whose unique needs were being ignored in the regular system or whose special problems would otherwise cause them to drop out.[5]

Some free schools, reflecting the youth counter-culture of a decade ago, were begun in hopes of creating a learning environment adapted specifically for self-exploration, for "doing one's own thing" outside the constraints of the traditional middle-class lifestyle. Some were designed to appeal to inner-city blacks or other racial and ethnic minorities. Still others scarcely resembled schools at all in their efforts to bring incidental and formal learning closer together. Permutations on the theme of educational alternatives was seemingly endless, with organizational formats ranging from the highly structured to the chaotic: multicultural schools, bilingual schools, street academics, dropout centers, and schools without walls. Physical facilities ranged the gamut from urban streetfront or warehouse loft to rural commune. Although the publicity accorded free schools was out of all proportion to their numbers, it seemed obvious that they represented an important, legitimate response to the question of radical educational reform.

Nevertheless, from the very outset the independent school movement of the late 1960's and early '70's encountered serious difficulties. One problem, as Jonathan Kozol perceptively noted in his important critique, *Free Schools* (1972), was intellectual imprecision. Many who aspired to create new alternatives proved themselves surprisingly dogmatic in their imposition of modish slogans on the real world they entered. Unwilling to confront squarely problems involving the role of authority or the place of objective knowledge in learning, they tended to reflect a kind of "siege mentality" which substi-

[5] Cf. Donald W. Robinson, "Alternative Schools: Do They Promise System Reform?" *Phi Delta Kappan*, Vol. **LIV**, No. 7 (March 1973), 433.

tuted radical revolutionary rhetoric and clichés for reasoned statements of purpose, process, and organization. Unless the sponsors of free schools came to terms with hard questions concerning the problems of leadership, structure, and power in a humane learning environment, Kozol warned prophetically, they would condemn themselves to impotence and eventual irrelevance.

An equally serious problem was money. It quickly became apparent that so long as independent free schools were denied access to public revenues, they could never serve more than a miniscule percentage of the school-age population or compete effectively with tax-supported public schools. At best, they could extend the promise of "freedom" in learning only to those able to afford the necessary tuition fees. Why, many critics asked rhetorically, in a democratic society, should only those parents with sufficient funds have freedom of educational choice for their children? Given the fact that everyone pays taxes to sustain the present monopolistic public system, would it not be possible to allow for some genuine democratic pluralism in education by ending that monopoly?

An affirmative response was forthcoming in proposals for a so-called "voucher plan," which, ideally, would provide freedom of educational choice for both children and parents. University of Chicago economist Milton Friedman, an early advocate of the idea, suggested that with the pupil would go a voucher entitling the school he attended to an amount of money equal to the average per capita expenditure for public education in the local school budget. By thus expanding the options available to parents, private independent schools could be supported, thereby ending the entrenched educational bureaucracy's long-standing monopoly over schooling. Friedman held that the poor and disenfranchised especially would have far better opportunities in an open, competitive educational structure than under the present closed, paternalistic system. The result, he predicted, would be to give more power to parents and students and, quite possibly, at the same time to stimulate reform in those public schools faced with a precipitate loss of pupils and funds.

Christopher Jencks of the Center for the Study of Public Policy at Harvard, another advocate of vouchering, advanced a similar argument for breaking up the existing pattern of school control. Despite the enrollment of a sizable minority of children in nonpublic schools, Jencks pointed, elementary and secondary education in the United States has been, for all practical purposes, a public monopoly.[6] Aside from the 10 or 11 percent preferring religious schools, the sole course

[6] Cf. Christopher Jencks, "Giving Parents Money for Schooling: Education Vouchers," *Phi Delta Kappan*, Vol. **LII**, No. 1 (September 1970), 49–52; and John H. Fischer, "Who Needs Schools?" *Saturday Review*, Vol. **LIII**, No. 38 (September 1970), 79.

available to most families has been to send their offspring to the
public school designated by the local schoolboard. Nor, in most
school districts, has a parent been able to exercise any effective influence on what his child learns, how he is taught, or how he is treated.
Only through the stimulus of real competition provided through
vouchers, Jencks and his supporters argued, could schools be rendered more responsive to the diverse needs of learners. "Today's
public school has a captive clientele," Jencks wrote in defending his
scheme. "As a result, it in turn becomes the captive of a political process designed to protect the interests of its clientele. The state, the
local board, and the school administration establishes regulations to
ensure that no school will do anything to offend anyone of political
consequence. By trying to please everyone, however, the schools
often end up pleasing no one. The voucher system seeks to free
schools from these managerial constraints by eliminating their monopolistic privileges." [7]

Criticism of the proposals of Friedman, Jencks, and other advocates of vouchers was swift and occasionally vituperative.[8] Charges
were heard that an unregulated "free market" in education would invite the worst kind of economic and racial segregation, encourage
hucksterism as schools competed for students, and exacerbate the
problems of existing public schools without offering any offsetting
advantages. At yet another level, critics questioned whether there was
any substantial reason to believe that a voucher plan would succeed
where integration, compensatory education, and local community
control had failed. The fact that existing private schools, which presently have to compete for students, had not engaged in widespread
experimentation or offered substantially different alternatives to public schools, was advanced as a counter-argument to the claim that a
voucher plan would stimulate innovation and diversity.[9] Except in
isolated cases, the argument continued, private educational agencies
do not mount programs or devise curricula materially different from
those available through the public school system, because both public and private educators inevitably respond to the same set of societal forces and influences with predictably similar results. The dises-

[7] Jencks, op. cit., p. 50.
[8] For a representative sample of more temperate and thoughtful criticism, consult Harry S. Broudy, "Educational Alternatives—Why Not? Why Not," Phi Delta
Kappan, Vol. LIV, No. 7 (March 1973), 438–440; and by the same author, The Real
World of the Public Schools (New York: Harcourt Brace Jovanovich, 1972), pp.
133 ff. Cf. also Robert J. Havighurst, "The Unknown Good: Education
Vouchers," (52–53) and A. Stafford Clayton, "Vital Questions, Minimal Responses: Education Vouchers," (53–54), both in Phi Delta Kappan, LII, No. 1
(September 1970).
[9] James J. Shields, Jr., The Crisis in Education Is Outside the Classroom (Bloomington, Ind.: Phi Delta Kappa Educational Foundation, 1973), pp. 27–28.

tablishment of the public school by means of vouchers, therefore, was not likely to alter that basic political reality.

THE RETREAT FROM SCHOOLING

Still another factor contributing to the erosion of public confidence in formal education was the appearance of a body of sociological research which seemed to strike hard at long-cherished assumptions about the effects of schooling. Utilizing data from the massive Coleman Report [10] of 1966, Christopher Jencks and his associates concluded six years later that "the evidence suggests that equalizing educational opportunity would do very little to make adults more equal." Moreover, "the character of a school's output depends largely on a single input, namely the characteristics of the entering children." Finally, according to Jencks, "everything else—the school budget, its policies, the characteristics of the teachers—is either secondary or completely irrelevant." [11] In other words, there seemed to be little or no correlation between educational expenditures and student achievement and even less connection between quality of schooling and level of support. Popular beliefs that schools foster equality, creativity, or anything else now seemed to be open to question.[12] In point of fact, the evidence was not nearly so clear-cut as it had been represented. Nor was there unanimity of opinion as to the meaning of the data employed in the Coleman and Jencks studies, much less its implications for long-range educational policy and planning. Nevertheless, by the mid-1970's, the weight of popular opinion seemed to have shifted discernibly away from what Gunnar Myrdal once termed the traditional faith in education "as a part of, or a principle conclusion from, the American Creed." [13]

More or less coincident with that shift was a major reinterpretation of the educational past which posed a major challenge to accepted views of the development of schooling in the United States.[14] Mainstream historiography, as represented in the writings of Bernard Bailyn, Lawrence Cremin, Richard Hofstadter, and Rush Welter, had always tended to look favorably upon the rise of the common school

[10] James J. Coleman, *Equality of Educational Opportunity* (Washington, D.C.: U.S. Government Printing Office, 1966).
[11] Christopher Jencks, et al., *Inequality: A Reassessment of Family and Schooling in America* (New York: Basic Books, 1972), pp. 255, 256.
[12] Rand Corporation, *How Effective Is Schooling?* (Santa Monica, Calif.: The Corporation, 1972), p. xiii. For an excellent criticism, consult Daniel Tanner, "The Retreat from Education—for Other People's Children," *Intellect,* Vol. **102**, No. 2354 (January 1974), 222–225.
[13] Gunnar Myrdal, *An American Dilemma* (New York: Harper & Row, 1962), p. 709.
[14] Lucas, op. cit., 357 ff.

movement, regarding the subsequent expansion of institutionalized education to the lower classes as an almost unmitigated triumph of human freedom and progress. But to a new generation of historians, most notably Michael Katz, Colin Greer, and Joel Spring, the growth of public schooling was something less than an unalloyed good. Greer, for example, in a 1972 study entitled *The Great School Legend*, was to argue that far from being an expression of burgeoning egalitarian sentiment, early efforts to acculturate immigrant children in school were expressly calculated to keep them in a subordinate position within a social hierarchy. More broadly, Greer alleged that schools past and present have always performed the same basic task: selecting out individuals for opportunities according to a hierarchical schema which runs closely parallel to existing social class patterns.[15]

Similar in tone was Joel Spring's *Education and the Rise of the Corporate State*, published the same year as Greer's analysis. Spring argued at length to show that an image of society as a corporate structure requiring a high degree of social control and organization played a decisive role in the shaping of the schools by an emergent elite of business and labor leaders, politicians, and pedagogical theorists. In response to the importunate needs of urban life, industrialization, and an expanding technology, schools distorted the original meaning of freedom and individualism, denied democracy, and slavishly served the interests of the corporate state.[16] Although no intentional conspiracy may have been involved, the consequences were the same: schools came to play a major role in educating people to a new corporate form of existence demanded by urban life. In practical terms, this meant the replacement of an individualism stressing autonomy and independence with one emphasizing self-subordination, social adjustment, and cooperation. In addition, the schools were expected to train workers with the correct social attitudes and skills needed for effective assimilation into the industrial system: thrift, obedience, respect for authority, group consciousness, and loyalty.

According to Spring, the rise of the vocational guidance movement early in the twentieth century was essentially an expression of the same desire to make institutionalized education serve simultaneously as a mechanism of social control and as a feeder system to the industrial complex.[17] By analyzing abilities and gearing instructional programs to future vocations, student clients could more readily be prepared for slots within the corporate state. Vocational counselors thus joined with teachers, administrative bureaucrats, and

[15] Colin Greer, *The Great School Legend, A Revisionist Interpretation of American Public Education* (New York: Viking Compass (Basic Books), 1972), p. 152.
[16] Joel H. Spring, *Education and the Rise of the Corporate State* (Boston: Beacon Press, 1972), pp. 2–6 ff. and *passim*.
[17] Ibid., chapter five.

outside business interests to make the schools over into smoothly functioning machines that stamped out human "raw material" in the corporate mold.

It can be argued that the revisionist historical analysis developed by Spring, Greer, Katz, and others was almost certainly as one-sided and unbalanced as the older interpretation it was intended to supplant. Yet for all its faults, the thesis that schools have always been employed as instruments of social and political control has had the practical effect of rendering more persuasive current allegations that such control is *intrinsic* to the nature of institutionalized schools. In a sense, modern revisionism in educational history complements the entire deschooling thesis advanced by such radical critics as Paul Goodman, John Holt, Carl Bereiter, Everett Reimer, and Ivan Illich.

THE DESCHOOLING MOVEMENT

The basic thesis of those who urge the deschooling of society is devastatingly simple: the school as an institution has lost its formerly unchallenged claim to educational legitimacy. Accordingly, critics who still persist in demanding, according to their lights, modest changes or radical reforms *within* schools miss the point. By its very nature, institutionalized schooling is an organized enterprise designed to reproduce the established order by perpetuating its dominant values, ideology, and forms of organization. In order to bring about true reform, nothing less will suffice than the prohibition of compulsory school attendance and the elimination of all academic certificates and credentials. Most of the traditional functions served by the school can and should be eliminated or reallocated to other agencies in society. "We are witnessing the end of the age of schooling," writes Ivan Illich. "School has lost the power, which reigned supreme during the first half of this century, to blind its participants to the divergence between the egalitarian myth its rhetoric serves and the rationalization of a stratified society its certificates produce." [18]

Among the earliest critics to argue that schooling impedes education was Paul Goodman (1911–1973), self-styled anarchist, psychologist, linguist, novelist, philosopher, poet, and social theorist, who in a succession of incisive critiques of American life inveighed against coercive institutions, the broad separation of schools from life, while arguing for the need to create a culture in which children did not "grow up absurd." Education in the sense of socialization, Goodman asserted in *Compulsory Mis-education* (1964), is a natural and inevitable process to which formal schooling is a reasonable auxiliary whenever

---

[18] Ivan Illich, "After Deschooling, What?" in Alan Gartner, et al. (eds.), *After Deschooling, What?* (New York: Perennial Library, 1973), pp. 5–6.

an activity is best learned by singling it out for special attention under the tutelage of someone else. But it by no means follows "that the complicated artifact of a school system has much to do with education, and certainly not with good education." [19] In both primitive and highly civilized societies, until very recently, Goodman pointed out, most education occurred incidently rather than in schools specifically established for the purpose. Learning of social tasks and economic skills took place through direct first-hand observation and experience: in families and peer groups, community labor, master-apprentice arrangement, games, play, and rituals.[20] As was the case among the Greeks, the surrounding culture, or *paideia*, was thought to be inherently educative. So also today, "ideally, the *polis* itself is the educational environment; a good community consists of worthwhile, attractive, and fulfilling callings and things to do, to grow up into." [21]

Repeatedly, Goodman stressed the point that only in the last century in industrialized countries has a majority of children gotten much formal teaching, and only in the past few decades has formal schooling been extended into adolescence and adulthood. In the United States in 1900, only six per cent completed high school and roughly one-quarter of one per cent finished college. Thus, the provision of incidental education by extended formal schooling is a very recent phenomenon. Schooling today, Goodman noted, "serves mainly for policing and for taking up the slack in youth unemployment." More precisely, he explained, schools play two roles: one noneducational and the other educational. The first and more important of the two is custodial. Elementary schools provide a baby-sitting service necessitated by the decay of the extended family and urban mobility. Junior and senior high schools are basically an arm of the police, providing wardens (teachers) and concentration camps (schools) through the budget of the local board of education.[22] The educational role, further, is by and large to provide at public expense apprentice-training for corporations, government, and the teaching profession itself, as well as to train the young to adjust to authority. "To a remarkable degree," Goodman claimed, "vital functions of growing up have become hermetically redefined in school terms: being a good citizen is doing homework; apprenticeship is passing tests for jobs in the distant future; sexual initiation is high school dating; rites of passage are getting diplomas." [23]

[19] Paul Goodman, *Compulsory Mis-education and the Community of Scholars* (New York: Vintage, 1964), pp. 16–17.
[20] Paul Goodman, *The New Reformation: Notes of a Neolithic Conservative* (New York: Random House, 1970), p. 69.
[21] Paul Goodman, "Freedom and Learning: The Need for Choice," in Frank R. Krajewski and Gary L. Peltier (eds.), *Education, Where It's Been, Where It's At, Where It's Going* (Columbus, Ohio: Charles E. Merrill, 1973), p. 179.
[22] *Compulsory Mis-education*, p. 18.
[23] *New Reformation*, p. 70.

The real question is whether formal schooling, representing a deliberate imposition upon informal learning, can be adequately justified. For example, is it true, as the popular wisdom has it, that a highly technological social order cannot be sustained without extended periods of book-learning for every child and adolescent? Goodman's answer was the evidence is strong that there is little correlation between school performance and life achievement in any of the skilled professions and that so far as performance in more modest clerical, technological, or semiskilled factory jobs is concerned, there is no substantial advantage accrued by years of schooling or number of diplomas gained. The belief that industrialism necessitates a dozen or more years of formal schooling, he avowed, is a myth, a hoax, an illusion. "In licensing professionals," Goodman insisted, "we have to look more realistically at functions, drop mandarin requirements of academic diplomas that are irrelevant, and rid ourselves of the ridiculous fad of awarding diplomas for every skill and trade whatever." [24]

Goodman did not go so far as to suggest the total elimination of schools. But he did suggest that on-the-job training, apprenticeships, innovative community activities in "a protective and life-nourishing environment," and independent auto-tutorial study should be explored as alternatives to formal schooling. We can educate the young entirely in terms of their free choice, he suggested, with no processing whatever. "Our aim should be to multiply the paths of growing up, instead of narrowing the one existing school path. There must be opportunity to start again after false starts, to cross over, take a moratorium, travel, work on one's own." [25] On the whole, education should be voluntary rather than compulsory, with diverse educational opportunities, variously administered. The monolithic school system should be broken down rather than expanded. "Every part of education can be open to need, desire, choice, and trying out," Goodman emphasized. "Nothing needs to be compelled or extrinsically motivated by prizes and threats."

Specifically, Goodman's program for educational reformation called for the following: (1) making incidental education the chief means of learning and teaching; (2) the elimination of most high schools, with other kinds of youth communities taking over their socializing functions; (3) direct grants to adolescents for any plau-

---

[24] "Freedom and Learning: The Need for Choice," op. cit., p. 180. ". . . Where jobs exist and there is need for technical training," Goodman argued, "the corporations ought to spend more money on apprenticeships. We are an affluent society and can afford it. And the conditions of modern life are far too complicated for independent young spirits to get going on their own. They need some preparation, though probably not as much as is supposed; but more important, they need various institutional frameworks in which they can try out and learn the ropes." *Compulsory Mis-education*, p. 59. Cf. Ivar Berg, *Education and Jobs: The Great Training Robbery* (New York: Praeger, 1970).
[25] *New Reformation*, p. 87.

sible, self-chosen educational proposal such as purposeful travel or individual enterprise; (4) college training to follow, rather than precede, entry into the professions; and (5) more on-the-job apprenticeship training. Nowhere did Goodman take what Ivan Illich called the only true "revolutionary" position: he did not argue for the abolition of schooling. He did claim, however, that only those capable of profiting by learning through books in an academic setting (not more than fifteen percent by his estimation) should be encouraged to patronize schools. "Forcing the nonacademic to attend school breaks the spirit of most and foments alienation in the best," he asserted. "Kept in tutelage, young people, who are necessarily economically dependent, cannot pursue the sexual, adventurous and political activities congenial to them. Since lively youngsters insist on these anyway," he added, "the effect of what we do is to create a gap between them and the oppressive adult world, with a youth subculture and an arrested development." [26]

Finally, to the charge that his proposals were unrealistic or prohibitively expensive, Goodman replied: "I do not know [if my ideas] would cost more than our present system—though it is hard to conceive of a need for more money than the school establishment now spends." What would be saved, he suggested, is "the pitiful waste of youthful years—caged, daydreaming, sabotaging, and cheating—and the degrading and insulting misuse of teachers." [27]

Very similar in its approach and style was the argument advanced by John Holt, a one-time practicing teacher who was led step by step from acvocacy of classroom reforms *within* existing schools to the proposition that attendance at schools should be completely voluntary. Like Goodman, Holt observed that throughout history most children have been educated by the whole community, the wider society they lived in. Nothing else, he alleged, makes any sense. Compulsory attendance laws should be abolished because schools are only one place among many where young people can learn about the world. "Let them compete with other educational resources for the time and attention of children," he advised.[28] Secondly, Holt advocated the abolition of all teacher certification requirements. They do not make teachers better, he alleged, but often make them worse, and have the additional defect of keeping out or driving away many otherwise qualified people. Those who run a school should be free to use anyone as instructors they think can be helpful to the learners. For the most part, teachers and parents should control schools, rather than professional administrators.

[26] "Freedom and Learning: The Need for Choice," op. cit., p. 179.
[27] Ibid., p. 181.
[28] John Holt, "Why We Need New Schooling," in Stephen C. Margaritas (ed.), *In Search of a Future for Education* (Columbus, Ohio: Charles E. Merrill, 1973), p. 60. Cf. also his *Freedom and Beyond* (New York: E. P. Dutton and Company, 1972).

Thirdly, Holt urged the elimination of any required curriculum. "Children want to learn about the world and grow into it; adults want to help them," he stated. "Let them get together, and the proper curriculum will grow out of what children need and want, and what the adults have to give." [29] In a similar vein, all compulsory grading and testing should be done away with unless a student desires to be tested so that his teacher can help him improve. Otherwise, all assessment and evaluation is "destructive" and "inexcusable." Students should refuse to take examinations, Holt suggested; and teachers should refuse to administer them. Finally, if schools are retained as educational institutions, their traditional constraints and regulations should be abolished: entrance requirements, attendance rules, achievement standards, grades, diplomas, all the paraphernalia of external authority. Like Friedenberg and Jencks, Holt also urged the enactment of a voucher system. Any school that is free and open to all should be entitled to tax support on the same basis as state-run institutions. The state's monopoly on public education should be outlawed. Lastly, Holt endorsed the concept of life-long, self-directed learning. "For part of people's lives," he noted, "we tell them they can't get out of school, and once they're out, we tell them they can't get back in. Let people, of whatever age, go in and out of school when they see fit, using it when it seems most useful to them. Let the learner direct his own learning." [30]

Psychologist Carl Bereiter, who first won national prominence for his development with Siegfried Engelmann of preschool curricula and teaching programs for disadvantaged children, took an opposing tack in his controversial *Must We Educate?* (1973). The elementary school, he conceded, is bound to continue to exist, not because it performs a vital function but because it is a convenience as a custodial baby-sitter. Its sole responsibility beyond baby-sitting should be limited to "training in well-defined, clearly teachable skills," with children free the rest of the time "to do what they want." Schools should stop trying to educate; furthermore, they should abandon all pretense of doing so. "What I propose that schools should be," Bereiter explained, "is essentially what they are now, only better. For there is no evidence that schools accomplish anything beyond training and child care. Education amounts to an empty claim, but in trying to make good on the claim, schools waste money and energy, subject people to endless tedium, and end up doing an inferior job. . . ." [31]

We must distinguish carefully between child care and deliberate training. Informal, humane schools after the open education model

---

[29] Ibid., p. 60.
[30] Ibid., p. 62.
[31] Carl Bereiter, *Must We Educate?* (Englewood Cliffs, N.J.: Prentice-Hall, 1973), p. 81.

are fine, Bereiter claimed, *as child care centers* insofar as they provide a suitable environment for children. The child's life should be more or less his own, the teacher serving as an adjunct to nature rather than an agent of society charged with shaping the child to a preformed pattern. Good training, however, has little in common with good child care, and they should be clearly separated. Schools should be downgraded to the status of centers where training in reading and numerical skills would be provided "with a minimum of fuss and bother." Incidental learning, education in the more generous sense of the term, can and must occur elsewhere. Schools could still be useful and enjoyable places, but not very important ones: most children could afford to stay away most of the time without loss. As for cultural resources to complement schooling, Bereiter advised that vigorous efforts be undertaken to create recreational centers, library media centers, user-programmed facilities, in brief, a multitude of socially engineered ways of inducing people to become more active participants in their own self-development and growth.

With respect to adolescence, Bereiter suggested that many ways should be provided for growing up, learning, and for entering adulthood. A minority of academically-inclined students could be given the opportunity to pursue their interests within independent centers of higher learning similar to liberal arts colleges. For the majority who are not academically oriented, "it would seem immensely more sensible and humane to allow this large group of young people to enjoy their adolescence without the burden of formal academic work. All they need is money." [32] An ideal arrangement, to Bereiter, would be to give every citizen four years of unrestricted support: that could be used by those under twenty-one for academic pursuits or for doing nothing in particular. Or, some youth might prefer significant work in the company of peers through some type of service corps. Work, vocational training, apprenticeships, and other kinds of on-the-job training might offer attractions for still other students. At the very least, the traditional functions performed by the old-fashioned high school (except possibly meeting the social needs of adolescents) could easily and more effectively be assumed by other agencies and institutions in society.

The best-known and in some ways the most radical of the deschooling advocates has been Ivan Illich, a disestablishmentarian Catholic priest, formerly Vice-Chancellor of the Catholic University at Ponce, Puerto Rico, and subsequently founder and director of the Centro Intercultural de Documentación, (CIDOC), an independent language training research, and publication center in Cuernavaca, Mexico.[33] The public school system of most industrialized nations,

[32] Ibid., p. 115.
[33] For a description of CIDOC, cf. Howard Ozmon, "The School of Deschooling," *Phi Delta Kappan*, Vol. LV, No. 3 (November 1973), 178–179.

Illich claimed, might be likened to the advertising agency that makes people believe they need society as it is presently constituted. The public is systematically indoctrinated to believe, for example, that skills are valuable and reliable only if they are the result of formal schooling and only if they find practical application in the existing social order. Because the formal educational system has a monopoly on access to opportunity in society, the school as the single major vehicle of social selection replaces other-worldly promises of the good life with immediate promises of social mobility and prosperity. "School appropriates the money, men, and good will available for education and in addition discourages other institutions from assuming education tasks," Illich argued in his best-selling book, *Deschooling Society* (1970). "Work, leisure, politics, city living, and even family life depend on schools for the habits and knowledge they presuppose, instead of becoming themselves the means of education. Simultaneously both schools and the other institutions which depend on them are priced out of the market." [34]

Schools by their very nature are unmitigatedly bad in Illich's view. Students within them are led to confuse teaching with learning, grade advancement with education, a diploma with competence, and fluency with the ability to say something novel or different.[35] Formal educational institutions—the world-wide "sacred cow" of industrialism—monopolize opportunity, standardize norms, and deny individual human differences while delaying need gratification and stifling creativity. They repress love and encourage fear; they teach alienation and encourage competition; and they discourage sharing and cooperation. In their practical effects, they act to preserve privilege and power for the schooled; reinforcing rather than minimizing social stratification. "Equal educational opportunity is, indeed, both a desirable and a feasible goal," Illich argued, "but to equate this with obligatory schooling is to confuse schooling with the Church. School has become the world religion of a modernized proletariat, and makes futile promises of salvation to the poor of the technological age. The nation-state," he noted, "has adopted it, drafting all citizens into a graded curriculum leading to sequential diplomas not unlike the initiation rituals and hieratic promotions of former times." [36] What the modern state has done, Illich claimed, is to assume responsibility for enforcing the judgments of its educators through truant officers and job requirements, much as did the Spanish monarchs who enforced the judgments of their theologians through the conquistadors and the Inquisition.

Trying to improve schools is a hopeless delusion, Illich insisted. Those who seek to reform schools by introducing new curricula or

[34] Ivan Illich, *Deschooling Society* (New York: Harrow Books, 1972), p. 11.
[35] Ibid., p. 1.
[36] Ibid., p. 15.

pedagogical techniques, who would transform basic objectives, who want to substitute local community control for centralized authority or to introduce free choice among alternate schools, those who would like to "electrify" the classroom with computerized and electronic gadgetry, all miss the point. Their nostrums issue from an inadequate analysis of the nature of schooling and only postpone the facing of deeper underlying issues. All such critics miss the point because they fail to attend to the "ritualistic" aspects of schooling, what Illich called "hidden curriculum"—the structure of schooling as opposed to what goes on in school.

Institutionalized education in the West, according to Illich, has been tainted with a technocratic orientation based upon the psychology of a consumer society.[37] Knowledge defined in terms of accredited, prepackaged curricula and educative action is circumscribed by tightly regulated, professionalized role structures. Schooling accentuates the fundamental inaccessibility of modern institutions in the sense that one is taught to distrust one's own experience. Worse yet, knowledge is organized in forms that make it impermeable in terms of active participation in the world. The "hidden curriculum," Illich asserted, fosters the myth that certified teacher-bureaucrats alone command worthwhile knowledge and that they alone are entitled to impart it on restrictive terms to the uninitiated. As Illich phrased it, "The hidden curiculum teaches all children that economically valuable knowledge is the result of professional teaching and that social entitlements depend on the rank achieved in a bureaucratic process. The hidden curriculum transforms the explicit curriculum into a commodity and makes its acquisition the securest form of wealth."[38] Extensive accumulation of knowledge thus converts into guaranteed privilege and high personal consumption. Small wonder then that the school is accepted as the avenue to greater power, to self-enlightenment, and to social legitimacy.

The translation of the need for learning into a demand for schooling has thus altered the meaning of "knowledge" from "a term that designates intimacy, intercourse, and life experience into one that designates professionally packaged products, marketable entitlements, and abstract values."[39] Schools convert knowledge to power and parlay consumption of knowledge into the exercise of privilege and status in the social hierarchy. It becomes clear then, on Illich's analysis, why schooling is an elitist institution structured to undermine learner sovereignty: the "free determination by each learner

[37] Note the analysis in Manfred Stanley, "Illich Defrocked," in Cornelius J. Troost (ed.), *Radical School Reform, Critique and Alternatives* (Boston: Little, Brown and Company, 1973), pp. 74–80.
[38] Ivan Illich, "After Deschooling, What?" in Gartner, et al., loc. cit., pp. 8–9.
[39] Ibid., p. 10.

of his own reason for living and learning—the part that his knowledge is to play in his life." The only remedy is to abolish all formal schools and with them all compulsory education.

According to Illich, a good educational system should have three purposes: it should provide people with unrestricted access at all times to needed learning resources; it should engage all who wish to share knowledge with those who want to acquire it from them; and it should afford all who want to present an issue to the public with the opportunity to make their viewpoint known. It follows that a necessary first step is to enact laws making schooling optional rather than compulsory. Further, there should be legislation forbidding discrimination in hiring, voting, or admission to centers of learning based on previous attendance or performance at some school. Only by creating a society that is totally noncoercive educationally, can people be free to decide what they shall learn, what skills they wish to acquire, and under what conditions. Because bureaucratized schools have always socialized the public into assuming that knowledge is worthwhile only as a specialized, technologically produced commodity the individual ceases to engage in autonomous effort once trapped by this imposed "commodity consciousness." He has been made over to all intents and purposes into a consumer of predefined value-products and knowledge-commodities. The only true path leading to liberation is to deprive people of institutionalized definitions of commodities to consume—then and only then will they make knowledge their own and devise values for themselves.

Illich advanced a number of proposals designed to end man's alienation from learning and his dependence on institutionalized schooling. To grow up decently, he said, a person needs access to things, places, processes, events, and records. To guarantee such access is primarily a matter of unlocking the privileged storerooms, or schools, to which they are presently consigned. A major goal should be the prevailing practice of restricting access to teaching or learning. Secondly, a learner must have access to persons who can teach him skills or impart information. Incentives need to be provided, Illich urged, to encourage the sharing of acquired skills, as opposed to the existing situation in which professional teachers monopolize instruction, restrict initiation into the various fields of knowledge, and exert political influence to disqualify unauthorized teaching. Thirdly, people need access to what Illich referred to as "convivial tools" or instrumentalities through which people can relate freely to one another, sharing, teaching, and learning from one another.

Reliance upon "self-motivated" learning and self-instruction, upon natural associations of learners and teachers, can be greatly facilitated in Illich's scheme by interrelated networks or "learning webs": arrangements whereby students are furnished essential materials and resources for learning, are enabled to exchange skills, are "peer matched" so that partners can learn together to their mutual advantage, and, finally, are afforded access to data banks or "reference services" supplying knowledge on where and how to obtain needed information. The technology to create such learning webs already exists, Illich avowed, all that is lacking is the will to use it.

Still another proponent of deschooling deserving brief mention is Everett Reimer, a one-time executive secretary of the Committee on Human Resources of the Commonwealth (Puerto Rico) and adviser to the Alliance for Progress, who later served as consultant and frequent lecturer at Cuernavaca. "Our views are very close," Illich told an interviewer. "We have a real academic relationship and see each other several times a year." [40] Reimer's *School Is Dead, Alternatives in Education* (1970) was, like *Deschooling Society*, an eloquent and spirited defense of the thesis that schools have outlived their usefulness. After presenting at length the case against compulsory schooling, Reimer went on to outline strategies for its replacement by universal access to informal learning resources. School, he argued, has become "the universal church of a technological society, incorporating and transmitting its ideology, shaping men's minds to accept this ideology, and conferring social status in proportion to its acceptance." It is too late to reject technology, but time still remains to escape enthrallment with the monolithic secular orthodoxy represented by schooling. "There are," Reimer claimed, "many roads to enslavement, only a few to mastery and freedom. . . . Our major threat today is world-wide monopoly in the domination of men's minds. We need effective prohibition of scholastic monopoly, not only of educational resources but of the life chances of individuals." [41]

REACTION AND RESPONSE

Initial reaction to the Illich-Reimer thesis ranged from incredulity to disbelief. Typical was philosopher Sidney Hook's dismissal of *Deschooling Society* as a "smart, silly book . . . whose absurd criticism warrants little attention from anyone endowed with a normal portion of common sense." [42] Mortimer Smith termed Illich's argument utopian, sentimental, and "the ultimate cop-out." Because schools at present are not the voluntary, noncoercive centers of innocence and pleasure deschoolers want them to be is sufficient reason for scrapping them. It is pure romantic anarchism, Smith insisted, to suppose

[40] Quoted in Ozmon, op. cit., p. 179.
[41] Everett Reimer, *School is Dead, Alternatives in Education* (Garden City, N.Y.: Doubleday & Company, 1971), p. 30.
[42] Sidney Hook, "Illich's De-Schooled Utopia," *Encounter*, Vol. **38**, No. 1 (January 1972), pp. 54 ff.

that learners can acquire knowledge and skills "by poking around in libraries and museums, by watching craftsmen in tool shops" or by "watching surgeons and fiddlers in action, a practice bound to set back the clock in medicine and music." [43] Similarly, Philip W. Jackson of the University of Chicago assailed advocates of deschooling for their seeming naiveté. In a postschool era, he wondered, is it realistic to expect that school-age children, liberated from the artificial constraints of the classroom, will be enthusiastically engaged in learning through contact with real-life situations? "Guided by nothing more than natural curiosity and an instinctual love for learning." Jackson mused, "our children will presumably wander over the streets and fields of our land, gathering rosebuds of wisdom along the way. Adults, gladdened by the sight of these wandering scholars, will hail them as they pass and will invite them into the shops and factories and offices and hospitals, where they will become apprentices and learn at the feet of their elders those skills and trades that will equip them to take a productive place within our society." [44] It was highly improbable, he concluded, that such an idyllic state of affairs would ever come to pass.

Many hostile respondents denied that schools are as bad as deschooling critics claimed. "Much as it might dampen the critic's flame," Jackson argued, "a calm look at what goes on in our classrooms reveals them to be neither Dickensian nor Orwellian horrors. They are neither prisons, presided over by modern-day Fagins who take delight in twisting ears and otherwise torturing children, nor are they gigantic Skinner boxes, designed to produce well-conditioned automatons who will uncritically serve the state." [45] Those who believe otherwise are simply misinformed or irresponsible in their attacks. Having begun with an exaggerated picture of how bad things are in the schools, critics asserted, the deschoolers end up with an unrealistic and highly romanticized notion of the alternatives. Their image of a schooled society is too pessimistic; their ideal of a deschooled society too optimistic. Not all schools deserve to be charged with totalitarian oppressiveness. There is a difference between reasonable demands that they be reformed and an unreasonable demand that they be abolished.

Some opponents of deschooling fastened on what they charged was Illich's overly simplistic view of learning. It would be criminally negligent, they argued, to rely on the chance, casual encounters of

[43] Mortimer Smith, "The Romantic Radicals—A Threat to Reform," in Daniel U. Levine and Robert J. Havighurst (eds.), *Farewell to Schools???* (Worthington, Ohio: Charles A. Jones, 1971), pp. 74–75.
[44] Philip W. Jackson, "A View from Within," in Levine and Havighurst, op. cit., pp. 62–63.
[45] Ibid., p. 62.

the young, or upon the unrestricted exercise of uninformed free
choice. Certain skills, for example reading, if not learned early preclude or render infinitely more difficult other kinds of subsequent
learning experiences. Young children, especially, are not always
aware of what they need to know or how skills and values acquired at
present can enhance learning in the future. The cumulative effect of
wrong choices or too many missed opportunities could be extremely
serious, particularly for children who are not self-motivated learners.
Teaching as the art of arranging subject matter in sequential patterns
so as to facilitate learning and make it more accessible ought not be
disparaged. Until learners arrive at the point where they can *knowl-
edgeably* direct their own patterns of growth, the counsel and direction of teachers is always helpful and occasionally essential. Like good
health care of dental hygiene, for example, schooling *is* a legitimate
form of coercion designed to introduce and reinforce habits subsequently valuable to a mature adult.[46] Besides, the fact of the matter
is that not all learning can be intrinsically interesting and immediately
attractive. Some schooling is drudgery and it is foolish to suppose
otherwise.

Critics further charged that a more sensible view of teaching and
learning would acknowledge the vital role explicit instruction plays in
education. "To claim that we will all learn from and teach one another
as need and interest manifest themselves is to invoke pious hope that
flies in the face of overwhelming evidence. Not everyone who knows
something, even when he knows it well, can teach it, not to mention
teach it effectively. Not everyone who is able to teach is willing or in a
position to do so." [47] Furthermore, while Illich, Reimer, and others
have claimed correctly that people learn most of what they know outside the school, the skills, knowledge, and training acquired in a formal instructional situation frequently furnish the necessary prerequi-
sites for meaningful incidental learning. Experience, in other words,
is not of itself necessarily educational. Schooling potentially makes a
difference insofar as it contributes to what the learner brings *to* his
outside experiences in order to make them educationally significant.

One frequent criticism of deschooling centers on the question
of whether human freedom and individuality should be looked upon
as an unconditional absolute. Through the school a society represents
itself, extending its traditions, values, mores, and patterns of living.
Such social standards inevitably pose certain limits upon the degree
of uniqueness permitted each person within society; in fact, they
help define the terms under which participation in society is possible.
The question then is whether individualism is not itself partly a social

---

[46] Stanley, in op. cit., p. 76.
[47] Hook, op. cit., p. 55.

concept, and whether or not society has a right to impose through its institutions some obligations and responsibilities upon its separate constituent members. For example, schools traditionally have been thought to serve as a cohesive, integrative force within society. If schools are abolished, will the concept of a common core of values and learning also be destroyed? Would deschooling further fragment and divide society, rendering the proliferating social subcultures within it ever more isolated in the absence of a shared culture as transmitted through the schools? [48] Closely related is the objection raised by those critics who wonder whether Illich's proposed legal prohibition on any standards for employability except specific job-task skills might not hasten undue technical specialization and utterly destroy both the concept of general liberal education and the associated social values.

While the reaction to the position developed by Illich and Reimer has not been uniformly hostile, it *has* tended to be overwhelmingly critical.[49] Interestingly, some theorists take deschooling proponents to task for not being "radical" enough in the etymological sense of getting to the root causes of the matter. More than a few commentators have observed that Illich offers little that is really new among recent criticisms of American education.[50] Herbert Gintis was the first of many to point out that Illich's indictment of educational bureaucracies and institutions utterly ignores the more fundamental socio-economic factors nurturing socialization institutions.[51] Others, Sizer among them, regard Illich's advocacy of "learning webs" with their master-disciple dyads or groupings as positively medieval in character:

For Illich, it appears, left-convivial institutions and mendicant scholars are neither abberations nor simply a nostalgic search for gemeinschaft that some contemporary counterculturists seek. Rather, Illich's entire commentary may be viewed as an instance of a traditional protest against modern societies, with their emphases on technology and science, middle class or socialist economies, and large scale political, welfare, and educational structures, characteristic of *philosophia perennis*.[52]

[48] The point is developed by Stanley, op. cit., pp. 79–80.
[49] For example, consult the bibliographic compilations and writings of John Ohliger, especially his "The Educational Future of the Incipient Revolution: Total Manipulation or Faith in Man's Ability to Choose?" in Levine and Havighurst, op. cit., pp. 65–71.
[50] Theodore R. Sizer, "Deschooling Society," *Comparative Education Review*, Vol. **16**, No. 2 (June 1972), 359.
[51] Herbert Gintis, "Toward a Political Economy of Education: A Radical Critique of Ivan Illich's *Deschooling Society*," *Harvard Education Review*, Vol. **42**, No. 1 (February 1972), pp. 76–77 ff.
[52] Francis R. McKenna, "Problems with Deschooling," unpublished paper presented at the annual meeting of the American Educational Studies Association, San Antonio, Texas, (March 1973), p. 2.

It would serve no good purpose to develop in further detail the litany of complaints lodged against Illich: that his discussion of the operation of skill centers, peer-matches, and learning exchanges is fleeting and superficial; that he neglects in Neo-Marxist terms any coherent analysis of the relationship between the social superstructure of schools and the underlying socio-economic substructure; that he neglects to note difficulties of access to learning that might arise from economic, political, or social differences within a deschooled society; that he fails to appreciate the impact of geopolitical factors relating to imbalances of human or physical resources upon the development of learning webs; or that his conception of learning is too intellectualist and rational. More significant, perhaps, is the extent to which his deschooling thesis has provoked serious discussion of obstacles to social and educational reform, has focused attention upon undesirable characteristics seemingly intrinsic to institutions of socialization, and has stimulated interest in the search (on a limited basis to be sure) for nontraditional alternatives to formal education.

Deschooling today is less an organized movement than a conceptual point of contact, one which practially all contemporary educational theorists must take into account if they expect serious consideration. The invectives of hostile critics discounted, Illich, Reimer, Holt, Spring, Greer, and others have raised an important set of issues and concerns which educational planners and policy-makers must confront now and in the future. If the criterion for the success enjoyed by advocates of deschooling is the degree to which there has been a precipitate abandonment of formal institutions of learning, then their efforts must be said to have met with abysmal failure. But if the proper standard for judging their importance is the extent to which major questions, otherwise neglected or glossed over, have been brought to the fore for discussion and open debate, then controversy over deschooling has been of incalculable benefit to investigations of the nature and purpose of education in contemporary society. If nothing else, the deschooling thesis is likely to exert a salutory, astringent influence upon the bombastic rhetoric of school reform for years to come. That in itself must be counted no small achievement.

No School?

GEORGE B. LEONARD

The most obvious barrier between our children and the kind of education that can free their enormous potential seems to be the educational system itself: a vast, suffocating web of people, practices, and presumptions, kindly in intent, ponderous in response. Now, when true educational alternatives are at last becoming clear, we may overlook the simplest: no school.

This means just what it says: the elimination of educational institutions housed in separate buildings with classrooms and teachers. At the least, it involves the end of all compulsory school attendance. The idea may seem entirely impractical. But the recent development of a technology of individualized learning has changed things. "No school" has now become feasible. The case may be stated as follows: Practically everything that is *presently* being accomplished in the schools can be accomplished more effectively and with less pain in the average child's home and neighborhood playground.

The man who first brought this proposal to my attention is Dr. M. W. Sullivan, an educational programmer. Sullivan is an outspoken and passionate man, and he argues with the prejudice of one who has seen the power of well-designed self-instructional materials. But I doubt if there is anyone who can state the case better.

Sullivan first began mulling over the "no school" idea in the late 1950s, when he and others at Hollins College in Virginia were developing some of the earliest programmed instruction. Why ship the bodies of our children through crowded streets to overstuffed schools, he wondered, when we can much more easily ship instructional materials to homes?

> In the entire psychological literature [Sullivan says], you can find no evidence that the teacher *per se* helps learning. You can find much evidence that the teacher does harm to the learning process. The average school, in fact, is no fit place to learn in. It is basically a lock-up, a jail. Its most basic conditions create a build-up of resistance to learning. Physically, the child is worn down by the fatigue of sitting in one position for inordinate lengths of time. Mentally, he is stunned by the sameness of his surroundings and the monotony of the stimuli that bombard him. Can you imagine the amount of energy it takes just to sit still, waiting, against every impulse, for your turn to respond?
>
> When *you* think, you want to get up, move, pace around. But most schoolrooms are set up to *prevent* thinking, learning, creativity—

whatever you want to call it. You'd be surprised how many new teachers are told, "Classroom control must come first. The most important thing the child has to learn is how to take instructions, so if you spend the first two months, or two years, teaching them to take instructions, it will be well worth while."

The average kid gets few chances to respond during the school day. And when he does get a chance, it's generally an echoic response. He just gives the teacher back what the teacher wants to hear. And you end up with an organism that has no integrity at all. Too often, when the organism does break through and start responding, he gets slapped down. He learns to sit still, to line up in orderly rows, to take instructions, to feel guilt for his natural impulses—and perhaps to do a few simple things that he could learn to do one-fiftieth—yes, *one-fiftieth*—of the time it usually takes him.

Now what would happen if you shipped the learning materials to the child rather than shipping the child to the dungeon? Let's assume no technological advances—no computers or electronic consoles. All you'd have to have would be the present form of programmed textbooks plus tapes that could be played on $24.95 Japanese tape recorders equipped with foot pedals. We already have programs for teaching languages and other auditory subject matter; the child goes through a written program, turning on the recorder with a foot pedal wherever stars appear in the program. Thus we can combine all the needed written, visual, auditory stimuli. We can provide any learning of importance that goes on in most present classrooms.

So I would have to say that, even with the present rather primitive programs, even the worst ghetto home can be a better learning environment than most schools. At least in the ghetto home, the child can get up and run around when he wants to. If he can just be kept out of school, he won't be taught that learning is dull, unpleasant work. He'll just assume it's what it is: the greatest pleasure in human life. There'll be no guilt and fear. He'll play with his learning materials when he feels like it. And if it's only a half hour a day, he'll be *far* ahead of school learning in all the basic subjects.

But what of social contacts, I asked Sullivan? What of "learning to get along with others in the peer group?" Sullivan replied:

Is there any indication that such a thing takes place in school? What is this *getting along* or *making out* with others? Why can't children learn that much better in neighborhood playgrounds or on the sidewalks or even in the streets? These bowling-alley places where you leave kids. They're good. Much better than schools where children are subjected to a totally false discipline and totally artificial relationships with each other.

In my own case, I was the only kid in my neighborhood who was sent to kindergarten. It was optional then in Connecticut. So for almost a year my peer group was out playing, learning, creating their own very exciting world while I was being tortured in school. They built a treehouse. They built a hut. And what did I do? I learned how to lie on a mat, how to listen to stories, how to line up, how to sit still. Finally, I figured how to escape. I wet my pants and they sent me home. *They sent me home.* The first time was an accident, but after that I made sure to do it every day. And I was free to learn again.

School is a terrible thing to do to kids. It's cruel, unnatural, unnecessary.

Many people would argue, I reminded Sullivan, that the school is a model of the world. Eventually, the child probably will have to face unpleasant working situations, narrow competition. There will be unreasonable deadlines, hasty instructions that will have to be understood and heeded—all sorts of hardships.

Yes, I know. The old idea was, if you want the kid to get along in life, you put him in that situation as soon as possible. If he's going to be in a lousy situation where he feels inadequate later, you put him in a lousy situation where he feels inadequate now. It just doesn't work that way. There was a very interesting study made on those Marines in World War II who went through the worst campaigns of the war, the ones who hit Guadalcanal and went through the whole thing— boredom, jungle rot, water up to the waist in foxholes, people dying all around them. As it turned out, the guy who stands up under all this is the one who would be considered to have had a very fortunate childhood, the good boy who was always told he was good. And who cracks wide open? The person who had been up against tough conditions in his childhood, with all sorts of hardships, the guy who had never had a chance at success.

You see, the whole argument falls apart however you look at it, even in the extreme case of the Marines in combat. But the world is generally not that extreme. The world isn't any damned way. It's what people make it. You can go a long way toward making your world. And that's just where the school steps in. It warps your expectations so that you'll see the outside world like the school and then you'll tend to make your world that way. You'll be trained to see learning as hard and painful. And you'll go out and perpetuate a world in which those conditions exist.

You know, you have to *teach* any organism how to be unhappy. And the human being is the only organism that has *learned* unhappiness— except maybe some of his has spilled over onto his dog. I must insist that schools as they now exist are well-designed to produce unhappiness and little else.

At this point, I felt constrained to raise the most powerful objection of all. "Whatever you say," I told Sullivan, "the mothers won't buy it. They just don't want their kids around the house, under their feet all day."

You're probably right. It's strange. They're so anxious to have the kids, then they seem to want to get them out of sight as quickly as possible. We'd have to teach the mothers a different attitude toward their children, not so much goddess and slave as playmates. We'd have to relieve their nervousness about the whole area of book learning. We'd have to show them how to reinforce their children's exploratory behavior whenever possible. Most of all, we'd have to teach them to spend a lot more time just leaving them alone—and perhaps enjoying them.

The trouble is that the parents have been to school, too. If we could just get the kids *out* of school for one generation, we'd solve the whole problem.

Parents who would reject Sullivan's views as extreme have a simple way of checking them out. Arrange for a visit to your child's school—but not on the usual parents' visiting day. (Go then, too, if you wish, but don't expect to find out what really goes on; the teacher and class have probably spent several days or weeks preparing for this charade.) Arrive early in the morning, with your child. Chat for a few moments with the teacher to put him at ease, and allow him to introduce you to the class. Assure him that you plan to create no disturbance whatever but simply to melt into the woodwork. Then take a chair near the back of a room at a position where you have an oblique view of your child. Be natural, casual, friendly. When children turn to look at you, smile slightly in acknowledgment and reassurance, then turn away. If you are natural and at ease, you will probably be surprised at how quickly you are ignored. And, though the teacher may tend to be on guard, his basic style of teaching and relating with the children is generally too deeply ingrained to allow for very much dissembling. You will have the opportunity of experiencing what your child experiences.

Take the opportunity. Focus in on your child. Try to assume his viewpoint, feel what he feels, learn what he learns. Become sensitive to his body positions; see when he sits straight, when he hunches over, when he squirms, when he languishes. Balance the weight of the teacher's words against the pressure on your seat. Try not to daydream. Remember that time goes more slowly for a child than for an adult.

Now are you ready for a little walk? A cup of coffee? A visit to the restroom? A cigarette? Forget it. Stay with your child. Stand only when he stands. Leave the room only when he leaves the room. Concentrate on him. *Become* your child.

Bored beyond endurance? Let us hope not. Let us pray for our children and for all children that you have found one of those master magicians who, in spite of every obstacle, manages to pull each unlikely new moment out of a hat, wiggling and full of life. If not, be easy on yourself for a little while; steal a few moments from the day (though your child has no such opportunity) for a modest experiment.

Take out a watch with a second hand. Mark the lines of a sheet of notebook paper with tiny crosshatches, each representing ten seconds. An hour's worth will fit neatly on a single sheet of notebook paper. Select a typical period, say, arithmetic instruction. During this period, mark each ten-second interval during which your child is really *learning* something. Leave the other intervals blank. . . . Bear in mind that true learning is change (not needless repetition of something already known) and that the learning has to do with the response of the child, not with the presentation of the teacher.

This little exercise will take sensitivity; you will have to be, in a sense, inside your child's mind. It will be more easily accomplished in the lower grades than in high school (or college, for that matter), where the lecture system makes it virtually impossible to know if learning is taking place. It will involve some guessing and can under no circumstances be termed "scientific." Nonetheless, it will most likely prove a revelation to you. I have tried it with my own children and with scores of others in all sorts of schools. The results are discouraging. Even marking with a kind of desperate generosity, I have rarely been able to fill in more than a third of the intervals. Often I have found that "classroom control" plus waiting for other children to recite plus all the other unwieldy manipulations demanded by the usual classroom environment leave less than ten percent of any child's time for anything that can remotely be termed "learning."

When you have had enough of this exercise, *stay where you are.* No coffee, no cigarettes, no moving around to relax your body and stimulate your thoughts.

Playtime. *Freedom.* Not so fast. First (if you are in a typical classroom), the entire class must come to order. That means stillness, silence. Perhaps each row of children will be pitted against the others; the row achieving submissive nonactivity first gets to line up first at the door. After all the children, again, have come to order and after teacher, again, orders the class to walk, not run, down the stairs, the door is opened. The children explode onto the play yard.

Go with them. Sit down somewhere among them so that you can experience the child's world at the child's level. True learning can take place under the conditions of play. But are you observing *play?* Probably not, unfortunately. The children are likely to be merely letting off steam, with shrill yells and frenetic running about. It has been my experience that, wherever the classroom situation is repressive and antithetical to learning, the playground situation, in direct ratio, is hyperactive and equally antithetical to learning. In true play, the child is intent, responsive, unhurried, completely involved. There is a lovely seriousness about it. The child who explodes out of and in reaction to a static, nonlearning environment is hurried, unresponsive, indeed almost spastic. This is not delight; it is desperation. After experiencing the playground situation. ask yourself, "Is this the kind of social interaction for which I'm sending my child to school?"

Back in class again, then to lunch. And then the afternoon. Does the classroom seem stuffy? Watch the eyes of your child and all the others. Are they becoming heavy with incipient sleep? Are the tender half-moons of delicate skin just beneath them becoming puffy and discolored? Look closely. And how about your own eyes? Do you find yourself stifling yawns? Let us hope not. Let us hope the day has been an exhilarating one.

If not, however, don't hasten to blame the teacher. The environment in which he works, the expectations he tries to fulfill, the techniques generally offered him are woefully inadequate to the human potential. The teacher who prevails over such conditions is an artist, a hero of our times.

And yet do not let compassion for the teacher soften the sense of tragedy that you may feel. The world is filled with wrongs—war, disease, famine, racial degradations and all the slaveries man has invented for his own kind. But none is deeper or more poignant than the systematic, innocent destruction of the human spirit that, all too often, is the hidden function of every school. And do not think that your child can escape unscathed. There has been a lot of speculation lately about LSD's permanently altering the brain structure. This is a naïve way of putting it. First, the brain does not have a set "structure." Second, there is very little that is entirely "permanent" about the behavior of the central nervous system. Learned behavior is generally reversible, though reversing a behavior learned early in life takes a great deal more energy at a later stage than was originally needed to establish the behavior. Still, it might well be said that a number of LSD trips do alter the brain, if only because of the changes wrought through the behaviors engaged in during those trips. This being the case, it must be said that the typical first-grade experience probably alters the brain of your child even more than would many LSD trips, doing untold violence to his potential as a lifelong learner.

"Tragedy" is a strong word, but I can think of no other to describe what happens to most children during the early elementary years. Visiting schools around the country, I have shuttled again and again from a kindergarten room to, say, a fourth grade. (If you have the chance, you might try this for yourself.) And I have talked with hundreds of teachers about the seemingly mysterious human discrepancy revealed on that short journey. It is almost as if you are viewing specimens of two different species. Teachers are the first to agree that this is so. Nor did I receive a single letter of dissent when I described the trip in a *Look* magazine story called "What Your Child Can Teach His Teacher," in December of 1966:

> Go into a kindergarten room. By and large, the five-year-olds are spontaneous, unique. Tell them to dance, and they move naturally with a sort of unorganized grace. Read them a story, and their eyes give you back its suspense, fear, laughter. We like to say their faces light up (a particularly telling phrase), and when we look into this illumination, we are not ashamed to let our own faces glow in return. All of this, we assume, is a natural condition of the very young.
>
> Walk down the hall to a fourth-grade classroom. Very quickly, you will notice that something has been lost. Not so many eyes are alight. Not so many responses surprise you. Too many bodies and minds seem locked in painful self-awareness. This, too, we carelessly attribute to the natural order. It's just part of growing up.
>
> But is it really? Is it really necessary for the human animal to lose in spontaneity and imagination as it gains in knowledge and technique? Must we shed the brightness of childhood as we put on the armor plating of age?

Perhaps it is no coincidence that the growth rate of intelligence falls off so rapidly just at the point when the child enters school. Older concepts of how the brain works offered physiological explanations for the startling fact that most humans have achieved eighty percent of their intelligence growth by their eighth birthday. Each new fact, it was said many years ago, makes a little crease or rut in the gray matter. After so long, there is no space for any more ruts. In more recent times, the synapses were said to be somehow "filled up," or the brain cells were "committed." The best recent research, however, suggests that the brain can never be "filled up." But it can be *taught* to stop learning—that is, changing. It can be *taught* to stop exploring, to reject the unfamiliar, to focus on a limited number of stimuli, to make repetitive, standard responses.

Indeed, the entire education process as it is usually constituted in our schools may best be viewed as a funnel through which every child is squeezed into an ever-narrowing circle; at the end there is room only for a single set of "right answers." The funnel does not stop constricting at the end of the lower grades, or even at high-school graduation. Educator Harold Taylor told me of what he called "four of the most depressing days of my life," with students from each of the four classes of a small, elite Eastern college—one day for each class, starting with freshmen. The experience had the quality of stop-action photography, in which the effects of four years of college were compressed into that many days. The freshmen, Dr. Taylor said, were still, to some extent, open and inquisitive, ready for new ideas. Each subsequent class was less so, with the seniors seeming bored, cynical and interested only in "How will this help me get a better grade?" or "What's in it for me?"

Professor William Arrowsmith goes another step, in writing of his preference for teaching the undergraduate in the humanities rather than the graduate student, whom he finds

> already half-corrupted by the fate he has chosen, the fate which makes him a graduate student. He wants knowledge and information. He has examinations on his mind, and hence tends to conform to his professor's expectation of him—the fate they have jointly chosen and now jointly enforce. The resentment they both frequently feel is their resentment of this mutual fate. For the graduate student, the undergraduate's lucky integration is no longer possible—or if it is, God help him! The present is now less insistent for him. He has chosen to *know* rather than to *be*. For a man with a gift of life, that loss is like castration; the best leave rather than suffer it. Others grit their teeth and will their way through.

It is not that the "product" of our education system is not "capable." He comes out with "skills." He may be a usable component in the social machine. But he is just about finished as a learner.

Only the inefficiency of the present school system and the obdurance of certain individuals can account for the creativity, the learning ability that survives after age twenty-five. Dr. Harold G. McCurdy of the University of North Carolina has studied the childhood patterns of those historical geniuses about whose childhood most is known. Seeking factors common to the early life of the twenty geniuses he selected, Dr. McCurdy came up with three: "(1) a high degree of attention focused upon the child by parents and other adults, expressed in intensive educational measures and, usually, abundant love; (2) isolation from other children, especially outside the family; and (3) a rich efflorescence of phantasy, as a reaction to the two preceding conditions." McCurdy concludes that "the mass education of our public school system is, in its way, a vast experiment on the effect of reducing all three of the above factors to minimal values, and should, accordingly, tend to suppress the occurrence of genius."

When McCurdy refers to public education as an "experiment," he is, unwittingly, taking educators into dangerous territory. For if we *did* consider schooling as experimental in nature, educators might well stand indicted under at least five of the ten essential principles of the Nuremberg Code for research involving human subjects. Imagine your children as the subjects:

1. The voluntary consent of the human subject is absolutely essential.

2. The experiment should be such as to yield fruitful results for the good of society, unprocurable by other means of study, and not random and unnecessary in nature.
3. The experiment should be designed and based on the results of animal experimentation and a knowledge of the natural history of the disease or other problem under study, so that the anticipated results will justify the performance of the experiment.
4. The experiment should be so constructed as to avoid all unnecessary physical and mental suffering and injury.
5. During the course of the experiment, the human subject should be at liberty to bring the experiment to an end if he has reached the physical or mental state where continuation of the experiment seems to him impossible.

The first and last provisions cited here would seem to be the most grossly violated by the present system of compulsory mass education. That children should be forced by law to stay in school until late adolescence may someday be perceived as outrageous. The current series of public-service advertisements urging adolescents to remain even longer already reveals the crux of the matter:

EDUCATION IS FOR THE BIRDS
The birds that get ahead
or
BOY.
Drop out of school now and that's what
they'll call you all your working life.

Behind the words, society's naked face—patronizing, insulting, ultimately utterly cynical.

But the slogans are true, aren't they? Yes. And there's the trouble. Jobs *are* withheld from those who don't possess a certain diploma. The diplomas, however, are screening devices. The job-dispensing agencies are not really interested in what the job seeker has learned in the school, but merely that, for whatever reason, he has survived it.

When you come right down to it, the amount of learning that goes on in high school, even in the simplest and most explicit techniques of our civilization, is minuscule. Look, for example, at the English textbooks from seventh grade through twelfth. They are basically the same book. And the student who writes and comprehends skillfully in the seventh grade will most likely be doing equally well at high-school graduation and forever after. To quote the recent president of the National Council of Teachers of English, Dr. Alfred H. Grommon: "Forty years of teaching traditional English grammar to

American students of varying backgrounds has failed to improve their ability to speak or write it."

Perhaps we should be glad that schools do generally fail in their present task, which is, as I have said before and undoubtedly will say a few more times, to teach a few tricks and otherwise limit possibilities, narrow perceptions and bring the individual's career as a learner (changer) to an end. Such a task may have seemed necessary, if ignoble, in the precarious fragmented society of the past, when individuals, as components, had to prop up the great social machine.

It is [my] basic premise, however, that the highly interactive, regenerative technological society now emerging will work best, indeed will *require* something akin to mass genius, mass creativity and lifelong learning. If this premise proves out, schools *as they now exist* are already obsolete. And, if someone like Sullivan can provide us with the wherewithal to do at home, easily, painlessly and quickly, what the schools attempt presently to do, in pain and failure, then perhaps we should consider ending the affliction, the tyranny that for so long has entrapped schoolchild and schoolmaster alike—and save billions of dollars in the process. (Linguistic note: The only two entries under the word "disciplinarian" in the index of Roget's *Thesaurus* are "tyrant" and "teacher.")

But let me hasten to stress again that what is usually being taught in school today makes up only a tiny fraction of man's education, present or potential. Nor does programmed instruction offer salvation; it will soon become outmoded. But this mode of learning—and others, such as the new speed-reading technique—provides hope and confidence to those who would expand education's domain and pursue ecstasy in learning. It proves that, *if need be,* we can even now remedy most educational ills that have plagued our children and confounded the "experts" over the years. Excepting the severely handicapped (possibly less than one percent of the population), *every* child can learn to read, to write, to spell, to manipulate quantities, to learn all the hard stuff of present-day schooling—in less than one-third the present time.

We might end schools rather than let them remain as they are today. Except for the legal difficulties, I would prefer having my own children learn at home; I have seen what schools, in spite of every good intention, have subtracted from their lives. But, instead of taking that alternative, we can move on into the unexplored lands of the human potential. We can take that extra two-thirds of present school time available to us right now (as a few experimental schools already are doing) and get on with the most exhilarating experiment in man's history: to help every child become, *in his own way,* an artist; to help every child become, *in his own way,* a genius; to see just how far toward ecstasy and accomplishment every human being can go.

About that day in class, your visit to school: I was not being hypothetical. I seriously recommend that you do it. Most teachers and administrators will probably welcome you. If, however, some administrator should bridle, remind him that you have every educational, moral and legal right to be there. The kind of visit outlined above, one parent a day, creates far less disruption than does a mass visitation on special days or weeks. And anyway (we keep forgetting) the schools belong to us. If they are failing to educate, it is, ultimately, because we don't care enough.

The Alternative to Schooling

IVAN ILLICH
CIDOC

For generations we have tried to make the world a better place by providing more and more schooling, but so far the endeavor has failed. What we have learned instead is that forcing all children to climb an open-ended education ladder cannot enhance equality but must favor the individual who starts out earlier, healthier, or better prepared; that enforced instruction deadens for most people the will for independent learning; and that knowledge treated as a commodity, delivered in packages, and accepted as private property once it is acquired, must always be scarce.

In response, critics of the educational system are now proposing strong and unorthodox remedies that range from the voucher plan, which would enable each person to buy the education of his choice on an open market, to shifting the responsibility for education from the school to the media and to apprenticeship on the job. Some individuals foresee that the school will have to be disestablished just as the church was disestablished all over the world during the last two centuries. Other reformers propose to replace the universal school with various new systems that would, they claim, better prepare everybody for life in modern society. These proposals for new educational institutions fall into three broad categories: the reformation of the classroom within the school system; the dispersal of free schools throughout society; and the transformation of all society into one huge classroom. But these three approaches—the reformed classroom, the free school, and the worldwide classroom—represent

From "The Alternative to Schooling," *Saturday Review* (June 19, 1971), 44–48, 59–60. © 1971 by Saturday Review, Inc. Reprinted with permission.

three stages in a proposed escalation of education in which each step threatens more subtle and more pervasive social control than the one it replaces.

I believe that the disestablishment of the school has become inevitable and that this end of an illusion should fill us with hope. But I also believe that the end of the "age of schooling" could usher in the epoch of the global schoolhouse that would be distinguishable only in name from a global madhouse or global prison in which education, correction, and adjustment become synonymous. I therefore believe that the breakdown of the school forces us to look beyond its imminent demise and to face fundamental alternatives in education. Either we can work for fearsome and potent new educational devices that teach about a world which progressively becomes more opaque and forbidding for man, or we can set the conditions for a new era in which technology would be used to make society more simple and transparent, so that all men can once again know the facts and use the tools that shape their lives. In short, we can disestablish schools or we can deschool culture.

In order to see clearly the alternatives we face, we must first distinguish education from schooling, which means separating the humanistic intent of the teacher from the impact of the invariant structure of the school. This hidden structure constitutes a course of instruction that stays forever beyond the control of the teacher or of his school board. It conveys indelibly the message that only through schooling can an individual prepare himself for adulthood in society, that what is not taught in school is of little value, and that what is learned outside of school is not worth knowing. I call it the hidden curriculum of schooling, because it constitutes the unalterable framework of the system, within which all changes in the curriculum are made.

The hidden curriculum is always the same regardless of school or place. It requires all children of a certain age to assemble in groups of about thirty, under the authority of a certified teacher, for some 500 to 1,000 or more hours each year. It doesn't matter whether the curriculum is designed to teach the principles of fascism, liberalism, Catholicism, or socialism; or whether the purpose of the school is to produce Soviet or United States citizens, mechanics, or doctors. It makes no difference whether the teacher is authoritarian or permissive, whether he imposes his own creed or teaches students to think for themselves. What is important is that students learn that education is valuable when it is acquired in the school through a graded process of consumption; that the degree of success the individual will enjoy in society depends on the amount of learning he consumes; and that learning *about* the world is more valuable than learning *from* the world.

It must be clearly understood that the hidden curriculum translates learning from an activity into a commodity—for which the school monopolizes the market. In all countries knowledge is regarded as the first necessity for survival, but also as a form of currency more liquid than rubles or dollars. We have become accustomed, through Karl Marx's writings, to speak about the alienation of the worker from his work in a class society. We must now recognize the estrangement of man from his learning when it becomes the product of a service profession and he becomes the consumer.

The more learning an individual consumes, the more "knowledge stock" he acquires. The hidden curriculum therefore defines a new class structure for society within which the large consumers of knowledge—those who have acquired large quantities of knowledge stock—enjoy special privileges, high income, and access to the more powerful tools of production. This kind of knowledge-capitalism has been accepted in all industrialized societies and establishes a rationale for the distribution of jobs and income. (This point is especially important in the light of the lack of correspondence between schooling and occupational competence established in studies such as Ivar Berg's *Education and Jobs: The Great Training Robbery.*)

The endeavor to put all men through successive stages of enlightenment is rooted deeply in alchemy, the Great Art of the waning Middle Ages. John Amos Comenius, a Moravian bishop, self-styled Pansophist, and pedagogue, is rightly considered one of the founders of the modern schools. He was among the first to propose seven or twelve grades of compulsory learning. In his *Magna Didactica,* he described schools as devices to "teach everybody everything" and outlined a blueprint for the assembly-line production of knowledge, which according to his method would make education cheaper and better and make growth into full humanity possible for all. But Comenius was not only an early efficiency expert, he was an alchemist who adopted the technical language of his craft to describe the art of rearing children. The alchemist sought to refine base elements by leading their distilled spirits through twelve stages of successive enlightenment, so that for their own and all the world's benefit they might be transmuted into gold. Of course, alchemists failed no matter how often they tried, but each time their "science" yielded new reasons for their failure, and they tried again.

Pedagogy opened a new chapter in the history of Ars Magna. Education became the search for an alchemic process that would bring forth a new type of man, who would fit into an environment created by scientific magic. But, no matter how much each generation spent on its schools, it always turned out that the majority of people were unfit for enlightenment by this process and had to be discarded as unprepared for life in a man-made world.

Educational reformers who accept the idea that schools have failed fall into three groups. The most respectable are certainly the great masters of alchemy who promise better schools. The most seductive are popular magicians, who promise to make every kitchen into an alchemic lab. The most sinister are the new Masons of the Universe, who want to transform the entire world into one huge temple of learning. Notable among today's masters of alchemy are certain research directors employed or sponsored by the large foundations who believe that schools, if they could somehow be improved, could also become economically more feasible than those that are now in trouble, and simultaneously could sell a larger package of services. Those who are concerned primarily with the curriculum claim that it is outdated or irrelevant. So the curriculum is filled with new packaged courses on African Culture, North American Imperialism, Women's Lib, Pollution, or the Consumer Society. Passive learning is wrong—it is indeed—so we graciously allow students to decide what and how they want to be taught. Schools are prison houses. Therefore, principals are authorized to approve teach-outs, moving the school desks to a roped-off Harlem street. Sensitivity training becomes fashionable. So, we import group therapy into the classroom. School, which was supposed to teach everybody everything, now becomes all things to all children.

Other critics emphasize that schools make inefficient use of modern science. Some would administer drugs to make it easier for the instructor to change the child's behavior. Others would transform school into a stadium for educational gaming. Still others would electrify the classroom. If they are simplistic disciples of McLuhan, they replace blackboards and textbooks with multimedia happenings; if they follow Skinner, they claim to be able to modify behavior more efficiently than old-fashioned classroom practitioners can.

Most of these changes have, of course, some good effects. The experimental schools have fewer truants. Parents do have a greater feeling of participation in a decentralized district. Pupils, assigned by their teacher to an apprenticeship, do often turn out more competent than those who stay in the classroom. Some children do improve their knowledge of Spanish in the language lab because they prefer playing with the knobs of a tape recorder to conversations with their Puerto Rican peers. Yet all these improvements operate within predictably narrow limits, since they leave the hidden curriculum of school intact.

Some reformers would like to shake loose from the hidden curriculum, but they rarely succeed. Free schools that lead to further free schools produce a mirage of freedom, even though the chain of attendance is frequently interrupted by long stretches of loafing. Attendance through seduction inculcates the need for educational treatment more persuasively than the reluctant attendance enforced by a truant officer. Permissive teachers in a padded classroom can easily render their pupils impotent to survive once they leave.

Learning in these schools often remains nothing more than the acquisition of socially valued skills defined, in this instance, by the consensus of a commune rather than by the decree of a school board. New presbyter is but old priest writ large.

Free schools, to be truly free, must be run in a way to prevent the reintroduction of the hidden curriculum of graded attendance and certified students studying at the feet of certified teachers. And, more importantly, they must provide a framework in which all participants—staff and pupils—can free themselves from the hidden foundations of a schooled society. The first condition is frequently incorporated in the stated aims of a free school. The second condition is only rarely recognized, and is difficult to state as the goal of a free school.

It is useful to distinguish between the hidden curriculum, which I have described, and the occult foundations of schooling. The hidden curriculum is a ritual that can be considered the official initiation into modern society, institutionally established through the school. It is the purpose of this ritual to hide from its participants the contradictions between the myth of an egalitarian society and the class-conscious reality it certifies. Once they are recognized as such, rituals lose their power, and this is what is now beginning to happen to schooling. But there are certain fundamental assumptions about growing up—the occult foundations—which now find their expression in the ceremonial of schooling, and which could easily be reinforced by what free schools do.

Among these assumptions is what Peter Schrag calls the "immigration syndrome," which impels us to treat all people as if they were newcomers who must go through a naturalization process. Only certified consumers of knowledge are admitted to citizenship. Men are not born equal, but are made equal through gestation by Alma Mater.

The rhetoric of all schools states that they form a man for the future, but they do not release him for his task before he has developed a high level of tolerance to the ways of his elders: education *for* life rather than *in* everyday life. Few free schools can avoid doing precisely this. Nevertheless they are among the most important centers from which a new life-style radiates, not because of the effect their graduates will have but, rather, because elders who choose to bring up their children without the benefit of properly ordained teachers frequently belong to a radical minority and because their preoccupation with the rearing of their children sustains them in their new style.

The most dangerous category of educational reformer is one who argues that knowledge can be produced and sold much more effectively on an open market than on one controlled by school. These people argue that most skills can be easily acquired from skill-models if the learner is truly interested in their acquisition; that individual entitlements can provide a more equal purchasing power for education. They demand a careful separation of the process by which knowledge is acquired from the process by which it is measured and certified. These seem to me obvious statements. But it would be a fallacy to believe that the establishment of a free market for knowledge would constitute a radical alternative in education.

The establishment of a free market would indeed abolish what I have previously called the hidden curriculum of present schooling—its age-specific attendance at a graded curriculum. Equally, a free market would at first give the appearance of counteracting what I have called the occult foundations of a schooled society: the "immigration syndrome," the institutional monopoly of teaching, and the ritual of linear initiation. But at the same time a free market in education would provide the alchemist with innumerable hidden hands to fit each man into the multiple, tight little niches a more complex technocracy can provide.

Many decades of reliance on schooling has turned knowledge into a commodity, a marketable staple of a special kind. Knowledge is now regarded simultaneously as a first necessity and also as society's most precious currency. (The transformation of knowledge into a commodity is reflected in a corresponding transformation of language. Words that formerly functioned as verbs are becoming nouns that designate possessions. Until recently dwelling and learning and even healing designated activities. They are now usually conceived as commodities or services to be delivered. We talk about the manufacture of housing or the delivery of medical care. Men are no longer regarded fit to house or heal themselves. In such a society people come to believe that professional services are more valuable than personal care. Instead of learning how to nurse grandmother, the teen-ager learns to picket the hospital that does not admit her.) This attitude could easily survive the disestablishment of school, just as affiliation with a church remained a condition for office long after the adoption of the First Amendment. It is even more evident that test batteries measuring complex knowledge-packages could easily survive the disestablishment of school—and with this would go the compulsion to obligate everybody to acquire a minimum package in the knowledge stock. The scientific measurement of each man's worth and the alchemic dream of each man's "educability to his full humanity" would finally coincide. Under the appearance of a "free" market, the global village would turn into an environmental womb where pedagogic therapists control the complex navel by which each man is nourished.

At present schools limit the teacher's competence to the classroom. They prevent him from claiming man's whole life as his domain. The demise of school will remove this restriction and give a semblance of legitimacy to the life-long pedagogical invasion of everybody's privacy. It will open the way for a scramble for "knowledge" on a free market, which would lead us toward the paradox of a vulgar, albeit seemingly egalitarian, meritocracy. Unless the concept of knowledge is transformed, the disestablishment of school will lead to a wedding between a growing meritocratic system that separates learning from certification and a society committed to provide therapy for each man until he is ripe for the gilded age.

For those who subscribe to the technocratic ethos, whatever is technically possible must be made available at least to a few whether they want it or not. Neither the privation nor the frustration of the majority counts. If cobalt treatment is possible, then the city of Tegucigalpa needs one apparatus in each of its two major hospitals, at a cost that would free an important part of the population of Honduras from parasites. If supersonic speeds are possible, then it must speed the travel of some. If the flight to Mars can be conceived, then a rationale must be found to make it appear a necessity. In the technocratic ethos poverty is modernized: Not only are old alternatives closed off by new monopolies, but the lack of necessities is also compounded by a growing spread between those services that are technologically feasible and those that are in fact available to the majority.

A teacher turns "educator" when he adopts this technocratic ethos. He then acts as if education were a technological enterprise designed to make man fit into whatever environment the "progress" of science creates. He seems blind to the evidence that constant obsolescence of all commodities comes at a high price: the mounting cost of training people to know about them. He seems to forget that the rising cost of tools is purchased at a high price in education: They decrease the labor intensity of the economy, make learning on the job impossible or, at best, a privilege for a few. All over the world the cost of educating men for society rises faster than the productivity of the entire economy, and fewer people have a sense of intelligent participation in the commonweal.

A revolution against those forms of privilege and power, which are based on claims to professional knowledge, must start with a transformation of consciousness about the nature of learning. This means, above all, a shift of responsibility for teaching and learning. Knowledge can be defined as a commodity only as long as it is viewed as the result of institutional enterprise or as the fulfillment of institutional objectives. Only when a man recovers the sense of personal responsibility for what he learns and teaches can this spell be broken and the alienation of learning from living be overcome.

The recovery of the power to learn or to teach means that the teacher who takes the risk of interfering in somebody else's private affairs also assumes responsibility for the results. Similarly, the student who exposes himself to the influence of a teacher must take responsibility for his own education. For such purposes educational institutions—if they are at all needed—ideally take the form of facility centers where one can get a roof of the right size over his head, access to a piano or a kiln, and to records, books, or slides. Schools, TV stations, theaters, and the like are designed primarily for use by professionals. Deschooling society means above all the denial of professional status for the second-oldest profession, namely teaching. The certification of teachers now constitutes an undue restriction of the right to free speech: the corporate structure and professional pretensions of journalism an undue restriction on the right to free press. Compulsory attendance rules interfere with free assembly. The deschooling of society is nothing less than a cultural mutation by which a people recovers the effective use of its Constitutional freedoms: learning and teaching by men who know that they are born free rather than treated to freedom. Most people learn most of the time when they do whatever they enjoy; most people are curious and want to give meaning to whatever they come in contact with; and most people are capable of personal intimate intercourse with others unless they are stupefied by inhuman work or turned off by schooling.

The fact that people in rich countries do not learn much on their own constitutes no proof to the contrary. Rather it is a consequence of life in an environment from which, paradoxically, they cannot learn much, precisely because it is so highly programed. They are constantly frustrated by the structure of contemporary society in which the facts on which decisions can be made have become elusive. They live in an environment in which tools that can be used for creative purposes have become luxuries, an environment in which channels of communication serve a few to talk to many.

A modern myth would make us believe that the sense of impotence with which most men live today is a consequence of technology that cannot but create huge systems. But it is not technology that makes systems huge, tools immensely powerful, channels of communication one-directional. Quite the contrary: Properly controlled, technology could provide each man with the ability to understand his environment better, to shape it powerfully with his own hands, and to permit him full intercommunication to a degree never before possible. Such an alternative use of technology constitutes the central alternative in education.

If a person is to grow up he needs, first of all, access to things, to places and to processes, to events and to records. He needs to see, to touch, to tinker with, to grasp whatever there is in a meaningful setting. This access is now largely denied. When knowledge became a commodity, it acquired the protections of private property, and thus a principle designed to guard personal intimacy became a rationale for declaring facts off limits for people without the proper credentials. In schools teachers keep knowledge to themselves unless it fits into the day's program. The media inform, but exclude those things they regard as unfit to print. Information is locked into special languages, and specialized teachers live off its retranslation. Parents are protected by corporations, secrets are guarded by bureaucracies, and the power to keep others out of private preserves—be they cockpits, law offices, junkyards, or clinics—is jealously guarded by professions, institutions, and nations. Neither the political nor the professional structure of our societies, East and West, could withstand the elimination of the power to keep entire classes of people from facts that could serve them. The access to facts that I advocate goes far beyond truth in labeling. Access must be built into reality, while all we ask from advertising is a guarantee that it does not mislead. Access to reality constitutes a fundamental alternative in education to a system that only purports to teach *about* it.

Abolishing the right to corporate secrecy—even when professional opinion holds that this secrecy serves the common good—is, as shall presently appear, a much more radical political goal than the traditional demand for public ownership or control of the tools of production. The socialization of tools without the effective socialization of know-how in their use tends to put the knowledge-capitalist into the position formerly held by the financier. The technocrat's only claim to power is the stock he holds in some class of scarce and secret knowledge, and the best means to protect its value is a large and capital-intensive organization that renders access to know-how formidable and forbidding.

It does not take much time for the interested learner to acquire almost any skill that he wants to use. We tend to forget this in a society where professional teachers monopolize entrance into all fields, and thereby stamp teaching by uncertified individuals as quackery. There are few mechanical skills used in industry or research that are as demanding, complex, and dangerous as driving cars, a skill that most people quickly acquire from a peer. Not all people are suited for advanced logic, yet those who are make rapid progress if they are challenged to play mathematical games at an early age. One out of twenty kids in Cuernavaca can beat me at Wiff 'n' Proof after a couple of weeks' training. In four months all but a small percentage of motivated adults at our CIDOC center learn Spanish well enough to conduct academic business in the new language.

A first step toward opening up access to skills would be to provide various incentives for skilled individuals to share their knowledge. Inevitably, this would run counter to the interest of guilds and professions and unions. Yet, multiple apprenticeship is attractive: It provides everybody with an opportunity to learn something about almost anything. There is no reason why a person should not combine the ability to drive a car, repair telephones and toilets, act as a midwife, and function as an architectural draftsman. Special-interest groups and their disciplined consumers would, of course, claim that the public needs the protection of a professional guarantee. But this argument is now steadily being challenged by consumer protection associations. We have to take much more seriously the objection that economists raise to the radical socialization of skills: that "progress" will be impeded if knowledge—patents, skills, and all the rest—is democratized. Their argument can be faced only if we demonstrate to them the growth rate of futile diseconomies generated by any existing educational system.

Access to people willing to share their skills is no guarantee of learning. Such access is restricted not only by the monopoly of educational programs over learning and of unions over licensing but also by a technology of scarcity. The skills that count today are know-how in the use of highly specialized tools that were designed to be scarce. These tools produce goods or render services that everybody wants but only a few can enjoy, and which only a limited number of people know how to use. Only a few privileged individuals out of the total number of people who have a given disease ever benefit from the results of sophisticated medical technology, and even fewer doctors develop the skill to use it.

The same results of medical research have, however, also been employed to create a basic medical tool kit that permits Army and Navy medics, with only a few months of training, to obtain results, under battlefield conditions, that would have been beyond the expectations of fullfledged doctors during World War II. On an even simpler level any peasant girl could learn how to diagnose and treat most infections if medical scientists prepared dosages and instructions specifically for a given geographic area.

All these examples illustrate the fact that educational considerations alone suffice to demand a radical reduction of the professional structure that now impedes the mutual relationship between the scientist and the majority of people who want access to science. If this demand were heeded, all men could learn to use yesterday's tools, rendered more effective and durable by modern science, to create to-morrow's world.

Unfortunately, precisely the contrary trend prevails at present. I know a coastal area in South America where most people support themselves by fishing from small boats. The outboard motor is certainly the tool that has changed most dramatically the lives of these coastal fishermen. But in the area I have surveyed, half of all outboard motors that were purchased between 1945 and 1950 are still kept running by constant tinkering, while half the motors purchased in 1965 no longer run because they were not built to be repaired. Technological progress provides the majority of people with gadgets they cannot afford and deprives them of the simpler tools they need.

Metals, plastics, and ferro cement used in building have greatly improved since the 1940s and ought to provide more people the opportunity to create their own homes. But while in the United States, in 1948, more than 30 per cent of all one-family homes were owner-built, by the end of the 1960s the percentage of those who acted as their own contractors had dropped to less than 20 per cent.

The lowering of the skill level through so-called economic development becomes even more visible in Latin America. Here most people still build their own homes from floor to roof. Often they use mud, in the form of adobe, and thatchwork of unsurpassed utility in the moist, hot, and windy climate. In other places they make their dwellings out of cardboard, oildrums, and other industrial refuse. Instead of providing people with simple tools and highly standardized, durable, and easily repaired components, all governments have gone in for the mass production of low-cost buildings. It is clear that not one single country can afford to provide satisfactory modern dwelling units for the majority of its people. Yet, everywhere this policy makes it progressively more difficult for the majority to acquire the knowledge and skills they need to build better houses for themselves.

Educational considerations permit us to formulate a second fundamental characteristic that any post-industrial society must possess: a basic tool kit that by its very nature counteracts technocratic control. For educational reasons we must work toward a society in which scientific knowledge is incorporated in tools and components that can be used meaningfully in units small enough to be within the reach of all. Only such tools can socialize access to skills. Only such tools favor temporary associations among those who want to use them for a specific occasion. Only such tools allow specific goals to emerge in the process of their use, as any tinkerer knows. Only the combination of guaranteed access to facts and of limited power in most tools renders it possible to envisage a subsistence economy capable of incorporating the fruits of modern science.

The development of such a scientific subsistence economy is unquestionably to the advantage of the overwhelming majority of all people in poor countries. It is also the only alternative to progressive pollution, exploitation, and opaqueness in rich countries. But, as we have seen, the dethroning of the GNP cannot be achieved without simultaneously subverting GNE (Gross National Education—usually conceived as manpower capitalization). An egalitarian economy cannot exist in a society in which the right to produce is conferred by schools.

The feasibility of a modern subsistence economy does not depend on new scientific inventions. It depends primarily on the ability of a society to agree on fundamental, self-chosen anti-bureaucratic and anti-technocratic restraints.

These restraints can take many forms, but they will not work unless they touch the basic dimensions of life. (The decision of Congress against development of the supersonic transport plane is one of the most encouraging steps in the right direction.) The substance of these voluntary social restraints would be very simple matters that can be fully understood and judged by any prudent man. The issues at stake in the SST controversy provide a good example. All such restraints would be chosen to promote stable and equal enjoyment of scientific know-how. The French say that it takes a thousand years to educate a peasant to deal with a cow. It would not take two generations to help all people in Latin America or Africa to use and repair outboard motors, simple cars, pumps, medicine kits, and ferro cement machines if their design does not change every few years. And since a joyful life is one of constant meaningful intercourse with others in a meaningful environment, equal enjoyment does translate into equal education.

At present a consensus on austerity is difficult to imagine. The reason usually given for the impotence of the majority is stated in terms of political or economic class. What is not usually understood is that the new class structure of a schooled society is even more powerfully controlled by vested interests. No doubt an imperialist and capitalist organization of society provides the social structure within which a minority can have disproportionate influence over the effective opinion of the majority. But in a technocratic society the power of a minority of knowledge capitalists can prevent the formation of true public opinion through control of scientific know-how and the media of communication. Constitutional guarantees of free speech, free press, and free assembly were meant to ensure government by the people. Modern electronics, photo-offset presses, time-sharing computers, and telephones have in principle provided the hardware that could give an entirely new meaning to these freedoms. Unfortunately, these things are used in modern media to increase the power of knowledge-bankers to funnel their program-packages through international chains to more people, instead of being used to increase true networks that provide equal opportunity for encounter among the members of the majority.

Deschooling the culture and social structure requires the use of technology to make participatory politics possible. Only on the basis of a majority coalition can limits to secrecy and growing power be determined without dictatorship. We need a new environment in which growing up can be classless, or we will get a brave new world in which Big Brother educates us all.

Must We Educate?

CARL BEREITER
Ontario Institute for Studies in Education

For those who know of my earlier work on teaching disadvantaged children, some explanation is needed to relate what I am saying now with what I was saying seven years ago. The academic preschool that Siegfried Engelmann and I ran has been labeled a "pressure-cooker" and a "Marine drill-sergeant" approach to teaching. Those are exaggerated characterizations of a program that aimed at giving children lively, direct training in basic academic skills. It is fair, however, to say that our approach represented the very antithesis of the informal child-centered approach so dear to educational liberals and radicals.

I still think that if you want to teach a skill, the direct approach is the way to do it. That is how most training is carried out in the real world, where training works—in swimming classes, music lessons, and on-the-job training. The indirect approach favored by schools simply cheats kids by putting too much of the burden on their own initiative and ability to figure things out.

What I have never felt good about is making kids over in the interest of an educational program. Undiscriminating readers like Edgar Z. Friedenberg and William Labov saw our approach as imposing middle-class standards on lower-class kids. In fact, our approach does just the opposite—and that is both its strength and its weakness. It leaves kids alone. It doesn't try to alter their language or behavior in any general way but merely tries to teach skills and behaviors useful in a teaching situation.

From the Preface and Chapter 1 of Carl Bereiter, *Must We Educate?*, © 1973. Reprinted by permission of Prentice-Hall, Inc., Englewood Cliffs, New Jersey.

Lower-class black kids remain lower-class black kids, except that they become literate. We don't try to condition them in the process to some ideal of middle-class childhood or to some romanticized form of black culture. There may be some value in doing one or the other, but I don't see it as our prerogative or the prerogative of any public school system. The weakness of this hands-off approach is that children don't change in fundamental ways. If direct training ceases and children are left in the sink-or-swim environment of the modern classroom, they tend to sink as other children like them do. They haven't been made over into the kinds of children who fare well in such an environment.

What can we do? The options are fairly clear. Either make kids over or continue direct training or give up and say, "Who needs to read anyway?" The choice is a moral one, not a technical one. It is a moral dilemma that applies to all children, not only to the most needy. I see "making kids over" as another label for "educating the whole child." I'm opposed to it. To me it means forcing on all children the prevailing notions of how people should be. I see it as incompatible with the values of a free society.

THE RIGHT TO MAKE MISTAKES

Someone must educate children. It is sheer romance to imagine that they can grow into adequate adults without some guiding influence. Traditionally this guidance comes from the home, and even with universal compulsory schooling the home still appears to be the main educational influence on children. That is how it should be in a free society. A society that granted individuals the right to live according to their own values but did not grant them the right to raise their children according to those values would not be a free society—it would only be a society in which individual liberty was strangled slowly instead of abruptly.

How, then, does it happen in democratic societies that the state has assumed the right to educate children? There are fairly obvious reasons why the state should have an interest in how children turn out, but it does not immediately follow that the state has a right to do anything about it, beyond providing cultural resources and perhaps financial assistance to parents in educating their children. The answer seems to reside in a widespread conviction, shared by government officials and professional "helpers" of all kinds, that people must not be allowed to make mistakes. For parents and children, given the freedom to determine their own lives, will make mistakes. The need to keep people from making mistakes has been used for centuries to justify keeping people in bondage—slaves, women, whole nations. The argument has always proved to have some truth in it. When set free, people *have* made mistakes. But increasingly it is recognized that they have a right to freedom nevertheless. It would seem that this same recognition must eventually be made of the right of people to make mistakes in educating themselves and their children.

Even if the majority are satisfied to have educational choices made for them, it does not follow that the state should do so. Educational freedom and religious freedom are parallel cases in this regard. State schools and state churches both inevitably undermine freedom, even if they satisfy a large majority of the people. It seems clear that, from the standpoint of human rights, public education is an anachronism. Established at a time when individual liberties were not so clearly recognized and not so jealously defended, public education is grossly out of keeping with modern conceptions of freedom.

The most difficult issue of rights is not the issue of parents versus the state but the issue of parents versus their children. The issue is difficult because the child cannot exercise rights from birth but must somehow at some time in his development accede to rights that were previously held by his parents. There is no neat solution to the problem of transfer of rights. What I suggest is that children should not necessarily acquire all rights of citizenship at the same time, and that they should acquire educational rights at an earlier age than some other rights. It seems that it is around the age of 13 or 14 that children begin to take a conscious interest in their own development, and so it would be reasonable for them to have the right to begin making their own educational decisions at about that time. Parents would still have influence, of course, but they would not have authority supported by law. This is a hard nut to swallow, for most parents too are infected with an unwillingness to let people make mistakes, particularly their own children. But I don't see any other way to give full meaning to the right of people to determine their own course of development, and this is a right without which most other rights become meaningless.

IS INEQUALITY HERE TO STAY?

The strongest argument against leaving educational decisions in the hands of parents and children is that poorly educated parents will have poorly educated children. Thus, the argument runs, the price of educational freedom will be that the poor get poorer and the rich get richer.

It is difficult to write this argument off by saying that freedom always has its price. If the costs fall mainly on the poor, that is not a good thing. It is true, of course, that the poor come off badly even now under a system of universal compulsory education, but it is still possible that they could come off worse. If, however, we look dispassionately at why the poor come off badly under the present system, the evidence is clear that they are deficient in a variety of intellectual and motivational characteristics that constitute scholastic aptitude (of which IQ is only one component).

To remedy all of these deficiencies would be to make poor people over into quite different kinds of people. They might then be better equipped to succeed in school, but in the process whole subcultures would have been destroyed. That is an intolerably high price to pay for something that in the end would make at best a modest contribution to equality in the things that really count, such as income. Recent studies such as those of Ivar Berg and Christopher Jencks indicate that education has been greatly overrated as a basis for social success. Our concern with educational equality has produced no tangible gains and has served only to deflect us from more positive social actions in the interests of equality.

A more reasonable goal in the area of education would be to make it possible for all children, regardless of background and regardless of scholastic aptitude, to acquire adequate levels of skill in reading, writing, and practical arithmetic. The means to do this are available, or are becoming available, through careful training. There is no reason to suppose that if the training opportunities were available poor people would not take advantage of them. Such training would not achieve social equality for poor people, but it could do more than any mild sort of educational treatment could do, and perhaps as much as can be done in any way that respects the right of people to be different.

INSTITUTIONALIZING PERSONAL CHOICE

How is one to draw the line between public services and public imposition of goals on individuals? The two cannot be entirely separated, because in providing any public service decisions have to be made that may influence the development and destinies of people. There are some principles, however, that can be applied to minimize the extent to which public institutions take over the lives of people. One principle, stressed by Ivan Illich, is that institutions should not generate needs for their services and other services, thus leading to an ever-increasing dependence on institutions. Illich has proposed radical redesign of institutions, including educational ones, so that they leave people alone, the way public utilities do, instead of absorbing them, the way the welfare system does.

I suggest that the key point is to limit the means by which institutions are able to create needs for their services. Schools make people dependent on schooling through monopoly, compulsory attendance, and by issuing credentials that have become requirements of employment. Other institutions create needs by attaching strings to benefits, as the welfare system does, and by advertising, as private industry does. These methods of generating needs are all, in their various ways, disreputable, and could in all justice be limited by law. That would leave the way open for services to be offered to the public, but they would have to stand on their merits and would no longer be such a threat to individual responsibility and freedom.

At present we are so committed to a belief in public education that a parks commissioner or a welfare director is considered to be operating in the best of faith if he uses his office to advance generally acceptable notions of how people should be. If we looked at it differently, however, if we saw public education as a dangerous intrusion into the lives of individuals, we would kick out public officials who acted that way, as readily as we now kick out those who use their offices for graft. The responsible official would be one who regarded his power to educate in the same way as he regarded his power to make people rich—as a power not to be abused, but to be exercised with as much fairness, impartiality, and restraint as possible.

SCHOOLS WITHOUT EDUCATION

Perhaps the greatest obstacle to fundamental criticism of education is that there are no immediately obvious alternatives except doing nothing. It is hard to imagine a child doing anything worthwhile that is not educational, and hard to imagine an adult relating to a child in any worthwhile way except to educate him. Let us look more carefully, however, at what public services children actually need.

Children need to be taken care of when they are away from their parents and they need training in some basic skills, mainly the three Rs. Elementary schools exist mainly to serve these two needs, but they have subordinated them to an overall objective of educating the child, for which there is no clearly established need. Training in the schools has been poor. Substantial numbers of children have failed to learn the rudimentary skills to an adequate level. The quality of child care has varied. In the days of the birch rod it was abominable. More recently it has been not bad, but its ritualistic form is becoming too evidently absurd to survive. Informal education shows promise of being a superior form of child care, although it does not appear to be any improvement as far as training is concerned.

I suggest that both training and child care can be done better if they are handled separately by different people according to different styles. By unpackaging them, moreover, education as the all-embracing function of schools becomes lost. I do not think it will be missed. The alternative system would find the typical child involved for a couple of hours a day in lively sessions of training in basic skills, carried out by people who did not fancy themselves to be educators but capable imparters of competence. For the rest of the time the child would be in the care of people similar to camp counselors who would help children avail themselves of opportunities inside and outside of school for activities that were worthwhile in their own right rather than for some supposed educational effect.

A BETTER LIFE FOR CHILDREN

What are activities for children that are worthwhile in their own right? They are not merely activities that are fun. I suggest as a criterion that child care should be concerned with increasing the quality of children's immediate experience. By whose standard? Inevitably, by the standard of the people who have control. These will be mainly adults, although children can enter into the process of proposing and judging alternatives.

What I am proposing, thus, is not a neutral or value-free treatment of children, which would be impossible in any event. I am proposing that the cultural life of children should be treated like the cultural life of adults, as something that should have quality, meaning, and moral value in the here and now rather than in some future state of development. Cultural facilities and activities should be designed to enable children to make fuller use of the human qualities they already have rather than to develop new qualities. It might be argued that this is simply education under a different guise, but I think the intention is fundamentally different.

Some specific suggestions: Provide intellectual recreation in place of schooling; make it easier for children to do things rather than merely watch; provide quiet places without prescribed activities; encourage age intermixing; and provide resources that can be used in a variety of unprogrammed ways so as to balance the resources that program the user. There is room for a great deal of creative thinking in planning cultural resources for children, once it is recognized that the talents of the educator are not the main talents to be employed.

OPTIONAL ADOLESCENCE

As children grow into adolescence, their needs diverge. Some are ready to move directly into adult jobs and marriage. Others need an extended period of career training, but want little else in the way of education. Then there are others—the most conspicuous, but actually a minority—who value a lengthy period of freedom from work in order to pursue their own development and to do any of a variety of nonvocational things. If we define adolescence as this in-between period of freedom from vocational responsibility, then it is obvious that some want it and others do not.

At the present time the choice is not a free one. If you want to be an adolescent you have to be a student, and vice versa. Consequently, our high schools and colleges are glutted with young people who don't particularly want schooling but who want the kind of adolescent life and the kinds of future careers that schooling makes possible. The U.S. Supreme Court has already judged that competence, not schooling, should be the criterion for employment. If this judgment were applied fully, it would relieve one of the binds that young people are in. But to make adolescence truly optional it should also be possible for young people to enjoy their freedom without having to go to school. I suggest unrestricted grants for this purpose, to be repaid through a surtax on income in later years.

Other options to meet other needs are university-type schooling for the minority seriously interested in studying academic disciplines, a service corps to provide socially meaningful work, and opportunities for vocational training and on-the-job training. This set of options may raise fears of the emergence of a caste system, but such fears I think are realistic only under a system where academic education is the sole route to social status. When that is not the case, optional adolescence would make it possible for more people with nonacademic inclinations to experience the period of adolescent development that so sharply separates the social classes in contemporary society.

To permit young people to be adolescents without going to school would be to turn them loose on a world that is afraid of them. But it appears that the world is going to have to come to terms with adolescents as a subcultural group anyway. Society could stand to benefit from what adolescents have to offer instead of fighting a losing battle to keep them in a check.

EDUCATION AND SOCIETY'S NEEDS

What education does for the individual is one thing; what it does for society is another. We look to education to solve social problems by changing people. It does not work very well, and in general problems of human behavior are better dealt with by changing the incentives according to which people act. There are times when a whole population might need to be changed—for instance, to make people less inclined toward violence. Such changes, however, would require a great deal more than schooling. They would require overhauling virtually every aspect of societal functioning. It is unlikely that a free society would ever take such a change upon itself. To support public education as a partial measure is simply to feed an expensive illusion.

We also look to education to provide a productive work force. What has happened, however, is that educational processing has taken the place of competence. If the emphasis were shifted back to demonstrated ability, with opportunities available for training and testing, the likely result would be a general increase in competence.

Finally, education has often been looked to as a means of keeping the classical heritage alive. What is at issue here is not only preservation of the old but infusion of the present with wisdom and with ideas of greatness. To many people, giving up on the effort to educate means consigning modern society to mediocrity, materialism, and short-sightedness. I sense this danger very strongly, but it seems to me that mass education has not been and cannot possibily be the answer. Its effect is to dilute the classical tradition to the point where it is ineffectual. I would rather put my faith in serious humanistic study for the few who want it and, for society as a whole, to trust that high ideals will ultimately prove more attractive than low ones. That is a slim hope, but I do not see that we have any other.

WILL ANYTHING HAPPEN?

What will happen to education is anybody's guess, but there are definite trends suggesting eventual decline of public education. Rising costs, together with a declining public concern for education as knowledge becomes less of a scarce commodity, may lead to schooling's being pared down to training in basic skills. High schools may become more like colleges and other options may have to be established as more rapidly maturing adolescents insist on their rights. If the trend toward more experimentation in life-styles continues, we will have a new kind of cultural pluralism that will make mass education less acceptable. Many of the new life-styles stress values of life in the here and now, values that run counter to educational values. Finally, as more powerful techniques for changing people develop, education is likely to be seen as dangerous rather than as the benign, unobjectionable thing it is now. These trends suggest changes in the directions of ones I have proposed, but all outcomes are in doubt. Therefore it is worth giving some serious thought to whether we want the lives of our children to be dominated by education in the future and to whether there are alternatives that we should be working toward.

Public Education Reconsidered

JOHN H. FISCHER
Teachers College, Columbia University

Although neither the outcome nor the process can yet be described with certainty, it is clear that the American system of universal education has entered a period of profound change. What we face, what indeed we are already involved in, is much more than another of the shifts of emphasis that have marked the history of our schools since the turn of the century. We are in the beginning stages of a sweeping redefinition of the purposes and functions of education in our society. Before the task is finished, we shall have to reconsider not only the nature and operation of existing institutions but also the entire question of how multiple means of education, old and new, can best be used to liberate the possibilities of individuals and to enhance the scope and meaning of human life.

For a generation, educational criticism has focused upon the shortcoming of schools as they are conducted and has produced numerous proposals for improving or redirecting them. More recently we have seen the arguments—philosophical, political, and financial—in support of institutions to offer alternatives to the public schools or the traditional types of private schools. The most radical and most provocative of all the reforms being put forward are those calling for the abolition of schools and the total "deschooling" of society.

Outrageous though the idea seems, deschooling deserves examination. Would the end of schools really further the cause of freedom? Would it increase the chances for personal fulfillment for a larger fraction of humanity?

To Ivan Illich, the most widely publicized proponent of deschooling, the school is the prime example of the damaging effect of institutions on man. The essence of his argument is that in the developed countries as well as in the newly developing ones "the institutionalization of values leads inevitably to physical pollution, social polarization, and psychological impotence: three dimensions in a process of global degradation and modernized misery."

Universal schooling as Illich sees it, and most particularly compulsory schooling, far from equalizing opportunity, monopolizes access to it and further deprives the poor. The school's traditional

From "Public Education Reconsidered," *Today's Education*, Vol. 61, No. 5 (May 1972), 22–31. © 1972 by the National Education Association of the United States. Reprinted with the permission of the publisher and author.

processes of promotion, classification, and certification, he argues, divide individuals into classes and subject nations to an international caste system. Illich sees no hope in efforts to improve existing schools since he believes increased expenditures on formal education only increase its destructiveness.

The cure, as Illich sees it? First we must recognize that not only education but society must be deschooled. Second, the school's monopoly of teaching must be disestablished. (The first article in Illich's new Bill of Rights would be an analogue of the First Amendment: "The state shall make no law with respect to the establishment of education.") Third, we must create new educational systems free of any obligation to learn but providing access for all to "learning webs" designed to facilitate inquiry, expression, association, and skill development.

There would be four of these webs or networks of resources:

1. Reference services to educational objects in order to facilitate access to things used for formal learning, such as libraries, museums, laboratories, airports, factories, farms.
2. Skill exchanges through which persons possessing skills may be put in touch with others who want to learn those skills.
3. Peer matching—a communication network to enable persons to describe learning activities they want to pursue and to locate partners similarly interested.
4. Reference services to educators-at-large—a network to provide access to professional educators with the competence to create and operate exchanges, to offer individual guidance in the use of the networks, and to act as first-among-equals for persons undertaking "difficult intellectual exploratory journeys."

Whether Illich's proposals would actually remedy the ills he deplores, whether they would enlarge possibilities for human fulfillment, is extremely unlikely. The abolition of schools, far from solving the problems of poverty, would widen the gulf between the advantaged and the disadvantaged.

It would be patently absurd to contend that compulsory schooling and universal education pose no problems. But to ignore the humane social purposes for which the public school system was created would be as irresponsible as to deny the benefits that the system, despite all its weaknesses, has brought to millions of people. When Horace Mann described education as "the great Equalizer of the conditions of men—the balance wheel of the social machinery," he forecast what the public schools have in fact become for the vast majority of the American population.

The advocates of deschooling want no balance wheels. They

oppose all institutional intervention in education except such assistance as the individual wants and can seek out on his own initiative. In their romantic enthusiasm, the deschoolers fail to consider a well-documented truth of social and political history. No society can provide opportunity for personal fulfillment on a universal scale except through institutions explicitly designed for that purpose.

Like so many proposals calling for the end of inclusive institutions, deschooling would be elitist in its effect. If the world were populated by human beings totally unselfish in respect to their goals and in their aspirations for children, if the available resources for learning and teaching were sufficient to meet all demands, and if the distribution of these resources corresponded exactly to the pattern of demand for them, unrestricted freedom of access would assure equality of opportunity. But in the only world in which Illich's "learning webs" can be created, their existence would by no means assure their actual availability on anything like an equal basis to all children.

From the outset, the child of knowledgeable and sophisticated parents would enjoy an enormous advantage. His family, not only able to understand the child's needs in the social context but capable of manipulating the system in his interest, would soon find the persons and agencies best adapted to cultivate his talents and to serve his aspirations. For the child whose parents had themselves been victimized by deprivation, the absence of institutional support would mean that the inequalities of earlier generations would be compounded and projected into the child's own life. In order to argue that learning opportunities would be improved if all institutional structure, protection, and assistance were removed, one must posit fundamental changes not only in society but in human nature.

While Illich's advocacy of the total abolition of schools is the most extreme, it is by no means the only proposal for sweeping alterations in the patterns and programs of educational institutions. (See, for example, the proposals of his colleague, Everett Reimer, in *School Is Dead: Alternatives in Education.*) Paul Goodman, in *The New Reformation,* finds that "the present extended tutelage is against nature and arrests growth," and argues that formal schooling should be drastically cut back. For children between six and 11, he favors a system of small schools (two or four rooms), but he would replace most high schools with other types of youth communities.

As the chief means of teaching and learning, Goodman would rely on incidental education gained through participation in ongoing social activities. If activities currently available failed to provide enough such situations for the education of young people, he would expect educators to make it their business to invent new activities to furnish the opportunities needed.

Goodman's indictment of schools is perceptive and often persuasive. The failure of many schools and teachers to reach large numbers of young people in any useful way is appallingly plain. It is equally clear that one reason for this failure is that much of the curriculum is irrelevant to students' experiences or to their purposes. When Goodman insists that there should be multiple paths for growing up, he is on sound ground, and while his imaginative educational alternatives can be criticized in some respects as utopian, they do take account of social and psychological realities far better than Ivan Illich's romanticism.

Goodman accepts, for example, the need to protect young children and to provide for them a "life-nourishing environment." (One cannot imagine that following Goodman's prescription a Harlem youngster would, as one fully "on the community" recently did, fall into drug addiction, become a heroin pusher, and be found in an abandoned house dead of an overdose at the age of 12.) One looks in vain among Illich's proposals for any responsible calculation of the risks entailed in leaving children to learn from their own experience with no regular institutional protection. Self-motivation is an essential element in learning, but one may question whether an eight-year-old's involvement in reading should be determined by his own evaluation of the cultural significance of print.

Most critics and reformers, however, want neither to abolish schools nor to remove large numbers of learners from them. What they want is better schools. They argue for more humane treatment of children and for curriculums that reflect the nature of children and of the world they inhabit. They advocate more effective control by parents and an end of bureaucracies that are benevolently benighted at best and dictatorially arrogant at worst. They insist upon teachers who are able to accept children where they find them, to help them widen their awareness, and to make the most of their capabilities and encounters.

The question that cannot be avoided is whether the changes that growing numbers of thoughtful people consider necessary are posible within the American system of public education. This query is more than one of operational detail, for it would be difficult to cite any proposition that is supported as widely or with as much conviction as is that of the relation between the common school and the fundamental principles of liberty, equality, and open opportunity. It would be unwise to minimize the crises our schools have faced—and in some cases caused— in recent years, but it would be no less foolish to concentrate so much attention upon these traumatic eruptions as to overlook the long-term development of education in this country and the depth of its roots in American society. . . .

Although a few insist that formal education has become too dominant a feature of our culture, the common consensus and an impressive body of well-informed opinion assert the need for strong schools and universal access to them. Since George Washington, the leaders of the United States have affirmed the dependence of democracy on the enlightenment of the people. Lyndon Johnson put the relationship in quite inclusive terms. "One great truth" he had learned, he said in 1964, was "that the answer to all of our national problems, the answer to all the problems of the world comes down, when you really analyze it, to one simple word—education."

Ten years earlier, the United States Supreme Court in its historic *Brown* decision called education "perhaps the most important function of state and local governments."

"It is required," the Court said, "in the performance of our public responsibilities . . . it is the foundation of good citizenship . . . a principal instrument in awakening the child to cultural values, in preparing him for later professional training and in helping him to adjust normally to his environment. In these days it is doubtful that any child may reasonably be expected to succeed in life if he is denied the opportunity of an education."

The Court, it is to be remembered, was dealing here specifically with public schools. In contrast to these assertions of confidence in the schools and dependence upon them there stands a formidable body of comment on the schools' failure to perform the tasks laid upon them. This criticism began to take form shortly after World War II. In 1949, Bernard Iddings Bell published his *Crisis in Education*, soon to be followed by Mortimer Smith's *And Madly Teach*. In 1953 came Albert Lynd's *Quackery in the Public Schools* and Arthur Bestor's *Educational Wastelands*.

This postwar criticism centered largely on what was regarded as the debilitating consequences of progressive education and opposed the growing influence of professional educators and colleges of education. The authors, expressing views shared by a substantial number of citizens, urged greater attention to the academic disciplines, more rigorous standards, and heavier emphasis in teacher education upon subject matter, with less attention to professional courses.

Our national embarrassment when the Russians orbited their first Sputnik ahead of our satellite provided another opportunity to fault the schools, which was readily seized by Admiral Hyman Rickover, among others. Few bothered to note that the pace of the American space program was not determined by the schools but by high-level governmental decisions with regard to allocation of money and manpower.

By the late fifties, the schools were under pressure to produce what was being called with steady insistence but little clarity "quality education."

Defining in particular the qualities of a curriculum that will produce quality education in general calls for much more than rousing clichés, but at first the task seemed easy. Still smarting from the irritation of Sputnik, Americans, or many of them at least, appeared to agree on what they wanted when they demanded "quality education." They wanted more math, more science (especially physics), more foreign languages, and a guidance program which guaranteed that square pegs got into square holes.

During that period, school people were asked such questions as "Whatever happened to trigonometry?" "What are you doing about physics in the fourth grade?" "When do you begin French?" Rarely were the questions, to say nothing of the issues, put in terms of children's development, the significance of their cultural backgrounds, or the part parents should play in the educational process—beyond making sure that homework was faithfully done.

With the emergence of the civil rights movement in the early sixties, the spotlight of educational concern began to focus again on people. In the South, efforts centered upon desegregation, at first with less success in schools than on buses, in terminals, and at lunch counters. As successive suits worked their slow way through the courts, dual school systems began to yield reluctantly and grudgingly in the beginning but with inescapable and growing momentum. If the pace of change was more often deliberate than speedy, it became plainer every year that the force of law was finally to prove irresistible despite the massiveness of the early resistance.

In the North, where school segregation lacked legal sanction, it nevertheless persisted as a result of residential patterns. While Northern de facto segregation was due in part to the inability of Negroes to afford the cost of homes in which neighborhoods, the separation of races, if not required, was often encouraged by the design of school attendance areas, the classification of pupils, and the choice of housing sites by private and public agencies.

On educational and social grounds, de facto segregation is no more defensible than de jure discrimination. However, the existence of de facto segregation, especially in the large cities, has focused attention on the conditions minority children face. With black, Puerto Rican, and Chicano children concentrated in particular schools, the extent of their educational deprivation is undeniable. And with that revelation, the obligation of corrective action has become as inescapable as it is visible.

While much of the action to promote justice for Negroes was centered in the South, parallel movements developed in other parts of the country, especially in the larger cities. Increasing concentrations of black and Puerto Rican children in the central cities accentuated what the Educational Policies Commission called in one of its reports the problem of "cultural incompatibility." Conditions in slum schools became a matter of growing concern to the residents of those neighborhoods themselves and to others troubled by the deterioration of the core cities.

Out of this complex of old trouble and new awareness came another flood of school criticism with a very different orientation. The earlier criticism had reflected the conservatives' view of the consequences of progressive education and dealt mainly with the alleged failure of the schools to stress fundamental skills and the traditional academic disciplines. The new attacks charged the schools with prejudiced and inhumane treatment of poor and minority children, disrespect for the culture of these children and systematic rejection of their special needs.

Despite the efforts of writers and activists, the sixties saw little basic change in most schools. The atmosphere surrounding the schools and sometimes the tone within them changed, however. Thanks to the ubiquitous influence of television and the frequent presence of cameras on university campuses, collegiate fashions in hairstyles, clothing, and language were effectively communicated to the high schools. Teachers, tired of being taken for granted, organized themselves more strongly; spoke out more freely; and, in general, together with the students, made life less agreeable for administrators and board members. Nevertheless, at the beginning of the 1970's, the essential character of most schools—in purpose, in form, and in function—appeared to be very much as it had been in the early sixties.

Behind an apparently unchanged facade, however, forces that had been set in motion during the 1960's were beginning to produce significant changes (in some cases, profound and sweeping reforms) in the American school system. Not least among the new influences were the pressures from the poor and the minorities, who in the past had been almost totally powerless in school policy. The principal thrust of these new pressure groups has been to broaden and deepen the concept of universality in American education and to require quite different approaches to the equalization of opportunity.

The visibility of the injustice, insensitivity, and failure in numerous schools has not, however, been enough to bring about reforms on the scale necessary to bridge the gulf between the traditional promise of the American system and its present performance. Reasons given are manifold, but in too many cases, neither critics nor defenders of the school establishment distinguish as clearly as they should between feeble excuses and valid reasons for failure. The result is that both groups multiply misunderstanding and diminish the chances for constructive change.

The indiscriminate indictment of all inner-city schools as monolithic citadels of reaction controlled by bureaucratic monsters is so patently exaggerated as to approach the absurd. But while such overstated criticism arouses predictable defensiveness among school people, it also often produces acknowledgment of shortcomings that can be neither concealed nor explained. Frequently, these are due to conditions that teachers and administrators have themselves tolerated out of a mistaken sense of public relations or misguided institutional loyalty. Many a school staff, forced by a disorderly demonstration to yield on some point of policy or procedure, has come later to realize that the change was indeed for the better and long overdue. Not infrequently, the consequence is increased awareness among the staff of other needs for a change and a keener sensitivity to the perceptions, feelings, and rights of pupils and parents. But while partisan and hostile criticism can serve as a sharp stimulus, durable improvement in institutions becomes possible only with a rational understanding of problems, objective analysis of relevant facts, and the identification and marshaling of the resources required for a constructive response.

It would be an error to equate the whole of education with schooling or to treat the problems of schooling as though all were soluble through the public system. It would be no less mistaken, however, to ignore the imperative requirements for systematic learning imposed by the culture, the society, and the economy.

The utopian visions of the romantic radicals are alluring, but they offer no escape from certain stubborn truths. Unless we choose to do away with most of present civilization, there will be no escaping the requirement for large numbers of people to learn a great many things, only some of which "come naturally." To be sure, a good deal of the knowledge and skill children need will be acquired where it always has been—in the family, in the community, in peer groups, and in a wide variety of other informal relationships, some voluntary and some mandatory. But much that human beings must know to survive as persons or to maintain a workable social order is too important for random encounters or accidental rediscovery.

Only at our peril and that of our posterity can we ignore the essential if difficult task of conserving our laboriously accumulated cultural heritage and the instruments for transmitting it. The danger is not so much that we shall toss out the baby with the bathwater; babies have ways of announcing where they are. The more apt caution is that in disposing of handiwork we judge too imperfect to keep, we not throw away with it the only tools we have for building something better. Not even the most primitive society has any hope of continuing unless it can systematize the transmission of its culture to successive generations. As cultures grow in content and complexity, so, too, must the institutions that serve them.

Except among a miniscule group of radical reformers, there is now little actual support for the abolition of schools. The vehemence of advocates notwithstanding, deschooling offers little promise of becoming the wave of the future. The focus of current controversy is not on that issue at all but on how to design educational programs to be responsive to people's needs and on how to make such education available equally to all.

To attain these ends, efforts are going forward along three fairly well-defined lines. One group of enterprises is directed toward making the educational system more responsive and more accountable. The second, now moving with increasing momentum through the courts, is to equalize educational opportunity by ending the discriminatory variations that are caused by differences in the wealth of school districts. The third is directed toward creating "free schools" intended either to replace public institutions or to induce change in them.

The so-called "free schools" gain special significance because of their new approaches to curriculum and teaching procedures and because they enroll larger proportions of minority students than do typical private schools.

Their curriculums frequently differ radically from customary patterns; their staffs, typically augmented by volunteers, seldom conform to the professional criteria for selecting or certificating teachers; their physical settings are often makeshift and their financial support uncertain. Yet because of the sensitivity, enthusiasm, dedication, and hard work of their sponsors and staffs, many of these schools show promise and some have attained remarkable results.

They should be welcomed by the broader educational community both for the benefits they bring to the children and families they serve and for what they can teach other schools about the possibilities of new approaches.

Unfortunately, their principal advantages (flexibility, originality, and freedom) are all but inseparable from their chief difficulties (instability, high staff turnover, and financial uncertainty). Characteristically, free schools are the lengthened shadows of the individuals or groups who initiate them, and few have been able to attract sustained financial support. Public funds are seldom available to them, and their pupils' parents often are unable to afford tuition fees. While a few have been able to cultivate loyal groups of donors, the heavy dependence of most on unpredictable contributions means a precarious, hand-to-mouth existence. By choice, almost by definition, they avoid connections with any sort of establishment, but they are discovering that sustained fiscal support, whether in the form of public money or private gifts, requires durable relationships.

The free schools are a valuable addition to the pluralism of American education, but their leaders will probably find that complete freedom is hard to reconcile with solvency. The price of maintenance will almost surely turn out to be some form of institutionalization involving at least minimal accommodation to a constituency that can supply money. It would be a serious loss, however, if survival were to require the sacrifice of their most distinctive qualities. Since the chief asset of the free schools is their founders' courage to break with customary procedures, their experiments and experience should prove of great interest and value.

The most widely available longstanding alternative to American public education has been, of course, the system of Roman Catholic parochial schools. That system expanded in all parts of the country but its greatest growth occurred where Catholic immigrant families settled in the largest numbers, mainly the Eastern and North-Central industrial centers.

As parochial schools grew in size and their constituencies grew in political influence, it was predictable that claims would be advanced for public funds to support them. The parochial schools now educate at private expense about 8 percent of the total school population of the United States, and a majority of the school population in some communities. All of these children are legally entitled to public education and, except for the voluntary action of their parents, they would be enrolled in public schools.

Although the courts have repeatedly affirmed the right of parents to choose nonpublic education, the same courts have ruled with equal consistency that the First Amendment prohibits the use of public funds for religious purposes.

A number of states do supply tax money for transportation, health services, books, and other auxiliary services to parochial pupils, and federal funds are made available through programs for disadvantaged children and for school lunches. But public funds are not available to meet the principal instructional costs of church schools. In the most recent decisions on direct state financial support in Pennsylvania and Connecticut, the U.S. Supreme Court has held that appropriations for teachers' salaries and other general expenses require "excessive entanglement" of government in church affairs and are therefore unconstitutional.

While the controversy over public aid to church schools has proceeded, these schools have been encountering several problems, such as the need to employ increasing numbers of lay teachers because of the decrease in the number of young people entering religious teaching orders. These teachers expect salaries comparable to those paid in public schools and organize unions to obtain them. The consequent increases in tuition fees have been a factor causing Catholic parents to reconsider the tradition of church-school attendance. Among other factors are the exodus of Catholic families from city parishes and the fact that second- and third-generation Irish, Italian, Polish, and other groups are being assimilated into an increasingly homogenized suburban middle class.

Vigorous efforts by church authorities and political leaders in a number of states to use public funds for parochial schools have met with some success in the legislative halls but little support in the courts. When President Nixon appointed his Commission on School Finance in 1970, he specifically directed it to study the financial difficulties of the nonpublic schools. Of the 18 specifications in the Commission's charge, no less than six dealt with that problem.

After two years of research and deliberation, the Commission was able to produce little more than a hortatory recommendation that "governmental agencies promptly and seriously consider additional and more substantive forms of assistance" to such schools. The First Amendment remains a formidable obstacle to any form of federal aid to schools whose essential purpose is to promote a religious doctrine.

Two facts are now quite clear: One is that a decline in the availability or viability of parochial schools will diminish the pluralistic character of American education; the other is that the fewer pupils these schools serve, the greater will be the enrollment and financial pressure upon public schools. At the same time, however, it is to be noted that as these changes occur—and it is plain that they are occurring—a significant group of parents who heretofore have had little personal stake in the public schools will have strong reasons for interesting themselves in the problems of the public sector.

The so-called voucher plan is one proposal that might unite supporters of free schools, church schools, and independent schools and the many who continue to favor public education but are unhappy with its present performance. As proposed for experiment by the Office of Economic Opportunity, it is a device to distribute public funds in the form of vouchers to parents who would then be free to enroll their children in any school approved by the community. When a child is enrolled, the voucher would be used to meet all of the school's tuition charges. The value of the voucher would equal the amount per pupil appropriated to support the local public school system, except that its value would be supplemented with federal funds for children from poor families. It would be cashable by the school receiving it.

The voucher plan is the most obvious and direct answer to the plight of the free schools, but the OEO proposal would not help relieve parents of children in independent schools of high tuition charges, since the voucher cannot be used to pay for only part of a tuition charge. Subject to the outcome of inevitable court tests, it might, however, solve the financial problem of church schools.

A fear that troubles some of its advocates and many of its critics is that it might be equally useful to the white segregated private schools of the South. The possibility that vouchers might destroy the public school and end a major unifying influence in a society already plagued by divisive forces worries a number of thoughtful observers [including members of the NEA Representative Assembly who passed Resolution 71–13, calling for legislation to prohibit establishment of voucher plans].

The voucher plan would undoubtedly increase options for some parents and their children. The contest for pupils and their voucher dollars might also increase beneficial competition among existing schools and stimulate the founding of new ones. But, the skeptics point out, it might also generate practices as questionable as those the consumer-protection movement opposes in competitive corporations.

By expanding possibilities for innovation, the plan would create rich new opportunities for children. It would enlarge freedom of choice for pupils, parents, and schools. But the result of voluntary selection by both sides could leave a residue of pupils whom no school would welcome. In most communities, it seems reasonable to predict, there would be parents so lacking in initiative or sophistication as to be unable to find the school most likely to serve their children's needs.

The proponents of the voucher plan recognize these dangers and propose protective devices in the form of quota requirements, prohibitions against racial discrimination, and similar safeguards. But despite these assurances, no state legislature has yet passed the enabling legislation necessary for getting local experiments under way.

Possibly the most promising of all the new trends is the growing interest in the concept of accountability in education and the search for ways to translate an unexceptionable principle into acceptable procedures. It is inconceivable that anyone would suggest, much less argue, that teachers, administrators, or school boards should not be accountable for their performance as professionals or public officials. The disagreements begin only when practical questions are raised. Who should be accountable to whom? For what? In what terms? Who shall audit the accounts, according to what legal standards, and with what sort of expertise?

The wholly admirable concept of accountability has unfortunately begun to suffer the fate that befalls so many admirable ideas, especially in education. It is being reduced to a cliché—undefined, sloganized, and hucksterized. And, in my opinion, the blame rests in large part upon the shoulders of professional educators in schools, universities, and professional organizations who have been reluctant to come to grips with the difficulty of defining the task and accepting the responsibility it implies.

The heart of the accountability problem is to find the means of determining what difference a school or a teacher makes in the learning and development of a child, distinguishing the effects that are fairly attributable to the school from those produced by the other influences in the child's life.

Obviously, this is no easy undertaking, but there is no reason to assume it is impossible aad certainly no excuse for an unwillingness to attempt it. Admittedly, there are complications. Schools dealing with different types of learning problems should not be expected to produce identical or perhaps even directly comparable results. Faculties teaching advantaged students should not be evaluated by the same criteria as those whose pupils are educationally handicapped. The situations of poverty-stricken schools must be differentiated properly from those of affluent institutions.

But these questions are hardly beyond the mind of man or the competence of social and psychological science. They call for specification of purpose, clear definition, fair distinction, and objective rationality. They also call for sensible collaboration by all who are concerned with the problem and able to contribute experience, insight, and skill to its solution.

As my colleague, Frank Jennings, puts it, "Accountability, whatever meaning we infuse it with, refers essentially to moral behavior. . . . To be accountable is to use and to tolerate certain uniform or regular accounting procedures and to accept stoically the tyranny of the bottom line."

It is, he suggests, the cost of living, "the examined life." When all of us in education are willing to examine what we do as impartially as we can and to invite similar examination by other honest people, we shall be on the way to a far better system of education than we have ever known.

As American public schools move through this new period of reconsideration, the reappraisal of their purposes and their performance may well prove painful for many involved in the process. The chief hazard is not that society is about to be deschooled. Short of nuclear catastrophe, the probability seems fairly remote that the cultures we have been building for 10 millennia will be abandoned. Man's disposition to use his mind is well ingrained and is likely to persist. While it does, the chances are good that parents will want their children to learn and to be inducted systematically into the culture of their forebears.

Given the character of modern civilization, which for all its frustrating weaknesses also possesses a stubborn durability, the need for the acquisition of certain kinds of knowledge—and the teaching to promote that acquisition—is clear. But what is equally evident is the inadequacy of our present institutions to further individual development and to promote the general welfare in ways sufficiently responsive to the conditions of modern life.

American schools have never lacked for critics, but the criticism has reflected special concerns more often than widespread popular dissatisfaction. For most of their history, the schools, particularly the public schools, have enjoyed not only strong but remarkably stable public support. To question their value has seemed to many tantamount to challenging the rightness of religion. The behavior of large segments of the public toward these schools has been analogous to the acceptance in some societies of officially established religious institutions. Indeed, D. W. Brogan, the British historian, once called American public schools our "formally unestablished national church."

What now troubles the schools and a substantial fraction of their once unquestioning adherents is something closely akin to a crisis of faith. At the root of this condition lies a growing awareness that for large numbers of young people the public school system has provided neither the opportunity for personal fulfillment nor the foundation for productive participation in an open society that we have long regarded as its promise and commitment.

The failure has been in part a failure of pedagogy. The teachers and managers of schools have not yet learned how to make enough schools both soundly educational and broadly universal. Centuries of experience have prepared the teaching profession to teach tolerably well the young who come to them already oriented toward formal learning and conscious of its place in lives like theirs. But for those whose families have been deprived not only of education but of any acknowledged claim to its benefits, the schools, in general, have been unprepared. For pupils whose backgrounds differ from the dominant culture, the curriculum is too often without meaning and the teaching procedures without stimulus.

Part of the task now facing the schools and bearing directly upon the teaching profession is to devise new approaches to make the schools genuinely and fully inclusive. No longer may schools assume that their function is to identify those most apt to learn under the schools' familiar practices and to screen out and reject the remainder.

The pyramidal model of an educational system in which the total population is admissible at the base but only the ablest survivors are permitted to reach the apex has ceased to correspond to the conditions of our society. Equality of educational opportunity can no longer be defined as merely an open chance to enter a uniform system which provides a convenient exit for those who fail. While differences in special talent and general ability must be recognized and the requirements for specified levels of competence must be regarded realistically, we can no longer discard those who fall outside traditional academic stereotypes.

Now we must guarantee every individual a setting designed to respect his potentialities and the assistance needed to make the most of them. In addition, we must provide such supplementary help as each individual requires to compensate for those conditions beyond personal control that prevent the full use of the individual's opportunities.

The generous publicity regularly given conflict and crisis in the public schools has often obscured significant improvements that have gone forward in those schools throughout the country. The changes range from a steady expansion of preschool education to new high school programs like Philadelphia's Parkway School or Cleveland's Vocational Education Centers. The new enterprises combine imaginative use of community resources with sensitive respect for young people's concerns.

Not least among the recent gains has been the sound and therefore quiet progress in genuine racial and cultural integration in public schools. Despite formidable economic, political, and social difficulties, thousands of these schools are demonstrating the capacity not only to meet change responsively but, in many instances, to lead it constructively.

A new sequence of decisions now accumulating in the state and federal courts appears likely to produce changes in the American public school system more sweeping and more consequential than any comparable course of events in the past if they are upheld by the U.S. Supreme Court. The decisions that began with the *Serrano* case in California and have since been reinforced by other cases in Minnesota, Texas, and New Jersey seem destined to affect the structure of American education even more than the decisions that forbade racial segregation.

The thrust of these new cases is to assert that education, like the right to vote, is a "fundamental interest" and accordingly a right that, in the language of the earlier *Brown* decision, "must be made available to all on equal terms."

With the exception of a decision in New York, the courts have consistently held in these cases that the quality of a child's educational opportunity may not be inferior to that of others in the state because of the relative poverty of the district in which he happens to attend school. The positive result is that the state, which holds constitutional authority in education and, with it, the residual responsibility for assuring equal treatment, is required to provide equality of opportunity to every child.

The direct projection of this principle would imply the collection of all school tax funds at the state level and their distribution throughout the state on an equal per capita basis. Even the most superficial examination, however, soon reveals that so simplistic a solution will not equalize educational opportunities.

We have already recognized, in countless ways, that "the equal treatment of unequals produces neither equality nor justice." In virtually every state, special allocations of funds are made for the education of physically or mentally handicapped pupils. Increasingly in recent years the same kind of attention has been paid to the educational needs of children who are handicapped by social and economic conditions. Now adjustments will undoubtedly have to be devised to meet differential cost levels in regions within states and to deal with the unusual and costly problems of inner-city schools.

We shall probably discover, however, that devising fair statewide taxing programs and equitable distribution formulas are the least of the problems flowing from state-level funding of education. As the responsibility for financing schools is transferred from the local district to the state, questions will inevitably arise regarding the degree to which the control of schools should be transferred to the state level.

Although the American tradition of locally controlled schools has led to indefensible differences in the quality of education, it has also created thousands of relatively independent centers of initiative and has protected their freedom to meet varied local needs. For at least the next decade, a major task of policy makers and practitioners in American education will be to find workable ways to eliminate inequality without imposing uniformity and without destroying opportunity for local initiative.

This is one reason that the aggressive movements in support of community control in large cities should be welcomed and nurtured. Those movements are a necessary counterforce to the equally necessary trends toward metropolitan regionalism, statewide funding, and national programs. Our main hope for a school system that will be strong, equitable, and responsive lies in the creative and balanced interrelationship of all of these developments.

For all our disillusionment with schools as they are, despite our disappointment at the persistent gulf between promise and performance, and notwithstanding the shocking evidence of the neglect of our schools and the neglect in them, we still know how great a force for good schools can be. The role schools have played in building the better qualities of our society is undeniable. The more admirable aspects of American life that are directly traceable to the influence of educational institutions are visible all about us. But we have allowed the urgency of our shortcomings to divert attention from the importance of our achievements and the promise of possibilities still unrealized.

The only reasonable assumption for policy makers and practitioners in American education to act upon is that the public schools are here to stay. If that is true—and it is as close an estimate of truth as we require—we should get on with the work before us.

Whether our national purpose is described as pulling the country together, getting it moving again, or mounting the new American revolution, we shall find the need for education close to the heart of any sound effort. Whatever other means of education our ingenuity may devise, we can predict with some confidence that the need for a system of schools free, open, and hospitable to all will still be with us.

Deschooling? No!

PHILIP W. JACKSON
University of Chicago

The criticism of schools is a profitable pastime, as a visit to our local bookstore or a glance at a current issue of almost any of our most widely circulated magazines will quickly show. There, in volume after volume and article after article, some of our most well-schooled and well-read journalists, novelists, academicians, ex-teachers, and just plain critics describe the evils of our educational system and discuss what should be done about them. The quality of the writing and the sharpness of the criticism vary from one author to the next, but the overall tone is one of uniform dissatisfaction with things as they are.

Despite the up-to-the-minute freshness of much of this writing, the fact that many people seem to be unhappy with current educational practices is not exactly new. Our schools have long been the target of critics from all walks of life. Moreover, it would be surprising if this were not so, given the centrality of schooling in the lives of our citizens and the complexity of the institution designed to perform this important service.

What *is* new in the current situation is a marked increase in the

From "Deschooling? No!" *Today's Education*, Vol. **61**, No. 8 (November 1972), 18–22. © 1972 by the National Education Association of the United States. Reprinted with the permission of the publisher and author.

amount of criticism, reflecting a corresponding growth in the size of the critics' audience. What is also new and even more important in the current scene is a marked radicalization of the critics' proposals for change.

Until quite recently, the desirability of schools and of compulsory attendance by the young were more or less taken for granted by friend and foe alike. The aim of both, even of those who were most unhappy with the status quo, was not to do away with schools as we now know them, but somehow to improve their operation.

Now from a growing number of writers—including such prominent critics as Ivan Illich, Everett Reimer, John Holt, and the late Paul Goodman—the message is that improving what we presently have is not enough. Today's schools, so the argument goes, have outlived or outgrown their usefulness. They are institutional dinosaurs that should either be hunted down or allowed to sink of their own dead weight into the swamps of academia.

The aggressive brashness of such a charge, with its not-so-subtle promise of a good old-fashioned free-for-all between defenders of our schools and their attackers, is bound to generate excitement and to bring out crowds of onlookers. And, clearly, the school-is-dead argument has done just that. Its proponents appear on talk shows, testify before Congressional committees, are given front-page space in Sunday magazine sections, and are even in demand as speakers at educational conventions!

For those of us who work in these allegedly dead or dying institutions, living, as it were, like parasites ecologically tied to the fate of our dinosaur hosts, there is the serious question of what to do in the face of such allegations. Should we simply ignore them and get on with our work? Should we pause to reply? Might we, in a more hopeful vein, actually learn something from those who would have us go out of business and, armed with that new learning, return with even greater strength and deepened conviction to the task at hand? In my judgment, there is someting to be said on behalf of each of these alternatives.

At first glance, the strategy of simply ignoring the deschoolers does seem a bit foolhardy, if not downright stupid. It brings to mind images of Nero with his legendary fiddle or of ostriches with their heads stuck in the sand.

How dare we ignore the enemy veritably clamoring at our gates? The answer, in part, depends on how serious we judge the threat to be, a judgment that requires a detailed examination of the critics' charges. If Rome is *really* burning or if the ostrich hunters are *really* nearby, then larger numbers of us had better turn from whatever we are doing and consider what should be done about the disturbance. This involves becoming critics of the critics, so to speak, an alternative about which more will be said later.

But even if the threat is real, the fact remains that we do have schools that have to be run as best we know how. No matter what the future holds, millions of students and the public at large are counting on us to perform those duties for which we are being paid. Teaching, if it is done well, and school administration, if it is done at all, are full-time jobs, requiring almost all the available time and energy of those who engage in them.

What with daily classes, preparing lessons, grading papers, attending meetings, consulting with parents, and all the other things he is expected to do, there is not much time left for the average teacher to man the barricades, even if the will and ability to do so were strong.

And most school administrators are in a similar fix. Even as I write this, during the final days of my summer vacation, I realize that it is a great luxury for me to have the time to turn my attention to what critics are saying about our schools and to compose, however sketchily, a reasoned reply. Next week, the demands of school administration will descend with a dull thud, and I will look back on this moment and this activity with a feeling akin to nostalgia.

The truth is that most of us who work in schools are (or should be!) too busy to be more than casually engaged in listening to the school-is-dead critics or in responding to what they say. Teaching is a serious undertaking, as is the job of administering a school.

If those who are engaged in these pursuits take their work seriously, they often find little time for anything else. Yet, there may be teachers and administrators who, for a variety of reasons, have energy and time to spare, or there may be persons from other walks of life, such as university professors, who feel sufficiently incensed to take arms, as it were, against a sea of troubles.

Theirs is the strategy of countercriticism or, if you prefer, counterattack. Fortunately for those of us who are interested in preserving our school system, the writings of most critics reveal weaknesses that seriously damage the force of their argument. The most blatant of these is surely to be found in the demagogic style that characterizes so much of the school-is-dead literature. The tone throughout is strident and at times borders on hysteria.

We are told that our present schools are little more than prisons or concentration camps for the young. Teachers (*all* teachers, presumably) are depicted as mindless and inhumane, and administrators are described as pigheaded and petty tyrants whose main purpose in life seems to be to keep the halls clean and the cafeteria running smoothly. Students, poor things, are crushed by their exposure to these horrible conditions and leave school much worse off than when they entered—with psyches destroyed, spirits sagging, and minds devoid of any true knowledge. It is enough to make the blood boil, which is precisely the intended effect of the authors who write in such a style.

It does not require much analytic power to discern the emotionalism and propagandistic aims of such prose. Hopefully, even the casual reader will take these qualities into account as he judges the critics' case. What does require closer analysis is the detection of flaws in the critics' logic or the scantiness of the evidence they present. Also, more than a casual reading is required to reveal deficiencies in the historical perspective of those who criticize today's schools and in the reasonableness of the alternative proposals they put forth.

Let us consider one or two quick examples of what such an analysis might yield.

Take, for instance, the following statement by John Holt that appeared in a recent issue of *Harper's Magazine* in an article entitled, significantly enough, "The Little Red Prison."

"Thus, as more people learn in school to dislike reading, fewer buy books from bookstores and borrow them from libraries. The bookstores close and the libraries cut back their services, and so we have fewer places in which people outside of school can have ready access to books. This is just one of the ways in which too much school works against education."

A grim picture, indeed. It makes a person want to run out and buy or borrow a couple of books while they are still to be had! But we must ask: Is it true? *Are* more people learning to dislike reading in school? Is the sale of books *really* declining? Are libraries across the nation cutting back their services because of a shorage of interest in their wares? The answer, as all the statistics on publishing and library usage clearly indicate, is emphatically "No!"

Or take another instance, this one chosen almost at random from Ivan Illich's book, *Deschooling Society*. In attempting to analyze what he calls "the phenomenology of school," Illich offers his readers the following gem of syllogistic reasoning:

"School groups people according to age. This grouping rests on three unquestioned premises. Children belong in school. Children learn in school. Children can be taught only in school. I think these unexamined premises deserve serious questioning."

Indeed they do, Mr. Illich. But so does the logic by which the premises are said to lead to the conclusion: "School groups people according to age." We can begin with the assumption that Illich was referring not to the system of grades by which students customarily are grouped *within* school, but rather to the fact that children go to school and adults, for the most part, do not. School, in other words, segregates children from adults. Fair enough, but how does that fact "rest" on the premises? And, further, are the premises themselves seriously held by a significant segment of our population, including, incidentally, our professional educators? Who among us seriously believes that children can be taught only in school?

Other instances of illogic or scant evidence or unreasonable assumptions are easy to come by in the writings of the deschoolers, but these two will have to suffice as illustrations of the kind of detailed criticism that must surely come if we are to take such writings and the proposals contained with them seriously. Some of this counter-criticism is already beginning to appear in print, and more is bound to be written.

The chief danger in focusing on flaws in the deschoolers' argument is that such a strategy may blind us to the strengths that are also there. In our zest to prove them wrong, in other words, we may overlook the extent to which the critics are right. And, let's face it: There *is* basis for concern about what our schools are doing and how their operation might be improved. Perhaps, contrary to what John Holt contends, more and more students are not being taught to dislike reading by their school experience, but a goodly number *are*, and we should be worried about that.

Obviously our high schools are *not* the concentration camps that some critics would have us believe, but many students within them do feel constrained and bridled by their experience, and that fact should trouble us.

Certainly the vast majority of our teachers and school administrators are *not* the mindless and unfeeling creatures depicted by some of the less responsible attackers of our schools, but too many of them *are* halfheartedly engaged in what they are about, more concerned with the benefits of their position than with the services they perform. We cannot rest easy so long as this is true.

The list could be extended, but the point is already obvious: There is serious work to be done within our schools.

This brings us to the third and last of the alternative responses educators might presumably take in the face of the deschooling argument. The first was to ignore the critics and get on with our work. The second was to expose weaknesses in the critics' argument, to counterattack, so to speak. The third is to learn from the critics, not simply by having them reinforce our awareness of our schools' shortcomings, but by seeing where their efforts fall short of perfection and by trying to avoid similar pitfalls as we go about trying to improve our schools. Two such shortcomings are worthy to mention and serve well as examples of lessons to be learned from those who would bring lessons, as such, to an end.

As I study the contemporary critics of our schools, it becomes increasingly evident to me that most of them are animated more by a sense of what is *wrong* with our present system than by a conception of what education is all about and how it might proceed. They lack, in other words, a vision of the good in educational terms. What they are *against* is more evident than what they are *for*.

This same tendency, incidentally, is also apparent within the ranks of professional educators as they impatiently work to reduce the abrasiveness of schooling without pausing to give sufficient thought to the educational purpose of the institution. I plead as guilty as the rest in yielding to the natural appeal of such a tactic. After all, it is easier to put oil on squeaky wheels than to ask about where the vehicle is headed in the first place and to ponder the necessity of a change in direction. The danger, of course, is that by so doing we may create a smoothly running machine that is moving in the wrong direction or not at all.

And this is precisely the likelihood we face if we only ask: What is wrong with our schools and how can we correct those faults? In answering such questions, we may indeed produce conditions in which students and teachers are happier and more contented than is presently true, but will those happier and more contented people still be students and teachers in the educational sense of those terms?

Our goal, in other words, cannot simply be to eliminate the discomfort of schooling, though certainly there is much that should be eliminated. Nor can it even be simply to provide environments in which students are learning things they *want* to learn—a favorite image of many of the romantic critics. It must be to create environments—institutions, if you like—in which students are being educated, a different matter entirely.

This last point deserves elaboration, for it contrasts nicely with one of the major premises in the deschooling argument. Many of the more radical critics are fond of reminding their readers that education involves more than schooling—that it can occur in the absence of teachers and courses and classrooms and all of the paraphernalia that we have come to associate with formal schooling. The same argument, incidentally, has recently been adopted as the slogan of several not-so-radical researchers and professors of education who use it to justify turning their attention away from schools and toward other institutions and agencies within our society that perform an educative function.

Now no one can dispute the truism that reminds us of differences between the concepts of education and schooling. Perhaps such a reminder needs to be presented more frequently and more forcefully today than in the past. But there is another truism that needs to be stated with equal force, for it often seems to be overlooked by friend and foe alike. It is that education, in addition to being more than schooling, is also more than learning.

John Dewey, more than any other educator with whom I am familiar, understood supremely both of the cautions to which I have now made reference: that the foundations on which to build a new and constructive view of schooling cannot simply be a reaction to the ailments of our present system and that education involves much more than letting students "do their thing" even when the latter results in significant learning.

Disturbed by the excesses of the reform movement carried out in his name, Dewey pointed out:

"There is always the danger in a new movement that in rejecting the aims and methods of that which it would supplant, it may develop its principles negatively rather than positively and constructively. Then it takes its clew in practice from that which is rejected instead of from the constructive development of its own philosophy."

And, in my judgment, this seems to be precisely what today's would-be reformers are doing. They are saying, in effect, "Here are the features of schooling that are unpleasant. Let us, therefore, make the absence of those features our goal in the design of alternate forms of schooling." The missing element, of course, is a conception of what the process of education leads *toward*, and this can only be supplied by an ethic and a psychology which are conjured in a coherent philosophy or *theory* of education.

The closest today's critics seem to come to such a conception is their insistence on individual choice and their celebration of man's natural curiosity and his desire to learn. Apparently, if unfettered by institutional constraints, the human spirit will spontaneously seek and achieve those ends that schools are designed to serve. Such is the hope, at any rate. Nor are the critics alone in holding to this belief. Even within our schools themselves a number of persons who call themselves educators seem to be arguing for such a hands-off policy.

Again, it is Dewey who blows the whistle of alarm better than most. Almost 50 years ago he wrote:

> There is a present tendency in so-called advanced schools of educational thought . . . to say, in effect, let us surround pupils with certain materials, tools, appliances, etc., and then let pupils respond to these things according to their own desires. Above all, let us not suggest any end or plan to the students; let us not suggest to them what they shall do, for that is an unwarranted trespass upon their sacred intellectual individuality since the essence of such individuality is to set up ends and aims.
>
> Now such a method is really stupid. For it attempts the impossible, which is always stupid; and it misconceives the conditions of independent thinking. There are a multitude of ways of reacting to sur-

rounding conditions, and without some guidance from experience these reactions are almost sure to be casual, sporadic, and ultimately fatiguing, accompanied by nervous strain. Since the teacher has presumably a greater background of experience, there is the same presumption of the right of a teacher to make suggestions as to what to do, as there is on the part of a head carpenter to suggest to apprentices something of what they are to do.

Coming from as mild-mannered a man as Dewey, those are strong words indeed. Yet the fact that they are as applicable today as when they first were written suggests that the message they contain remains unheeded by many educational critics both inside and outside the schools. And, I suspect, a major reason why this is so is because to take Dewey's admonition seriously would entail an enormous amount of work and thought on the part of everyone connected with schooling.

It is no easy task to keep our educational purpose in mind while carrying out our day-to-day responsibilities in classrooms and administrative offices; in short, to blend theory and practice. To achieve that end requires nothing less than that each of us, again in Dewey's words, be "possessed by the spirit of an abiding student of education."

Such is the challenge that lies before us if we are to learn from our critics to sidestep some of the pitfalls into which they themselves appear to have fallen. Only then will we truly be able to respond with conviction to those who would claim that schools are passé. Moreover, if we are to avoid a tone of defensiveness and apology, our conviction must be voiced in the language of educational purpose. This means more than empty slogans cloaking an absence of thought, but, rather, a lively and tough-minded discourse that means what it says, that changes as schools change, and that mirrors the reality within them.

Our schools are neither dead nor dying, but neither, unfortunately, are they marked by a degree of vitality and energy that befits the grandeur of their mission. Paradoxically, and even ironically, the writings of those who would bury us may well stimulate such an infusion of new life.

The Role of Public Education

ROBERT MAYNARD HUTCHINS
Center for the Study of Democratic Institutions

The Constitution of the United States contemplates government by discussion, with all citizens participating in it. The members of a political community do not have to agree with one another—the First Amendment, which deals with freedom of speech, assumes that Americans will not—but they do need to understand one another. The aim is twofold, unity and diversity, an aim we see reflected in John Stuart's Mill's argument for public education in his essay, *On Liberty.*

If this is the ideal, what part does public education have to play in it? Those who have been leading the antischool campaign have ignored this question. Yet it is, after all, *the* question. It cannot be answered by saying that we should have no schools at all or that we should let our children go or that we should encourage them to pursue their own interests or that we should have schools they could drop into and out of as they pleased or that the schools should be turned over to parents or private businesses, for such decisions would promote cultural, social, and economic segregation and the kind of individualism Tocqueville saw as a danger to every democracy.

The doctrine of every man for himself, or every nation for itself, loses its charm in an interdependent world. This doctrine has to give way before the idea of a world community. We have to understand and rely on our common humanity if we are to survive in any condition worthy to be called human. Everything else sinks into triviality in comparison with this task. To consider most of the topics of current education discussion is irrelevant to the real issue we face. So is the great antischool campaign, except that if it succeeds, we shall be deprived of the one institution that could most effectively assist in drawing out our common humanity.

Democracy is the best form of government precisely because it calls upon the citizen to be self-governing and to take his part in the self-governing political community. This is the answer to the individual/community dilemma. The individual cannot become a human being without the democratic political community; and the democratic political community cannot be maintained without in-

From "The Role of Public Education," *Today's Education*, Vol. **63**, No. 7 (November–December 1973), 80–83. © 1973 by the National Education Association of the United States. Reprinted with the permission of the publisher and author.

dependent citizens who are qualified to govern themselves and others through the democratic political community.

The primary aim of the educational system in a democratic country conscious of the impending world community is to draw out the common humanity of those committed to its charge. This requires careful avoidance of that which may be immediately interesting but which is transitory, or that which is thought to have some practical value under the circumstances of the time but which is likely to be valueless if the circumstances change.

The most elementary truth about education is the one most often disregarded: It takes time. The educator must therefore remember that unless he wants to be a custodian or a sitter or a playmate, he must ask himself whether what he and his pupils are doing will have any relevance 10 years from now. It does not seem an adequate reply that they were having fun, any more than it would be to say they were learning a trade. Nor would it be much more adequate to say they were learning what their parents wanted. The community includes parents but is not confined to them. Taxes for the support of schools are paid by bachelors, spinsters, childless couples, and the elderly on the theory that the whole community is interested in and benefits from its schools.

The first object of any school must be to equip the student with the tools of learning. "Communication skills," which is the contemporary jargon for reading, writing, figuring, speaking, and listening, appear to have permanent relevance. These arts are important in any society at any time. They are more important in a democratic society than in any other, because the citizens of a democratic society have to understand one another. They are indispensable in a world community: They are arts shared by people everywhere. Without them the individual is deprived and the community is too. Learning these arts cannot be left to the choices of children or parents.

The second object of any school—and this is vital to a democratic community—should be to open new worlds to the young.

Whatever the charms of the neighborhood school, whatever the pleasures of touring one's native city, whatever the allure of the present, emphasis upon the immediate environment and its current condition must narrow the mind and prevent understanding of the wider national or world community and any real comprehension of the present. Hence, those who would center education on the interests of children and on their surroundings are working contrary to the demands contemporary society is making upon any educational system.

The third object of any education institution must be to get the young to understand their cultural heritage, This, too, is in the interest of the individual and the community. Comprehension of the cultural heritage is the means by which the bonds uniting the community are strengthened. The public school is the only agency that can be entrusted with this obligation.

Within the limits set by the Constitution and by the necessity of allocating resources in the most economical way, school districts, schools, and classes should be as small as possible. Even if, according to the Coleman Report, such changes would not materially affect the achievement of children, they would facilitate variety and experimentation, and they would make schools less formidable to those who must attend.

Ways must be found to break the lockstep, the system by which all pupils proceed at the same pace through the same curriculum for the same number of years. The disadvantages of small schools can be overcome by building them in clusters, each with somewhat different courses and methods and permitting students to avail themselves of anything offered in any one. This is an extension of the idea of dual enrollment or shared time, which now exists everywhere, and which allows students in one school to take advantage of what is taught in another, even if one is private and the other public.

Variety in the methods and curriculum is one way of breaking the lockstep. Another is allowing the student to proceed at his own rate of speed. Under the present system the slow learner is eventually thrown into despair because he cannot keep up, and the fast learner is in the same condition because he has "nothing to do." If we are to have a graded curriculum, we can overcome some of the handicaps it imposes by substituting examinations for time spent and encouraging the student to present himself for them whenever in his opinion he is ready to take them.

It is self-evident that if a course of study is designed to provide the minimum requisites for democratic citizenship, nobody can be permitted to fail. If, then, the basic curriculum is revised as proposed above, so that it is limited to studies essential to the exercise of citizenship, it follows that grades would be eliminated and with them the invidious distinction between winners and losers. We have reason to believe that everybody is educable. The rate and method of education may vary; the aim of basic education is the same with all individuals, and the obligation of the public schools is to achieve it with all. On this principle, if there is failure, it is the failure of the school, not of the pupil.

I take for granted the adoption or adaption of many of those reforms about which so much noise has been made of late. The critics of the schools have performed a public service in calling attention to shortcomings that can be repaired by keeping them in mind and working on them. Interest, for example, can be restored to schooling without coming to the indefensible conclusion that whatever is not immediately interesting to children should be omitted from their education.

About some other matters, the elementary and secondary schools can do little or nothing. They cannot do much to change parental attitudes, though they should certainly try by keeping in touch with the families of pupils. They can do nothing about the socioeconomic status or the slum environment of the children in their charge. The present efforts in pre-school education have a trifling effect in improving the conditions of the earliest years in the lives of slum children. The schools can do nothing about the high taxes that infuriate their no-nonsense, hardheaded critics. They can see to it that money is not wasted, but the definition of waste depends upon an understanding of the purpose of the activity and the best methods of accomplishing it.

The purpose of the activity is the crucial question. The purpose of the public schools is not accomplished by having them free, universal, and compulsory. They may do many things for the young: They may amuse them, comfort them, look after their health, and keep them off the streets. But they are not public schools unless they start their pupils toward an understanding of what it means to be a self-governing citizen of a self-governing political community.

The conclusion of Christopher Jencks's book, *Inequality,* is that schools should be pleasant places for children. Because one child's pleasure is another child's poison, schools should vary according to the preferences children display. Why the power of the state should be invoked to compel children to enjoy themselves remains obscure. If a child and his parents agree that he has a better time at home than he has at school, why should he not stay home? If he and his parents have no interest in education, and if the community has no interest in having him educated, why not simply give up education?

This is in effect what Carl Bereiter advocates in an article in the *Harvard Educational Review,* called, in all seriousness, "Schools Without Education." I can understand him only as proposing the abandonment of all institutions he calls educational.

To Mr. Bereiter education is "the deliberate development of human personality, the making of citizens. . . . Schools cannot cease to be places where intellectual growth and personality development go on, but they can cease to be places where an effort is made to direct or shape these processes. . . . Parents typically educate, and it's my contention . . . that they are the only ones who have a clear-cut right to educate."

If parents are the only ones who have a clear-cut right to educate, the interest of the community in education or in "the making of citizens" is at best unclear, Bereiter, like Jencks, favors voucher plans that would enable parents to decide how tax dollars would be spent on their children.

He proposes to retain schools, apparently compulsory, for two purposes: child care and training in reading, writing, and arithmetic. If parents have the only clear-cut right to educate their children, one would think they have the only clear-cut right to determine what care their children had outside the home or indeed whether they needed any at all. If compulsory education is unjustifiable, compulsory child care seems less so.

If parents are for any reason not interested in having the child learn to read, write, and calculate, why should the state assert the right to "train" him to do so? Reading, writing, and arithmetic are the essential tools of education. They have other uses, but a parent unconcerned about education might feel that he did not want his child to waste much time acquiring them. If education is the exclusive territory of the parent, his conclusion on reading, writing, and arithmetic should have great weight.

Since reading and writing, if not arithmetic, are certain to have an educational effect, depending on what is read and written in learning to read and write, training in these activities comes dangerously close to the process that parents, and parents only, have a right to direct.

Mr. Bereiter says, "The need for training arises from the incompleteness of normal experience." This is precisely the way the need for education arises. To intimate that the normal experience of a slum child does not teach him arithmetic, whereas it does "make a citizen" out of him is to display a lamentable ignorance of the facts of life. Consider the implications of Bereiter's recommendation that after training is completed, we should "then simply provide enough resources in the environment that the child can put the skills to use if he feels inclined."

The conclusions of Jencks and Bereiter are based on the proposition that schools make no difference. The logical result would be to abolish them or at least any compulsion to attend them. This would also be the result of the opposite argument, advanced by Joel H. Spring: that schools make too much difference. In his book, *Education and the Rise of the Corporate State*, the community is the villain. It uses the schools as an "instrument of social control," to fit the young into the established social, economic, and political structure. The power of the school is enormous, and it must be broken in order to achieve democracy, which means "freedom to choose one's own goals and the opportunity to develop one's own life-style."

Whereas Jencks and Bereiter ignore the community and make light of schools as ineffective, Spring thinks of the community as the modern Medusa and finds the schools all too effective in her service. He cannot stand "socialization." Neither can I, chiefly because I do not know what it means. When it appears, as it often does, to be synonymous with Carl Bereiter's definition of the purpose of education—making citizens—it seems sensible enough.

According to Spring: "The solution is not to change the goals and directions of socialization and social control. This is impossible. As long as the public schools take responsibility for the socialization of the child, social adaptation to the institution becomes inevitable. . . . The only possible solution is to end the power of the schools." If "socialization" as Spring uses the word can be equated with "education" as Bereiter uses it, then the way to end the power of the schools is to restrict their educational efforts along the lines Jencks and Bereiter propose. This means the community would have no interest in what went on in the schools.

The novel definition of democracy put forward by Spring— freedom to choose one's own goals and the opportunity to develop one's own life-style—leads to the conclusion, by what it omits as much as by what it contains, that there can be no such thing as a democratic community anyway. A community of any kind must impose some limits on the freedom to choose one's own goals and develop one's own life-style. Those who talk about a community at all, even those who refer to it in the most high-minded, disinterested, and (it seems to me) reasonable way, play a consistently fiendish role in Spring's book.

There is no easy way by which a political community can make itself better. It seems doubtful that it can do so by leaving education, "the making of citizens," to chance. The whims of children are unreliable guides and the vagaries of parents not much better. There is some evidence that compulsory schooling came to existence to rescue children from their families, and neglect and exploitation by parents are visible in every American city.

How, then, do we change the status quo? If I understand the authors discussed here, they hold we can do nothing about it through educational institutions. Jencks and Bereiter believe these institutions can make no difference. Spring says they can do nothing but sustain the existing order. What would happen if the schools or compulsory attendance at them were abolished and "the making of citizens" were left to parents? The status quo would be maintained—or would deteriorate.

This must be so because those who had the power would start with all the advantages, and their children would end with them. The restraints now placed on snobbishness and exclusivity, on prejudice, would disappear and any idea of the common good would vanish into thin air.

But perhaps there is nothing in that idea or in the idea of community, anyway. Since there is no space for argument, I shall have to content myself for the moment with the assertion that man has never been able to live without the community and that, if he is to live well, he must try to make the community as good as it can possibly be.

The American political community is based on the notion of the continuous engagement of all the people in dialogue about their common concerns. I am aware of the obstacles that make this dialogue an ideal rather than a reality. I am also aware that an educational system operates within severe limitations. It cannot proclaim a revolution and survive.

But to proclaim rededication to basic American principles, to announce a commitment to prepare the rising generation for that dialogue which it should carry on, to enunciate the reasons why the rising generation should be prepared, and to work out the methods by which it could be is within the scope—and I hope the competence—of American educators.

American citizens have an awful responsibility: They have to try to understand the world. Of course the public schools cannot provide this understanding. But statistics showing the dubious results of our present efforts will not convince me that it is impossible to formulate an educational program that will make a difference in the degree of understanding the citizen achieves.